World Social Science Report

**2016 | Challenging Inequalities:
Pathways to a Just World**

Published by the United Nations Educational, Scientific and Cultural Organization (UNESCO),
7, place de Fontenoy, 75352 Paris 07 SP, France
and the International Social Science Council (ISSC),
1 rue Miollis, 75732 Paris Cedex 15, France.

© ISSC, the Institute of Development Studies (IDS) and UNESCO, 2016

ISBN 978-92-3-100164-2

This publication is available in Open Access under the Attribution ShareAlike 3.0 IGO (CC-BY-SA 3.0 IGO) licence (*http://creativecommons.org/licenses/by-sa/3.0/igo/*). By using the content of this publication, the users accept to be bound by the terms of use of the UNESCO Open Access Repository (*http://www.unesco.org/open-access/terms-use-ccbysa-en*).

The designations employed and the presentation of material throughout this publication do not imply the expression of any opinion whatsoever on the part of UNESCO, the ISSC or the IDS concerning the legal status of any country, territory, city or area or of its authorities, or concerning the delimitation of its frontiers or boundaries.

The *World Social Science Report 2016* editorial team is responsible for the choice of articles and the overall presentation. Each author is responsible for the facts contained in his/her article and the opinions expressed therein, which are not necessarily those of UNESCO, the ISSC or the IDS and do not commit these Organizations.

Cover photo: © Suso33. All rights reserved.
AUSENCIAS ('Absences'), Suso33 (Logroño, Spain, 2008)
Third-party use or commercial redistribution of all or part of this image is subject to the prior permission of Suso33 Studio, which should be requested by email to *info@suso33.com*

Graphic and cover design: Corinne Hayworth

Typeset and printed by: UNESCO

Printed in France

The Report is available online at: *en.unesco.org/wssr2016*
Hard copies are available from UNESCO Publishing:
http://publishing.unesco.org/details.aspx?&Code_Livre=5160&change=E

This report should be cited as follows: ISSC, IDS and UNESCO (2016), *World Social Science Report 2016, Challenging Inequalities: Pathways to a Just World*, UNESCO Publishing, Paris.

The Report is supported by The Swedish International Development Cooperation Agency (Sida)

Foreword

The world is converging around high levels of inequalities. And they matter.

Inequalities in individual living standards have, on average, declined between countries. Sustaining this progress and extending it to those countries that have not yet benefited is crucial. But this should not come at the cost of neglecting inequalities within countries, the level and progression of which undermine economies, social inclusion and environmental sustainability.

The international community is committed to meeting this challenge, which we see expressed in demands for greater equity and inclusion rising all over the world – and which is embodied in the *2030 Agenda for Sustainable Development*, and specifically Sustainable Development Goal 10 to reduce inequalities.

For this, resources are needed, and so is political will. The world also needs improved understanding, which the *World Social Science Report 2016* is designed to provide.

Inequalities are multi-dimensional, multi-layered and cumulative. The Report makes clear that understanding and acting effectively upon inequalities requires looking beyond income and wealth disparities to capture their political, environmental, social, cultural, spatial, and knowledge features. Untangling such complexity is a challenge we must fully take on – if we are to develop policies and solutions that are feasible and sustainable.

The Report also emphasizes that the costs of inequalities are very high and borne by all – not just by the deprived and the excluded, but collectively, by current and future generations, in the form of heightened conflict and instability, economic and fiscal losses, environmental degradation, and political tensions. Reducing inequalities is thus everyone's concern.

Countering inequalities requires robust knowledge – but knowledge alone is not enough. The challenge is to improve the connection between what we know and how we act: to mobilize the knowledge of the social and human sciences to inform policies, underpin decisions and enable wise and transparent management of the shift towards more equitable and inclusive societies. In this sense, investment in knowledge is a down-payment for informed change.

And in some respects, even the knowledge we have is not fully adequate. Social science research agendas equally require revisiting. The Report calls for a step change towards a research agenda that is interdisciplinary, multiscale and globally inclusive, creating pathways for transformative knowledge.

Inequalities are a major concern for social science today. That is reflected by a fivefold increase in studies of inequality and social justice in academic publications from 1992 to 2013. However, the Report highlights two major knowledge divides in research into inequality. Firstly, too many studies are too narrow in focus. There is too little attention to the overlapping inequalities that go beyond income and wealth, such as health, knowledge, and gender. Secondly, the Report shows that the focus of social science research into inequality tends to be concentrated in the countries of the North, where a reliable knowledge base already exists, to the detriment of the countries of the Global South without similarly robust data. Over 80 per cent of publications on inequalities come from the North.

To overcome these knowledge divides, we need more cooperation across disciplines and across borders to help governments develop more effective and inclusive policies, North and South. International networks, open data sources, co-creation of knowledge, open access to publishing and software – these are all vital to achieving this.

UNESCO's longstanding cooperation with the International Social Science Council stands at the heart of our efforts to promote social science to address the world's problems. The World Social Science Reports are a cornerstone of this collaboration, and I wish to thank the Council for its intellectual and editorial efforts to produce the 2016 Report, in collaboration with the Institute of Development Studies, based at the University of Sussex in the United Kingdom.

This Report is a wake-up call. Let there be no doubt: investing in and closing the knowledge gap in social science research into inequalities will be vital to achieve the cross-cutting ambitions of the *2030 Agenda for Sustainable Development*. Let's work together now – to 'leave no one behind' tomorrow.

Irina Bokova
Director-General of UNESCO

Preface

The coexistence of deep and persistent inequalities as well as increasing prosperity is a paradox of our time, a paradox that calls into question global development and processes of modernization in today's world. Despite a fall in global levels of economic inequality, driven in part by the reduction of poverty in India and China, inequality within countries has risen over the past forty years and has recently accelerated further, especially following the 2008 financial crisis.

Economic inequalities in income and wealth, social inequalities in health, education and access to welfare services, gender and racial inequalities, cultural and religious discrimination, barriers to political participation, all are main instances of inequalities, global in scope, often intertwined and influencing each other. All these inequalities go against widely shared values of social justice, equitable and sustainable development, individual freedom and collective empowerment, cultural pluralism and peaceful coexistence. As a matter of fact, deep inequalities among social classes and groups undermine social cohesion and the legitimacy of political institutions. High differences in educational and health levels, and discrimination based on gender, dramatically reduce the potentiality for individual self-realization, as well as the amount of human resources available for societal progress. Uneven income distribution hinders economic growth as it implies a reduction of the consumption power of majority of the population that cannot be compensated for by the extra spending of the wealthiest 1 per cent. Repression of ethnic, religious and political minorities fosters waves of exploited migrants and asylum-seekers. While the processes influencing declines or increases in inequality are global and interlinked, the responses to these processes are specific, heterogeneous and uneven.

Inequality is a longstanding – and even foundational – topic of research for the social sciences. Rousseau's discourse on the origins of inequality, Marx's critique of capitalism, Weber's analysis of class, status and party, Pareto's theory of elites, Keynes's general theory of employment and others are classical examples of the centrality of the interest in this subject. Social science literature on the manifestations, causes and consequences of inequality is vast and multidisciplinary, spanning sociological research on social stratification and mobility, economic analysis of labour markets and income distribution, gender studies, and also comparative research on welfare policies. However, social research on inequality is flourishing particularly now, with new studies opening up new perspectives. The increasing availability of big datasets used to analyse inequalities over time and space helps the advancement of knowledge on the reproduction of inequality, and its effects. Major recent theories of inequality, such as those outlined in Deaton's *The Great Escape* (2013) and Piketty's *Capital in the Twenty-First Century* (2013), have reignited debate on the origins and causes of inequality, as well as on the impact of inequality on growth, patterns of modernization and models of development. These questions are central. The sunset of trickle-down economics and the 2008 financial crisis have laid bare the need for a new examination of understandings of growth and progress, and of the confluences of global challenges we are facing. Which models of growth, production patterns and consumption styles are sustainable in a world with limited natural resources? Will emerging economies follow the same development patterns as those that went before them, and how will inequalities be affected? The comparative analysis of different modernity paths in the contemporary globalized world can be of help in answering these questions.

Social scientists have long been studying the various dimensions of inequality both among and within countries, with the help of different theoretical paradigms and research methods. But more and more political leaders and concerned citizens are now becoming aware of the relationships and intersections between different forms of inequality and also other global challenges, including climate change and sustainable development, peace and conflict, corruption and crime, education and health. The Sustainable Development Goals (SDGs) adopted in September 2015 helped formally recognize the intersectionality of these challenges, while achieving a crucial step towards a new global agenda for development. In addition to specific goals relevant to inequality, the articulation of the agenda, and indeed the overall commitment to 'leave no one behind', illustrate the extent to which inequality is understood as a multifaceted, urgent problem that requires our joint efforts as a global community.

Preface

Much of the knowledge needed in achieving the SDGs is generated by increasing inter- and cross-disciplinary work, and articulates the social, economic and biophysical dimensions of human development.

Inequality is a crucial economic and political concern which is also rising up on the agenda of public discourse. A 2014 Pew Research Center survey found that a majority of people in all of the forty-four countries polled described the gap between rich and poor as a problem for their country. In twenty-eight nations, the majority of those polled found that the wealth gap was a very serious issue. Public concern about inequality is also translating into visible action. According to a working paper by the Initiative for Policy Dialogue and Friedrich-Ebert-Stiftung (2013), between 2006 and mid-2013, over 13 per cent of all protests worldwide were mainly about economic inequality.

At the heart of this Report is a call for a revitalized research agenda on inequality, one that is global in its outlook and participation, and that draws from across the disciplines. This call means recognizing and challenging inequalities in social science research itself. While they draw on a long legacy of research on inequality, many of the key thinkers, and the vast majority of publications, come from the global North. Divides in knowledge production on inequalities constitute a real challenge to our understanding of inequalities and to the development of appropriate responses. This Report aims to correct the scale, through the inclusion of a wider range of voices, and a deliberate effort to highlight aspects of inequality that have hardly ever been featured in the many reports and think pieces published on inequality in recent years.

As the primary body representing the full scope of social scientists at the global level, the ISSC is uniquely positioned in bringing together research communities to co-develop research agendas around the most pressing issues of our time. The evidence presented in this Report makes it clear that social scientists, as a global community, must keep their attention on inequality in the years to come. The agenda for future research presented indicates the kinds of priorities that may lead such efforts.

Through its various programmes and activities, the ISSC aims to provide global leadership on advancing the social sciences in all parts of the world. This Report, which brings together the contributions of over 100 authors from some forty countries worldwide, is the culmination of a much larger discussion with many hundreds of social scientists worldwide that began to take shape at the 2013 ISSC General Assembly, where the topic of this Report was chosen by the ISSC's members. An international consultation of scientists followed. An international expert meeting, co-organized with UNESCO in 2014, started the process of identifying the topics that a new Report on inequality had to cover. The 2015 World Social Science Forum on the topic of Transforming Global Relations for a Just World was also critical in identifying further topics and potential contributors. The Forum took place in Durban, South Africa, under the leadership of my predecessor as ISSC president, Olive Shisana. To her we express our appreciation for overseeing this thought-provoking gathering.

Our work on the Report has been greatly enriched by our collaboration with the Institute of Development Studies (IDS), based at Sussex University (UK), and most of all by the professionalism, networking and collegiality of Melissa Leach, John Gaventa and Patricia Justino. It is the first time that the ISSC has invited a research institute to help coordinate one of its reports, and it has been a very rewarding decision.

I wish to thank the various funding agencies who have made this World Report possible: **the European Science Foundation (ESF), the Netherlands Organisation for Scientific Research (NWO), the Research Council of Norway, Riksbankens Jubileumsfond, the Swedish International Development Cooperation Agency (Sida), the Swedish Research Council, and the Swiss Agency for Development and Cooperation (SDC).**

As with the previous editions, the 2016 *World Social Science Report* is co-published with UNESCO. I therefore wish to thank Nada Al-Nashif, Assistant Director-General of the Social Science and Humanities sector, and her team, as well as Ian Denison and the team from UNESCO Publishing, for their support in the production process.

Alberto Martinelli

President, International Social Science Council

Bibliography

Deaton, A. 2013. *The Great Escape*. Princeton, N.J., Princeton University Press.

Initiative for Policy Dialogue and Friedrich-Ebert-Stiftung. 2013. *World Protests 2006–2013*. New York. http://policydialogue.org/ (Accessed 13 July 2016.)

Keynes, J. M. 1936. *General Theory of Employment. Interest and Money*, London, Palgrave Macmillan.

Martinelli, A. 2005. *Global Modernization: Rethinking the Project of Modernity*. London, Sage.

Marx, K. 1867. *Das Kapital* [*Capital*], 3 vols. Hamburg, Germany, Verlag von Otto Meisner.

Pareto, V. 1916. *Trattato di sociologia generale* [*The Mind and Society*]. Florence, Italy, G. Barbéra.

Pew Research Center. 2014. *Emerging and developing economies much more optimistic than rich countries about the future*. www.pewglobal.org/ (Accessed 13 July 2016.)

Piketty, T. 2013. *Le capital au xxie siècle* [*Capital in the Twenty-First Century*]. Paris, Seuil.

Rousseau, J.-J. 1755. *Discours sur l'origine et les fondements de l'inégalité parmi les hommes* [*Discourse on the Origin and Basis of Inequality Among Men*]. Amsterdam, Marc-Michel Rey.

Weber, M. 1922. *Wirtschaft und Gesellschaft* [*Economy and Society*], Tübingen, Germany, Mohr.

This article features in the *World Social Science Report 2016*, UNESCO and the ISSC, Paris. Click *here* to access the complete Report.

WSS Report Editorial Team

Report directors (IDS):	Melissa Leach, John Gaventa, Patricia Justino
Report director (ISSC):	Mathieu Denis
ISSC senior adviser:	Françoise Caillods
Researcher, IDS report manager:	Bruno Martorano
ISSC report manager:	Lizzie Sayer

WSS Report 2016 Scientific Advisory Committee

Alberto Martinelli, *Chair*	University of Milan, Italy
Elisa Reis, *Vice-Chair*	Federal University of Rio de Janeiro, Brazil
Seyla Benhabib	Yale University, United States
Joshua Castellino	Middlesex University, London, UK
Juliana Martinez Franzoni	University of Costa Rica, Costa Rica
Achille Mbembe	Witwatersrand University, South Africa
Jamie Peck	University of British Columbia, Canada
Ingrid Schoon	Institute of Education, United Kingdom
Ismail Serageldin	Bibliotheca Alexandrina, Egypt
Olive Shisana	Evidence Based Solutions, South Africa
Joseph Stiglitz	Columbia Business School, USA
Michel Wieviorka	École des hautes études en sciences sociales, France
Jijiao Zhang	Chinese Academy of Social Sciences, China
John Crowley, *observer*	UNESCO
Mathieu Denis, *ex-officio*	Executive director, International Social Science Council (ISSC)
Adebayo Olukoshi, *observer and Chair of the Scientific Committee of the 2015 World Social Science Forum*	International IDEA, and University of Johannesburg, South Africa

Acknowledgements

The *World Social Science Report 2016* is a collaborative effort made possible by the support and contributions of many individuals and organizations worldwide.

Thanks are due to all ISSC members around the world who have contributed to the development of the Report, nominating people for the Scientific Advisory Committee, reaching out to authors, and supporting its dissemination and discussion through their international networks.

The *World Social Science Report 2016* was prepared in partnership by the ISSC and the Institute of Development Studies (IDS) at the University of Sussex, and has been greatly strengthened by the engagement and contributions of its leadership team and its wider international network.

The Report was financed by generous contributions from:

- the Swedish International Development Cooperation Agency (Sida)
- UNESCO, as part of its framework agreement with the ISSC
- the Swiss Agency for Development and Cooperation (SDC)

Other generous contributors include European Science Foundation (ESF), Netherlands Organisation for Scientific Research (NWO), Research Council of Norway, Riksbankens Jubileumsfond and the Swedish Research Council.

The ISSC is very grateful for this support, without which the report would have not been possible. The ISSC also wishes to acknowledge Sida's invaluable contribution to the Report through the World Social Science Fellows programme.

The Report was prepared under the guidance of a Scientific Advisory Committee, who provided advice on the structure and content, as well as providing expert counsel on the development of its key messages and recommendations for research. The editorial team would particularly like to thank the chair of the Committee, Alberto Martinelli.

We would also like to thank Nada Al-Nashif, Assistant Director-General for Social and Human Sciences, and her team at UNESCO, as well as the team from UNESCO Publishing, for their support throughout the production process. We are also grateful for the provision of statistical data by the UNESCO Institute for Statistics.

The editorial team is indebted to the many colleagues who peer-reviewed contributions, as well as those who provided ideas and advice on specific sections. There are simply too many to name, but a specific thank you goes to Veronica Amarante, Bob Deacon, William Gumede, Elisa Reis, Daniel Waldenström and Iulia Sevciuc for their detailed comments on the manuscript.

The Report also benefited from the editorial expertise of Martin Ince, Alison Clayson, Anita Craig, Susan Curran, Ilse Evertse, Carmen Scherkenbach and Dee Scholey. We are appreciative of the support and assistance provided by the ISSC Secretariat, as well as by Corinne Hayworth for the graphic design and Katerina Markelova for project management support.

We would like to thank all the authors for their insightful contributions and patient cooperation throughout the editorial process.

A special tribute goes to our dear colleague Louise Daniel, who passed away in February 2015, and who initiated the work on this Report with great enthusiasm and devotion.

Contents

Foreword 3
Preface 5
Acknowledgements 9
List of figures and tables 14

Introduction and key messages

1. Social science challenges inequalities: general introduction,
   Françoise Caillods and Mathieu Denis 18
2. Challenging inequalities: pathways to a just world.
   Key messages and main contributions, *Melissa Leach, John Gaventa,
   Patricia Justino, Françoise Caillods and Mathieu Denis* 26

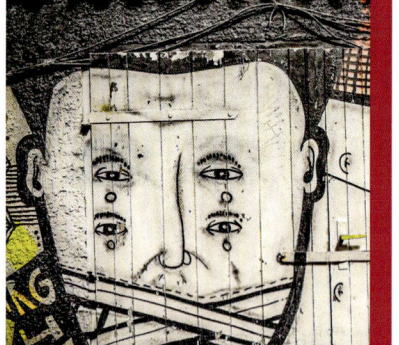

PART I • CURRENT TRENDS IN INEQUALITIES   33

3. Drivers and dynamics of inequalities worldwide (an introduction to Part I),
   Patricia Justino and Bruno Martorano 34

Chapter 1 • Inequalities: many intersecting dimensions   41

4. Global versus national inequality, *François Bourguignon* 42
5. Global inequality and the middle classes, *Branko Milanovic* 47
6. Wage and income inequality, *Patrick Belser* 49
7. Horizontal inequalities, *Frances Stewart* 51
8. 'Leaving no one behind': the challenge of intersecting inequalities, *Naila Kabeer* ... 55
9. Inequality and natural resources in Africa, *James C. Murombedzi* ... 59
10. Inequality in education: the challenge of measurement,
    Manos Antoninis, Marcos Delprato and Aaron Benavot 63
11. POSTCARD • The multiple forms of digital inequality, *Ben Ramalingam and Kevin Hernandez* ... 68
12. Untangling economic and political inequality: the case of South Africa,
    John Gaventa and Carin Runciman 70
13. Grounding justice and injustice, *Ruth Fincher* 74
14. Rising economic inequality and gender inequality: intersecting spheres of injustice, *Shahra Razavi* ... 78

Chapter 2 • Inequalities in different parts of the world   83

15. Recent changes in income inequality in China, *Li Shi* 84
16. Inequality in India: drivers and consequences, *Jayati Ghosh* 89
17. Social justice and equality/inequality issues in modern-day Russia, *Natalia Grigorieva* ... 93
18. Inequality in sub-Saharan Africa: dimensions and drivers, *Jimi O. Adesina* ... 96
19. Inequalities in the Arab region, *Adam Hanieh* 101
20. The invisible hands of racial inequality in the USA, *Fredrick C. Harris* ... 104
21. Income inequality in Brazil: new evidence from combined tax and survey data, *Marcelo Medeiros* ... 107

Contents

PART II • THE CONSEQUENCES OF INEQUALITIES — 111

22. Consequences and futures of inequalities (an introduction to Part II), *John Gaventa* 112
23. POSTCARD • Inequality: a historical issue within the United Nations System, *Richard Jolly* 118

Chapter 3 • Consequences and interactions of multiple inequalities — 121

24. Economic growth and poverty reduction: the inequality connection, *Ravi Kanbur* 122
25. Inequality and political conflict, *Gudrun Østby* 126
26. POSTCARD • Perceived inequalities among Lebanese nationals and Syrian refugees, *Charles Harb* 129
27. Inequality and sustainability, *Melissa Leach* 132
28. POSTCARD • Challenging intersecting inequalities around access to water, *Tahseen Jafry, Blessings Chinsinga, Lilian Zimba and Ted Scanlon* 135
29. Poverty and environmental inequality in India, *Sunita Narain* 137
30. Health and social justice in Egypt: towards a health equity perspective, *Soha Bayoumi* 140
31. POSTCARD • The Ebola crisis: inequality and distrust, *Annie Wilkinson and Abu A. Brima* 144
32. The spatial patterning of exposure to inequality and its social consequences in South Africa: work in progress, *David McLennan* 146
33. POSTCARD • Food rights and wrongs, *Naomi Hossain* 150
34. The role of aspirations in the exclusion of Peruvian indigenous children, *Laure Pasquier-Doumer* ...151
35. POSTCARD • Social inequality and young people in Europe: their capacity to aspire, *Evelyne Baillergeau and Jan Willem Duyvendak* 155
36. POSTCARD • Consequences of inequality for persons with disabilities – experience of ADD International, *Emma Cain* 157

Chapter 4 • Inequality futures — 159

37. Inequality, economic democracy and sustainability, *Madeleine Power, Richard Wilkinson and Kate Pickett* 160
38. Malaise in the Western middle classes, *Louis Chauvel and Anne Hartung* 164
39. BRICS and global inequality, *Jing Gu, Alex Shankland, Anuradha Chenoy and Gerry Bloom* 170
40. Inequalities and social progress in the future, *Marc Fleurbaey and Stephan Klasen* 173
41. Inequality in an increasingly automated world, *Lizzie Sayer* 177
42. POSTCARD • Digital connections in the face of inequality, *Charles Onyango-Obbo* 180

Contents

PART III • TRANSFORMATIVE RESPONSES, TRANSFORMATIVE PATHWAYS   183

43. Towards equality: transformative pathways (an introduction to Part III), *Melissa Leach* 184

Chapter 5 • Changing the rules   191

44. Labour market institutions and inequality, *Janine Berg* 192
45. Inequality and global social policy: policies, actors and strategies, *Bob Deacon* 197
46. The decline and recent uptick of income inequality in Latin America, 2002–13, *Giovanni Andrea Cornia* 201
47. Taxation and inequality: lessons from Latin America, *Juan Carlos Gómez Sabaíni, Bruno Martorano and Dalmiro Morán* 206
48. Global instruments for tackling inequality: the African experience, *Adebayo O. Olukoshi* 211
49. POSTCARD • Financial liberalization and global inequality, *Stephany Griffith-Jones and E.A. Brett* 215
50. POSTCARD • Could changes in the international tax system be a strategy for dealing with inequality? *Mick Moore* 217
51. A seat at the table is not enough: gender and political inclusion, *Sohela Nazneen* 219
52. POSTCARD • Land redistribution: opportunities and traps, *Michael Lipton* 223
53. Legal rights as instruments for challenging inequality, *Celestine Nyamu Musembi* 225
54. POSTCARD • Reducing inequality through transformative institutional policies: the case of the industrial court of Nigeria, *Caroline Joelle Nwabueze* 229
55. Social protection, inequality and social justice, *Keetie Roelen, Rachel Sabates-Wheeler and Stephen Devereux* 231
56. POSTCARD • Unconditional basic income, *Erik Olin Wright* 237
57. POSTCARD • Universal health coverage as a powerful social equalizer, *Rüdiger Krech* 239
58. Critical elements for ensuring the success of more inclusive social policies, *Michael Woolcock* 241
59. Inequality and corruption, *Bo Rothstein* 245

Chapter 6 • Mobilizing for change   249

60. Why social movements matter for addressing inequalities and ensuring social justice, *Leandro Vergara-Camus* 250
61. POSTCARD • Inequalities and protests, *Isabel Ortiz and Sara Burke* 254
62. POSTCARD • Africa's uprisings: no end in sight, *Adam Branch and Zachariah Mampilly* 256
63. POSTCARD • Representing inequality: film, literature and the arts, *Mike van Graan* 257
64. Grass-roots pathways for challenging social and political inequality, *Alison Mathie with E. Alma, A. Ansorena, J. Basnet, Y. Ghore, S. Jarrín, J. Landry, N. Lee, B. von Lieres, V. Miller, M. de Montis, S. Nakazwe, S. Pal, B. Peters, R. Riyawala, V. Schreiber, M.A. Shariff, A. Tefera and N. Zulminarni* 259
65. POSTCARD • Equality as a valued social norm, inequality as an injustice, *Sakiko Fukuda-Parr* 263
66. A historical view of the politics of inequality, *Duncan Green* 265
67. POSTCARD • Rising extreme inequality is a concern for us all, *Winnie Byanyima* 269

PART IV • TRANSFORMATIVE KNOWLEDGE FOR A JUST WORLD   273

68. A global research agenda on inequality for the next ten years, *The* World Social Science Report *2016 Editorial Team* 274
69. Knowledge divides: social science production on inequalities and social Justice, *Françoise Caillods* 280
70. The use of big data in the analysis of inequality, *Mike Savage* 286
71. Tax and legal havens: a priority for inequality research, *Alain Deneault* 289
72. POSTCARD • Increasing childhood equality in cities: a practical intervention through policy, research and advocacy, *Alberto Minujin* 291
73. POSTCARD • Local knowledge as a common good, *Kemly Camacho Jiménez* 293
74. POSTCARD • A proposal to monitor intersecting inequalities in the post-2015 Agenda, *Deborah S. Rogers* 294

ANNEXES   297

Annex A • Basic statistics on the production of social science research   299

Annex B • Bibliometric analysis of social and human science research into inequalities and social justice   345

Annex C • Acronyms and abbreviations   355

Annex D • Glossary   357

Contents

List of figures and tables

Figures

Figure 1.1	Evolution of Gini coefficients, high-income countries.	18
Figure 1.2	Evolution of Gini coefficients, middle-income countries	19
Figure 3.1	Wealth of bottom 50 per cent versus wealth of richest sixty-two people	34
Figure 3.2	Income share of the top 1 per cent of earners	35
Figure 3.3	Gini trends in sub-Saharan Africa and Latin America and the Caribbean, 1993–2011	37
Figure 4.1	The evolution of global inequality of living standards from 1988 to 2010	44
Figure 5.1	Variation of real income across different percentiles of global income distribution, 1988–2008	47
Figure 5.2	Countries with more than 30 per cent of their population in the bottom global decile (below $PPP 450 per capita in 2008 prices)	48
Figure 10.1	Lower secondary education completion rate by location, selected low and middle income countries, 2008–14	64
Figure 10.2	Lower secondary education completion rate by location, wealth and gender, Nigeria and the Philippines, 2013	65
Figure 10.3	Primary education completion rate and wealth parity index, selected low and middle income countries, 2008–14	66
Figure 10.4	Concentration curve of the lower secondary education completion rate, sub-Saharan Africa, 2000 and 2010	66
Figure 15.1	Gini coefficient of income inequality in China, 1981–2014	85
Figure 15.2	Number of workers in state-owned and urban collective enterprises as a percentage of all workers in urban China	85
Figure 15.3	Income gap between urban and rural areas in China	86
Figure 15.4	Number of rural–urban migrant workers in China	87
Figure 18.1	Income share of the top 1 per cent and 5 per cent in South Africa	97
Figure 22.1	Interaction of Inequality Goal 10 and the other SDGs	113
Figure 26.1	Time series of Syrian refugees registered by cadastral in Lebanon as of 30 April 2014	130
Figure 32.1	a) Neighbourhood poverty rates across Johannesburg and surrounding areas, 2001; b) Neighbourhood 'exposure to inequality' scores across Johannesburg and surrounding areas, 2001	148
Figure 38.1	The shrinking middle in the USA during times of economic crisis: percentage of adults identifying themselves as each social class	164
Figure 38.2	The shrinking middle: the changing shape of income distribution in Denmark, Germany, France, the UK, the USA and Israel – six typical stroboloids	165
Figure 38.3	Diverging cost of housing (real housing price index) and real household incomes index in Germany, France, the UK, Australia, Canada and the USA	166
Figure 40.1	World income distribution (with absolute population numbers) at three dates	174
Figure 44.1	The different policy areas that shape labour market outcomes	192
Figure 44.2	Components of disposable income, working-age population, mid-2000s, thirty OECD countries	194
Figure 46.1	Trend in the average regional Gini index, early 1980s to 2012	201
Figure 46.2	Trends in ideological orientation of eighteen Latin American governments, 1990–2013	202
Figure 49.1	Bank failures, regulation and inequality in the USA	215

Figure 55.1	Social assistance programmes in the 'developing world', 1990 to 2012	232
Figure 55.2	The impact of social grants on income inequality in South Africa	233
Figure 61.1	Number of protests by grievance or demand, 2006–13	255
Figure 69.1	a) Worldwide publications on inequality and social justice per year, 1991–2014; b) Number of social science and humanities publications on inequalities and social justice produced worldwide per year, 1992–2013	281
Figure 69.2	Number of SHS publications produced worldwide on inequality and social justice per subfield, 1992–2013 (fractional counting)	282
Figure 69.3	a) Number of social and human science publications on inequality and social justice per region, 1992–2013 (fractional counting); b) Number of social and human science publications on inequality and social justice per region for two periods, 1994–2003 and 2004–13	283
Figure 69.4	Number of social science and humanities publications on inequality and social justice per country, 1992–2013 (fractional counting)	284
Figure 70.1	Health and social problems are worse in more unequal countries	286
Figure 70.2	Income inequality in the USA, 1910–2010	287
Figure 72.1	Under-5 mortality rate: local inequities	292

Tables

Table 2.1	Policies identified by authors as having contributed to reducing or curbing inequalities in specific countries in specific time periods	29
Table 47.1	Tax composition evolution in Latin American and OECD countries	207
Table 47.2	Change in RS indices for taxes in selected Latin American countries	208
Table A1	Socio-economic indicators, 2014 or latest available year	300
Table A2	Expenditure on research and development, 2014 or latest available year	304
Table A3	Researchers by sector of employment and field of science (in headcounts - HC and full-time equivalents, FTE), 2014 or latest available year	308
Table A4	Student enrolments, by level, total, social science, business and law, and gender for three years circa 2006, 2011, 2014	322
Table A5	Student graduation, by level, total, social science, business and law, and gender, selected years circa 2001, 2006 and 2011	330
Table A6	Number of publications of the highest-producing countries in natural sciences, social sciences, arts and humanities, 2009 to 2013	338
Table A7	Number of social science publications per country, Scopus and Web of Science (2008–13)	339
Table B1	Evolution in the number of publications on inequalities and social justice per domain of study, 1991–2014	347
Table B2	Number of publications in the social and human sciences on inequalities and social justice produced per year worldwide, 1992 to 2013	347
Table B3	Number of publications in the social and human sciences on inequalities and social justice produced worldwide per subfield (according to the Science-Metrix classification), 1992–2013	348
Table B4	Number of publications (fractional counting) on inequalities and social justice produced worldwide per region, country and time period, 1992–2013	350
Table B5	Number of social and human science publications (full and fractional counting) on inequalities and social justice produced worldwide by region and time periods 1992–2013	352
Table B6	Number of social and human science publications (fractional counting) on inequalities and social justice produced worldwide per subfield (according to the Science-Metrix classification) and region for the entire period, 1992–2013	353

Introduction & key messages

INTRODUCTION AND KEY MESSAGES

1. Social science challenges inequalities: general introduction
   Françoise Caillods and Mathieu Denis

2. Challenging inequalities: pathways to a just world.
   Key messages and main contributions
   Melissa Leach, John Gaventa, Patricia Justino, Françoise Caillods and Mathieu Denis

28 Millimètres, Women are Heroes. Action in Kibera slum, general view, JR (Nairobi, Kenya, 2009)
© JR-ART.NET
Third-party use or commercial redistribution of all or part of this image is subject to the prior permission of JR.

Introduction and key messages

1. Social science challenges inequalities: general introduction

Françoise Caillods and Mathieu Denis

The 2008 economic crisis, the popular uprisings of the so-called 'Arab spring', food riots in Mexico, and the Occupy movement, have put inequality back on the global political agenda in the second decade of the twenty-first century. The headlines on inequality are well known, but they remain striking. Various evaluations conclude that in 2015 almost half of all household wealth was owned by 1 per cent of the global population (Crédit Suisse, 2015) and that the sixty-two richest individuals owned as much as the bottom half of humanity (Oxfam, 2016). In the USA, the top 1 per cent captured 55 per cent of the total growth produced in the country between 1993 and 2014, and this trend is on the rise (Saez, 2014).

The recent increase in economic inequalities seems to find its origins in the 1980s and 1990s, when the neoliberal paradigm became dominant in western countries. During the same period, the interaction of international organizations like the International Monetary Fund (IMF) and the World Bank with states and private sector actors also saw neoliberalism take root in other parts of the world, in the context of the globalization and financialization of the global economy after the fall of the Eastern Bloc. The assumption behind this shift in the logic of economic development was that the benefits of growth generated by market forces would ultimately 'trickle down' to poor and vulnerable populations.

However, this neoliberal 'virtuous circle' effect did not take place on a large scale. Following the liberalization of their economies, and in an increasingly globalized world, several countries – both developed and emerging – did indeed record high rates of economic growth. Yet inequality, and especially income inequality, increased rapidly. With the adoption of the Millennium Development Goals by the international community in 2000, a strong emphasis was placed on the reduction of extreme poverty and hunger, primary education for all, gender equality and women's empowerment, and health.

Figure 1.1 **Evolution of Gini coefficients, high-income countries**

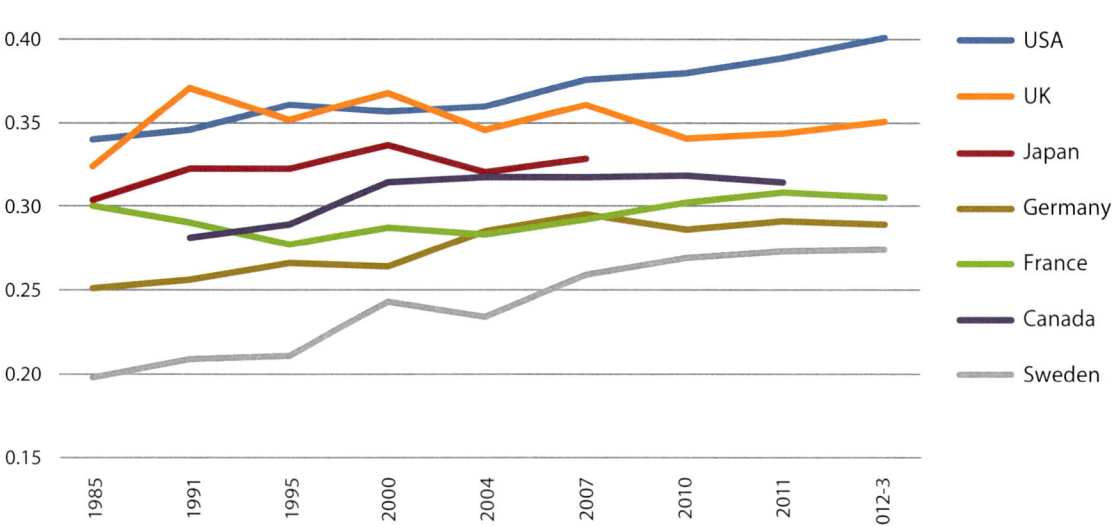

Sources: OECD Income Distribution Database (retrieved 3 March 2016).

Despite undeniable results on all of these fronts, economic inequality continued to increase within countries.

The data in Figure 1.1 confirm the considerable increase in income inequality in Northern countries such as the USA and the UK over the period. Even countries with low levels of income inequality before the 1980s, such as Sweden, have recorded substantial increases. Emerging economies such as Colombia, Brazil and India seem to have a higher level of income inequality, although the data is scarcer and time series shorter. Today, South Africa has the world's highest income inequality, despite a decrease in recent years.

The context

On 25 September 2015, and following a globally inclusive consultation process, the UN Assembly adopted the Sustainable Development Goals (SDGs), which aim to end poverty, protect the planet and ensure prosperity for all as part of a new sustainable development agenda. Challenging inequality is at the heart of the SDGs, with their commitment to 'leave no one behind'. One specific Goal (10) is devoted to 'Reducing inequality within and among countries'. Goal 10 has ten targets, some of which emphasize the economic dimension of inequality, such as Target 1, to promote faster than average income growth for the bottom 40 per cent of the population.

Target 2 stresses the need to promote the social, economic and political inclusion of all, irrespective of age, sex, disability, race, ethnicity, origin, religion or economic or other status. Reaching these goals will require macroeconomic, fiscal, financial, legal and political instruments.

Beyond SDG 10, several other SDGs encompass the need to reduce inequalities and promote inclusiveness by 2030 (see Box 1). They include Goal 1 (End poverty in all its forms everywhere), Goal 2 (End hunger, achieve food security and improved nutrition and promote sustainable agriculture), Goal 3 (Ensure healthy lives and promote well-being for all at all ages), Goal 4 (Ensure inclusive and equitable quality education and promote lifelong learning opportunities for all), Goal 5 (Achieve gender equality and empower all women and girls), Goal 6 (Ensure availability and sustainable management of water and sanitation for all), Goal 7 (Ensure access to affordable, reliable, sustainable and modern energy for all), Goal 8 (Promote sustained, inclusive and sustainable economic growth, full and productive employment and decent work for all), Goal 11 (Make cities and human settlements inclusive, safe, resilient and sustainable) and Goal 16 (Promote peaceful and inclusive societies for sustainable development, provide access to justice for all and build effective, accountable and inclusive institutions at all levels).

Figure 1.2 **Evolution of Gini coefficients, middle-income countries**

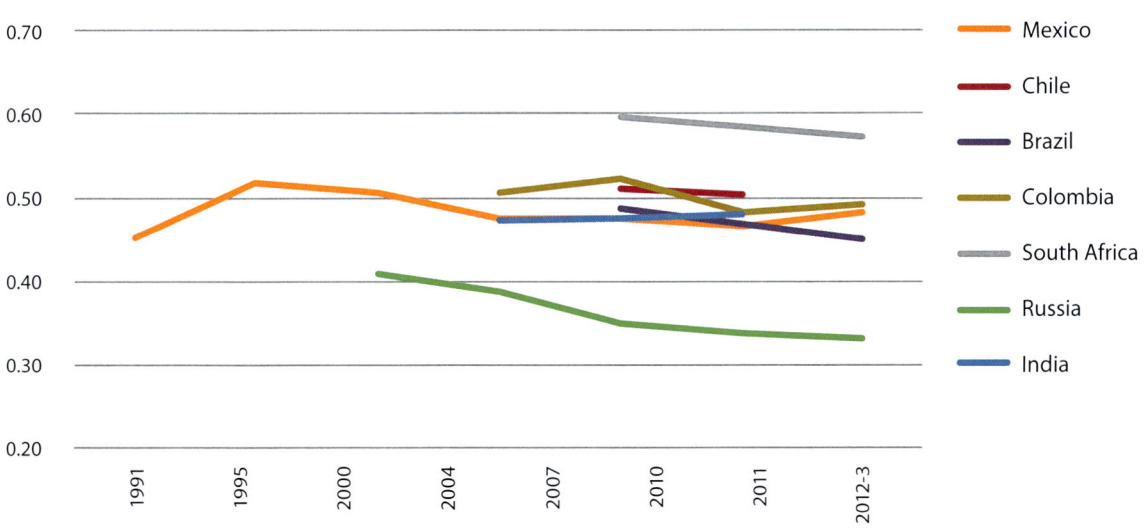

Sources: Luxembourg Income Study (LIS) Database (retrieved 3 March 2016).

Introduction and key messages

Concurrently with the development of the SDGs, several important studies over the past decade or so have confirmed that some dimensions of inequality are reaching levels unheard of in recent decades. Some of these accounts have become best-sellers.

Granted, inequality stands very high in the list of classic social science topics. Sociology was largely born out of efforts to understand new forms of inequality associated with the industrialization of European countries. Over the past two centuries, social theories have focused continuously on inequality in one way or another, and the number of studies dealing with issues and aspects of inequality is probably incalculable. Inequality never entirely disappeared from the radar of the social sciences. Yet until recently it had ceased to be a trend-setter in most disciplines. The incredible success of Thomas Piketty's *Capital in the Twenty-First Century* (close to 2 million copies sold in its various translations) and Wilkinson and Pickett's *The Spirit Level* (translated into twenty-four languages), the awarding of the Sveriges Riksbank Prize in Economic Sciences in Memory of Alfred Nobel to inequality specialists Joseph Stiglitz (2001) and Angus Deaton (2015), and the publication of numerous world reports, confirm that inequality has once more become a critical field of concern and of vibrant, innovative research.

The objectives of the *2016 World Social Science Report*

Does the world need a new global report on inequality? This Report adds to the existing literature by filling several important gaps. First is the insufficient consideration given in many of these studies to forms of inequality beyond economic ones such as income, consumption and assets. Less attention has been paid to other forms of inequality, including in health and education and with regard to gender, and still less to further dimensions such as environmental and knowledge inequalities. Even when these other dimensions are recognized, studies usually focus on one or another, missing the interactions between them. Then the partition of research on inequality into subfields of specialization, or silos, creates a second gap, namely the over-representation of certain disciplines, and insufficient recognition of the potentially much broader scope of social science contributions and perspectives on inequality. A third, additional gap results from the dominant focus on quantifiable indicators to the detriment of analytical approaches combining quantitative and qualitative analytical frameworks. Closely linked with the preference for quantifiable data is the focus on those countries and regions where reliable data are available, mainly OECD countries, to the detriment of other countries without similarly reliable statistics and data, typically low to middle-income countries.

A fourth gap concerns the insufficient consideration given to the multiple consequences of inequality, beyond the study of the levels of inequality, and how they affect different groups of people. Finally, studies and reports on inequality do not by and large identify potential solutions and responses to multiple inequalities which are adapted to specific contexts, and which help to provide pathways to more equitable futures.

These gaps help us determine the six objectives of this Report. They are:

- to look beyond economic inequality and into the interactions between multiple dimensions of inequality;
- to document the trends in inequality in several countries and in all world regions; providing data and information on less well-researched countries, notably low-income countries in Africa and Asia;
- to analyse the consequences of inequalities in different countries and regions, and for different groups of people;
- to identify strategies to reduce inequalities;
- to provide a multidisciplinary contribution to the study of inequality, with inputs from a large range of social sciences such as economics, political science, sociology, psychology, anthropology, legal studies and development studies, as well as from other disciplines and outside academia;
- to identify critical knowledge gaps and propose a global research agenda on inequality.

Box 1 Illustrative list of recent books and reports on inequality

Books and papers

Atkinson, A. 2015. *Inequality – what can be done?* Cambridge, Mass., Harvard University Press.

Berg, A. and Ostry, J. D. 2011 *Inequality and Unsustainable Growth: Two Sides of the Same Coin?* Washington DC, International Monetary Fund.

Deaton, A. 2013. *The Great Escape: Health, Wealth, and the Origins of Inequality*. Princeton, N.J., Princeton University Press.

Milanovic, B. 2016. *Global Inequality: A New Approach for the Age of Globalization*. Cambridge, Mass., Belknap Press.

Piketty, T. 2014. *Capital in the Twenty-First Century* (first published in French in 2013). Cambridge, Mass., Harvard University Press.

Stiglitz, J. E. 2012. *The Price of Inequality: How Today's Divided Society Endangers Our Future*. New York, W.W. Norton & Company.

Wilkinson, R. and Pickett, K. 2009. *The Spirit Level: Why More Equal Societies Almost Always Do Better*. New York, Bloomsbury.

Reports

ILO (International Labour Office). 2015. *Global Wage Report 2014/15: Wages and Income Inequality*. Geneva, ILO.

OECD. 2011. *Divided We Stand. Why Inequality Keeps Rising*. Paris, OECD Publishing.

OECD. 2015. *In It Together: Why Less Inequality Benefits All*. Paris, OECD Publishing.

Ostry, J. D., Berg, M. A. and Tsangarides, M. C. G. 2014. *Redistribution, Inequality and Growth*. Washington DC, IMF.

Oxfam. 2016. *An Economy For the 1%: How Privilege and Power in the Economy Drive Extreme Inequality and How this can be Stopped*. Oxfam Publishing.

UNDP (UN Development Programme). 2014. *Humanity Divided: Confronting Inequality in Developing Countries*. New York, UNDP Publishing.

UNESCO. 2004. *Gender and Education for All – The Leap to Equality. Education for All Global Monitoring Report 2003/4*. Paris, UNESCO Publishing.

UNESCO. 2009. *Inequality: Why Governance Matters. Education for All Global Monitoring Report 2009*. Paris, UNESCO Publishing.

World Bank. 2005. *World Development Report 2006, Equity and Development*. Oxford, World Bank and Oxford University Press.

World Bank. 2013. *The World Development Report 2013: Jobs*. Washington DC, World Bank.

An inclusive analytical framework

The starting point of this Report is a recognition of the need for holistic approaches to the study of inequality, and for analyses of its many interacting dimensions. The Report recognizes that the issues of poverty, inequality and social justice are very much related. Although inequality will be the main entry point to the analysis, issues related to poverty, inequity and injustice are also considered, as are responses to those issues. The Report covers seven dimensions of inequality, and studies their configurations in different contexts. They are:

Economic inequality – refers to differences between levels of incomes, assets, wealth and capital, and living standards, including inequalities in employment. Whereas poverty and extreme poverty are usually determined according to a threshold (such as 60 per cent of median income, or US$1.90 or less per day), inequality is a relative appreciation of the economic situation of individuals and groups within societies.

Social inequality – is defined as the differences between the social statuses of different population groups such as classes, castes, or age groups. It refers to systemic imbalances rooted in the functioning of social institutions, such as education, health, justice and social protection. These disparities in roles, functions, decisions, rights and their determinants affect the level and quality of access to services and protection for different groups, as well as life chances and the capacity to aspire to and attain certain outcomes.

Cultural inequality – refers to differences in status between identity-based groups (self-determined, socially constructed or both). Cultural inequalities encompass discriminations based on gender, ethnic and racialized categorizations, religion, disability and other group identities, rooted in cultural justifications and historic practices. For analytical purposes in this Report, social institutions are associated primarily with the production of social inequality, yet their role in maintaining and reproducing inequality between identity-based groups is also important.

Political inequality – is defined as the differentiated capacity for individuals and groups to influence political decision-making processes and to benefit from those decisions, even in political systems with open processes and procedural equality between citizens. Political inequality also refers to unequal opportunity to enter into political action. It typically refers to the idea that certain 'voices' resonate louder in political debates, and others are not heard at all.

Environmental inequality – covers the full range of differences and disparities in the quality of the environment to which individuals and groups have access. It refers to levels of environmental protection, access to natural resources and opportunities to benefit from their exploitation, and exposure to pollution and to risks of natural hazards and disasters. It also covers capacities to adapt to climate change and to adopt more sustainable ways of living, and the capacity to influence and shape decision-making relating to environmental issues.

Spatial inequality – is used to describe disparities in economic activity and income across spaces, typically between centres and peripheries, between urban and rural areas, and between regions with more or less useful resources. It often entails unequal access to services and knowledge, and discriminations and inequities in political influence. Spatial and regional divisions may interact with economic, political or ethnic divisions, and foster social and political protest.

Knowledge inequality – comprises the numerous factors influencing access to different sources and types of knowledge, as well as the consequences of these disparities, as was addressed in the International Social Science Council (ISSC) *World Social Science Report (WSSR) 2010: Knowledge Divides*. It also includes the question of whose knowledge counts and what types of knowledge are considered most important. Knowledge inequalities between individuals and groups affect the capacity to make informed decisions, to access services and to participate in political life. There is often a correlation with spatial inequality, whereby peripheries with lesser access to knowledge are also less known (subjects of fewer studies, with poorer data, and so on).

This conceptual framework is not rigid. There are overlaps between the definitions, and authors also offer their own interpretations. By drawing attention to and addressing these seven dimensions of inequality, this Report captures a large set of unequal dynamics, and the analysis contained within it reaches beyond that of many recent studies.

Justice and equality, opportunities and outcomes, and equity

The study of inequality in social science and philosophy has also embraced broader conceptual debates and ambiguities. Among them are the distinction between equality and justice, and equalities of opportunities and of outcomes. These terms are often used differently in different contexts and academic disciplines. Where economists tend to focus on equality of opportunity, equality of outcomes and equity, philosophers and political scientists tend to frame their discussions in terms of justice, equity and fairness.

Equality and justice. The question of equality refers to the distribution of resources within a particular social setting and to the meaning given to the resources and their distribution: both subjectively, from the perspective of individual agents, and socially, as a pattern that forms part of a collective understanding. Considerations of fairness, justice, equity and so on are part of the subjective dimension of equality, which has been highly variable historically within and between societies. Equality refers to three interlocking sets of issues: to what extent distribution matters; what is important in distributional terms; and how much inequality is tolerable for any given resource. A broadly egalitarian conception of social justice – as illustrated in Goal 16 of the SDG – is one that states that distribution matters, that all issues that bear on the realization of human rights matter in distributional terms, and that current levels of inequality are excessive.

Equality of opportunities and outcome. Equality of opportunity posits that all individuals should have equal chances according to their individual capacities, talents and merit, regardless of where they live, their socio-economic background, gender, origin, cultural identity and so on. Equality of outcome pertains to income, wealth, employment and learning achievements. Conceptually, the principle of equality of opportunity is simple. But defining it precisely and measuring it is much more difficult, as inequalities of opportunities can often only be detected by the outcomes they produce.

For many observers and analysts, aiming for equality of opportunity is not enough. Obstacles and practices may remain that prevent people from succeeding in life. For them, the goal must rather be equality of outcome, so that all those with similar talents and abilities – and the willingness to use them – are able to achieve equally in terms of learning achievements, health, income and so on, independently of their circumstances at birth. What should be developed are not policies focusing on equal access to services and opportunities, but policies to support those who were less advantaged to start with. This is done, for example, in policies of affirmative action. But the question still remains: what should be equalized? This depends on how equity is understood in each society. According to the prevailing understanding at a specific time and place, the accent will be placed on one or several dimensions, and the level of inequity deemed acceptable will differ.

There are longstanding debates on these terms and their meaning. This report engages with these long-running debates, leaving authors free to take their own positions on these definitions and their application, rather than imposing any single set of definitions.

Plurality of voices

The 2016 *WSSR* aims to be inclusive with regard to the multiplicity of disciplinary outlooks and approaches, the countries and regions observed and the voices represented. It brings together original works from a diverse mix of social scientists, practitioners, activists and other thought leaders with expertise on the issue of inequality. In commissioning authors for the Report, the editorial team sought to involve a wide range of social scientists from within and outside academia, and to involve stakeholders and activists, as well as voices that may be less frequently heard in academic debates on inequalities. It also brings together global social science expertise from across the disciplines. The *WSSR* counts amongst its contributors 107 social scientists, originating from some forty countries, from different disciplinary backgrounds, of whom 46 per cent are women. The diversity of perspectives represented here is arguably greater than in most reports on inequality.

Audiences

The Report was prepared with the following audiences in mind:

● Students and experts on inequalities, who will find an up-to-date review of influential approaches and data; an encompassing portrait of the state of inequalities worldwide through multidisciplinary insights from several countries and all world regions; and cutting-edge studies that are opening new fields for inequality research. Most articles are short, and designed to provide brief and compelling insights across a range of subjects related to inequality.

● Decision-takers, policy-makers and practitioners from developed and developing countries, who are increasingly concerned with rising inequalities. The Report highlights learnings about policy solutions and responses to inequality developed and implemented by different kinds of policy and civil society actors worldwide.

● Research councils and agencies organizing, financing and evaluating social science research everywhere. Here they will find a proposed research agenda for the next decade, allowing for comparisons of inequality research in their countries with the key areas and priorities for future research globally identified by the report authors.

● Civil society and all potential 'users' of social science knowledge, including non-governmental and similar organizations, the media and the general public. All are increasingly concerned with the consequences of inequalities. Here they will find studies exploring some of those consequences at different levels and in various parts of the world, as well as prospective essays about inequality's possible futures, and articles on strategies to achieve greater equality.

Preparation and structure of the Report

The 2016 *WSSR* was prepared by the ISSC and the Institute of Development Studies (IDS) under the guidance of a Scientific Advisory Committee (SAC) composed of renowned scholars who have written on inequality from different disciplinary backgrounds and come from all parts of the world. Most members of the SAC were nominated directly by their international disciplinary associations.

Discussions at the ISSC's Twenty-Ninth General Assembly, held in September 2013, resulted in agreement by ISSC members that the 2016 *WSSR* should focus on issues of inequality. As always when a new topic is decided by its members, the ISSC secretariat launched an international consultation and review process in collaboration with its members and partners, to define the specific contribution that we wish to make, to select issues to cover, and to start approaching potential contributors. An international expert meeting on 'Global justice, poverty, inequality and the post-2015 development agenda', co-organized with UNESCO in April 2014, provided some initial inputs and recommendations on the kind of specific contribution that a *WSSR* could make on the topics of inequality, poverty reduction and justice. To further this discussion, twenty internationally renowned social scientists were surveyed, and a review of the recent literature was conducted.

On the basis of these various inputs, an outline of potential issues was discussed at the first SAC meeting, which took place in January 2015 in Paris. At this meeting the SAC also recommended that the Report should analyse the multiple dimensions of inequalities, mobilize all social science disciplines, and cover all countries and world regions, as well as providing concrete examples of responses and solutions.

In May 2015 a grant agreement for research collaboration was signed between the ISSC and the IDS, whereby a team of IDS researchers and research leaders would become part of the team of Report directors. IDS, as a world-leading institution in development studies, with a large international network of researchers, was particularly suitable to help produce a global social science report on inequality. A first outline of the Report was developed jointly, and responsibilities for the different parts and chapters were shared between ISSC and IDS. The team started to approach authors and commission articles.

The 2015 World Social Science Forum on 'Transforming Global Relations for a Just World', co-organized with South Africa's Human Sciences Research Council (HSRC) and the Council for the Development of Social Science Research in Africa (CODESRIA), was held in September in Durban, South Africa. It brought together close to 1,100 participants from eighty-four countries. In conjunction with the Forum, the SAC held its second meeting with the editorial team.

Several Forum keynote speakers and presenters were invited to contribute to the Report, specifically from regions that were less represented among the Report's authors, and additional topics were included. Finally, the SAC approved the Report's key messages and conclusions as well as the proposed research agenda.

The editorial team had decided early on to keep the Report to book size, and to provide a mix of shorter and longer articles, with shorter boxes providing a snapshot of a particular issue or response. Several of the articles have been written by international and multidisciplinary teams of authors. As always, hard choices had to be made. In the end, the editorial team is confident that it has achieved a good balance of research excellence, disciplinary diversity, regional coverage and gender diversity.

Each article was reviewed internally by the editorial team, and typically by two external reviewers. The entire Report was reviewed by four external reviewers, from different disciplinary backgrounds and regions of the world.

Structure

The Report is divided into four parts and seven chapters. Parts I, II and III are introduced by a synthesis article, discussing key points made in the various contributions to the Report, in the light of current academic discussions and societal debates. Each chapter includes a number of articles and boxes, providing state-of-the-art inputs and detailing specific cases and methodological points.

Part I opens with a discussion of current trends in economic inequality around the world, and then enlarges its scope to consider the other intersecting dimensions of inequality (*Chapter 1*). It then focuses on particular regions and countries, to analyse some specific configurations of inequality's many dimensions, and how inequalities can be rooted in history and culture (*Chapter 2*). *Part II* discusses the consequences of inequality for economic growth, poverty, conflicts, sustainability and more generally our collective capacity to address global priorities, such as through the 2030 Agenda. It also addresses the consequences of intersecting inequalities on certain groups (*Chapter 3*).

A chapter is dedicated to articles about possible futures for inequality, on the basis of some trends observed today (*Chapter 4*). *Part III* moves the discussion on to consider various pathways toward greater equality. It presents some instances where changes in rules (such as public policies and legal mechanisms) have contributed to reducing inequality or halting rising inequality (*Chapter 5*), and to the outcomes of mobilizations for change (*Chapter 6*). On the basis of all these contributions, new gaps are identified and recommendations made for future international research on inequality (*Part IV*). A bibliometric analysis of the research outputs on inequality and social justice serves to identify the disciplines and countries that produce the most (*Part IV, Annex*). As in the 2010 and 2013 *WSSR*s, the Report concludes with an Annex comprising updated statistical data on the state of global social science knowledge production.

Bibliography

Crédit Suisse. 2015. *Global Wealth Report 2015.* https://publications.credit-suisse.com/tasks/render/file/?fileID=F2425415-DCA7-80B8-EAD989AF9341D47E (Accessed 9 June 2016.)

Oxfam. 2016. An Economy for the 1%, Briefing Paper 210, 18 January. *https://www.oxfam.org/sites/www.oxfam.org/files/file_attachments/bp210-economy-one-percent-tax-havens-180116-en_0.pdf* (Accessed 9 June 2016.)

Saez, E. 2014. Income and wealth inequality: evidence and policy implications. Neubauer Collegium Lecture, October 2014. *https://eml.berkeley.edu/~saez/lecture_saez_chicago14.pdf* (Accessed 9 May 2016.)

■ ***Françoise Caillods*** *(France) is ISSC senior adviser to the 2016 World Social Science Report.*

■ ***Mathieu Denis*** *(Canada) is executive director, ISSC.*

Introduction and key messages

2. Challenging inequalities: pathways to a just world. Key messages and main contributions

Melissa Leach, John Gaventa, Patricia Justino, Françoise Caillods and Mathieu Denis

---

'We pledge that no one will be left behind' Preamble to the 2030 Agenda for Sustainable Development

'Inequality is one of the key challenges of our time. … Ranking second in last year's Outlook, it was identified as the most significant trend of 2015 by our Network's experts'
World Economic Forum Outlook on the Global Agenda 2015

'Rising extreme inequality is a concern for us all' Winnie Byanyima, Oxfam International.

The issue of rising inequality and what to do about it looms large in the minds of governments, businesses, civil society leaders and citizens around the world. Reducing inequality is first and foremost a question of fairness and social justice. Addressing inequality is key to eradicating extreme poverty, fostering transformations to sustainability, promoting social progress, reducing conflict and violence, and developing inclusive governance. The next few years comprise a key moment in which social science must up its game to address and challenge inequality, in alliance with other actors who are already raising their voices. The time is now.

Key messages

- Economic and political power are increasingly concentrated in the hands of a small number of people. This can threaten growth, social cohesion and the health of democracies;
- Global economic inequality declined during the first decade of this century, largely due to the reduction of poverty in countries like China and India. This favourable trend could however be reversed if inequality within countries continues to increase;
- Reducing inequalities is a requirement for human rights and justice, and is essential for success in other global priority areas, such as environmental sustainability, conflict resolution and migrations;
- Inequalities should not be understood and addressed only in relation to income and wealth. They interact across seven key dimensions: economic, political, social, cultural, environmental, spatial and knowledge;
- In recent years, some countries have succeeded in reducing or at least halting rising inequalities. Simultaneous, integrated policy actions in different spheres are needed to tackle multiple inequalities, and there is no one-size-fits-all solution;
- Responses to inequality must recognize and address the specific historical legacies and the deep-rooted cultural practices that shape inequalities in different places;
- While reducing inequalities is important everywhere, a clear priority for action lies in the poorest countries of sub-Saharan Africa, where poverty will continue to be concentrated in the coming decades if inequalities remain as high as they are;
- Collective action by citizens is opening spaces for additional solutions to inequality that can inspire inclusive policy innovation;
- A step change towards a research agenda that is interdisciplinary, multiscale and globally inclusive is needed to accompany and inform pathways toward greater equality.

Main contributions

1. This Report argues that understanding and acting effectively upon inequality requires us to look beyond economic inequality. It highlights seven dimensions of inequality, their interactions and cumulative effects.

While much of the recent debate on inequality focuses on economic disparities of income and wealth, inequality is multidimensional in nature. This Report therefore speaks of multiple inequalities. It explores seven dimensions of inequality in particular: economic, political, environmental, social, cultural, spatial, and inequalities based on knowledge. These dimensions are rarely experienced in isolation. Rather they intersect, often in accumulating and self-reinforcing ways that produce a vicious cycle of inequality. Those at the bottom economically may also be those who have the least voice; the least access to quality education, health care, knowledge and information; are the most powerless in their own cultures and societies; and face the greatest barriers to challenging their own positions.

● In many countries, economic and political resources are concentrated in the hands of a small elite (see Medeiros on Brazil, 21), threatening the health of democracies (Byanyima, 67) and widening social and economic inequalities, especially when these inequalities are combined with autocratic and non-representative political systems (Hanieh, writing on the Arab region, 19);

● Inequalities in access to knowledge remain significant, and interact with other dimensions of inequality. In Nigeria, just 3 per cent of the poorest girls living in rural areas completed lower secondary school in 2013, compared with 17 per cent of the boys. In contrast, 95 per cent of the richest boys in urban areas completed lower secondary school (Antoninis, Delprato and Benevot, 10). Adesina (18) notes that although greater gender equality in education has been attained in Africa – the Gender Parity Index in primary education having increased from 0.85 to 0.93 between 1999 and 2011 – this improvement has not yet translated to greater equality in other domains;

● Life in the Anthropocene is creating new inequalities on environmental lines, and exacerbating existing inequalities in some settings. The development of markets for natural resources has increased poverty and inequality in certain places (Fincher, 13). Less equal societies have greater carbon emissions per dollar of GNP (Power, Wilkinson and Pickett, 37). Inequality and environmental unsustainability are deeply interlinked, so that tackling one without addressing the other is unlikely to succeed (Leach, 27; Narain, 29).

2. Shared and context-specific dynamics each play a role in creating, maintaining and reproducing inequalities in different regions and countries

Many drivers operating at different levels interact to create the current scale and shape of inequality that we observe in different regions and countries of the world. They include processes operating at the global level, such as financialization and changes in trade patterns, as well as the role of national regulations on environmental resources, health and education, and the reduction or absence of regulation. Within a country, inequalities are typically distributed unevenly between regions, and between urban, peri-urban and rural areas. History, culture and norms also affect the level and reproduction of inequalities. They often maintain and even reinforce social exclusion based on gender, race, class, caste, ethnicity, disability and other axes of difference.

● There was a fall in global inequality in the first decade of the 2000s, due to a decline in inequality between countries. However, this decline in global inequality might slow down, or possibly be reversed, if inequality within individual nations continues to increase (Bourguignon, 4). The reduction in income inequality between countries is largely the result of growth in China and India, which lifted large numbers of people out of poverty. However, inequality was not eradicated in either of these countries, and indeed, new inequalities were created there. Redistributive policies have contributed to reducing economic inequality significantly in some Latin America countries, yet with a limited effect at the global level. Levels of economic inequality remain consistently higher in developing countries than in developed countries, most notably in Africa and Latin America;

Introduction and key messages

● Inequalities and discriminations based on gender, such as gender violence, and constraints on voice and participation, continue to exist in every country and socio-economic group, cutting across all other forms of inequality. Men continue to comprise the majority of high earners and political elites. Even when formal rules guarantee a 'seat at the table' for women, informal rules may impede their participation in political debates and decision-making (Razavi, 14; Kabeer, 8; Mathie et al., 64; Nazneen, 51);

● Like other disadvantaged groups, minorities are less likely than others to earn a decent wage (Belser, 6). Ethno-racial discrimination, which can be internalized by indigenous groups, is leading to lower aspirations, lower educational achievements and eventually lower incomes than for non-indigenous groups. Despite a significant reduction in extreme poverty, the income gap between indigenous and non-indigenous people in Peru has not changed over ten years (Pasquier-Doumer, 34);

● While a century of democratization has made the USA more politically equal for black people and other minorities, the disparity in income between black and white households has been remarkably stable over the past forty years. Racial disparity remains significant in other domains, such as access to education, health and justice (Harris, 20).

● In Africa as elsewhere, control of and access to natural resources has for centuries underpinned social stratification and the production of inequalities (Murombedzi, 9; Olukoshi, 48);

● The increase of economic inequality in the period from 1998 to 2008 resulted primarily from the growth in incomes of the top 1 per cent, particularly in rich countries (Milanovic, 5). At the same time, globalization, deindustrialization and the polarization of the labour market in Western economies mean that the middle classes are experiencing a slow but consistent erosion of their standard of living (Chauvel and Hartung, 38).

3. Current levels of inequality threaten our capacity to address other global priorities

Inequalities matter, not just intrinsically as issues of fairness and social justice, but also because of their impact on other priority issues. In recent years, research has focused largely on economic inequality. Yet because of the connections between its many dimensions, inequality also engages issues of gender equity, future growth, poverty reduction, health, education, nutrition and environmental sustainability. Changes in inequality also have impacts on migration, peace-building and conflict resolution, and for building inclusive and accountable institutions. While the trends in economic and other inequalities are not uniform, the evidence presented in this Report suggests significant consequences in all these areas if current trends remain unchecked. Our collective capacity to achieve the Sustainable Development Goals (SDGs) is at stake. Unless addressed urgently, these inequalities will make the cross-cutting ambition of the SDGs to 'leave no one behind' by 2030 as an empty slogan.

● High and rising inequality can act as an impediment to economic growth, and dissipates the impact of growth on poverty reduction (Kanbur, 24);

● There is now a large body of evidence that health and social problems are worse in countries with higher income inequality. Health inequalities have grown in many countries, often intersecting with political inequalities. In Egypt, health inequalities have increased because of a combination of authoritarian politics, corruption, and brain drain of health workers (Bayoumi, 30);

● Inequalities can limit our ability to respond to crises. The effective management of the Ebola crisis was hindered by visible inequalities between local and expatriate medical staff, and between communities and elites, which undermined trust between them (Wilkinson and Brima, 31). In Lebanon, the arrival of large numbers of refugees from Syria has put an already-stretched infrastructure under further pressure, creating perceptions of unequal treatment, and increasing support among the local population for restrictive human rights policies (Harb, 26);

● There is a growing consensus that systemic inequality between identity groups may spur conflict, and evidence that countries with high levels of group-based inequalities are more likely to experience civil war (Østby, 25);

● Current affluent lifestyles depend upon an unsustainable use of fossil fuels and raw materials, and remain incompatible with the survival of ecosystems. Reducing inequalities requires using resources differently (Fleurbaey and Klasen, 40).

Table 2.1 **Policies identified by authors as having contributed to reducing or curbing inequalities in specific countries in specific time periods**

Policy type	Examples of policies and measures that contributed to reducing inequality in specific contexts and settings	Countries/regions where implemented	See article by
Macroeconomic policies	Investment in infrastructure	China	Li (15)
	Reduction of large balance of payments deficits and debt accumulation	Latin America	Cornia (46)
	Fiscal policy and better management of public spending leading to reduced budget deficit	Latin America	Cornia (46)
Providing quality education for all; investing in human capital	Increased public expenditure on education and massive increase in secondary education enrolment	Latin America	Cornia (46) Medeiros (21)
	Abolishing fees in public primary education; school feeding programmes	Sub-Saharan Africa	Adesina (18)
Regulating the marketplace and strengthening labour market institutions	Minimum wage policy	Latin America	Belser (6) Berg (44) Cornia (46) Medeiros (21)
	Reduction of the wage gap between skilled and unskilled labour (linked to massive investment in education) between urban and rural areas	Latin America China	Cornia (46) Li (15)
	Active role for labour market institutions (unions, collective bargaining)		Berg (44)
Fiscal redistribution mechanisms	Reforming tax rates to emphasize more progressive taxation, increasing revenue collection, and reducing exemptions for top incomes	Latin America	Cornia (46) Gómez et al. (47)
	Changing fiscal policy, with more progressive taxation of farmers in rural areas	China	Li (15)
Social protection policies	Conditional cash transfers	Brazil's Bolsa Familia, Mexico's Opportunidades	Roelen et al. (55) Cornia (46) Medeiros (21)
	Unconditional cash transfers	South Africa (Social Grant programme) China 'Dibao programme' (guaranteeing a minimum income for poor households)	Roelen et al. (55) Li (15)
	Social pension schemes	Latin America	Roelen et al. (55) Cornia (46)
	Rural pension scheme Rural social protection network and medical scheme	China	Li (15)
	Food security programme	Ethiopia (Productive Safety Net Programme)	Roelen et al. (55)
Anti-discrimination legislation	Civil Rights Acts and antidiscrimination laws	USA	Harris (20)
	Affirmative action in access to education, employment, political positions	Malaysia India USA	Roelen et al. (55) Stewart (7) Nazneen (51)
Improved governance	Clearly identified implementation agencies working as 'learning organizations'	Education programmes implemented by Pratham in the state of Bihar (India)	Woolcock (58)
	Improved accountability and transparency	Scandinavian countries as the model	Rothstein (59)
	Automatic exchange of financial accounts information to reduce tax evasion	Being implemented by OECD and G20	Moore (50) Deacon (45)

Note: The authors cited in this table discuss the limitations and unintended consequences of some of these policies (e.g. levels of minimum wage). Some also note the context-specificity of their application, including the difficulty of ending or changing these measures, even when they are no longer necessary or fulfilling their purpose. In addition, policies may have significant symbolic importance, yet have limited effects in substantially changing social practices (see Harris, 20, on anti-discrimination laws). Policies not yet implemented such as universal health coverage (Krech, 57), or not yet tested on a large scale, such as unconditional basic income (Wright, 56), are not included in the table.

In this table Latin America refers to Latin American countries with elected governments pursuing progressive policies.

Introduction and key messages

4. The Report reminds us that the future of inequality is unwritten. It details cases of changes in rules, and of initiatives at various levels, that are building a fairer world.

A central challenge is to understand how inequality futures could become 'equality' futures, and how action by governments, civil society, businesses and citizens can make a difference. This Report helps to widen the focus on inequality and its consequences to encompass greater equality and how it can be achieved, pointing to a number of transformative pathways which can help move us towards a fairer world.

We have several examples from around the world of rule-changing measures in trade and finance, taxation and asset distribution, work and employment, education, health care, social protection and housing that can contribute to reducing inequalities. *Table 2.1* presents policies which have been implemented recently in countries and regions that have undergone a reduction or stabilization of rising inequalities, mainly in Latin America and China. These countries have targeted several dimensions of inequalities by combining measures that nevertheless may have differed from one country to another. These countries also benefited from positive conditions including economic growth (which is often a prerequisite for governments to have the capacity to mount major new programmes), political stability, and a shared concern for rising inequalities.

The overall effectiveness of the measures adopted seems to depend on their coherence and coordination, the combination of policies with short-term impact (such as social protection and fiscal policy) and longer-term impact (such as education), and the regional and global conditions in which they are implemented. To remain effective, a policy mix developed in a specific context will require adaptation to the conditions of the country to which it is transferred. The social sciences should be prepared to assess the effectiveness of different policy approaches in addressing the complex and intersecting nature of inequality.

However, changes to policy and regulation are not the only responses to inequality. While the vicious circle of multiple inequalities can create a sense of powerlessness leading to inaction, it can also create its own response. There can be calls for transparency and accountability from powerful elites and institutions, demands for new policies and rights, and the growth of seeds and visions for new alternatives. Such efforts from below may start small, but they may multiply, spread and scale up to have large-scale impacts, especially when combined with rule changes and actions involving states and market actors. More significantly perhaps, they also set the discursive foundations for future struggles for equality and social justice.

- In India, Indonesia, Ethiopia and Brazil, local initiatives empower poor and vulnerable adults, especially women, to diversify their income sources and access microcredit. They are instrumental in the development of solidarity and self-help networks among the individuals concerned (Mathie et al., 64);

- Grass-roots mobilization and political action can often be effective in breaking down deeply connected economic, social and political inequalities (see Gaventa and Runciman, 12, on South Africa);

- Public participation can increase the political will to reduce inequality. A high level of public participation in Brazil's 'Zero Hunger' effort was crucial to the country's turnaround to reduced inequality (Green, 66);

- New alliances of stakeholders can build broad support for change. The mobilization of doctors, patient groups and political forces around the design of a Patient's Bill of Rights was a significant contributor to a new Health Insurance Law on universal coverage in Egypt (Bayoumi, 30);

- Pratham, a non-governmental organization (NGO) based in India, worked with local officials and schools to develop tailored pedagogical strategies for each child, and was successful in improving learning outcomes in Bihar, the poorest state in India (Woolcock, 58).

5. The Report proposes seven priority areas for a new global social science agenda on understanding and challenging inequalities; it also calls for a more transformative social science to achieve this

The level and consequences of the inequalities documented in this Report, by experts from across regions, methods and traditions, produce a clear demand for more research. They also call for greater collaboration and cross-fertilization between researchers, policy-makers and civil society actors to support change. There has been a fivefold increase in studies of inequality and social justice in academic publications since 1992. Numerous international reports and books on inequality have been published, some of them bestsellers. However, simply continuing with more and more specific studies, without developing robust theories of inequality and without rising to the larger challenges discussed above, will make only marginal contributions to our understanding. Furthermore, over 80 per cent of the publications on inequality are by researchers based in North America and Western Europe, an enduring and fundamental inequality in the production of knowledge about inequality that must itself be addressed.

The social science community, including its funders and supporters, can take the following actions:

Priority 1 – Increase support for knowledge production about inequality, and processes of social inclusion and exclusion, in those places most affected by them.

Priority 2 – Improve our ability to assess, measure and compare the dimensions of inequality over time and across the world.

Priority 3 – Deepen our understanding of diverse experiences of inequality.

Priority 4 – Deepen our understanding of how multiple inequalities are created, maintained and reproduced.

Priority 5 – Deepen our understanding of how local and global forms of inequality connect and interact.

Priority 6 – Promote research on how to move towards greater equality.

Priority 7 – Support cross-cutting syntheses and theory on inequality and equality.

The change needed should result in a truly global research agenda that is far more interdisciplinary, methodologically pluralistic, multiscaled and globally inclusive than we see today. It should contribute towards more equal and just futures. Moreover, there is a need for a transformative social science, one that treats inequality and equality not just as a matter for analysis, but also as a normative concern, seeking to inform struggles for social justice, and engaging with those in society positioned to bring about change.

■ **Melissa Leach** *(UK) is director of the Institute of Development Studies (IDS), Brighton, UK.*

■ **John Gaventa** *(UK/USA) is director of research at IDS, Brighton, UK.*

■ **Patricia Justino** *(Portugal) is a professorial fellow at IDS, UK.*

■ **Françoise Caillods** *(France) is ISSC senior adviser to the 2016 World Social Science Report.*

■ **Mathieu Denis** *(Canada) is executive director, ISSC.*

Part I

CURRENT TRENDS IN INEQUALITIES

Introduction

Chapter 1 ■ Inequalities: many intersecting dimensions

Chapter 2 ■ Inequalities in different parts of the world

Street artwork by iRG
(Berlin, Germany, 2015)
© Margie Savage

PART I · CURRENT TRENDS IN INEQUALITIES | Introduction | Drivers and dynamics of inequalities worldwide

3. Drivers and dynamics of inequalities worldwide (an introduction to Part I)

Patricia Justino and Bruno Martorano

Introduction

After decades of neglect, inequality is now firmly at the centre of research and policy agendas. This renewed interest is a response to increases in income and wealth inequality observed in a number of industrialized and developing countries (Milanovic, 5; Piketty, 2014; UNDP, 2013). In the USA, the top 1 per cent owns around 20 per cent of total national income and over 30 per cent of the country's wealth (Piketty, 2014). About 9 per cent of the world population receives one half of global income (Milanovic, 2011), while only sixty-two individuals own the same wealth as the bottom half of the world population (Oxfam, 2016) (*Figure 3.1*).

These overall trends mask important differences between countries. For instance, while the middle class in developed countries has experienced a continuous decline in relative living standards over the past decades, the middle class in emerging economies has benefited from global economic change (Milanovic, 5). Overall global inequality has decreased due to rapid economic growth in several African, Asian and Latin American countries, even though global inequalities are still dramatically high (Bourguignon, 4).

This Part of the report discusses the recent evolution of economic inequality around the world. It starts by summarizing recent trends and drivers of inequality in the 'old industrialized countries'. It then provides a brief analysis of recent patterns and trends in Africa, Asia and Latin America, regions that have not received enough attention in recent studies of inequality.

Yet inequality is not only a matter of income and wealth. *Part I* emphasizes the point that it has many intersecting dimensions, and discusses the challenges of measuring the aspects of inequality that intersect to produce and reproduce social, economic and political relations across space and time (Kabeer, 8). Seven key dimensions of inequality are introduced: economic, social, cultural, spatial, environmental, political and knowledge inequalities.

This Part of the report also offers the foundations for a further understanding of how inequalities are experienced across different sections of society (dealt with in more detail in *Part II*), and what policies and politics can be used to deal with inequalities (*Part III*).

Figure 3.1 **Wealth of bottom 50 per cent versus wealth of richest sixty-two people**

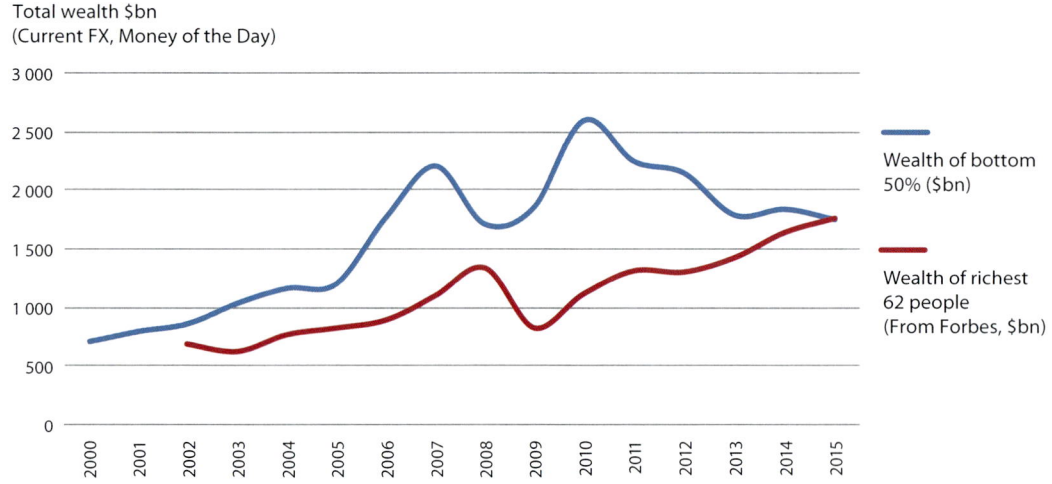

Source: Oxfam (2016).

Figure 3.2 **Income share of the top 1 per cent of earners**

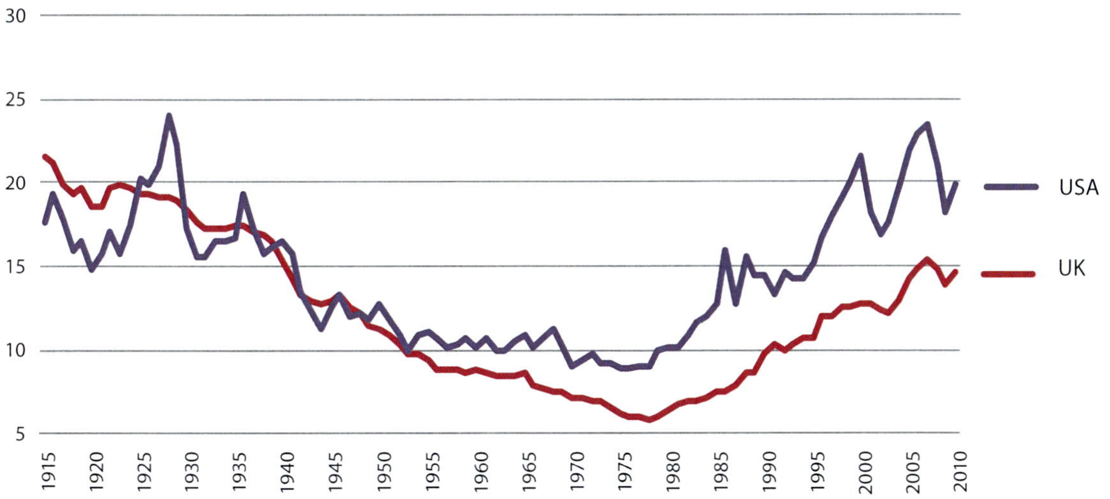

Source: Authors' elaboration on data available from Piketty (2014).

Current trends in economic inequality

Drivers of inequality vary considerably across countries and are context-specific. Inequality in the old industrial countries increased drastically in the later twentieth century, especially from around 1970 (Piketty, 2014; Stiglitz, 2013). Technological innovation increased wage disparities between skilled and unskilled workers, while deindustrialization and globalization led to shifts of employment out of factories and manufacturing. These processes weakened trade unions and exposed the labour force to wage competition from elsewhere in the world, through both the shift of industrial production to Asia and the increased scope for immigration into the old industrialized countries.

The financialization of the economy has resulted in growing economic inequalities. As Piketty (2014) has shown, the rate of return on capital has been higher than the rate of economic growth. Since capital is increasingly concentrated in the hands of few people, this process has contributed to the worsening of economic inequality in the last decades. The recent economic crisis has further shown that financial markets are beyond the control of many state governments. In particular, the lack of proper financial market regulation has been a source of economic instability, further fuelling economic inequalities (Galbraith, 2012).

The intensity and nature of these processes has varied between the old industrialized countries, and between regions within individual nations. Several of these processes have affected the UK and the USA most intensively, and these are the two countries in which recent increases in inequality have been especially marked (*Figure 3.2*).

The biggest uncertainty about the future of inequality in the 'old industrialized countries' lies in the effect of technological change on the demand for labour. Many jobs have been eliminated through recent changes in technology. These have generally been low-skilled jobs, and the effect on income distribution is likely to be negative. But labour-displacing technology is not in itself new, and it is still unclear whether the net effect of recent technological change on employment – once we take into account the ways in which it generates employment directly and indirectly – will be positive or negative.

What about Africa, Asia, Latin America and Eastern Europe? Some of the factors that explain the evolution of inequality in the old industrialized countries are valid too in other parts of the world. Notably, the adoption of new technologies has led in recent decades to a rise in the demand for skilled workers, pushing their wages up in those regions and widening inequality (see, for instance, Ghosh, 16). Trade liberalization introduced under the aegis of the Washington Consensus in many African and Latin American countries has also been a factor contributing to the increase of inequality, in contrast to early predictions of Heckscher–Ohlin theory.[1] In particular, free trade policies adopted since the 1980s have led to technological upgrading that has in turn caused growing wage disparities. In addition, the process of capital account liberalization fuelled increases in inequality and promoted economic instability (Griffith-Jones and Brett, 49). The dominance of neoliberal perspectives since the early 1980s has further reduced concerns about inequality. In many countries, redistribution has become a secondary goal for domestic policy in areas such as taxation, welfare and the labour market.

Overall, levels of inequality in wealth and income have been consistently higher in Africa, Asia and Latin America than in North America and Europe. There are two important reasons for this. First, the contemporary political and economic institutions of many developing countries were constructed under colonial rule in a context in which relatively small elites dominated their societies and economies, and accumulated wealth and power (Murombedzi, 9). Second, elites maintained their power to act as political and economic gatekeepers between their own populations and global institutions and markets in the post-colonial era, solidifying their power and maintaining social, economic and political inequalities.

The levels of inequality in Africa, Asia and Latin America are however the source of ongoing debate in the literature. For instance, UNDP (2013) reports that income inequality increased by 11 per cent in countries within these regions between 1990 and 2010. In contrast, Ravallion (2014) shows that inequality in these regions is lower now than it was thirty years ago, although he acknowledges high variations within and between different areas. The main reason behind these different conclusions is the use of different samples, depending on how different researchers deal with data limitations. Less data has been collected, and for fewer years, in Africa, Asia and Latin America than in the USA and Europe. This Report partly fills this gap, by providing recent evidence for selected countries.

Two important countries for this discussion are India and China. Both countries have experienced increases in inequality in recent years. The Gini coefficient in China rose by eleven points over the period 1985–2008 (Li, 15), although a decline of about two points in the subsequent six years could mark a turning point. Inequality in India has increased since the 1980s as a result of processes of internal and external economic liberalization. India's extraordinary economic performance in recent decades has generated only small amounts of decent work, leaving around half of the workforce employed in the low-productivity agriculture sector (which now accounts for less than 15 per cent of gross domestic product, GDP), in handicrafts and in low-remuneration services (Ghosh, 16).

Central and Eastern European countries have also experienced a dramatic increase in inequality after the transition to the market economy of the former Soviet bloc. For example, Russia has experienced a rise of almost twenty points in its Gini coefficient over the past twenty-five years. In 2014, nearly 10 per cent of the population in Russia received around 30 per cent of total national income, with the top 1 per cent owning around 70 per cent of all personal assets (Grigorieva, 17).

Trends in inequality have varied in sub-Saharan Africa (SSA) and Latin America. On average, inequality has decreased in SSA countries since the mid-1990s (*Figure 3.3*) (Adesina, 18), but with important variations across time and between countries: while inequality decreased in half of the region's countries, it rose or stabilized at high levels in the rest of the region.

In Latin America, almost all countries recorded a reduction of inequality in the first decade of the new century (*Figure 3.3*). For instance, the Gini coefficient decreased in Argentina and Brazil by around twelve points. Several factors have contributed to the reduction of inequality in Latin America. These include new macroeconomic policies (Cornia, 46), changes in the labour market such as increased minimum wages (Belser, 6), the introduction of progressive tax reforms, and the introduction of conditional cash transfers and social pensions. Yet these trends have reversed in recent years as a result of factors such as the recent economic crisis. After years of decline, inequality levels in Brazil have stabilized over the period 2006–13 (Medeiros, 21).

These differentiated regional and country trends account for contrasting trajectories of economic inequality at the global level. While inequality is increasing in the old industrialized countries, global inequality is decreasing, partially due to the good economic performance recorded by Latin American and SSA countries in the past fifteen years (Bourguignon, 4). The rapid economic growth experienced by two of the most unequal countries, China and India, has also contributed greatly to reductions in global inequality – what Bourguignon (2015) calls the 'paradox of inequality'.

According to Milanovic (5), three factors that emerge from recent global change are central to explaining future trends in inequality. These are the income growth of the top 1 per cent and the stagnation of the middle class in developed countries; the appearance of a new global middle class thanks to the rapid economic growth experienced by emerging countries; and the fact that SSA countries are still left behind, which calls for further efforts to continue reducing poverty there.

Figure 3.3 **Gini trends in sub-Saharan Africa and Latin America and the Caribbean, 1993–2011**

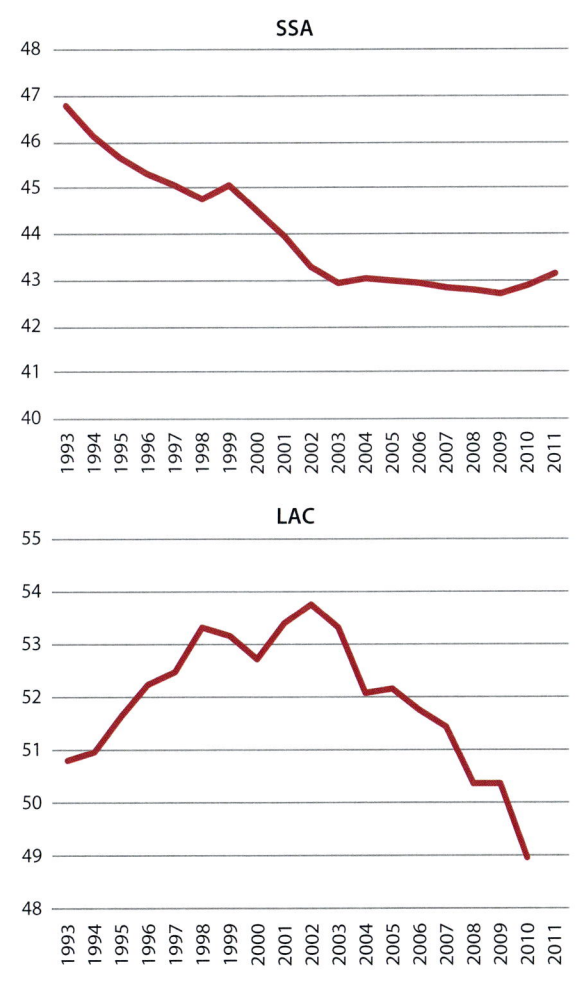

SSA = sub-Saharan Africa; LAC = Latin America and Caribbean.

Source: Cornia and Martorano (2012).

Beyond economic inequality

Inequalities can be measured vertically across all people in society, or between social groups. These latter 'horizontal inequalities' are often ignored in discussions of inequality, which tend to focus on differences between the 'rich' and the 'poor'. However, they have a considerable amount of relevance for social justice, political stability and economic development. Horizontal inequality refers to disparities between culturally defined or constructed groups with shared identities (Stewart, 7). Groups are usually defined according to ethnicity, gender, religion, language and other cultural or social identities, which may evolve across time and in different contexts. As argued in Kabeer (8), there may be several intersections and interactions between horizontal and vertical inequalities, and between different forms of inequality.

A growing number of studies have highlighted the crucial importance of social, cultural, spatial, environmental, political and knowledge inequalities. Social inequalities include differences across population groups in access to health and other services, as illustrated by the case of Egypt in Bayoumi's article (30). Circumstances at birth matter substantially for social inequalities experienced throughout life, particularly in terms of determining access to education for children born in deprived households (Antoninis et al., 10).

Lack of access to education also creates and perpetuates knowledge inequalities,[2] which today are also affected by disparities in access to new communications technologies. About 2 billion people – largely living in poorer countries or deprived areas – do not have access to basic mobile phones (Ramalingam and Hernandez, 11). Four billion people lacked access to the internet in 2015.[3]

All the multiple inequalities described above are closely related to spatial inequalities, as people living in different places (inner cities or remote rural areas, for instance) can experience different and sometimes unjust access to resources, opportunities and services not because of who they are, but because of where they live, as emphasized by Fincher (13). Environmental inequalities and the issue of access to natural resources further strengthen these intersecting patterns of deprivation and discrimination, as noted by Murombedzi (9).

Social, knowledge, cultural, spatial and economic inequalities in turn shape civic and political participation, thereby intersecting with forms of political inequality. Social and economic inequalities affect the capacity of people at the bottom of the distributions to mobilize, weaken group-level cooperation and coordination, hamper their capacity to engage in social and political decision-making processes, and reduce their trust in institutions (Gaventa and Runciman, 12). Socially excluded groups are usually poorer and less engaged in social and political activities, but they also face additional forms of discrimination as a result of their identity. Exclusion along gender lines resulting from formal rules, social norms and informal practices (Razavi, 14) is an important case in point.

Gender inequality intersects with and may be compounded by other dimensions of inequality. For instance, access to educational or health services is more problematic for indigenous women living in rural areas in Latin American countries than for white men living in urban areas in the same region. Wage discrimination against women is also common in many parts of the world. Young women in particular face many difficulties in finding jobs in the Arab region, where economic and political life is still dominated by men and elders (Hanieh, 19). Formal rules, social norms and informal practices are considered the most powerful driver for gender inequality in African countries (Adesina, 18). In India, rapid economic growth has been associated with an increase in gender disparities (Ghosh, 16). Racial inequality in the USA is another interesting case. Although there have been legislative interventions and efforts to modify anti-black attitudes, racial inequality is still an important variable shaping a variety of inequalities across the USA (Harris, 20). Invisible practices operating in different institutional domains (e.g. education, criminal justice, consumer markets, employment and housing) perpetuate racial inequality, for example in employment opportunities and income.

The challenges of measuring intersecting and multidimensional inequalities

The discussion above highlights two important points. First, inequality is not only an economic issue: it is also multidimensional. Second, forms of inequality intersect. Multidimensional, intersecting inequalities call for collaboration between different disciplines to understand their causes and implications, and to develop the possible solutions needed to challenge them.

Our knowledge about inequality across the social sciences is very much shaped by our ability to measure inequality across countries, within countries, among and across different population groups, and across time. The availability of information and high-quality data on different forms of inequality is therefore a key goal in tackling inequality.

The literature on the measurement of inequality is vast, and has changed considerably through time (Atkinson and Bourguignon, 2015). Most measurements of global and national-level inequality (whether on income or other underlying variables) have been based either on household surveys or on administrative data such as censuses and national accounts. Some of these data have suffered from limitations, well documented in the literature (Atkinson and Bourguignon, 2015), notably in terms of historical perspective and the under-representation of top incomes and wealth. Recent work by Atkinson and colleagues (2011) has sought to address some of these limitations. Piketty's book *Capital in the Twenty-First Century* (2014) in particular has brought this work to the forefront of academic and policy discussions and the public arena.

This body of research has led to significant new advances in our understanding of trends and determinants of inequality. In particular, it has led to substantial advances in inequality measurement by making use of previously unused (and often inaccessible) data on tax returns. In this Report, Medeiros (21) combines tax and survey data to show how the Gini coefficient in Brazil during the 2006–12 period was higher than that reported by other empirical results based on survey data (López-Calva and Lustig, 2010).

Tax data has important advantages over household survey-based data in that it provides arguably more accurate – although still incomplete – information about the incomes of very wealthy people.

A new strand of the literature has started to examine the importance of perceptions of inequality, arguing that these may matter more for a variety of outcomes and decision-making processes than actual levels of inequality. Some emerging studies have shown that judgements about levels of inequality rarely match real levels of inequality (Gimpelson and Treisman, 2015; McLennan, 32).

Finally, given the multidimensional and intersectional nature of inequality, we cannot focus only on one indicator or dimension of inequality. Rather, inequality must be monitored across the full spectrum of factors that contribute to human well-being. A substantial body of research has developed theoretical frameworks for the measurement of multidimensional inequality (Kolm, 1977; Atkinson and Bourguignon, 1982). Thanks to the availability of new data – including household-level data – there is now growing interest in the construction of multidimensional indicators (Aaberge and Brandolini, 2015). Yet the theoretical literature, and in particular its empirical application, are still very much work in progress. Real challenges remain for continued advances in understanding inequality within the social sciences.

Notes

1 According to Heckscher–Ohlin theory (and in particular the Stolper–Samuelson corollary), trade promotes the equalization of the remuneration of production factors, leading in the case of developing countries to an increase of unskilled labour wages.

2 See ISSC and UNESCO (2010).

3 The theme of knowledge inequalities will be developed further in *Part IV*.

Bibliography

Aaberge, R. and Brandolini, A. 2015. Multidimensional poverty and inequality. A. B. Atkinson and F. Bourguignon (eds), *Handbook of Income Distribution*, Vol. 2. Amsterdam, Elsevier.

Atkinson, A. B. and Bourguignon, F. 1982. The comparison of multi-dimensioned distributions of economic status. *Review of Economic Studies,* Vol. 49, pp. 183–201.

Atkinson, A. B. and Bourguignon, F. (eds). 2015. *Handbook of Income Distribution*, Vol. 2. Amsterdam, Elsevier.

Atkinson, A. B., Piketty, T. and Saez, E. 2011. Top incomes in the long run of history. *Journal of Economic Literature,* Vol. 49, pp. 3–71.

Bourguignon, F. 2015. *The Globalization of Inequality*. Princeton, N.J., Princeton University Press.

Cornia, G. A. and Martorano, B. 2012. *Development Policies and Income Inequality in Selected Developing Regions, 1980–2010*. Discussion Paper 210. Geneva, UN Conference on Trade and Development (UNCTAD).

Galbraith, J. K. 2012. *Inequality and Instability*. Oxford, Oxford University Press.

Gimpelson, V. and Treisman, D. 2015. *Misperceiving Inequality*. NBER Working Paper 21174. Cambridge, Mass., National Bureau of Economic Research (NBER).

ISSC and UNESCO. 2010. *World Social Science Report 2010: Knowledge Divides.* Paris, UNESCO.

Kabeer, N. 2000. *The Power to Choose. Bangladeshi Women and Labour Market Decisions in London and Dhaka*. London and New York, Verso.

Kolm, S. C. 1977. Multidimensional egalitarianisms. *Quarterly Journal of Economics*, Vol. 91, No. 1, pp. 1–13.

López-Calva, L. and Lustig, N. 2010. *Declining Inequality in Latin America: A Decade of Progress?* Washington DC, Brookings Institution Press.

Milanovic, B. 2011. *The Haves and Have-Nots: A Brief and Idiosyncratic History of Global Inequality*. New York, Basic Books.

Oxfam. 2016. *An Economy for the 1%: How Privilege and Power in the Economy Drive Extreme Inequality and How this can be Stopped*. Briefing Paper 210. Oxford, Oxfam.

Piketty, T. 2014. *Capital in the Twenty-First Century* (trans. A. Goldhammer from the French). Cambridge, Mass., Harvard University Press. (Originally published 2013.)

Ravallion, M. 2014. Income inequality in the developing world. *Science*, Vol. 344, No. 6186, pp. 851–55.

Stiglitz, J. 2013. *The Price of Inequality*. London, Penguin.

UNDP (UN Development Programme). 2013. *Humanity Divided: Confronting Inequality in Developing Countries*. New York, UNDP.

■ **Patricia Justino** *(Portugal) is a professorial fellow at the Institute of Development Studies (IDS), UK. She is a development economist specializing in applied microeconomics. Her research focuses on the impact of violence and conflict on household welfare and local institutional structures, the measurement of multidimensional inequality and poverty and their effects on social development and economic growth, the measurement and modelling of poverty, and the role of redistribution and welfare policies on economic growth and household welfare. Patricia convenes the Conflict and Violence cluster at the IDS.*

■ **Bruno Martorano** *(Italy) holds a PhD in development economics from the University of Florence. He is currently based at the Institute of Development Studies (IDS) as ISSC-IDS Report Fellow, in charge of co-coordinating the preparation of this Report; and a research associate at Consortium pour la recherche économique et sociale (CRES) in Dakar, Senegal. Prior to this, Bruno worked at the UNICEF Office of Research in Florence and the University of Florence, and has held consultancies for the University of North Carolina at Chapel Hill, UNCTAD, UNU-WIDER and the World Bank. His research interests lie in the fields of development economics, fiscal policy, taxation, social protection, poverty and inequality.*

Chapter 1

Inequalities: many intersecting dimensions

4. **Global versus national inequality**
   François Bourguignon

5. **Global inequality and the middle classes**
   Branko Milanovic

6. **Wage and income inequality**
   Patrick Belser

7. **Horizontal inequalities**
   Frances Stewart

8. **'Leaving no one behind': the challenge of intersecting inequalities**
   Naila Kabeer

9. **Inequality and natural resources in Africa**
   James C. Murombedzi

10. **Inequality in education: the challenge of measurement**
    Manos Antoninis, Marcos Delprato and Aaron Benavot

11. **POSTCARD • The multiple forms of digital inequality**
    Ben Ramalingam and Kevin Hernandez

12. **Untangling economic and political inequality: the case of South Africa**
    John Gaventa and Carin Runciman

13. **Grounding justice and injustice**
    Ruth Fincher

14. **Rising economic inequality and gender inequality: intersecting spheres of injustice**
    Shahra Razavi

4. Global versus national inequality

François Bourguignon

This contribution analyses the evolution of the global inequality of individual living standards, and discusses whether the fall of global inequality witnessed over the past decades, largely based on a decline of inequality between countries, is likely to be permanent or temporary, in view of the opposite evolution in a number of countries.

The concept of the global inequality of living standards that is so often heard in international circles is ambiguous. Sometimes it refers to inequality between the nations of the globe, and at other times to inequality within nations. Yet such an expression should clearly relate to the whole human population as a single community – rich Americans, poor Ethiopians or middle-class Brazilians alike.

But why should global inequality be studied? Don't people tend to compare themselves with people close to them and with whom they share characteristics, in particular their geographical location, citizenship and major societal values, rather than with people living on the other side of the planet? There is a national and possibly local component to the way people feel about inequality.

If global inequality may not be a big concern to the citizens of a specific country, it matters as soon as we adopt global values. The Millennium Declaration of the United Nations, which launched the Millennium Development Goals (MDGs) fifteen years ago, started with the following sentences (my emphasis):

> We, heads of State and Government, have gathered at United Nations Headquarters in New York, at the dawn of a new millennium, to reaffirm our faith in the Organization and its Charter as indispensable foundations of a more peaceful, prosperous and **just** world. We recognize that, in addition to our separate responsibilities to our individual societies, we have a collective responsibility to uphold the principles of human dignity, **equality and equity at the global level**.

The resolution of the United Nations that launched the Sustainable Development Goals (SDGs) as the successor of the MDGs in September 2015 reaffirmed this commitment to improved global equality.

In that context, this article analyses the evolution of the global inequality of individual living standards of recent decades. It stresses several important facts. First, global inequality is much higher than the level of inequality most commonly observed in individual countries. This is to be expected, as global inequality combines the average inequality within countries, for example between poor and rich Americans, and the average inequality between countries, for example between the average American and the average Vietnamese person. Second, global inequality has substantially declined since the turn of the millennium, possibly marking a dramatic reversal of historical trends. Third, this reversal appears to be essentially due to lower inequality between countries, rather than to lower average inequality within them. Fourth, however, it is also true that the available statistics contradict this generally accepted view and suggest that inequality within nations has tended to increase without neutralizing the overall fall in global inequality. As there are reasons to believe that this rise in within-country inequality is underestimated, it is quite possible that the lower global inequality is less pronounced than it appears. If so, we would be witnessing a partial substitution of inequality within countries for the inequality between countries, which is a concerning perspective.

This contribution begins by outlining the way global inequality is measured. The analysis then focuses on the level and evolution of global inequality over the past two decades and its decomposition into between-country and within-country inequality, going over the four preceding points. It will also allude to globalization as a possible major cause of these changes in global and national inequality, before some concluding comments.

Difficulties in measuring global inequality

Global inequality is estimated by merging household survey samples regularly taken in individual countries, in order to estimate the distribution of living standards in that population. In this way, a sample of the global population is obtained that can be used to estimate inequality among world citizens. In some countries, surveys are unavailable or unreliable, which means there is less than full coverage of the world population, but most available estimates cover more than 95 per cent of it.

Problems arise when trying to compare national survey data. Three issues are particularly important. First, standards of living in national surveys are reported in the local currency and need to be converted to a common currency, say the US dollar. But a US dollar converted to currencies such as rupees or pesos at the official exchange rate does not buy the same quantity of goods in New York, Delhi or Mexico City. 'Purchasing power parities' (PPP) obtained from an international price comparison programme are used to make that correction, but disparities among household consumption baskets are ignored, as is the consequent inequality in the comparison between them.

Second, individual standards of living are not measured in the same way across countries. Some countries use household disposable income, while others use consumption expenditure; some divide the corresponding amounts by the size of households to approximate individual living standards, while others adjust the amount for the composition of the household. Rough approximations are needed to make national data more or less homogeneous, but the results are far from perfect.

Third, there are differences in the coverage of national surveys. When comparing surveys with national accounts, a sizeable gap generally appears in the total income or consumption expenditure recorded in surveys. It is generally the case that property income is underreported and/or that wealthy people are undersampled. It is therefore most likely that surveys tend to underestimate the actual degree of inequality and that the degree of underestimation varies between countries.

One way of reducing heterogeneity across countries is to proportionally scale up all personal income or consumption figures in national surveys in order to fit the aggregate amounts reported in national accounts, and to keep the survey distributions unchanged. Such a normalization of something as arbitrary as national accounts may not be more precise than household surveys, and often relies on income or consumption definitions that cannot fully be compared with surveys.

Although somewhat technical, these remarks about the disparities in measuring individual living standards across countries, and of missing income and people in household surveys, are important. They make it clear that estimates of global inequality may vary among authors, depending on the choices they have made to ensure maximum comparability across countries, and point to a negative bias in the estimation of both national and global inequality.

Various estimates of shifts in global inequality over recent decades are available in the literature (e.g. Anand and Segal, 2014; Bourguignon, 2015; Lakner and Milanovic, 2015). They essentially differ in the databases that are used, as various sources may be available for the same country, and in corrections applied to the original data aimed at making them as comparable as possible across countries, for instance through normalizing them to national accounts. Fortunately, they paint a uniform picture.

Figure 4.1 shows the movements in global inequality between the late 1980s and the late 2000s, as obtained from averaging and interpolating three recent sets of estimates. Global inequality is measured by the Gini coefficient. This most frequently used measure of inequality varies between 0 (no inequality) and 1. Actually, it currently ranges from between 0.25 and 0.30 in continental Europe to slightly below 0.40 in the USA and slightly above 0.60 for the most inegalitarian countries in the world, for example South Africa.

As expected, the Gini coefficient of global inequality is even higher, being above 0.70 at the beginning of the period under review, a level rarely witnessed at the country scale. The most noticeable feature of the chart is the fall in global inequality over the past two decades, mostly during the 2000s. This is substantial, as it amounts to 3 or 4 percentage points depending on whether we scale national household survey data by national accounts. The other remarkable aspect is that this fall occurs after a roughly continuous rise that lasted from the industrial revolution in the early nineteenth century in Europe until the last quarter of the twentieth century (Bourguignon and Morrisson, 2002).

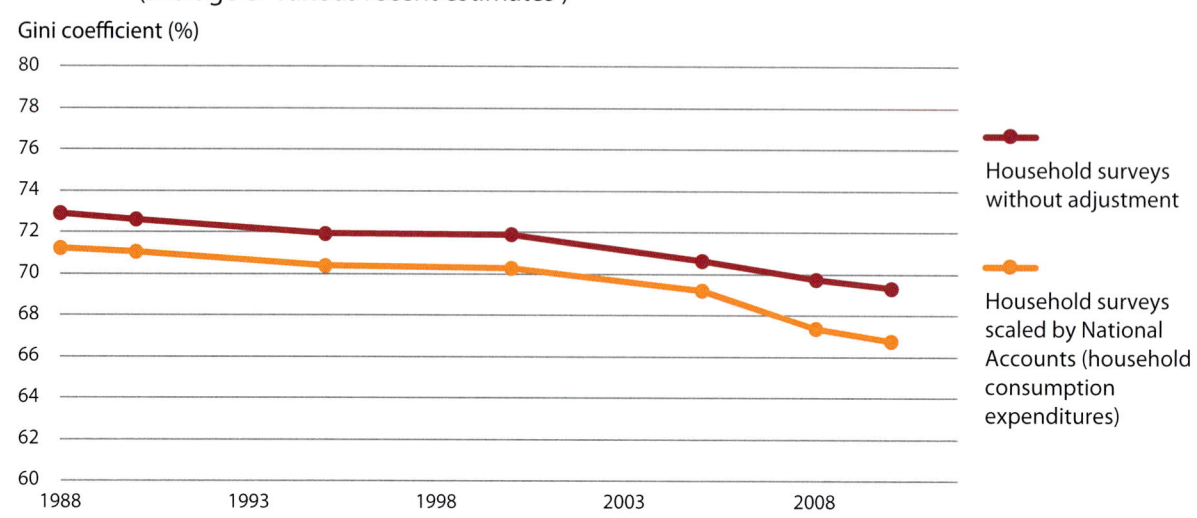

Figure 4.1 **The evolution of global inequality of living standards from 1988 to 2010**
(average of various recent estimates*)

Gini coefficient (%)

— Household surveys without adjustment
— Household surveys scaled by National Accounts (household consumption expenditures)

* Averaging requires interpolation across estimation years in various cases. Only the last two references provide estimates after 2008.

Sources: Anand and Segal (2014), Bourguignon (2015), Lakner and Milanovic (2015).

A decomposition of this downward shift in global inequality shows that it essentially comes from a decline in inequality between countries. In contrast, the inequality within countries increases slightly over the period.

The asymmetry between these two components of global inequality is easily understood. The dominant factor in the fall in inequality between nations is the dramatic catching-up process between the developed and the developing world over the past twenty to thirty years. The outstanding growth performance of China and India played a major role. However, it is quite remarkable that the accelerated fall of inequality in the 2000s is to a large extent due to better growth performances in other developing regions, for example sub-Saharan Africa and Latin America.

The roots of the increase of the within-country component of global inequality are in the rise of inequality observed in several countries with a significant weight in the global economy: the USA in the first place, but also China and India, and to a lesser extent several European countries. On the basis of the available estimates, this effect pales in comparison with the decrease in between-country inequality.

A first key question about this evidence is whether we are indeed witnessing a historic trend reversal, or whether the decline in global inequality will be temporary.

Looking at the giant Asian emerging countries, China and India, there are reasons to believe that this change will be permanent. Both will most likely continue to catch up with developed countries thanks to the growth potential of their huge domestic market. Things are less clear for smaller countries, whose development relies primarily on commodity exports. World commodity prices may be low for some time and growth perspectives may be much less favourable for these countries than in the first decade of this century. A prudent forecast is that global inequality may indeed keep declining in the coming decades, but at the slow pace of the 1990s rather than the high speed of the 2000s.

A second important question concerns the issue of underestimating top incomes, and therefore national inequality, in household surveys. Tax data sources in developed countries suggest that top earners are underrepresented in income surveys, and the rising share of the top 1 per cent observed in such data over the last twenty years or so in several countries has attracted a lot of public attention (e.g. Atkinson and Piketty, 2010).

As no comparable change was observed in the household surveys, it may be that standard survey data underestimate the rise in inequality in a number of countries. By ignoring top incomes, the preceding estimates would tend to overestimate the fall in global inequality. In one of the papers cited above, a simulation was undertaken where the observed gap between the mean income or consumption expenditure per capita in household surveys and in national accounts was ascribed to underreporting of the top income decile in each country in the global sample. This correction leads to global inequality estimates that are higher than in the preceding chart, and to a less steep fall at the end of the period.[1]

This possible overestimation of the size of the fall in global inequality because of the likely imprecision of survey data raises an important issue: the possibility that a partial substitution is taking place between the within-nation and between-nation components of global inequality. The underestimation of national inequality, and the possible recent rise in this form of inequality, do not affect the conclusion that the inequality between countries has fallen substantially over recent decades. But it does suggest that the increase in within-country inequality might not be as minor as it appeared to be in available estimates, and might partly compensate for the fall due to between-country inequality. In other words, part of the inequality between the rich average American and the poor average Chinese person would be replaced by an increasing inequality between rich and poor Americans and between rich and poor Chinese people. Some inequality between countries would thus be transferred to national inequality, and this is a concerning perspective if such a process persists.

Globalization might be the main mechanism for this substitution, as it has facilitated the catching-up of Asian emerging countries with the developed countries at the same time as it has tilted the functional distribution of income in favour of capital and against labour in most countries. Of course there are many other reasons why inequality may have increased throughout nations, including technical change in favour of skilled labour and, in a number of countries, a shift towards liberal policies, even though those two factors may not always be independent from the globalization process itself.

At this stage, the magnitude of the substitution of between-country by within-country inequality is quite uncertain, and it must be viewed more as a hypothesis to be investigated than as a fact. Even under rather extreme assumptions to correct survey data for missing top incomes, the substitution is incomplete and global inequality keeps falling.

Concluding comments

To conclude this short review of global inequality issues in our globalizing world, three basic points may be stressed.

First, in line with objectives to which the global community has repeatedly committed, it is essential that the inequality in individual living standards across countries keeps falling. From that perspective, the priority for global poverty action now clearly lies in sub-Saharan Africa, where global poverty will tend to concentrate in the coming decades.

Second, to keep global inequality falling, national inequality must be prevented from rising and must be cut down in countries where it is high. Failure to do so in major economies could endanger not only their functioning and efficiency, but also the positive aspects of globalization, by increasing resistance to further progress by those who are hurt by it.

Third, there is the issue of whether global inequality can be further reduced without increasing national inequality, contrary to what may have happened in recent decades. In theory, both objectives can be pursued independently through policies aimed at controlling national levels of inequality. Redistribution is essential, but redistributive instruments seem to be impaired by the enhanced mobility of capital and income associated with globalization. From that point of view, international agreements such as the recent G20 one about the transparency of bank accounts held by non-residents, and the operations of multinationals, are encouraging initiatives that may help countries to recover some autonomy in this key policy area.

Note

1. Lakner and Milanovic (2015) p. 25. Anand and Segal (2014) reach analogous results with another type of correction for underrepresented top incomes.

Bibliography

Anand, D. and Segal, P. 2014. The global distribution of income. A. Atkinson and F. Bourguignon (eds), *Handbook of Income Distribution*, Vol. 2. Amsterdam, Elsevier, pp. 937–79.

Atkinson, A. and Piketty, T. (eds). 2010. *Top Incomes: A Global Perspective*. Oxford and New York, Oxford University Press.

Bourguignon, F. 2015. *The Globalization of Inequality*, Princeton, N.J., Princeton University Press.

Bourguignon, F. and Morrisson, C. 2002. Inequality among world citizens: 1820–1992. *American Economic Review*, Vol. 92, No. 4, pp. 727–44.

Lakner, C. and Milanovic, B. 2015. Global income distribution: from the fall of the Berlin Wall to the Great Recession. *World Bank Economic Review*. http://wber.oxfordjournals.org/content/early/2015/08/12/wber.lhv039 (Accessed 9 June 2016.)

■ ***François Bourguignon*** *(France) is professor of economics and emeritus chair at the Paris School of Economics, France. He is a former World Bank chief economist and senior vice-president. He was director of studies in the Ecole des hautes études en sciences sociales (EHESS). He has written widely on issues of poverty and income distribution and on the globalization of inequality.*

5. Global inequality and the middle classes

Branko Milanovic

This short contribution reports on trends of global income distribution between 1988 and 2008.

In recent years, a growing number of works have focused on the evolution of inequality within specific countries. This article investigates the evolution of inequality from a different perspective, the trend of global income distribution between 1988 and 2008 as shown in *Figure 5.1*.

Figure 5.1 provides a number of interesting insights. First of all, top incomes have risen both in relative and absolute terms over the period 1988–2008. This result is consistent with recent studies reporting evidence that the increase of inequality has been driven by the income growth of the top 1 per cent, especially in rich countries. Second, *Figure 5.1* shows the poor performance of income at the bottom of the global income distribution. This group mainly comprises people living in sub-Saharan Africa. *Figure 5.2* shows that in fourteen countries, more than one-third of the population occupies the bottom decile of the global distribution.

The most significant case is the Democratic Republic of the Congo, where this figure reaches 86 per cent (*Figure 5.2*).

Third, *Figure 5.1* shows that income in the middle of the global distribution performed better than in other areas. This group essentially comprises the Chinese, or more broadly Asian, middle classes, who have experienced massive improvements in living standards. Yet many have incomes just above the global poverty line, and a significant economic slowdown could mean that many of them slip back into poverty. Lastly, upper middle-class incomes (around the eightieth and ninetieth global percentiles) remained stagnant or recorded the lowest growth rate (*Figure 5.1*). This group is composed of the lower middle classes living in Western economies, who have experienced a clear stagnation of their incomes in recent decades.

Figure 5.1 **Variation of real income across different percentiles of global income distribution, 1988–2008**

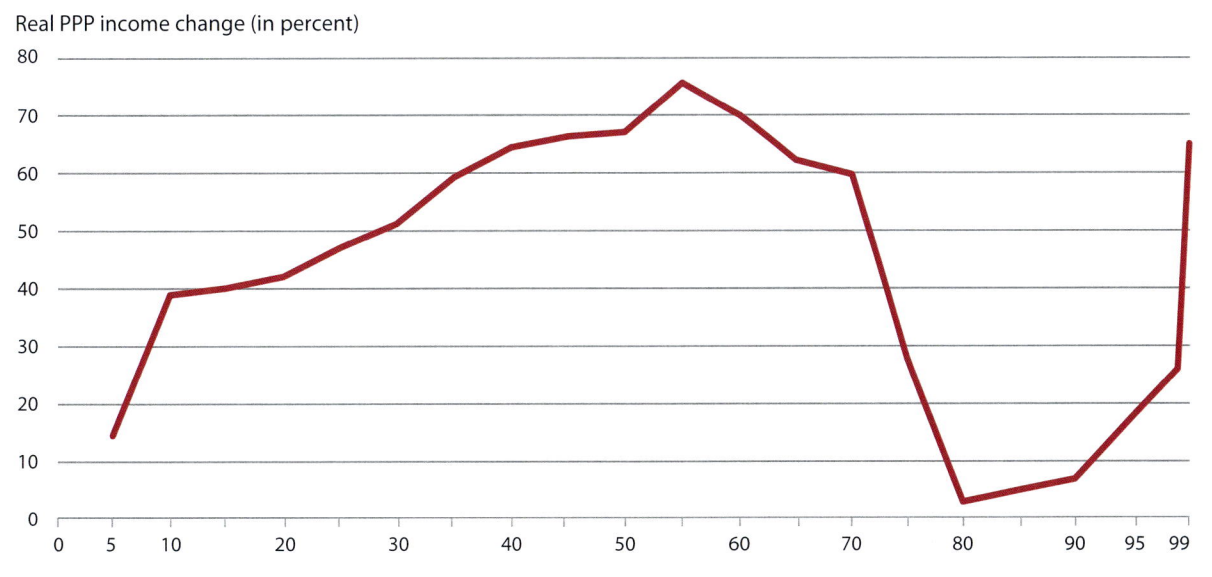

Source: Lakner and Milanovic (2015). Reprinted from Christoph Lakner and Branko Milanovic. Global Income Distribution: From the Fall of the Berlin Wall to the Great Recession. World Bank Econ Rev (2016) 30 (2): 203-232 doi:10.1093/wber/lhv039, by permission of Oxford University Press on behalf of the World Bank. This image/content is not covered by the terms of the Creative Commons licence of this publication. For permission to reuse, please contact the rights holder.

Figure 5.2 **Countries with more than 30 per cent of their population in the bottom global decile (below $PPP 450 per capita at 2008 prices)**

Country	%
Mali	36
Ghana	40
Guinea	42
Niger	45
Liberia	46
Mozambique	47
Nigeria	49
Central African Republic	50
Kenya	50
Tanzania	50
Swaziland	60
Côte d'Ivoire	72
Madagascar	80
Congo, Dem. Rep.	86

Source: Author's own calculations.

Overall, we can extract two main results. First, globalization has generated winners and losers. While top incomes as well as the middle class in emerging economies have benefited disproportionally from these conditions, most African countries have been left behind. The second result refers to the political consequences of globalization in Western economies; the lower middle or middle class is observing a slow but continuous decline in relative living standards. The increasing gap between the highest incomes in the rich countries and the stagnant incomes of the middle class in those same countries could fuel discontent and social tension in the 'rich' world which would translate into politically explosive resentment.

As a result, there are two dangerous phenomena at the national level. One is populism and the other is plutocracy. Populism refers to an ideology supporting the power of the people against the 'corrupt' elite. In the real world, however, populist governments use policies to appeal to the masses more than to pursue people's interests. Plutocracy refers to a society controlled by a few, and in particular by the richest. While in the first case the process of globalization could be rolled back with negative consequences for emerging economies (and in particular for the new middle class), the most important cost in the second scenario is the end of democracy in rich countries, even in a context of an open economy.

Bibliography

Lakner, C. and Milanovic, B. 2015. Global income distribution: from the fall of the Berlin Wall to the Great Recession. *World Bank Economic Review*. http://wber.oxfordjournals.org/content/early/2015/08/12/wber.lhv039.abstract (Accessed 9 June 2016.)

■ **Branko Milanovic** *(Serbia) is presidential professor at the Graduate Center, City University New York and senior fellow at Luxembourg Income Study. He was lead economist in the World Bank Research Department for almost twenty years and senior associate at the Carnegie Endowment for International Peace, Washington DC.*

6. Wage and income inequality

Patrick Belser

A recent International Labour Organization (ILO) report found that changes in the distribution of wages and paid employment are key factors behind recent inequality trends in both developed and developing countries.

What role have labour markets had in shaping recent trends in household income inequality? This question is little discussed in the literature on the topic. But a recent International Labour Organization (ILO) report, excerpted below, shows that changes in the distribution of wages and paid employment have been key factors behind recent inequality trends in both developed and developing countries.

The report highlights a number of major trends concerning wages, with important consequences for the evolution of income inequality between and within countries. It argues that in many countries, inequality starts in the labour market. This is because wages are a major source of household income, particularly in developed, but also in developing, economies.

Global trends in wages

Changes in wages and paid employment throw some light on recent trends in inequality between countries. Global wage growth in recent years has been mainly driven by developing economies, where real wages have been rising since 2007, in some cases very rapidly. In 2013 real wage growth reached 6 per cent in Asia and nearly 6 per cent in Eastern Europe and Central Asia, but was less than 1 per cent in Latin America and Africa. China accounted for much of the global wage growth, due to both the high rate of real wage growth and its size.

In developed countries, on the other hand, real wages have not increased very much since the financial crisis, rising particularly slowly in 2012 and 2013. As a result, average wages in developing economies are slowly converging toward those in developed economies, even though they remain considerably lower.

Trends in income within countries

Within countries, income inequality is much higher in developing economies than in developed ones. Yet over the period 2006–10 overall inequalities increased very fast in some developed countries. This was mainly owing to a combination of job losses and increasing wage disparities. In Spain and the USA, the two countries where inequality increased most, job losses and changes in the distribution of wages accounted for 90 per cent of the increase in inequality in Spain and 140 per cent of the increase in the USA – meaning that in Spain inequality was further increased by changes to other income sources, while in the USA (as in some other countries) other income sources partially offset the increase in inequality caused by the labour market.

Taken together, the evidence from developed economies shows that the labour market was the largest force contributing to inequality over the period 2006–10. Other income sources, such as transfers, offset some of these increases in some countries. Earlier evidence shows that in the three decades before the 2008 crisis, increases in inequality were also largely driven by changes in the distribution of wages.

The labour market is an important factor in explaining income inequality trends in developing economies too. Although the contribution of wages to household income is smaller, and self-employment income larger, than in developed economies, no country has succeeded in reducing income inequality over the past decade without also reducing inequality in the labour market. Argentina and Brazil are among the countries where inequality fell most. More paid employment and reductions in wage inequality, including through a minimum wage policy, accounted for 87 per cent of the reduction in inequality in Argentina between 2003 and 2012, and for 72 per cent in Brazil between 2001 and 2012.

Conditional or unconditional cash transfers have made further contributions to the incomes of low-income groups. In many other countries, such as India, inequality increased around the same period.

Explaining wage inequality between groups

One element of inequality lies in the wage gaps between different groups of workers. In order to close these wage gaps, it is important to understand why they exist. The ILO report shows that women, migrants and workers in the informal economy sometimes incur 'wage penalties' for multiple and complex reasons which differ from one country to another, and that the penalty occurs at different places in the overall wage distribution. In general, a proportion of the wage gap can be explained by differences in observable individual and labour market characteristics which we would expect to determine wage levels.[1] Unfortunately, the part of the wage gap that cannot be explained by these characteristics remains substantial in many countries, and points towards continued wage discrimination against some categories of workers.

Acknowledgement

This contribution is excerpted from ILO (2015).

Note

1. Differences that are taken into account to explain the wage gap include experience; education; occupational category (managerial, high-skilled, semi-skilled, low-skilled and unskilled); economic activity (about ten categories, including manufacturing, services, and public administration); location (urban, rural); and work intensity (hours worked).

Bibliography

ILO. 2015. *Global Wage Report 2014/15: Wages and Income Inequality*. Geneva, ILO.

■ *Patrick Belser (Switzerland) is senior economist at the ILO in Geneva, and is the principal editor of the ILO* Global Wage Report, *an ILO flagship report published every two years since 2008.*

7. Horizontal inequalities

Frances Stewart

This contribution explains what horizontal inequalities are and why they are important. It argues that horizontal inequalities – group inequalities in a wide range of political, economic and cultural dimensions – are not only unjust, but may lead to violent conflict and can reduce the efficiency of resource allocation as well as lessening societal achievements on health and education. Most horizontal inequalities emerge from historical biases, often as a result of colonialism. They tend to persist over many generations because of manifold connections between dimensions of deprivation and privilege. The paper briefly reviews policies aimed at reducing horizontal inequalities, differentiating between direct (or targeted) and indirect (or universal) policies.

Horizontal inequalities are inequalities among groups with a shared identity. They constitute one of the most important types of inequality, notably because of their implications for justice and social stability, where relevant group categories include among others race, ethnicity, religion, class, gender and age. They are a neglected aspect of inequality. Most assessments of income distribution (or other resources or outcomes) are concerned with distribution among individuals or households, termed vertical inequality.

People can be grouped in many ways, and most people are members of many groups. In assessing a country's horizontal inequalities, the first question to be considered is which group classification to follow. The appropriate classification is the one (or ones) that reflect the identity distinctions that are important to people, in terms of both their own perceived identity and how they perceive others. Some group categories may be transient or unimportant – for example, membership of a particular club. But other categorizations shape the way people see themselves and how they are treated and behave.

Societies differ as to which are the salient identities at any time. Some identities persist over a long period; others may become of less significance; and, of course, the social, political and economic context varies across time and place. For example, race is clearly an important identity distinction in South Africa and the USA, while ethnicity is relevant in the politics of many African countries. Religion was critically important historically in Europe, with religious differences leading to much violence, but is of less importance today. However, it constitutes a critical dividing line in many countries in Africa, the Middle East and Asia. Caste is an extremely important category in South Asia. And class is of recurring significance, varying with the nature of the economic system and how far people identify with their class position. Age and gender distinctions are universally important.

While people have multiple identities, the ones that matter to them most can vary according to the politics of the time and the issue being considered. Overlapping group membership, sometimes described as 'intersectionality' (Kimberle, 1989), is often used to depict multiple sources of discrimination and oppression of females in minority groups. Other types of category overlap include religion and ethnicity; such overlapping can reinforce deprivation or privilege and may strengthen divisions between groups.

Invariably, then, there is no single 'correct' group classification, but a number of relevant ones, each important in relation to particular issues. The significance of particular categorizations varies according to the rigidity of group boundaries. If people can move from one group to another freely, group inequalities may be inconsequential. Though most group distinctions are socially constructed and many are blurred at the edges – for example, ethnic distinctions – they are nonetheless felt very strongly in some situations. Group classifications may also be more salient, the more the overlap of membership along different categorizations.

Vertical distribution is mostly considered unidimensionally – notably in income space. Sen (1980) has argued that this is inappropriate and that distribution should be measured in relation to a range of capabilities, or what people may do or be. Similarly, an essential feature of horizontal inequalities is their multidimensionality. Their prime dimensions are economic, social, political and cultural recognition. For each there is an array of elements. Economic inequalities include inequalities in economic resources – income, assets, employment, and so on. Social inequalities cover inequalities in access to basic services – education, health, water. In the political dimension, it is a matter of representation at the top levels of government, in the bureaucracy, the military and local government as well as in political parties and civil society. Relevant inequalities in the cultural dimension include recognition, use and respect for a group's language, religion and practices.

There are many causal connections across the various dimensions. For example, educational inequalities may be responsible for economic inequalities, with reverse causality as children from low-income households tend to receive less education. Inequalities in cultural recognition can lead to educational and economic inequalities, for example, if a group's language is not used in government business. The tighter the causal connections, the more consequential the inequalities are. Again, the relevant dimensions vary across societies. While land inequalities are of major significance in agrarian societies, they matter little in advanced economies, where inequalities in financial asset ownership and skills determine life chances.

The sources of horizontal inequality are generally historical. Many are a product of colonial policy favouring particular groups or regions, or are the outcome of contemporary migration. An important feature is their persistence. Peruvian indigenous people have been relatively impoverished in multiple dimensions since the conquest. Successive generations of the non-indigenous have largely monopolized land ownership, technology and education, so that the indigenous have mainly been excluded from the modern economy altogether or incorporated on adverse terms (Thorp and Paredes, 2010). Many other indigenous groups have suffered from persistent deprivation as a result of their cumulative disadvantage in multiple dimensions. This persistence is created by the manifold connections across dimensions which hold back progress, enforced by asymmetrical social networks and compounded by tenacious discriminatory practices. This suggests that horizontal inequalities are important in themselves; and also instrumentally, because they affect other objectives (see Loury, 1988).

Above all, any significant horizontal inequality is unjust. There is no reason why people should receive unequal rewards or have unequal political power merely because they are black rather than white, women rather than men, or of one ethnicity rather than another. While it can be argued that some vertical inequality is justified to reward effort and merit, there is no reason to believe there are any major differences in either effort or merit between large groups of people. Anti-discrimination law is justified on this principle. Such legislation typically requires that a person's group identity is not relevant to decisions, for example, on employment or educational admissions. But centuries of discrimination cannot be offset by such a requirement alone.

Another reason for concern with horizontal inequality is that individual well-being is frequently affected not only by a person's individual circumstances, but also by how well their group is doing. This occurs partly because group membership can form an integral part of a person's identity, and partly because relative impoverishment of the group increases people's perceptions that they are likely to be trapped permanently in a poor position. It seems probable that the well-being of Muslims in Western Europe, Afro-Americans in the USA, and Africans in apartheid South Africa, is deeply affected by the relative impoverishment of the group over and above the position of the individuals within it. Psychologists have suggested that Afro-Americans suffer from psychological ills owing to the position of their group (Broman, 1997). Hence it has been argued that the relative position of the group should enter into a person's welfare function (Akerlof and Kranton, 2000). The weight to be given to this element is an empirical matter on which more research is needed.

Apart from these intrinsic reasons for concern with horizontal inequalities, there are instrumental reasons because they may also affect the achievement of other objectives. One way is by impeding efficiency. If a group is discriminated against, production is likely to be less efficient than in the absence of discrimination, since talented people in the group discriminated against will be held back, while too many resources, or too high a position, will go to less talented people in the favoured group.

For example, Macours (2004) has argued that ethnic diversity often leads to suboptimal allocation of property, drawing on evidence from Guatemala, and many studies show that affirmative action for Afro-Americans in the USA has had a positive impact on economic efficiency (Badgett and Hartmann, 1995). Similarly, evidence indicates that greater average achievements in health and education are associated with more equal distributions. It may also be difficult to attain certain targets, such as poverty elimination or universal education, without tackling horizontal inequality, because deprived groups often find it particularly difficult to access state services.

The third and most powerful instrumental reason to oppose horizontal inequality is that it has been shown to raise the risk of violent conflict significantly (Stewart, 2008; Cederman et al., 2011). Group inequalities provide powerful grievances which leaders can use to mobilize people to political protest, by calling on cultural markers (a common history, language or religion) and pointing to group exploitation. This type of mobilization is especially likely to occur where there is political as well as economic inequality, so that the leaders of the more deprived groups are excluded from political power and therefore have a motive for mobilizing. Group inequalities have been a contributory factor to conflicts in Côte d'Ivoire, Rwanda, Northern Ireland, Chiapas and the Sudan, for example (Langer, 2005; Stewart, 2001). Sharp horizontal inequality within countries is an important source of grievance and potentially of instability, independently of the extent of vertical inequality. Indeed, most econometric investigations have shown little connection between vertical inequality and conflict (Collier and Hoeffler, 2004).

Given their significance, systematic measurement and monitoring of horizontal inequality is needed. Global datasets do not include relevant measures, apart from gender and age categories. However, ethnic, racial and regional data are increasingly collected by national governments. Many national censuses and some household surveys collect data that permit analysis of a variety of socio-economic horizontal inequalities. But data on political forms of horizontal inequality, arguably the dimension most relevant to social stability, are very rare, estimated only by some individual scholars (e.g. Gurr, 1993; Langer, 2005; Wimmer et al., 2009). Finally, there are very few attempts to collate data on inequalities in cultural recognition. As for political data, it is difficult to collect this information, which requires detailed knowledge of complex matters in a society, while presenting the data in summary form is also problematic (but see Gurr, 1993). Yet information on inequalities in cultural recognition is critically important, since such inequalities reinforce group boundaries and stimulate mobilization. Indeed cultural events (such as the destruction of a religious building) often provide the trigger for violence.

A range of policies address horizontal inequalities. They include direct approaches, often termed affirmative action, which target deprived groups in a variety of ways: for example, by giving preferences in employment and education, or political representation. Such policies require a supporting national consensus if they are not to provoke hostility among more privileged groups. They also need to be comprehensive, addressing a range of deprivations, as unidimensional interventions are unlikely to be effective. Malaysia is a successful example of such policies, having introduced them comprehensively after riots in the late 1960s. Although these policies are increasingly opposed by the richer Chinese group, strong interest in their maintenance is making it difficult to end them. This appears to be a general problem with direct policies.

In contrast, indirect policies are universal policies which by design benefit poorer groups disproportionately. Where poorer groups are regionally concentrated, policies to promote the development of poorer regions generally reduce horizontal inequality. Progressive taxation, and policies targeting resources towards lower-income individuals, also do this. These policies work more slowly and with greater leakage in terms of reducing horizontal inequality. But they have the advantage of reducing vertical inequality as well. Anti-discrimination legislation is another general policy for reducing horizontal inequality, but it requires a strong legal system for enforcement, which makes it less suitable for many developing countries. It was an important contributory factor in reducing horizontal inequalities in Northern Ireland (McCrudden et al., 2004). Effective reduction of horizontal inequality may require a combination of direct and indirect policies, as exemplified in Malaysia, Northern Ireland and South Africa.

Despite the clear importance of keeping horizontal inequalities low in the interest of justice and social stability, this priority has not formed part of the norms or policies of the most powerful international actors, for example the World Bank. A more overt and direct approach is needed if these severe and persistent inequalities are to be overcome.

Bibliography

Akerlof, G. A. and Kranton, R. E. 2000. Economics and identity. *Quarterly Journal of Economics*, Vol. 115, No. 3, pp. 715–53. *http://qje.oxfordjournals.org/content/115/3/715. abstract* (Accessed 3 February 2016.)

Badgett, M. V. L. and Hartmann, H. L. 1995. The effectiveness of equal employment opportunity policies. M. C. Simms (ed.), *Economic Perspectives on Affirmative Action*. Lanham, Md., University Press of America.

Broman, C. 1997. Race-related factors and life satisfaction among African Americans. *Journal of Black Psychology*, Vol. 23, No. 1, pp. 36–49. *http://jbp.sagepub.com/content/23/1/36. abstract* abstract (Accessed 3 February 2016.)

Cederman, L.-E., Weidmann, N. B. and Gleditsch, K. S. 2011. Horizontal inequalities and ethno-nationalist civil war: a global comparison. *American Political Science Review*, Vol. 105, No. 3, pp. 478–95. *http://journals.cambridge.org/ action/displayAbstract?fromPage=online&aid=8368186* (Accessed 3 February 2016.)

Collier, P. and Hoeffler, A. 2004. Greed and grievance in civil war. *Oxford Economic Papers*, Vol. 56, pp. 563–95. *www. econ.nyu.edu/user/debraj/Courses/Readings/CollierHoeffler.pdf* (Accessed 3 February 2016.)

Gurr, T. R. 1993. *Minorities at Risk: A Global View of Ethnopolitical Conflicts*. Washington DC, Institute of Peace Press.

Kimberle, C. W. 1989. Demarginalizing the intersection of race and sex: a black feminist critique of antidiscrimination theory and antiracist politics. *Chicago Legal Forum: Feminism in the Law, Theory Practice and Criticism,* Vol. 1989, No. 1, pp. 139–67. *http://chicagounbound.uchicago.edu/cgi/ viewcontent.cgi?article=1052&context=uclf* (Accessed 3 February 2016.)

Langer, A. 2005. Horizontal inequalities and violent group mobilization in Côte d'Ivoire. *Oxford Development Studies*, Vol. 33, No.1, pp. 25–45. *http://www.tandfonline. com/doi/abs/10.1080/13600810500099634*. (Accessed 3 February 2016.)

Loury, G. C. 1988. Why we should care about group equality. *Social Philosophy and Policy*, Vol. 5, No. 1, pp. 249–71.

http://journals.cambridge.org/action/displayAbstract? fromPage=online&aid=3093076&fulltextType=RA&file Id=S0265052500001345 (Accessed 3 February 2016.)

Macours, K. E. D. 2004. *Ethnic Divisions, Contract Choice and Search Costs in the Guatemalan Land Rental Market*. Washington DC, Paul H. Nitze School of Advanced International Studies (SAIS), Johns Hopkins University. *http://papers.ssrn.com/sol3/papers.cfm?abstract_id=647065* (Accessed 3 February 2016.)

McCrudden, C., Ford, R. and Heath, A. 2004. Legal regulation of affirmative action in Northern Ireland: an empirical assessment. *Oxford Journal of Legal Studies*, Vol. 24, No. 3, pp. 363–415. *http://ojls.oxfordjournals.org/ content/24/3/363.abstract* (Accessed 3 February 2016.)

Sen, A. K. 1980. Equality of what? S. McMurrin (ed.), *The Tanner Lecture on Human Values*, Vol. 1. Cambridge, Cambridge University Press, pp. 197–220. *http://ictlogy. net/bibliography/reports/projects.php?idp=845* (Accessed 3 February 2016.)

Stewart, F. 2001. *Horizontal Inequality: A Neglected Dimension of Development*. WIDER Annual Development Lecture 2001, Helsinki, 14 December 2001. *https://www.wider.unu.edu/ publication/horizontal-inequality* (Accessed 3 February 2016.)

Stewart, F. (ed.) 2008. *Horizontal Inequalities and Conflict: Understanding Group Violence in Multiethnic Societies*. London, Palgrave Macmillan.

Thorp, R. and Paredes, M. 2010. *Ethnicity and the Persistence of Inequality: The Case of Peru*. Basingstoke UK and New York, Palgrave Macmillan.

Wimmer, A., Cederman, L.-E. and Min, B. 2009. Ethnic politics and armed conflict: a configurational analysis of a new data set. *American Sociological Review*, Vol. 74, No. 2, pp. 316–37. *http://asr.sagepub.com/content/74/2/316.abstract* (Accessed 3 February 2016.)

■ ***Frances Stewart*** *(UK) is emeritus professor of development economics, University of Oxford. She was director of the Centre for Research on Inequality, Human Security and Ethnicity (2003–10). She has an honorary doctorate from the University of Sussex and received the Leontief Prize for Advancing the Frontiers of Economic Thought from Tufts in 2013. Among many publications, she was the leading author of* Horizontal Inequalities and Conflict: Understanding Group Violence in Multiethnic Societies *(Palgrave Macmillan, 2008).*

8. 'Leaving no one behind': the challenge of intersecting inequalities

Naila Kabeer

This contribution deals with the durable forms of inequality which result when economic deprivation intersects with identity-based discrimination and spatial disadvantage. Groups located at these intersections tend to be worse off than the rest of the poor in their societies, in both the multiple dimensions of poverty and their voice and influence in the political process. Conventional approaches to poverty reduction have left these inequalities largely intact. The author suggests a number of basic principles that could lead to more transformative forms of public action.

Conceptualizing intersecting inequalities

A key principle of the Sustainable Development Goals (SDGs) is 'to leave no one behind': no goal is considered to be met unless it is met for everyone. More specifically, SDG 10 commits the international community to the reduction of inequality within and between countries, and to the promotion of 'the social, economic and political inclusion of all'. These commitments are unlikely to be realized without policies that ensure that the socially excluded among the poor, those who are hardest to reach, are part of the transformations aimed at by the SDGs. The focus on intersecting inequalities in this article seeks to illuminate the nature of this challenge.[1]

Inequality has been conceptualized in a number of ways. The dominant approach in economics is based on the ranking of individuals (or individual households) by income or wealth to capture what have been described as 'vertical inequalities'.

A second approach revolves around the analysis of social discrimination. The focus here is on identity-based discrimination operating at group level rather than against individuals. These 'horizontal' inequalities cut across the distribution of income and wealth, and are the product of social hierarchies which define certain groups as inferior to others through the devaluation of their socially ascribed identities.

While the identities in question take different forms in different societies, the most enduring forms of group-based disadvantage are associated with identities ascribed from birth such as race, caste and ethnicity.

Gender inequalities cut across all other forms of inequality, so that within most socio-economic groups, women and girls are positioned as subordinate to men. Unlike many socially subordinate groups, women and girls are distributed fairly evenly across different economic classes, so gender on its own does not constitute a marker of deprivation. However, the overlap between gender and other forms of inequality generally positions women and girls from poor and socially marginalized groups as the most disadvantaged in their society.

Finally there are spatial inequalities, which tend to affect poor and socially marginalized groups to a disproportionate extent. In rural areas, they may relate to the remoteness of a location or the nature of the terrain, which makes it physically difficult for its inhabitants to participate in broader socio-economic processes. In urban areas, they are likely to be associated with slum neighbourhoods which are poorly served by infrastructure and social services, and are characterized by high levels of violence, criminality and drug dependence.

These vertical, horizontal and spatial conceptualizations describe the different ways in which inequalities are manifested in society.

Where they overlap with each other, they give rise to an intersecting, rather than an additive, model of inequality, where each fuses with, and exacerbates, the effects of the other. This helps to explain why certain groups in society are systematically left behind, or left out of any progress experienced by the wider society. A concern with intersecting inequalities encourages us to pay attention to those whose economic disadvantages are intensified by the discriminations they face on the basis of their identity, as well as by their greater concentration in the least favourable locations in their society.

Thus we find that even when poverty is in decline, the persistence of intersecting inequalities means that it declines more slowly in some groups than in others. In India, for instance, it fell by 40 per cent between 1983 and 2004/05 for the overall population but by just 31 per cent for indigenous groups and 35 per cent for Dalit castes, leading to a widening of economic inequality over time. In Nepal, the overall decline in poverty between 1995 and 2003 varied from 46 per cent for the Brahmin/Chhetri castes to 21 per cent among Dalits and just 10 per cent among indigenous groups living in the hills. In South Africa, while per capita income has risen for all groups between 1917 and 2008, it increased for whites from an average of ZAR13,069 (at constant 2000 values) to ZAR75,297, while average incomes of Black Africans rose from 9 per cent of white income to just 13 per cent. In Nigeria, the northern, predominantly Hausa-Fulani states reported poverty levels of over 70 per cent, while the southern, predominantly Yoruba states reported levels of 30 per cent or less.

In Latin America, moderate and extreme forms of poverty have decreased since the 1990s, but both have remained considerably higher for ethnic and racial minorities in all countries for which disaggregated data are available. Thus, white people made up 88 per cent of the richest 1 per cent of the population of Brazil in 2005 and just 27 per cent of the poorest 10 per cent, while Afro-descendants made up 12 per cent of the richest 1 per cent and 74 per cent of the poorest 10 per cent.

Gender, as noted earlier, intensifies the disadvantages associated with income inequality and social identity. So for instance, the incidence of workers earning 'poverty wages' in Bolivia rose from 50 per cent among non-indigenous men to 55 per cent of non-indigenous women to 80 per cent of indigenous men and 86 per cent of indigenous women.

In Brazil, the incidence of poverty wages rose from 35 per cent of white men to 43 per cent of white women to 60 per cent of Afro-Brazilian men and 67 per cent of Afro-Brazilian women. Similar patterns were reported for Peru and Guatemala, for which comparable data were available (Duryea and Genoni, 2004). Poverty data for 1993, 2000 and 2008 in South Africa show that the incidence and share of poverty were higher for Black Africans as a group than for other groups in the population, and that among Africans, both the incidence and share of poverty were consistently higher for women than for men.

Groups at the intersection of inequalities are also likely to be disadvantaged in relation to other measures of deprivation. Their education levels are lower, infant and child mortality rates higher, and they are less well served in the distribution of social services, reflecting the difficulties of the terrains in which they are located as well as the discriminations built into policy decisions and market provision.

When intersecting inequalities are reproduced in the exercise of political power and access to public institutions, they undermine the confidence of socially disadvantaged groups in the government's ability to rule fairly. Excluded groups are often minorities, and there is little incentive for political parties to take their interests into account.

The conflicts, group violence, riots and civil wars that feature in the literature on horizontal inequalities can be seen as the 'noisy' consequences of social exclusion, but there are other more 'silent' and ongoing consequences. Denied a voice in the affairs of their communities, and overlooked in the provision of basic services and social protection, these groups are often characterized by high rates of crime, alcoholism and other forms of addiction, violence, depression and alienation. Such behaviour undermines the democratic process and serves to reproduce divided and fragmented societies over time.

Responsive states and active citizens

The intersecting nature of the inequalities under discussion makes it clear that they have to be tackled on a number of different fronts – political, economic, spatial and cultural. While different institutions in society can all play a role, the role of the state is central because it is the only institution with the mandate to respond to the claims of all citizens. At the same time, not all states are equally or always responsive to these claims.

Citizens have an indispensable part to play in exercising pressure to hold their government accountable. Intersecting inequalities are most likely to be addressed when responsive states act in tandem with active citizens.

Macroeconomic policies could create an enabling economic environment for tackling inequalities at sectoral and local levels. Broad-based, employment-centred patterns of growth are a critical precondition, but have to be accompanied by redistributive measures if they are to address the hardest-to-reach sections of the poor. Similarly, measures to decentralize and democratize local government must be accompanied by special measures which seek to increase the political participation of excluded groups. Public policies could also be made more inclusive through the targeting of social services to underserved areas or underserved groups. Most governments committed to overcoming historically entrenched patterns of inequality have made use of affirmative action in education, politics, employment and development programmes to help kick-start a process of change.

Such policies rarely occur without active mobilization of marginalized groups. They are most in evidence where such mobilizations have helped to put in power regimes which are representative of their needs and interests. Mobilization and collective action have also been important at the level of micro-politics, acting as a powerful countervailing force against the arbitrary use of power on an everyday basis.

Conclusion

Socially diverse societies do not have to be socially divided societies. But left to themselves, group-based differences can harden into inequality, exclusion and conflict in the face of systematic discrimination. At the same time, there are enough examples of progress around the world to suggest that change is possible.

These efforts may need to be framed in the language of rights. The rights discourse has proved to be a powerful mobilizing force in bringing marginalized groups together in their search for justice. In contexts where intersecting inequalities run deep, and are reinforced on an everyday basis by culture, religion and long-standing traditions, the language of rights may be the only one available to excluded groups to articulate their demand for equality.

While building inclusive forms of citizenship requires the transformation of the relationship between state and citizens, it also requires a transformation of relations between citizens themselves. Along with changing laws and policies, efforts to tackle exclusion must also challenge taken-for-granted norms and practices that make up the mindset of a society.

It is also essential to balance equality and difference. Universalist approaches are essential to building a sense of social solidarity and citizenship, particularly critical for excluded groups. Universal coverage also gives privileged groups more of a stake in policy outcomes, a greater willingness to contribute to them, and hence the possibility of cross-subsidizing marginalized groups. At the same time, 'universality' should not be taken to imply 'uniformity'. There are strong grounds for plurality and diversity within universal frameworks of provision.

It is important to go beyond ameliorative approaches that address the symptoms of the problem to multi-pronged transformative approaches that address its root causes. Transformation is more likely to be achieved by using group-based approaches to tackle group-based problems. This calls for approaches that can help challenge the internalization of inferiority, to create a shared understanding of oppression and the solidarity necessary to challenge existing systems of power.

Finally, we need to work towards a new social contract that recognizes the increasingly interconnected nature of the world we live in. The problems of poverty and social exclusion are not confined to the individual, and are not purely national in their scope. They are also the product of structural inequalities at the global level. The new focus on sustainability in the SDG agenda highlights the stake that all countries have in the future of the planet. An explicit concern with inequality in all its forms, both within and between countries, can unify countries around a shared agenda at global, national and subnational levels. A concern with sustainability and social justice would remind us of the common challenges we face and provide the basis for a more genuine collaboration across national boundaries.

Note

1. The empirical findings cited in this paper can be found in Kabeer (2010), Paz Arauco et al. (2014), Kabeer (2014) and Duryea and Genoni (2004).

Bibliography

Duryea, S. and Genoni, M. E. 2004. Ethnicity, race and gender in Latin American labour markets. M. Buvinic and J. Mazza (eds), *Social Inclusion and Economic Development in Latin America*. Washington DC, World Bank, pp. 247–60.

Kabeer, N. 2014. Social justice and the Millennium Development Goals: the challenge of intersecting inequalities. *Equal Rights Review*, Vol. 13, pp. 91–116.

Kabeer, N. 2010. *Can the MDGs Provide a Pathway to Social Justice? The Challenge of Intersecting Inequalities*. Brighton, UK, IDS/MDG Achievement Fund.

Paz Arauco, V., Gazdar, H., Hevia-Pacheco, P., Kabeer, N., Lenhardt, A., Quratulain Masood, S., Naqvi, H., Nayak, N., Norton, A., Sadana Sabharwal, N., Scalise, E., Shepherd, A., Thapa, D., Thorat, S. and Hien Tran, D. 2014. *Strengthening Social Justice to Address Intersecting Inequalities in the Post-2015 Agenda*. London, Overseas Development Institute (ODI).

■ **Naila Kabeer** *(Bangladesh) is professor of gender and international development at the Gender Institute, London School of Economics and Political Science, UK.*

9. Inequality and natural resources in Africa

James C. Murombedzi

The control of natural resources and access to them has underpinned processes of social stratification and class formation in Africa, and indeed elsewhere. Nascent African nations and states were coalescing around control over natural resources at the moment they encountered colonialism. Colonialism, itself constructed on the control of natural resources, created new forms of inequality and exacerbated existing ones. Today's globalized natural resource extraction processes are defined by the logic of 'accumulation by dispossession,' including land grabs, climate change and natural resource concessions built around lucrative commodity markets and labour migration. They entrench historical vulnerabilities and set the stage for unprecedented inequalities.

Natural resources and the historical origins of inequality in Africa

The use and governance of natural resources is among the most central of issues for the daily lives of the majority of Africans. Patterns of rural resource use are fundamental to rural and national economies, as well as to local and global concerns about sustainability. Institutional histories and political interests fundamentally shape rights over natural resources, and rights are central to the ways in which those resources are used. In this regard, the desire of European powers to capture and exploit African resources played a key role in the transformative process of colonialism. The core characteristic of the colonial project was the alienation of natural resources and the imposition of new forms of centralized political authority over land and resources that previously had been controlled by more localized institutions. The expropriatory processes associated with the imposition of new forms of resource ownership and control occasioned the creation, or in some cases the exacerbation, of inequalities which have endured into the present day. Colonialism was about controlling natural resources, and many of the inequalities on the continent today are reflected in unequal access to the continent's natural resources.

Today, extreme global economic inequality is at an all-time high, largely as a result of corporate-led globalization. The causes of inequality are many, but are mostly located in the historical process of production and distribution. In Africa, while precolonial forms of inequality have influenced the continent's encounter with colonialism and been reproduced and sometimes exacerbated in the colonial period, colonialism itself created new and more extreme forms of inequality that define the continent's social condition today. Colonial dispossession, particularly pronounced in settler colonial societies (Boone and Moyo, 2012), has led to enclosures, created poverty, and exacerbated inequalities.

The colonial state in Africa was established to control labour, capital and resources for external European purposes. This set of political objectives resulted in the concentration of central bureaucratic and executive power. The state's powers of coercion were used to limit independent forms of social organization. Governance was not democratic, representative or accountable. States claimed wide powers over natural resources, particularly land, which was generally placed under discretionary bureaucratic control, with customary rights subordinated to claims explicitly recognized by the colonial administration. Even under indirect British rule, this meant concentrating fused executive, legislative and judicial powers in externally recognized local authorities which bolstered what Mamdani (1996) has called 'the fist of colonial power'.

Shivji (1998) notes that 'There is a deep structural link between the use and control of resources and the organization and exercise of power. Control over resources is the ultimate source of power.'

The colonial incorporation of Africa into the global economy saw it primarily as a source of raw materials. This immediately shaped the continent into a series of enclave economies structured around the control of land and mineral resources, and their supply to the colonial centres. These enclave economies have other fundamental characteristics. They are based on the exploitation of a single resource, and its exportation in raw unprocessed form, or in partially processed form, for value addition in another economy. Many African economies are exporters of a single dominant mineral ore, such as iron ore or copper, or an agricultural commodity, such as cotton or palm oil. A second key characteristic is the creation of a small formal labour force within the enclave, and the consignment of reproduction of labour to locations outside the formal economy. This pattern is particularly pronounced in the former settler colonial societies which were structured on an ideology of white supremacy (South Africa, Rhodesia, South West Africa, Portuguese East Africa and Angola), creating an enclave formal economy employing one-fifth of the labour force (Kanyenze and Kondo, 2011).

The informal sector is characterized by 'customary land tenure' systems where land ownership is effectively vested in the state and land use is subject to a high level of state intervention. The state can control commodity and labour markets through economic and extra-economic means of coercion. The formal sector, on the other hand, is characterized by private land tenure systems (freehold or leasehold) which give rights holders a higher degree of control and flexibility regarding land use.

The formal/informal dichotomy in turn informed the huge disparities between the unskilled and semi-skilled native labour force, and the skilled non-native labour force. Control over land and mineral resources became the basis on which equity and equality of opportunity – access to nutrition, education and job opportunities – were constructed, and highly skewed in favour of the formal sector. This has resulted in a highly underdeveloped informal sector characterized by low pay, low nutrition, high unemployment and high poverty.

Contemporary natural resources control and inequality

Most African economies are predominantly agrarian. The bulk of the population is rural and depends on agriculture. These economies are based on the super-exploitation of peasant labour in order to subsidize labour reproduction for the formal sector. In turn, the exploitation of peasant labour becomes increasingly feminized as male labour is absorbed into the formal sector to the exclusion of female labour. This gendered exploitation is reflected in the extreme inequality between men and women, urban and rural, and black and white in the colonial and postcolonial African economies.

Natural resources governance issues such as land and resource tenure continue to underpin evolving relations between states and citizens in the postcolonial era. Post-independence African governments tended to reinforce centralized authority over natural resources as states sought to consolidate the political authority needed to drive modernization processes and control resources for patronage. Postcolonial Africa has continued on a neoliberal development trajectory which not only creates unsustainable use of natural resources, but also exacerbates the historical inequalities of colonial exploitation.

Natural resources, with their historic grounding in the public domain and their high economic values, are central to the patronage interests that allow governing elites to maintain powers and privileges. This political logic shapes natural resource governance patterns across the continent. For example, agricultural policy in agrarian nations has evolved according to political interests bent towards controlling producers' access to markets and inputs in order to extract rent. Similarly, forestry policy and management institutions across the continent are crafted according to central patronage interests in controlling and extracting rents from both formal and informal patterns of trade, and the utilization of products such as timber and charcoal (Oyono, 2004).

While the continent is engaged in various projects to restructure economies away from their historical limitations, and towards more inclusive and equitable trajectories, such transformational initiatives rarely seek to transcend the neoliberal hegemony. Various attempts have been made to promote equitable access to land and natural resources through redistributive processes such as land reform (Boone and Moyo, 2012), economic empowerment programmes such as in South Africa, and so on. However, these policy reforms are occurring in contexts characterized by the enclosure and privatization of public lands (Harvey, 2003). In Africa, this phase of globalization is creating new enclosures and dispossessions, and thus exacerbating the natural resource-based inequalities of the colonial era.

Natural resource degradation contributes to growing inequality. Conservative estimates show that industrial gas emissions have increased by almost 50 per cent; more than 300 million hectares of forest have been cleared; and many communities in developing countries have lost rights and access to lands and forests to large multinational corporations acting in collaboration with national governments. Although poverty has been reduced in a few industrializing countries, nearly 20 per cent of the world's population remain in absolute poverty (Watts and Ford, 2012; Global Race Equality Action Trust, 2012), and more continue to be impoverished through land and resource expropriations. The commodification and privatization of the environment has accelerated through increased 'green grabs', carbon sequestration schemes such as REDD+, water privatization, and the creation of new protected areas on lands expropriated from the poor and marginalized, as well as the suppression of indigenous forms of production and consumption.

Climate change and inequality

Many countries, particularly the most vulnerable, are already experiencing the negative impacts of climate change. Many poor countries are already affected by frequent floods, storms and droughts. Even if the Paris Agreement and other measures succeed in keeping temperature rises below 1.5 degrees, these impacts will continue and even worsen for several decades to come. Recent estimates suggest that climate change will reduce GDP per capita in Africa by between 66 per cent and 90 per cent by 2100 (Houser et al., 2015).

Climate change has also become the defining context of natural resources use and control in recent times. An inescapable irony of climate change is that those economies whose development has led to climate change are the least vulnerable to its impacts, while countries that emit the least are the most vulnerable to climate change. This exacerbates inequality between the nations of the developed north and those of the global south. 'Climate change is inextricably linked to economic inequality: it is a crisis that is driven by the greenhouse gas emissions of the "haves" that hits the "have-nots" the hardest' (Oxfam, 2015). GDP growth can be linked directly to carbon emissions, and those economies with the highest rates of GDP are also those that have historically had the highest rates of greenhouse gas emissions.

Climate change not only exacerbates inequalities between nations, but also amplifies the vulnerabilities of those communities whose livelihoods are directly dependent on access to natural resources. Most of Africa's rural households have livelihoods that are based on access to agricultural land, and associated natural resources such as forests and water. Access to these resources is already inequitable because of historical factors. Climate change not only increases these challenges, but also creates new competition for natural resources. Pastoral and sedentary communities compete for water and grazing lands, and within sedentary communities, access to vital forest products is increasingly contested. As rainfall patterns vary, competition for access to land is also increasing. Climate change will affect the productivity of the land, change access to natural resources, and create new conditions for further primitive accumulation, already seen in the expansion in land acquisitions for biofuel production on lands belonging to vulnerable communities.

Conclusions: towards an equitable world order

The use and control of natural resources has historically generated inequality in Africa. Climate change and the responses to it have exacerbated these inequalities. The dominance of the market, representing corporate interests over social and environmental interests, is clearly socially, economically and environmentally unsustainable. Instead of the current production system which emphasizes market mechanisms to allocate the costs and benefits of nature, what is required is a social structure of accumulation that places economic justice over profit and, more practically, institutes an inclusive, sustainable model for growth (Tabb, 2012). With reference to climate change, the Intergovernmental Panel on Climate Change (IPCC) notes that 'equitable socioeconomic development in Africa may strengthen its resilience to various external shocks, including climate change' (2013, p. 1121).

There are many processes around the world today seeking alternatives to the destructive logic of the hegemonic models of production and consumption. These are evident in a wide range of rich experiences in alternative technology, renewable energy and new regulatory regimes that exist in different parts of the world.

Bibliography

Boone, C. and Moyo, S. 2012. The politics of land in contemporary Africa. London School of Economics and Political Science Africa Talks Public Lecture, 12 November. *www.lse.ac.uk/publicEvents/events/2012/11/20121112t1800vU8.aspx* (Accessed 3 March 2016.)

Global Race Equality Action Trust. 2012. Rio+20 Earth Summit: Campaigners Greenpeace, GREAT Trust, Council for Afrika International & Afrika Liberation Society Decry Final Document, 23 June. *https://sites.google.com/site/greattrustspace/home/great-news-1/* (Accessed 3 March 2016.)

Harvey, D. 2003. *The New Imperialism*. Oxford, Oxford University Press.

Houser, T., Hsiang, S., Kopp, R. and Larsen. K. 2015. *Economic Risks of Climate Change: An American Prospectus*. New York, Columbia University Press.

IPCC. 2013. *Climate Change 2013: The Physical Science Basis*. Contribution of Working Group I to the Fifth Assessment Report of the Intergovernmental Panel on Climate Change (IPCC). *http://www.climatechange2013.org/* (Accessed 2 March 2016.)

Kanyenze, G. and Kondo, T. (eds). 2011. *Beyond the Enclave. Towards a Pro-Poor and Inclusive Development Strategy for Zimbabwe*. Harare, Weaver Press.

Mamdani, M. 1996. *Citizen and Subject: Contemporary Africa and the Legacy of Late Colonialism*. Princeton, N. J., Princeton University Press

Oxfam. 2015. Extreme carbon inequality: why the Paris climate deal must put the poorest, lowest emitting and most vulnerable people first. Media Briefing, 2 December. *http://policy-practice.oxfam.org.uk/publications/extreme-carbon-inequality-why-the-paris-climate-deal-must-put-the-poorest-lowes-582545* (Accessed 2 March 2016.)

Oyono, P. R. 2004. Assessing accountability in Cameroon's local forest management: are representatives responsive? *African Journal of Political Science*, Vol. 9, No. 1, pp. 125–36. *www.cifor.org/library/1723/assessing-accountability-in-cameroons-local-forest-management-are-representatives-responsive/* (Accessed 3 March 2016.)

Shivji, I. G. 1998. *Not Yet Democracy: Reforming Land Tenure in Tanzania*. Dar es Salaam, University of Dar es Salaam.

Tabb, W. K. 2012. *The Restructuring of Capitalism in Our Time*. New York, Columbia University Press.

Watts, J. and Ford, L. 2012. Rio+20 Earth Summit: campaigners decry final document. *Guardian*. www.guardian.co.uk/environment/2012/jun/23/rio-20-earth-summit-document (Accessed 28 August 2012.)

■ *James C. Murombedzi (Zimbabwe) is senior political affairs officer, climate change with the Africa Climate Policy Centre (ACPC) at the UN Economic Commission for Africa (ECA), Ethiopia.*

10. Inequality in education: the challenge of measurement

Manos Antoninis, Marcos Delprato and Aaron Benavot

Education is essential to economic growth, poverty reduction, gender equality, public health, conflict resolution and the transformation to sustainable production and consumption. Ensuring equality in education can further accelerate the achievement of these and other Sustainable Development Goals (SDGs). This contribution discusses how to monitor progress toward reducing inequality in education, which indicators can be used, and what the challenges are for communicating these results.

Economic inequality within countries is rising (Milanovic, 2013). This explains why one of the new SDGs is dedicated to reducing income inequality. Beyond this specific goal, the desire to 'leave no one behind' permeates the entire 2030 Agenda. The result is an unprecedented global commitment to monitoring progress using data disaggregated 'by income, gender, age, race, ethnicity, migratory status, disability, geographic location, and other characteristics relevant to national contexts' (United Nations, 2015). In the case of education (SDG 4), Target 4.5 focuses exclusively on the need to 'ensure equal access to all levels'.

Education is a fundamental human right which countries have committed to uphold since they signed the 1948 Universal Declaration of Human Rights. Education is also a key driver for attaining most SDGs by 2030, whether these concern gender equality, healthy families, poverty reduction, sustainable consumption, resilient cities or peaceful societies. Yet for education to have a positive impact in advancing these goals, it is necessary to first ensure equality of opportunity for learning. Given that individuals have varying abilities and competences, it is unrealistic to expect equality of education outcomes. However, such differences should not be amplified by individual circumstances at birth.

In practice, education remains a social institution that reflects and reproduces the socio-economic and cultural disadvantages that prevail in the rest of society (Bourdieu and Passeron, 1977). For instance, students from economically poor families are more likely to attend schools characterized by worse infrastructure, fewer qualified teachers, less ambitious peers and outmoded pedagogical practices compared with those in more affluent areas. Hence they are more likely to end up with lower learning outcomes.

Eliminating inequality in education will amplify the positive influence of education on the achievement of other development outcomes. For example, for a given level of average education in the population, a more equal distribution has an additional impact on economic growth. An equitable delivery of education is critical for tackling the roots of discontent in cities. And studies of low and middle-income countries have shown that increased educational inequality is linked with a higher probability of conflict (UNESCO, 2014).

Multiple ways of measuring inequality

The monitoring of inequality in education is critical to understanding how, and how much, education contributes to more equitable societies. This necessarily calls for a series of choices to be made.

First, educational inequality can be examined using indicators that capture different aspects of education ranging from resources to access, participation and attainment. These may, for example, include the percentage of individuals who have attained a particular level of education, or the number of years of education attained (e.g. Morrisson and Murtin, 2013; Meschi and Scervini, 2014). The increasing availability of national and international learning achievement surveys further enables the measurement of inequality in learning outcomes (e.g. OECD, 2010; Fereira and Gignoux, 2014).

Second, different inequality measures can be used to summarize the degree of dispersion for a given educational indicator. Each measure has advantages and disadvantages, in both its technical qualities and the ease with which it can be communicated to non-specialist audiences and policy-makers. However, different inequality measures can also lead to different conclusions about the degree of inequality and its change over time for the same educational indicator (as illustrated in *Figure 10.4*).

Third, while it may be interesting to view the distribution of an education indicator throughout the population, policy-makers need to know how its value varies by individual characteristics if they are to address issues of inequality. The most important markers of potential disadvantage include gender, location, income or wealth, ethnicity and disability. To measure progress over time, inequality can also be examined across generations (e.g. Blanden, 2013).

Fourth, different data sources are available that measure different aspects of the education process and provide information on background characteristics. However, close attention needs to be paid to whether they are representative of the general population, and are sufficiently reliable to be used for the reporting of trends over time.

Communicating about inequality in education

To illustrate inequality in education, the Global Education Monitoring Report developed the World Inequality Database on Education (WIDE), using demographic and health surveys (DHS), multiple indicator cluster surveys (MICS) and national household surveys (UNESCO, 2015).[1] It also developed accompanying graphics to help visualize the extent of inequality and facilitate comparisons between countries or between groups within countries.

For example, the percentage of young people who have completed lower secondary school varies from 6 per cent in Niger to 100 per cent in Armenia. It can also vary by more than 40 percentage points within countries – for example, between rural and urban areas in Laos and Namibia (*Figure 10.1*).

Overlapping markers of disadvantage show how disadvantages can cumulate, seriously affecting certain groups. In Nigeria, just 3 per cent of the poorest rural girls completed lower secondary school

in 2013. By comparison 17 per cent of the poorest rural boys and 95 per cent of the richest urban boys completed this level. In the Philippines, gender disparities worked in the opposite direction for lower secondary education, with a 25 percentage point advantage for the poorest females over the poorest males in both urban and rural areas (*Figure 10.2*).

Figure 10.1 **Lower secondary education completion rate by location, selected low and middle-income countries, 2008–14**

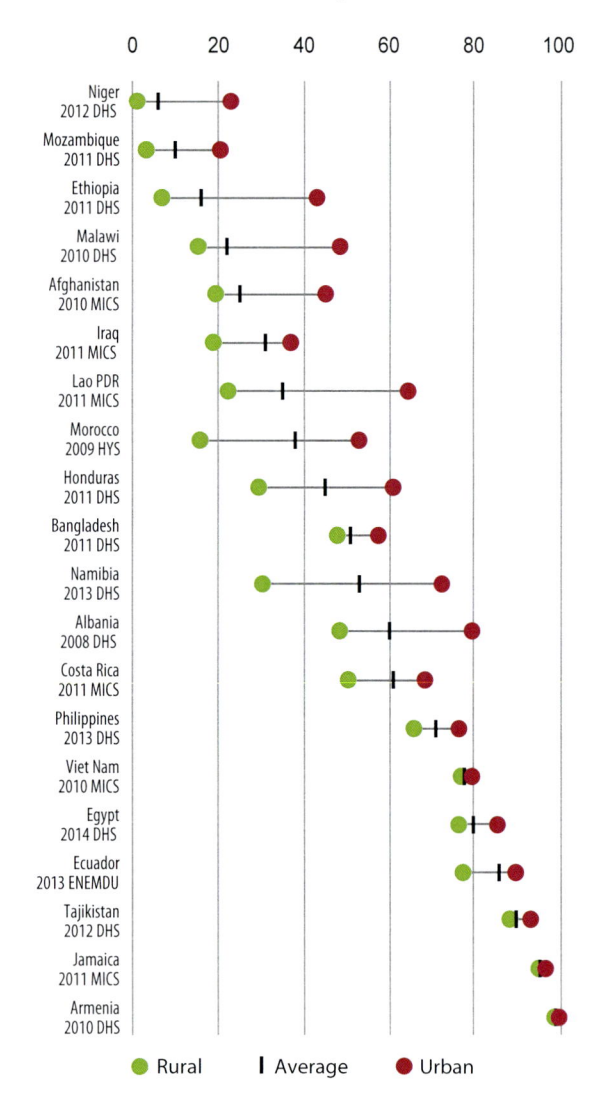

● Rural | Average   ● Urban

Note: The lower secondary completion rate is the percentage of young people (aged 3–5 years above lower secondary school graduation age) who had completed lower secondary school. See www.education-inequalities.org/indicators

Source: World Inequality Database on Education.

Inequality in education: the challenge of measurement | *Manos Antoninis, Marcos Delprato and Aaron Benavot*

Figure 10.2 **Lower secondary education completion rate by location, wealth and gender, Nigeria and the Philippines, 2013**

Source: World Inequality Database on Education

The Inter-Agency and Expert Group on SDG indicators has proposed the 'parity index' as the global measure of inequality in education. This is the ratio between the education indicator values of two population groups,[2] and ranges from 0 (extreme inequality at the expense of one group) to 1 (parity) (extreme inequality at the expense of the other group). For example, if 30 per cent of the poorest and 60 per cent of the richest have completed primary school, then the wealth parity indicator is 0.5. The measure has been proposed because it is the easiest to communicate to a broad audience.

However, the parity index has to be interpreted cautiously. In *Figure 10.3*, the horizontal axis shows the primary completion rate in selected countries, while the vertical axis shows the primary completion rate wealth parity index. On average, the index is higher – and therefore inequality lower – when the completion rate is higher (and vice versa). In other words, there is a risk that simple measures of inequality may be misleading if used out of context. In particular, it would be misleading to compare the value of the index of two countries at different levels of educational development, such as Honduras and Mauritania, and conclude that the latter is more unequal. However, the index is useful to analyse inequalities between countries at the same level of educational development: for example, for every 100 rich children who completed primary school, only 28 poor children did so in Pakistan compared with 51 poor children in Malawi.

If we want to show how an education indicator is distributed in a population ranked by a characteristic such as wealth (from poorest to richest) then the concentration index can be used. This index is calculated as being twice the area between the concentration curve (which shows the actual distribution) and the diagonal line (which shows perfect equality): the farther a line is to the right of the diagonal, the higher the inequality.

For example, regarding the lower secondary education completion rate in sub-Saharan Africa by wealth in both 2000 and 2010, the poorest 40 per cent of young people represented less than 20 per cent of lower secondary school completers. But while inequality fell overall between 2000 and 2010, the concentration curves highlight that it is the middle classes that benefited most, while the poorest have done worse. Clearly, it behoves us to develop and use measures that are sensitive to the educational progress of all groups (*Figure 10.4*).

Conclusion

The increasing availability of household and school-based surveys has made it possible to do more high-quality, in-depth analyses of inequality in education both within and between countries. However, distinct challenges remain for the monitoring of progress toward the global target of achieving equal access to all education levels by 2030, including the need to articulate clear messages for broad policy audiences.

PART I • CURRENT TRENDS IN INEQUALITIES | Chapter 1 | Inequalities: many intersecting dimensions

Figure 10.3 **Primary education completion rate and wealth parity index, selected low and middle income countries, 2008–14**

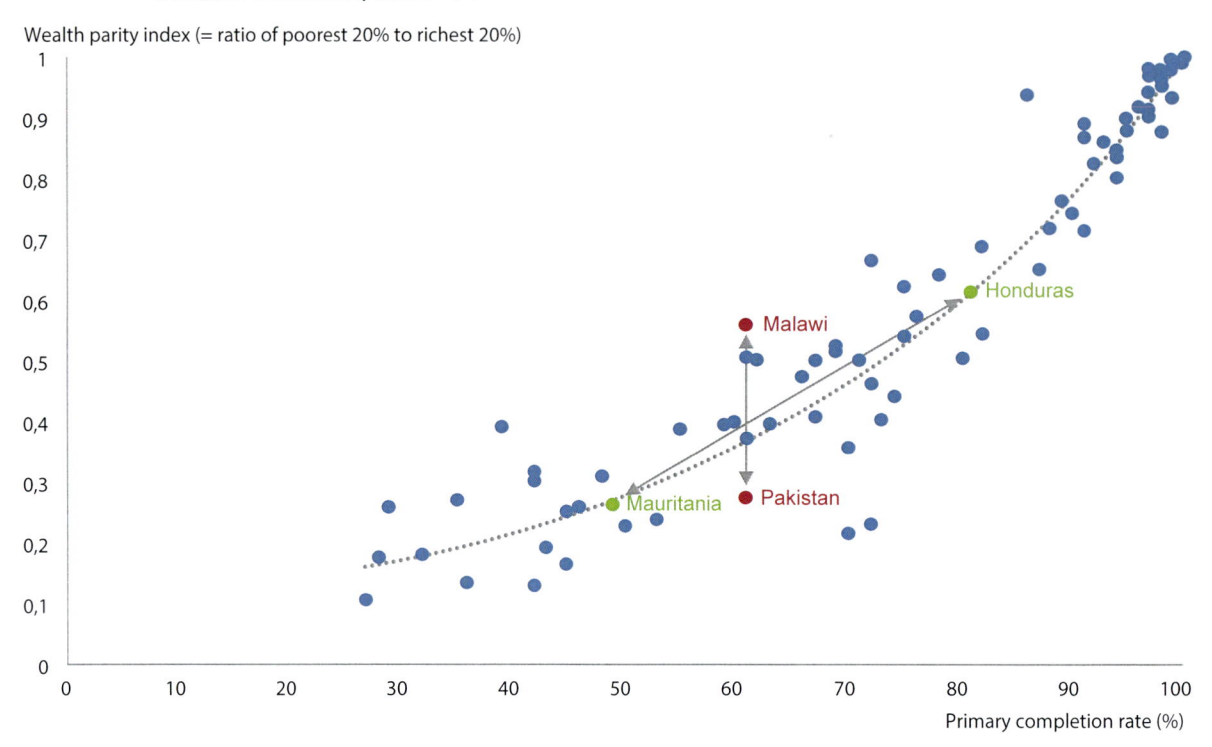

Wealth parity index (= ratio of poorest 20% to richest 20%)

Source: Global Education Monitoring Report team analysis using household surveys

Figure 10.4 **Concentration curve of the lower secondary education completion rate, sub-Saharan Africa, 2000 and 2010**

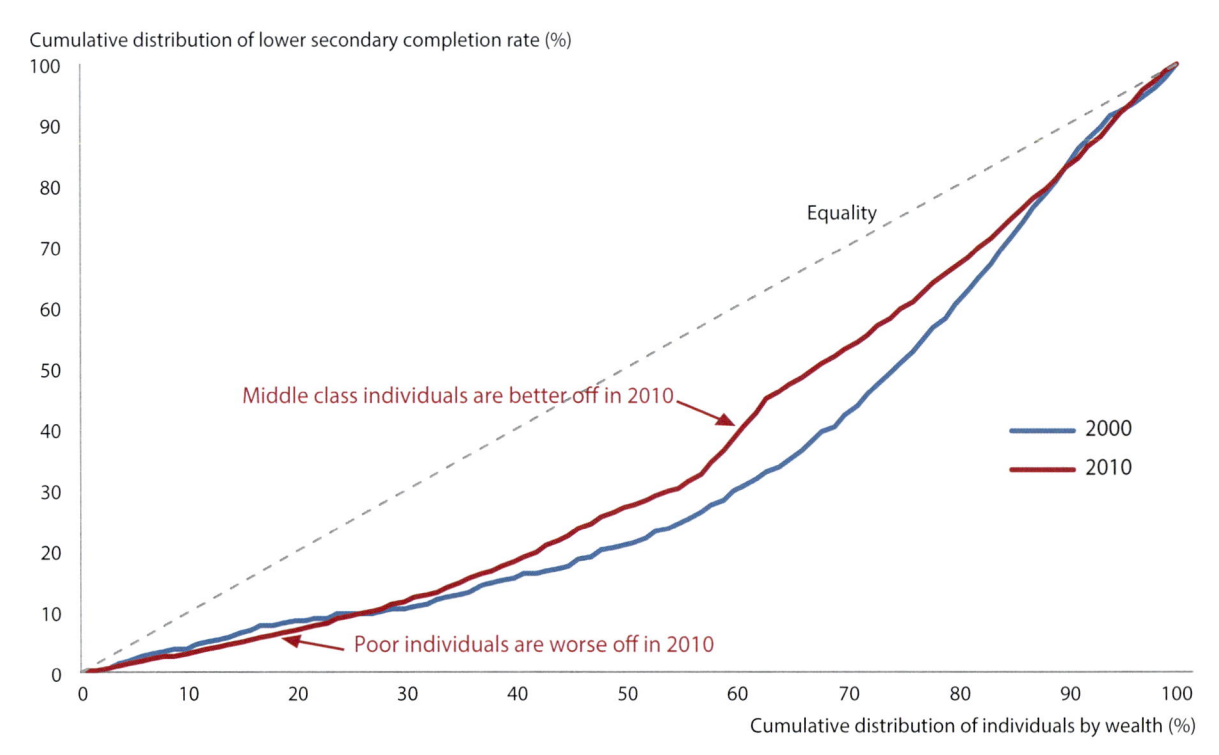

Cumulative distribution of lower secondary completion rate (%)

Source: Global Education Monitoring Report team analysis using household surveys

Greater consensus is needed among the international community as to which education indicators, inequality measures, individual characteristics and data sources should be emphasized.

Notes

1. See www.education-inequalities.org/
2. Such as female over male for the gender parity index or the poorest over the richest for the wealth parity index.

Bibliography

Blanden J. 2013. Cross-country rankings in inter-generational mobility: a comparison of approaches from economics and sociology. *Journal of Economic Surveys*, Vol. 27, No. 1, pp. 28–73.

Bourdieu, P. and Passeron, J. C. 1977. *Reproduction in Education, Society and Culture.* London, Sage.

Fereira, F. H. G. and Gignoux, J. 2014. The measurement of educational inequality: achievement and opportunity. *World Bank Economic Review*, Vol. 28, No. 2, pp. 210–46.

Meschi, E. and Scervini, F. 2014. Expansion of schooling and educational inequality in Europe: the educational Kuznets curve revisited. *Oxford Economic Papers*, Vol. 66, No. 3, pp. 660–80.

Milanovic, B. 2013. Global income inequality in numbers: in history and now. *Global Policy*, Vol. 4, No. 2, pp.198–208.

Morrisson, C. and Murtin, F. 2013. The Kuznets curve of human capital inequality: 1870–2010. *Journal of Economic Inequality*, Vol. 11, No. 3, pp. 283–301.

OECD. 2010. *PISA 2009 Results: Overcoming Social Background – Equity in Learning Opportunities and Outcomes*, Vol. 2. Paris, OECD.

United Nations. 2015. *Transforming Our World: The 2030 Agenda for Sustainable Development.* New York, United Nations.

UNESCO. 2014. *Sustainable Development Begins with Education: How Education Can Contribute to the Proposed Post-2015 Goals*, Global Education Monitoring Report. Paris, UNESCO.

UNESCO. 2015. Education in 2030: equity and quality with a lifelong learning perspective. Insights from the EFA Global Monitoring Report's World Inequality Database on Education (WIDE), Global Education Monitoring Report Policy Paper 20. Paris, UNESCO.

■ ***The authors*** *work in the Global Education Monitoring Report team at UNESCO, Paris.*
Manos Antoninis *(Greece) is senior policy analyst,* ***Marcos Delprato*** *(Argentina) is research officer, and* ***Aaron Benavot*** *(Israel) is director of the Global Education Monitoring Report.*

11. The multiple forms of digital inequality

Ben Ramalingam and Kevin Hernandez

The digital revolution, like every other revolution, has produced winners and losers. As of 2015, nearly 60 per cent of the world's population – 4 billion people – lack access to the internet, while 2 billion lack access to basic mobile phones (World Bank, 2016). These digitally excluded 4 billion are unable to access income-generating opportunities, goods and services based on information and communications technologies (ICT), and cannot fully engage and participate in the digital economies, societies or polities that shape their lives. As Manuel Castells predicted (in 1996), the digital revolution divides the world into two populations: the interacting and the interacted.

The opportunities and challenges of digital technology have not gone unrecognized in development policy and practice. The most salient illustration is Sustainable Development Goal (SDG) 9 on infrastructure and innovation, which calls for enhanced ICT access and affordable internet access worldwide by 2020.[1] This target, and the decades of work leading to it, are laudable and important. It has the potential to make a difference to millions of lives, especially in the rapidly changing context of digital technology. But this won't happen unless some of the important lessons that have been learned about the reality of existing digital inequalities are taken into account.

Tangible dimensions of digital inequality include apparatus inequality and spatial inequality. Apparatus inequality relates to differing levels of physical and technological ownership and access, based on the presence and adequacy of hardware, software and connectivity. Owners of basic mobile phones – with no alternative internet access – have been described as 'stuck' in text and voice (Zainudeen and Ratnadiwakara, 2011). Spatial inequality concerns differences in digital coverage and participation between urban and rural areas, city centres and outskirts, and developed and developing countries.

This has both global and local manifestations. Developing countries are less likely to have their contexts and histories represented on Wikipedia, and developing country citizens are much less likely to contribute articles (Graham et al., 2014). Looking at contemporary attempts to increase digital access, it is fair to conclude that the focus has been on addressing these tangible inequalities in a relatively superficial manner, as if they can be divorced from socio-economic realities.

However, there are also various intangible forms of digital inequality that should not be overlooked or dismissed. For example, inequality of autonomy concerns the degree of control individuals have over their digital access: owners of personal equipment exert more control than users of shared or public equipment. Inequality of skills concerns digital literacy levels: some people can only consume information, some can produce and upload new content, while others understand how to manage data, programme applications, or build networks and platforms. Generally, intangible digital inequalities cannot be separated from socio-economic forms of inequality, including economic status, education, class, gender and age. Intangible inequalities are those that see people excluded because of who they are.

Tangible and intangible dimensions are intricately interwoven and cannot easily be tackled in isolation from each other, or from other forms of inequality. Inequalities stemming from social stratification are strongly correlated with digital inequalities: the digital world frequently mirrors the analogue one and reinforces it. For example, inadequate infrastructure in remote areas makes internet access expensive and inefficient, which excludes the poor, while the lack of basic digital skills and access in disadvantaged areas further entrenches inequalities of opportunity. As well as being complex, digital inequalities are not static.

The form of digital inequality that exists today, when billions of people have access to a mobile phone, is naturally very different to that of 1995, when almost no one had a mobile phone.

We conclude by making three specific suggestions to ensure that the global community doesn't hit the SDG target while missing the point about inequality.

First, a better understanding of the many forms of digital inequality requires collaboration between social, computing, humanities and physical sciences to understand and anticipate the dynamic consequences of technological change. There is also potential to engage scientists from future 'game-changing' revolutions such as biotechnology and nanotechnology (DiMaggio and Hargittai, 2001).

Second, tackling digital inequalities requires broader societal, political and economic engagement. Leaving digital development to digital scholars, practitioners and policy-makers alone perpetuates narrow views of both problems and potential solutions. The drivers shaping digital access extend well into the analogue world, and we need to account for this in our policy and practical frameworks.

Third, we must relinquish views of the digital bottom 4 billion as passive agents waiting to be reached through elaborate technological innovations. Just as broader debates and efforts on inequality are moving beyond notions of 'reaching the poor' and towards empowering them, we must start thinking and doing more in the emerging realm of digital empowerment.

Why is this important? The risk is that by hitting the SDG 9 target by 2020 only by focusing on tangible indicators of access, we will address only technological forms of digital inequalities, to the detriment of millions if not billions of people.

Note

1. See *https://sustainabledevelopment.un.org/sdgs*.

Bibliography

Castells, M. 1996. *The Rise of the Network Society, The Information Age: Economy, Society and Culture, Vol. I.* Cambridge, Mass. and Oxford, Blackwell.

DiMaggio, P. and Hargittai, E. 2001. From 'digital divide' to 'digital inequality': studying internet use as penetration increases. Working Paper No. 15. Princeton, N. J., Center for Arts and Cultural Policy Studies, Woodrow Wilson School, Princeton University.

Graham, M., Hogan, B., Straumann, R. and Medhat, A. 2014. Uneven geographies of user-generated information: patterns of increasing informational poverty. *Annals of the Association of American Geographers*, Vol. 104, No. 4, pp. 746–64.

Hernandez, K. 2015. Connectivity flying high: bridging the digital divide from the sky. Master's thesis. Brighton, UK, IDS.

Schradie, J. 2011. The digital production gap: the digital divide and Web 2.0 collide. *Poetics*, Vol. 39, No. 2, pp.145–68.

World Bank. 2016. *World Development Report 2016: Digital Dividends.* www.worldbank.org/en/publication/wdr2016 (Accessed 9 June 2016.)

Zainudeen, A. and Ratnadiwakara, D. 2011. Are the poor stuck in voice? Conditions for adoption of more-than-voice mobile services. *Information Technologies and International Development*, Vol. 7, No. 3, pp. 45–59.

■ **Ben Ramalingam** *(UK) is a researcher, author, advisor and facilitator focusing on global development and humanitarian issues. He is currently leader of the Digital and Technology Cluster at the Institute of Development Studies (IDS).*

■ **Kevin Hernandez** *(USA) is currently a research assistant at IDS. His main areas of interest include digital technology, the role of business and markets, and the use of foresight methodology in development.*

12. Untangling economic and political inequality: the case of South Africa

John Gaventa and Carin Runciman

This contribution proposes three lenses through which political inequality can be understood: voice, representation and influence. Using the example of South Africa, the contribution goes on to explore how political inequalities are created and reinforced. The analysis demonstrates how socio-economic inequalities powerfully shape all three dimensions of political inequality. Poor communities have responded to this exclusion through the use of protest in order to disrupt their political marginalization as well as their socio-economic exclusion. South Africa illustrates the deep interconnections of economic, social and political inequalities, ones which can only be broken through new forms of political action.

Introduction

Understanding the interrelationships between political and other forms of inequality is a critical challenge for social scientists, policy-makers and activists alike. For those concerned with building and deepening democracy, a fundamental premise is that while broad social and economic inequalities may exist in society, they will be countered by the relative equality of all citizens to exercise voice in the future of their own affairs. From a rights perspective, the provision and protection of equal political rights is seen as a prerequisite to the realization of other socio-economic rights. And from a development perspective, the recently approved Sustainable Development Goal (SDG) 10 on reducing inequality includes the objectives of achieving political inclusion and voice within and between countries, as well as those that speak to countering economic and social inequality alone.

But while the normative imperatives for political equality are high, our empirical understanding of where, when and how social and economic inequalities affect the distribution of political inequality is relatively limited. Social science research is largely based in Western democracies, particularly the USA. Against this backdrop, this article seeks to review the meanings of political inequality. We then consider South Africa to understand further how intersecting social, economic and political inequalities affect political voice, representation and power today.

What do we mean by political inequality?

Unlike economic inequality, with its widely understood measures of inequality such as the Gini coefficient of income, there are few common measures of political inequality across contexts (Dubrow, 2010). At least three different measures are commonly used.

The most common approach is to understand political inequality as differences in political voice and participation (sometimes also referred to as civic or voice inequality). These are often measured through indicators of who votes or otherwise participates in both formal and informal processes of governance. Such literature usually argues that economic and social inequalities impede political voice and participation in a number of ways. They may weaken subjective incentives to participate, through eroding trust in government institutions, or contribute to a sense of powerlessness or an internalized acceptance of the status quo. They may weaken group-level cooperation and coordination, reducing the possibilities of collective action and mobilization (Justino, 2015). Or they may contribute to the creation of external obstacles to participation, through the lack of resources of those at the bottom to engage, the creation of political and administrative barriers, or through the hard powers of coercion and violence against those who would challenge inequities in the status quo.

For others, however, political inequality is understood less in terms of who participates and more in terms of political representation and inclusion, for instance who gets to the political table. Measures of political inequality in this area point to a lack of representation in political office on the basis of race, gender, class, ethnicity, disability or other forms of discrimination. Regarding intersecting inequalities, this body of work argues that even though voice may be exercised, it fails to translate into real presence at key forums and arenas of power. Other studies also highlight the point that elected representatives, many of whom are themselves very wealthy, overwhelmingly respond more favourably to those at the more affluent end of the economic ladder than to those at the bottom, making the imperative of more equal and inclusive forms of representation even more critical if more equal outcomes are to be achieved.

A third, more fundamental measure of political inequality has to do with inequalities of power and influence in determining decisions about the distribution of social and economic resources. Here, inequality is seen in terms not just of who participates or is represented in political processes, but of who benefits. As Robert Reich, former US secretary of labor, puts it, growing inequality is shaped less by the market, technology or the behaviour of ordinary citizens, and more by 'the increasing concentration of political power in a corporate and financial elite that has been able to influence the rules by which the economy runs' (Reich, 2015, p. 27). As their influence often exists beyond nation states, these elites have the ability to shape patterns of inequality not only within countries, but across countries as well.

In reality, these three ways in which economic and social inequalities shape political inequality are mutually reinforcing: who gets into the game and who sits at the table affect how the game is played, who wins and who loses. Inequalities of political opportunity shape inequalities of outcomes, and unequal outcomes allow the powerful more scope to restrict opportunities, leading a UN Special Rapporteur on Human Rights to comment, 'Material deprivation and disempowerment create a vicious circle: the greater the inequality, the less the participation; the less the participation, the greater the inequality' (Carmona, 2013, p. 5).[1]

If this is the case, how then is the 'vicious circle' of political and economic inequality to be broken? Despite the ability of elites to shape both political opportunities and outcomes, there are political counter-narratives in the face of rising inequality, such as the Occupy movement, landless people's movements, food riots and youth revolts. These examples suggest that the relationships of economic and political inequality are not one-way or linear. What is needed though is a far more nuanced and developed understanding of the new politics of inequality in the face of its contemporary forms.

South Africa

South Africa offers one important arena to understand how social, political and economic inequalities interact. Over the course of the past twenty years of democracy, South Africans have become less poor but more unequal. More than half of the population survives on less than R779 (US$67) a month, or R26 (US$2.20) per day, and patterns of poverty and inequality continue to be heavily racialized. Black African households, which account for more than three-quarters of all households, earn less than half of the country's total annual household income.

While poverty has endured and inequality has deepened, the African National Congress (ANC) has at the same time fostered the development of a new Black elite through the Black Economic Empowerment (BEE) programme. This programme has attempted to deracialize the economy but as many commentators have observed, it has also been part of a strategy to forge an economic elite loyal to the ANC (Southall, 2004). It means that economic power and political influence are often closely tied to connections with the ANC. Such relations, often referred to as patronage or clientelism, not only exist in the political elite but permeate everyday lives, affecting patterns of participation and representation in the new democracy.

Since 1994 the government and civil service have been deracialized, and women account for 40 per cent of seats in parliament, a proportion that ranks South Africa among the best in the world for the representation of women. Furthermore, multiple levels of participatory governance have been created in recognition of the key role civil society has in the democratization process. However, there have been limits to the effectiveness of the participatory model in promoting political voice and genuine inclusion.

Participatory mechanisms are largely confined to local governance, and civil society is generally excluded from shaping macro-level policy. While statutory bodies such as the National Economic Development and Labour Council (NEDLAC) were established as forums in which government, labour, business and civil society could negotiate on national-level economic and development issues, government has the discretion to appoint who represents civil society within the chamber, and consequently which voices are heard.

At the local level, ward committees, non-partisan advisory bodies to local councillors, were introduced to strengthen political voice and representation. Data from Afrobarometer suggests that South Africa can be characterized as having an 'active' citizenry, with over half of those surveyed in 2011 reporting they had attended at least one community meeting in the last year. However, spaces of participatory governance have increasingly become channels for party political interests in which local political rivalries and factionalism predominate, allowing little room for alternative community voices to contribute to the development agenda (Ngamlana and Mathoho, 2013). The ANC's political dominance means that there is a danger that political power is taken for granted and less consideration is given to the need to be responsive and accountable to constituents. This, coupled with deepening economic inequalities, means that many South Africans, particularly Black South Africans, feel deeply estranged from democracy. A common theme, recurrent in interviews with Black South Africans living on the socio-economic margins, is that 'democracy is only for the rich'.

As a result, alternative political expression and voice are being found increasingly through protest. South Africa has been dubbed the 'protest capital of the world'. Protests commonly emanate from impoverished townships and informal settlements concerned with the inadequate provision of public goods such as housing, water and electricity, and often involve marches to local municipalities, the focal point of much protest activity. A growing proportion of protests have also embarked on disruptive or even violent tactics, including the barricading of roads and the burning down of local amenities such as clinics. While the protests centre on demands for public goods, they are often an expression of the democratic deficit that is particularly acute in areas of poverty. They often seem to be partly a reaction to frustrated attempts to exercise political voice in institutional channels (Alexander et al., 2014).

While protest is frequent in South Africa, it is commonly fractured and disconnected. Unlike elsewhere in the world, protesters rarely gather in central urban spaces, the result of the enduring legacy of apartheid geography, and protests are rarely coordinated across different areas despite the common elements of their demands. One of the reasons for this is the acute resource challenges, material and otherwise, which mainly unemployed community activists face. A common strategy to disrupt community mobilization is for politically connected local elites to offer employment opportunities to activists. As one activist explained, 'That is why we have lost many cadres that are strong leaders because stomach politics at the end of the day is a bigger issue. I can be an activist but at the end of the day I have to eat.'[2] This highlights the point that the ability to challenge economic inequality requires political voice, but the ability to forge this voice is intersected by the very same inequalities.

Conclusions

The example of South Africa illustrates all three forms of political inequality discussed earlier. Citizens participate, yet increasingly it seems that the democratic measures to deepen voice and representation have themselves been captured by elites in the new system. In the midst of such political capture, new formations are emerging such as the Economic Freedom Fighters and the United Front, which seek explicitly to challenge economic inequalities. Yet their challenges from below may well be limited. South Africa's growing inequalities are shaped and maintained by rules of the game over which local citizens have little influence. South Africa illustrates the deep interconnections of economic, social and political inequalities, links which can only be broken through new forms of political action.

Notes

1. Quoting Council of Europe (2013, p. 125).
2. Interview by C. Runciman, February 2010.

Bibliography

Alexander, P., Runciman, C. and Ngwane, T. 2014. *Community Protests 2004–2014: Some Research Findings.* https://www.youtube.com/watch?v=XqwBSNBMPCU (Accessed 22 February 2016.)

Carmona, M. S. 2013. *Report of the Special Rapporteur on Extreme Poverty and Human Rights.* Geneva, UN Human Rights Council. www.un.org/esa/socdev/egms/docs/2013/EmpowermentPolicies/Report%20of%20the%20Special%20Rapporteur%20on%20extreme%20poverty%20and%20human%20rights.pdf (Accessed 9 May 2016.)

Council of Europe. 2013. *Living in Dignity in the XXIst Century, Poverty and Inequality in Societies of Human Rights: The Paradox of Democracies.* Paris, Council of Europe.

Dubrow, J. K. 2010. Cross-national measures of political inequality of voice. *Research and Methods*, Vol. 19, No. 1, pp. 93–110. http://politicalinequality.org/2010/12/13/cross-national-measures-of-political-inequality-of-voice/ (Accessed 20 February 2016.)

Justino, P. 2015. Inequality, social cooperation and local collective action. Working Paper 457. Brighton, IDS. www.ids.ac.uk/publication/inequality-social-cooperation-and-local-collective-action (Accessed 20 February 2016.)

Ngamlana, N. and Mathoho, M. 2013. *Examining the Role of Ward Committees in Enhancing Participatory Local Governance and Development in South Africa.* www.afesis.org.za/local-governance/local-governance-reports/36-examining-the-role-of-ward-committees-in-enhancing-participatory-local-governance-and-development-in-south-africa.html (Accessed 8 January 2016.)

Reich, Robert. 2015. The political roots of widening inequality. *American Prospect*, Vol. 26, No. 2, pp. 27–31. http://prospect.org/article/political-roots-widening-inequality (Accessed 20 February 2016.)

Southall, R. 2004. The ANC and black capitalism. *Review of African Political Economy*, Vol. 31, No. 100, pp. 313–28.

■ **John Gaventa** (UK/USA) is director of research at the Institute of Development Studies (IDS), Brighton, UK.

■ **Carin Runciman** (UK/South Africa) is senior researcher, South African Research Chair in Social Change, University of Johannesburg, South Africa.

13. Grounding justice and injustice

Ruth Fincher

Justice and injustice, equality and inequality, occur in places and only in places. Here are some ways to think about this reality.

Justice and injustice are produced through social practices in places and times, and are usefully explained with reference to those practices in those places, rather than solely with reference to formal, unsituated philosophical norms. This basic understanding about the nature of justice and injustice, drawn from developments in critical human geography over many decades (Harvey, 1973, 1996), is in sympathy with important recent writings from other disciplines (from economics, see Sen, 2009; from feminist political philosophy, see Young, 1990). In this contribution, several concepts are described that illuminate the ways in which justice and injustice are grounded in contexts and take on particular forms in different settings: the dispossession or displacement of nomadic peoples in China's Inner Mongolia, the absence of local people's views from planning responses to anticipated sea level rise in south-eastern Australia, and the material impediments to the right to the city in Cape Town, South Africa. In each of these examples, the stances taken by governments, at different levels and scales, are pivotal to local experiences of justice or injustice in places.

Grounded, justice-seeking, concepts: place, scale, environment, mobility, difference

For powerful thinking about the grounded production of justice and injustice, and of inequalities, the following five concepts provide a useful framework.

Locating justices and injustices in *places*. Place does more than describe variations in the lifestyles and landscapes of different locations. It includes a 'sense of place' that is basic to people's feelings of belonging and self-worth in a location of meaning to them. The idea of place also causes us to consider, as Harvey (1996) has it, 'the just production of just geographical differences', and how this might happen: how we might be different one from another and yet equal.

It makes the matter of displacement a central question of justice and injustice: are conditions in some contexts separating people unjustly from their links to place?

Identifying the *scales* at which processes giving rise to justices and injustices in places occur and intersect. They are interrelated, too. We no longer refer to different 'scales' such as the global and the local uncritically. Rather, it is now recognized that the global is local and vice versa. But the concept of scale does cause us to investigate the production of processes that shift power from actors and institutions at one scale, to those at another – and how just or unjust this shifting of control over economies and people might be. In the example of the dispossession of nomadic people, the shift in the scale at which control over herders' lives exists is evident.

Taking up questions of *environment* as a way to make us conscious that the human world links with the non-human world and must respect it. In this, there are major issues of injustice and justice. Recognizing that what we see as 'nature' and 'the environment' is socially produced, critical social science now understands that markets have caused natural resources to be used in ways that give rise to hunger and poverty in certain places. Climate change is posing new questions about the distribution of justice and injustice: what new global inequalities will be associated with the Anthropocene?

The concept of *mobility* gives a different view of the production of justice and injustice, one that treats places as origins and destinations. Justice and injustice can be present in multiple ways as we think about mobility in places, including the institutional settings that give opportunities for mobility or deprive people of them. Mobility can be a justice-creating force and can prevent fixity in communities and places from being restrictive and unjust. A very visible mobility now is that of migrant and refugee movements from certain disadvantaged places to certain more advantaged ones. The implications of these mobilities are profound.

Finally, *difference* is central to a grounded imagining of justice and injustice. It involves the recognition that any society contains different social groups whose varied interests need to be considered, and the understanding that difference can create a politics for unjustly segregating people. Power relations thread through and between these groups, as they exist in places, and may or may not assess people of different characteristics as equals. In each of the three examples discussed below, the views and lives of some groups of people are given priority over others. An awareness of the need to recognize difference helps us see that the favouring of certain interests over others may be unjust.

Key examples in grounding justice and injustice

Dispossession/displacement of nomadic people

To see the importance of place and also scale in the production of injustice and in the possibilities for justice, consider the dispossession and displacement of nomadic people. Such dispossession renders them sedentary and fixed in certain locations that are more limited than those on which their lives had previously been built. Examples of this practice abound – for example in attempts to close down services in tiny Indigenous communities in northern Australia, requiring people to obtain services from designated major towns and so to relocate there. There is the example of the Israeli government's attempts to 'settle' Bedouin people in the Negev desert region, by declaring small Bedouin settlements 'unrecognized' and requiring people to obtain services from centrally recognized townships. I focus below on analyses of the Chinese northern steppes of Inner Mongolia, conducted by the economic geographer Michael Webber (2012), that reveal the situated complexity of finding injustice and justice in the changes in this place.

Since 1998, forced ecological migration has occurred in northern China including Inner Mongolia, in light of the central government's view that land use practices by herders have resulted in degraded grasslands and increased desertification. Bans on grazing have meant that herders, almost all of them Mongols, have had to relinquish traditional ways and migrate to central towns, where they are encouraged to develop non-agricultural work such as animal processing and tourism. Those forced to migrate do not know whether they will ever be permitted to return to their old ways of life and places. Most were unhappy about the programme of migration, regretting the ensuing reduction in their self-sufficiency. Decision-making over their lives has been moved from the scale of their local group to that of government at a range of higher levels. Officials claim that people are richer than they were before they were moved, now that their livelihoods are more oriented to commercial markets. Presumably this constitutes 'justice' in the official view. The goals of conservationists wanting to protect the grasslands are also served. A goal of national ethnic unification has also been served by longstanding migration of Han Chinese into Mongol cultural zones. Yet many dispute the logics of justice and injustice at play here – the logic that good outcomes always derive from entering the market more thoroughly, and that ending traditional grazing practices is the way to protect the grasslands. Mongol critics observe that land degradation now exists because of crop farming introduced to the grasslands. They can no longer make their own decisions and live their lives self-sufficiently through mobility.

Climate change adaptation strategies in the times of places

Climate change and the scales of the processes contributing to it are tremendously significant in current discussions of environmental justice and injustice. The scales of relevance here are temporal as well as spatial. Global atmospheric processes affect everyone everywhere, but global warming has been caused by the actions of some people in some places whose economic development has benefited from these actions, and the negative outcomes are not falling solely on them in spatial terms. Nor is the harm of global warming falling justly in generational terms. Future generations are likely to face the consequences of the actions of their predecessors.

To these global and local dilemmas have come social scientific discussions of climate change adaptation, in which the focus is on resilient action rather than solely on mitigation. Of course that action must be taken in places, locally. In those local places, forms of science and policy usually made at different scales need to be considered.

One study (Barnett et al., 2014) of tiny, disadvantaged coastal communities in south-eastern Australia that are subject to sea-level rise in a future of global warming has made suggestions about responding to this situation in a fair or just way. Its proposal is to align official policies for planning for climate change with local knowledge and practices for dealing with extreme environmental events that already exist in those places. Local knowledge, as expressed in everyday practices, often diverges from expert scientific opinion formed at larger scales (often the national and planetary) and the adaptation actions it suggests.

Residents of these small settlements build their environmental knowledge on the basis of known family and community histories, and make clear their understanding of the similarities between these experiences in the past, present and anticipated future. In this context, popular messages of permanent, climate-driven catastrophe that draw on 'the science' are incommensurable with residents' local time-spaces. The urgency that many decision-makers express for taking action now that will be appropriate for a future of higher sea levels and more frequent flooding is not shared by local residents. The official future-makers in senior levels of governments do not seem at present to be hearing the stories that local people are telling about what their futures could and should include. This is not to suggest that local people should be the sole arbiters of knowledge, or overly privileged in decision-making, but it is to say that effective planning for adaptation requires the inclusion of the varied perspectives of local people. Justice for local people is in part the way in which their everyday practices and understandings of time are included in adaptation to climate change

The 'right to the city'

As the urbanization and mobility of the world's population increases, we see people clamouring for access to the services and opportunities of the city, and especially to those parts of cities that are well provided with public services, public spaces and the civilities of community development. The right to the city is a notion (drawn from the writings of French philosopher and urbanist Henri Lefebvre) that is strongly held in discussions of the injustices and justices associated with urbanization. It means the right of all to the benefits that an adequately resourced urban life can have, and that they have a collective role in determining.

Life in the good city also recognizes difference and inequalities, where there will be a commitment to creating cosmopolitanism as well as providing infrastructure and employment.

Since 2001, when a world charter of the right to the city was developed at the first World Social Forum in Brazil, international meetings of urbanists and urban planners have been underpinned by the notion of the right to the city, amid concerns that privatization policies are reducing the public realm of cities (Harvey, 2008). The idea of the right to the city applies to existing inhabitants of urban areas, and to those who are part of national and international population movements, whose search for a better life is usually a search for a better life under modern urban conditions.

In their analysis of the urban injustices of the contemporary South African city, Parnell and Pieterse (2010) take up 'the issue of the universal right to the city as the moral platform from which the developmental role of the state should be defined' (Parnell and Pieterse, 2010, p. 147). They take the example of Cape Town, a large and well-resourced city which nevertheless has a considerable, spatially concentrated group of residents in poverty. They stress sensitivity to local scale and locational context in achieving poverty reduction as an expression of the right to the city. Local levels of the state are significant players here, not just national governments, as they have the close knowledge needed to improve the conditions of households and neighbourhoods.

Despite good intentions politically, the complex material conditions of Cape Town limit governmental capacity to deliver services to poor households and areas. In the past ten years, barriers to providing subsidies for services to poor households have been administrative. Many households are not present on the city's billing system for household infrastructural services because they are in areas never serviced, or in locations where bulk delivery of services had been made rather than delivery to households. Many households had no postal addresses and were thus invisible to agencies trying to get service subsidies to them. Things are gradually improving, but of course, 'the issue of informality lies at the core of this unspoken discussion of an alternative governance framework' (Parnell and Pieterse, 2010, p. 155).

This example highlights the point that governmental bodies with the potential to be helpful and enabling may have limited capacity to be so. All states are not equal in their capacity. But a focus on the right to the city leads us to consider the complex situation in which governmental practices occur, at the scale of the lived everyday in a place. The mitigation of injustice relies on small steps as well as on large pronouncements to do with national policies and constitutions.

Conclusion

New forms of injustice and justice are being made all the time, in places, and old forms can persist just as inequalities can persist. Knowing how this happens requires us to ground our thinking and analysis of justice and injustice in situated contexts that are often local and multi-scaled, rather than relying solely on overarching understandings that are only vaguely related to the actual places in which people live and interact. As Harvey put it, 'the question of justice falls squarely into the middle of the tension between particularity and universalism' (Harvey, 1996, p. 332). We can have universal notions of justice, but these need to be situated in space and time, and grounded in contexts. A conceptual strategy that highlights place, scale, environment, mobility and difference can go a long way towards revealing not only what is happening and why, but what interventions might usefully enhance just outcomes there and reduce inequalities.

Bibliography

Barnett, J, Graham, S, Mortreux, C, Fincher, R, Waters, E. and Hurlimann, A. 2014. A local coastal adaptation pathway. *Nature Climate Change*, Vol. 4, pp. 1103–08.

Harvey, D. 1973. *Social Justice and the City*. Baltimore, Md., Johns Hopkins University Press.

Harvey, D. 1996. *Justice, Nature and the Geography of Difference*. Oxford, Blackwell.

Harvey, D. 2008. The right to the city. *New Left Review*, Vol. 53, pp. 23–40.

Parnell, S. and Pieterse, E. 2010. The 'Right to the City': institutional imperatives of a developmental state. *International Journal of Urban and Regional Research*, Vol. 34, No.1, pp. 146–62.

Sen, A. 2009. *The Idea of Justice*. Cambridge, Mass., Belknap Press of Harvard University Press.

Webber, M. 2012. *Making Capitalism in Rural China*. Cheltenham, UK, Edward Elgar.

Young, I. M. 1990. *Justice and the Politics of Difference*. Princeton, N.J., Princeton University Press.

■ **Ruth Fincher** *(Australia) is distinguished professor emeritus in geography at the University of Melbourne. An urban and social geographer, her research interests have long been in questions of social and spatial justice and the production of difference in the city.*

14. Rising economic and gender inequality: intersecting spheres of injustice

Shahra Razavi

The evidence for rising income inequality over the past four decades has triggered an array of analytical work, and has also resonated with the wider public. However, gender inequalities have appeared only tangentially in these largely 'malestream' political economy debates. Approaching the issue of inequality from a gender perspective raises a number of different questions which are explored in this contribution. A gender perspective broadens the horizon by foregrounding the multidimensional nature of inequality. This involves socio-economic disadvantage, but also misrecognition as a result of discriminatory social norms and violence, as well as constraints on voice and participation.

The evidence on rising income inequality within developed and developing countries over the past four decades has triggered a rich array of analytical work by leading academics (Atkinson, 2015) and international organizations (UNDP, 2013), and has also resonated with the wider public and underlined the need for countervailing political and policy responses. Gender inequalities have appeared only tangentially in these largely 'malestream' political economy debates. There is some useful (though conflicting) analysis of how gender equality and inequality in paid work accentuates or mitigates income inequality, and whether the growth in female employment has had an equalizing or disequalizing effect on income distribution. Approaching the issue of inequality from a gender perspective, however, raises a number of different questions, which I explore briefly in this contribution. A gender perspective broadens the horizon by foregrounding the multidimensional nature of inequality, which includes not only socio-economic disadvantage or redistributive concerns, but also claims of misrecognition including stigma, stereotyping and violence, as well as constraints on voice, agency and participation. These three dimensions are recognized by human rights scholars as constituting the concept of 'substantive equality' (Fredman, 2011), and also reflect the integrated conception of justice by Fraser and colleagues (2004) as encompassing struggles for redistribution, recognition and representation.[1]

Gender inequality and class inequality: a view from the malestream

In the mainstream writings on inequality by political economists, some passing references are made to gender inequality (e.g. Atkinson, 2015). These refer for the most part to how women's labour force participation accentuates or mitigates income inequality. The earliest studies for the USA (from the 1950s up to 1980), for example, found that while the pay distribution was getting wider, it was not accompanied by a rise in the inequality of household incomes. A key factor explaining this seeming incongruence was the influx of women, especially married women with children, into the labour force, because their earnings moderated economic inequality (Atkinson, 2015, ch. 2). However, the impact of women's employment on household income inequality depended on who was entering the labour force. In the immediate post-war period it seems that increased participation by women had an equalizing effect on income distribution because the women who entered the workforce were married to (or cohabiting with) low-earning men. This is contrasted with the later period after 1970 when increased labour force participation largely came from women with above-average earnings who were often married to high-earning men – a trend that seems to have reversed again in recent years (Atkinson, 2015).

Taking a broader range of countries (seventeen industrialized countries from the Luxembourg Income Study database) Susan Harkness (2013) shows that while as a general rule women with higher earning power are most likely to work in all countries, employment rates among those who are less educated vary enormously, from under 40 per cent in Italy and Spain to over 70 per cent in Finland. While the unequal distribution of paid work among women might suggest that women's employment will reinforce income inequality, her detailed findings do not support this hypothesis. In fact, in all seventeen countries women's labour force participation had an equalizing effect on income inequality across households with couples, although in countries where women's participation rates are low, such as in Southern Europe, the equalizing effects are much smaller. However, as she notes in her conclusion, 'Perhaps one of the most surprising findings here is just how much lower women's earnings are relative to their partners across all of these countries, including the Nordic ones' (p. 228).

Socio-economic disadvantage from a gender perspective

Approaching the issue of socio-economic inequality from a gender perspective, as Harkness alludes to in her remarks above, would help us raise a different set of questions – not about how women's paid work contributes to income equality or inequality, but instead about the scale of gender inequalities in the economic domain and what its drivers are.

At a time when women's access to education has converged with, if not surpassed, men's, why have women's and men's economic opportunities and earnings not shown a commensurate degree of convergence? As feminist economist Stephanie Seguino puts it, why has equality in the 'capability domain' not been translated into equality in the 'livelihoods domain'? And 'why should women's economic activities on average attract a lower valuation in the market than men's, for example, if their capabilities are equal?' (Seguino, 2013, p. 7). To give a broad-brush global overview, the gap between women's and men's labour force participation stands at around 26 percentage points, but with significant variations across regions. Progress in closing this gap has stalled in most regions with the exception of Latin America and the Caribbean, and women on average earn about 24 per cent less than men (UN Women, 2015).

It is difficult to understand income inequalities between women and men without delving into the gendered arena of non-market work, including unpaid domestic and care work. This activity is essential for well-being and economic dynamism, and continues to shape and constrain women's engagement in paid work. On average women do nearly 2.5 times as much of this work as men, and the gender inequalities widen when there are young children in the household (UN Women, 2015). The domain of non-market work, however, remains as parenthetical to political economy today as it was in the past. The failure of labour markets to acknowledge the contribution of unpaid domestic and care work in reproducing labour and enabling the functioning of any economy is a reflection of the fact that labour markets are 'bearers of gender' (Elson, 1999).

In low-income countries in particular the lack of basic infrastructure, especially water and sanitation, contributes to the drudgery of the work involved in provisioning for households, work that is mainly done by women and girls on an unpaid basis (UN Women, 2015). This constrains women's time and energy for paid work, as well as in other activities, self-care and leisure. In countries where this infrastructure is largely in place, the lack of family-friendly policies to support women and men to combine paid and unpaid work can be a major constraint, especially for women who bear heavy care responsibilities. This points to the need for collectively financed paid maternity and parental leave, and for quality childcare services as a major enabler of women's economic participation. Comparative evidence from across Europe shows that countries that provide comprehensive support to working parents, including the provision of childcare services, have higher rates of female employment than countries without such policies (Thévenon, 2011). These policies may also help mitigate the 'motherhood penalty', which accounts for as much as 40 to 50 per cent of the gender gap in pay.

In developed and developing countries alike, public transfer payments such as child and family allowances and pensions tend to narrow, though not eliminate, the gender gap in personal income from paid employment (UN Women, 2015). Atkinson (2015) argues that while tax and transfer policies are clearly important means of redistributing income, today's high levels of inequality can only be reduced effectively if we also tackle head-on inequalities in the marketplace.

This is an important observation which should draw attention to the complex ways in which gender inequalities are embedded in markets, and the need for multi-pronged actions to address them.

Socio-economic disadvantage reinforced by discriminatory social norms

Gender pay gaps have often been attributed to women's lower educational achievements, which are seen as a contributor to 'human capital'. However, now that women's 'human capital investments' equal or surpass men's, attention has shifted from years of study to the subjects studied or to women's underlying 'motivations' and 'commitment' to paid work, shifting the goalposts and requiring women to change their 'commitments' to paid work to become more like men (Rubery and Grimshaw, 2015). This suggests that the previous focus on what we might term the 'supply-side' characteristics of workers may have been misplaced. Even economists are discovering that demand-side approaches, informed by sociological perspectives, may provide more useful insights into how labour markets operate and how they reproduce gender stratifications (Rubery and Grimshaw, 2015).

These more sociological approaches understand labour markets to be social institutions shaped by power dynamics, societal valuations, social norms and stereotypes. The persistence of the gender pay gap can be attributed in part to formal rules and informal practices that value male and female labour differently, regardless of the levels of 'human capital' they embody. These pay gaps are closely intertwined with gender-based occupational segregation which slots women and men into different occupations that are deemed suitable (horizontal segregation) and at different levels, grades or positions of seniority (vertical segregation). The low value attached to quintessentially female tasks performed in the private domain, such as domestic work, nursing and caring, is carried over into the labour market to devalue the jobs dominated by women. The assumption that these types of work somehow flow naturally from women's genetic endowment rather than from knowledge and skills acquired through education, training or experience lurks behind the low recognition and rewards they command, as does the continued treatment of women's wages as pin money to top up the male breadwinner wage.

Occupational segregation is widespread and persistent across both formal and informal labour markets. It is resistant to change, even as countries develop economically. Its most pernicious impact is in maintaining pervasive gender pay gaps, by making it hard for job evaluations to compare like with like when women and men are slotted into non-similar jobs. This applies especially in the current context of individualized pay setting under a broadly deregulation-oriented agenda (Rubery and Grimshaw, 2015). These issues of misrecognition are pervasive, and go beyond the ways in which discriminatory social norms and stereotypes shape labour market hierarchies and drive the undervaluation of women's paid work. Gender stereotypes, stigma and violence manifest themselves in a variety of settings, in both private and public life, including through intimate partner violence and sexual harassment in the workplace, all of which have the effect of reinforcing gender hierarchies of power.

Women's agency and collective action

Having access to an independent source of income can give women an exit option from intimate relationships that are abusive and unacceptable (Kabeer, 2000). There is also some evidence to suggest that beyond its impact at the individual level in terms of women's agency, women's increased access to economic resources can have the structural effect of shifting social norms and stereotypes in a gender-equitable direction (Seguino, 2007).[2]

Institutional and organizational characteristics can also make a difference. In particular, wage-setting policies, mechanisms and institutional practices that reduce overall wage inequalities influence gender pay gaps. Countries with statutory minimum wages that are set at a relatively high level, workplace agreements that protect low-income workers and higher trade union coverage are also associated with lower gender pay gaps and a lower wage penalty for workers in care-related occupations (Budig and Misra, 2010).

How can women create the countervailing forces needed to reduce gender inequality in livelihoods and access to resources? To build inclusive and effective movements, women have to confront tenacious hurdles stemming from gender-biased governance structures as well as the many cleavages that divide women along the lines of class, race and ethnicity, and immigration status, to name a few factors. In addition to organizing through their own movements and organizations, it is also critical for women's rights advocates to work with and through broader labour and social justice movements in order to amplify their voice and be heard.

While historically, trade unions have often failed to be inclusive of women, seeing women-specific concerns as less of a priority, there has been a sea change in their approach over the past couple of decades. Women's membership of trade unions has increased since the early 2000s, though their presence is not yet reflected at the leadership level, and there is also greater responsiveness to the kinds of issues that matter to women workers, such as the precariousness of jobs, equal pay, the importance of services, and sexual harassment at work.

As women have strengthened their foothold in the world of work, women's organizations have also been at the forefront of new forms of labour organization involving informal workers such as domestic workers, street traders and homeworkers. In the context of rising public concern about inequality, movements of domestic workers have been among the most vibrant parts of the labour movement. About 80 per cent of these workers are women, usually from marginalized racial, ethnic and immigrant backgrounds, and they are clustered at the bottom of the pay hierarchy. What is even more encouraging is the way in which domestic workers' organizations have built alliances across countries, while building relationships with established trade unions, other workers' groups and employers, to drive the agenda for social change at multiple levels including the local, national and global (Boris and Fish, 2014).

Notes

1. Substantive equality is often contrasted with formal equality, and refers to the concrete enjoyment of human rights.

2. Seguino's analysis uses responses from *World Value Surveys* over a fifteen-year period for seventy countries to analyse the determinants of changes in women's and men's attitudes regarding gender norms and stereotypes. Her regression results suggest that women's increased share of employment has a positive impact on attitudinal shifts in a gender-equitable direction.

Bibliography

Atkinson, A. B. 2015. *Inequality: What Can Be Done?* Cambridge, Mass. and London, Harvard University Press.

Boris, E. and Fish, J. N. 2014. Domestic workers go global: the birth of the International Domestic Workers Federation. *New Labour Forum*, Vol. 23, No. 3, pp. 76–81. *http://nlf.sagepub.com/content/23/3/76.full* (Accessed 16 February 2016).

Budig, M. and Misra, J. 2010. How care-work employment shapes earnings in cross-national perspective. *International Labour Review*, Vol. 149, No. 4, pp. 441–60. *http://onlinelibrary.wiley.com/doi/10.1111/j.1564-913X.2010.00097.x/abstract* (Accessed 16 February 2016).

Elson, D. 1999. Labor markets as gendered institutions: equality, efficiency and empowerment issues. *World Development*, Vol. 27, No. 3, pp. 611–27.

Fraser, N., Dahl, H. M., Stoltz, P. and Willig, R. 2004. Redistribution, recognition and representation in capitalist global society: an interview with Nancy Fraser. *Acta Sociologica*, Vol. 47, No. 4, pp. 374–82. *www.jstor.org/stable/4195051?seq=1#page_scan_tab_contents* (Accessed 16 February 2016).

Fredman, S. 2011. The potential and limits of an equal rights paradigm in addressing poverty. *Stellenbosch Law Review*, Vol. 22, No. 3, pp. 566–90. *http://reference.sabinet.co.za/sa_epublication_article/ju_slr_v22_n3_a9* (Accessed 16 February 2016).

Harkness, S. 2013. Women's employment and household income inequality. Janet C. Gornick and Markus Jantti (eds), *Income Inequality: Economic Disparities and the Middle Class in Affluent Countries*. Redwood City, Calif., Stanford University Press, pp. 207–33.

Kabeer, N. 2000. *The Power to Choose. Bangladeshi Women and Labour Market Decisions in London and Dhaka*. London and New York, Verso.

Rubery, J. and Grimshaw, D. 2015. The 40-year pursuit of equal pay: a case of constantly moving goalposts. *Cambridge Journal of Economics*, Vol. 39, No. 2, pp. 319–43. *http://cje.oxfordjournals.org/content/39/2/319* (Accessed 16 February 2016).

Seguino, S. 2007. Plus ca change: evidence on global trends in gender norms and stereotypes. *Feminist Economics*, Vol. 13, No. 2, pp. 1–28. *https://www.uvm.edu/~sseguino/pdf/plus_ca_change.pdf* (Accessed 22 February 2016).

Seguino, S. 2013. Toward gender justice: confronting stratification and unequal power. *Generos Multidisciplinary Journal of Gender Studies*, Vol. 2, No. 1, pp. 1–36. *http://hipatiapress.com/hpjournals/index.php/generos/article/view/277* (Accessed 16 February 2016).

Thévenon, O. 2011. Family policies in OECD countries: a comparative analysis. *Population and Development Review*, Vol. 37, No. 1, pp. 57–87. *www.vasa.abo.fi/users/minygard/Undervisning-filer/Th%C3%A9venon%202011.pdf* (Accessed 16 February 2016).

UNDP. 2013. *Humanity Divided: Confronting Inequality in Developing Countries*. New York, UNDP.

UN Women. 2015. *Progress of the World's Women 2015/2016: Transforming Economies, Realizing Rights*. New York, UN Women.

■ **Shahra Razavi** *(Iran) is chief, research and data at UN Women.*

World Social Science Report

Chapter 2

Inequalities in different parts of the world

15. **Recent changes in income inequality in China**
    Li Shi

16. **Inequality in India: drivers and consequences**
    Jayati Ghosh

17. **Social justice and equality/inequality issues in modern-day Russia**
    Natalia Grigorieva

18. **Inequality in sub-Saharan Africa: dimensions and drivers**
    Jimi O. Adesina

19. **Inequalities in the Arab region**
    Adam Hanieh

20. **The invisible hands of racial inequality in the USA**
    Fredrick C. Harris

21. **Income inequality in Brazil: new evidence from combined tax and survey data**
    Marcelo Medeiros

15. Recent changes in income inequality in China

Li Shi

During the past three decades China's economic growth has been among the fastest in the world. At the same time the country experienced one of the fastest increases in income and wealth inequality in the world. Since 2008, however, the Gini coefficient measuring income inequality seems to have stabilized and may even have started to decline. This contribution looks at recent data and underlines the policy measures that may explain this new trend.

Since the end of the 1970s China has undergone dramatic changes in its economic structures, institutions and social policies, and in the composition of its employment. During the past three decades China's economic growth has been among the fastest in the world. Yet China also experienced one of the fastest increases in income and wealth inequality in the world over the same period. While the rate of annual GDP growth was close to an average of 10 per cent between 1985 and 2014, the Gini coefficient of income distribution increased from 0.38 to 0.47[1] during the same period.

Despite this change, official statistics also show a more recent declining trend in income inequality in China over the past five to six years. The Gini coefficient of national income inequality reached its highest level in 2008 (0.491), and has been declining ever since. It seems that 2007–08 was a turning point for income inequality trends.

However, questions have been raised recently about whether income inequality really has decreased. This contribution attempts to provide explanations for the latest changes in income inequality in China by providing new evidence from the 2013 China Household Income Project (CHIP) survey.[2] Increasing income inequality and disequalizing forces are briefly discussed, and some explanations are provided for the decrease in national income inequality over the past few years.

Economic transition and disequalizing forces

Income inequality has increased considerably since the beginning of the Chinese economic transition that started in the early 1980s. China had previously been an egalitarian society with a planned economy and low income inequality,[3] particularly in urban areas where the government strictly controlled the wage system and wage distribution. The National Bureau of Statistics China (NBS) estimated the urban Gini coefficient at 0.16 in the early 1980s.

Income distribution gradually became less equal from the mid-1980s. Income inequality increased in the country as a whole, both between and within urban and rural areas.[4] According to official statistics, the Gini coefficient of income inequality reached 0.35 in urban areas and 0.38 in rural areas in 2008, while the national figure climbed to 0.491 (see *Figure 15.1*), the highest level in the history of the Chinese communist regime.

Of all the economic transition processes, the development of the private sector and the privatization of state-owned enterprises (SOEs) were the most important. At the beginning of the economic transition, almost all urban employees worked for either SOEs or urban collective enterprises (UCEs, a type of urban public enterprise). In 1988 more than 90 per cent of all urban workers were employed in SOEs or UCEs (see *Figure 15.2*). However, the percentage of SOE and UCE employees decreased dramatically in the following years, falling to less than 25 per cent in 2007. Wage and income inequality also increased significantly in public sector enterprises such as SOEs and in the government institutions (Gustafsson and Sicular, 2008).

Along with decreasing public-sector employment, employment in private enterprises, foreign enterprises and joint-venture firms increased very rapidly, as did self-employment. Consequently, private-sector employment exceeded public-sector employment at the end of the century, which contributed to increased inequality of wages and incomes.[5]

Figure 15.1 **Gini coefficient of income inequality in China, 1981–2014**

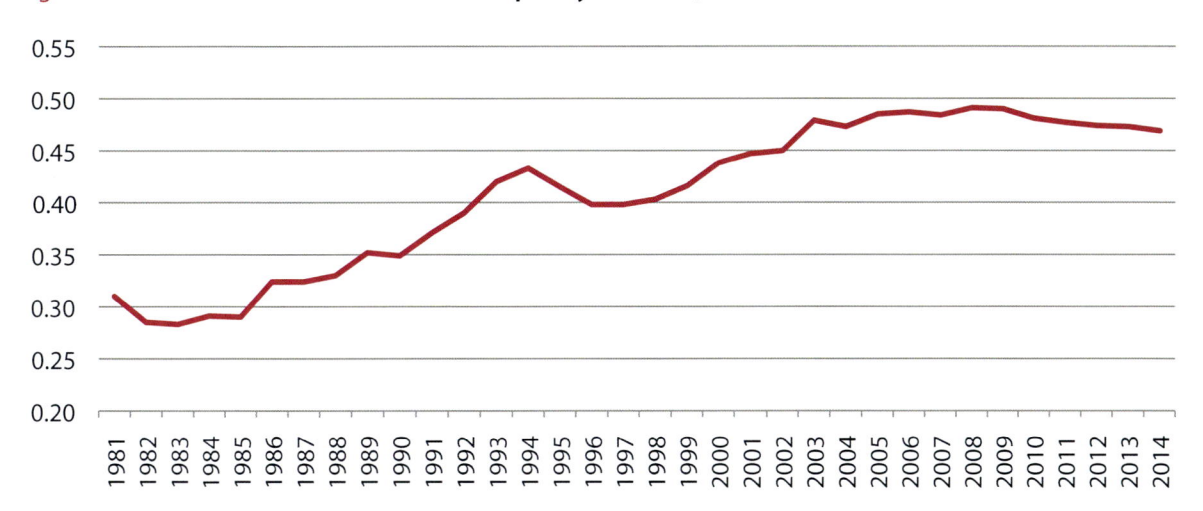

Sources: The Gini coefficients for 1981–2001 are by Ravallion and Chen (2007), who calculated them using the income data from the NBS urban and rural household surveys. The Gini coefficients for 2003–14 are from NBS (2015). The 2002 Gini coefficient is from Gustafsson and Sicular (2008).

Figure 15.2 **Number of workers in state-owned and urban collective enterprises as a percentage of all workers in urban China**

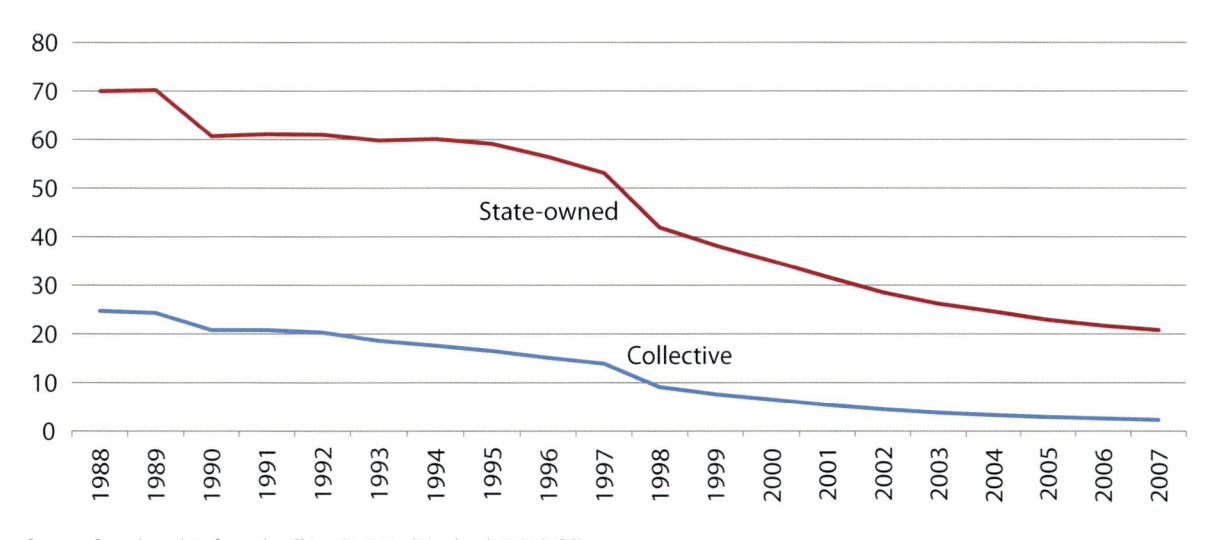

Sources: Based on data from the *China Statistical Yearbook 2008* (NBS).

Urban–rural disparity

The income gap between urban households and rural households increased significantly from the mid-1980s, and particularly between 1997 and 2008. As shown in *Figure 15.3*, the ratio of urban household income per capita to rural household income increased from 2.5 in 1997 to 3.0 in 2009, so that income per capita is three times higher in urban areas than in rural areas. This urban–rural income gap has played an increasingly important role in income inequality in China as a whole. An analysis based on the decomposition of Theil indices[6] indicates that the urban–rural income gap contributed 37 per cent, 41 per cent and 46 per cent to national income inequality in 1988, 1995 and 2002 respectively (Sicular et al., 2007).

Income inequality also increased in rural China. With the collapse of the rural collective economy, the privatization of land, the emergence of family farms and the growth of township-village enterprises (TVEs), it increased particularly in the 1990s. TVEs first emerged in the coastal regions, where they grew more quickly than elsewhere (Khan and Riskin, 1998), leading to an imbalance in regional growth that became one of the major contributors to increasing income inequality. As a result, non-agricultural incomes and wage incomes from employment in TVEs were concentrated in rural households in the coastal region rather than in the central and western regions.

Declining income inequality in recent years

Figure 15.1 presents changes in national income inequality, showing that the income inequality increased until 2008, and began to decrease afterwards. Between 2008 and 2014, the Gini coefficient declined by a total of 2.3 percentage points, a small but significant change.

It is often argued that the official estimates of income inequality are biased towards a lower figure, because extremely rich households are less likely to figure in the NBS household survey. In spite of this, it is possible that national income inequality has shown a declining trend over the past few years. The data from the last two waves of CHIP surveys – 2007 and 2013 – also indicate that national income inequality decreased by 3 percentage points in this period (Li et al., 2015). A decomposition analysis of the data implies that the decreasing income inequality in the country as a whole is due to the narrowing income gap between urban and rural households. Nonetheless, income inequality within urban and rural areas has risen since 2007. The urban Gini coefficient increased from 0.34 in 2007 to 0.36 in 2013, while the rural one increased from 0.36 to 0.37 (Li et al., 2015).

Why has the urban–rural income gap narrowed during the last few years? There are several answers to this question.

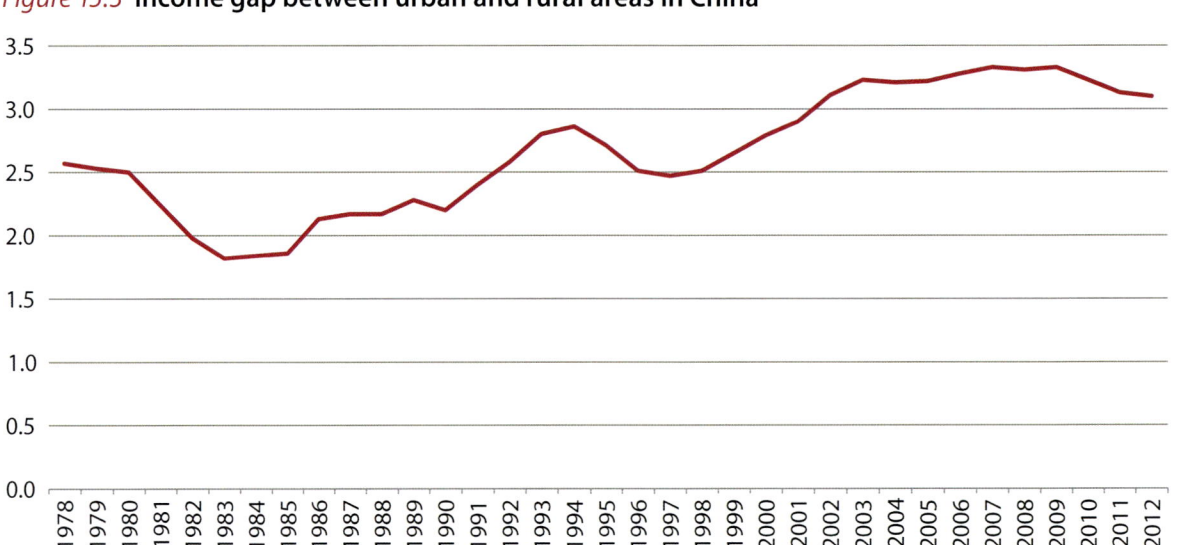

Figure 15.3 **Income gap between urban and rural areas in China**

Sources: *China Statistical Yearbook* (NBS) for relevant years.

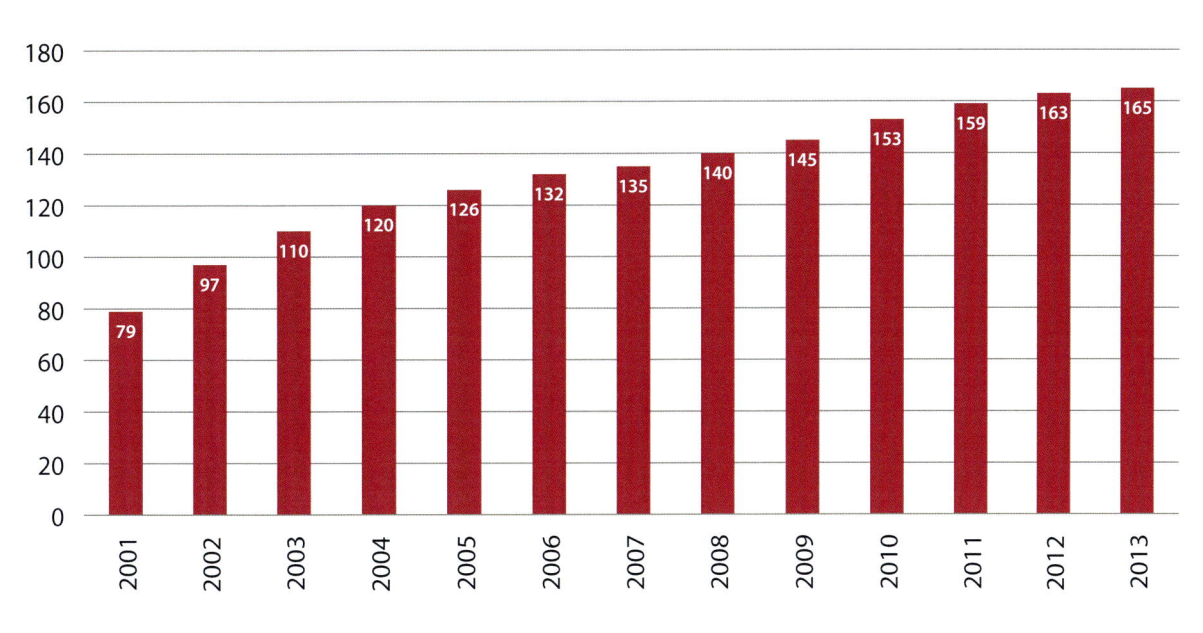

Figure 15.4 **Number of rural–urban migrant workers in China (in millions)**

Year	Millions
2001	79
2002	97
2003	110
2004	120
2005	126
2006	132
2007	135
2008	140
2009	145
2010	153
2011	159
2012	163
2013	165

Source: *Monitoring Report of Rural Migrant Workers* for various years (NBS).

The increasing number of rural–urban migrant workers has led to faster wage income growth for this group, increasing their remittances to rural areas. There were close to 170 million rural–urban migrant workers by the end of 2013 (see *Figure 15.4*), compared with fewer than 80 million in 2001. And after almost twenty years of rural–urban migration, the wages of unskilled workers – including migrant workers – have started to increase[7] more rapidly than the wages of skilled urban workers. The real wages of rural–urban migrant workers increased by 16 per cent in 2010 and 15 per cent in 2011(Li et al., 2015).

Although Chinese economic growth slowed after the international financial crisis in 2008, this slowing-down did not have a negative impact on employment in urban areas. The number of urban employees increased by 24 per cent during the 2007–13 period, even though the economic growth rate fell by 2–3 percentage points. To deal with the shock of the international financial crisis, the Chinese government instigated a stimulation package in 2009, including large investments in infrastructure which generated increasing demand for unskilled and migrant workers.

Since 2003, the Chinese government has issued new policies to increase the income of rural households and of low-income groups. These policies have played a very important role in reducing the income gap between urban and rural households (Li and Sicular, 2014). Since 2006 they have included an exemption from agricultural taxes and fees for rural households. These taxes and fees had been a huge burden for rural Chinese households, particularly in the 1990s when they accounted for around 10 per cent of rural households' average income. Moreover, rural taxes and fees were regressive rather than progressive, with lower-income groups taxed at higher rates than higher-income households. This exemption from agricultural taxes and fees has had a positive impact on reducing income inequality in rural areas and between urban and rural areas, and taxes have become more progressive since the reforms.

Since 2002, policies have also included agricultural subsidies for farming households. This policy was initiated partly to offset the potential shock effect of China joining the World Trade Organization (WTO) on rural household incomes. Nevertheless, the subsidies led to a narrowing of the income gap between urban and rural households. In addition, the Dibao Program, a cash transfer programme guaranteeing a minimum income for poor and low-income households, which started in the mid-1990s, was expanded very rapidly from 1999 onwards to cover rural as well as urban areas. By the end of 2013, nearly 54 million rural people were receiving Dibao funds.[8]

Finally, the rural social protection network has gradually expanded during the past ten years to cover all people living in rural areas. The New Rural Cooperative Medical Scheme, a type of health insurance initiated in the late 1990s, has seen its coverage grow rapidly since 2005. By the end of 2013, more than 800 million rural people were participating in the programme, with a participation rate close to 99 per cent in rural areas. This programme has had important indirect effects on rural incomes. Further, the New Rural Pension Scheme was established around 2010 and has expanded rapidly. In most counties, all rural people aged 60 and above receive 65 yuan per month, equivalent only to one-third of the rural poverty line in 2010.

To conclude, China experienced rapid economic growth and a swift increase in income inequality in the first three decades of its economic transition. However, income inequality has narrowed since 2008 due to a reduction in the income gap between urban and rural households. This reduction was mainly due to rural migrant workers' wages increasing more quickly than those of skilled urban workers, and to the social policies implemented in rural areas. These trends have to be placed in the context of China's new social and economic policies. In recent years, China has changed its social policy with the aim of reducing disparities in income distribution. The government's economic policy has also changed, from a focus on economic growth and efficiency to equal sharing of the outcomes of growth and a harmonious society; from stimulating investment and export growth to encouraging an increase in consumption.

Notes

1. In this article, China refers to mainland China. If Hong Kong, Macau and Taiwan, China were to be included, income inequality would be much greater.

2. The CHIP survey was conducted in five waves, in 1988, 1995, 2002, 2007 and 2013. The 2013 CHIP survey was conducted in the spring of 2014, collecting information on household income and consumption expenditures in the previous year.

3. The Gini coefficient of income inequality was estimated around 0.3 in the early 1980s (Ravallion and Chen, 2007).

4. It should be noted that urban–rural division in China is administrative rather than demographic. Some rural areas in the coastal region are in fact peri-urban areas.

5. Wage inequality is higher in the private sector than in the public sector, as wage distribution in the public sector continues to be largely controlled by the government.

6. The Theil index is a weighted average of the inequality within subgroups, as well as of the inequality between these subgroups. For example, income inequality in China is measured as the average inequality in urban and rural areas, plus the inequality between urban and rural areas.

7. As an economy develops, labourers in the subsistence sector move into the modern sector and a point is reached at which excess labour is fully absorbed into the modern sector, and further capital accumulation and economic growth begin to increase wages. This is called the Lewis turning point.

8. See China National Bureau of Statistics, *http://data.stats.gov.cn/easyquery.htm?cn=C01*

Bibliography

Gustafsson, B., Li, S. and Sicular, T. 2008. *Income Inequality and Public Policy in China*. Cambridge, Cambridge University Press.

Khan, A. and Riskin, C. 1998. Income and inequality in China: composition, distribution and growth of household income, 1988 to 1995. *China Quarterly*, Vol. 154, pp. 221–53.

Li, S., Luo, C., Sicular, T. and Yue, X. 2015. The latest changes in income inequality in China. Presented at the International Conference on China: Accountability and Control in the Xi Jinping Era, organized by the Centre for Contemporary Chinese Studies, University of Melbourne, 21–22 August 2015.

Li, S. and Sicular, T. 2014. The distribution of household income in China: Inequality, poverty, and policies. *China Quarterly*, Vol. 217, pp. 1–41.

National Bureau of Statistics. Various years. *China Statistical Yearbook*.

National Bureau of Statistics. Various years. *Monitoring Report of Rural Migrant Workers*.

National Bureau of Statistics. 2013. Ma Jiantang's press conference. *www.stats.gov.cn/was40/gjtjj_detail.jsp?searchword=%BB%F9%C4%E1%CF%B5%CA%FD&channelid=6697&record=4*

National Bureau of Statistics. 2015. *Statistical Bulletin of China's Economic and Social Development 2014. www.stats.gov.cn/tjsj/zxfb/201502/t20150226_685799.html*.

Ravallion, M. and Chen, S. 2007. China's (uneven) progress against poverty. *Journal of Development Economics*, Vol. 82, No. 1, pp. 1–42.

Sicular, T. Yue, X., Gustafsson, B. and Li, S. 2007. The urban–rural income gap and inequality in China. *Review of Income and Wealth*, Vol. 53, No. 1, pp. 93–126.

■ *LI Shi (China) is professor of economics in the School of Economics and Business, and acting director of the China Institute for Income Distribution and Poverty Studies, at Beijing Normal University. www.iza.org/en/webcontent/personnel/photos/index_html?key=161*

16. Inequality in India: drivers and consequences

Jayati Ghosh

Inequalities in India increased following the internal and external economic liberalization measures of the 1980s. Since then, the country's economy has expanded very rapidly, particularly after 2002, reaching an average annual growth of about 6–8 per cent. Yet the benefits of growth remain very unevenly distributed across the population. Existing sociocultural divisions – such as those operating on gender, caste and community lines – have been strengthened through intersections with new economic drivers. Inequality constitutes a real challenge for India's future development.

India is often mistakenly seen as a country with relatively low economic inequality. In fact, the country's inequalities widened after the internal and external economic liberalization measures from the 1980s, which attracted global financial investors and boosted economic growth considerably. The economy had been growing at an average annual rate of about 3 per cent in the years after independence in 1947. It started to expand rapidly, particularly after 2002, reaching an average annual growth of about 6–8 per cent. But the benefits of growth remain very unevenly distributed across the population. Old sociocultural divisions, such as gender and caste, have been strengthened, because the new economic drivers build on them, posing a real challenge for the future.

Economic inequalities

Official survey data indicate that the Gini coefficient increased from 0.31 in 1993–94 to around 0.34 in 2011–12, clearly an underestimate. The only large-scale survey data available in India relate to consumption expenditure, which tends to understate the extent of inequality by underestimating the distribution tails, which exclude the very rich and the very poor. Further, the poor are more likely to consume their income or spend more than they earn, while the rich can save. The first detailed income distribution estimates for India (Desai et al., 2011) reveal rather high income inequality, with a Gini coefficient of 0.54, almost the same as for Brazil (based on survey estimates of gross income).

Estimates based on village surveys derive an even higher Gini coefficient of around 0.60 or more (Rawal and Swaminathan, 2011).

Even consumption data suggest increasing consumption inequality, both across regions and states and within regions (Vanneman and Dubey, 2011). Along with the increase in the national Gini coefficient for consumption, the ratio of urban to rural consumption increased from 1.62 to 1.96 between 1993–94 and 2009–10. The largest increases in consumption expenditure were concentrated in the top decile of the urban population. In the same period, the income of the top urban decile increased from 7.14 times to 10.33 times that of the bottom urban decile and from 10.48 times to 14.32 times that of the bottom rural decile. The shift in incomes between classes confirms the tendency towards greater inequality: the wage share of national income fell from 40 per cent at the start of the 1990s to only 34 per cent by 2009–10. In the organized sector (referring to registered enterprises that are subject to various laws), the wage share fell from 69 per cent to 51 per cent in the same period. The unorganized sector's share of the national income fell from 64 per cent to 57 per cent, although it continues to comprise the overwhelming majority of workers in the country, including the self-employed (CSO, 2012).

A major reason for this decrease is that the economic growth has not generated enough employment. About half of the workforce remains in low-productivity agriculture (which now accounts for less than 15 per cent of GDP), and another quarter in low-paid services. India's recent high economic growth was related to financial deregulation, combined with tax concessions and credit to stimulate consumption by the richest sections of the population, especially in urban areas. This led to a substantial rise in profits and the spread of financial activity. The earlier emphasis was on public spending as the Indian economy's principal growth stimulus – primarily in the form of public investment, but also other spending designed to improve the living standards of the poor. In the past two decades, this engine has been replaced by debt-financed housing investment and private consumption by the elite and the growing middle classes (Ghosh and Chandrasekhar, 2009).

Employment and wages inequalities

The economy's capacity to create jobs has been low even during periods of rapid growth. It has declined further as a result of India's exposure to global competition, which forced enterprises to adopt the latest labour-saving technologies developed in the advanced economies. In addition, a significant portion of the GDP increase was due to services that are not very employment-intensive, such as financial services and telecommunications. Manufacturing's share in both economic output and employment has not moved from rather a low level. Low-paid, low-productivity work continues to dominate employment; on the whole, there is little evidence of labour moving to higher-productivity activities. Interestingly, this is true across all sectors: low-productivity employment coexists with some high value-added activities in all of the major sectors. Further, there are extremely wide variations in productivity across enterprises and even within the same subsector.

Most remarkable of all is that the period of rapid GDP growth has been marked by low and declining workforce participation rates of women. This pattern is unlike that in almost any other rapidly growing economy in any phase of history over the past two centuries. This is significant for the following reasons.

Women largely (although not solely) do the tasks associated with social reproduction and the care economy, which, as in many other societies, are not counted as economic or productive activities. Similarly, many women are engaged in productive work as unpaid household helpers, who are barely seen as workers. As some younger women engage in education, older female workers have shifted from paid or recognized employment to unpaid household-related work.

The general invisibility of women's work is an indication of their status in society. Where women's official work involvement is low, this is usually a sign of their lack of freedom and progress, low status and low empowerment. Where more women are active in the labour market and are employed (especially in formal activities), the share of unpaid work tends to fall and even this work is more likely to be recognized and valued. Female labour participation rates in India have historically been significantly lower than male rates, and are among the lowest rates in the world, even the developing world.

Intersecting inequalities

In India, the power of the state has been used to advance the accumulation project by various means. These include land use changes that displace people from their land, from their livelihood and from access to natural resources, as well as substantial fiscal transfers and indirect subsidies to large capitalists. In addition, Indian capitalism has exploited specific sociocultural features, such as caste, community and gender differences, to enable greater labour exploitation and generate higher surpluses. It has been argued (Harriss-White, 2005) that social institutions stemming from a 'primordial identity', such as gender, caste and community, indirectly regulate or determine most of the modern Indian economy. These institutions interact with political forces, generating forms of patronage, control and clientelism that vary across regions. This leads to unexpected outcomes from government strategies, including those connected with liberalization, privatization and deregulation.

Thus we see that the biggest Indian firms are typically part of diversified family-owned conglomerates extending across different economic sectors.

Even in the globalization phase, caste, region and linguistic community were crucial in shaping these groups, determining their behaviour and influencing their interaction with each other as well as with global capital (Damodaran, 2008). The emergence of such capital often reflects social forces. There are no major business groups in the north and east that are not from 'traditional' business communities. Nationally, there is no significant Dalit (lowest or Scheduled Caste) business group. Corporate behaviour has often reinforced existing practices, such as gender discrimination in property ownership and control. An example of such corporate behaviour is the use of legal methods (such as the Hindu undivided family form of ownership) that deny women a role (Das Gupta, 2012). These practices add to the weight of socially discriminatory practices, and affect how large and medium-sized businesses deal with purely economic forces and their attitudes to investment, employment and output.

These features of the Indian economic landscape have been crucial in generating the recent phase of rapid growth, but they have also allowed backwardness and accentuated inequalities to persist despite that expansion. The ability of employers in India to utilize social characteristics to ensure lower wages for certain categories of workers has greatly assisted the direct and indirect subsidization of the corporate sector's costs. Caste and other forms of social discrimination, which have a long tradition in India, have therefore interacted with capitalist accumulation to generate particular forms of labour market segmentation that are unique to Indian society (Thorat, 2010; Human Rights Watch, 2007).

This suggests that exclusion was a basic feature of the recent economic development process. It involves exclusion from control over assets, exclusion from the benefits of economic growth, exclusion from the impact of physical and social infrastructure expansion, and continued exclusion from education and from income-generating opportunities. This exclusion has been along class or income lines, by means of geographical location, caste and community, and gender. However, exclusion from these benefits has not meant exclusion from the system. Rather, those who are supposedly marginalized or excluded have been affected precisely because they have been incorporated into the market.

Peasants, for example, have been integrated into a system that has made them more dependent on purchased inputs in deregulated markets, which in turn has made them more dependent on unpredictable output markets in which state protection is very poor.

It may not be surprising, then, that private investors find little value in accumulation strategies designed to further structural transformation. Such transformation may even harm investors' short-term interests if it reduces their bargaining power. Capitalism in India, especially in its most recent globally integrated form, has used past and current modes of social discrimination and exclusion to its own benefit, in order to make the obtaining of surpluses easy and ensure employers' greater flexibility and bargaining power when they deal with workers. The ability to benefit from socially segmented labour markets has, in turn, created incentives for surplus extraction by suppressing the wages of some workers, rather than through productivity increases.

Increasingly visible social and political problems accentuate the unsustainable nature of these processes. Extremist movements are powerful, and dominate in 150 backward and undeveloped districts where extractive industries are located. The lack of more productive employment has led to powerful demands for regional autonomy and for the exclusion of 'non-natives' from other states. Various forms of criminality are increasing, and there is widespread public anger at the corruption that has characterized this phase of Indian development as well as the other ways in which state policy has favoured the rich. These forces create potent sources of instability that may harm the growth process in unpredictable ways.

Bibliography

CSO (Central Statistical Office). 2012. *National Income Accounts, 2012*. Delhi, Government of India.

Damodaran, H. 2008. *India's New Capitalists: Caste, Business and Industry in a Modern Nation*. Basingstoke, UK, Palgrave Macmillan.

Das Gupta, C. 2012. Gender, property and the institutional basis of tax policy concessions: investigating the Hindu undivided family. *www.macroscan.net/index.php?view=search&kwds=Chirashree%20Das%20Gupta* (Accessed 10 June 2016.)

Desai, S. and Amaresh, D. 2011. Caste in the 21st century India: competing narratives. *Economic and Political Weekly*, Vol. 46, No. 11.

Ghosh, J. 2009. *Never Done and Poorly Paid: Women's Work in Globalising India.* New Delhi, Women Unlimited.

Ghosh, J. and Chandrasekhar, C. P. 2009. The costs of coupling: the global crisis and the Indian economy. *Cambridge Journal on the Financial Crisis*, Vol. 33 (July), pp. 725–39.

Harriss-White, B. 2005. *India's Market Economy.* Delhi, Three Essays Collective.

Human Rights Watch. 2007. *India: Hidden Apartheid. Caste Discrimination against India's 'Untouchables,'* Shadow Report to the UN Committee on the Elimination of Racial Discrimination. *https://www.hrw.org/report/2007/02/12/hidden-apartheid-caste-discrimination-against-indias-untouchables* (Accessed 10 June 2016.)

Rawal, V. and Swaminathan, M. 2011. Income inequality and caste in village India. *Review of Agrarian Studies*, Vol. 1, No. 2. *http://ras.org.in/income_inequality_and_caste_in_village_india* (Accessed 10 June 2016.)

Thorat, A. 2010. Ethnicity, caste and religion: implications for poverty outcomes. *Economic and Political Weekly*, 18 December.

Vanneman, R. and Dubey, A. 2011. Horizontal and vertical inequalities in India, Indian Human Development Survey Working Paper No. 16. *www.vanneman.umd.edu/papers/VannemanD13.pdf* (Accessed 10 June 2016.)

■ ***Jayati Ghosh*** *(India) is professor of economics at Jawaharlal Nehru University, New Delhi, India, and executive secretary of International Development Economics Associates (www.networkideas.org).*

17. Social justice and equality/inequality issues in modern-day Russia

Natalia Grigorieva

This contribution examines inequality in modern-day Russia. It discusses different types of inequality, including income and economic disparities, regional imbalances, and differences in access to social services such as health and education.

Justice and equality after the fall of communism

The challenge of social justice and inequality in Russia has to be placed in historical context. As part of the socialist doctrine of the former Soviet Union, equality was ensured through the distribution of goods and services by governmental institutions. Social policies were developed to support an equal – although by European norms rather poor – sustainable standard of living, promoting equal access to a wide range of social benefits such as housing, education, health and leisure, which lessened social inequality. The difference between the poorest and the richest did not exceed a ratio of 1 to 5 or 6.

The reforms of the 1990s completely changed this approach, with most people being unprepared for a market system (Kosova, 2012). The gap widened between expectations based on perceptions of social equality rooted in the Soviet egalitarian legacy, and the real state of affairs. Excessive income differences inflamed a feeling of social injustice in many Russians.

Almost all surveys demonstrate that justice is one of the five most important issues for Russians, and it is regarded as an element of social harmony (Gorshkov et al., 2013). For example, in a survey entitled 'Social justice and how we understand it', which the Russian Public Opinion Research Center conducted on 13 and 14 April 2013, only 7 per cent of the respondents thought 'high income inequality is good'; 66 per cent were ready to accept inequality, 'but only if the rich/poor divide is not too wide'; and 23 per cent believed that 'any income inequality is harmful, and people should strive to eradicate it'. Every fifth respondent (20 per cent) assumed that social justice would be achieved when the 'standards of living of each person are nearly the same, there are neither poor nor rich'.[1]

Inequality in modern-day Russia: the poor and the rich

It is conventional to distinguish between wealth inequality (referring to a stock) and income (a flow). Over the past twenty-five 'post-USSR' years, growing income inequality has been one of the most significant changes in Russia. During this period, the Gini coefficient of disposable income increased from 0.26 to 0.42. By 2014, the richest 10 per cent of people accounted for 30.6 per cent of total cash income,[2] while the poorest 10 per cent of people accounted for 1.9 per cent. In other words, the richest 10 per cent received almost seventeen times more than the poorest 10 per cent. They received only four times more at the end of the 1980s (Rosstat, 2013).

With the collapse of the Union of Soviet Socialist Republics (USSR), the poverty rate in Russia rose to a high of 33.5 per cent in 1992. By 2013 it had decreased to 11.2 per cent, which still means that 15.8 million Russians are living below the poverty line.

Wealth inequality is even greater than income inequality. Currently, 1 per cent of the population possess more than 70 per cent of all personal assets in Russia (Oxfam, 2014).

Regional economic inequalities are also high, having increased sharply in the 1990s. Later on, income and consumption inequality diminished as a result of various state social policy measures, and the redistribution of oil revenue. After the 2008 crisis, income growth in specific regions slowed down and regional budgets appeared to be overburdened by social obligations. Against this background, regional disparities grew again.

According to official statistics, the residents of the richest region are fifteen times wealthier than those in the poorest region (Zubarevich and Safronov, 2013). The 'rich' regions have the means to introduce policies of income equalization, such as pension supplements in Moscow, which in 2011 formed 10 per cent of the city budget. Regional disparities can be observed in all social sectors, such as health and education.

From economic inequality to inequality of opportunity?

Economic inequality is aggravated by other kinds of disparities, such as unequal access to health and social services (Chubarova and Grigorieva, 2015), and this has become a matter of serious concern. A sociological survey revealed that Russians' well-being is strongly affected by two forms of inequality: income inequality (72 per cent of the respondents) and unequal access to health care (27 per cent of the respondents) (Oxfam, 2014).

Health care and education, which used to be free, are increasingly being funded by private sources. The share of private funding of health-care expenses increased to 41.2 per cent in 2003. This figure was significantly reduced after an increase in public spending on health care, but started to increase again after 2009. Public expenditure, covered by tax and compulsory health insurance, accounts for only about 3 per cent of GDP. The role of income as an important factor governing access to medical care is increasing.

People usually perceive having to pay more for health-care services as negative. Paying for education seems to be more acceptable, probably because education is still considered a necessary and worthwhile investment. According to a recent survey, most parents interviewed (75 per cent) are ready to give up important life benefits for the development of their children, and 65 per cent are ready to pay, or have already paid, tuition fees for supplementary classes. Almost 40 per cent of the poorest people are considering paying for their children's studies, and 13 per cent have already paid.

Inequality and politics

The post-Soviet focus on economic growth has made social equality a low-priority issue. However, several researchers have recently identified a growing number of social tensions linked to high income inequality, and to the fact that high incomes have not been used to support investment in the national economy, so that new jobs have not been created and there are limited prospects of income growth for the economically active population at a time of economic stagnation. These researchers attribute high income inequality to flawed distribution mechanisms, the flat personal income tax (with a relatively low 13 per cent rate having been introduced in 2001), regressive social insurance contributions, and low property and inheritance tax.

The challenges of equality and inequality, and the fair or unfair distribution of resources and tax, are the focus of several academic discussions and political debates (Divina, 2011). The country's leadership, including President Vladimir Putin, has recognized that the scale of wealth inequality in Russia is a huge challenge (Putin, 2011). Measures such as a wealth tax and progressive income tax have been considered to redress the situation, but no practical steps have yet been taken.

Conclusions

Throughout the period of reform in Russia, the levelling of social inequality was linked to the growth of macroeconomic indicators. This point of view has dominated discussions about social policy reforms over the years. However, theoretical and practical research in this area shows the fallacy of such representations. Rising inequality, unrestrained by progressive taxation or other means of income redistribution, is leading to a significant social divide in Russian society that is likely to hinder the country's social and economic development. High social inequality and unequal access to health care and education are also obstacles to human development (Human Development, 2014, p. 82).

In Russia, there is no broad discussion on how to overcome inequality, which is not addressed as an urgent problem. However, mobilizing civil society could make a difference in addressing these challenges, and more research and action is required in this area.

Notes

1. About 1,600 respondents were interviewed at 130 sampling points in forty-two Russian regions.
2. The method of calculating inequality in Russia is different from those used in other countries. Official statistics use model assessments based on per capita income before any payments. Cash income includes labour remuneration, pension, allowances, scholarships and other social transfers.

Bibliography

Chubarova, T. and Grigorieva, N. 2015. The Russian Federation. K. Fierlbeck and H. Pally (eds), *Comparative Health Care Federalism*. Farnham, UK, Ashgate, pp. 195–213.

Divina, L. E. 2011. Ploskaya shkala nalogoobIozheniya [The flat tax scale]. *KANT*, No. 3. (In Russian.)

FOM (Public Opinion Foundation). Rezultati pervogo vserossiyskogo issledovaniya otnosheniya grazhdan k talantam [Results of the first nationwide study on the relationship between citizens and talent]. *http://fom.ru/special.html* (Accessed 10 June 2016.)

Gorshkov, M., Krumma, R. and Tikhonova, N. (eds) 2013. *O Chem Mechtayut Rossiyane: Ideal i Realnost* [*What Russians Dream About: Ideal and Reality?*] Moscow, Ves mir. (In Russian.)

Gorshkov M. and Tikhonova N. (eds). 2014. *Bogatie I bednie v sovremennoy Rossii: 10 let spustya* [*Poverty and the Poor in Modern Russia: 10 Years Late*]. Moscow, Ves mir. (In Russian.)

Human Development. 2014. *Doklad o Chelovecheskom Razvitii v Rossiyskoy Federacii, 2014* [*Report on Human Development in the Russian Federation, 2014*]. Moscow, Ves mir. (In Russian.)

Kosova, L. 2012. Pro ravenstvo i neravenstvo [About equality and inequality]. *Otechestvennie zapiski* (Moscow), Vol. 5, No. 50.

Oxfam. 2014. Znak neravenstva: Problemi neravenstva i puti ih resheniya v sovremennoy Rossii. [After equality: inequality trends and policy responses in contemporary Russia]. Doklad OKSFAM [Oxfam report]. *http://fom.ru/Economika/11089* (Accessed 10 June 2016.)

Putin, V. V. 2011. Glavniy vopros zapros grazhdan Rossii obespechit spravedlivost [The main demand of the Russians is to ensure justice]. http://media-mera.ru/politics/putin/2011-11-27 (Accessed 31 August 2015.)

Rosstat. 2013. *Socialnoe Polozhenie i Uroven Zhizni Naseleniya v Rossii, 2012. Statisticheskiy Sbornik.* [Social *Status and Standards of Living in Russia in 2012: Statistical Yearbook*]. Moscow, Rosstat.

VCIOM (Russian Public Opinion Research Centre). 2013. Socialnaya spravedlivost kak mi ee ponimaem [Social justice and how we understand it]. No. 2346. *http://wciom.ru/index.php*&uid+114297 (Accessed 10 June 2016.)

VSHE (Higher School of Economics, Moscow). Ediniy arhiv ekonomicheskih i sociologicheskih dannih [Joint economic and social data archive, HSU]. *http://sophist.hse.ru* (Accessed 10 June 2016.)

Zubarevich, N. V. and Safronov, S. G. 2013. Neravenstvo socialno-ekonomicheskogo razvitiya regionov i gorodov Rossii 2000-h godov: rost ili snizhenie? [The inequality of the social and economic development of Russia's regions and cities in 2000s: Growth or decline?]. *Obschestvennie nauki i sovremennost* [*Social Sciences and Modernity*], No. 6, pp. 15–20.

■ ***Natalia Grigorieva*** *(Russia) is professor of political science and head of the Centre of Comparative Social Policy at the School of Public Administration at the Lomonosov Moscow State University (MGU), Russia. Her professional interests cover social and health policy and gender issues.*

18. Inequality in sub-Saharan Africa: dimensions and drivers

Jimi O. Adesina

The average Gini index for sub-Saharan Africa is one of the world's highest. However, since 2000 inequalities in education, health and gender have been significantly reduced, and this might eventually lead to improvement in people's well-being. This contribution explores these four important dimensions of inequality in sub-Saharan Africa.

Introduction

Over the past two decades, evidence from all over the world has shown the harmful effects of high levels of inequality on everything from economic growth to poverty reduction, social unity and public health. A similar pattern has been shown in sub-Saharan Africa, especially regarding the influence of growth on reducing poverty. Reducing inequality is not only helpful but essential. High inequality is 'divisive and socially corrosive', Wilkinson and Pickett (2010, p. 195) remind us.

The economy of sub-Saharan Africa has grown at an exceptional pace over the past decade. Seven of the ten countries with the highest growth rates worldwide are in Africa. However, growth has been concentrated in particular sectors of the economy and in specific geographical areas within countries. The benefits of this growth have not been broadly shared, and have left out large sections of the population. Poverty has not fallen as much or as fast as expected and economic inequalities have remained high. There are, of course, significant differences between the countries in the region and their directions of inequality.

In this contribution, I explore four important dimensions of inequality in sub-Saharan Africa and some of the reasons for their evolution.

Economic inequality: consumption, income and wealth

There is broad agreement that the average economic inequality in sub-Saharan Africa is the highest in the world after Latin America (Milanovic, 2003, p. 10; ADB, 2012). The average rate of income inequality in sub-Saharan Africa declined from 1960 to the 1980s, before rising in the 1990s and declining again in the 2000s.

Using consumption data for the period 1991–93 to 2011, Cornia and Martorano (2015) found four trends in twenty-nine sub-Saharan African countries with at least four observation data points. In thirteen countries, the Gini index fell between 1991–93 and 2011. Some of these countries experienced high growth rates during the last decade sampled. Four countries show an inverted U-shaped trend, with the Gini index rising before falling. In seven countries, the Gini index rose during the period. In the last group of five countries, the Gini trend showed a U shape, with income inequality falling before rising over the period. Of the twenty-nine countries, Ethiopia (2011) had the lowest Gini index at 33.6, while the Gini indices for Botswana (2009) and South Africa (2011) were the highest, at 68.6 and 65.0 respectively.

A somewhat different picture appears when we consider wealth inequalities. Again, Africa's[1] wealth inequality level is the highest after the Asia-Pacific region,[2] at 89.2. The countries with the highest wealth Gini index include South Africa (84.0), Botswana (81.7), Namibia (81.6) and Nigeria (81.4), all mining or oil-producing countries.

In South Africa, the income and wealth indices of inequality have worsened since 1994. Using tax-income data, *Figure 18.1* shows the income share of the top 1 per cent and top 5 per cent of adults between 1990 and 2011. Using wealth data, in 2015, the share of the top 1 per cent was 42.8 per cent, and 75.9 per cent for the top 10 per cent (Shorrocks et al., 2015). The average income of a male-headed household is nearly twice that of a female-headed household (SSA, 2011).

Figure 18.1 **Income share of the top 1 per cent and 5 per cent in South Africa**

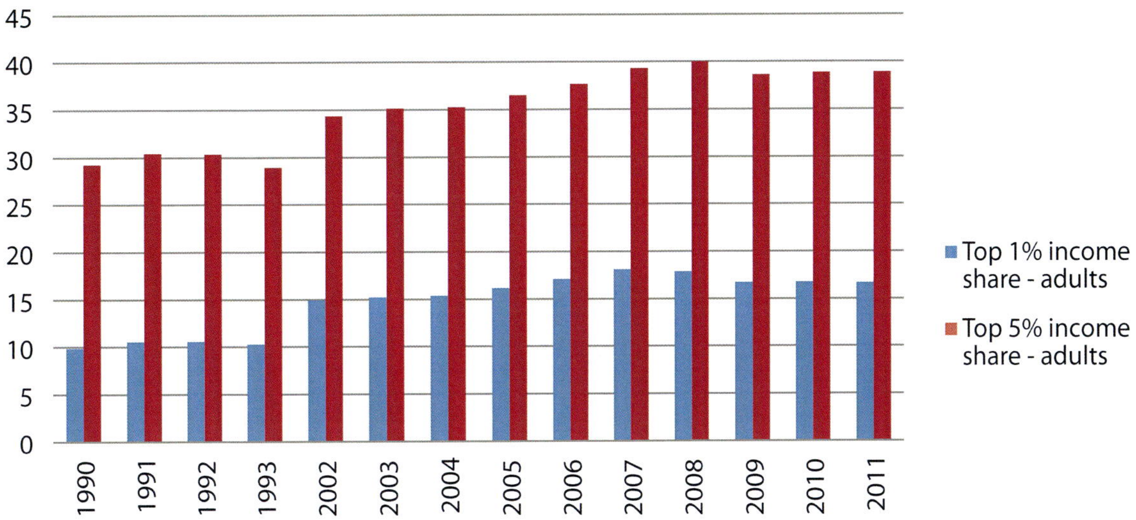

Source: Paris School of Economics Dataset (*http://topincomes.g-mond.parisschoolofeconomics.eu/*).

The fall and rise in economic inequality

The reasons behind changes in economic inequality differ between countries. The overall fall in average income inequality across the region from 1960 to 1980, and its subsequent rise, reflect the serious shift in the economic and social roles of the state in the region. The fall in inequality before 1980 reflects the growth of economic opportunities and social mobility in postcolonial Africa. A higher level of investment and broader participation in education led to a much higher level of social mobility. Economic liberalization, deregulation and other neoliberal policies were the main reason for inequality increasing in the post-1980 period, as in other regions of the world.

The decline in inequality that some countries experienced in the 2000s is probably related to their good economic performance and to favourable external conditions such as improvements in terms of trade. But not all countries that experienced fast economic growth have seen a reduction in levels of inequality (for example, Botswana and Ghana have not). On the whole, we have too little information to identify the reasons for the decrease or increase in economic inequality in many countries during those years.[3]

It is often easier to identify drivers of income inequality at the national level than across the continent as a whole. In South Africa, race and labour market location are the most significant drivers of inequality, and combined, they lead to the highest level of inequality.

Other dimensions of inequality: education, health and gender

Improvement in the education sector

Between 1999 and 2011, sub-Saharan Africa showed improvements in several education indicators, from net enrolment ratio in primary school (58 per cent to 77 per cent) to gender parity (0.85 to 0.93). The youth literacy rate also increased. However, the region lagged behind other regions in the world, and there is wide variation between different countries. Across the region, 16.6 million girls and 13 million boys in the primary school age cohort did not attend school in 2012 (UNESCO, 2015). Two out of three illiterate adults in the region are women.

Within-country indicators also vary widely by gender, by location (urban, rural) and by income group. Disadvantages often accumulate and lead to high levels of inequality. Inequality of learning also increases when moving up the educational ladder.

Unless public authorities actively promote and fund education, wealth inequalities and spatial location will continue to shape inequalities in education. The direct and indirect costs of education often discourage or prevent poor households from investing in the education of their children.

Over recent years, public authorities' active efforts to reduce the financial burden of education (abolishing fees, introducing school feeding programmes and in some cases cash transfers)[4] have helped to improve enrolment rates at primary school level. This has helped lessen the influence of social norms that discriminate against women and girls. The problems of low-quality education and early drop-outs remain an object of concern, as is the high inequality at the post-primary level.

The following examples highlight the differences between and within countries. In 2013, a child from the poorest quintile in Nigeria was more than twenty-three times more likely to have never attended school than a child from the richest quintile; this figure was nine times in Ghana in 2011 and two in South Africa in 2013. Forty per cent of children in rural areas in Nigeria had never been to school, compared with 10 per cent in urban areas. The primary school completion rate varies similarly.

Only 15 per cent of girls in Niger complete primary school education compared with 30 per cent of boys, while the completion rate is 91 per cent for girls and 86 per cent for boys in Zimbabwe; and 95 per cent for girls and 91 per cent for boys in South Africa.

Again, in Nigeria 98 per cent of children from the richest quintile complete primary school, compared with 20 per cent of children from the poorest quintile (UNESCO, 2015). The difference increases at higher educational levels. Eighty-nine per cent of adolescents from the richest quintile complete lower secondary school compared with only 9 per cent of those from the poorest quintile.

In Niger, only 4 per cent of females, 1 per cent of rural adolescents and 1 per cent of those from the poorest quintile complete lower secondary school (UNESCO, 2015). But in Namibia, Lesotho, South Africa and Zimbabwe, more girls complete lower secondary education than boys.

Health

Sub-Saharan Africa witnessed improvements in several health indicators between 1990 and 2012, although at lower levels than the global average.

Once again there are differences at the national level (WHO, 2014). While life expectancy is increasing across the region, it varies at birth from 74 years in island states such as Cape Verde, Mauritius and Seychelles to 46 years in Sierra Leone. These three island states have some of the most developed social policy structures in the region. The infant death rate declined between 1990 and 2012, but again differed between countries, ranging from thirteen deaths for every thousand live births in the Seychelles to 182 in Sierra Leone.

According to various indicators, the main factors influencing health inequalities (WHO, 2014) are wealth, spatial location (rural/urban), and mothers' educational level. But the extent to which public authorities help promote and enable the wellness of citizens influences these factors.

In Nigeria the main drivers of health inequality, far more than spatial location, are mothers' educational level and wealth inequality. The DTP3[5] immunization coverage of the poorest quintile is more than eight times lower than that of the richest quintile. In contrast, these quintiles exhibit parity or near parity in immunization, and at high levels of coverage (between 89 per cent and 99 per cent) in Burundi and Rwanda (WHO, 2014).

In South Africa, significant health inequalities exist along wealth lines. In 2015, total health-care expenditure was 8.5 per cent of the GDP. Of this, less than half (4.1 per cent) was public health-care spending, covering 84 per cent of the population. The remaining balance of the GDP dedicated to health care (4.4 per cent, or more than half) was used by the 16 per cent of the population who have private health insurance and mainly use private health-care facilities. The top two quintiles form the majority of health insurance membership, which is 'almost non-existent in the other quintiles' (Ataguba and McIntyre, 2013, p. 37). These two quintiles receive just slightly less than 60 per cent of the total benefits of the health-care system compared with a health-care need share of just over 25 per cent (Ataguba and McIntyre, 2013).

Gender equity and inequity

Gender inequity merits distinct exploration. The Global Gender Gap Report (World Economic Forum, 2014) provides a snapshot of the gender gap in sub-Saharan Africa according to four fields: economic participation and opportunity, educational achievement, health and survival, and political empowerment. As with other aspects of inequality, there are enormous differences between countries in the region. Rwanda, Burundi and South Africa are the three top-performing countries on the overall gender-gap index, while Côte d'Ivoire, Mali and Chad are the worst. However, the countries' performance varies across the subindexes. In 2015, Rwanda ranked highest in political empowerment, which was partly because it had the highest percentage of female legislators in the world: 63.8 per cent of its parliamentarians are women (International Parliamentary Union, 2016). Burundi, with a score of 0.86, topped the global subindex for economic participation and opportunity, followed by Malawi (0.829), Botswana (0.816) and Kenya (0.81).

The difference in the gender gap scores shows that gender equality in education does not automatically translate into gender equality in other domains. Globally, and across the region, social institutions (including norms, practices and law) remain the most powerful drivers of gender inequality (OECD, 2015). Here, policy and leadership again matter. Reducing gender inequality is often a result of focused activism and strong public leadership.

Conclusion

While growth is important for reducing inequality and poverty, sub-Saharan Africa's experience with growth fuelled by the commodity super-cycle shows that growth alone is not enough to reduce poverty. In the past, orthodox pro-market policies which boosted economic growth also increased inequality. Reducing inequality in sub-Saharan Africa would require a publicly driven programme of inclusive development, active social policy (combining redistribution and growth in productive capacity) and tackling the norms and practices that sustain gender discrimination.

Notes

1. The Global Wealth Databook (2015) covers fifty-two African countries, forty-seven of which are in sub-Saharan Africa.
2. Asia-Pacific minus China and India.
3. It is to be remembered that the statistical database on output, consumption and income can be weak in some countries, casting doubt on the level and evolution of some indices.
4. These programmes were often organized with the support of development agencies.
5. Three doses of diphtheria–tetanus–pertussis vaccine.

Bibliography

ADB (African Development Bank). 2015. Data Portal. *http://dataportal.afdb.org/DataQuery.aspx* (Accessed 20 November 2015.)

Ataguba, J. E.-O. and McIntyre, D. 2013. Who benefits from health services in South Africa? *Health Economics, Policy and Law*, Vol. 8, No. 1, pp. 21–46.

Cornia, G. A. and Martorano, B. 2016. Building the integrated inequality database and the seven sins of inequality measurement in Sub-Saharan Africa, UNDP Africa Policy Notes 2016-02, UNDP Regional Bureau for Africa. New York, UN Development Programme (UNDP).

Fosu, K. 2008. Inequality and the impact of growth on poverty: comparative evidence for sub-Saharan Africa. Research Report no. 2008-107. Helsinki, United Nations University World Institute for Development Economics Research (UNU-WIDER).

International Parliamentary Union. 2016. Women in national parliaments. *http://www.ipu.org/wmn-e/classif.htm* (Accessed 28 June 2016.)

Milanovic, B. 2003. Is inequality in Africa really different? Working Paper no. 3169, Washington DC, World Bank.

OECD. 2015. Social Institutions and Gender Index Database. *www.genderindex.org/* (Accessed 2 December 2015.)

Okojie, C. and Shimeles, A. 2006. Inequality in sub-Saharan Africa: a synthesis of recent research on the levels, trends, effects and determinants of inequality in its different dimensions. London, Overseas Development Institute Inter-Regional Inequality Facility.

Ravallion, M. and Chen, S. 2012. Monitoring inequality. *http://blog.worldbank.org/developmenttalk/monitoring-inequality* (Accessed 2 October 2015.)

Shorrocks, A., Davies, J. and Lluberas, R. 2015. *Global Wealth Databook 2015*. Zurich, Switzerland, Credit Suisse Research Institute.

SSA (Statistics South Africa). 2011. South Africa 2011 census data. Pretoria, SSA.

UNESCO. 2015. World Inequality Database on Education. *www.education-inequalities.org* (Accessed 25 November 2015.)

WHO (World Health Organization). 2014. *The Health of the People: What Works. The African Regional Health Report 2014*. Brazzaville, WHO Regional Office for Africa.

Wilkinson, R. and Pickett, K. 2010. *The Spirit Level: Why Greater Equality Makes Societies Stronger.* New York, Bloomsbury Press.

World Economic Forum. 2014. Global Gender Gap Report 2014. *http://reports.weforum.org/global-gender-gap-report-2014/* (Accessed 10 June 2016.)

■ ***Jimi Adesina*** *(Nigeria) is a professor at the College of Graduate Studies, University of South Africa and holder of the South African Research Chair in Social Policy. The South African National Research Foundation supports his work.*

19. Inequalities in the Arab region
Adam Hanieh

Social and economic inequalities remain among the most pressing developmental issues for the Arab region. These inequalities are indicated by the large and persistent disparities that exist in ownership and control of economic wealth, access to resources and markets, and the exercise of political power. They are found both within and between states, and have profound and complex connections to violence and conflict. This contribution examines some of the quantitative and qualitative trends in inequality for the Arab world, and explores their relationship to contemporary political dynamics.

Numerous scholars and development institutions have pointed to the widening social and economic inequalities that have characterized the Arab world for two decades. These inequalities are indicated by large and persistent disparities in the ownership and control of economic wealth, access to resources and markets, and the exercise of political power. They also have significant political implications: the popular uprisings that spread across the region in 2011 were in large part triggered by perceptions of inequality, reflected in the ubiquitous cries of '*aish, hurriyah, 'adalah ijtima'iyah*' (bread, freedom, social justice). The longstanding denial of basic social rights remains a potent contributor to violence and conflict in the region. Challenging inequality must therefore be at the forefront of any sustainable development strategy for the Arab world.

Inequalities are found within and between Arab states and they manifest themselves differently across a range of social markers including gender, national origin, age and citizenship status. One important illustration of these differences can be seen in labour market outcomes. Before the global economic downturn of 2008, the average official unemployment rate across Egypt, Jordan, Lebanon, Morocco, Syria and Tunisia was higher than in any other region in the world (IMF, 2011, p. 39). Young people and women are most affected by unemployment. Around 19 per cent of all Arab women are unemployed, as are 26 per cent of the young people in the region (ESCWA, 2013, p. 10). These figures hide large regional disparities: In the Mashreq sub-region (Egypt, Jordan, Iraq, Syria, Lebanon and the West Bank and Gaza Strip) over 45 per cent of all young females were unemployed in 2011, more than double the rate for young men (UNDP, 2011, p. 41).

The Arab region also ranks bottom of the world for labour market participation rates, with less than half of the region's population considered part of the labour force (IMF, 2011, p. 39). Only about one-third of young people and 26 per cent of women are in work, or are actively seeking employment (ESCWA, 2013, p. 9). This profound marginalization of young people and women has deep social implications in countries where elderly men still dominate political power.

Unlike in many other countries, university graduates do particularly poorly in Arab labour markets. Recent reductions in public sector spending and state employment mean that many young people graduating from tertiary education find themselves without suitable job opportunities. In 2012, more than 30 per cent of university graduates in Egypt, Tunisia and Jordan were unemployed. In the latter two countries, the proportion of unemployed graduates has more than doubled since 2004 (World Bank, 2014). Again, women tend to be disproportionally represented in these statistics: more than 60 per cent of women with tertiary education are unemployed in Jordan, while in Egypt the figure reaches 40 per cent.

Elusive formal employment

The widespread prevalence of informal and precarious work across the region also reflects its lack of stable job opportunities. In 2009 the UN Development Programme (UNDP) reported that the growth of informal work in Egypt, Morocco and Tunisia was among the fastest in the world, and totalled between 40 and 50 per cent of all non-agricultural employment (UNDP, 2009, p. 111).

In Egypt, three-quarters of new labour market entrants from 2000–05 joined the informal sector, up from only one-fifth in the early 1970s (Wahba, 2010, p. 34). Not only do these trends affect the character of employment, they also have important implications for the way urban space is used and the kinds of social and political movements that have emerged in the Arab world. The residents of densely packed informal settlements across cities such as Cairo, Casablanca, Algiers and Beirut are viewed by governments with deep mistrust and suspicion.

These highly unequal employment and labour market outcomes have contributed to worsening overall poverty in the region. The proportion of the population without the means to acquire basic nutrition and essential non-food items (the 'upper poverty line') has averaged close to 40 per cent across Jordan, Morocco, Syria, Tunisia, Mauritania, Lebanon, Egypt and Yemen in the past decade (Achcar, 2013, p. 31). An August 2013 UN report on the MDG in the Arab world notes that when measured by regression-based poverty estimates, more than 20 per cent of people in the Arab region are poor, and that this figure has not changed since the 1990s (ESCWA, 2013, p. 5). According to these figures, the Arab region is the only area of the developing world in which poverty levels remained stagnant through the 1990s and 2000s.

Health and education

Health and educational outcomes also show unequal access to state services and social support. Between 2000 and 2006, around one-fifth of all children in Egypt and Morocco exhibited stunted growth as a result of malnutrition (UNDP, 2009, p. 137). Across the Mashreq countries, undernourishment increased from 6.4 per cent in 1991 to 10.3 per cent in 2011 (ESCWA, 2013, p. 14). Illiteracy remains at strikingly high levels in Morocco (33 per cent of the adult population), Egypt (25 per cent) and Tunisia (20 per cent) (UNESCO database, figures for 2013). Educational access is also clearly marked by sharp inequalities. The Economic and Social Commission for Western Asia (ESCWA) notes, for example, that '20 per cent of the poorest children [in Egypt] do not enter primary school, while almost 100 per cent of rich children complete upper-secondary education. Around 25 per cent of poor families spend money on supplementary tuition for their children, compared to 47 per cent of the richest families. The richest households spend around four times the amount of the poorest households' (ESCWA, 2013, p. 17).

The self-reinforcing effects of poverty and of harmful educational and health conditions raise serious concerns for social development in the Arab world.

Who benefited from economic growth?

The widespread deterioration in social conditions described above occurred during a period of relatively strong economic growth between 2000 and 2008, which again reflects the high levels of inequality in the region. The United Nations recently described this divergence in the case of Egypt as a 'paradox' – national poverty rates rose from 16.7 per cent in 2000 to 21.6 per cent in 2008, while GDP per capita rose consistently and rapidly over the same period (ESCWA, 2013, p. 6). In Lebanon, Morocco, Tunisia and Jordan, real GDP per capita rose by between 14.7 and 23 per cent in constant US dollars over the period 2003–08 (figures from the World Bank database). This indicates that any benefits from economic expansion and growth were not experienced evenly across all layers of the population.

Widening gaps

Widening gaps in power and wealth are not only apparent within countries. They are also seen at the regional level, most notably between the Gulf Cooperation Council (GCC) states and the rest of the Arab region. According to an October 2014 report by the Institute of International Finance, the net foreign assets (gross foreign assets minus external debt) of the GCC states rose from $878 billion in 2006 to a forecast $2.27 trillion by the end of 2014 (IIF, 2014, p. 32). This compares with a decline in the net foreign assets of Egypt, Syria, Jordan, Lebanon, Tunisia and Morocco from a surplus of $11 billion in 2006 to a forecast deficit of $46.7 billion by the end of 2014 (IIF, 2014, p. 34). Alongside the high levels of state wealth in the Gulf, privately held wealth has also increased very rapidly. According to one estimate, private wealth in the Gulf rose by 17.5 per cent each year from 2010 to 2014, with the total dollar amount doubling from $1.1 trillion to $2.2 trillion over this period (Strategy&, 2015, p. 3).

The fate of migrant workers

Despite these high levels of wealth in the GCC states, it is important to remember that more than half of the Gulf's workforce is made up of migrant workers, mostly from South Asia or other Arab countries.

In some states, notably the United Arab Emirates, Kuwait, Oman and Qatar, more than 80 per cent of the workforce consists of non-citizens (GLMM, 2014). These workers cannot become permanent residents or citizens, and are systematically denied their political, civil and social rights. As a consequence, reports of human rights abuses are common, including the payment of very low wages, confiscation of passports, restrictions on movement, unsafe working and living conditions, and physical and sexual assault (Hanieh, 2013). All these examples point to the hidden inequalities that lie behind the Gulf region's glittering towers and fanciful projects: inequalities that are demarcated and reproduced through differential rights associated with citizenship.

There is no single cause of these inequality trends across the Arab region. In some countries (Iraq, Syria, the West Bank and Gaza Strip, Lebanon and Yemen), high levels of violence and conflict have played a major role in contributing to social polarization and exclusion. Military occupation – in Iraq as well as the West Bank and Gaza Strip – has worsened poverty and exacerbated inequality. Conflict-ridden areas also tend to have large numbers of displaced persons and refugees, placing even more strain on social support systems and state capacities. Other countries, notably Egypt, Jordan, Morocco and Tunisia, have seen inequality levels increase during periods of economic liberalization and the adoption of market-led development strategies (Hanieh, 2013). As noted above, reductions to state and social spending have reinforced the marginalization of poorer communities, young people and women. Moreover, all Arab states have suffered from autocratic and non-representative political systems, which have compounded social, political and economic inequalities. Despite these different contributory factors and the variety of development patterns seen throughout the region, inequality remains a constant and commonly held grievance, and forms part of the shared experience of social injustice across the Arab world. Addressing these inequalities remains an urgent task for development organizations, policy-makers, and social movements throughout the region.

Acknowledgement

This contribution draws on the author's keynote presentation at the Arab Council for Social Science (ACSS) Second Biannual Conference, Beirut, 13–15 March 2015.

Bibliography

Achcar, G. 2013. *The People Want*. London, Saqi Books.

ESCWA. 2013. *The Arab Millennium Development Goals Report: Facing Challenges and Looking Beyond 2015*. www.undp.org/content/dam/rbas/doc/MDGS%20publications/Arab_MDGR_2013_English.pdf (Accessed 10 June 2016.)

ESCWA. 2014. *Arab Integration: A 21st Century Development Imperative (AI)*. New York, UN Regional Commissions Office, www.regionalcommissions.org/arab-integration-a-21st-century-development-imperative-escwa-publication/ (Accessed 10 June 2016.)

GLMM (Gulf Labour Markets and Migration). 2014. Percentage of nationals and non-nationals in employed population in GCC countries. http://gulfmigration.eu/percentage-of-nationals-and-non-nationals-in-employed-population-in-gcc-countries-national-statistics-latest-year-or-period-available/ (Accessed 10 June 2016.)

Hanieh, A. 2013. *Lineages of Revolt: Issues of Contemporary Capitalism in the Middle East*. Chicago, Ill., Haymarket.

IIF (Institute of International Finance). 2014. MENA region: recovery buffeted by geopolitical risks, 8 October.

IMF. 2011. *Regional Economic Outlook: Middle East and Central Asia*. World Economic and Financial Surveys, Vol. 39, 11 April. Washington DC, IMF. www.imf.org/external/pubs/ft/reo/2011/mcd/eng/pdf/mreo0411.pdf (Accessed 10 June 2016.)

Strategy&. 2015. GCC private banking study 2015: Seizing the opportunities. www.strategyand.pwc.com/media/file/GCC-private-banking-study-2015.pdf (Accessed 10 June 2016.)

UNDP. 2009. *Arab Human Development Report: The Challenge to Human Security*. New York, UNDP.

UNDP, 2011. *Arab Development Challenges Report 2011*. Cairo, UNDP.

Wahba, J. 2010. Labour markets performance and migration flows in Egypt. *Labour Markets Performance and Migration Flows in Arab Mediterranean Countries: Determinants and Effects*. European Commission Occasional Papers 60, Vol. 3. Brussels: European Commission.

World Bank. 2014. Unemployment in the Middle East and North Africa explained. blogs.worldbank.org/arabvoices/problem-unemployment-middle-east-and-north-africa-explained-three-charts (Accessed 10 June 2016.)

■ *Adam Hanieh (Australia) teaches in the Development Studies Department, SOAS, University of London. He is author of* Capitalism and Class in the Gulf Arab States *(Palgrave-Macmillan, 2011) and* Lineages of Revolt: Issues of Contemporary Capitalism in the Middle East *(Haymarket, 2013).*

20. The invisible hands of racial inequality in the USA

Fredrick C. Harris

This contribution explores how institutional practices perpetuate racial inequality in the United States of America. It explores how hidden mechanisms – which are on the surface thought to be 'race neutral' – actually produce racially unbalanced outcomes that privilege white people and disadvantage black people and other stigmatized minorities. The author calls for looking beyond the conscious and unconscious racial bias of individuals to consider how institutional practices and rules continue to perpetuate racial inequality, even without the backing of state-sanctioned racial discrimination.

Although state-approved racial discrimination has been outlawed, and anti-black public attitudes have decreased for more than half a century, racial inequality remains a key feature of overall inequality in the USA. Unrestricted market forces have deepened income and wealth inequality worldwide, and those forces, together with hidden institutional practices, have accelerated and intensified deep-seated racial inequality in US society.

For more than a century, democratization has been making US society more politically equal for black people and other minorities. Most black people were not allowed to vote and were openly discriminated against in employment, housing and access to public spaces until the 1960s. Reforms carried through then brought legal protection that advanced the social and economic opportunities of black people and other racial minorities. The state introduced laws that protected voting rights, and established anti-discrimination legislation to eliminate racial bias in education, employment and housing. But despite these reforms, racial inequality has persisted for half a century. It might even have become worse, despite anti-discrimination laws, better access to education for minorities, and the incorporation of black people and other minorities into the political mainstream.

A large gap – in education, income, wealth, health and justice – persists particularly between white and black Americans, whose history of slavery, legalized segregation and state-approved terror partly accounts for their ongoing stigmatized status in society. These disparities have largely remained the same over the years, or have sharpened, especially since the 2008 recession. For decades, the rate of black unemployment has been twice or nearly twice that for the white population, and black people are overrepresented among the underemployed and workers who have given up seeking work, believing they have no prospects for attaining stable or viable employment. And a small though significant gap in unemployment persists between college educated black and white people.

The racial gap is especially acute when it comes to income and wealth. Although inflation-adjusted wages have decreased for all US workers, the disparity in incomes between black and white households has been remarkably stable over the past forty years (Desilver, 2013). Today, the black median household income is roughly 60 per cent of the white median household income, a figure that has changed little since 1967. Net worth, a measure of wealth, is thirteen times bigger for white people than for black people, a gap that has grown since the early 1990s and accelerated since the end of the Great Recession (Kochhar and Fry, 2014).

Perhaps the most critical disparity, one with social as well as economic implications for minority communities, is the wide gap in incarceration rates across race.

The US criminal justice system has a higher proportion of incarcerated individuals than any other advanced industrial nation, with 2.2 million people in federal, state and local prisons and jails (The Sentencing Project, 2013). Black and Hispanic people make up a quarter of the population, but represent nearly 60 per cent of all incarcerated people.

To understand the persistence of racial inequality in the absence of state-approved discrimination, we have to unravel everyday social practices which seem 'race neutral' but which produce racially unequal outcomes (Harris and Lieberman, 2015). Invisible practices, understood as hidden mechanisms that sustain and perpetuate racial inequality, are vast and cannot really be pinpointed. They are embedded in economic, social and political institutions, and are largely overlooked as enablers of racial bias because they do not explicitly reveal how they advantage white people and disadvantage black people and other stigmatized minorities. The bias operates in several institutional domains, such as education, criminal justice, consumer markets, employment and housing.

One set of institutions where the invisible hands of racial inequality operate in various ways is the criminal justice system. For example, the mechanism of federal sentencing rules has contributed to the wide racial disparity in incarceration. Mandatory sentencing requirements have specified longer sentences for using and distributing crack cocaine, a cheaper form of cocaine circulated in black and poor communities, than for powder cocaine, a more expensive form of cocaine used more often in whiter and more affluent communities.

This discrepancy – which was narrowed in 2010 but has not been eliminated – has for over twenty years sent hundreds of thousands of black and Latino people to prison to serve long sentences for non-violent offences. On average, black non-violent offenders have served just as much time in prison as white offenders convicted for violent crimes (The Sentencing Project, 2013). These sentencing requirements have further disadvantaged communities by weakening families, increasing the probability that the children of the incarcerated will engage in criminal behaviour, and by stigmatizing ex-offenders who attempt to re-enter society after serving their terms.

In many ways, ex-offenders become second-class citizens (Alexander, 2012). They are denied government-subsidized housing and education grants and loans to pursue higher education. Employment applications ask job seekers whether they have ever been convicted of a felony. This practice lowers the chances of ex-offenders being interviewed for jobs, as those who check the felon box are usually eliminated as serious applicants.

The stigma of being an ex-offender also weighs more heavily on black ex-offenders than on their white counterparts. As researchers have shown, black men with a high school education and without criminal records are less likely to be called back for a job interview than similarly educated white men with criminal records, which gives black ex-offenders virtually no chance of being employed (Pager, 2009).

These invisible practices may not have been intentionally designed to adversely affect black and Latino people. But they perpetuate racial inequality by lessening the employment opportunities of ex-offenders, thereby increasing the probability that ex-offenders will return to a life of crime and imprisonment. Institutional practices also protect racially biased and unconsciously biased police officers who use police brutality against people of colour. Union rules in some police departments allow officers to avoid speaking to investigators for days, and sometimes weeks, after they have been accused of misconduct. This gives biased and corrupt officers time to have their version of events match the physical evidence from investigations of misconduct. In many police jurisdictions across the USA, prosecutors, who are elected by voters, are reluctant to charge police officers accused of misconduct. Prosecutors work closely with the police in criminal investigations, and face pressure from officers to not send brutality cases to a grand jury, a procedural judicial process that decides, via a panel of citizens, whether individuals should be indicted for a crime. It is extremely rare that police officers are indicted in cases before grand juries, and when they are they tend not to be convicted.

The invisible hands of inequality may be more difficult to uproot than the old regime of legalized racial discrimination that marked out the USA as a racist state alongside apartheid South Africa and fascist Germany. Since the effects of racially infected institutional practices are far less visible, the 'race-neutral' mechanisms of bias, and future inventions that may replace them, will continue to perpetuate racially unequal outcomes in a society where many people erroneously believe the USA to be a 'post-racial' nation.

Bibliography

Alexander, M. 2012. *The New Jim Crow: Mass Incarceration in the Age of Colorblindness.* New York, New Press.

Desilver, D. 2013. Black income is up, but not wealth. Pew Research Center. 30 August. *www.pewresearch.org/fact-tank/2013/08/30/black-incomes-are-up-but-wealth-isnt/* (Accessed 10 June 2016.)

Harris, F. C. and Lieberman, R. C. 2015. Racial inequality after racism: how institutions hold back African Americans. *Foreign Affairs,* March/April.

Kochhar, R. and Fry, R. 2014. Wealth inequality has widened along racial, ethnic lines since end of Great Recession. Pew Research Center. 12 December. *www.pewresearch.org/fact-tank/2014/12/12/racial-wealth-gaps-great-recession/* (Accessed 10 June 2016.)

Pager, D. 2009. *Marked: Race, Crime, and Finding Work in an Era of Mass Incarceration.* Chicago, Ill., University of Chicago Press.

The Sentencing Project. 2013. Report of The Sentencing Project to the United Nations Human Rights Committee Regarding Racial Disparities in the United States Criminal Justice System. August. *http://sentencingproject.org/doc/publications/rd_ICCPR%20Race%20and%20Justice%20Shadow%20Report.pdf* (Accessed 10 June 2016.)

■ ***Fredrick C. Harris*** *(USA) is professor of political science and director of the Center on African-American Politics and Society at Columbia University. He is the co-author, with Robert C. Lieberman, of* Beyond Discrimination: Racial Inequality in a Post-Racist Era. *Harris is a non-resident senior fellow at the Brookings Institution in Washington DC and former visiting professor at the Pantheon-Sorbonne University in Paris.*

21. Income inequality in Brazil: new evidence from combined tax and survey data

Marcelo Medeiros

Inequality in Brazil fluctuates over time, but has been high since at least 1928, as a result of an impressive concentration of income among the rich. This contribution analyses the viability of commonly proposed strategies to reduce inequality. It argues that a realistic expansion of education, the eradication of poverty, the expansion of social assistance programmes, economic growth and a more efficient management of current policies will not have major impacts on inequality within a reasonable time frame of, say, two decades.

For many decades of the twentieth century, Brazil was ranked among the most unequal countries in the world. In the mid-1990s, household surveys showed that this was changing. Inequality in labour earnings began to decline and after 2001, household per capita income inequality fell systematically for eleven years. A combination of the labour market's good performance, systematic increases in the minimum wage, increases in the coverage of social assistance programmes and a better distribution of pensions were the cause of these changes. Encouraged by political campaigns, a triumphalist discourse of good government greeted the decline in the inequality that the household survey data showed. The Bolsa Familia programme,[1] a trademark of Brazilian President Lula's administration, was especially emphasized.

This apparent decline in Brazilian income inequality drew attention: a large economy could reduce inequality while it was increasing in various other countries. Nevertheless, it was not an exception in the region. Income inequality was declining in several South American countries, suggesting that changes in the region were affecting the way income was distributed.

However, household surveys only tell part of the story. They do not accurately measure top incomes, and as a consequence they underestimate total inequality. Income tax data painted a different picture. It showed that inequality in Brazil was higher than previously thought and remained stable, at least between 2006 and 2013.

The top 1 per cent of the richest people in Brazil accrued 25 per cent of all incomes, with only minor changes, during this period. Over a longer period, income inequality has gone up and down since 1928, reaching a peak when Brazil entered the Second World War, followed by a long decline. This decline was completely reversed when a coup d'état led to two decades of dictatorship. Since the country's return to democracy, inequality seems to be fluctuating within a relatively narrow band (Souza and Medeiros, 2015). Given this evidence, we must revise what we know about inequality, its determinants and the policies that could help reduce it.

Yet, while tax data are better than survey data at measuring what happens to the distribution of top incomes, they give no information about the distribution of the bottom incomes, since people with low incomes in Brazil do not have to submit tax returns. Moreover, tax tables offer almost no information on who falls into the top income group, making it impossible to compare this group with those at the bottom. Much more could be done if the Brazilian tax agency were to give researchers access to unidentified microdata (personal data that cannot be linked to specific persons). Until this happens, methods that correct surveys by using tax data are one of the few alternatives to cope with the underestimation of incomes. These methods are still being developed and because their results are preliminary, they should be used with caution.

The corrected survey data point out that occupational and educational elites contribute disproportionally to the inequality between adult individuals. In this context, 'contribution' is a statistical measure calculated as the product of the income of a social group, as a share of total income, and its concentration coefficient.[2] These contributions are higher than the household surveys estimate. Employers, who are only 1 per cent of the population, make up 13 per cent of the inequality; workers with an 'elite education' – those with university degrees in professional areas (medicine, engineering and law, for example), and those with Master's degrees and PhDs – who represent no more than 3 per cent of the population, are responsible for 25 per cent of the inequality. Those with any type of university education, who represent about 8 per cent of the adult population, contribute half of all the inequality. Gender, racial and generational inequalities are also higher than commonly estimated: this is not a surprise, as the rich are often white men older than 45 (Medeiros, Galvao et al., 2015).

A large mass of low-income people, separated from a small, but quite rich, elite, characterize the Brazilian income distribution. Economic and political powers are intermingled and this elite controls both.

Which policies would be suitable to reduce inequalities?

A survey by Elisa Reis (2005) on what elites think of inequality, and the public policies that would be required to reduce it, shows that in general, the rich tend to confuse the reduction of inequality with anti-poverty policies. They also believe that equality should be achieved without redistribution or any radical changes in the status quo: that is, without immediate losses for those at the top. Elites explain the failure of policies aimed at reducing inequality in terms of mismanagement or issues of attitude, rather than in terms of structural constraints. As in many other countries, Brazilian elites believe that the solution for inequality is a combination of education, growth and efficient public administration, but without a major increase in taxes to fund these policies.

A quick look at the data suggests that the solutions these elites envisage are not sufficient to reduce inequality considerably and cannot be implemented without a reasonable amount of redistribution. Data and research suggest that without important changes in the status quo, inequality will take a very long time to decline.

Poverty is morally unacceptable and should therefore be eradicated

The concentration of incomes in Brazil is so great that simple calculations show that even if poverty was eradicated, inequality would remain very high. Brazil was very successful in expanding its two main cash transfer programmes to fight poverty during the first decade of the twenty-first century. Consequently, the number of poor people declined and so did their degree of poverty. But the effect of these transfers on inequality is very small. Even though the cash transfers reach the poor very well, they contribute to reducing the concentration of income much less than people think[3] (Medeiros and Souza, 2015). Compared with poverty eradication, equality is harder to achieve and costs more, both economically and politically.

More and better quality education for all is a priority

Not only is education intrinsically necessary for a good life, it also may help lower income inequality.

Education in Brazil is very unequally distributed, and the majority of adults do not have any secondary schooling. Public education is free at all levels but the quality of public basic education is low, making a good education highly dependent on students' social origin. Richer families send their children to private schools for their basic and secondary education so that they will have a better chance of passing the higher education entrance exam and enter the far better public university system. This unequal access to quality education is a major driver of the country's inequality in the long run. The resulting structure for career opportunities is the most obvious result of this inequality. In addition, education is strongly related to labour earnings as well as to social and cultural capital. This means that there is an educational inequality trap that reproduces social status over generations. Long-distance social mobility – that is, mobility from the bottom to the higher levels of the social pyramid – is very low (Ribeiro, 2012).

As a result, it is not sufficient that the country give lower-class students access to education; it must also compensate them for their disadvantages. This implies providing public education that is better than private schools offer. Obviously, this will be very expensive and even if such an ideal settlement is possible, it will probably take years to implement. Even under a perfect, classless educational system, it will take decades before a generation of properly educated children begin their working lives and become a majority in the labour force. Therefore, education is necessary, although it will probably not be enough to reduce the country's inequality to acceptable levels within a reasonable time frame.

'Growth is the best social policy' is a good slogan. It sounds particularly good to elites, because it dismisses the need for redistribution. After all, the saying is that a rising tide lifts all boats. This image is not only old-fashioned, but also wrong. Growth can actually increase inequality. There are different types of growth that benefit different types of people. If the country wants to use growth as a policy tool to reduce inequality, this growth must be much better explained, making clear who is to get what. In Brazil, the top 1 per cent accumulated 28 per cent of all personal income growth between 2006 and 2012 (Medeiros, Souza et al., 2015). The poor would have to benefit from much faster growth for inequality to decrease within a reasonable time frame.

Finally, the perception of elites that the good management of public policies is necessary to reduce inequality is correct, if we understand this belief in broad terms. It is always possible to make the administration of social expenditures more efficient, but we should not expect too much from it. Pensions are the most important social expenditure, but in this area it is difficult to reduce expenditure significantly even if administrative efficiency is improved. In fact, better management of public affairs would have stronger effects on inequality if it were focused on redesigning policies and their funding. For example, interest paid to creditors of the public debt amounts to 5 per cent of GDP, almost half the cost of the entire pension system. If management has room for improvement, it is definitely in this area and in other macroeconomic policies.

A complicated web of taxes and required contributions funds all these payments. They are all very complex, but they share one characteristic: they are neither socially progressive nor economically efficient. Brazil has an outdated taxation system inherited from the time when the country was still industrializing. The system has been adjusted several times, but never reformed. Progressive personal income taxes are actually a minor part of the system, and taxation on property and inheritances is limited.

Expanding education, solving debt problems and reforming the pension and taxation systems will require huge efforts. Yet without such efforts, Brazilians will have to cope with inequality for a long time to come.

Notes

1. Bolsa Familia is a poverty alleviation programme consisting of targeted transfers conditional on school attendance and health checks for family members if these apply. Together with the BPC – the targeted unconditional social cash transfer for older people or those with disabilities – it forms the core of the Brazilian social assistance policy. The BPC was included in the 1988 Constitution and cannot therefore be associated with a single government. Bolsa Familia was created during President Lula's administration and became one of his trademarks. Bolsa Familia came from the Bolsa Escola of President Cardoso, which in turn had its origin in previous city-level programmes.

2. The concentration coefficient is a measure of the concentration of one source of income on the distribution of incomes from all sources. The share of a social group's contribution to total income is the share of the income of that group's members compared with the total income of the population. We calculate a source of income's contribution to inequality by multiplying this source's concentration coefficient by the share of that income in the total income. A group's contribution to inequality is a measure of how the income of this group's members contributes to the composition of the total inequality. It cannot be interpreted in counterfactual terms: that is, if a group's contribution to inequality is 10 per cent, inequality would not decline by 10 per cent if the group ceased to exist. This is because removing such a group would affect the total income and therefore all the concentration coefficients.

3. More specifically, the static contribution of all cash-transfer programmes together to the Gini index is not even minus 1 per cent (Medeiros and Souza, 2015).

Bibliography

Medeiros, M., Galvao, J. C. and Nazareno, L. 2015. A composição da desigualdade no Brasil: conciliando o Censo 2010 e os cados do Imposto de Renda [The composition of inequality in Brazil: conciliating the 2010 census and income tax data]. Social Science Research Network (SSRN) Scholarly Paper. Rochester, N.Y., SSRN. *http://papers.ssrn.com/abstract=2636586* (Accessed 30 September 2015.)

Medeiros, M. and Souza, P. H. G. F. 2015. State transfers, taxes and income inequality in Brazil. *Brazilian Political Science Review*, Vol. 9, No. 2, pp. 3–29.

Medeiros, M., Souza, P. H. G. F. and Castro, F. A. de. 2015. The stability of income inequality in Brazil, 2006–2012: an estimate using income tax data and household surveys. *Ciência & Saúde Coletiva*, Vol. 20, No. 4, pp. 971–86.

Reis, E. P. 2005. Perceptions of poverty and inequality among Brazilian elites. E. P. Reis and M. Moore (eds), *Elite Perceptions of Poverty and Inequality*. New York, Zed Books, pp. 26–51.

Ribeiro, C. A. C. 2012. Quatro décadas de mobilidade social no Brasil [Four decades of social mobility in Brazil]. *Dados*, Vol. 55, No. 3, pp. 641–79.

Souza, P. H. G. F. and Medeiros, M. 2015. Top income shares and inequality in Brazil, 1928–2012. *Sociologies in Dialogue*, Vol. 1, No. 1, pp. 119–32.

■ *Marcelo Medeiros (Brazil) is professor in the Department of Sociology of the University of Brasilia and senior researcher at Ipea, the Institute for Applied Economic Research. He studies income inequality in developing countries, both today and in historical perspective.*

Part II

THE CONSEQUENCES OF INEQUALITIES

Introduction

POSTCARD • Inequality: a historical issue within the United Nations System

Chapter 3 ■ Consequences and interactions of multiple inequalities

Chapter 4 ■ Inequality futures

COLOUR RAIN, Icy and Sot
(New York, USA, 2013)
© Icy and Sot

22. Consequences and futures of inequalities (an introduction to Part II)

John Gaventa

Introduction

Inequalities matter for many reasons. To some, inequalities – especially the extreme examples we see across the world – are intrinsic issues of fairness and social justice. For others, they are important because of their consequences for the critical global issues of our times, for the voice and inclusion of particular groups, and for the well-being of societies as a whole. As is shown throughout this report, these inequalities are not only economic. They have social, cultural, spatial, environmental, political and knowledge dimensions. The rapid rise of these multiple forms of inequality, and the interactions between them, have galvanized new debates on inequality and its consequences among businesses, politicians, civil society and development actors worldwide.

In this section, we explore further how these multiple forms of inequality intersect with one another, with what consequences, and for whom. We turn then to the question, 'What are the consequences of transitions towards greater equality?' Recognizing that we live in a world full of uncertainty, we conclude by exploring relatively unknown inequality futures. If we continue on the pathway of growing inequality, what will the consequences be? What are the possibilities of alternative pathways which take us to a fairer world? What will be the critical tipping points along the way?

While inequality has long been a concern in the global arena (Jolly, 23), the Sustainable Development Goals (SDGs) 2015–30 represent a new strategic opportunity to place inequality and social justice at the centre of local, national and global strategies and priorities. Not only is 'reducing inequalities' a standalone goal (Goal 10), but the cross-cutting commitment of the SDGs to 'leave no one behind' provides a normative framework for the inclusion of groups affected by these inequalities. The universal framing of the goals also has implications for inequality discourses and actions for all countries, crossing old divides of North and South, and opening up new possibilities for a truly global agenda.

However, the inequality-related commitments of the SDGs cannot be dealt with in isolation, as they interact deeply with the other goals as well. Examining these interactions provides a useful lens through which to understand the consequences and interactions of multiple forms of inequality more generally.

The interactions of inequalities: the example of the Sustainable Development Goals

Multiple inequalities have multiple consequences. Their simultaneous intersections and interactions make it difficult to distinguish causes from effects. Nevertheless, certain patterns do emerge. Inequalities tend to associate with each other, and their impacts and effects accumulate for certain groups more than others. Drawing on the evidence from the longer analytical articles and the shorter case studies in this part, as well as on other parts of this report, we highlight here the consequences of multiple inequalities for four broad development outcomes: poverty and growth; conflict and access to justice; health, nutrition and education; and environment and sustainability. Cross-cutting each of these are consequences for a fifth, gender equality and inclusion. Each of these areas is critical to the success of the SDGs, as seen in *Figure 22.1*. Yet each is also deeply interconnected with the specific standalone goal of reducing inequality.

Inequality, poverty and growth

Goal 1 of the SDGs has to do with the elimination of poverty, while Goal 8 refers to decent work and growth, and Goal 9 to the pattern of growth. The question of whether and how inequality affects economic growth, and the ability to reduce or eliminate poverty, has long been debated in social science. The seminal works of Lewis (1954) and Kuznets (1955) argue that a certain degree of inequality is inevitable during the process of economic development.

Figure 22.1 **Interaction of Inequality Goal 10 and the other SDGs**

Source: Author's illustration.

Distribution does not matter – according to neoclassical theory – because benefits will be shared by all in the long term. In recent years, however, growing evidence has challenged this assumption of the trickle-down effects of economic growth (Ravallion, 2005; Ostry et al., 2014) and has also shown that distribution matters in terms of poverty reduction (Bourguignon, 2004). In this report economist Ravi Kanbur (24) reviews these controversial debates on the relationships between inequality, economic growth and poverty reduction, while also examining the mechanisms through which they occur. Recognizing that there are a variety of views on the theme, he finds the conclusion quite clear: 'high and rising inequality dissipates the impact of growth on poverty, it can act as an impediment to growth, and is ethically objectionable in itself'.

Inequality, conflict and access to justice

SDG 16 highlights the importance of reducing conflict and of building peaceful and inclusive societies. Social science research suggests that violence and conflict are deeply related to multiple forms of inequality. For instance, Østby (25) examines the relationship between inequality and political violence, noting the importance of horizontal inequalities for conflict as well as the role of 'sheer inequality between rich and poor nations'.

McLennan (32) points to the impact of spatial patterns of inequality, arguing that it is the proximity of the haves and have-nots that affects patterns of crime and violence (although he also argues that more research is needed on this theme). In their summary of future scenarios of inequality, Fleurbaey and Klasen (40) similarly argue that inequalities separate social groups, leading to reduced empathy, which in turn contributes to 'gratuitous violence' among the disadvantaged and feelings of insecurity among the elites. In areas affected by mass migration, perceptions of inequalities may also lead to violence, or at least the fear of violence, between refugees and others. For instance, as Harb (26) discusses in relation to the mass influx of Syrian refugees into Lebanon, 90 per cent of those in the receiving country (Lebanon) saw refugees as an existential threat to their value system and worldview, as well as to their economic opportunities. Goal 16 also speaks to the access of justice for all, yet achieving these goals is linked to the challenge of confronting other social, cultural and economic inequalities, as is illustrated in an earlier chapter of this volume on the deep inequalities experienced by African Americans in the penal system in the USA (Harris, 20).

Inequality, health, nutrition and education

Another set of the SDGs has to do with broader social goals, including zero hunger (Goal 2), health (Goal 3) and quality education (Goal 4). Yet engaging with each of these also means engaging with multiple inequalities. For instance, as Hossain points out (33), the area of hunger is witnessing new manifestations of inequality related to nutrition – the '"stuffed and starved" phenomenon of chronic undernourishment alongside rising obesity' (quoting from Patel, 2013) – as well as other food insecurities related to finance, trade and climate shocks. Bayoumi (30) explores the evidence on health inequities in Egypt, arguing that these are very much based on a 'complex web' of other intersecting inequalities, which can be political, economic, educational and spatial. Wilkinson and Brima (31) elaborate on how the 'corrosive effects' of inequality contributed to the Ebola crisis. A lack of access to health care is part of the problem, but there are also deeper issues such as the impact of inequality on trust in institutions, their motivations and their ability to respond effectively. Attempts to ensure 'inclusive and equitable quality education' (Goal 4) are also affected by multiple forms of inequality, as Antoninis, Deprato and Benavot reminded us in Chapter 1 (10).

Inequality and environmental sustainability

The year 2015 was a deeply significant one for those concerned for environmental sustainability, as well as for those concerned with social development. No fewer than seven of the nineteen SDG goals link to issues of sustainability. In addition, the world celebrated in December as COP 21 established the first ever global framework for dealing with climate change. While each framework is significant in its own way, their success will be deeply affected by how successful they are in tackling intersecting inequalities. As Leach points out in Chapter 3 (27), inequality and environmental unsustainability are not only defining challenges of our age, they are also deeply interlinked in multiple ways. For instance, the earlier article by Murombedzi (9) in Part I argues that inequality of land and natural resources in the hands of the few has not led only to inequalities of wealth. It also allows the few to clear-cut, mine or farm the land in ways that may be ecologically unsustainable. Unless curbed, inequality is likely to continue to drive consumption of global resources in ways that are unsustainable, as Power, Wilkinson and Pickett describe (37). Focusing more on the experiences of those living in urban poverty, Narain (29) graphically describes how poor people are most exposed to air pollution, including the use of inefficient and dirty cook stoves and their exposure to emissions from the rising number of cars on the road, most of which are owned by the well-off. Strategies to provide clean water for all, she argues, must also be linked to strategies for affordable and equitable sanitation and waste management for all. Similarly, drawing on their research in Zambia and Malawi, Jafry and colleagues show how access to water in rural areas is a critical daily issue of survival (28) for millions in sub-Saharan Africa, one that is likely to be exacerbated if temperatures continue to rise due to climate change.

Consequences for whom? Gender equality and inclusion for all

The consequences of inequality affect economic, social, environment and peace-building goals. But they also raise the question of 'consequences for whom?' The SDGs speak strongly to the importance of addressing issues of gender equality and the empowerment of women and girls, in the standalone Goal 5 and across other goals. They also speak strongly to issues of greater inclusion and the need to overcome discrimination for other groups.

Subgoal 10.2 is concerned with the 'social, economic and political inclusion of all irrespective of age, sex, disability, race, ethnicity, origin, religion or economic or other status'.

Achieving the gender equality and inclusion goals of the SDGs will perhaps be the most challenging target of all. Multiple inequalities not only intersect, but also affect and accumulate for some groups more than others. For instance, the problem of access to water for farmers in Malawi and Zambia discussed above particularly affects women, and is deeply rooted in other cultural and gendered inequalities and forms of exclusion from decisions that affect their lives (28). Exclusion at the local level is reinforced by the challenges of women's representation and inclusion in the formal political process, as Nazneen discusses further in the next part of the report (51).

Women and girls have multiple identities as members of excluded groups. Growing up in an increasingly unequal world has enormous consequences for children, both girls and boys, for their education, employment and nutrition, and for their aspirations and identities (Pasquier-Doumer, 34; Minujin, 72). People with disabilities continue to experience discrimination, which in turn affects their economic status as well as their access to resources, food, health care, personal development and well-being (Cain, 36). Refugees and displaced peoples also experience growing forms of hostility and discrimination, exemplified by the situation of Syrian refugees in Lebanon (Harb, 26). And in many parts of the world, race and ethnicity operate as strong axes of inequality and exclusion, as seen in South Africa (McLennan, 32) or the United States (Harris, 20). This list is not exhaustive, and could include the particular experiences of intersecting inequalities on other groups as well.

Such intersecting inequalities contribute to a lack of material well-being, and also have more psychological and intangible consequences, not only for those at the bottom of the inequality ladder, but also for the middle classes as well (Chauvel and Hartung, 38). For many it may be the lived experience of inequality, rather than the inequality itself, which affects people's attitudes towards it, as McLennan argues (32). The experience of inequality may also affect aspirations to challenge or move out of inequality. Pasquier-Doumer (34) explores the links between inequality and the aspirations of indigenous children in Peru, which in turn contribute to disparities in educational outcomes.

Building upon Appadurai's work in India on the 'capacity to aspire' (2013), Baillergeau and Duyvendak (35) demonstrate how social inequality affects not only the educational and occupational aspirations of young people in Europe, but also broader aspirations around consumption or social identity. Lower aspirations help reinforce other inequalities, leading to the acceptance and internalization of an unjust or unequal status quo, the reproduction of inequalities over time, and thus to a vicious circle of inequality which is hard to break.

The impact on particular groups of these enduring and intersecting inequalities provides huge challenges for SDG 10. For many commentators, the unequal accumulation and experience of inequalities raises fundamental moral questions of fairness and social justice. As Fleurbaey and Klasen argue (40), inequalities are unfair to those involved, but also have consequences for society as a whole, representing 'a huge waste of human potential'.

What difference does a transition to greater equality make?

While a large number of empirical studies in the social sciences outline the consequences and interactions of inequality on certain issues and for certain groups, we also can ask the counterfactual: what difference does greater equality make? Can the transition to more equal societies contribute to a reversal of some of these negative consequences?

In Chapter 4, Power, Wilkinson and Pickett (37) argue that a reduction in income inequality will lead to positive gains in other areas related to heath, social well-being and sustainability as well. At a very general level, this argument seems to be supported by looking at what has happened at key moments of political and economic transition. For instance, from the 1960s to the mid-1990s, countries such as the Republic of Korea and Taiwan, China, experienced a rapid reduction of inequality, often referred to as the 'East Asian Miracle' (World Bank, 1993). At the same time, they recorded impressive results in terms of growth and nutrition. Kanbur (24), Cornia (46) and several other authors also refer to more recent cases, such as the extraordinary performance of Latin America during the first decade of the 2000s, during which Latin American countries recorded extraordinary rates of growth and a substantial decline in poverty and inequality. Over the same period, these economies reported interesting progress in other dimensions such as education, health and social well-being, as well as in sustainability and the quality of institutions (Cornia and Martorano, 2012).

By contrast, a rise of income inequality as experienced by some Eastern European states after the dismantling of the Soviet bloc was associated with a parallel rise of poverty (Grigorieva, 17), decline of social well-being, and decline in life expectancy at birth (Leon and Walt, 2000; Nolte et al., 2005). In China and India, rapid economic growth has contributed to social gains in several areas. But this has occurred alongside rising income inequality, and the gains are experienced unequally (Ghosh, 16; Knight, 2013). These inequalities may in turn contribute to other negative outcomes in the longer term.

While further research would be needed to develop this argument, we can see in the above examples that there are some cases of a strong association between greater income equality and greater progress on other social and economic indicators, and vice versa. This suggests that while multiple inequalities are experienced in an intersecting and cumulative way, transitions towards greater equality can also have intersecting and cumulative effects. Yet far more needs to be understood about the sequence and complexity of these interactions. This in turn requires new data sources and new forms of investigation, a challenge that will be taken up in *Part IV*.

Inequality futures

The discussion above points to two contrasting futures for the impacts of inequality. On the one hand, there is a great deal of evidence to suggest that growing inequality will have negative consequences on other economic, social, environmental, peace-building and inclusion goals. On the other hand, there is at least some associational evidence at both country and regional levels to suggest that if one form of inequality can be reversed, then there is the likelihood of positive progress in other areas as well.

This then brings us to the question, 'What is the future of inequality?' In contrast to work on climate change, where thousands of studies have helped to develop a global consensus on the impact of a 2 °C rise in temperatures, we have no such consensus on either where the tipping points are for inequality, or indeed what would be necessary for its reduction (although this theme is picked up in *Part III*).

PART II · THE CONSEQUENCES OF INEQUALITIES | Introduction

If inequality continues to grow unabated, what might be the further and broader consequences? What broad forces might drive the reduction of inequality, and with what alternative consequences?

We know from the social science literature that the large-scale social changes that would be required to reduce multiple inequalities around the world are likely to be uncertain, complex and nonlinear, making firm predictions risky. But while we have not found a great deal of social science research specifically on inequality futures, the articles in *Chapter 4* offer some basis for us to begin this discussion. Fleurbaey and Klasen (40), for instance, offer several possible scenarios, one of business as usual; a second in which countries do take action against inequalities at home, partly due to rising public concern; a third (geographic) scenario in which globalization and technical transfers contribute to declining inequality between countries; and a fourth more ideal scenario which combines intra-country action with a growing convergence between the regions of the world.

Much speculation on the future of inequality has argued that it depends in a globalized world on what happens with the BRICS countries (Brazil, Russia, India, China and South Africa), especially China and India. Gu and colleagues (39) reflect on this theme, looking at inequality futures within and across BRICS and in other parts of the world. Chauvel and Hartung (38) focus on the consequences of inequality on the Western middle classes, arguing that the gap between their aspirations and the reality of stagnant or downward mobility will contribute to greater frustration, loss of social cohesion, and political instability, which in turn will add to economic decay. Power, Wilkinson and Pickett (37) argue that a key strategy for constructing alternative futures has to do with economic democracy. This can contribute to lowering economic inequality, which in turn will have positive consequences for sustainability and well-being.

Others have argued that technology will play a key role, but debate what that role will be. Digital communications have the potential for increasing agency and action by those affected by the consequences of inequality, as the example in Uganda by Onyango-Obbo suggests (42). But they also pave the way for automation (Sayer, 41). The uncertain impacts of automation led Stephen Hawking to quip that 'Everyone can enjoy a life of luxurious leisure if the machine-produced wealth is shared, or most people can end up miserably poor if the machine-owners successfully lobby against wealth redistribution' (2015).

While inequality futures are unclear, there is evidence that we have a choice of pathways to those futures. A pathway of growing inequality will have serious negative consequences on other social, economic, environmental, peace-building and inclusion goals. A pathway of diminishing inequality offers greater prospects for progress on these and other indicators of well-being and social justice. Both pathways are possible, with many variations and crossroads along the way. Which we take will depend a great deal on how political will and pressure are developed to form policy. An elaboration of these transformative policy and political pathways is the focus of *Part III*.

Bibliography

Appadurai, A. 2013. *The Future as Cultural Fact: Essays on the Global Condition.* London and Brooklyn, N.Y., Verso.

Bourguignon, F. 2004. The poverty–growth–inequality triangle, paper presented at the Indian Council for Research on International Economic Relations, New Delhi, 4 February. *http://siteresources.worldbank.org/INTPGI/Resources/342674-1206111890151/15185_ICRIER_paper-final.pdf* (Accessed 25 February 2016.)

Cornia, G. A. and Martorano, B. 2012. *Development Policies and Income Inequality in Selected Developing Regions, 1980–2010,* Discussion Paper no. 210. Geneva, UNCTAD.

Hawking, S. 2015. Quoted in the *Huffington Post*, 10 August, *www.huffingtonpost.com/entry/stephen-hawking-capitalism-robots_us_5616c20ce4b0dbb8000d9f15* (Accessed 26 February 2016.)

Knight, J. 2013. Inequality in China: an overview. Policy Research Working Paper 6482. Washington DC, World Bank.

Kuznets, S. 1955. Economic growth and income inequality. *American Economic Review*, Vol. 65, No. 1, pp. 1–29. *https://www.aeaweb.org/aer/top20/45.1.1-28.pdf* (Accessed 25 February 2016.)

Leon, D. A. and Walt, G. 2000. The health consequences of the collapse of the Soviet Union. D. A. Leon and G. Walt (eds), *Poverty, Inequality and Health: An International Perspective.* New York, Oxford University Press, pp. 1–19.

Lewis, A. W. 1954. Economic development with unlimited supply of labour. *The Manchester School*, Vol. 22, No. 2, pp. 139–91. *http://onlinelibrary.wiley.com/doi/10.1111/j.1467-9957.1954.tb00021.x/abstract* (Accessed 25 February 2016.)

Nolte, E., McKee, M. and Gilmore, A. 2005. Morbidity and mortality in the transition countries of Europe: the new demographic regime. *Population Challenges and Policy Responses*, Vol. 5, pp. 153–76.

Ostry, J. D., Berg, A. and Tsangarides, C. G. 2014. Redistribution, inequality, and growth. Staff Discussion Note 14/02. Washington DC, IMF. *https://www.imf.org/external/pubs/ft/sdn/2014/sdn1402.pdf* (Accessed 25 February 2016.)

Patel, R. 2013. *Stuffed and Starved. From Farm to Fork: The Hidden Battle for the World Food System,* 2nd rev. exp. edn. London, Portobello.

Ravallion, M. 2005. A poverty-inequality trade-off? *Journal of Economic Inequality*, Vol. 3, No. 2, pp. 169–81. *http://link.springer.com/article/10.1007/s10888-005-0091-1* (Accessed 25 February 2016.)

World Bank. 1993. *The East Asian Miracle: Economic Growth and Public Policy.* Oxford, Oxford University Press.

■ ***John Gaventa*** *(UK/USA) is director of research at the Institute of Development Studies (IDS), Brighton, UK.*

POSTCARD

23. Inequality: a historical issue within the United Nations System

Richard Jolly

Inequality has been a major concern for the United Nations since 1945. The preamble of the UN Charter reaffirms faith in fundamental human rights and the equal rights of men and women. Article 55 explicitly states that the United Nations 'shall promote higher standards of living, full employment and conditions of economic and social progress and development [with]… universal respect for and observance of human rights and fundamental freedom for all' (United Nations,1945).

Between 1949 and 1951, the United Nations issued three pioneering economic reports – on national and international measures for full employment, for the economic development of under-developed countries, and for maintaining economic stability (Jolly et al., 2009). This choice of themes indicated direct concern for conditions within and between countries in which both inequalities and poverty needed to be reduced, nationally and internationally. After careful analysis, these reports called for measures such as diminishing the high concentration of land ownership, reducing discrimination in banking systems, and prompt counter-cyclical action by the World Bank and the IMF in the event of recessions.

In 1961 the UN General Assembly (GA) adopted proposals for a 'Development Decade'. This set a target for accelerating the rate of economic growth in developing countries between 1961 and 1970 to reach a self-sustaining rate of 5 per cent per year by 1970. This goal was initially dismissed as unrealistic, but it was more than achieved over the 1960s as a whole. Although the resolution made no mention of income distribution, the Secretary-General's accompanying report elaborated the need for 'improvements in internal income distribution' to go hand in hand with growth, if other elements of social progress were to be achieved (United Nations, 1962, p. 9).

Income distribution emerged as a key element in development strategy in the 1970s when the ILO launched a series of country missions, each making country-specific proposals for actions required to deal with unemployment, poverty and lack of employment opportunities. Inequality of income distribution was identified as an important cause of employment problems in all these missions. The Kenya Report (ILO, 1972), which gathered major international attention, contained recommendations for 'redistribution from growth'. This strategy was subsequently generalized in an IDS/World Bank study, *Redistribution with Growth* (Chenery et al., 1974).

By the early 1980s, concern for inequality was largely abandoned, sidelined by rising debt and structural adjustment in many countries and displaced by the ideological triumph of Thatcher-Reaganism. The World Bank and the IMF introduced structural adjustment policies as conditions for receiving loans. Free-market liberalization and the Washington consensus became the dominant influence on most of the countries of Africa and Latin America.

The 1990s brought back inequality as part of three major UN initiatives. The UNDP Human Development Report, launched in 1990, emphasized the importance of tackling extremes of income distribution, nationally and internationally. The 1993 Conference on Human Rights gave a new impetus to international action for human rights, with the creation of a High Commissioner for Human Rights and an Office in support. And the World Summit for Social Development (WSSD) in 1995 called on all countries to conduct 'regular national reviews of their economic policies and national budgets to orient them towards eradicating poverty and reducing inequalities' (United Nations, 1995, ch. 2, para 25).

The Millennium Declaration, adopted at the Millennium Summit in 2000, included strong and eloquent words on new global challenges including poverty reduction, but was cautious on inequality. It did state that 'only in societies with the greatest inequalities does growth fail to benefit the poor' (Annan, 2000, p. 21). The Millennium Development Goals (MDGs) did not include specific reference to reducing inequalities, except in relation to gender.

In contrast, the Sustainable Development Goals (SDGs), adopted in September 2015, underlined inequality via specific Goal 10, to reduce inequality within and among countries, while also asserting a general goal to 'leave no one behind'. The targets elaborating Goal 10 emphasized that income inequality in developing countries had increased since 1990 and that more than 75 per cent of the world's population now live in households where income is more unequally distributed. Targets also focused on diminishing extreme inequalities in relation to under-5 child mortality, maternal mortality and people living with disabilities. The targets stressed examples of country success, to emphasize that there is nothing inevitable about growing inequalities (United Nations, 2015).

Bibliography

Annan, K. A. 2000. *We the Peoples: The Role of the UN in the 21st Century*. New York, United Nations.

Chenery, H., Ahluwalia, M. S., Bell, C. L. G., Duloy, J. H. and Jolly, R. 1974. *Redistribution with Growth*. Oxford, Oxford University Press.

ILO. 1972. *Employment, Incomes and Equality: A Strategy for Increasing Productive Employment in Kenya*. Geneva, ILO.

Jolly, R., Emmerij, L. and Weiss, T. G. 2009. *UN Ideas that Changed the World*. Bloomington, Ind., Indiana University Press.

United Nations. 1945. The United Nations Charter. *www.un.org/en/charter-united-nations/* (Accessed 10 June 2016.)

United Nations. 1962. *The United Nations Development Decade*. New York, United Nations.

United Nations. 1995. Programme of Action of the World Summit for Social Development, *www.un-documents.net/poa-wssd.htm* (Accessed 10 June 2016.)

United Nations. 2015. Sustainable Development Goals. *www.un.org/sustainabledevelopment/sustainable-development-goals/* (Accessed 10 June 2016.)

■ *Richard Jolly (UK) is honorary professor at the Institute of Development Studies (IDS), UK and research associate. He was co-director of the UN Intellectual History Project at the Graduate Center, City University New York from 2000–10. He was an assistant secretary general of the United Nations as deputy executive director of UNICEF from 1982–95, and in UNDP from 1996–2000 as principal coordinator of the widely acclaimed* Human Development Report. *He has written or co-authored many books on development and UN history, including* UN Contributions to Development Thinking and Practice *(Indiana University Press, 2004) and* UNICEF: Global Governance that Works *(Routledge, 2014).*

**World
Social
Science
Report**

Chapter 3
Consequences and interactions of multiple inequalities

24. Economic growth and poverty reduction: the inequality connection
   Ravi Kanbur
25. Inequality and political conflict
   Gudrun Østby
26. POSTCARD • Perceived inequalities among Lebanese nationals and Syrian refugees
   Charles Harb
27. Inequality and sustainability
   Melissa Leach
28. POSTCARD • Challenging intersecting inequalities around access to water
   Tahseen Jafry, Blessings Chinsinga, Lilian Zimba and Ted Scanlon
29. Poverty and environmental inequality in India
   Sunita Narain
30. Health and social justice in Egypt: towards a health equity perspective
   Soha Bayoumi
31. POSTCARD • The Ebola crisis: inequality and distrust
   Annie Wilkinson and Abu A. Brima
32. The spatial patterning of exposure to inequality and its social consequences in South Africa: work in progress
   David McLennan
33. POSTCARD • Food rights and wrongs
   Naomi Hossain
34. The role of aspirations in the exclusion of Peruvian indigenous children
   Laure Pasquier-Doumer
35. POSTCARD • Social inequality and young people in Europe: their capacity to aspire
   Evelyne Baillergeau and Jan Willem Duyvendak
36. POSTCARD • Consequences of inequality for persons with disabilities: experience of ADD International
   Emma Cain

24. Economic growth and poverty reduction: the inequality connection

Ravi Kanbur

Global trends in technology and trade are pushing towards greater inequality within countries. The policy responses to rising inequality have varied, and explain differing outcomes in inequality around the world. Policy in China and some other Asian countries has internalized these trends, while policy in the USA and the UK has exacerbated global tendencies. But policy in Latin America has mitigated global forces of rising inequality. High and rising inequality needs to be addressed by policy-makers because it dissipates the impact of growth on poverty, it can act as an impediment to growth, and it is ethically objectionable in itself.

Income inequality is directly objectionable from an ethical point of view. But my focus here is on inequality as being instrumentally relevant to economic growth and poverty. Take any distribution of income across individuals (or a distribution of consumption or expenditure) and specify three summary statistics: the average (or mean), a measure of spread, and a measure which aggregates information on incomes below a specified poverty line. The rate of change of the first (average income) is of course what is commonly known as the rate of economic growth. The second can be captured through a range of inequality indices such as the Gini coefficient. The most commonly used summary measure of the third is the fraction of individuals below the poverty line, or the head count ratio, although there are a suite of indices which weight depth of poverty to different degrees. How does inequality come into the picture in the connection between economic growth and poverty reduction?

It should be clear intuitively that an increase in the average holding inequality constant will reduce poverty. This is the case of 'distribution neutral growth' which is a benchmark in many poverty projection exercises, and leads to the often cited 'growth elasticity of poverty reduction': put simply, the responsiveness of poverty to growth. On the other hand, increasing inequality while holding the mean constant will usually increase poverty. Thus, if a rising mean is accompanied by rising inequality, the poverty reduction impact from growth will be attenuated.

But if growth is accompanied by reduced inequality, the impact of growth on poverty reduction will be heightened. These effects constitute the first channel through which inequality mediates the impact of growth on poverty.

The above scenarios are not merely statistical artefacts, but correspond to real phases of history for many countries. Thus the 'East Asia miracle' in the 1960s and 1970s was one where countries such as the Republic of Korea had both growth and falling inequality, leading to a 'double blessing' for poverty reduction. During the period of 'shock therapy' in the 1990s, some East European transition economies experienced a declining average income and rising inequality at the same time, with disastrous consequences for poverty. From the late 1990s onwards, a group of large Latin American economies have seen growth along with falling inequality. According to one estimate, economic growth would have had to be 4 percentage points higher to achieve the same rate of poverty reduction for Brazil over this period without the fall in inequality (Barros et al., 2010). But for many other countries, especially in Asia, growth has been accompanied by rising inequality. It has been estimated that had rising inequality not accompanied high growth in developing Asia in the 1990s and 2000s, that growth would have lifted 250 million more people out of poverty (Kanbur and Zhuang, 2012).

Even when inequality does not change with growth, its overall level can affect the relationship between growth and poverty reduction. It is well established that distribution-neutral growth starting at a higher level of inequality will reduce poverty by less. In other words, the responsiveness of poverty reduction to growth is lower when initial inequality is higher. This is the second channel through which inequality connects growth and poverty reduction, even if inequality stays constant with growth.

There is a third inequality channel through which growth and poverty reduction are connected, and which follows from those mentioned above. In fact it is a channel through which the impact of growth on poverty reduction can be overestimated. Standard national statistical sources usually do not, and cannot, produce information on intra-household inequality. In effect, it is assumed that there is no inequality within households and that inequality between individuals is purely the result of inequality in household per capita income or consumption. But there is considerable corroborative evidence that resources within the household are themselves distributed unequally, for example between men and women. Thus standard income and expenditure distributions understate inequality. And for this reason they overstate the responsiveness of poverty reduction to growth, with the overstatement being greater the larger is the degree of intra-household inequality.

These three channels can explain why poverty can persist as the result of inequality despite sustained economic growth. To gain more insight into inequality and its evolution, we can think of income as the returns on assets. The assets can be physical, financial or human. The return on human capital, for example, could be thought of as the wage premium for every additional year of schooling. From this perspective, overall inequality is composed of the inequality of assets and the inequality of returns on assets. The evolution of inequality is a combination of the evolution of these two types of inequality.

Differential rates of return from assets can be the result of technological or market forces, for example when technological change leads to increased demand for skilled labour relative to unskilled labour. They can also be the result of market imperfections, or of discrimination and social norms, for example when men and women are paid different wages for the same work. Social norms are more likely to explain the level of inequality, since they change slowly.

As already noted, gender inequality and intra-household inequality are well corroborated empirically. Technology and trade, however, are more likely to explain short to medium-term changes in inequality. Indeed, it has been argued that the forces of labour-displacing technical change are behind much of the increasing share of capital income, and are the cause of rising income inequality between skilled and unskilled labour (Autor, 2014).

If technical change is causing a global trend to rising inequality in the rate of return on assets, particularly human capital, one response is to reduce the inequality of assets. Clearly this would mitigate the impact on overall inequality of income for any given increase in the inequality of rates of return. For human capital, the impact on inequality of increasing wage premiums for more skilled workers would be mitigated by reducing inequality in skill levels. But it would also increase the supply of skilled labour. So reducing inequality in skills would hold back the premiums for skill offered by the demand side of technical change. Indeed, this effect is argued to have been a key mechanism through which Latin American inequality was held in check from the late 1990s onwards.

In this framework, then, the level of inequality can be lowered through asset redistribution, which can be done all at one time as in the case of land reform in the Republic of Korea or Taiwan, China, or over time as was done through the more equitable spread of education in East Asia in the 1960s and 1970s, and in Latin America from the 1990s onwards. Addressing other structural factors such as gender disparities can also lower the level of inequality. But trends in inequality are affected by trends in relative demand for factors of production, such as the disparity between demand for skilled labour versus unskilled labour as the result of technical change. These forces can be mitigated by counteracting expanding demand with expanding supply, which is what Latin American education policies did. Other interventions such as minimum wage policies can also shore up the bargaining power of workers. But they have to be applied with caution, taking into account their possible unemployment consequences. Finally, redistribution of market income through taxation and transfers may also be needed. All of these strands of intervention came together in Latin America in the 1990s and 2000s, not just to hold inequality in check but to reduce it – an unprecedented outcome (López-Calva and Lustig, 2010).

So far we have looked at inequality as the connector between growth and poverty, but have taken growth itself as being unconnected to inequality. However, there is vigorous debate on whether rising inequality is a necessary condition for higher growth, or whether in fact higher inequality is causally linked to lower growth. There are good theoretical arguments on either side. Arthur Lewis, the father of modern development economics, wrote that 'Development must be inegalitarian because it does not start in every part of an economy at the same time' (Lewis, 1976). The rural–urban migration aspect of increasing inequality was emphasized by Kuznets (1955). A standard argument also bases itself on the empirical regularity which the share of savings out of income rises with income, so that greater inequality will raise the aggregate share of saving and thus make more resources available for investment.

The counters to these arguments are more recent. One strand is based on the role of credit constraints in limiting the capacity of the less wealthy to invest, in their own human capital or in enterprises, together with a minimum size requirement for investment (Banerjee, 2010). In this scenario it is intuitive that greater inequality will inhibit a greater number at the bottom from investing, and that this will impede growth. A second strand is oriented towards political economy. The simplest framework is one where greater inequality in income leads to a divergence between median and mean income. The median voter theorem in political economy would then suggest that policies would be chosen to raise median income, whereas those that raised mean income would be growth-enhancing by definition (Alesina and Rodrik, 1994).

Another entry point is via the following sequence of arguments. All economies are hit by shocks. Economies that change policies to present the most efficient response to these shocks will show the greatest growth of total income. But if the policy response involves major losses as well as gains, the losers can block the efficient outcome unless redistribution provides adequate compensation. Once again, then, distribution and growth are intricately connected.

So much for the theoretical argument. Empirical support for the thesis that greater inequality is detrimental to growth has always been sketchy.

Kanbur and Lustig (2000) in their survey concluded that 'the jury is still out'. However, strong support has recently come from an IMF study. In a remarkable piece of ongoing analysis, the authors draw three major conclusions:

> First, *more unequal societies tend to redistribute more* … Second, *lower net inequality is robustly correlated with faster and more durable growth, for a given level of redistribution* … And third, *redistribution appears generally benign in terms of its impact on growth; only in extreme cases is there some evidence that it may have direct negative effects on growth.*
> (Ostry et al., 2014, emphasis in the original)

There are of course econometric questions to be raised on these results, which are based on cross-country regression analysis. But it does seem as though the pendulum is swinging in the direction of an assessment of inequality as a causal factor impeding growth, or at least towards the position that redistribution in the direction of greater equality is not necessarily an impediment to economic growth.

What then explains different policies on inequality? The answer is not easy, and lies deep in the political economy and history of a society. An interesting case in point is China. Here, inequality fell in the early phase of post-1978 reform, as rural incomes were expanded through the policy allowing peasants to keep a larger and larger share of the output they produced. After a few years, however, China entered into a two-decade-long period of rising inequality, associated particularly with the opening-up and rapid growth of the coastal regions relative to the inland provinces. However, inequality has plateaued since the mid to late 2000s, and by some estimates has begun to turn down.

Each of these phases is associated with specific policy choices. An intriguing historical explanation is provided by Bin Wong (2011). He identifies the historical roots of Chinese rulers' concerns with inequality, particularly regional inequality, in the setting of a large land empire whose outermost provinces were always vulnerable to temptation from competing polities. In this view the seeming lack of concern with inequality over a quarter of a century spanning the 1980s, 1990s and early 2000s was the aberration rather than the rule, and the traditional concern with inequality, which predated communist rule and was in some sense 'hardwired' into Chinese rulers, would assert itself sooner or later.

This it did from the second half of the 2000s onwards through investment in the inland provinces, the development of health insurance, and a range of other measures.

Thus high and rising inequality dissipates the impact of growth on poverty; it can act as an impediment to growth; and it is ethically objectionable in itself. Global trends in technology and trade are pushing for greater inequality within countries, but whether these will elicit policy responses to mitigate rising inequality remains to be seen on a country-by-country basis.

Bibliography

Alesina, A. and Rodrik, D. 1994. Distributive politics and economic growth. *Quarterly Journal of Economics*, Vol. 109, No. 2, pp. 465–90.

Autor, D. 2014. Skills, education, and the rise of earnings inequality among the other 99 percent. *Science*, Vol. 344, No. 6186, pp. 843–51.

Banerjee, A. V. 2010. Investment efficiency and the distribution of wealth. R. Kanbur and M. Spence (eds), *Equity and Growth in a Globalizing World*. Washington DC, World Bank on behalf of the Commission on Growth and Development, pp. 71–102.

Barros, R., De Carvalho, M., Franco, S. and Mendonça, R. 2010. Markets, the state and the dynamics of inequality in Brazil. L. F. Lopez-Calva and N. Lustig (eds), *Declining Inequality in Latin America: A Decade of Progress?* New York and Washington DC, UNDP and Brookings Institution Press, pp. 134–74.

Kanbur, R. 2014. Globalization and inequality. A. B. Atkinson and F. Bourguignon (eds), *Handbook of Income Distribution*, Vol. 2B. Amsterdam, Elsevier, pp. 1845–81.

Kanbur, R. and Lustig, N. 2000. Why is inequality back on the agenda? *Proceedings of Annual World Bank Conference in Development Economics*, Washington DC, World Bank, pp. 285–313.

Kanbur, R. and Zhuang, J. 2012. Confronting rising inequality in Asia. *Asian Development Outlook 2012*. Mandaluyong City, Philippines, Asian Development Bank.

Kuznets, S. 1955. Economic growth and income inequality. *American Economic Review*, Vol. 45, No. 1, pp 1–28.

Lewis, W. A. 1976. Distribution and development. A. Cairncross and M. Puri (eds), *Employment, Income Distribution and Development Strategy: Problems of the Developing Countries. Essays in Honour of H. W. Singer*. London, Macmillan, pp. 26–42.

López-Calva, L. F. and Lustig, N. (eds). 2010. *Declining Inequality in Latin America: A Decade of Progress?* New York and Washington DC, UNDP and Brookings Institution Press.

Ostry, J. D., Berg, A. and Tsangarides, C. G. 2014. Redistribution, inequality, and growth. Staff Discussion Note SDN14/02. Washington DC, IMF.

Wong, B. 2011. Historical lessons about contemporary social welfare: Chinese puzzles and global challenges. C. A. Bayly, V. Rao, S. Szreter and M. Woolcock (eds), *History, Historians and Development Policy*. Manchester, Manchester University Press.

■ *Ravi Kanbur (UK) is T. H. Lee Professor of World Affairs at Cornell University, N.Y. He is president-elect of the Human Development and Capabilities Association and past president of the Society for the Study of Economic Inequality. He has published in leading economics journals and is ranked in the top 0.5 per cent of academic economists in the world. He has also served on the senior staff of the World Bank, including as chief economist for Africa.*

25. Inequality and political conflict

Gudrun Østby

This contribution summarizes the literature on how inequality relates to political conflict. It reviews the most central theoretical arguments and empirical findings concerning this relationship. Most importantly, there is a growing consensus that whereas inequality between individuals (vertical inequality) does not affect the risk of conflict, systematic inequality between identity groups (horizontal inequality) indeed does. Further, the article discusses various approaches to measuring horizontal inequality. It ends by discussing some avenues for policy and future research.

Introduction

At least since Aristotle, political theorists have proposed that political discontent and its consequences – protest, instability and violence – depend not only on the absolute level of economic wealth, but also on its distribution, or in other words the inequality between the rich and poor.

While the number of armed conflicts worldwide has decreased steadily since the Cold War, in 2014 the Uppsala Conflict Data Program (UCDP) recorded forty armed conflicts with a minimum of twenty-five battle-related deaths each (Themnér and Wallensteen, 2014), the highest number of conflicts reported since 1999.

Whether or not income inequality in the world has increased is subject to debate. If we weight countries by their population size, inequality between states is decreasing, mostly owing to economic growth in large countries such as China and India. But at the same time many countries are experiencing rising internal inequality: this is true for large states such as China and India, but also for smaller African states.

Does inequality breed political conflict? For almost half a century, scholars have sought to test this assumption, but the empirical literature remains inconclusive. However, there is increasing evidence that suggests that group-based inequalities are particularly linked to conflict. Here, I review central theoretical arguments and empirical findings concerning the relationships between various forms of economic inequality and violent political conflict. I conclude by discussing some avenues for policy and future research.

The inequality–conflict nexus: arguments and empirical evidence

Different theoretical approaches to inequality and conflict include the Marxist theory of class struggle and revolution, relative deprivation theory, and theories of ethnic conflict and structural inequality. These theories share the interpretation of conflict as a result of widely felt grievances among the relatively disadvantaged in society.

Advocates of the mobilization opportunity approach criticize the explanation of collective violence and protest offered by the theory of relative deprivation. They reject grievances hypotheses, because inequality and discontent are more or less always present in all societies. They argue that we should focus on the roles of financial and political opportunities to mobilize a rebel organization.

In theory, there are five possible relationships between economic inequality and political conflict: positive, negative, convex (inverted U-shaped), concave (U-shaped) or null. Reviewing the empirical literature, we find examples of all five (Lichbach, 1989). However, the more recent empirical conflict literature, with Collier and Hoeffler (2004) at the forefront, has largely dismissed grievances as causes of conflict, finding no cross-national relationship between inequality and the onset of conflict.

Horizontal inequality and conflict: findings and measurement

The weak empirical evidence for the inequality–conflict link may stem from the use of individual-level measures of inequality, such as the Gini coefficient.

In contrast to the statistical rejection of the link between inequality and conflict, a case-based literature has emerged, spearheaded by the Oxford-based development economist Frances Stewart. Stewart focuses on the role of horizontal inequalities, systematic economic and political inequalities between ethnic, religious or regional groups, arguing that such group-based inequality is more likely to trigger conflict than vertical or individual-based inequalities (Stewart, 2008). According to this argument, it is not only resentment on the part of relatively deprived groups that causes political instability. Privileged groups may also attack the less privileged, fearing that they might demand more resources, or might try to break away.

Most research on the relation between horizontal inequality and conflict has relied on qualitative case studies (e.g. Stewart, 2008). The picture that emerges from these studies is mainly that horizontal inequalities are associated with increased risks of political violence.

However, there have been few efforts to study the conflict potential of horizontal inequalities systematically and quantitatively. Until recently, most researchers exploring the consequences of intergroup inequalities have relied on Ted Gurr's Minorities at Risk (MAR) dataset (see *www.cidcm.umd.edu/mar*), which provides indicators of group-based disparities. However, the various indicators of relative group grievances provided by MAR are quite crude, and are largely based on statements and actions by group leaders and members, which produce fairly subjective evaluations of group deprivation.

More recently, some conflict studies have sought to measure horizontal inequality on the basis of data from national household surveys, such as the demographic and health surveys (DHS) (e.g. Østby, 2008). These studies largely support the validity of the positive relationship between conflict and various forms of horizontal inequality. Further, Cederman and colleagues (2011) reported support for the horizontal inequality–conflict nexus. They provided the first global dataset on economic horizontal inequality, combining their own data on ethnic groups' settlement areas (Min, Cederman and Wimmer, 2008) with Nordhaus and colleagues' (2006) G-Econ dataset (Geographically based Economic data) on local economic activity. The latter covers the gross cell product for all regions for 1990, 1995, 2000 and 2005, and includes 27,500 terrestrial observations (see *http://gecon.yale.edu*). In order to proxy horizontal inequality, they use these sources to calculate wealth estimates for each ethnic settlement group, and compare them with the average wealth of all groups in a country. In line with their expectations, they find that groups with wealth levels far below the country average are more likely to experience an outbreak of civil war, measured by whether a group has links to a rebel organization actively involved in fighting. Although this research offers an interesting empirical contribution to the horizontal inequality–conflict debate, a potential warning about Cederman and colleagues' analysis is that the G-Econ data have certain limitations, such as low-quality data in many developing states.

Given that there is no one perfect way to measure horizontal inequality, Cederman, Weidmann and Bormann (2015) introduced a new composite indicator that explores and combines the strengths of three different sources of data on local wealth: the G-Econ data, survey data on household durables, and night lights emissions data from satellites combined with geographical data on the settlement of ethnic groups. Their combined index confirms the previous findings that horizontal inequalities do spur conflict in the case of groups that are poorer than the country average.

Conclusions

As has been demonstrated in this literature review, what seem to matter for conflict are horizontal inequalities – systematic economic disparities between identity groups, and not only inequality between rich and poor individuals.

A main challenge for future research in this field is to provide better data on horizontal inequalities for various group identifiers and dimensions. A point of departure can be to identify more sophisticated ways to merge different data sources, as Cederman and colleagues (2015) do. Another important future research task should be to better account for the causal mechanisms that underlie the horizontal inequality–conflict nexus.

This requires extensive theorizing and carefully selected micro-level studies, such as Hillesund's (2015) analysis of how horizontal inequalities affect support for violent and nonviolent resistance among Palestinians in the West Bank and Gaza. Furthermore, we need to better understand the relationship between objective and perceived inequalities (e.g. see Must, 2013). Finally, we need to better understand whether and how various dimensions of horizontal inequality lead to different forms of conflict. For instance, Buhaug and colleagues (2014, p. 419) found that horizontal economic inequality is primarily associated with separatist attempts, while widespread ethno-political discrimination seems to motivate attempts to target central governmental power. On a related note, while most studies of inequality and conflict have tended to focus on civil conflict, we need to get a better understanding of whether and how horizontal inequalities influence other forms of political violence, such as urban violence (see Østby, 2015).

Where horizontal inequalities are found to be severe, policies are needed to correct them. In our increasingly pluralistic societies, development policies should seek to reduce horizontal inequalities in all countries, not only those currently in conflict. Such policies should include both the elimination of discrimination and affirmative action, providing a positive bias in favour of relatively deprived groups. However, policies developed to correct horizontal economic inequality can be tricky, and in the worst case can provoke rather than lessen or avoid conflict (see Stewart, 2008).

Bibliography

Buhaug, H., Cederman, L.-E. and Gleditsch, K. S. 2014. Square pegs in round holes: inequalities, grievances, and civil war. *International Studies Quarterly*, Vol. 58, No. 2, pp. 418–31.

Cederman, L.-E., Gleditsch, K. S. and Weidmann, N. B. 2011. Horizontal inequalities and ethno-nationalist civil war: a global comparison. *American Political Science Review*, Vol. 105, No. 3, pp. 478–95.

Cederman, L.-E., Weidmann, N. B. and Bormann, N.-C. 2015. Triangulating horizontal inequality: toward improved conflict analysis. *Journal of Peace Research*, Vol. 52, No. 6, pp. 806–21.

Collier, P. and Hoeffler, A. 2004. Greed and grievance in civil war. *Oxford Economic Papers*, Vol. 56, No. 4, pp. 563–95.

Hillesund, S. 2015. A dangerous discrepancy: testing the micro-dynamics of horizontal inequality on Palestinian support for armed resistance. *Journal of Peace Research*, Vol. 52, No. 1, pp. 76–90.

Lichbach, M. I. 1989. An evaluation of 'Does economic inequality breed political conflict?' studies. *World Politics*, Vol. 41, No. 4, pp. 431–70.

Min, B., Cederman, L.-E. and Wimmer, A. 2008. Ethnic Power Relations (EPR) [data file], Harvard Dataverse, V1. Accessed 28 June 2016 *http://hdl.handle.net/1902.1/11796*,

Must, E. 2013. Perceptions, horizontal inequalities and conflict outbreak: a global comparison. Paper presented at the annual Midwest Political Science Association (MPSA) conference, Chicago, Ill., 11–14 April.

Nordhaus, W., Azam, Q., Corderi, D., Hood, K., Victor, N. M., Mohammed, M., Miltner, A. and Weiss, J. 2006. The G-Econ database on gridded output: methods and data. Unpublished manuscript, New Haven, Conn., Yale University, 12 May.

Østby, G. 2008. Polarization, horizontal inequalities and violent civil conflict. *Journal of Peace Research*, Vol. 45, No. 2, pp. 143–62.

Østby, G. 2015. Rural–urban migration, inequality and urban social disorder: evidence from African and Asian cities. *Conflict Management and Peace Science*, forthcoming. Published online first on 20 July 2015, doi: 10.1177/0738894215581315.

Stewart, F. 2008. *Horizontal Inequalities and Conflict: Understanding Group Violence in Multiethnic Societies*. Basingstoke, UK, Palgrave Macmillan.

Themnér, L. and Wallensteen, P. 2014. Armed conflicts, 1946–2013. *Journal of Peace Research*, Vol. 51, No. 4, pp. 541–54.

■ *Gudrun Østby (Norway) (PhD, 2011) is a senior researcher at the Peace Research Institute Oslo (PRIO) and associate editor of the* Journal of Peace Research. *Her research interests include how conflict relates to inequality, gender-based violence and health.*

POSTCARD

26. Perceived inequalities among Lebanese nationals and Syrian refugees

Charles Harb

The wars in the Eastern Mediterranean region are drastically changing its demographic profile, with large-scale migration of people within and between nations. The wars in Iraq and Syria alone have displaced more than 12 million Syrians and 4 million Iraqis (Yahya, 2015), with 4 million Syrians finding shelter in the neighbouring countries of Jordan, Lebanon and Turkey. Lebanon, a small country with about 4 million inhabitants, is hosting more than 1.2 million Syrian refugees. This is 25 per cent of its population – 'the world's highest number of refugees per inhabitant' (UNHCR, UNICEF, WFP, 2015, p. 1).

This sudden influx of a large number of Syrian refugees into a small country that already had a challenged infrastructure is straining Lebanon's socio-economic fabric. With most refugees settling in some of Lebanon's poorest areas, there is fierce competition for employment, basic services and provisions, which are seen as existential requirements. Severely diminished water supplies, daily power outages, higher unemployment rates,[1] rising poverty,[2] and the inability of health-care providers and educational institutions to cope with demand are exacerbating perceived inequalities and inter-group tension.

Research on intercommunity relations and perceptions by Harb and Saab (2014) showed large discrepancies in perceptions of inequality and threats between Syrian refugees and Lebanese nationals.[3] Many refugees complained of widespread bias and inequality in their treatment by local businesses (such as being charged higher prices than for locals), health-care services (for instance, restricted access to emergency hospital services), property owners (such as inflated rental costs), community officials and the police. Perceptions of inequality also applied to international NGOs, which were seen as corrupt and biased in their treatment of refugees.[4]

These perceptions are compounded by the deteriorating conditions of life for Syrian refugees over time,[5] as donor fatigue and high levels of food insecurity[6] further affect this already vulnerable population.

Some Lebanese nationals saw Syrian refugees as disproportionately benefiting from international aid and attention, including housing subsidies, cash stipends, employment opportunities and basic health-care services, while disadvantaged local communities did not receive such treatment. These experiences of inequality heighten perceptions of threat, with more than 90 per cent of the nationals surveyed reporting refugees as a symbolic threat. That is, they were seen as a threat to their basic value system and worldview as well as an economic threat by competing with locals for jobs and economic opportunities. More than two-thirds of the respondents also saw refugees as an existential threat. These elevated threat perceptions were accompanied by equally high levels of support for restrictive policies against Syrian refugees, including support for policies that violated basic human rights,[7] such as the rights to freedoms of movement and assembly.

While there has been sporadic and isolated violence against Syrian refugees,[8] no organized collective action against them has been recorded to date. Similarly, while isolated incidents between refugees and NGO workers have been noted, no collective action against NGOs has been recorded. Recent cuts to international aid, and the ongoing lack of action by Lebanon's central government, contribute to worsening quality of life indices for both communities, indicating a significant human security threat for the country and the wider region.

PART II · THE CONSEQUENCES OF INEQUALITIES | Chapter 3 | Consequences and interactions of multiple inequalities

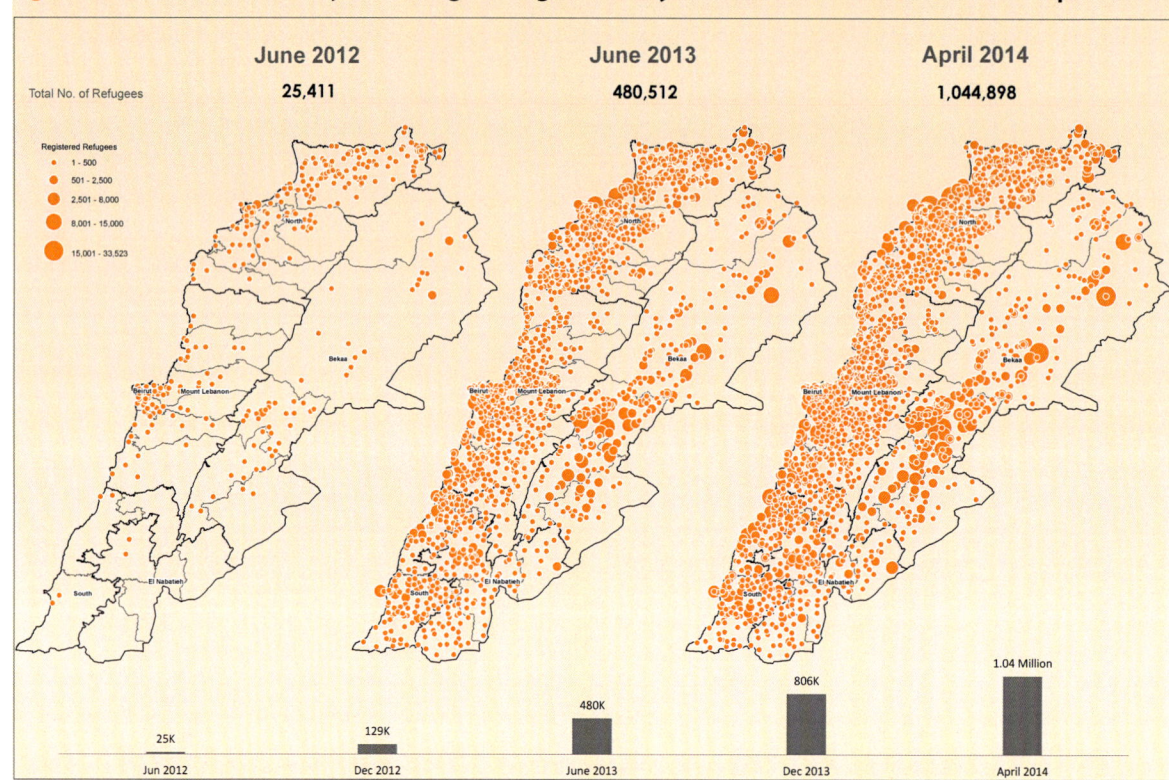

Figure 26.1 **Time series of Syrian refugees registered by cadastral in Lebanon as of 30 April 2014**

Note: The boundaries, names and designations used on this map do not imply official endorsement of the United Nations or UNHCR. All data used were the best available at the time of map production.

Source: Refugee population and location data by UNHCR as of 30 April 2014.
http://reliefweb.int/sites/reliefweb.int/files/resources/UNHCR_LBN_REF_MAP_2014_06_06_TimeSeries_RefugeesRegisteredInLebanon.pdf

Notes

1. An assessment of socio-economic conditions in some of the affected areas shows unemployment rates averaging around 40 per cent, with a range between 23 per cent and 58 per cent (Harb and Saab, 2014).

2. More than a million Lebanese nationals live below the poverty line, and it is estimated that a further 170,000 have been pushed into poverty by the unfolding Syrian crisis (World Bank, 2013).

3. The multi-stage multi-method study involved seventeen focus group discussions and a representative sampling survey of 600 Syrian refugees and 600 Lebanese nationals in some of the more affected areas.

4. A third of the refugees perceived aid organizations as corrupt, whereas 25 per cent of the refugees are not registered with the UN High Commissioner for Refugees (UNHCR) and are therefore denied refugee status and assistance.

5. A 2015 assessment found that more than two-thirds of Syrian refugees are living below the minimum expenditure basket (MEB). This is worse than for 2014, when less than half of the refugees were assessed below the MEB. The MEB is a way of establishing poverty lines for refugee populations (*https://data.unhcr.org/syrianrefugees/download.php?id=9098*).

6. Refugees' average monthly household income was a third of their Lebanese counterparts' average monthly income (Harb and Saab, 2014), while only 10 per cent of refugees were seen to have food security (Aktis, 2015).

7. About 90 per cent of the surveyed participants would support nightly curfews and restricted political freedom, while 75 per cent want Lebanon to stop receiving refugees and forbid those who are already there from finding a job.

8. There have been forced evictions in several areas (OCHA, 2015).

Bibliography

Aktis. 2015. Monitoring stability in Lebanon. Report submitted to the UNDP Lebanon office, Beirut.

European Commission. 2015. Humanitarian aid and civil protection (Echo factsheet). *http://ec.europa.eu/echo/files/aid/countries/factsheets/syria_en.pdf* (Accessed 30 November 2015.)

Harb. C. and Saab, R. 2014. *Social Cohesion and Intergroup Relations: Syrian Refugees and Lebanese Nationals in the Bekaa and Akkar*. Save the Children and UNHCR. *https://data.unhcr.org/syrianrefugees/download.php?id=5807* (Accessed 10 June 2016.)

OCHA (UN Office for Coordination of Humanitarian Affairs). 2015. *Humanitarian Bulletin (Lebanon Issue)*, Issue 13. *http://reliefweb.int/sites/reliefweb.int/files/resources/Humanitarian%20Update%20-%20Issue%2013%20%281%20September%20-%2015%20October%202015%29_EN.pdf* (Accessed 30 November 2015.)

UNHCR. 2014. Syria regional refugee response. *http://data.unhcr.org/syrianrefugees/country.php?id=122* (Accessed 30 November 2015.)

UNHCR, UNICEF (UN Children's Fund) and WFP (World Food Programme). 2015. *Vulnerability Assessment of Syrian Refugees in Lebanon (VASyR)*. *http://reliefweb.int/sites/reliefweb.int/files/resources/VASyR2015_ExecutiveSummary.pdf* (Accessed 30 November 2015.)

World Bank. 2013. *Lebanon: Economic and Social Impact Assessment of the Syrian Conflict*. www.worldbank.org/content/dam/Worldbank/document/MNA/LBN-ESIA%20of%20Syrian%20Conflict-%20EX%20SUMMARY%20ENGLISH.pdf (Accessed 30 November 2015.)

Yahya, M. 2015. *Refugees and the Making of an Arab Regional Disorder*. Beirut, Carnegie Middle East Center. *http://carnegieendowment.org/files/CMEC57_Yahya_final.pdf* (Accessed 10 June 2016.)

■ **Charles Harb** *(Lebanon) is a social and political psychologist at the American University of Beirut, Lebanon, interested in research on identities, group dynamics, and social cohesion in the Arab world. He has also consulted on several UN-related projects.*

27. Inequality and sustainability

Melissa Leach

As the Sustainable Development Goals (SDGs) make clear, inequality and environmental unsustainability are both defining challenges of our age. They are also deeply linked in multiple ways, so that tackling one without addressing the other is unlikely to succeed.

In the Anthropocene, humans are the defining force shaping environmental change, from the global to the local scale, whether it concerns climate, biodiversity, the oceans, fresh water, or rural or urban landscapes (Steffen et al., 2015). Social–ecological systems, or coupled human–natural ones, can move along pathways that are unsustainable – leading to stresses, shocks and irreversible and damaging climate change, for instance – or sustainable, securing the integrity of ecosystems, and human well-being for current and future generations. In differing ways, current definitions of sustainability emphasize the integration of environmental, social and economic dimensions, and the need to steer within a 'safe' or 'safe and just' operating space for humanity, or to combine ecological integrity, well-being and social justice (Leach et al., 2013). To some extent, these definitions internalize a concern with equality as being intrinsic to sustainability. But understanding and action demand further unpacking of the ways in which multiple dimensions of inequality interact with different dimensions of environmental change, and of the distributional implications of different pathways towards sustainability or away from it. Deeply relevant here are 'environmental inequalities' – inequalities in access to and control over ecological space and resources, in experiences and impacts of environmental change, and in agency to shape environmental futures.

Inequalities affect how the ecological space and resources of a finite planet are shared. Debates over the limited carbon emissions budget that the world can afford if climatic warming is to be kept below 2 or 1.5° Celsius, for instance, highlight unequal shares in the past, and the challenge of building fair emissions regimes into the future among countries with different development paths and different stakes in an economically unequal world (Bulkeley et al., 2014).

On the global, national and local scales, environmental and resource scarcities are rarely problems of overall availability, but rather of distribution amid economic and political inequalities. For instance, threats to the sustainability of food systems for growing populations relate less to the overall availability of productive land and water and more to how these are distributed and used, especially the dominance of unsustainable industrial production and wasteful consumption practices. Global food production (and the global cropland it requires) is theoretically sufficient to feed twice the planet's current population (Lundqvist et al., 2008), but access is deeply unequal. And as has long been known, hunger and food insecurity are principally matters of access and entitlement, not availability. In relation to land, water and other resources, scarcities are often manufactured, as elites with economic and political power command and concentrate resources at the expense of others (Mehta, 2011). Environmental inequalities in resource access and control, shaped by various forms of social, economic and gender inequality and discrimination, can create deprivation, driving downward spirals that in turn intensify inequalities further.

Exposure and vulnerability to environmental stresses and shocks are also affected by inequalities. As the environmental justice literature has long made clear, the impacts of climate change, pollution, or degradation of land, vegetation, water or fisheries are often experienced differently according to differences of class, ethnicity, or where people live. The costs of environmental change also fall differentially between women and men, affected by gender inequalities in control over labour, land and decision-making. Women often bear the brunt of coping with declining water, food or fuel resources, and with the health effects of climate change and pollution, adding to their burdens of care work, and undermining opportunities for empowerment and economic advancement (Leach, 2015).

Inequalities also undermine sustainability, and compromise the addressing of environmental challenges. Economic, social and spatial inequalities, and discrimination against certain groups, can push those at the bottom into unsustainable practices that worsen environmental degradation, inequality and unsustainability. For instance, where land and water grabs linked to elite-driven commercial developments dispossess indigenous people onto marginal lands, they can be forced to 'mine' soils and vegetation unsustainably merely to eke out a livelihood. Environmental inequalities can work directly against sustainability, for instance when people deprived of secure tenure over natural resources lack incentives and abilities to conserve them for the future. More significant, though, are the ways in which inequalities of wealth, privilege and power have enabled those at the top – wealthy businesses and consumers – to pollute and degrade environments with impunity, confident that they will have the wealth and alternatives to escape the consequences. A growing awareness that in a deeply interconnected world, unsustainability will undermine economies and societies for everyone everywhere – wealthy and poor alike – is only just beginning to impinge on this pattern.

Meanwhile, inequalities of many kinds work against sustainability by making cooperation more difficult. Environmental issues require cooperative institutional arrangements to manage public goods at different scales. Effective local regimes to manage common property resources such as forests or fisheries have often been undermined by horizontal inequalities or class differences (Ostrom, 1990). Globally, inequalities between countries have compromised cooperation on challenges such as climate change and biodiversity. Nationally, unequal societies are less able to address sustainability challenges in the long term, as their ability to form a common commitment or compact for change is compromised (Wilkinson et al, 2010). Inequalities can also drive competition for status, which if linked to material consumption can drive unsustainable practices and lifestyles.

Underpinned by growing environmental concerns, policies and interventions to address unsustainability and build more sustainable paths are multiplying. These too interact with inequalities, so that tensions and trade-offs, as well as synergies and alignments, are evident. For instance state, market or technology-led approaches to the 'green economy' are a major focus of much sustainability policy and investment in areas like renewable energy and payments for ecosystem services. These initiatives may reduce employment for some, increase the costs of resources and environmental services, encourage elite capture, and divert resources and create barriers to poverty-reducing livelihood change (Levidow, 2014). As Dercon (2012, p. 17) argues, the poor 'should not be asked to pay the price for greening the planet'.

Market-led schemes to conserve forest carbon through selling credits and offsets, in Africa and beyond, have been associated with 'green grabs' that dispossess local forest users of livelihoods and resource rights (Leach and Scoones, 2015). These build on a long history of interventions in the name of environmental sustainability which misinterpret the dynamics of change and label people as resource destroyers, in turn justifying restrictions that contribute to social and economic inequalities. Such processes often increase knowledge inequalities. Local ways of knowing and living with environments – whether in rural or urban settings, or among pastoralist, agricultural or forest communities – are ignored or undermined. Yet approaches that build respectfully on local knowledge, practices and institutions in managing forest landscapes offer the prospects of enhancing both climate change mitigation, and environmental and economic equalities.

Policies that are good for sustainability and economic equality may also have gender-differentiated effects. A focus on women can risk casting them as 'sustainability saviours', adding 'environment' to women's already heavy unpaid care and work burdens, but without conferring rights, resources and benefits. Yet gender equality and sustainability can also reinforce one another in alternative pathways built on women's knowledge, agency and collective action. Forms of local forest governance in India and Nepal, involving women's full participation, have been shown to improve conservation, livelihoods and gender equality simultaneously (Agarwal, 2010).

Sustainability can thus be achieved through different means and pathways, each with their own synergies and trade-offs with different dimensions of inequality; the choices amongst these are deeply conditioned by political economy (Schmitz and Scoones, 2015).

Arguably the dominance of political and economic decision-making by powerful elites, driven by market profit at the expense of the environment, has underlain our planetary predicament. Citizen-led movements and claims to voice and power have been central in pushing for pro-sustainability change. Yet some argue too that effective sustainability will only be realized at the scale, depth and urgency required if there is strong, directive, top-down leadership (Hickman, 2010), prioritizing environmental sustainability above political inclusion and democracy. Counter-arguments are that non-inclusive sustainability solutions will ultimately flounder or be resisted, and that effective, long-term sustainability will only emerge when democratic inclusion and citizen participation are assured (Stirling, 2015). Tackling political inequalities emerges as a crucial contributor to sustainability, intrinsic to notions of sustainability that also encompass social justice.

Bibliography

Agarwal, B. 2010. *Gender and Green Governance: The Political Economy of Women's Presence Within and Beyond Community Forestry*. Oxford, Oxford University Press.

Bulkeley, H., Andonova, L., Betsill, M. M., Compagnon, D., Hale, T., Hoffmann, M. J., Newell, P., Paterson, M., Roger, C. and Van Deveer, S. 2014. *Transnational Climate Change Governance*. Cambridge, Cambridge University Press

Dercon, S. 2012. Is green growth good for the poor? Policy Research Working Paper 6321. Washington DC, World Bank.

Hickman, L. 2010. 'James Lovelock: humans are too stupid to prevent climate change'. *Guardian*, 29 March.

Leach, M. 2015. *Gender Equality and Sustainable Development*. London, Routledge.

Leach, M., Raworth, K. and Rockström, J. 2013. Between social and planetary boundaries: navigating pathways in the safe and just space for humanity. Introductory keynote chapter, *World Social Science Report*. Paris, International Social Science Council.

Leach, M. and Scoones, I. (eds). 2015. *Carbon Conflicts and Forest Landscapes in Africa*. London, Routledge.

Levidow, L. 2014. What green economy? Diverse agendas, their tensions and potential futures. IKD Working Paper 73, Innovation Knowledge Development, Open University, www.open.ac.uk/ikd/publications/working-papers/ (Accessed 3 August 2015.)

Lundqvist, J., de Fraiture, C., and Molden, D. 2008. Saving water: from field to fork – curbing losses and wastage in the food chain. Policy brief. Stockholm, Stockholm International Water Institute (SIWI).

Mehta, L. 2011. *The Limits to Scarcity: Contesting the Politics of Allocation*. London. Earthscan

Ostrom, E. 1990. *Governing the Commons: The Evolution of Institutions for Collective Action*. Cambridge UK, Cambridge University Press.

Schmitz, H. and Scoones, I. 2015. Accelerating sustainability: why political economy matters, Evidence Report 152. Brighton, UK, IDS.

Steffen, W., Richardson, K., Rockström, J., Cornell, S. E., Fetzer, I., Bennett, E. M., and Sörlin, S. 2015. Planetary boundaries: guiding human development on a changing planet. *Science*, 1259855.

Stirling, A. 2015. Emancipating transformations: from controlling 'the transition' to culturing plural radical progress. I. Scoones, M. Leach and P. Newell (eds), *The Politics of Green Transformations*. London, Routledge/Earthscan.

Wilkinson, R.G., Pickett, K.E. and De Vogli, R. 2010. Equality, sustainability, and quality of life. *British Medical Journal* 341, doi: 10.1136/bmj.c5816.

■ **Melissa Leach** (UK) is the director of the Institute of Development Studies (IDS). A geographer and social anthropologist, her interdisciplinary, policy-engaged research in Africa and beyond links environment, agriculture, health, technology and gender, with particular interests in knowledge, power and the politics of science and policy processes. She is vice-chair of the Science Committee of Future Earth; a member of the International Panel of Experts on Sustainable Food Systems (IPES-food); and was lead author of UN Women's World Survey on the Role of Women in Economic Development 2014. She co-founded the Ebola Response Anthropology Platform and was lead social scientist in the UK and WHO Ebola scientific advisory committees during 2014–15.

POSTCARD

28. Challenging intersecting inequalities around access to water

Tahseen Jafry, Blessings Chinsinga, Lilian Zimba and Ted Scanlon

Around the world, inequalities in access to water remain a critical daily issue of survival. Challenging cultural values, gendered roles and power structures is critical to reducing intersecting inequalities of access to water. In turn, these inequalities are exacerbated in many places by climate change. Climate variability via severe drought or flooding is predicted to bring about significant changes to food production systems in sub-Saharan Africa, leading to millions of people being threatened by hunger if the temperature rises by between 2.5 and 4.0 °Celsius. In this scenario, access to water is critical for survival.

However, marginalized groups, and women and children from within these groups, particularly in rural communities, suffer from appallingly low levels of access to safe water. They continue to face major challenges; walking 3–4 km daily to public water points, carrying 20–25 litre containers on their heads, and having to stand and wait in long queues. There is an urgent need for a collective voice calling for dignity, compassion and solidarity for access to water for all.

In Siavonga, Zambia, in a village known as Sanjemuleke, women wake up at 5 a.m. and queue for water. This can take up to five hours and may not guarantee that they will access water, as it is not shared equally but on a first come, first served basis.

In the Chirundu District, in Lusitu Village, the Siavonga River has dried up and people rely on digging scoop holes in the dry river bed. Pregnant women going to deliver their babies have to bring their own water to be accepted onto the maternity ward in the local clinic.

Water from the scoop holes makes our children sick and when we go to the clinic sometimes there is no medicine to treat them (from a focus group discussion with women, Namasheshe Village, Zambia, August 2015).

The water from the scoop holes is never enough … we have to ration how we draw water (from a focus group discussion with women and men, Chinkome Village, Zambia, August 2015).

Our research in Zambia and Malawi suggests that such inequalities regarding access to water are deeply rooted in cultural and gendered inequalities and power structures.

It would be good to see more men helping us with this chore because the 20-litre containers are heavy to carry (from a focus group discussion with women, Chitete Village, Zambia, August 2015).

'Getting water is women's work – a man will never do this job if he wants to keep his reputation.' The reasons for this, described by Ruth Mwyene, a farmer from Malawi attending the World Social Sciences Forum in Durban in 2015, come down to 'cultural values and traditional belief systems. Men are "providers" of the household with women's roles being described as "caring" for the house: cooking, collecting water, looking after children.'

Feedback from poor and marginalized groups in these communities also indicates their feelings of being helpless and worthless, which implies being seen as low-class people by the headman, and considering themselves abandoned by society. There is also a sense of being cut off from government interest as if they are an 'insignificant' people.

In this village, we live like orphans. We are like refugees in our own country. The government doesn't seem to care about us and our welfare. They only think about us during elections when they come to beg for our votes (from a focus group discussion with women and men, Suluba Village, Zambia, August 2015).

Challenging such deep-seated social inequalities will require a collective voice. Our evidence from dialogue and discussion with marginalized farmers in Malawi and Zambia suggests that this voice will require demands for greater access to water supply services, but also demands for dignity, compassion and solidarity, with the aim of reducing deeper forms of intersecting inequalities.

■ **Tahseen Jafry** (UK) *is director and professor at the Centre for Climate Justice, Glasgow Caledonian University.*

■ **Blessings Chinsinga** (Malawi) *is deputy director and professor at the Centre for Social Research (CSR), a research arm of the Faculty of Social Science, and a professor at the Department of Political and Administrative Studies, Chancellor College, University of Malawi.*

■ **Lilian Zimba** (Zambia) *is a lecturer in the School of Education, Social Sciences and Technology, University of Lusaka, Zambia.*

■ **Ted Scanlon** (UK) *is an educator at the Centre for Climate Justice, Glasgow Caledonian University.*

Acknowledgements

This contribution is based on research under the Water for ALL project. For more details see *www.gcu.ac.uk/climatejustice/research/researchthemeprojects/waterforall/*

The authors would like to acknowledge financial support from the Scottish Government's Climate Justice Fund. The views given are those of the authors and not of the Scottish Government.

29. Poverty and environmental inequality in India

Sunita Narain

In considering pollutants, it is important to distinguish between the 'survival' emissions of the poorest – for example, their use of polluting cookstoves which cause severe health damage – and the 'luxury' emissions generated by rich and powerful elites to maintain their consumer lifestyles. It is also important to acknowledge that current systems of water and waste management are capital-intensive and create divisions between rich and poor. The current discourse on environment and development must be reframed so that it is built on the premise that sustainable development needs to be equitable. In other words, growth has to be affordable and inclusive.

The world's poor are the worst affected by environmental degradation. They live in poverty. They have the highest exposure to pollution; the world's highest mortality rates in children are attributed to drinking dirty water. They breathe polluted air. And forest degradation leads to the exacerbation of poverty as the poor cannot get the materials they need for survival. Yet researchers maintain that the poor, despite their intensive use of natural resources, are not responsible for environmental degradation. It is the extensive use of resources for commerce by the rich, involving energy-intensive and extractive industrial methods, that is primarily responsible for degradation (Agarwal, 1985).

Today's question is different: can environmental management work if it does not address inequality?

We need to distinguish between the 'survival' emissions of poor people with no alternative but to walk long distances to collect firewood, sweep the forest floor for leaves and twigs, and do back-breaking work to collect and dry cow-dung, all for some 'oil' to cook their food, and the 'luxury' emissions of those who drive to work and live in air-conditioned comfort.

This distinction is necessary for policy and action. Otherwise, an important opportunity – provided to us by the poorest of the world – to reduce emissions in the future will be lost. Lost, once again, to the ignorance of the international community regarding how the other half lives and the arrogance of powerful polluters.

Cookstoves

Let us be clear: the poorest of the world, who use polluting cookstoves because they cannot afford commercial fossil fuel, provide our only real space today to avert climate change. The energy trajectory is such that these families, when they move out of poverty, will also move out of cooking on this biomass stove. They will walk up the fossil-fuel stairway to liquefied petroleum gas (LPG). Every time they move away, as they must, one less family will be using renewable energy; one more family will begin polluting with long-term greenhouse gas emissions. The difference is that black soot pollutes locally – it literally kills the women who cook – but has a relatively short life in the atmosphere. Unlike carbon dioxide, it disappears in a few weeks.

The poorest people, therefore, provide the world with the perfect opportunity to leapfrog from using polluting but renewable energy, to using energy that is renewable, but clean for them and the world. It is this objective that must drive our efforts, not a plan to pick on the poorest so that we can continue to pollute.

Urban air pollution: equity in road space

It is also clear that solutions to urban air pollution cannot be viable unless they take into account the inequities in current policy.

Today a small but growing number of people in the cities of the South drive a car. In Delhi, for instance, it is only 15 per cent (Wilbur Smith Associates, 2008). But the cost of their driving is high in terms of air pollution, and the congestion is crippling. The question is how to combat air pollution as more and more people drive in Delhi and other increasingly car-clogged cities. Is it possible to plan for the remaining 85 per cent? Is there space on the road, or in the already polluted 'air shed', for the cars of the many?

Clearly there is not. Unless we reinvent urban mobility on an unprecedented scale, we cannot have clean air. Understanding this, the Delhi High Court ruled in 2010 that Delhi roads need to be planned taking into account 'equity of use' (Manushi Sangathan *v.* Govt of Delhi, 2010). Today, the bulk of Delhi's population walks, cycles or takes a bus. Most people do this because they are poor. The question is whether these poor-rich cities of the emerging world can reinvent, upgrade and greatly improve urban public transportation systems so that the majority won't need to use cars so much. In this way, cities do not become car-clogged and then attempt to accommodate buses. They build differently today, for tomorrow.

In short, the policy approach to combat air pollution must move from cleaning the tailpipe to planning for affordable and inclusive mobility solutions. This is not easy. But what is clear is that solutions must work for the poor, for them to work for the rich.

Water pollution: the sewage of all must be treated to clean the rivers

Indian rivers are increasingly polluted, but the question is, how can we clean up when large numbers of people are unconnected to sanitation and do not have access to clean water? Our report, *Excreta Matters* (Narain, 2012) showed why policy needs to be changed. We find that current systems of water and waste management are capital-intensive and create divisions between rich and poor.

The state has limited resources and can only invest in providing for some people – invariably the rich and not the poor. But if only part of the city has access to sanitation and underground sewage disposal, pollution control will not work. The treated waste of the few will be mixed with the untreated waste of many. The end result is pollution.

The standard technocratic response to fixing this requires providing sanitation and connected drainage, so that waste is intercepted and taken to a sewage treatment plant, which is designed to clean waste and discharge the effluents to a river or water body, which in turn has the ability to assimilate and clean the residue. This is very complex and expensive. Current financial and technical constraints will not allow this to happen for all. This is because the more water we use in our houses, the more waste we discharge. The water inequity in Delhi is legendary. Parts of the city are flush with over 200 litres of water per capita, and the rest get a few drops. But what we don't realize is that those who use water, and discharge the waste which ends up in the river, do not pay for the full cost of water or its treatment. In other words, we do not internalize the negative externalities of our water pollution, its economic, social and environmental costs.

The fact is that most governments are designing expensive and technically inappropriate water and waste systems for their teeming cities. These unaffordable systems pipe water for long distances, which adds to the costs of distribution and worse, increases water loss. Then they take back the waste, clean it and pipe it even longer distances. The cost of electricity for pumping, and even more for the exorbitant cost of building and then maintaining this elaborate infrastructure, means that only a small proportion of the urban population will ever be served by adequate water and waste services of this type.

In many cases, municipal governments do not charge enough for the water they supply, or for the waste they collect or treat. The relatively rich users of this system of underground drainage are then subsidized. But this also means that governments do not have sufficient resources to build, operate or maintain the system for all. This is the 'political economy of water supply and defecation' where the rich are subsidized in the name of the poor.

If this approach is not reworked and the technology for water supply and waste management is not reinvented, it will not meet the needs of all. As a result, rivers will continue to be polluted and there will be a higher health burden of polluted water on poor users, while the rich will have to pay higher costs for treating waste water for their drinking water needs. The answer is to have affordable solutions which are also environmentally, socially and technologically sustainable.

In this way, the current discourse on environment and development must be reframed on the premise that sustainable development is not possible if it is not equitable. In other words, growth has to be affordable and inclusive. This also means that the developing world cannot follow the incremental route of the rich world, which has invested in pollution control as it has discovered problems.

But the most important priority is to rearticulate that the environmental challenge is not technocratic but political. We cannot neuter the politics of access, justice and rights and hope to fix environmental problems.

Bibliography

Agarwal, A. 1985. *The Politics of Environment in the State of India's Environment Report.* New Delhi, Centre for Science and Environment.

Manushi Sangathan v. Govt. of Delhi. 2010. WP(C) No. 4572/2007, February. Delhi High Court.

Narain, S. 2012. *Excreta Matters.* New Delhi, State of India's Environment, Centre for Science and Environment. *www.cseindia.org/content/excreta-matters* (Accessed 24 February 2016.)

Wilbur Smith Associates for the Ministry of Urban Development (MOUD). 2008. *Study on Traffic and Transportation Policies and Strategies in Urban Areas in India.* New Delhi, Ministry of Urban Development, Government of India.

■ **Sunita Narain** (India) is the director general of the Centre for Science and Environment (CSE), New Delhi, India.

30. Health and social justice in Egypt: towards a health equity perspective

Soha Bayoumi

This contribution highlights Egypt's striking health inequities. They intersect with other inequities related to gender, socio-economic status, education levels, employment status and geographical location. It argues that efforts to improve the health sector in Egypt need to embrace health equity as an ideal and as a guiding principle for all attempted reforms.

Egypt's health sector has been in a state of crisis for decades. Run-down public hospitals, rampant corruption, lack of accountability, inadequate health insurance, poor-quality public health care and unaffordable and sometimes unreliable private health care have resulted in hardship and even death for many Egyptians (Rafeh et al., 2011).

A look at a number of health indicators is telling. In 2013, Egypt ranked 118th among the 193 member states of the World Health Organization (WHO), and 15th among Arab countries, in life expectancy at birth (WHO, 2013). It is 117th in hospital beds per capita and faces a severe shortage of intensive care units (Kaiser Family Foundation, 2013). Families cover 72 per cent of health-care costs in Egypt (Rafeh et al., 2011). In 2015, the health sector accounted for 5.4 per cent of the total government budget, compared with 12 per cent for education, one of the lowest rates in the Middle East and North Africa region (Ministry of Finance, 2014).

The state of health care in Egypt has in the past become a major cause of social and political discontent among Egyptians, leading up to the political uprising in January 2011 that called for 'bread, freedom, social justice and human dignity'. From January to February 2011, chants lamenting the deplorable health conditions of the Egyptian population echoed in Tahrir Square.[1]

Intersecting inequalities, intersecting causes

There have been some improvements in aggregate health indictors over the past few decades. However, they mask striking inequalities among Egyptians by gender, income level, education and geographic location.

For instance, child mortality is twice as high in rural upper Egypt (thirty-eight deaths per 1,000 births) as in lower urban Egypt (twenty deaths per 1,000 births) (El-Zanaty and Associates, 2014).

Stunting among children aged 0–4 varies tremendously by governorate, from around 12 per cent in Suez to nearly 85 per cent in the Red Sea governorate (El-Kogali and Krafft, 2015). A recent study estimated that 96 per cent of women from the most advantaged group (MAG) (defined as urban, educated and belonging to the highest wealth quintile) receive prenatal care, compared with only 60 per cent from the least advantaged group (LAG) (defined as rural, uneducated and belonging to the lowest wealth quintile). Similarly, births attended by a skilled professional range between 97 per cent for the MAG to 54 per cent for the LAG. Infants born to the LAG are more than twice as likely to die in their first month of life than are those born to the MAG (1.9 and 0.8 per cent respectively: El-Kogali and Krafft, 2015). Health-care financing is also inequitable. Families in the lowest income quintile spend 21 per cent of their income on health-care-related costs, versus 13.5 per cent for those in the highest income quintile (Rafeh et al., 2011).

These examples highlight the fact that health inequities intersect with inequities among income groups and those related to gender, education and geographical location. The deterioration of the health system in Egypt, and its accompanying health inequities, is the outcome of a complex web of authoritarian politics, crony capitalism and corruption, which among other results has led to a brain drain of health-care workers.

The struggle for reform

Efforts have been made to reform the situation in Egypt. The most prominent voices in the fight to overhaul the health system have been medical doctors, who have coupled their professional demands for better wages, working conditions and training opportunities with social and political demands to improve the health-care system and increase public spending on health. Among various other efforts, doctors staged two long strikes, in 2012 and 2014, which lasted for nearly three months each.

These mobilizations have been largely unsuccessful, leading, even by the most optimistic accounts, to only modest increases in doctors' salaries. The deterioration of the public health system and the limited success of protest efforts cannot be understood outside the context of the state of Egyptian politics over the past several decades, characterized by authoritarian leadership, a downtrodden public sphere, a stifled civil society, a neutered opposition and a widespread crackdown on any anti-government social activism or popular mobilization.

It is also relevant to note that doctors in Egypt have historically been shaped by a modernizing project in a colonial and postcolonial setting that is articulated around 'the rule of experts' – including natural scientists, social scientists, economists, engineers, and physicians – who not only make sense of the world, but also shape it. Egyptian doctors historically have been shaped to play that role. Today theirs are the only audible voices in the contested space of health politics in Egypt, where, as Timothy Mitchell puts it, 'nobody listens to a poor man', and where experts have the most leverage to redirect the conversation (Mitchell, 2002). Health system reform has turned into what Matthieu Fintz calls 'a reform for the poor without them' (Fintz, 2006).

These political and historical realities are combined with political and economic factors that have allowed successive Egyptian regimes to maintain the status quo. Corruption, favouritism and crony capitalism are rampant in the health system. Private health-care industry moguls stand to benefit from maintaining the status quo of dilapidated public hospitals, which patients of means do their best to avoid, and of underpaid public-sector doctors who often end up taking second or third jobs at pitiful rates in private hospitals (Berman and Cuizon, 2004).

A brain drain of health workers has exacerbated the crisis. According to some estimates, more than 60 per cent of Egyptian doctors now work outside of the country, mostly in Gulf countries. Here they represent a significant percentage of the health workforce, despite being paid far less than local nationals or colleagues from other countries, and only slightly more than they would earn in Egypt (Fathi, 2012).[2]

While it is true that the crisis in the health sector is representative of a general crisis in the public sector (Shukrallah and Khalil, 2012), each sector has its own specific issues. For instance, despite the equally dismal state of the educational sector in Egypt, teachers' strikes in recent years have been more successful than doctors' strikes. This can be explained by structural factors in the two sectors. In the Egyptian education sector, as in the health sector, there is a two-tiered system of an expensive, relatively high-quality private sector operating in parallel to a nominally free, low-quality public sector. However, in the education sector the two tiers are almost mutually independent, because the private sector, which recruits highly skilled professionals, does not compete with or rely upon the public sector for teachers. In the health sector, the two tiers are much more interconnected, as the private sector exploits public-sector doctors who have to supplement their work with private-sector moonlighting to make ends meet.

The same can be said of demand from the Gulf countries. While they increasingly rely on teachers with higher qualifications than those currently possessed by most public school teachers in Egypt, they still rely on Egyptian doctors as a relatively cheap source of staff for health facilities. We might expect that this situation would enabled medical doctors to be more effective in their demands against the government. However, the government's interest in keeping doctors' salaries low coincides with that of the private-sector magnates and of the foreign employers.

It is not only the government, but also the private sector and oil-rich Gulf neighbours, which stand to benefit from maintaining the status quo.

Ways forward

Through the fieldwork I have conducted in Egypt since 2013 among health-care professionals, especially those who fight to reform the health system, I have noticed that the themes motivating their struggle revolve around resisting corruption, inefficiency, misguided spending priorities and exploitation, while health inequities were not as prominently or consciously cited. As has been shown above, health inequities exist in Egypt. However, a lack of epidemiological studies documenting inequitable health outcomes across geographic, gender and class lines has perhaps prevented the struggle for reforming the health system from being conceived of, first and foremost, as a fight against health inequities.

As Dr Hoda Rashad, director of the Social Research Center of the American University in Cairo, observes, Egypt still follows a 'health systems approach' which 'allows you to see the big picture, but not the inequities in different social groups or the structural determinants beyond the health system', such as poverty, unemployment and lack of education. As a result, we lack knowledge 'about the cumulative effect of deprivation'. A health equity approach, in that view, would prioritize the most vulnerable groups and those who are most in need, and would shed light on the suffering of some social groups that are completely invisible today (WHO, 2011).

Interest in this health-equity approach is slowly burgeoning in Egypt. This makes it incumbent upon the advocates of health-care reform there to adopt a more expansive concept of health, one that incorporates an account of the social determinants of health and which explicitly aims to reduce health inequalities. This would allow us to gauge the multifarious effects of all policy – and not just 'health policy' strictly defined – on different segments of the population. The problem of health in Egypt is not simply a technical issue that requires technical solutions, but rather a social and political one that requires social and political solutions. This understanding warrants an opening-up of the reform movement to engage the efforts of citizens, stakeholders, patient groups, civil society organizations and political parties.

A perhaps promising recent push in that direction is the effort of a group of doctors, in collaboration with civil society organizations, political parties and a patient advocacy group, and engaged ordinary citizens, to produce an Egyptian 'Patient Bill of Rights'. The current discussions about a new health insurance law that aims to guarantee universal coverage should also be inclusive of citizens and other stakeholders. Such efforts are indispensable if the mobilization to reform the health system in Egypt is to make strides on the path towards health equity, social justice and human dignity.

Notes

1. Examples of such chants were '**bā'ū dimānā wi bā'ū kalāwīnā wi binishḥat iḥnā wi ahālīnā**' (They sold our blood, and sold our kidneys, and we beg, we and our families) and '**is-saraṭān fī kull makān wi-l-ghāz mitbā' bil-maggān**' (cancer is everywhere, and the [natural] gas is sold for free), in reference to the deals that Egypt had with Israel to export natural gas to it at lower-than-market prices. For slogans, see *http://angryarab.blogspot.com/2011/01/egyptian-slogans.html* (Accessed 31 August 2014.)

2. The Egyptian Medical Syndicate laments the fact that Egypt is losing its health-care workforce in that brain drain. Despite the lack of exact figures, it estimates that around 100,000 Egyptian doctors work outside the country, almost as many as the total of Egyptian doctors working in Egypt (Egyptian Medical Syndicate, 2014). Sylvia Chiffoleau (2005) sheds light on other global factors and international dynamics that shape and hamper the reform of the Egyptian health system.

Bibliography

Berman, P. and Cuizon, D. 2004. *Multiple Public–Private Jobholding of Health Care Providers in Developing Countries: An Exploration of Theory and Evidence. www.hrhresourcecenter.org/node/270* (Accessed 14 January 2016).

Chiffoleau, S. 2005. La réforme du système de santé égyptien? Entre logique internationale et enjeux nationaux [The reform of the Egyptian health care system? Between international logic and national interests]. S. Chiffoleau (ed.), *Politiques de Santé Sous Influence Internationale. Afrique, Moyen-Orient* [*Health Care Politics under International Influence in Africa and the Middle East*]. Paris and Lyon, France, Maison de l'Orient et de la Méditerranée/Maisonneuve et Larose, pp. 213–36.

Egyptian Medical Syndicate. 2014. Report on the Activities of the Foreign Relations Committee [in Arabic]. *www.ems.org.eg/our_news/details/2828* (Accessed 15 January 2016.)

Egyptian Patient. n.d. The patient's right [in Arabic]. *http://egyptianpatient.org/* (Accessed 24 November 2015.)

El-Kogali, S. and Krafft, C. 2015. *Expanding Opportunities for the Next Generation: Early Childhood Development in the Middle East and North Africa.* World Bank. *https://openknowledge.worldbank.org/bitstream/handle/10986/21287/9781464807367.pdf?sequence=5&isAllowed=y* (Accessed 13 January 2016.)

El-Zanaty and Associates. 2014. *Egypt Demographic and Health Survey 2014*. Cairo, Ministry of Health and Population. *http://dhsprogram.com/pubs/pdf/PR54/PR54.pdf* (Accessed 13 January 2016.)

Fathi, Y. 2012. Egypt's public hospitals: from bad to worse. Ahram Online, 25 November. *http://english.ahram.org.eg/NewsContent/1/64/58686/Egypt/Politics-/Egypts-public-hospitals-From-bad-to-worse.aspx* (Accessed 15 January 2016.)

Fintz, M. 2006. A reform for the poor without them? The fate of the Egyptian health reform programme in 2005. Centre d'Études et de Documentation Économiques, Juridiques et Sociales (CEDEJ) Égypt and Sudan. *www.cedej-eg.org/spip.php?article134&lang=fr* (Accessed 19 February 2015,)

Kaiser Family Foundation. 2013. Hospitals (per 100,000 population). *http://kff.org/global-indicator/hospital-beds/* (Accessed 15 January 2016.)

Ministry of Finance (Egypt). 2014. *Egypt's State Budget 2014–2015* [in Arabic]. *www.budget.gov.eg/Budget20142015/Budget/2ca0bea2-0bc8-453f-adb7-cb1de74ce781* (Accessed 15 January 2016.)

Mitchell, T. 2002. *Rule of Experts: Egypt, Techno-Politics, Modernity*. Oakland, Calif., University of California Press.

Rafeh, N., Williams, J. and Nagwan, H. 2011. *Egypt Household Health Expenditure and Utilization Survey 2009/2010*. USAID Egypt. *https://www.hfgproject.org/egypt-household-health-expenditure-utilization-survey-2010/* (Accessed 13 January 2016.)

Shukrallah, A. and Khalil, M. H. 2012. Egypt in crisis: politics, health care reform, and social mobilization for health rights. S. Jabbour, R. Giacaman, M. Khawaja and I. Nuwayhid (eds), *Public Health in the Arab World*. Cambridge UK, Cambridge University Press, pp. 447–88.

WHO. 2011. Will the Arab Spring bring better health to Egyptians? *Bulletin of the World Health Organization*, Vol. 89, No. 11, pp. 786–87. *www.who.int/bulletin/volumes/89/11/11-041111/en/* (Accessed 10 June 2016.)

WHO. 2013. Life expectancy at birth, 1990–2013. *http://gamapserver.who.int/gho/interactive_charts/mbd/life_expectancy/atlas.html* (Accessed 15 January 2016.)

■ ***Soha Bayoumi*** *(Egypt) is a lecturer in the Department of the History of Science at Harvard University, Mass. Her research addresses the question of social justice with a thematic focus on health, biomedical ethics and the links between medicine and politics, a geographic focus on the Middle East and a special interest in postcolonial and gender studies. She is currently finishing a book manuscript (with Sherine Hamdy, Brown University) on the role of doctors in the Egyptian revolution, and starting a book project on health and social justice and the social roles of doctors in postcolonial Egypt.*

POSTCARD

31. The Ebola crisis: inequality and distrust

Annie Wilkinson and Abu A. Brima

In December 2013 the largest ever Ebola outbreak began in Guinea, spreading to neighbouring countries, the USA and Europe. Guinea, Liberia and Sierra Leone were most severely affected. The outbreak was declared over on 14 January 2016, after 28,637 cases had been recorded and 11,315 deaths (WHO, 2016).

These official figures are known to be underestimates. The Ebola crisis highlights key dimensions of the correlation between inequality and mistrust, and its significance for global health. It reveals how dramatic inequities in wealth, often sustained by corruption and poor governance but not limited to these causes, corrode the social fabric by establishing divisions which exacerbate crises and weaken collective responses to them.

Lack of trust has been noted as a pervasive and damaging feature of the epidemic. Yet fear and avoidance of hospitals were understandable and remediable when the conditions in treatment facilities were taken into account. Other developments, however, revealed less tangible issues, for example a belief that the government had started the epidemic for political gain, that it was allowed to spread in order to make money, that it was the doing of witches, or that health workers were infecting people and stealing organs.

When evoking trust, an essential distinction is the difference between having faith in a particular person or thing, based on direct experience, and having faith in strangers, which is generalized and reflects a confidence in a shared moral community. Many West Africans did not have this confidence.

Levels of generalized trust are lower in more unequal societies (Alesina and La Ferrara, 2002; Rothstein and Uslaner, 2005). Low trust and high inequality also hinder cooperation, collective action, inclusive politics and economic development (Justino, 2015). Centuries of slavery, wars, colonialism and resource exploitation have produced huge economic disparities and unequal power relations in the Mano River region. In Sierra Leone, resource distribution is patrimonial and space for civil society activity is limited and diminishing. Suspicion is natural and normal in this world of ambiguous and unequal opportunities. Recent development trends reproduce these dysfunctional patterns, which erode trust and produce inequality. In pre-Ebola Liberia and Sierra Leone, mining and bioenergy projects resulted in double-figure growth rates, but the profits were captured by foreign investors and local elites, while rural livelihoods were undermined by the annexing of land.

With Ebola, mistrust ruled as outreach workers and nurses struggled to convince communities that they were not profiting from Ebola, often against evidence that others were. Funds were centrally siphoned, or diverted into personal networks away from frontlines and local authorities. Liberian nurses protested about their unpaid salaries, pointing to the higher wages of expatriate staff and noting that school closures did not affect those in power because their children attended private schools abroad (see Samura and Patterson, 2016). In the face of such inequalities, it was hard to maintain the idea of a moral community who were 'all in it together'.

Levels and histories of inequality, and their impact on trust, need to be considered in outbreak response and in other emergencies. Resources should be directed towards affected communities and personnel. In the long term, reducing inequality alongside establishing a more inclusive national political process is vital to building trust both between citizens, and between authorities and their publics.

Bibliography

Alesina, A. and La Ferrara, E. 2002. Who trusts others? *Journal of Public Economics*, Vol. 85, pp. 207–34. *http://scholar.harvard.edu/alesina/publications/who-trusts-others* (Accessed 5 February 2016.)

Justino, P. 2015. *Inequality, Social Cooperation and Local Collective Action*. Working Paper 457. Brighton, UK, IDS. *https://opendocs.ids.ac.uk/opendocs/bitstream/123456789/6289/1/Wp457.pdf* (Accessed 5 February 2016.)

Rothstein, B. and Uslaner, E. M. 2005. All for all: equality, corruption, and social trust. *World Politics*, Vol. 58, No. 1, pp. 41–72. *www.jstor.org/stable/40060124?seq=1#page_scan_tab_contents* (Accessed 5 February 2016.)

Samura, S. and Patterson, C. 2016. *Africa Investigates*, movie. *http://africainvestigates.insighttwi.com/episode-one-liberia.html*

WHO. 2016. Ebola situation reports. *http://apps.who.int/ebola/ebola-situation-reports* (Accessed 10 June 2016.)

■ **Annie Wilkinson** *(UK) is a research fellow at the Institute of Development Studies (IDS), Brighton, UK.*

■ **Abu A. Brima** *(Sierra Leone) is executive director, Network Movement for Justice and Development (NMJD), Freetown, Sierra Leone.*

32. The spatial patterning of exposure to inequality and its social consequences in South Africa: work in progress

David McLennan

The author has developed a neighbourhood measure of exposure to socio-economic inequality in South Africa and argues that it better reflects people's actual lived experience of inequality than a national-level Gini coefficient. He explores associations between exposure to inequality, social attitudes and violent crime.

I would argue that economic measures of income inequality do not capture enough of the dynamic relationship between inequality and other social problems such as crime. I therefore propose a measure on another scale – the lived experience of inequality at a detailed, neighbourhood level. Getting the scale of measurements right is more than an academic exercise. Crime is costly, and inequality, poverty and unemployment obstruct development (NPC, 2014). The inequalities between people, between places and between people-in-places, are increasingly regarded as major drivers of social problems, such as violent crime and social unrest in urban areas (Bundy, 2014).

Inequality in South Africa

South Africa has undergone a remarkable political transformation since the birth of democracy in 1994. Successive African National Congress (ANC)-led governments have tried to remedy the harmful disadvantage and injustice inherited from the colonial, segregationist and apartheid eras. During the very first year of democracy, the government acknowledged that economic and social transformation had to accompany political freedom if the country was to prosper. A broad range of programmes aimed at removing disadvantages and injustices has been implemented (Bundy, 2014). At a national level, absolute levels of poverty and deprivation have fallen slightly over the past two decades (Leibbrandt et al., 2010; Noble et Wright, 2013) with some evidence that this is due at least in part to government intervention (Harrison and Todes, 2015).

But despite these advances, there are still extremely high levels of social and economic inequality in South Africa. In terms of income inequality, South Africa's 2008 Gini coefficient of 0.7 was one of the highest in the world (Leibbrandt et al., 2010). Furthermore, the country's inequality shows strong and continuing racial and spatial components (Noble and Wright, 2013a). The minority white population still enjoys higher living standards than non-white population groups (Wright, 2008). Urban and suburban residents generally enjoy greater economic opportunities and better services than people in townships (specified urban areas where non-white people were permitted to live during the apartheid regime) and in rural areas (Noble and Wright, 2013b; Turok and Borel-Saladin, 2014). In this respect, there has been very little change over the past twenty years.

Measuring the lived experience of inequality in South Africa

Despite discussions of inequality by the government, in academia and in society at large, evidence of intervention and transformation has remained quite limited. To date, most quantitative research on inequality in South Africa has utilized the classical measures of income inequality, for example, the Gini coefficient, General Entropy measures and the Atkinson Index, expressed at the national or occasionally provincial level. Although these measures are powerful tools for measuring change in inequality in South Africa over time, or for international comparisons, they say little about people's day-to-day lived experience of inequality and how it influences them.

My colleagues and I propose that in order to understand how inequality affects people's lives, how it contributes to and interacts with social problems, and general attitudes towards it, we also need to understand how people actually experience it.

I would argue that an individual's experience of inequality is mainly shaped by two interrelated factors: the degree to which an individual routinely comes into personal contact with people from the other end of the socio-economic spectrum (for instance, a poor person from a poor neighbourhood working or seeking work in a wealthy setting and who encounters wealthy people daily); and the degree to which an individual sees severe visual signs of inequality which do not involve direct personal contact (for instance, a wealthy person driving along a highway who notices very poor informal settlements, but does not come into personal contact with their inhabitants).

People from across the entire income spectrum can experience inequality in these ways, by personal contact or by observing the visual signs of inequality. Although this is my main focus here, I also acknowledge that inequality may be experienced in other, less tangible ways, such as via the media.

I would argue that the geographical settings in which people live, work, socialize, travel and so on will contribute to their first-hand experience of inequality. In my team's research, we propose that the experience of inequality is dependent on the neighbourhood in which a person lives and the spatial interrelationships between the home neighbourhood and other nearby neighbourhoods in which daily activities are carried out.

To date, we have used our measure in two separate but complementary pieces of research. The first involved exploring the relationship between the experience of inequality and attitudes to inequality in South Africa.[1] The second involved exploring the associations between the rates of violent crime and the levels of poverty and exposure to inequality across South Africa.[2] In the latter study, we developed a number of statistical models to explore whether the rates of violent crime at the police district level were associated with a range of social, demographic and economic variables, including exposure to inequality.[3]

Findings

In general, we found that the poor population's exposure to inequality is highest when a poor person lives within, or close to, a wealthy neighbourhood. Similarly, exposure to inequality is usually lowest when a poor person lives in a poor neighbourhood surrounded by many other poor neighbourhoods.

It is immediately obvious from *Figure 32.1a* that a mix of neighbourhood poverty rates, with some areas of concentrated poverty (as are found in the Alexandra township) very close to wealthy areas (such as Sandton), are characteristic of Johannesburg.

A poor person living within the largely affluent areas of Sandton experiences some of the highest levels of exposure to inequality in the country. However, residents of the Alexandra Township, which has very high levels of poverty, also experience very high levels of exposure, as shown in *Figure 32.1a*. These high levels of exposure are mainly due to the township being very close to wealthy Sandton.

In contrast, the former homeland areas are typically rural, and remote from major urban centres. While the vast majority of their inhabitants are extremely poor, they experience less exposure to inequality. However, important differences in exposure are also apparent within specific municipalities, depending on the neighbourhood in which people live and carry out their daily activities. Our neighbourhood-level measure of exposure to inequality is therefore more geographically refined than most other measures of inequality in use in South Africa.

In both studies, we found evidence of associations between exposure to inequality and specific dependent variables, such as violent crime and attitudes to inequality. However, the size of the effect, although significant, was typically quite small. This may be because of the limitations of the dependent variables, such as the under-reporting and under-recording of violent crime. Two main concerns for future research in this field are to test for associations between exposure to inequality and other social outcomes, such as fear of crime (using victimization surveys), in South Africa and internationally; and to develop time series of exposure measures on consistent spatial scales to allow us to assess the impact that changing socio-spatial dynamics have on the dependent variables of interest.

PART II · THE CONSEQUENCES OF INEQUALITIES | Chapter 3 | Consequences and interactions of multiple inequalities

Figure 32.1a **Neighbourhood poverty rates across Johannesburg and surrounding areas, 2001 (left);**
Figure 32.1b **Neighbourhood 'exposure to inequality' scores across Johannesburg and surrounding areas, 2001 (right)**

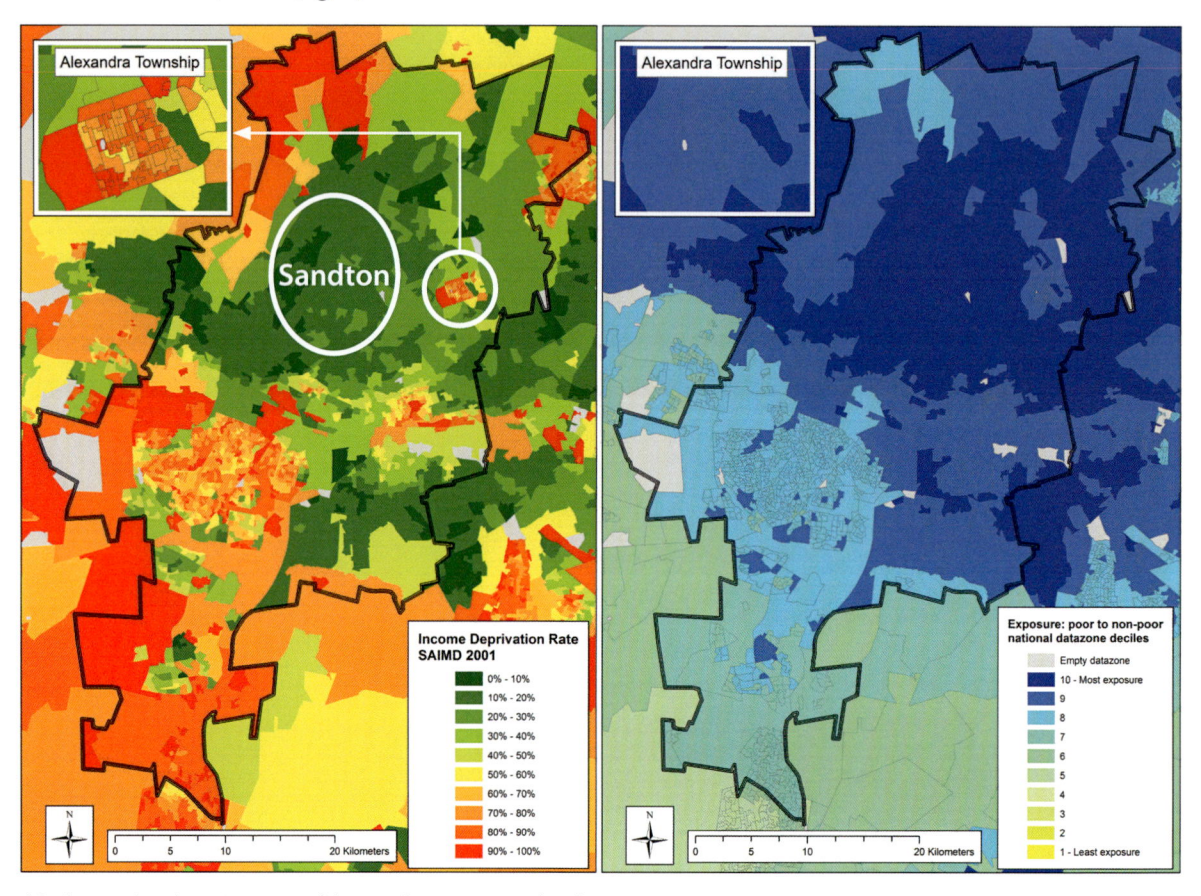

a) Dark green: less than 10 per cent of the population was considered poor in 2001;

b) Dark blue: highest exposure decile to inequality in 2001.

Sources: Author's elaboration of data supplied by Statistics South Africa and the Chief Directorate of Surveys and Mapping; and derived from the South African Index of Multiple Deprivation (SAIMD) 2001.

In summary, the spatially refined consideration of inequality described here offers a potentially useful way to identify neighbourhood-level associations between inequality and social problems, such as violent crime, and to build a strong evidence base for interventions that will help reduce inequality, poverty, and crime.

Notes

1. For this, we developed an exposure measure, using neighbourhood-level data derived from the South African Index of Multiple Deprivation 2001 (Noble et al, 2009), which was based on the 2001 census data. For the method used in developing this index see McLennan et al (2015). DOI: 10.1080/03736245.2015.1028980.

2. In this second research project, we developed the exposure measure using data from the 2011 South African Index of Multiple Deprivation (Noble et al., 2013a), which was based on 2011 census data.

3. For a project aimed at disaggregating relevant variables, see Pare and Felson (2014).

Bibliography

Bundy, C. 2014. *Short-Changed? South Africa since 1994.* Johannesburg, Jacana.

Harrison, P. and Todes, A. 2015. Spatial transformations in a 'loosening state': South Africa in a comparative perspective. *Geoforum*, Vol. 61, pp. 148–162.

Leibbrandt, M., Woolard, I., Finn, A. and Argent, J. 2010. Trends in South African income distribution and poverty since the fall of apartheid, Social, Employment and Migration Working Paper No. 101. Paris, OECD Directorate for Employment, Labour and Social Affairs.

McLennan, D., Noble, M. and Wright, G. 2015. Developing a spatial measure of exposure to socio-economic inequality in South Africa. *South African Geographical Journal*, Vol. 98, No. 2, pp. 254–74.

NPC (National Planning Commission). 2014. *National Development Plan 2030: Our Future – Make It Work.* Pretoria, The Presidency, Republic of South Africa.

Noble, M., Barnes, H., Wright, G., McLennan, D., Avenell, D., Whitworth, A., and Roberts, B. 2009. *The South African Index of Multiple Deprivation 2001 at Datazone Level.* Pretoria, Department of Social Development.

Noble, M. and Wright, G. 2013*a*. Using indicators of multiple deprivation to demonstrate the spatial legacy of apartheid in South Africa. *Social Indicators Research*, Vol. 11, No. 1, pp. 187–201.

Noble, M. and Wright, G. 2013*b*. Ring of fire – socially perceived necessities in informal settlements in South Africa. *Policy and Politics*, Vol. 4, No. 2 pp. 259–77.

Pare, P.-P. and Felson, R. 2014. Income inequality, poverty and crime across nations. *British Journal of Sociology*, Vol. 65, No. 3, pp. 434–58.

Turok, I. and Borel-Saladin, J. 2014. Is urbanization in South Africa on a sustainable trajectory? *Development Southern Africa*, Vol. 31, No. 5, pp. 675–91.

Wright, G. 2008. *Findings from the Indicators of Poverty and Social Exclusion Project: A Profile of Poverty Using the Socially Perceived Necessities Approach.* Key Report 7, Pretoria, Department of Social Development, Republic of South Africa.

■ ***David McLennan*** *(UK) is a senior research fellow at Southern African Social Policy Research Insights (SASPRI). Between 2002 and 2015 he was a senior research fellow in the Department of Social Policy and Intervention at the University of Oxford. His primary research interests are in the spatial configurations of poverty, deprivation and inequality in South and southern Africa.*

POSTCARD

33. Food rights and wrongs

Naomi Hossain

The green revolution and integrated world food markets were supposed to relegate scarcity to the history books, yet food riots erupted in dozens of countries in 2008 and 2011. These events starkly dramatized the inequalities built into the world food system, in which food and commodity corporations profit from the price spikes that put people at risk of hunger and malnutrition. While the spectre of starvation through famine has largely receded, food injustice has a new face – the phenomenon of chronic undernourishment alongside rising obesity, as calorie-dense 'Western' diets spread to societies that until recently grew their own plant-based foods. While ancient problems of seasonal hunger and crop failure still plague the smallholders of the world, poor people now buy more food than they grow, exposing them to finance, trade and climate shocks. In terms of control over the food people eat, the system is growing ever more unequal, increasingly dominated by big food corporations and the international commodity trade.

Understandings of the world's globalizing food system are polarized, and the changes are themselves contradictory. The extent to which the world food system is contributing to inequalities in livelihoods, nutrition, food quality and human well-being can be concealed by the abundance of cheap staple and processed foods. Is global food security improving thanks to open trade regimes, agricultural modernization and nutrition science? Should we celebrate the fact that fewer than 1 billion people are hungry (FAO, 2012)? Or should we worry that food regimes during the past century have increased food inequalities, industrialized food production, commodified eating, and eradicated peasantries and cuisines (McMichael, 2009)? While there is little agreement about the effects of financialization, all observers worry that food insecurity could worsen with climate change and water and energy crises.

But while the US$8 trillion agro-food industry grows apace, so too does resistance to the increasing lack of control that most people have over this fundamental aspect of everyday life (Clapp, 2012).

Broad international movements with wide popular support are mobilizing around food sovereignty, peasant rights, and the right to food, while numerous consumer movements campaign on issues from food safety and food justice to 'slow food', localism and fair trade (Holt-Giménez and Patel, 2009). People across the globe seem willing and able to organize against growing inequality in the food system, as they have done throughout history (Bohstedt, 2014).

Acknowledgement

This contribution is based on a larger research programme funded by the UK Department for International Development (DFID) and Economic and Social Research Council (ESRC) grants scheme. For more details see www.ids.ac.uk/project/food-riots-and-food-rights.

Bibliography

Bohstedt, J. 2014. *Food Riots and the Politics of Provisions in World History*, Working Paper no. 444. Brighton, UK, IDS.

Clapp, J. 2012. *Food*. Cambridge UK, Polity.

FAO (Food and Agriculture Organization of the United Nations). 2012. *State of Food Insecurity in the World: Economic Growth Is Necessary but Not Sufficient to Accelerate Reduction of Hunger and Malnutrition*. Rome, FAO.

Holt-Giménez, E. and Patel, R. 2009. *Food Rebellions: Crisis and the Hunger for Justice*. Oxford, Pambazuka Press.

McMichael, P. 2009. A food regime genealogy. *Journal of Peasant Studies*, Vol. 36, No. 1, pp. 139–69.

■ **Naomi Hossain** *(Bangladesh) is a political sociologist at the Institute of Development Studies (IDS), currently focusing on the political economy of subsistence crises. Recent projects include comparative research on adjustment to the food crisis (www.ids.ac.uk/project/life-in-a-time-of-food-price-volatility, funded by UK Aid and Irish Aid) and food riots (www.ids.ac.uk/project/food-riots-and-food-rights, funded by DFID/ESRC). Her book about the consequences of Bangladesh's 1974 famine,* The Aid Lab: Explaining Bangladesh's Surprising Success, *will be published by Oxford University Press in 2016.*

34. The role of aspirations in the exclusion of Peruvian indigenous children

Laure Pasquier-Doumer

This contribution highlights a particular mechanism which underlies the exclusion of indigenous people in Peru. More precisely, it analyses how aspirations contribute to the persistence of inequality between ethnic groups. Relying on the Young Lives dataset, I find that indigenous children do not limit their aspirations when compared with non-indigenous children with the same socio-economic background. Findings suggest that they do not have internalized racial schemas about their opportunities. However, aspirations are a channel through which inequality persists between ethnic groups, exacerbating the effect of socio-economic status on educational achievement. Indeed, socio-economic status predicts levels of aspiration, which in turn affects progress in language mastery.

This contribution highlights a particular mechanism which underlies the exclusion of indigenous people in Peru. To be precise, it analyses how aspirations contribute to the persistence of inequality between ethnic groups.

With the adoption of the UN Declaration on the Rights of Indigenous Peoples in 2007, and the first World Conference on Indigenous Peoples in 2014, the international community has shown a strong commitment to ensuring the rights and well-being of indigenous people. Although progress has been made, recent evidence has disclosed the large disadvantage that affects indigenous people worldwide, and in Latin America in particular.

Peru has the highest proportion of indigenous people in Latin America, along with Bolivia, Ecuador, Guatemala and Mexico. This plurality of cultures, including languages, is associated with large differences in income and economic opportunity. Despite significant poverty alleviation overall, the gap between indigenous and non-indigenous people remains as high as it was ten years ago. Indigenous people have less access to education, particularly good education, and opportunities for indigenous people in the labour market are even more limited. Although inequalities that affect indigenous people are widely documented, the mechanisms at play in the persistence of these inequalities remain poorly understood.

My aim is to contribute to understanding these mechanisms by scrutinizing the role played by aspirations in the generation of educational inequality.

Assumptions concerning the cause of low aspiration

Aspiration is commonly understood as the desire or ambition to achieve something. This concept suggests that some effort might be exerted to realize the desired aim. This suggests that aspirations are likely to determine the level of effort provided for educational attainment. If indigenous people suffer from low aspiration, they may underinvest in their education. Two reasons may explain why they can suffer from aspiration failure.

The first is that being indigenous may lead to lower aspiration if indigenous people internalize the discriminatory values of the *criolla*[1] elite. If so, their chances of attaining a high socio-economic status would be reduced. Racial categorization used during the colonial period, when white people dominated indigenous people, has generated stigma and stereotypes (Portocarrero, 1993). From the cognitive sociology perspective, stereotypes are an 'outgrowth of ordinary cognitive processes ... Stereotypes, once activated, can subtly influence subsequent perception and judgment without any awareness on the part of the perceiver' (Brubaker et al., 2004).

They can affect the decision-making processes of indigenous people, who may adapt their behaviour to the expectations embedded in the stereotypes. Indigenous children may lower their aspirations by comparison with other children with the same socio-economic background, because the discriminatory values which they have internalized negatively affect their self-esteem and their perception of their opportunities in the labour market. This can lead them to underinvest in their education. This is what I call the 'internal channel' hypothesis.

The second mechanism derives from the fact that being indigenous is associated with other forms of disadvantage, such as being poor or living in a rural environment. These 'external constraints' largely result from the colonial period (1514–1821) when the Spaniards introduced discriminatory practices and developed extractive institutions in Peru. These institutions concentrated power, land ownership and access to education in the hands of a small elite. By contrast, indigenous people have been confined to the poorest parts of society, with limited access to education and other opportunities to develop their human capital, which has impeded their entrance to the modern sector and their political participation. These external constraints may be the main determinant of aspiration failure, as they limit access to information and to opportunities to invest in the future. For example, indigenous children are more likely to live in remote areas, where information about occupational opportunities and access to quality education are limited. They may receive less support for their education from their parents, who are themselves poor. As a result, they may stop aspiring to high levels of education, and to prestigious occupations that can only be reached with family support. In addition, they are often growing up in poorer neighbourhoods. The peers visible in their 'aspiration window' are more likely to have occupations providing low socio-economic status.

On the external channel hypothesis, indigenous children may not aspire to become doctors because they know their chance of continuing on to further study is limited, partly because their parents would not have the funds to pay for their studies. With the internal channel hypothesis, they will not aspire to become doctors because they think that a doctor has to be 'white' or that they are not smart enough to succeed at medical school.

The policy implications of these two hypotheses are dramatically different. 'Levelling the playing field' for indigenous people – to quote the metaphor that Roemer (1998) used to define ensuring equality of opportunity – would reduce inequalities only if the external channel hypothesis is correct. If the 'internal channel' is predominant, policies providing equal access to human and physical capital to indigenous people would not be sufficient to break the vicious circle of poverty for them.

The research carried out

Based on these perspectives, this research investigated first whether the aspirations of indigenous people differ from those of non-indigenous people in Peru. If it found that they do, it planned to seek to identify the respective relevance of the internal and external channel hypotheses in the Peruvian context, while acknowledging that these two channels are not mutually exclusive. Then it addressed the question of whether low aspiration leads to personal underinvestment in education.

To tackle these issues, I relied on a very rich data set, the Young Lives data,[2] for which 678 children and their main caregiver were interviewed three times, when the children were 8, 12 and 15 years old.

The analysis of this data showed that indigenous children aspire on average to occupations providing lower socio-economic status than non-indigenous children at age 8 or 12. However, the aspirations of indigenous children are quite similar to those of non-indigenous children if children of the same socio-economic status are compared.[3] This last finding would not support the internal channel hypothesis. Being at the bottom of the socio-economic stratification negatively affects aspirations for indigenous and non-indigenous children alike. This shows that ethnic discrimination is not important in the development of aspiration today. But over the long term, it has shaped socio-economic stratification, which seems to be the main predictor of children's occupational aspirations.

In addition, the analysis of data collected suggests that high aspirations at age 12 have a positive impact on progress in the mastery of Spanish, the official teaching language, for children between ages 12 and 15. Progress in Spanish is measured by the variation between the beginning and the end of the academic year in a score measuring vocabulary acquisition in

Spanish (the Peabody Picture of Vocabulary Test, or PPVT test). To identify the causal effect of aspiration on these educational outcomes, we adopted an identification strategy based on the method of instrumental variable (IV).[4] Our estimates indicate that the lower the aspiration of the children, the lower their progress in language. This means that aspiration failure is an additional channel for the persistence of inequality between ethnic groups, exacerbating the effect of socio-economic background on educational achievement. Indeed, the socio-economic background of indigenous children affects their school learning in a direct way, as demonstrated in the literature, but it also has an indirect effect by shaping the aspirations driving their effort to study in school.

Consequently, policies that aim at alleviating the external constraints faced by indigenous people are likely to contribute to enhancing their aspirations. They could have an incentive effect on the effort that children make to improve their socio-economic status, as well as a direct effect on their educational achievement. In other words, influencing aspiration may have a multiplier effect on policy which seeks to break the vicious circle of poverty for indigenous people by levelling the playing field for them.

Policies that act directly on the aspirations of indigenous children could also contribute to filling the gap in education between indigenous and non-indigenous people in Peru. Expanding indigenous children's perception of the opportunities for their lives could positively affect their educational outcomes.

The validity of our results should be tested in other contexts. The challenges that indigenous people face in Peru are shared with other indigenous populations in Latin America, and evidence for the internalization of ethno-racial discrimination in aspiration formation may be found in other countries. But the prevalence of a contemporaneous hierarchy mostly based on socio-economic status could be specific to Peru, where the concept of ethnic identity is particularly fluid. Peru has a low level of politicization of ethnic cleavages, and by comparison with Mexico, Guatemala, Bolivia and Ecuador, has few important social movements based on ethnic identity (Sulmont, 2011). Peru's low levels of mobilization on the basis of ethnic identity may be associated with a lack of resonance of the ethnic group notion among indigenous people themselves.

This would suggest that ethnic-based hierarchy is unimportant in shaping aspiration. This article opens up a new research avenue in order to understand the persistence of major disadvantage among indigenous people worldwide, and calls for empirical studies of their aspiration in other contexts.

Acknowledgement

This research has received funding from the NOPOOR project (*www.nopoor.eu*) under the FP7 of the European Commission. Full results of this research have been published in the review *World Development* (see Pasquier-Doumer and Risso Brandon, 2015).

Notes

1. Referring to people who are of Spanish descent but born in America.

2. Young Lives is a longitudinal study of childhood poverty led by a team at the University of Oxford and funded by UK aid from the DFID and by the Netherlands Ministry of Foreign Affairs (see *www.younglives.org.uk*). The data are collected in four countries: Ethiopia, India (Andhra Pradesh), Peru and Viet Nam, with two cohorts of children being surveyed, a younger cohort and an older cohort, born in 2001–02 and 1994–95 respectively. They were first surveyed in 2002, and then every four years. Twenty districts in fourteen regions are included in the sampling in Peru.

3. More precisely, the level of aspiration is estimated with ordinary least squares (OLS) and probit models to test whether the internal channel hypothesis is verified. Ethnic group and proxies of external constraints are introduced in the models as explanatory variables. If ethnic belonging determines youngster behaviour and decision-making as a result of the internalization of discriminatory values (the internal channel hypothesis), being indigenous should negatively and significantly affect aspirations, once external constraints are taken into account. We found that the coefficient of being indigenous becomes non-significant when proxies of external constraints are introduced into the models.

4. See Pasquier-Doumer and Risso Brandon (2015) for more details.

Bibliography

Brubaker, R., Loveman, M. and Stamatov, P. 2004. Ethnicity as cognition. *Theory and Society*, Vol. 33, No. 1, pp. 31–64. *http://link.springer.com/article/10.1023%2FB%3ARYSO.0000021405.18890.63* (Accessed 11 February 2016.)

Pasquier-Doumer, L. and Risso Brandon, F. 2015. Aspiration failure: a poverty trap for indigenous children in Peru? *World Development*, No. 72, pp. 208–23. *www.sciencedirect.com/science/article/pii/S0305750X15000601* (Accessed 11 February 2016.)

Portocarrero, G. 1993. *Racismo y mestizaje* [*Racism and Miscegenation*]. Lima, SUR Casa de Estudios del Socialismo. *http://trove.nla.gov.au/work/30365335?selectedversion=NBD11003333* (Accessed 11 February 2016.)

Roemer, J. E. 1998. *Equality of Opportunity*. Cambridge, Mass., Harvard University Press.

Sulmont, D. 2011. Race, ethnicity and politics in three Peruvian localities: an analysis of the 2005 CRISE perceptions survey in Peru. *Latin American and Caribbean Ethnic Studies*, Vol. 6, No. 1, pp. 47–78. *www.tandfonline.com/doi/abs/10.1080/17442222.2011.543873* (Accessed 11 February 2016.)

■ **Laure Pasquier-Doumer** (France) holds a PhD in development economics and is researcher at DIAL, a research unit of the French Research Institute for Development (IRD) and the University of Paris Dauphine. Her research focuses on the mechanisms underlying the reproduction of inequality in developing countries. She applies her research to the labour market and the education process in the contexts of West African countries, Peru and Viet Nam.

POSTCARD

35. Social inequality and young people in Europe: their capacity to aspire

Evelyne Baillergeau and Jan Willem Duyvendak

Diverse resources can be used to achieve social position. While we immediately think of material, economic resources in this context, there are others as well, notably aspirations. As a projection of the self in a desirable future, aspirations are inspiring emotions that guide individuals' commitments, whether these relate to work, school, sport or citizenship.

Aspirations draw upon personal characteristics and preferences, but they are also socially constrained. They depend on which opportunities are available, the future that is imagined and desired as a result of these opportunities, and thus, on the choices that can be made. As such, aspirations are affected by social inequality. As aspirations can influence future achievement, differences in aspirations can contribute to deepening social inequality, and can trigger corrosive disadvantage. Endeavours to research social inequality should therefore consider the social processes through which young people's aspirations develop and crystallize.

In our research, we consider the circumstances that lead young people to frame a desirable future, and the role of school, family and community in this process (Baillergeau et al., 2015). We do not measure aspirations, but we do analyse the capacity of young Europeans to aspire and the ways in which this capacity develops. Appadurai (2004, 2013) argues that the capacity to aspire is influenced by culture and social circumstances, and is therefore distributed unevenly in society, and suggests that this hampers the chances of the socially disadvantaged to improve their position.

However, Appadurai reports a case of slum dwellers in Mumbai in which their capacity to aspire is broadened thanks to the commitment of community-based agencies. This broadening of aspiration occurs in collective talks among slum dwellers so as to share, test and discuss their 'local horizons of hope and desire' (2004, p. 75).

This suggests that such community-based organizations are not fatalistic, and means that the capacity of the poor to aspire can develop, which in turn helps them improve their social position.

In our research, we have observed that disadvantaged young people in Europe do get opportunities, provided by schools or job guidance services, to discuss their aspirations. However, these discussions mainly address educational and occupational aspirations, and take the view that such aspirations are to be adjusted, either uplifted when deemed too 'low' or downsized when judged 'unrealistic'. We observe that just like more affluent young people, young people from disadvantaged backgrounds formulate all kinds of aspirations, some reaching beyond work. They are largely in line with what the mainstream projects as respectable aspirations, such as high purchasing power and social recognition.

This is not to claim that social inequality does not affect aspirations in Europe. It definitely does. But it affects the range of aspirations young people can have in different ways. For example, consumption aspirations are little affected by social inequality, influencing young people irrespective of their socio-economic position and their school achievements, while occupational aspirations of older adolescents are impacted by social inequality, so that older adolescents at the lower end of the scale have lower aspirations. As a consequence, it is certainly necessary to discuss occupational aspirations, but it is not sufficient. Leaving influential aspirations such as recognition unaddressed may lead disadvantaged young people to cope alone with highly contradictory aspirations, jeopardizing efforts to improve their social position and damaging attempts to reduce social inequality.

Acknowledgement

This research has received funding from the SocIEtY project (*www.society-youth.eu*) under the FP7 of the European Commission.

Bibliography

Appadurai, A. 2004. The capacity to aspire: culture and the terms of recognition. R. Rao and M. Walton (eds), *Culture and Public Action*. Stanford, Calif., Stanford University Press, pp. 59–84.

Appadurai, A. 2013. *The Future as Cultural Fact. Essays on the Global Condition*. London and Brooklyn, N.Y., Verso.

Baillergeau, E., Duyvendak, J. W. and Abdallah, S. 2015. Heading towards a desirable future: aspirations, commitments and the capability to aspire of young Europeans. *Open Citizenship*, Vol. 5, No. 2, pp. 12–23. https://www.researchgate.net/publication/275180045_Heading_towards_a_desirable_future_Aspirations_commitments_and_the_capability_to_aspire_of_young_Europeans (Accessed 15 February 2016.)

■ **Evelyne Baillergeau** *(France) is a senior researcher at the University of Amsterdam (Department of Sociology) and an associate researcher at the Centre de Recherches Sociologiques sur le Droit et les Institutions Pénales (Centre for Sociological Research on Law and Penal Institutions, CESDIP), CNRS, France.*

■ **Jan Willem Duyvendak** *(Netherlands) is distinguished research professor of sociology at the University of Amsterdam.*

36. Consequences of inequality for persons with disabilities – experience of ADD International

Emma Cain

Development interventions tend to focus on vertical inequalities, the link between economic status, income and assets. But it is often horizontal inequalities, linked to social status and identity, which lock individuals into marginalization and poverty. Without addressing horizontal inequalities, it is impossible to tackle vertical inequalities (Cain, 2012). This is the consistent message of work carried out by ADD International with persons with disabilities over thirty years, many of whom experience further marginalization because of their gender and age.

How the individual experiences disability depends not just on functional limitations relating to their impairment, but also on 'attitudinal and environmental barriers that hinder their full and effective participation in society on an equal basis with others' (United Nations, 2006). Negative attitudes towards disability mean that people with disabilities routinely experience discrimination which can deny them equitable access to resources, services and opportunities for personal development. This marginalization is exacerbated by environmental barriers such as inaccessible public buildings and services, and the lack of information in accessible formats.

There are close links between disabled people's social marginalization and economic inequalities, and this is consistently reflected in testimony from people with disabilities from all levels of society, including those who have managed to get an education despite their disability:

> *People without disabilities have alternative options if they can't get a job. They can be self-employed. But people with disabilities don't have as many alternatives. People with disabilities can't influence powerful people. In general, people have negative attitudes about disability, so they don't employ us. (Salamot Ullah, community peer researcher, Cox's Bazar, Bangladesh, quoted in Burns and Oswald, 2015, p. 29)*

There is also a growing body of empirical data demonstrating the link between disability and poverty, including a World Bank study of fifteen developing countries which found that people with disabilities were significantly worse off, were more likely to experience multiple deprivations, and had lower educational attainment and employment rates than non-disabled people (Mitra et al., 2011).

Through our work with disabled people's organizations (DPOs) in Africa and Asia, we have found that initiatives that promote the voice and empowerment of people with disabilities within their communities are effective at reducing social inequalities. In Cambodia, DPOs are working at village level to build understanding of intellectual disability: 'We didn't believe it was possible for them to change. We didn't know about the situation of people with intellectual disability so didn't know how to treat them,' said the relative of one person with intellectual disability in Svey Tayean Commune (ADD International, 2013, p.15). After efforts to identify and nurture the contributions they can make, people with intellectual disability are now being recognized as active community members: 'In farming work everyone helps one another – previously the people with intellectual disabilities just stood around, but now they help too. They are invited to help' (community member, Sam Ley Commune, quoted in ADD International, 2013, p.17). This recognition has paved the way for people with disabilities to become formally registered with local authorities, giving them access to development support including livestock and water and sanitation investments, and to basic services including free health care.

Bibliography

ADD International. 2013. *People with Intellectual Disabilities (PWID) Project Evaluation.* Cambodia, ADD International.

Burns D. and Oswald K. 2015. *We Can Also Make Change,* Report of Voices of the Marginalized participatory research project. Sightsavers, HelpAge International, ADD International and Alzheimer's Disease International. *www.add.org.uk/sites/default/files/Voices_of_the_Marginalised_FULL_2015.pdf* (Accessed 10 June 2016.)

Cain, E. 2012. *Voices of the Marginalized: Persons with Disabilities, Older People, People with Mental Health Issues.* UNICEF/UN Women. *www.addc.org.au/documents/resources/voices-of-the-marginalized-persons-with-disabilities-older-people-people-with-mental-health-issues_927.pdf* (Accessed 10 June 2016.)

Mitra, S., Posarak, A. and Vick, B. 2011. Disability and poverty in developing countries: a snapshot from the World Health Survey. Discussion Paper No. 1109. Washington DC, Social Protection and Labor, World Bank.

United Nations. 2006. Convention on the Rights of Persons with Disabilities – Preamble, Paragraph E. *www.un.org/disabilities/convention/conventionfull.shtml* (Accessed 10 June 2016.)

■ **Emma Cain** (UK) *is ADD International's learning and accountability advisor. She has over twenty years' experience of programme and policy work within development organizations and as a consultant. She has worked extensively on disability rights, inclusion and intersecting inequalities, supporting the development and evaluation of programmes in this area, and producing a number of key influencing papers, including submissions to the UK Parliament's International Development Sub-Committee.*

Chapter 4

Inequality futures

37. **Inequality, economic democracy and sustainability**
 Madeleine Power, Richard Wilkinson and Kate Pickett

38. **Malaise in the Western middle classes**
 Louis Chauvel and Anne Hartung

39. **BRICS and global inequality**
 Jing Gu, Alex Shankland, Anuradha Chenoy and Gerry Bloom

40. **Inequalities and social progress in the future**
 Marc Fleurbaey and Stephan Klasen

41. **Inequality in an increasingly automated world**
 Lizzie Sayer

42. **POSTCARD • Digital connections in the face of inequality**
 Charles Onyango-Obbo

PART II · THE CONSEQUENCES OF INEQUALITIES | Chapter 4 | Inequality futures

37. Inequality, economic democracy and sustainability

Madeleine Power, Richard Wilkinson and Kate Pickett

It is often feared that the transition towards environmental sustainability will depress living standards and reduce quality of life. But research shows that reducing income differences between rich and poor within each of the developed countries will remove important obstacles to sustainability and improve the real quality of life. The evidence suggests that the complementarity between greater equality and sustainability may be served best by policies to advance economic democracy.

Though far from universally accepted, the evidence for the consequences of high carbon emissions is scientifically incontrovertible. In May 2013 rising carbon concentrations in the atmosphere surpassed 400 ppm – 40 per cent higher than before industrialization, and higher than humans have ever breathed before. In 2007 Hansen (head of NASA's Goddard Institute of Space Studies) estimated that if we are to keep the rise in global temperatures to no more than 2 °C, atmospheric concentrations of carbon will have to be reduced to 350 ppm.

Yet the voluntary pledges to reduce carbon emissions made by 185 countries for the UN Paris summit in 2015 will not achieve the reductions needed to keep global warming within this less dangerous limit of 2 °C. Estimates are that global temperatures will rise by almost 3 °C even if countries live up to their promises. But unlike international trade agreements, the pledges are unenforced and the reality may be more like 3 to 4 °C.

Nor is the environmental crisis limited to climate change. It also includes soil erosion, deforestation, water salinization, the systemic effects of insecticides and pesticides, toxic waste, species loss, acidification of the oceans, decline of fish stocks, hormone discharges into the water, global food insecurity and so on.

Moves towards sustainability are widely regarded as an unwelcome belt-tightening exercise which will increase costs and threaten living standards as we are pushed into living within environmental constraints.

But rich societies are inefficient producers of well-being: economies that maximize consumption and profit not only fail to maximize quality of life but are obstacles to sustainability. With the right policies we can combine sustainability with higher standards of real human well-being.

A key is to reduce inequality. There is a large body of evidence that most of the health and social problems that tend to be more common lower down the social ladder – including infant mortality, mental illness, violence, teenage births, imprisonment, well-being, obesity, educational attainment and social cohesion – are substantially worse in societies with bigger income differences between rich and poor (Wilkinson and Pickett, 2010). Problems associated with low social status within societies tend to be more common in societies with larger income differences. And although inequality harms the poor most, it leads to worse outcomes among the vast majority of the population.

Time-series evidence and multilevel models strongly suggest causal relationships running from inequality to worse outcomes, mediated by poorer social relations as reciprocity and community life give way to mistrust, status competition, status insecurity and increased violence (Zheng, 2012; Lillard et al., 2015).

As we have become aware of the environmental costs of economic activity, we have also become aware that there are diminishing returns to human well-being from economic growth. Economic growth has transformed the real quality of life over the past couple of centuries, but in rich countries it has largely finished its work. Improvements in life expectancy are no longer related to economic growth even in analyses of ten, twenty or forty-year periods.

In the seventeen countries that it covers, the Genuine Progress Indicator has ceased to track growth. Similarly, measures of both adult and child well-being in the rich countries no longer respond to economic growth (Wilkinson and Pickett, 2010). Higher material standards continue to be needed in low-income countries where many people lack basic necessities, but in rich societies, having more and more of everything makes less and less difference.

But inequality continues to be a powerful driver of the desire for higher incomes. Community life atrophies in more unequal societies, and status anxieties increase across all income groups (Layte and Whelan, 2014). As a result, we worry more about the impression we create in the minds of others, and consumerism thrives as we try to communicate our self-worth to them. People in more unequal societies therefore spend more on status goods (Walasek and Brown, 2015), work longer hours, and get into debt more (Frank, 2007). Rather than being a reflection of a basic human acquisitiveness, consumerism is actually an alienated form of signalling, through which we try to maintain and communicate some sense of self-worth to each other (Frank, 2007; Dittmar et al., 2013). What the evidence suggests is that if we reduce inequality, we will also reduce consumerism.

Because consumerism and status competition are powerful drivers of our desire for ever higher incomes and our tendency to see sustainability as a threat to living standards, reducing inequality removes important obstacles to sustainability. And at the societal level, status competition is of course a zero sum game.

If the modern world is to move towards a sustainable way of life, it means acting as never before for the good of humanity as a whole. Greater equality makes an important contribution here too. Because it strengthens community life, people are two or three times as likely in equal societies to feel they can trust others (Wilkinson and Pickett, 2010). People in more equal societies are therefore more public spirited, have a stronger attachment to the common good and do more recycling. Business leaders give higher priority to environmental agreements, and more equal societies have lower carbon emissions per dollar of gross national product (GNP) (Wilkinson and Pickett, 2010).

We therefore particularly welcome UN Sustainable Development Goal (SDG) 10, which calls for the reduction of 'inequality within and among countries'.

Reducing income differences does not depend only on redistribution. It also means reducing differences before income transfers. We must undoubtedly tackle tax avoidance, end tax havens and make taxation more progressive, but there are two weaknesses to this approach. First, any progress on taxes and benefits can easily be reversed, and second, there is always the tendency for people to think that taxes are a kind of legalized theft, despite the fact that almost all production and wealth creation is a cooperative process. A much more fundamental approach to reducing inequality is to reduce differences in people's incomes before tax.

The rise in inequality since the 1980s is primarily the result of top incomes growing much faster than others. During the twentieth century, the decline in inequality between the 1930s and 1970s, and its subsequent rise, reflects a strong inverse relationship with the proportion of the labour force that is unionized (Gustafsson and Johansson, 1999). The tendency for income differences to widen in the absence of an effective labour movement reflects the loss of any constraint on top incomes. Part of the solution is to build effective new democratic constraints by embedding democracy into our economic institutions.

We need to increase employee representation on company boards and expand the share of the economy made up of mutuals, cooperatives, employee-owned companies and social enterprises. Around half the EU member countries have some – stronger or weaker – legal provision for employee representation on company boards. Countries with stronger legislation for employee representation have had smaller rises in inequality, and more democratic businesses tend to have smaller pay ratios among staff (Vitols, 2010). The Mondragon cooperatives in Spain employ about 80,000 people and have pay ratios of around 1:5 – rarely more than 1:9. This contrasts with ratios of 1:300 in many multinationals.

More democratic economic institutions have other social advantages. An employee buyout can turn a company from a piece of property into a community, so helping to offset the weakening of community life. It is also likely that less hierarchical structures improve the experience of work by enabling people to gain a sense of self-worth and to feel valued by colleagues.

The business case for more democratic companies is also strong. Companies that combine employee representation and participative management have higher productivity (Estrin et al., 1987). UK cooperatives have been outperforming the rest of the economy and the social enterprise sector has outperformed small and medium-sized businesses. Employee-owned companies have been creating new jobs faster than more traditional companies, and 76 per cent of the British public are in favour of board-level employee representation.

Economic democracy has other advantages too. Because investors with a long-term interest in companies have been largely replaced by computer-triggered short-term share trading, shareholder control has become an anachronism which should be replaced by the long-term interests of employees. Forms of economic democracy may also provide a partial response to the growing conflict between the public interest and the manipulative and anti-democratic power of multinationals. In *Lethal but Legal*, Freudenberg (2014) shows that profit-seeking in big corporations has become a major source of harm to public health. Similarly, Naomi Klein has shown how fossil-fuel companies have subverted responses to climate change. Where wage labour excludes employees from any ethical responsibility, more democratic models bring them centrally into decision-making at all levels. Perhaps as a result, evidence suggests that more democratic companies may perform better ethically (Weber et al., 2009).

Resurgent interest in the democratization of institutional structures needs to be turned into a publicly recognized political objective, advocated and defended by all progressive politicians as the next major step in human emancipation. We need to create a popular understanding that this is part of a gradual transition to high levels of sustainable well-being.

To this end, all but the smallest companies should be required to have employee representatives on company boards and remuneration committees. The proportion of employee representatives should be higher in larger companies and should increase over time, moving eventually to majority control. This could be achieved by legislation requiring that a small proportion of shares be transferred each year to employee-controlled trusts. Before these legal requirements enter force, employee representation could be made a condition of gaining public sector contracts and lower corporation tax rates.

Governments should also provide tax incentives for more democratic companies, and loans for employee buyouts. The widespread ignorance of democratic models among professional legal and financial advisers means that governments should promote and support routes to employee ownership. Governments should also provide training and advice in areas such as management, business law, accountancy and economics for employees of cooperative and employee-owned companies. The constitutions of democratic businesses should prevent employees from selling their companies back to external shareholders. Finally, we also need internet portals to help people shop from democratic businesses displaying a 'democratic company' logo such as Fair Trade.

Not to plan changes as sweeping as these may mean accepting that we will be defeated by climate change. And the longer we delay, the more sudden, difficult and traumatic the transition to low-carbon economies will be.

But the transition to sustainability could instead be a transition to a better society for all of us. By reducing inequality, we could make dramatic improvements in the social environment, strengthening community life and reducing a wide range of health and social problems.

A large body of research shows that the quality of social relationships is a crucial determinant of health and happiness. Reductions in status insecurity (Layte and Whelan, 2014) and consumerism would lead more people to use increases in productivity to create more leisure time rather than to increase consumption. As a means to achieving these ends, a transition to economic democracy would transform the experience of work, embed equality more deeply in society, and begin to tackle the growing power of multinational corporations to concentrate wealth and undermine democracy.

Bibliography

Note: A full bibliography can be found in R. Wilkinson and K. Pickett, *A Convenient Truth* (Fabian Society and Friedrich Ebert Stiftung, 2014), www.fabians.org.uk/publications/a-convenient-truth/

Dittmar, H., Bond, R., Hurst, M. and Kasser, T. 2013. A meta-analysis of the materialism literature. Unpublished manuscript. Brighton, UK, University of Sussex.

Estrin, S., Jones, D. C. and Svejnar, J. 1987. The productivity effects of worker participation: producer cooperatives in western economies. *Journal of Comparative Economics*, Vol. 11, No. 1, pp. 40–61.

Frank, R. H. 2007. *Falling Behind: How Rising Inequality Harms the Middle Class*. Berkeley and Los Angeles, Calif., University of California Press.

Freudenberg, N. 2014. *Lethal but Legal: Corporations, Consumption, and Protecting Public Health*. Oxford, Oxford University Press.

Gustafsson, B. and Johansson, M. 1999. In search of smoking guns: what makes income inequality vary over time in different countries? *American Sociological Review*, Vol. 64, No. 4, pp. 585–605.

Layte, R. and Whelan, C. T. 2014. Who feels inferior? A test of the status anxiety hypothesis of social inequalities in health. *European Sociological Review*, Vol. 30, No. 4, pp. 525–35.

Lillard, D. R., Burkhauser, R. V., Hahn, M. H. and Wilkins, R. 2015. Does early-life income inequality predict self-reported health in later life? Evidence from the United States. *Social Science and Medicine*, Vol. 128, pp. 347–55.

Vitols, S. 2010. Goodcorp: the research network on corporate governance. European Corporate Governance Institute and European Trade Union Institute. www.etui.org/Networks/GoodCorp-the-research-network-on-Corporate-Governance (Accessed 11 June 2016.)

Walasek, L. and Brown, G. D. 2015. Income inequality and status seeking searching for positional goods in unequal US states. *Psychological Science*, Vol. 26, No. 4, pp. 527–33.

Weber, W. G., Unterrainer, C. and Schmid, B. E. 2009. The influence of organizational democracy on employees' socio-moral climate and prosocial behavioral orientations. *Journal of Organizational Behavior*, Vol. 30, No. 8, pp. 1127–49.

Wilkinson, R. G. and Pickett, K. 2010. *The Spirit Level: Why Equality is Better for Everyone*. London, Penguin.

Zheng, H. 2012. Do people die from income inequality of a decade ago? *Social Science and Medicine*, Vol. 75, No. 1, pp. 36–45.

■ **Madeleine Power** *(UK) is a researcher in public health, working on health inequalities and food insecurity in the UK. She trained in social and political sciences at Cambridge and social policy at the London School of Economics and Political Science (LSE), and has experience of conducting quantitative and qualitative research in third-sector research organizations. Her research interests include food insecurity in developed countries and the social determinants of health. She is currently conducting a White Rose National Institute for Health Research (NIHR) funded project on the prevalence and experience of food insecurity in Bradford.*

■ **Richard Wilkinson** *(UK) is professor emeritus of social epidemiology at the University of Nottingham Medical School. His research has focused on health inequalities and on the health and social effects of income distribution. Before training in epidemiology he studied economic history at the LSE. He co-wrote* The Spirit Level *with Kate Pickett, which won the 2011 Political Studies Association Publication of the Year Award and the 2010 Bristol Festival of Ideas Prize. Richard is also a co-founder of the Equality Trust.*

■ **Kate Pickett FRSA FFPH** *(UK) is professor of epidemiology at the University of York and the university's champion for research on justice and equality. Her research focuses on the social determinants of health, in particular the effects of income inequality on well-being. She is co-author, with Richard Wilkinson, of* The Spirit Level, *which was winner of the 2011 Publication of the Year from the Political Studies Association, and translated into twenty-four languages. Kate is a co-founder and trustee of the Equality Trust.*

38. Malaise in the Western middle classes

Louis Chauvel and Anne Hartung

The living conditions and well-being of the middle class are traditionally considered an expression of how society is progressing. Yet growing inequality and the polarization of incomes observed in Western countries as a result of globalization, the recession and rapid technological change are leading to what has been described as a 'malaise of the middle class'. This contribution presents the evolution of the income distribution in selected Western countries, and discusses the possible impact of the threat created by downward mobility and the erosion of the middle class in today's society.

Fear among the middle classes, and the threat that this fear presents to the stability of democracies, is a recurrent theme in times of rising inequality and economic crisis. The living conditions and well-being of the middle class are traditionally considered an expression of how society is progressing. But the growing inequality and polarization of incomes observed in Western countries today can have corrosive effects. They can create a situation that has been described as a 'malaise of the middle class'. This is even more the case if globalization, stagnation and recession have a negative impact, leading to downward mobility and an erosion of the middle class.

The sociologist Theodor Geiger (1930) was the first to underline the importance of this type of distress – or 'panic in the middle class' – prophesying its potential consequences in the context of the German economic collapse after the First World War. When the middle class lacks class identity or cohesion, a negative economic context can generate anxiety and frustration, fear and phobias, which can in turn stimulate political unrest in the middle class, including populism and radical extremism. This vulnerability of the middle class implies the need for strong cohesive values to avoid centrifugal trends and the potential spread of violence.

Figure 38.1 **The shrinking middle in the USA during times of economic crisis: percentage of adults identifying themselves as each social class**

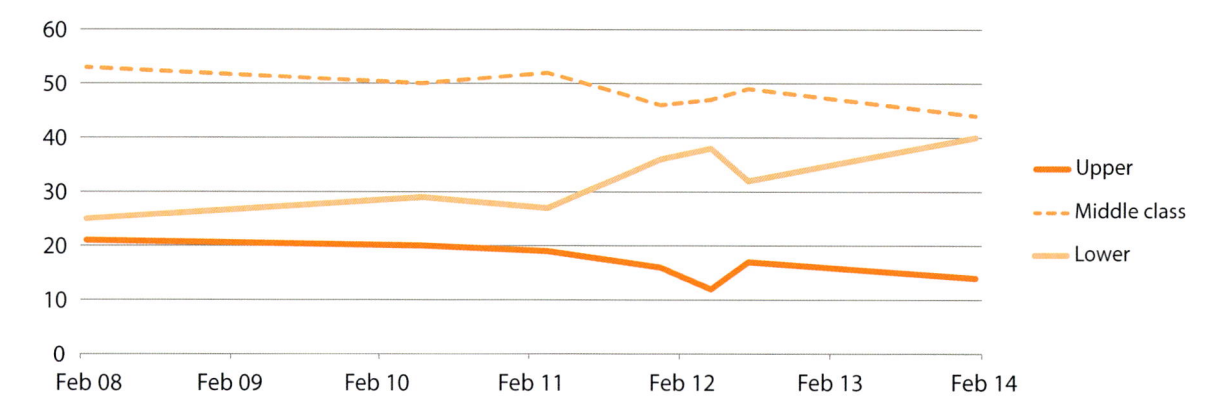

Note: 'Lower' includes lower-middle class and lower class; 'upper' includes upper-middle class and upper class.
Source: PEW Research Center.

Figure 38.2 **The shrinking middle: the changing shape of income distribution in Denmark, Germany, France, the UK, the USA and Israel – six typical strobiloids**

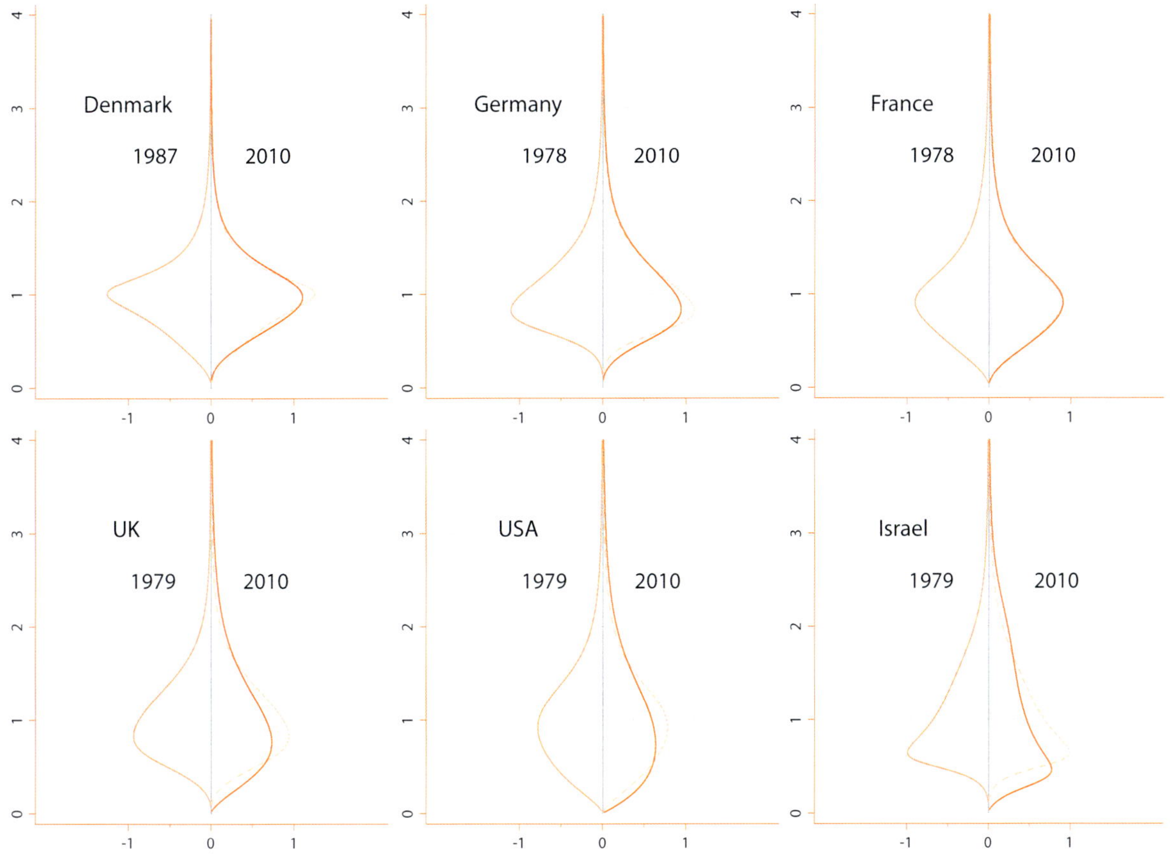

Note: The strobiloid shows the income hierarchy as a vertical axis (1 = country-year median). Exactly 50 per cent of the population is below versus above level 1. The larger the middle class, the larger the curve near level 1. Many individuals are at the intermediate level around the median and their number diminishes at the top (the rich, topped here at four times above the median, are not so many) and at the bottom (impossible to survive near income = 0). Thus, in strobiloids with a larger belly, the intermediate middle class is larger with a more equal distribution (as in Denmark). The Israeli and the US cases are very specific of massive erosion of the middle or median class. The dashed line mirrors the left-hand side of the curve to facilitate comparison over time.

Source: Luxembourg Income Study (Chauvel, 2016).

The sociological diagnosis for the middle class in Western society today is not so pessimistic – at least not yet. However, several empirical elements of socio-economic upheaval affecting the middle class need to be underlined to reassess the stability of the middle class in many Western industrialized countries.

The middle classes under pressure

Definitions of the middle class are a debated issue in the social sciences. While sociological approaches are typically based on social classes as defined by occupational characteristics, and those used by political scientists are based on belonging to particular social classes, economists prefer the measurement of income groups. The income-based approach we apply here allows for improved detection of massive local transformations in the shape of societies, and specifically whether and where on the income scale a 'hollowing of the middle class' happens (Chauvel, 2016).

Let's look briefly at class membership during the recent economic crisis. The share of people who consider themselves as part of the middle class in the USA decreased by 9 percentage points from 53 per cent to 44 per cent in only six years (*Figure 38.1*).

Figure 38.3 **Diverging cost of housing (real housing price index, dotted lines) and real household incomes index (thin lines) in Germany, France, the UK, Australia, Canada and the USA**

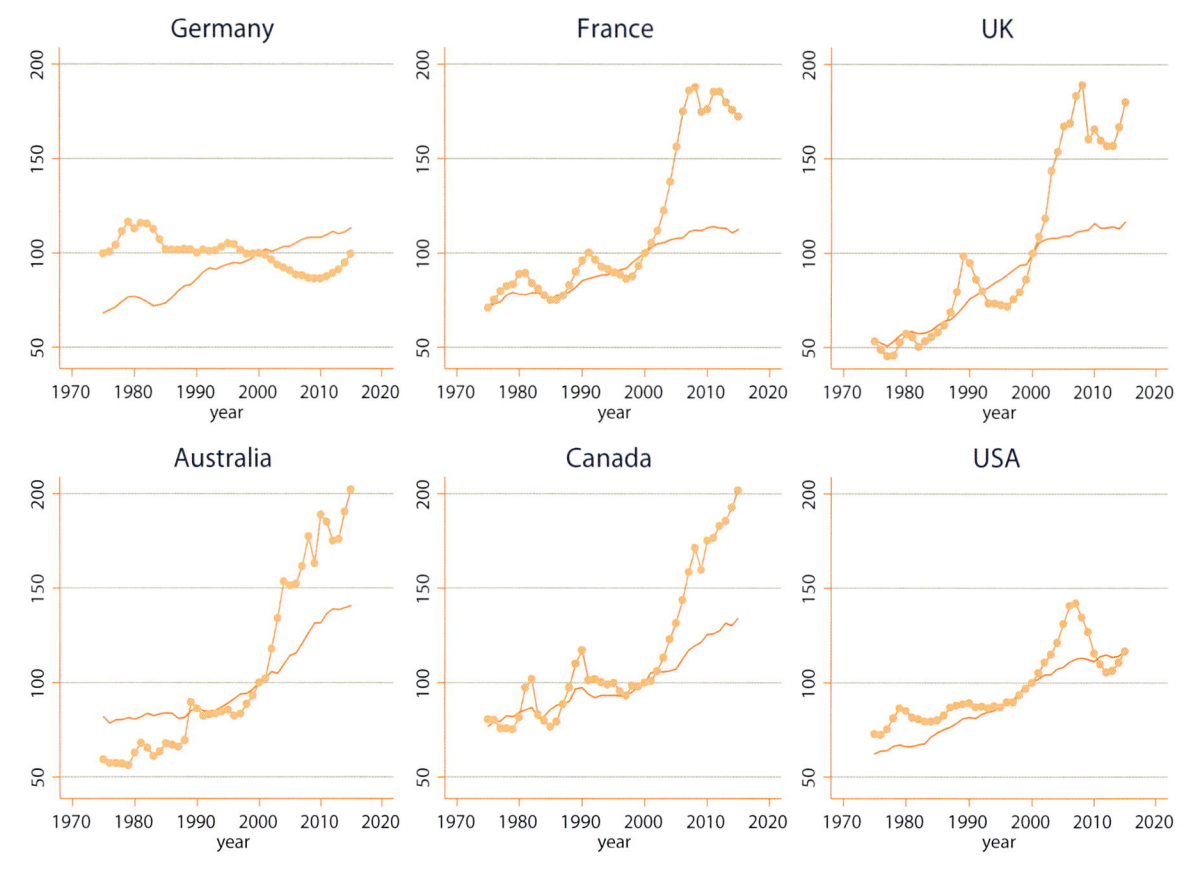

Note: y-axis: Housing index and household incomes adjusted for inflation, indexed to year 2000 (y = 100).
Source: International House Price Database, Federal Reserve Bank of Dallas. Data described in Mack and Martínez-García (2011).

The general diagnosis of the past decades is that the middle classes have been under pressure as a result of increasing economic inequality and polarization (Gornick and Jäntti, 2013; Piketty, 2014; Atkinson, 2016). This is true not only in the USA (Leicht and Fitzgerald, 2014), but also in many other Western countries.

This income polarization has led to a decline in the coherence of the middle classes as a large homogeneous group in the middle of the distribution. *Figure 38.2* compares the relative shape of the income distribution (relative to the median income of the country-year) in 1978/79 (left or dashed line on the right) and in 2010 (right), revealing the changing shape of societies and size of the income groups. In middle-class societies, such as in Germany and France, a large density or large area under the curve ('belly') around the median would be expected. In this respect, the USA and Israel are extreme cases, where the stretching movement of the middle class over these decades is obvious – if not alarming.

Conversely in France, the middle class remained stable between 1978 and 2010 (*Figure 38.2*). However, the skyrocketing trend of housing prices has almost halved the purchasing power of French wages in terms of square metres of housing since the end of the 1990s (*Figure 38.3*).[1] Wealth – and thus home ownership – is one of the most important drivers of middle-class dynamics.

The seven pillars of middle-class societies

A more systemic approach to understanding the middle class (rather than looking solely at measurements of inequality) can be achieved by incorporating a broader conceptualization of 'middle-class societies'. Drawing on various classical social science works (notably Galbraith), the typical middle-class societies of the industrial age that culminated in the Western world in the eve of the 1980s can be characterized by seven important parameters, or 'pillars' of 'middleization':

1. 'Wage-based middle-class society': permanent wage earners become a majority

Well above the level of the working class, a new group of wage earners has emerged with stable and predictable earnings, with controlled volatility around the median wage. This wage becomes a norm, or at least a typical model in the public sector which is imitated by large companies in the service sector such as banks and insurance companies. This model of average wage earners generates a pervasive model of wage-based middle-class society.

2. Wage incomes sufficient to live well: the affluent society

In Galbraith's model of the affluent society (1958), the standard of living increases over the course of a lifetime, leading to increasing levels of consumption as well as savings (in particular in home ownership). The wealth-to-income ratio is low and median earnings are sufficient for enjoying comfort. This is a new feature compared with former societies, where wealth was the nodal resource.

3. Generalization of social protection including labour stability: the spread of social citizenship

Welfare state development complements the protection provided by the permanent wage earner contract through lower earnings volatility. Major social risks (widowhood, retirement, illness, unemployment, old-age poverty and so on) are better covered by this developed social insurance. In this model, social protection is a form of depatrimonialization: wealth is no longer required for life stability.

4. Educational boom and upward social mobility: increasing belief in meritocratic society

Galbraith underlined the specific role of education, not only for obtaining selective skills that define the 'new middle class', but also for the values and identity of middle-class parents who measure their own social success on the basis of the educational performance of their children, itself an entry ticket to upward social mobility. A middle-class society is characterized by a growing tertiary education sector, able to offer younger generations increased educational capital.

5. Belief in progress

In the 1970s, middle-class societies were characterized by values of socio-economic progress and an optimistic vision of a never-ending search for personal and collective improvement in human development, as well as economic, technological and scientific progress. For the US middle class, the late 1960s were the climax of the belief in progress, exemplified by the Man on the Moon.

6. Political centrality of the middle class

In the context of the post-war Golden Age (in the USA and UK), *Miracolo economico* (Italy), *Rekordåren* (Sweden), *Wirtschaftswunder* (Germany) and *Trente glorieuses* (France), the middle class became an increasingly powerful political force. Traditional politics were based on the fight between the dominant bourgeois powers and the social critique of proletarian streams. Trade union forces were initially devoted to the defence of working-class interests, not the median wage earner. In this political model, the middle class had in many countries a very limited political choice and often joined the bourgeoisie in right-wing voting. Later, with its increasing size, the middle class gained political weight in democratic elections.

7. Middle-class moderate politics

Middle-class values in a middle-class society fit with the Aristotelian ideal of moderation, stability and rationality. As a result of progressive change in postmaterialist societies, the older political balance between proletariat and bourgeoisie gave place to the promotion of the middle class as a centred moderated actor, an idea shared by Aristotle and Simmel.

These seven parameters can generate a core of centripetal forces typical of 'middle-class societies'. These forces are defined by a large bulk of middle-class members, but rely too on the awareness of the bourgeoisie and the working class that their own social destination (or that of their children) is in the middle class. These centripetal forces are typical of the 1970s spirit where even non-middle-class actors, in the working class and elsewhere, share middle-class interests.

Diagnosis on the middle-class societies: are the seven pillars crumbling?

To date, the 'panic in the middle class' has not been assessed systematically. Instead, an array of potential trends of middle-class retrenchment has been observed by contemporary social scientists such as Piketty (2014), Therborn (2013) and Milanovic (2016). As a first step in this direction, we analyse here whether the seven trends mentioned above have gone into reverse with the end of the Golden Age.

1. Wage uncertainty: decline in predictability

The loss of stability in careers, and fluctuations in the labour market, generate wage uncertainty and thus make it difficult for the middle class to plan. This creates a new and massive precariat in middle-class societies.

2. Wage stagnation and increase in the real cost of life: the post-affluent society

A slowdown in economic growth negatively affects wage earners, even in 'affluent societies' where absolute levels of living are high. People search for other sources of income.

3. Destabilization of social protection and repatrimonialization

The model of wage earner protection faces welfare state retrenchment and the erosion of public insurance or its replacement by private insurances, with strong consequences for household incomes. Targeted and means-tested welfare regimes may exclude the middle class from social protection. Savings, business resources and capital gains make an increasing difference in the protection of individuals.

4. Mismatch between diploma and socio-economic position: over-education and downward social mobility

In several countries (for example in Southern Europe), even highly educated diploma holders face difficulties in entering the labour market, generating a mismatch between education and positions (*nimileuristas* in Spain). Beliefs in the intrinsic value of skills erode, and middle-class members become conscious of risks of social downward mobility.

5. New worries, declining beliefs in progress

Generalized distrust includes declining trust in the future, and new middle-class panic.

6. Loss of the political centrality of the middle class

Decline in social democracy; reflux of trade union participation of the middle class; development of lobbies.

7. Spreading populism

Problems that were previously limited to socially excluded groups or the working class spill over to the lower middle class. Populist parties progressively gain votes from the middle class.

The inversion of the seven Galbraith parameters is typical of the centrifugal dynamics that characterize today's middle classes. These new middle-class dynamics gain importance in periods of economic retrenchment, risking a social generation becoming marked by a pessimistic Zeitgeist. In Geiger's model, economic degradation, downward mobility and the lack of a reliable and stable regulating frame generate fear, frustration and social disorganization. A strong core of shared values and sense of solidarity can limit centrifugal trends but when they are absent, societies face the risk of anomie and social unrest.

Conclusion: systemic downward mobility and the risks for Western democracies

Later social transformations mean that the situation we face today is more complex than Geiger's seminal ideas suggest. The Western middle classes today are certainly more stable than in the 1930s. However, they also represent a larger share of the populace, and their destabilization could have significantly greater effects. Forecasts of labour market transformations caused by the 'Internet of Things' and by innovation in artificial intelligence suggest that 30 per cent of middle-income jobs could be eliminated (Autor, 2015). In the contemporary post-crisis shock, equality and the middle class are at risk (Atkinson, 2016; Mau, 2015) as a consequence of welfare state retrenchment, declining public employment, restrictive economic policies, unstable housing prices and uncertainty in the credit market, all of which directly affect the middle class.

The risk for today's middle classes involves a systemic threat created by the divide between a still-competitive upper middle class and a downwardly mobile lower middle class. This threat could spread stressors in the social system. The gap between aspirations to upward mobility and the realities of economic hardship, political tension, loss of social cohesion, frustration and support for undemocratic decisions might accelerate a vicious circle of economic decay, in turn exacerbating new social stressors. As Atkinson (2016) has said, a redeployment of the middle class in politics and democracy is the only route to stability.

Note

1. Note that the curves in *Figure 38.3* follow the dynamics of the two indices over years, contrary to *Figure 38.2*, which represents relative changes in the relative income distribution (shapes net of average transformations). The two figures may therefore reveal different aspects of the middle-class malaise.

Bibliography

Atkinson, A. 2016. How to spread the wealth: practical policies for reducing inequality. *Foreign Affairs*, Vol. 95, No. 1, pp. 29–33.

Autor, D. H. 2015. Why are there still so many jobs? The history and future of workplace automation. *Journal of Economic Perspectives*, Vol. 29, No. 3, pp. 3–30.

Chauvel, L. 2016. The intensity and shape of inequality: the ABG method of distributional analysis. *Review of Income and Wealth*, doi: 10.1111/roiw.12161

Geiger, T. 1930. Panik im Mittelstand. *Die Arbeit*, Vol. 7, No. 10, pp. 637–54: *library.fes.de/arbeit/pdf/1930/193010.pdf*

Galbraith, J. K. 1958. *The Affluent Society*. Boston, Mass., Houghton Mifflin.

Gornick, J. and Jäntti, M. (eds). 2013. *Income Inequality: Economic Disparities and the Middle Class in Affluent Countries*. Stanford, Calif., Stanford University Press.

Leicht, K. T. and Fitzgerald, S.T. 2014. *Middle Class Meltdown in America: Causes, Consequences, and Remedies*. New York, Routledge.

Mack, A. and Martínez-García, E. 2011. *A Cross-Country Quarterly Database of Real House Prices: A Methodological Note*. Globalization and Monetary Policy Institute Working Paper No. 99. Dallas, Tx., Federal Reserve Bank of Dallas.

Mau, S. 2015. *Inequality, Marketization and the Majority Class. Why Did the European Middle Classes Accept Neoliberalism?* Basingstoke, Palgrave Macmillan.

Milanovic, B. 2016. *Global Inequality: A New Approach for the Age of Globalization*. Cambridge, Mass., Belknap Press.

Piketty, T. 2014. *Capital in the Twenty-First Century*. Cambridge, Mass., Belknap Press.

Therborn, G. 2013. *The Killing Fields of Inequality*. London, Polity.

■ **Louis Chauvel** *(France) is professor of sociology at the University of Luxembourg (FNR-PEARL Chair), and Head of the Institute for Research on Socio-Economic Inequalities (IRSEI).*

■ **Anne Hartung** *(Germany) is researcher at the University of Luxembourg in IRSEI.*

39. BRICS and global inequality

Jing Gu, Alex Shankland, Anuradha Chenoy and Gerry Bloom

The original aim of the BRICS was to overturn inequality in international relations. They have been associated with breakthroughs in development finance without political conditions, and with increased shares of world trade. However, patterns of domestic inequality persist within the BRICS. This contribution asks whether the BRICS can be domestic models for the rest of the world, developed and developing. It explores patterns of inequality in each BRICS, and whether the BRICS elites contribute through capital transfer and trade to global domestic inequality. It concludes that the world can learn from the BRICS about how to tackle domestic inequalities.

The BRICS countries (Brazil, Russia, India, China and South Africa) matter for the future of global inequality. Together, they account for a huge proportion of the Earth's population and geographical space. Inequality and equality within the BRICS are therefore of global significance. The nature of economic growth within the BRICS nations has a significant impact on changes in inequality within other countries, both rich and poor.

They matter too because they are committed to challenging inequality among nations, having been drawn together by a shared sense of marginalization in the existing global architecture and a desire to advance what Russian foreign minister Sergei Lavrov described as 'a new polycentric system of international relations' (BBC, 2015). They also matter because their efforts to respond to their own domestic inequality challenges are an increasingly important source of innovation to which other countries can look for inspiration. Understanding how the BRICS will influence the different dimensions of inequality in future requires us to pay attention to the political economy of these processes, or in other words 'the politics of who gets what, when and how' as Harold Lasswell (1936) famously defined it. Any study of the prospects for global equity needs to pay serious attention to the political economy of the BRICS and to the forces likely to influence their domestic policies and international cooperation strategies.

The BRICS are highly heterogeneous in size, global economic impact, state resilience and domains of influence, and have very different 'inequality regimes' (Boyer, 2015). Their economic choices affect regions within and beyond the BRICS nations.

For example, falling Chinese commodity demand has had a severe effect on the economies of Brazil, Russia and South Africa, including their patterns of income distribution. As these three members of the BRICS group wrestle with complex domestic structural and political impediments, India and particularly China are likely to be the primary engines of growth among BRICS members.

The BRICS affect the wider global economy through their influence on the supply of and demand for commodities, goods and services, with different implications for inequality in richer and poorer countries. In the West, this influence has helped to intensify the established pattern of concentration of wealth through competition and accumulation (with the most successful accumulating more and more, and the weaker falling further behind), and most recently through societal dominance by finance capital. Indeed China, the largest BRICS economy, may have added to the dominance of finance in the West by encouraging its deindustrialization. This process has also driven down wage levels for relatively unskilled workers in the West. In future the BRICS (especially India) may play an increasing part in the technology-enabled erosion of the labour market for skilled workers. These processes have important political economy dimensions: the surplus invested by China in US Treasury bonds is taken out of the pockets of the general Chinese population and contributes to the running of the USA on credit instead of on taxes on the elites. What part does Indian, Russian, Brazilian or South African capital exported to the West contribute to the political dynamics that support the concentration of wealth in the West?

In recent years, the BRICS have reduced inequality among nations by driving economic growth through trade and investment in poorer regions of the world. In 2012 they collectively invested over US$6 billion in Africa, against US$3.7 billion invested by the United States (ActionAid, 2014). They have had contradictory effects on inequality in poorer countries, stimulating industrialization as well as commodity production, and generating jobs for many poor people at the same time as providing national elites with new opportunities for accumulation. They have helped to shift the balance of world trade, with South–South flows now playing a much more central role in global trade patterns. This effect is likely to persist despite the slowdown that several BRICS countries are currently experiencing.

Geopolitical shifts partly reflect those in the global economy. The BRICS have long had aspirations to challenge the global structural inequalities between the West and the Rest. A movement led by India and China, followed by many developing countries, ensured that there was always a 'third voice' that argued for a more equitable distribution of power, through the Non-Aligned Movement and then the G-77. This voice was maintained even in the 1990s when dominant narratives maintained that the collapse of the bipolar international system ensured the hegemonic status of a US-imposed collaborative framework. As the Asian Tigers, and then the BRICS, expanded their economic influence, they claimed a more equitable share in international economic policy-making institutions. The BRICS have greater leverage for negotiating their interests, which sometimes coincide with the interests of the global South as a whole. But their position is ambivalent and they may also align with the North through structures like the G-20, raising fears that they may be co-opted by the established powers.

However, and at a purely geopolitical level, increasing tensions between the USA on one side and China and Russia on the other, over the Ukraine and Crimea and over the South and East China Sea respectively, have led the USA to return to the pattern of 'alliances of democracies', especially in East Asia and Eastern Europe. These inevitably affect how the world sees the Russian and Chinese models of development.

But there is no doubt that the BRICS are increasingly influential over economics, trade and finance. India's objections to the global inequalities provoked by Western agricultural policies stopped the WTO in its tracks, albeit temporarily.

There are contradictions between the BRICS, and each member of the grouping has mostly wielded its influence individually, but their cooperation in global financial negotiations is growing, and they are building new collective institutions which may enable them to move forward with a shared global development agenda.

The BRICS' efforts to challenge the inequalities of today's international financial system include the creation of the BRICS' New Development Bank (NDB) and Contingent Reserve Arrangement (CRA), and the Chinese-led Asian Infrastructure Investment Bank (AIIB). The AIIB and the NDB offer loans without policy conditionalities, promising to change the institutional landscape of development finance. The BRICS proclaim a model of development assistance that is demand-driven, unconditional and horizontal; which combines grants, capacity-building and lines of credit for trade and business; and which gives more choices to the least developed countries. This approach has influenced OECD Development Assistance Committee (DAC) thinking on the future of aid and changed broader narratives on development.

However, the question that still needs to be confronted directly is whether the concept of a combination of states capable of steering their populations to greater welfare and equality is contradicted by the reality of a globally cohesive mega-rich class, whether state-based or in the private sector, which manages the global system to its own collective advantage, and not to that of the wider ethnic or national groups of which its members are a part culturally.

Across the BRICS, patterns of wealth inequality are converging as the proportion of the world's super-rich who are based in these countries continues to grow. However, patterns of income inequality across the BRICS vary widely, reflecting different drivers such as the Indian caste system, the role of the elites in China in monopolizing wealth, and the continuing significance of race in South Africa. Brazil is the only member of the grouping to have achieved a sustained fall in income inequality in recent years, but that was from a very high base, and Brazil remains more unequal than all the other BRICS except South Africa. In India income inequality has grown steadily from a low base, while in China it grew rapidly before beginning to moderate in recent years.

Despite these differences, the BRICS all face similar challenges in coping with the tensions that inequality presents for their political legitimacy, in sustaining political support for their development strategies and in ensuring that their populations benefit from development. This pressure has functioned as a powerful driver for innovation to meet at least some of the needs of most social groups. This driver is likely to persist, and we anticipate the emergence of new forms of organization to address rapidly changing patterns of inequality.

As the influence of the BRICS on the structure of global labour markets grows, many countries are likely to be torn over how to converge towards their social and economic models, given the split within the BRICS around the issues of democracy and civil liberties. It is true that the evolution of the political economy of these societies, and of the theories and practices they evolve for addressing inequalities, are likely to become increasingly important in all parts of the world. They are also likely to affect debates about global governance. However, these debates will be polarized because of the contrasting domestic images of the BRICS. This makes it especially important to establish a common language for understanding the options for addressing inequality.

Bibliography

ActionAid. 2014. The BRICS in 9 graphs. *www.actionaid.org/what-we-do/democratic-governance/brics* (Accessed 11 June 2016.)

BBC. 2015. Brics countries launch new development bank in Shanghai. *www.bbc.co.uk/news/33605230* (Accessed 7 March 2016.)

Boyer, R. 2015. A world of contrasted but interdependent inequality regimes: China, United States and the European Union. *Review of Political Economy*, Vol. 27, No. 4, pp. 481–517.

Gu, J., Shankland, A., and Chenoy, A. (eds). 2016. *The BRICS in International Development.* London, Palgrave.

Gu, J., Carey, R., Shankland, A. and Chenoy, A. 2016. International development, South-South cooperation and the rising powers. Gu et al. (eds), *The BRICS in International Development.* London, Palgrave.

Laswell, H. 1936. *Politics: Who Gets What, When, How.* New York, McGraw Hill.

■ ***Jing Gu*** *(China) is the director of the Centre for Rising Powers and Global Development at the Institute of Development Studies (IDS), Brighton, UK.*

■ ***Alex Shankland*** *(UK) is a research fellow in the Power and Popular Politics Research Cluster at IDS, Brighton, UK.*

■ ***Anuradha Chenoy*** *(India) is professor, Centre for Russian and Central Asian Studies, School of International Studies, Jawaharlal Nehru University (JNU), Delhi, India.*

■ ***Gerry Bloom*** *(UK) is research fellow and co-convenor, Health and Nutrition Cluster, IDS, Brighton, UK.*

40. Inequalities and social progress in the future

Marc Fleurbaey and Stephan Klasen

World inequalities have evolved in a complex way over the past few decades. The economic emergence of several developing countries with large populations has lowered global inequality, while the widening of inequalities within countries has served to increase it. Many future evolutions are possible. The baseline scenario would see the world go back to a nineteenth-century pattern of large social inequalities. Less unequal scenarios could involve political intervention to reduce inequalities domestically, or quicker convergence between countries. In all scenarios, the convergence of living standards will raise serious environmental challenges.

Inequalities in the world: stylized facts

The twentieth century saw many complex twists and turns as far as income inequalities are concerned. There are four main stylized facts to highlight.

First, the '*Great Escape*' (Deaton, 2014) of developed nations opened a gulf between the rich and the poor regions of the world, creating a bimodal distribution of incomes that was particularly large at the end of the colonial period. At the end of the twentieth century the catching-up initiated by several large emerging economies, particularly in Asia, brought the world distribution back to a unimodal pattern. This is shown in *Figure 40.1*.

The second important fact is that the shift of world income to a unimodal pattern has primarily been a movement of inequality reduction between countries rather than within countries. However, inequalities between countries have not been reduced by any decrease in the gap between their average incomes. In fact, the per-capita income gap between the world's richest and poorest countries today is as large as it has ever been. The real change is that a few countries with a large population, most notably China, but also India, Indonesia, Viet Nam and Thailand, have had high growth rates that lifted a large number of their citizens out of poverty and into the middle of the global income distribution. This reduction in inequalities between countries does not translate into a reduction of inequalities at the world level over the past two decades, because inequalities within countries have actually increased in many nations (though not all, Brazil being a notable exception).

The third fact is that in spite of the emergence of developing economies, and the high and rising inequalities within countries, the world is still one in which the widest gaps in living standards have to do with location, not with socio-economic status. According to Milanovic (2012), two-thirds of global inequalities at the end of the nineteenth century were socio-economic rather than geographical. Now geographical inequalities have become prominent. The global Gini coefficient is much higher, at about 0.7, than typical country coefficients (around 0.6 in Brazil, 0.4 in the USA and 0.3 in Scandinavia). Both inequalities have strong implications for social stability across the world. Large inter-country differences in incomes help promote large migration flows from poor to rich countries, which can put pressure on social provision there. At the moment, most migration is linked to civil conflict, wars and government repression in sending countries. However, the large income gaps in the world bring with them the potential for economic migration to increase. Increasing within-country inequality poses additional challenges for social stability.

The fourth fact (see *Figure 5.1* in article 5 in this volume) is that recent economic change has benefited a large portion of the lower middle class and the top elite of the world, but has left out the most disadvantaged and harmed the upper middle-class of the world, which consists largely of the lower-income groups in developed countries.

Globalization and technical progress have enabled the educated and globalized elite of the world to reap immense benefits. The elites of emerging countries are increasingly part of this global elite. Lower down, in the middle of the global income distribution, more educated blue-collar and white-collar workers have benefited tremendously from export-led growth in emerging economies, which has allowed them to increase their incomes. At the same time, social stratification in developed countries has widened, wages of less skilled workers have stalled, and the scarcity of decent jobs has had a deep impact on employees and blue-collar workers. People on these levels now think that their children will be worse off than they have been; a sad intergenerational perspective. The gathering of the world distribution into a single mode has been due to a combination of catching-up by some from the lower mode and a lack of movement among those in the upper mode.

The picture that results from combining these facts is complex, because geographic inequalities remain important in spite of emerging economies' catching-up movement. The socio-economic gaps have become increasingly worrying in spite of the geographic gaps being far larger.

What is wrong with inequalities?

What is the problem? Inequalities have three major undesirable features.

First, when the people at the lower end of the distribution fall into poverty, as has always happened throughout history, there is a huge waste of human potential. Further, high inequality reduces the impact of growth on poverty reduction. Reducing poverty is that much harder if inequality is large. This is why poverty was reduced so very fast in China in the early 1980s, when inequality was still low. With much higher inequality, poverty reduction has slowed considerably.

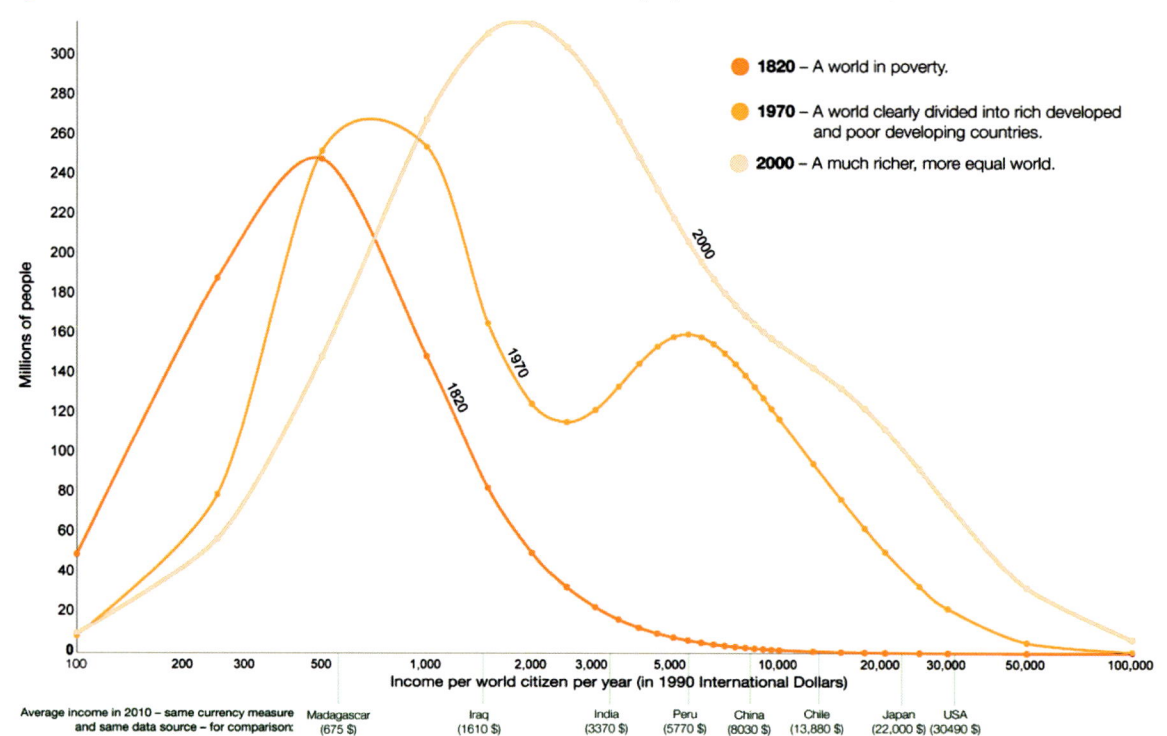

Figure 40.1 **World income distribution (with absolute population numbers) at three dates**

- **1820** – A world in poverty.
- **1970** – A world clearly divided into rich developed and poor developing countries.
- **2000** – A much richer, more equal world.

Note: The yearly income of all world citizens is measured in International Dollars. This is a currency that would buy a comparable amount of goods and services to those a US dollar would buy in the USA in 1990. Therefore incomes are comparable across countries and across time.

Source: Max Roser's elaboration on data available from www.Clio-Infra.eu via van Zanden et al. (2014) – *How Was Life ?*. OECD. The interactive data visualization is available at www.OurWorldinData.org.

Second, inequalities lead to social disintegration, unrest and violence.

The third undesirable feature of inequalities is that they are mostly very unfair. It is impossible to justify the unequal opportunities offered to the children of different socio-economic groups, or of different countries.

The duty to do something about inequalities, however, depends not just on the unfairness of the situation, but also on how effective the action will be.

Three – or four – scenarios

Examining how the trends observed in the first section may evolve in the twenty-first century, we can imagine three stylized scenarios.

In the first scenario, business as usual (BAU) continues, with the same policies: the sustained globalization of capital flows (but restricted migration), and low regulation of inequalities, financial risk and environmental externalities. Emerging economies will continue to catch up, while the most deprived countries might remain a long way behind. Inequalities within countries will continue to increase, at least in most of the developed nations, because of the inequality trap that allows the globalized and educated elite to tell national governments what to do. National governments then continue to lose their power to tax mobile inputs (capital and skilled workers) and have to reduce the welfare state. In this BAU scenario, world inequalities remain stable. Inequalities between countries continue to decrease, whereas inequalities within them rise. The world gradually returns to a situation where social inequalities become important and geographic inequalities lose their importance, although they remain substantial if some failed states fall behind. This scenario can be described as going back to the nineteenth century. It contains considerable potential for social unrest, which will have negative economic and political consequences. There is also significant potential for rebellion by Mother Earth, which could disrupt livelihoods in some areas and slow down or reverse the convergence in living standards between regions of the world.

In the second scenario, which may be called the 'social' scenario, many countries take drastic actions against inequalities at home, because a growing shared concern about inequalities brings a change in politics. While international coordination would make redistributive policies more effective, this scenario does not assume it, and substantial action on inequalities can happen on national grounds (Atkinson, 2015). This scenario actually favours the continued catching-up of emerging economies. Inequalities can be reduced in these countries and in developed nations. Capital is likely to flow away from developed nations, to avoid taxes and seek profitability in emerging economies. In this case, world inequalities would start to decrease, combining declining trends within and between countries. This social scenario would create a situation that is unlike both the nineteenth century, with its social inequalities, and the twentieth century, with its geographic inequalities. Instead, the scenario would combine the single mode situation of the nineteenth century with the social institutions of the twentieth century. An open question about this scenario is whether it would put more or less pressure on the environment than BAU. The international catching-up process adds pressure, while the impact of redistribution is unclear, and depends on consumer practices at different income levels.

In the third scenario, which may be called the 'geographic' scenario, national politics are unchanging, but globalization and technical transfers keep stimulating the catch-up process. Most developing countries benefit and raise their average living standards. Climate policies aimed at spreading clean energy throughout the world push the convergence process. Similarly, access to improved technologies in various sectors of production, agriculture and health promotes income growth in poor countries. Such policies may involve providing modern energy and technologies to currently deprived regions, which will increase economic development. In this scenario, inequalities between countries continue to decrease more sharply than in BAU. Inequalities might still increase in the developed countries, but global inequalities will decrease, slowly converging toward the level of within-country inequalities. Whether inequalities will increase or decrease in emerging countries depends on how new technologies and investments are spread. Complex patterns might develop in which the poorest populations (in particular, discriminated minorities) are left behind, with slightly less poor populations gaining. Different patterns may be observed in different countries, depending on their institutions and policies as well as on their trade and foreign investments.

This scenario is more favourable than the previous ones for one aspect of the environment: climate change. However, there is no guarantee that it will not create serious problems in resource depletion, biodiversity and pollution.

Of these three, the social scenario would be the most effective in protecting national societies against social unrest, but might not avoid destabilizing migration and other results of wide geographical wealth gaps. The geographic scenario will naturally control economic and refugee migration by ensuring better prospects at home for potential migrants. However, these prospects may become unstable at the national level if the elite 1 per cent and the remaining 99 per cent move further apart and end up living in such different conditions that the governing elite can no longer connect to the mass of citizens and satisfy their basic demands. The BAU scenario might combine both sources of instability, so that it is actually unlikely to unfold as described. It is quite possible that a mix of the social and the geographic scenarios could occur, with some countries turning to more redistribution, and a great effort being made internationally to combine climate policy and access to technologies and development.

The ideal scenario would develop this mix further, and combine internal and coordinated international action against inequalities with quicker convergence of living standards between regions of the world. Unfortunately, the degree of international coordination on tax policy that this scenario requires is quite unlikely. The promise of such a scenario is that it could generate a world free of absolute poverty, curable life-threatening illness, and poor education. Such an opportunity is only possible given the last century's large income growth and its associated improvements in health and education. It is less clear whether such a scenario would run up against environmental constraints without drastic changes in our production processes and consumption patterns (Rockström and Klum, 2015).

There are some encouraging facts. For instance, the quick convergence of living standards would make fertility rates converge and contribute to stabilizing the world population at lower levels, which is good for the environment. Likewise, spreading access to clean energy swiftly would enable poor populations to bypass older technology and raise their living standards in a much more environmentally friendly way than has happened previously.

But environmental problems could be worsened if the majority of the world's population imitate the damaging lifestyles of the rich in developed countries, with (for example) high levels of meat consumption, frequent tourism and large houses. Deep changes – not just in institutions, but also in technologies and norms of behaviour – would be required for such a scenario to fit planetary boundaries.

One key fact not mentioned in the first section is that the lifestyle of the affluent, which is based on fossil fuels and the extensive use of raw materials, was only sustainable for more than a century because of the worldwide inequalities we still have today. Spreading this lifestyle was and remains incompatible with the ecosystem. Reducing inequalities in the future, a key factor in social progress, will involve not just sharing resources, but also using them differently.

Bibliography

Atkinson, A. B. 2015. *Inequality: What Can Be Done?* Cambridge, Mass., Harvard University Press.

Deaton, A. 2014. *The Great Escape: Health, Wealth, and the Origins of Inequality.* Princeton, N.J., Princeton University Press.

Milanovic, B. 2012. Global income inequality by the numbers: in history and now. Policy Research Working Paper 6259. Washington DC, World Bank

Piketty, T. 2014. *Capital in the Twenty-First Century.* Cambridge, Mass., Harvard University Press.

Rawls, J. 1971. *A Theory of Justice.* Cambridge, Mass., Harvard University Press.

Rockström J. and Klum M. 2015. *Big World, Small Planet: Abundance within Planetary Boundaries.* New Haven, Conn., Yale University Press.

Roser, M. n.d. Our world in data. *https://ourworldindata.org/* (Accessed 11 June 2016.)

Van Zanden, J. L., Baten, J., Mira d'Ercole, M., Rijpma, A. Smith C. and Timmer, M. (eds). 2014. *How Was Life? Global Well-Being Since 1820.* Paris, OECD.

■ **Marc Fleurbaey** *(France), Robert E. Kuenne Professor at Princeton University, has published* Fairness, Responsibility and Welfare *(OUP, 2008) and* Beyond GDP *(OUP, 2013, with Didier Blanchet). He is coordinating editor of* Social Choice and Welfare.

■ **Stephan Klasen** *(Germany), professor of development economics at the University of Göttingen, is also director of the Ibero-America Institute for Economic Research and coordinator of the Courant Research Centre on 'Poverty, equity, and growth in developing and transition countries'.*

41. Inequality in an increasingly automated world

Lizzie Sayer

Technological advances are changing the way we live, work, spend and interact, with profound consequences for inequality.

77 per cent of existing jobs in China are susceptible to automation. Such was the conclusion of a 2016 World Bank *World Development Report*, which also found that 47 per cent of US jobs, 69 per cent of Indian jobs and an average of 57 per cent of jobs in OECD countries could be replaced by automated processes and robots.

While the debate about workers being replaced by machines is certainly not new, the accelerating pace and scope of technological change has led to claims that we have entered the 'Second Machine Age' (Brynjolfsson and McAfee, 2014). The 'Fourth Industrial Revolution'[1] is one in which technological advances are changing the way we live, work, spend and interact.

The rise of algorithms

The trend for technological change to replace routine manufacturing tasks and low-skilled jobs looks set to continue, and technological advances are also making it possible to automate a greater number of non-routine tasks. Advances in machine learning technology, coupled with increasingly available big data, could replace knowledge-intensive roles in sectors such as business and health care in the first half of the twenty-first century. Some estimate that machine learning algorithms could displace 140 million knowledge workers globally (McKinsey Global Institute, 2013), further contributing to a 'hollowing-out' of middle-income jobs (Frey and Osborne, 2013) and to growing polarization of the labour market. Added to this is the increasing availability of improved data-collecting sensors. These support mobile robotic development for use in a wide variety of settings, from elderly care to driverless cars and surgical robots.

Potential job losses in low and middle-income sectors, and the barriers to retraining and relocating workforces to suit the demands of new technology, mean that automation may generate unemployment and deepen existing economic and knowledge inequalities. In addition, automation may mean that wages continue to stagnate or even fall, meaning that the number of low-paid workers increases.

Increasing inequalities, diverging trends

While technological advances will shape employment opportunities and growth in future years, exactly what those advances look like and where they will happen is shaped by existing and future differences in labour and development patterns. Those without access to technological advances risk being left behind, and greater automation in the workplace without a corresponding rise in workers' skill levels risks increasing inequality. If productivity gains brought about by increased process efficiency do not occur in tandem with the creation of new jobs or with increased compensation for a broad spectrum of the workforce, they risk creating exclusion, reduction in demand and economic stagnation. Yet automation entails not only innovation in the development of existing products, but also the development of entirely new products and ways of working, and thus the creation of new jobs.

Ever since the Industrial Revolution, technological change has been an engine of income growth in developed countries. In more recent years there has been some convergence in how quickly countries worldwide adopt new technologies, but once those technologies have been taken up by a minority of users ('early adopters'), there is a divergence in how long they take to become widely used by large numbers of the population.

To see this latency in technology adoption as a reflection of widening income inequalities within countries may be a leap too far, but the present technological revolution is likely to make economic growth increasingly uneven, a worrying perspective for global inequality.

If the Industrial Revolution formed the building blocks of sustained growth in the developed world, more recent industrialization has allowed a number of emerging economies, particularly the so-called 'Asian tigers', to catch up rapidly. At the same time inequality declined, although this trend has reversed more recently in several of the countries, with the rich getting richer considerably faster than the poor. As technology advances, emerging market economies will need to keep pace with innovation in order to stay competitive.

Likewise, the rate of automation in manufacturing industries is contributing to concern over 'premature deindustrialization' in low-income countries, where jobs are relatively vulnerable to automation. An estimated 85 per cent per cent of jobs in Ethiopia could be automated (World Bank, 2016). Industrial automation also provides an increasingly cheap substitute for labour, meaning that low-wage countries may lose their cost advantage over time. As a result, companies in advanced economies may shift production to automated factories, or move manufacturing to 3D printing facilities located closer to their domestic markets. Furthermore, technological advances mean that industrialization is less likely to create jobs in manufacturing in the next generation of emerging economies. Low-income countries will no longer be able to follow the rapid growth trajectories that China has achieved by shifting workers from farms to higher-paying factory jobs. If export-led manufacturing growth is limited by technology-facilitated 'onshoring', and the automation of low-skill services means that service-led growth is limited, new models of growth will need to be found to ensure sustainable development in the world's poorest countries.

At a more local level, new product and process innovations have the potential to transform regions and cities. However, new jobs often emerge in different places from the ones in which old jobs disappear. This could cause uneven development and exacerbate regional inequalities.

The new jobs created by new technology will require highly skilled workers and computational literacy, while in some cases reducing demand for low-skilled workers. In the digital age, a focus on income-generating growth driven by access to data and connected devices (the 'internet of things') may deepen existing digital divides.

Where will workers hold the comparative advantage?

Frey and Osborne (2013) identify three human characteristics that currently appear difficult to automate: creative intelligence, involving the development of original ideas; social intelligence, relying on social interaction; and perception and manipulation, requiring manual dexterity and interaction with unstructured physical environments. Yet the rapid development of robotic technology and the potential of embodied artificial intelligence – based on an understanding of living organisms – may pose a challenge to at least two of these categories.

The knowledge-driven economy in a world of knowledge divides

One of the most commonly cited policy responses to automation is increasing innovation and upskilling of the workforce. However, ensuring that education systems produce the right mix of skills to respond to such a rapidly changing environment will remain a challenge.

With the pace of technological change now much faster than at any time in history, the future implications for life and work are far from certain. The advent of artificial intelligence and quantum computing to solve complex problems could create untold changes for the labour market.

Yet with prominent scientist Steven Hawking warning that the development of artificial intelligence 'could spell the end of the human race' (quoted in Cellan-Jones, 2014), and Google's director of engineering, Ray Kurzweil, stating that humans will have become immortal 'hybrids'[2] by 2030, perhaps it's not unrealistic to say that the future of inequality lies far beyond the scope of human understanding.

Notes

1. The focus of the 2016 World Economic Forum.
2. Speaking at the Exponential Finance conference in New York, 3 June 2015.

Bibliography

Brynjolfsson, E. and McAfee A. 2014. *The Second Machine Age: Work Progress, and Prosperity in a Time of Brilliant Technologies*. New York, W. W. Norton.

Cellan-Jones, R. 2014. Stephen Hawking warns artificial intelligence could end mankind. BBC, 2 December. *www.bbc.com/news/technology-30290540* (Accessed 11 June 2016.)

Citi GPS: Global Perspectives & Solutions. 2016. TECHNOLOGY AT WORK v2.0. The Future Is Not What It Used to Be. *www.oxfordmartin.ox.ac.uk/downloads/reports/Citi_GPS_Technology_Work_2.pdf* (Accessed 26 February 2016.)

Frey, C. B. and Osbourne, M. A. 2013. The future of employment: how susceptible are jobs to computerisation? *http://www.oxfordmartin.ox.ac.uk/downloads/academic/The_Future_of_Employment.pdf* (Accessed 28 June 2016.)

McKinsey Global Institute. 2013. Disruptive technologies: advances that will transform life, business, and the global economy. *www.mckinsey.com/~/media/McKinsey/Business%20Functions/Business%20Technology/Our%20Insights/Disruptive%20technologies/MGI_Disruptive_technologies_Full_report_May2013.ashx* (Accessed 3 March 2016.)

World Bank. 2016. Digital Dividends. Washington DC, International Bank for Reconstruction and Development/World Bank. *http://documents.worldbank.org/curated/en/896971468194972881/pdf/102725-PUB-Replacement-PUBLIC.pdf* (Accessed 26 February 2016.)

World Economic Forum. 2016. World Economic Forum Annual Meeting 2016: Mastering the Fourth Industrial Revolution. *www.weforum.org/reports/world-economic-forum-annual-meeting-2016-mastering-the-fourth-industrial-revolution* (Accessed 3 March 2016.)

■ **Lizzie Sayer** *(UK) is communications officer at the ISSC and manager of the 2016* World Social Science Report.

POSTCARD

42. Digital connections in the face of inequality

Charles Onyango-Obbo

On 4 August 2015 a popular Kenyan blogger, Jackson Biko, posted a *blog* about a student who was battling a brain tumour. Emmanuel Jadudi was desperately trying to raise $10,000 in a few days so he could fly to India for life-saving surgery. At the end of the blog, Biko made an appeal for donations of between US$1 and US$3 towards Jadudi's treatment. Donations could be sent via M-Pesa, the ground-breaking mobile payment system. Then he went to bed. By the time he checked next morning, the blog had gone viral and donations for Jadudi were flooding in. In just 48 hours, the appeal had raised $64,000 – more than six times what Jadudi was looking for.

For a nation ranked sixth in sub-Saharan Africa on the extreme poverty index (Turner et al., 2015), and where inequality remains deeply entrenched, that was astounding.

Biko was inundated with questions about the secret of raising so much money so quickly through a blog. His answer came in *an article* a week later. He said he could only speculate but, really, he didn't know. He is not alone. We know about the social and economic impact of digital media and mobile phone technology, but we are only beginning to figure out how it really works and why it succeeds.

Sometimes the insights come out of left field. On 18 February 2016 Uganda went to the polls, with President Yoweri Museveni seeking to extend his thirty-year rule. Ahead of the vote, the election commission announced a ban on taking mobile phones and other handheld devices into the polling stations. It relented in the face of a public outcry and allegations that it was trying to prevent people from recording vote cheating. But it had only retreated, not given up. On voting day access to Facebook and Twitter, and to mobile money platforms, was blocked. The industry regulator had ordered mobile phone companies and internet service providers to block the social media sites, upon the request of the election commission, for 'security reasons'. The opposition, for its part, alleged that their use was an attempt to prevent vote fiddling, in what ultimately turned out be a *very chaotic* election.

This suppression of social media had two unintended effects. One was to show how much the state saw them as a potentially subversive force. But it was also a measure of how much the people valued them as a tool for having their voices heard, and in this case, upholding vigilance at election stations.

There were many exchanges on both social media and messaging about how to work around the blockage using virtual private networks (VPNs). Use of the anonymous web-browsing network Tor, and Google searches for 'VPN' from Uganda, spiked dramatically.

Perhaps without these digital tools, the election wouldn't have trended as it did in all the neighbouring countries, shaping an *unflattering narrative* of an election dogged by protests and irregularities. Social media had given people a voice in the face of political inequalities, and a means to be heard across the world.

A discussion of digital media and access to it, however, would ultimately be meaningless without understanding the structural changes that are giving them important roles in organizing politics, activism, economics and society in new ways.

There is little research in this area in Africa, but I have a tentative theory.

The state of politics and of economies in Africa today owes its roots in part to the economic liberalization and privatization that followed the end of the Cold War. Before then, family and the 'village' (clan, ethnic community) were very important support systems. They were shattered from the end of the 1980s by one of the first things that hit on a scale that the support systems couldn't cope with – HIV/AIDS.

At about the same time, subsidies were being dismantled and fuel price controls lifted. State-run bus companies folded or were privatized as costs spiralled. Today, if you are a Tanzanian worker from the lakeside town of Mwanza working in Dar es Salaam, the cost of the nearly 1,200 km journey to the countryside every month is impossible unless you are highly paid. The very important connection to rural communities and family for Africans in urban areas frayed at the very moment when there was the greatest need for it.

The other pillar of African societies, patrilineality, which also defined systems of support, was weakened at the same time. The number of single mother-led families rose sharply, with one study (Clark and Hamplová, n.d., p. 1) finding that 'a substantial proportion of women experience at least one episode of being a single mother before the age of 45, ranging from 30 per cent in Ethiopia to nearly 70 per cent in Zimbabwe'.

In the face of these pressures and changes, a new marketplace of support, more rational and impersonal, arose to fill the vacuum. It coincided almost perfectly with the arrival of the mobile phone and the internet in Africa. It was a convergence made in heaven.

Bibliography

Clark, S. and Hamplová, D. n.d. Single motherhood in sub-Saharan Africa: a life course perspective (draft). Princeton, N.J., Princeton University. *http://paa2011.princeton.edu/papers/112136* (Accessed 28 February 2016.)

Turner, S., Cilliers, J. and Hughes, B. 2015. Reasonable goals for reducing poverty in Africa, African Futures Paper 13, February 2015. Pretoria, Institute for Security Studies and Frederick S. Pardee Center for International Futures. *https://www.issafrica.org/uploads/AF_Paper13.pdf* (Accessed 11 June 2016.)

■ **Charles Onyango-Obbo** *(Uganda) is editor of* Mail & Guardian Africa. *Twitter@cobbo3*

Part III

TRANSFORMATIVE RESPONSES, TRANSFORMATIVE PATHWAYS

Introduction

Chapter 5 ■ Changing the rules

Chapter 6 ■ Mobilizing for change

Street artwork by Ernest Zacharevic
(Georgetown, Penang, Malaysia, 2012)
© Ernest Zacharevic. All rights reserved.
Third-party use or commercial redistribution of all or part of this image
is subject to the prior permission of Ernest Zacharevic.

43. Towards equality: transformative pathways (an introduction to Part III)

Melissa Leach

Inequalities are accelerating across the world, with damaging consequences. Earlier parts of this report have explored how multiple inequalities – economic, social, cultural, spatial, environmental, political and knowledge – interact and often reinforce each other; their diverse configurations in different countries and regions; and their effects and implications – for different groups of people, but ultimately for us all.

Yet 'inequality is not inevitable' (Stiglitz, 2015). Current patterns and trends reflect particular social, economic and political structures and institutions. Sometimes deeply embedded and historically entrenched, they are also open to reshaping, choice and agency. There is much that can be done to reduce inequalities and move towards greater equality and social justice. This Part draws together an array of possible responses to different inequalities, in different spheres and contexts, and at local, national and global levels.

'Transformative pathways' towards equality are an organizing metaphor for this project. Pathways are particular directions of intervention, change and power relations (Leach et al., 2010, Scoones et al., 2015), while transformation implies deep, lasting change and the restructuring of power relations, rather than quick technical fixes. Power relations are important because although technical policies can be designed, whether they are chosen or implemented depends on political interests and discourses. Many current pathways reinforce inequalities; indeed, these pathways can be seen as the dominant motorways of the existing road system. Yet alternative routes towards greater equality are possible. These often start as small bush paths or even faint footprints, but can strengthen and converge over time, cutting into, redirecting or even replacing the highways. Such pathways towards greater equality may unfold at the local, national or international scale, or across these scales. Multiple inequalities require multi-dimensional responses. Yet, as contributions to this Part illustrate, powerful synergies are also possible in which tackling one sort of inequality enables others to be addressed, leading to broader pathways of change.

Current pathways are unfolding at a particular moment in twenty-first century capitalism. Rising inequalities are linked to the extension of unfettered markets and commodification, destabilizing economies, societies and indeed nature. Yet several influential analysts identify fundamental challenges to capitalism. They see the world as being on the brink of a postcapitalist age ushered in by information technologies (Mason, 2015) or as being gripped by a 'triple movement' struggle between actors and forces pushing for neoliberal marketization, social protectionism, and the recognition of identity-based groups (Fraser, 2013).

Contributions to this Part acknowledge these complex politics in a diversity of ways. They are broadly grouped into two chapters. *Chapter 5* (Changing the rules) focuses primarily on changes in policies, regulations and institutional arrangements that can help redress inequalities. *Chapter 6* (Mobilizing for change) shows the significance of social and political action in enabling and pushing for change.

Changing the rules

An array of policies and regulations can form part of a transformative pathway. Indeed, institutional design makes the critical difference between more and less unequal countries (Rothstein, 59). If economic inequalities stem from the power of moneyed interests to shape the rules of the market, then 'rewriting' those rules is essential to move towards equalities, as has been shown for the USA (Reich, 2015; Stiglitz, 2015). Multiple inequalities require different entry points and areas of rule-change, many of which have been rehearsed in international reports (Ortiz and Cummins, 2011). Less well-documented are the synergies and trade-offs between policies aimed at different dimensions of inequality, and the new and propositional ideas about equality now emerging from different country settings.

Work, decent pay, reduced wage disparity

The most effective and sustainable route out of poverty for the working-age population is a productive, fairly paid job (Berg, 44). Labour market institutions can be designed to support the creation of quality jobs with decent wages and working conditions. In Latin America, labour policies that sought explicitly to redress inherited problems of unemployment, job informalization and falling unskilled and minimum wages were central to the package of measures that reduced economic inequalities in the 2000s (Cornia, 46). In Nigeria, the Industrial Court supported conditions for reduced inequalities by implementing international labour standards that enforced decent labour practices and workers' rights (Nwabueze, 54). Although few countries have yet acted, global advocacy has turned to calls for the regulation of top salaries in the face of extreme inequalities driven by high incomes in the top 1 per cent.

Education is critical. Policies that enable high or universal access to quality education can enable previously unskilled workers to upgrade and access relatively higher-paying jobs, while offering synergies with reduced social and knowledge inequalities (Cornia, 46). However, a more educated workforce will only be effective in tackling economic inequalities if jobs are available. Approaches by which states offer guaranteed public employment have been effective at certain times and places, from the US post-recession 'New Deal' to the Maharashtra public works scheme in India, which guarantees paid work to the poorest and most socially marginalized.

There are many emerging examples around the world of new economic arrangements that link work and livelihoods with values of sharing and equity. These include various forms of 'economic democracy' that give workers shares in business fortunes (Power, Wilkinson and Pickett, 37), social and solidarity economies (Utting, 2015) and citizen-led alternatives (Mathie and Gaventa, 2015; Mathie et al., 64). Many involve synergies between greater economic equality and improvements along other dimensions including the social, cultural, environmental and political. For now, most are small, local and experimental, but they prefigure alternative ways of imagining and enacting economic relations which have the potential to scale up and out into bigger pathways of change.

Global policies and regulation, trade and aid

Macroeconomic policy and regulation can also play a key role in tackling inequalities. Since the rise of labour-displacing economic activity and technology contributes to economic inequality, industrial, trade and investment policies that affect this mix have a key role in reducing it. The innovation that drives technological change could be directed through regulation, incentives and policy frameworks towards forms that are more inclusive and job-creating.

Globalization, financialization and the associated boom-and-bust character of markets have contributed to instabilities and inequalities (Griffith-Jones and Brett, 49). To curb these negative dynamics requires effective regulation of financial institutions, while wise macroeconomic policies can mitigate the un-equalizing effects of financial crises.

More broadly, global economic interconnectedness means that rule changes cannot be confined to the national level. Reforms to global and regional governance and social policy are important to address globalized drivers of inequality within and between nations, such as those in the financial system, and to ensure that countries have the autonomy to enact inequality-reducing policies. Global policies might focus on more effective redistribution (for instance, via global tax cooperation and global funds), more socially responsible regulation (for example, in regional trade agreements) or strengthened social rights (Deacon, 45). Meanwhile carefully targeted aid packages and favourable trade regulations can have powerful effects on inequalities between and within countries (Olukoshi, 48).

Wealth and resource redistributive policies

Complementing policy mechanisms that equalize earnings are those geared towards redistribution.

Progressive income tax policies are a fundamental tool for tackling economic inequalities, for both reducing top incomes and enabling redistribution to those with bottom incomes (Sabaíni, Martorano and Morán, 47). Higher tax revenues make vital state finance available for social protection programmes, as well as for services like health and education. The so-called fiscal exchange bargain – whereby middle classes accept the need to pay higher taxes in exchange for improved social services – has been central to inequality reduction in many countries, including several in Scandinavia and Latin America.

Piketty (2014) drew attention to the entrenchment of inequalities through asset accumulation across generations – once via land, now more often finance. Wealth taxes appear an attractive solution. But if applied on a national scale, they run the risk that high net worth individuals or corporations will simply move elsewhere. Piketty therefore proposed a global tax on wealth. In the light of political challenges to the implementation of this idea, a pragmatic starting point might be a system of international tax information exchange (Moore, 50).

The redistribution of land, water and other natural resources is critical to redressing both economic and environmental inequalities in many local and national settings. Land reform programmes offer positive effects and opportunities (Lipton, 52), while regulation of international actors, and mechanisms to protect local resource rights, are crucial in the face of a new wave of global 'grabs' for land, water, carbon, minerals and other resources.

Social protection and services

Social protection policies can work hand-in-hand with progressive taxation to reduce economic inequalities. Services such as free and accessible health care, education, affordable housing and cash transfers are means of directly reducing social inequalities. They can also reduce economic inequalities by freeing up income that people would otherwise have spent on these essential forms of provision. Inclusive and accessible social protection schemes can be designed to address multiple dimensions of inequality, and to ensure the inclusion of marginalized groups. Because knowledge, social and political inequalities can restrict access to social protection, these need to be addressed if positive pathways are to unfold (Roelen, Sabates-Wheeler and Devereux, 55).

Some governments are now experimenting boldly with rights to a 'universal basic income' for all citizens (Wright, 56). This idea has a long history, with advocates from all parts of the political spectrum. Today, it implies genuine choice about how to live and work in contemporary contexts, and carries significant potential synergies for the fight for economic, social and cultural equalities.

The importance of access to quality education for reducing inequality across generations has been noted several times in this report. Care services for children and the elderly are critical if poor families are to work and earn income, and to address gender inequalities (Razavi, 14). Universal health coverage has great power as a strategy to tackle social inequalities (Krech, 57). These are entitlements due to all people via state financing, not commodities for sale only to those who can afford them.

However well designed, social policies will only be effective if they are properly financed and effectively implemented. Issues of which agencies take responsibility, their organizational capability, funding and staffing, and their local legitimacy are all critical in enabling implementation, and if they are lacking, they need to be built (Woolcock, 58).

Inclusive political and governance frameworks

Changing the rules towards reduced inequalities is more likely to be feasible if those with an interest in such change are included in rule-setting processes. Such processes may include laws and policies such as quotas to bring women, indigenous people or other politically marginalized groups into formal political arenas. But while their significance for gender equality is great, rules and formal representation are insufficient (Nazneen, 51). Promoting women's rights, and their inclusion in politics and policy-making, also depends on informal institutions and norms.

Meanwhile, the quality of political and government institutions is vitally important. If they are perceived as incompetent, or beset by favouritism or corruption, there will be declining support for rule changes that alleviate inequalities – even among the parts of a population that are politically included or ideologically in favour of such changes (Rothstein, 59).

Multiple inequalities need to be addressed by multiple policies. These in turn need to be designed and implemented in ways that acknowledge potential trade-offs and synergies between them. One size does not fit all; policy configurations can draw on general principles but to work, they must be adapted to real, diverse contexts, and applied with pragmatism.

Mobilizing for change

While changes in the rules are critical to creating transformative pathways towards greater equality, it is unlikely that they will take place without political pressure. Through what can be termed a 'paradox of power', those with most influence over the rules often have the least interest in changing them. Economic inequalities change the rules of the game, narrowing spaces and opportunities for decision-making. As Solt (2008, p. 48) puts it, 'the wealthy [are able] to shape politics in their own favor against rival arguments that focus on the effects of inequality on citizens' objective interests'.

The other part of the paradox is that those at the bottom of the inequality ladder may have the greatest interest in change, yet the least power and voice to influence it. Citizen participation is key yet it is often constrained by the interaction of economic, political, social and knowledge inequalities (Gaventa and Runciman, 12).

Put so crudely, this paradox invites hopelessness. But this reaction is clearly not justified. There is evidence of change. The paradox should be taken instead to signal the importance of challenges to power relations as an integral part of transformative pathways, and the importance of social and political action in mobilizing for change.

Such action may come from below, initiated by citizens, grass-roots groups and social movements, or from above, through enlightened global governance, political leadership or progressive political parties. Whether and how transformative pathways towards equality emerge depends on how these forces come together in complex alliances, combinations and sequences.

Social and political action from below

Social and political action against inequalities has long historical roots, but it has also shown dramatic recent increase. Today, three sorts of action can be distinguished: those demanding transparency and accountability from powerful institutions, those pushing for new policies and rights, and those offering the seeds of alternative arrangements and new pathways.

Mobilizations against economic, social and environmental inequalities have accelerated across the world over the past decade.

They have been prompted by grievances relating to economic and social justice, including demands for real democracy, public services, civil rights, and opposition to international financial institutions, corporate rent-seeking and corruption (Vergara-Camus, 60; Ortiz and Burke, 61). Africa has experienced youth uprisings in response to growing economic inequalities under neoliberalism and a crisis of electoral democracy (Branch and Mampilly, 62).

Movements such as Occupy, and 2015's climate marches, have united wide sections of society to protest against unfair, unsustainable economic and political systems. At the same time, we are also seeing particular social groups demanding rights and recognition (Fraser, 2013), based around gender, sexuality, indigeneity, disability or other forms of identity. Campaigns on gender and domestic violence, for instance, have challenged both laws and the discriminatory ideas and assumptions underpinning them (Nyamu Musembi, 53). Although such specific movements can strain and fragment the broader solidarities that are important for challenging economic and political inequalities, alliances between fragmented movements can emerge, such as those between feminist and economically based movements, and provide powerful ways to tackle intersecting inequalities and broader social injustice.

Contemporary movements take varied forms. Marches and protests on the street interact with those in law courts (Nyamu Musembi, 53), through the media and online. The digital era is providing new spaces for social and political action, for assembling transnational networks and alliances, and for citizen engagement and state accountability, as part of 'opening' governance (Ramalingam and Hernandez, 11; Edwards and McGee, 2016). Van Graan (63) highlights the role of the arts in participation and mobilization, drawing on powerful examples from South Africa. Yet as contributors to this volume remind us, these media carry dangers and can work in the political and economic interests of powerful elites, reinforcing and even adding to inequalities. To counter these requires policies and politics that ensure wide, public access to technologies, media and space.

At the extreme, protest can spill over into violence. Violent revolution has its place in the history of attempts to overturn inequality-supporting regimes (Vergara-Camus, 60). Conflict and civil war are not a consequence of inequality but a response to it.

Where people are severely disenfranchised both economically and politically, violent conflict can be their only recourse – something seen in recent violent extremism from the Middle East to North Africa.

Yet there are also positive examples where citizens have been able to marshal economic and political agency to protect their livelihoods and overcome inequalities. These amount to the precursors of a new political economy emerging at the grassroots (Mathie et al., 64). The steps are often small – involving new forms of community economic enterprise, for instance – but growing economic agency can help build wider awareness of rights, and deeper questioning of dominant forms of political and economic power.

Leadership from above

Transformative politics can also be driven from above. Progressive reforms in global governance and in global social, economic and sustainability policy are critical for tackling inequalities, and require international political alliances. Global agreements around the Sustainable Development Goals (SDGs) and climate change, and recent initiatives by the OECD and G20, show the potential for such initiatives, although complex geopolitics and concerns with national sovereignty often impede them (Deacon, 45).

Nationally, transformative politics towards equality may be driven by 'policy entrepreneurs'; governments and corporations; by the decisions and actions of enlightened leaders; and by progressive political regimes. It is no coincidence that many countries experiencing rising inequality have done so under conservative governments that have aggressively pursued neoliberal policies. By contrast, regime changes have often been catalytic in inequality reductions, in cases from Bolivia to Iceland.

Party political struggles around inequality have moved beyond simple dichotomies of left and right, as regimes of diverse political shades appreciate and respond to the harms that inequality brings to national economies and social stability. Governments may also pursue strategies that have the effect of reducing inequalities, even if this was not their prime motivation. For instance, many East Asian countries followed full employment regimes from the 1960s to the mid-1990s in the interests of industrial growth, with the spin-off of reducing economic inequalities – although notably not political or environmental ones. Emerging forms of state-supported capitalism in both democratic and non-democratic regimes are combining market regulation and social provision in diverse ways, with varied effects on different kinds of inequality. Examples include African countries pursuing vigorous state-led development, such as Ethiopia and Rwanda, and to some extent China, where economic inequality, which widened from the 1980s, has more recently declined amid policies to narrow the rural–urban gap and enhance social provision (Li, 15), though stark gender and environmental inequalities persist.

Alliances and shifting norms

Social and political protest has often helped bring about shifts in political leadership. For political action from below to combine effectively with political support from above, negotiation and alliances are often critical. While poor and marginalized people might appear politically weak, they can make themselves essential to elites, through electoral support or the threat of unrest. Political alliances and bargaining between private, public and civil society actors and interests shape pathways of change and the extent to which they are inequality-reducing or enhancing. Such bargaining is central to the politics of environmental inequalities, while political alliances can work well in favour of progressive tax regimes (Moore, 50).

Middle classes can be key to such alliances, whether in personal or group support to the struggles of the poor, or by eschewing narrow economic self-interest in favour of contributing to broader, collective solidarity and pathways towards equality (Rothstein, 59). The middle classes of today's rich countries experience declining living standards relative to both top incomes and the rising middle classes of Asia. Discontent and social tension could result (Milanovic, 5), with uncertain and potentially fast-moving political ramifications.

Individual and group action interacts with shifts in wider social and cultural norms. People's support for change seems to depend less on economic self-interest than on prevailing social attitudes and moral and ethical values. This includes judgements of whether extreme inequality is tolerated, or seen as wrong (Fukuda-Parr, 65). This suggests that building pathways towards equality may require sociocultural values to shift, through processes that will inevitably be complex and context-specific, and which will involve challenges to entrenched habits and perceptions.

Transformative pathways

In practice and over time, policies and politics interact. If we look at cases where inequalities have declined, it is combinations and sequences of rule changes and actions involving states, markets and citizens, involving top-down leadership and bottom-up action, that have made a difference. While reminding us of the importance of tackling the scourge of extreme economic inequality, Oxfam's work underlines too the importance of addressing power dynamics: citizens must be able to hold decision-makers to account, and governments must protect their rights against commercial and elite interests (Byanyima, 67).

Tracking the histories of countries that have successfully reduced inequalities and discussing their politics, Green (66) reveals important features of transformative pathways towards equality. First, they are non-linear. Pathways are rarely smooth and straight. There can be twists, turns and bumps along the way, with moments of abrupt advance combined with setbacks or periods of more gradual evolution. A specific change can open up possibilities for one group or close them down for another. Crisis can become an opportunity to challenge entrenched structures and provide a foothold for new ones. Multiple inequalities need to be tackled flexibly. The seven types of inequality addressed in this report require bundles of specific and intersecting policies and actions. Those related to particular inequalities will not move together at all times and in all contexts, and there can be tensions and trade-offs between them. Nevertheless some do align, and there is scope for policy and action to seek out and promote such synergies alongside broad forms of multidimensional change.

Small changes can add up to big transformations over space and time. The very idea of 'transformation' can imply the need to steer from above. But if we look back on some of the major transformations towards equality and social justice that have occurred historically – the ending of the slave trade and the granting of votes for women, for instance – it becomes clear that they unfolded through a multiplicity of smaller actions, by a range of dispersed people and groups (Stirling, 2015), scaling up and learning from each other (Speth, 2012). But 'flips' and 'tipping points' might also occur, fuelled by catalytic moments or actions, or as the result of accumulative change in complex systems. Such flips can be rapid.

Small changes in ways of doing things can also kindle new perceptions and imaginations of the possible, enabling pathways that might once have seemed unrealistic to be identified and pursued (Mathie et al., 64).

The dynamics of such transformative pathways are only just beginning to be understood, and this is an area where further research is needed. The future of inequality is unknown and uncertain, but what is clear is that extreme forms of inequality need to be avoided. Understanding how transformative pathways have unfolded in the past cannot dictate future action, but it can offer clues as to strategies that might work in different contexts. And it gives grounds for optimism. Major shifts in norms, policies and politics that add up to transformative pathways have occurred in the past. Today we are seeing rising inequalities, but also an unprecedented explosion of action and experimentation around the world. The broad direction is clear, and there is potential for small pathways to grow and coalesce into major roadways of transformative change towards greater equality for all.

Bibliography

Atkinson, T. 2015. *Inequality: What Can Be Done?* Boston, Mass., Harvard University Press.

Edwards, D. and McGee, R. (eds). 2016. Opening governance. *IDS Bulletin,* Vol. 47, No. 1.

Fraser, N. 2013. A triple movement? Parsing the politics of crisis after Polanyi. *New Left Review,* Vol. 81, May–June.

Leach, M., Scoones, I. and Stirling, A. 2010. *Dynamic Sustainabilities: Technology, Environment, Social Justice.* London, Routledge.

Mason, P. 2015. *Postcapitalism: A Guide to Our Future.* London, Allen Lane.

Mathie, A. and Gaventa, J. 2015. *Citizen-Led Innovation for a New Economy.* London, Practical Action Publishing.

Ortiz, I. and Cummins, M. 2011. *Global Inequality.* New York, UNICEF.

Piketty, T. 2014. *Capitalism in the Twenty-First Century.* Cambridge, Mass., Harvard University Press.

Reich, R. 2015. *Saving Capitalism: For the Many, Not the Few.* New York, Knopf.

Scoones, I., Leach, M. and Newell, P. 2015. *The Politics of Green Transformations.* London, Routledge.

Solt, F. 2008. Economic Inequality and Democratic Political Engagement. *American Journal of Political Science,* Vol. 52, pp. 48–60.

Speth, J. G. 2012. *America the Possible: Manifesto for a New Economy.* New Haven, Conn., Yale University Press.

Stiglitz, J. 2015. *Rewriting the Rules of the American Economy: An Agenda for Growth and Shared Prosperity.* Roosevelt Institute. *http://community-wealth.org/sites/clone.community-wealth.org/files/downloads/report-stiglitz.pdf* (Accessed 11 June 2016.)

Stirling, A. C. 2015. Emancipating transformations: from controlling 'the transition' to culturing plural radical progress. I. Scoones, M. Leach and P. Newell (eds), *The Politics of Green Transformations*. London, Routledge, pp. 39–53.

Utting, P. (ed.). 2015. *Social and Solidarity Economy: Beyond the Fringe.* London, Zed Books.

■ **Melissa Leach** (UK) is director of the Institute of Development Studies (IDS), Brighton, UK. A geographer and social anthropologist, her interdisciplinary, policy-engaged research in Africa and beyond links environment, agriculture, health, technology and gender, with particular interests in knowledge, power and the politics of science and policy processes. She is vice-chair of the Science Committee of Future Earth; a member of the International Panel of Experts on Sustainable Food Systems (IPES-food); and was lead author of UN Women's World Survey on the Role of Women in Economic Development 2014. She co-founded the Ebola Response Anthropology Platform and was lead social scientist in the UK and WHO Ebola scientific advisory committees during 2014–15.

Chapter 5
Changing the rules

44. Labour market institutions and inequality
    Janine Berg
45. Inequality and global social policy: policies, actors and strategies
    Bob Deacon
46. The decline and recent uptick of income inequality in Latin America, 2002–13
    Giovanni Andrea Cornia
47. Taxation and Inequality: lessons from Latin America
    Juan Carlos Gómez Sabaíni, Bruno Martorano and Dalmiro Morán
48. Global instruments for tackling inequality: the African experience
    Adebayo O. Olukoshi
49. POSTCARD • Financial liberalization and global inequality
    Stephany Griffith-Jones and E. A. Brett
50. POSTCARD • Could changes in the international tax system be a strategy for dealing with inequality?
    Mick Moore
51. A seat at the table is not enough: gender and political inclusion
    Sohela Nazneen
52. POSTCARD • Land redistribution: opportunities and traps
    Michael Lipton
53. Legal rights as instruments for challenging inequality
    Celestine Nyamu Musembi
54. POSTCARD • Reducing inequality through transformative institutional policies: the case of the Industrial Court of Nigeria
    Caroline Joelle Nwabueze
55. Social protection, inequality and social justice
    Keetie Roelen, Rachel Sabates-Wheeler and Stephen Devereux
56. POSTCARD • Unconditional basic income
    Erik Olin Wright
57. POSTCARD • Universal health coverage as a powerful social equalizer
    Rüdiger Krech
58. Critical elements for ensuring the success of more inclusive social policies
    Michael Woolcock
59. Inequality and corruption
    Bo Rothstein

44. Labour market institutions and inequality

Janine Berg

Throughout most of the world, earnings from work are the most important source of household income. While these earnings depend on where the person works and what the person does, they will also hinge on the governance of the labour market, through macroeconomic policies that support full employment and via the institutions that regulate the workplace, such as unions, collective bargaining, minimum wages and the regulation of employment contracts. Over the past several decades, many governments have neglected full employment as a policy objective, and these labour market institutions have been weakened.

Introduction

Among non-retired households, earnings from work are by far the most important source of household income. How much a person earns at work and how earnings are distributed across the labour market depends on labour market institutions. Labour market institutions – the laws, policies and practices – that govern the labour market can be designed to support the creation of quality jobs with decent wages and working conditions, and to support those who cannot work or who are unable to find work.

The erosion of labour market institutions, or in some countries the lack of them, has contributed to rising inequality in many countries across the world, including in North America, Europe, Asia and parts of Africa. In Latin America, on the other hand, many countries experienced a decline in inequality in the 2000s due in part to the strengthening of labour market institutions. Thus if a country wants to improve equity, it needs to strengthen its labour market institutions.

By labour market institutions, I am referring to the more familiar institutions that regulate the workplace such as unions, collective bargaining, minimum wages, the type of employment arrangement, and working time regulations, although other institutions also have a bearing on the operation of the labour market. In particular, macroeconomic policies in support of full employment are necessary for achieving more opportunities and higher earnings in the labour market, and social protection policies are necessary to support workers when they are no longer working, raise the incomes of those who are working, and improve workers' access to the labour market though social policies that provide child care, elder care and other forms of social support. *Figure 44.1* illustrates the different policy areas that shape labour market outcomes. As other articles in this report address social protection policies, the main focus of this article is on macroeconomic policies in support of full employment and labour market regulations.

Figure 44.1 **The different policy areas that shape labour market outcomes**

[Concentric circles diagram showing, from outermost to innermost: Social protection policies; Regulation of labour market; Full employment policies; Labour market outcomes]

Source: Author's illustration.

Macroeconomic policies are part of employment policy

Full employment policies are necessary for achieving equitable societies. Indeed, the OECD has found that a 1 percentage point decrease in the unemployed population reduces the overall Gini coefficient of the working-age population by 0.65 percentage points (OECD, 2011). Moreover, unemployment does not affect all workers equally. In industrialized countries, it is the less educated, poorer workers, as well as young people, women and minorities, who are more likely to be unemployed. In developing countries, it is the more educated who experience higher unemployment rates, as the less educated typically turn to self-employment in the informal economy and do not show up in unemployment statistics. This means that a policy of raising interest rates to contain inflation is particularly harmful to specific groups in the labour market.

Achieving full employment requires supportive monetary and fiscal policies that can stabilize the business cycle and support productive investment by the private and public sectors. In most countries, there are fewer jobs than there are workers. But unfortunately job creation has fallen off the macroeconomic policy agenda over the past several decades. Price stability has been the sole policy goal of monetary policy, and while controlling inflation is important, it should be considered alongside policies to boost investment and job creation (Islam and Kucera, 2014).

Fiscal policy is needed to boost aggregate demand during downturns, and to provide funds for public investment in physical and social infrastructure, which ultimately supports private enterprises. Unfortunately, tax-to-GDP ratios are low (in some cases around 10 per cent of GDP) in many developing countries, limiting the ability of governments to invest in infrastructure, which is fundamental for economic development as well as being an important source of direct and indirect job creation. Low tax revenues also limit the ability of governments to invest in public services such as education, training and care services, with implications for the quality of the labour force and workers' ability to access the labour market. In terms of equality, low tax revenues also limit the amount of redistribution that is possible. Moreover, fiscal policy has tended to be procyclical, augmenting boom and bust cycles and further exacerbating volatility in the labour market.

Income from work and the regulation of work

Income from waged work and self-employment accounts for the vast majority of individual and family incomes. According to the OECD (2011), 83 per cent of household disposable income among the working-age population is earnings from work, with 73 per cent stemming from waged work and 10 per cent from self-employment. The remaining income sources include rents (4.9 per cent) and government transfers (12.3 per cent) (see *Figure 44.2*).

This means that an individual's well-being is for the most part dependent on the income that the individual and the individual's family earn from work, which in turn depends on where the person works and what the person does, but also on the institutions that govern the labour market, including unions, collective bargaining, minimum wages and the regulation of employment contracts. In countries where labour markets are less regulated, or are regulated to allow employers more latitude in setting employment conditions, there is a wider dispersion of labour market earnings.

Unions influence the wage distribution through their engagement in broad economic and social policy debates, but also as parties to collective bargaining agreements negotiated at either the firm or sectoral level. The influence of collective bargaining will depend, however, on whether the system is 'narrow', limited to the parties or the immediate bargaining unit, or an 'encompassing system', whereby collective bargaining agreements are extended to workers in the broader economic sector who are not members of a union. Under both systems there will be wage compression, but because narrow systems are limited to unionized firms, the effect of the wage compression on broader wage inequality in the labour market will depend on the degree of unionization in the economy (Hayter, 2015).

Over the past several decades, trade union density has fallen in many (though not all) developed and developing countries (ILO, 2015a). As a result, the wage compression effects of the narrow systems have become even more limited. Under encompassing systems, collective bargaining agreements continue to be extended despite declines in trade union density, although even here, opt-out clauses and a movement from centralized to decentralized systems have eroded some coverage.

Nevertheless, extension has allowed these systems to have a greater effect on compressing wages in the overall economy (International Labour Organization (ILO), 2015a).

In some countries, unions have played an important role in influencing policies to the benefit of workers, particularly those at the bottom of the pay scale. This is particularly true for tripartite negotiations on the minimum wage as well as on social protection and social services. But the declining influence of labour has affected its ability to act as a countervailing force in many countries. The financial crisis of 2008, the ensuing Great Recession, the austerity measures being imposed in many parts of the world, and the deregulation of labour laws and collective bargaining in Europe in the 2010s, are all manifestations of its weakening voice.

Minimum wages by definition ensure a minimum level of earnings for those at the bottom of the pay scale, and are an effective tool for compressing the wage distribution as well as lessening the incidence of low pay in both developed and developing countries.[1] According to the ILO, approximately 90 per cent of countries have minimum wages. There is a wide diversity in the world's minimum-wage systems, including their wage-setting processes, their scope, complexity and effectiveness, and their absolute and relative values (ILO, 2008).

Figure 44.2 **Components of disposable income, working-age population, mid-2000s, thirty OECD countries**

- Government transfers: 12%
- Capital income: 5%
- Self-employment income: 10%
- Wages: 73%

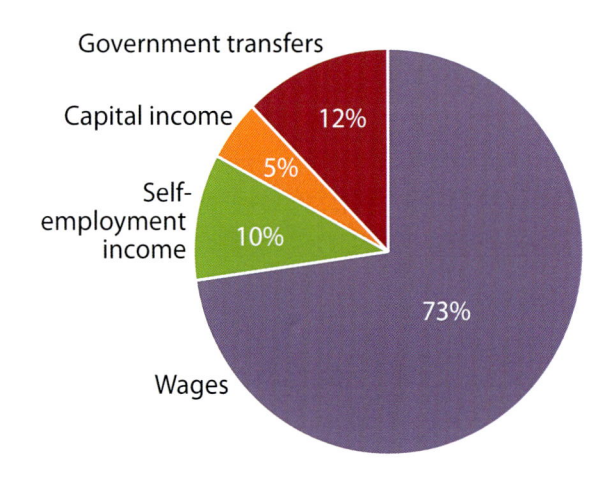

Source: OECD (2011, p. 230).

Minimum wages are particularly important in countries where collective bargaining is restricted to the firm level, as they ensure that all workers benefit from a wage floor. And even in developing countries where minimum wage laws are less enforced, empirical evidence demonstrates that minimum wages reduce inequality, in part due to 'lighthouse effects', whereby formal minimum wages provide a reference for bargaining among informal waged employees and their employers (Souza and Baltar, 1979).

Despite the benefit of minimum wages for equality, there has been considerable debate in the economics profession on their employment effects, specifically on whether raising the minimum wage leads to job losses, as the competitive labour market model suggests. Yet there exists substantial empirical evidence for negligible effects on employment, and sometimes for positive effects by encouraging workers to enter the labour market (Belser and Rani, 2015; World Bank, 2012). And at the macroeconomic level, higher minimum wages can stimulate consumption and aggregate demand. Nonetheless, minimum wages should not be set at a level that is too high, which promotes non-compliance, or at too low a level, which negates the effectiveness of this important policy tool.

The type of employment arrangement that a person works under also influences the pay and working conditions of the worker, including their sense of job and income security. The decline of the standard employment relationship, witnessed by the rise in temporary employment contracts, dependent self-employment, temporary agency work and other forms of subcontracted work, is just beginning to be understood (ILO, 2015b). Since the 1990s, temporary contracts have become a distinguishing feature of labour markets in Southern Europe, the Andean countries and parts of Asia. Temporary contracts entail significant wage penalties for individual workers. Moreover in countries with high shares of these contracts, such as Spain, where over a quarter of the labour force are on temporary contracts, workers are less likely to switch between fixed-term and indefinite contract jobs, and risk becoming trapped. This is problematic not just for the individual, but for the labour market as a whole. It inhibits investments in training which are important for improving productivity, and creates segmented labour markets, which constrains mobility and opportunities (ILO, 2015b).

Moreover, workers employed under temporary contracts often do not meet the requirements for receiving unemployment insurance benefits, and may not be covered by collective agreements.

Part-time work is another employment arrangement that has implications on inequality. Whether it is a source of inequality will depend largely on how it is regulated. In countries where the laws reflect the principle of equal treatment of part-time workers, wages and benefits will be on a pro rata basis. Moreover, some countries grant employees the right to switch into and out of part-time work, mitigating the risk of part-time jobs becoming a career trap. Under these conditions, part-time work can be an attractive option for workers who need to reconcile work with personal responsibilities, and who might not otherwise have participated in the labour market. But in some countries, unregulated part-time work is sometimes a strategy on the part of employers to evade paying social security contributions, health insurance or holiday pay, resulting in lower earnings, fewer training opportunities and poorer job quality. In developing countries, part-time work is common among informal, self-employed workers, at times reflecting a strategy for reconciling domestic responsibilities with work, but also reflecting insufficient work opportunities.

In countries with large informal economies, many workers have scant legal protection and poor access to social security. Institutions that regulate the workplace, such as the labour inspectorate and labour courts, as well as programmes to raise legal awareness among workers and employers, are needed to improve compliance with the law.

Accessing the labour market

Finally, institutions are needed to support access to the labour market for workers, especially for women, who typically shoulder the burden of care responsibilities. Public care services can facilitate women's ability to enter or remain in paid work, with consequences for both gender and income inequality. When care services are not provided publicly, workers are not able to enter the labour market, or have less flexibility, less choice and bargaining power when they do enter it. If they do enter, they might delegate their domestic responsibilities to other, usually female, members of the household, which explains in part the higher share of young females who are not in education, employment or training (NEET) in lower-income families.

Other institutions can also affect participation in the labour market, for example by ensuring that groups outside working age, such as adolescents and the elderly, have the option of not participating. There is a significant negative relationship between the coverage and benefit levels of pensions and labour force participation by the elderly.

Conclusion

As work is the source of most household income, the institutions that regulate work have important consequences for the distribution of income within a country. Over the past several decades in many countries around the world, there has been an increase in the pay of highly skilled workers along with a rise in the national share of income going to capital. In many countries, less-skilled workers have seen their wages and working conditions decline as unions have lost power, minimum wages have weakened and non-standard employment arrangements have proliferated.

Reversing the trend of increasing inequality, and ensuring just societies requires a wide range of policies, including explicit macroeconomic policies to support full employment, well-designed institutions that govern working arrangements, and social policies and public social services that support the working and non-working alike. There is no one-size-fits-all model; rather, policies should be designed to reflect the economic, social and institutional characteristics of the country concerned.

Acknowledgement

This text draws on Berg (ed.) (2015).

Note

1. See the two special editions of the *International Labour Review* on low-paid work in industrialized (Vol. 148, No. 4) and emerging economies (Vol. 151, No. 3).

Bibliography

Belser, P. and Rani, U. 2015. Minimum wages and inequality. J. Berg (ed.), *Labour Markets, Institutions and Inequality: Building Social Justice in the 21st Century*. Geneva and Cheltenham, UK, ILO and Edward Elgar, pp. 123–46.

Berg, J. (ed.). 2015. *Labour Markets, Institutions and Inequality: Building Social Justice in the 21st Century*. Geneva and Cheltenham, UK, ILO and Edward Elgar.

Hayter, S. 2015. Unions and collective bargaining. J. Berg (ed.), *Labour Markets, Institutions and Inequality: Building Social Justice in the 21st Century*. Geneva and Cheltenham, UK, ILO and Edward Elgar, pp. 95–122.

ILO. 2008. *Global Wage Report 2008/2009: Minimum Wages and Collective Bargaining, Towards Policy Coherence*. Geneva, ILO. *www.ilo.org/wcmsp5/groups/public/@dgreports/@dcomm/documents/publication/wcms_100786.pdf* (Accessed 19 February 2016.)

ILO. 2015*a*. Trends in collective bargaining coverage: stability, erosion or decline? Labour Relations and Collective Bargaining Issue Brief no. 1, October. Geneva, ILO. *www.ilo.org/wcmsp5/groups/public/---ed_protect/---protrav/---travail/documents/publication/wcms_409422.pdf* (Accessed 19 February 2016.)

ILO. 2015*b*. Non-standard forms of employment. Report for Discussion at the Meeting of Experts on Non-Standard Forms of Employment, Geneva, 16–19 February 2015. Geneva, ILO. *www.ilo.org/global/topics/employment-security/non-standard-employment/whatsnew/WCMS_336934/lang--en/index.htm* (Accessed 19 February 2016.)

Islam, I. and Kucera, D. 2014. *Beyond Macroeconomic Stability: Structural Transformation and Inclusive Development*. London, Palgrave Macmillan.

OECD. 2011. *Divided We Stand: Why Inequality Keeps Rising*. Paris, OECD.

Souza, P. and Baltar, P. 1979. Salário mínimo e taxa de salários no Brasil [The minimum wage and wage rates in Brazil]. *Pesquisa e Planejamento Econômico [Research and Economic Planning]*, Vol. 9, No. 3, pp. 629–60. *www.ppe.ipea.gov.br/index.php/ppe/article/viewFile/468/411* (Accessed 19 February 2016.)

World Bank. 2012. *World Development Report 2013: Jobs*. Washington DC, World Bank.

■ **Janine Berg** *(USA) is senior economist at the International Labour Organization, Geneva, Switzerland.*

45. Inequality and global social policy: policies, actors and strategies

Bob Deacon

This contribution briefly reviews the ways in which global processes of financialization, free trade and knowledge protection have been acting since the late 1970s to generate intra-national inequality and simultaneously deny national governments the autonomy to act to reduce them. It then reviews the ways in which potential reforms to global and regional social governance and global social policy might help reduce inequalities, both within and between countries. These include policies for more effective redistribution (for example global tax cooperation and global funds), more socially responsible regulation (in for example regional trade agreements) and strengthened access to social rights. Finally, the geopolitical obstacles to the implementation of these reforms are assessed and possible strategies to overcome them are discussed. The Sustainable Development Goals (SDGs), Agenda 2030 and the Addis Ababa Action Agenda (AAAA) are used to illustrate the discussion.

In the context of increased global economic interconnectedness, national social and economic policies alone cannot effectively address inequalities within and between countries. Existing global arrangements for economic and social governance prevent countries from having autonomy over some policy options that might increase equity. Global social policies that could contribute to the reduction of inequities are not always in place for various geopolitical reasons.

Competing advice on national social policy

The governance of the social at the global level is complex (Deacon, 2007, 2013a; Kaasch and Martens, 2015; Kaasch and Stubbs, 2014). A number of competing institutions help shape global social policy, through both policy advice to countries and constructing transnational economic and social policies for redistribution, regulation and rights. This competition between the International Monetary Fund (IMF), the World Bank, the UN Social Agencies and the Organisation for Economic Co-operation and Development (OECD) for the right to shape policy and its content passes for an effective system of international social governance.

The international non-governmental organization (INGO) community, transnational civil society movements and emerging club groupings, such as the G20, are also engaged. The struggle between the G77, which favour a greater role for the United Nations in global economic and social governance, and the European Union, the USA and other developed countries, which put more emphasis on the OECD, has generated a North–South stalemate, preventing the development of more effective institutions of global governance.

Existing global processes of financialization and free trade, combined paradoxically with the protection of intellectual property rights, often limit national governments' capacity to develop effective taxation and regulation policies to address inequality (George, 2015). Despite a short-lived interest in fiscal stimulus policies, the global financial crisis has led to austerity policies. The residual social policies that result are unable to counter structurally induced inequalities in most countries (McBride et al., 2015; Ortiz et. al., 2015).

The World Bank, the OECD and even the IMF increasingly regard widening inequities within countries as undesirable because of their negative impact on economic policy. This is a positive development. There is therefore some room for hope for the strand of global social policy that involves advice to governments on national social policies. Exemplifying this shift, the OECD argues that 'inequality hurts economic growth …. policies to reduce income inequalities should not only be pursued to improve social outcomes, but also to sustain long-term growth' (2014).

Competing institutions of global social governance

Stalemate at the United Nations?

Let me turn now to the strand of global social policy focused on transnational processes; to redistribution, social regulation and social rights policies; and to the global social governance institutions that might implement them. The SDGs, the associated Agenda 2030 (United Nations, 2015a) and the Finance for Development summit leading to the Addis Ababa Action Agenda (AAAA) (United Nations, 2015b) provide indications that global social policy and governance reform are undergoing only limited development. SDG 17, concerned with 'Strengthening the means of implementation', calls for better domestic resource mobilization, and for international support for improvements in domestic capacity for tax and other revenue collection. But as far as global redistribution is concerned, it simply repeats (17.2) the long-held aspiration that developed countries should provide 0.7 per cent of their GNI for official development assistance. Rather than tackling the issue of building a UN-based global tax authority, called for by the G77, or offering detailed reforms of the OECD's attempts to lessen the effectiveness of tax havens, the final document simply issues a vague call to 'mobilize additional resources for developing countries from multiple sources' (17.3) (see also Deacon, 2016). The AAAA also omits the G77 call for a UN-based tax authority.

On global social regulation, SDG 17 has even less to contribute. There is a general and unspecified call to 'promote a universal, rules-based, open, non-discriminatory multilateral trading system under the WTO (World Trade Organization)' (17.10). This call ignores the failure of the Doha round of trade talks and the bypassing of the WTO by intercontinental trade deals, which have been challenged for their potential impact on social provision. The contested issue of countries trading on their comparative advantage of low labour or social standards is not mentioned.

How the world might better realize global social rights is not mentioned in Agenda 2030. For example, it does not refer to the call by the Human Rights Special Rapporteurs on Food Security and Extreme Poverty to establish a global fund for social protection similar to the global fund for health (Schutte and Sepulveda, 2013).

So why is global social policy reform, and the strengthening of global social governance, in such a poor state, and what might be done? An explanation may be found in SDG Target 17.15, which calls for '[r]espect [for] each country's policy space and leadership to establish and implement policies for poverty eradication and sustainable development'. The Global South movement, forged in the struggle against the IMF and World Bank's imposition of a one-size-fits-all privatizing and residualizing social and economic policy in the 1980s and 1990s, strongly influenced the international and intergovernmental discussions around the SDGs and the AAAA. The priority of many governments and social movements in the Global South is to escape neoliberal globalization, which they perceive as Northern-driven. This makes it difficult for them to come together with progressive forces and countries in the Global North to fashion a new, socially just redistributive and regulatory global economic and social policy, with stronger institutions for global social governance. The call for a global tax authority is perhaps one exception to the Southern countries' demand for increased sovereignty. This does not mean that the conflict is only North–South. It is also about the power of global capital and global labour. The International Trade Union Confederation (ITUC) (2015) argued that 'the Addis Ababa Action Agenda (AAAA) is empty of ambition and achieves little in terms of identifiable and concrete commitment, especially in the areas of international cooperation on tax, financial, trade and systemic issues'.

Progress at the G20 and in world regions?

Is there a more optimistic story? Some suggest the G20 is central to a more positive assessment. Jiejin Zhu (2016) argues that the G20 is:

> *in transition from a short-term crisis institution to long-term steering institution, adopting a new 'G20 + established international organization' governance approach. In this approach, the main role of the G20 is to set the agenda and build political consensus for global economic governance. The established international organization provides the technical support and facilitates proposal implementation.*

Colin Bradford (2015) of the Brookings Institution has suggested that the task of implementing the SDGs falls to the G20. I have noted the G20's new role in working with the ILO to establish the Social Protection Inter Agency Cooperation Board (SPIAC-B), jointly chaired by the World Bank and ILO (Deacon, 2013b). Kirton and colleagues (2015, p. 112) note the G20's gradually increased role in the global governance of social policy, although its capacity to progress change is hindered by its lack of a permanent secretariat. The G20 meeting in Australia:

> *set up a 2-year tax reform program under the auspices of the OECD that would include several new requirements: (a) multinational disclosures to tax offices must detail their global activities country by country, (b) tougher rules so that digital multinationals will not be able to claim they are not operating in a country if they do not have a substantial number of employees located there, and (c) countries are to develop cross-border policies to harmonize tax breaks. (Bowers, 2015)*

Despite the European Union's current travails, the regional level of governance is also regarded as a policy space where cross-border redistribution, regulation and rights might be advanced to counter fundamentalist neoliberal free trade and financialization. Assessing the combination of the SDGs, Agenda 2030 and the AAAA from this standpoint, Yeates (2015) suggests that 'there are three principal conceptions of regional governance and policy instruments embedded in these frameworks'. These are regional fora for policy sharing, regional standard setting and regional resource mobilization and allocation.

Given the relative decline of the WTO, trade deals are increasingly inter-regional. Consequently, cross-border social regulations to help reduce inequities could also be discussed at the inter-regional level. Taking the Transatlantic Trade and Investment Partnership (TTIP) deal between the USA and the European Union as an example, De Ville and Siles-Brugge (2016, p. 138) find that the suggested Investor State Disputes Settlement processes within this deal threaten social standards. They also argue that in principle, the agreement could 'eliminate regulatory differences by consistently harmonising upwards. They [the USA and European Union] could also levy taxes at the border that would level the playing field in social, environmental and other areas not only among themselves but with the rest of the world.' They acknowledge that for this to happen, there would need to be a greater civil society push within the USA. In other words, they argue that the NGO lobby should change the terms of the debate so that 'trade policy becomes an instrument to achieve other policy goals' (De Ville and Siles-Brugge, 2015, p. 140). This suggests a return in effect to the WTO, to the global labour standards debate and to the defeated 'social clause' argument, but at the inter-regional level. Certain civil society actors from the Global South might, however, regard this argument as European social protectionism once again.

Conclusion

In sum, widening global inequities require action at the national and supranational level, as well as at the global and world regional levels. Policy instruments and governance arrangements to achieve this are easy to imagine. Regarding international organizations' advice to countries on overcoming inequality, there is an increased global policy synergy on strengthening tax capacity. At the transnational level, negotiating with global business and capital, as well as overcoming historically generated North–South differences about which agencies should be authorized to address the issues, is more difficult. This issue should be the strategic concern of all social movements and of all global policy entrepreneurs concerned with reducing world inequality.

Bibliography

Bowers, S. 2015. OECD hopes tax reforms will end era of aggressive avoidance. *Guardian*, 5 October. *www.theguardian.com/business/2015/oct/05/oecd-hopes-reforms-will-end-era-of-aggressive-taxavoidance* (Accessed 11 June 2016.)

Bracht, C. 2015. G20 governance of social policy: social protection, employment and education. Toronto, Canada, G20 Information Centre, University of Toronto. *www.g20.utoronto.ca/analysis/151113-bracht.html* (Accessed 23 November 2015.)

Bradford, C. 2015. Implementing the Post 2015 Agenda. Blog, Brookings Institution. *www.brookings.edu/blogs/up-front/posts/2015/09/14-implementing-post-2015-agenda-bradford* (Accessed 23 November 2015.)

De Ville, F. and Siles-Brugge, G. 2015. *The Truth about the Transatlantic Trade and Investment Partnership,* Cambridge, Polity.

Deacon, B. 2007. *Global Social Policy and Governance.* London, Sage

Deacon, B. 2013a. *Global Social Policy in the Making.* Bristol, Policy Press.

Deacon, B. 2013b. The social protection floor and global social governance: towards policy synergy and co-operation between international organisations. *International Social Security Review,* Vol. 66, No. 3–4, pp. 45–68.

Deacon, B. 2016. Assessing the SDGs from the standpoint of global social governance. *Journal of International and Comparative Social Policy,* No. 32, Vol. 2.

George. S. 2015. *Shadow Sovereigns: How Global Corporations are Seizing Power.* Cambridge, Polity.

ITUC. 2015. Trade Union reaction to the Addis Ababa Action Agenda (AAAA) on Financing for Development (FFD3). *www.ituc-csi.org/IMG/pdf/trade_unions_reaction_to_ffd3_action_agenda_final.pdf* (Accessed 23 November 2015.)

Kaasch, A. and Martens, K. 2015. *Actors and Agency in Global Social Governance.* Oxford, Oxford University Press.

Kaasch, A. and Stubbs, P. 2014. *Transformations in Global and Regional Social Policies.* Basingstoke, Palgrave Macmillan.

Kirton, J., Kulik, J. and Bracht, C. 2015. G20 social policy governance. A. Kaasch and K. Martens (eds), *Actors and Agency in Global Social Governance.* Oxford, Oxford University Press.

McBride, S., Mahon, R. and Boychuk, G. 2015. *After '08: Social Policy and the Global Financial Crisis,* Vancouver, UBC Press.

OECD. 2014. Inequality hurts economic growth, finds OECD research. *www.oecd.org/newsroom/inequality-hurts-economic-growth.htm* (Accessed 11 June 2016.)

Ortiz, I., Cummins, M., Capaldo, J. and Karunanethy, K. 2015. *The Decade of Adjustment: A Review of Austerity Trends 2010–2020 in 187 Countries.* Geneva, ILO.

Schutte, O. and Sepulveda M. 2013. Underwriting the poor: a global fund for social protection. Briefing Note no. 7. Geneva, Human Rights Council, UNHCR.

United Nations. 2015a. *Transforming Our World: The 2030 Agenda for Sustainable Development.* New York, United Nations.

United Nations. 2015b. *Addis Ababa Action Agenda (AAAA).* New York, United Nations.

Yeates, N. 2015. Southern regionalisms, global agendas. Background paper for international conference of the PRARI project, December. Open University, UK.

Zhu, J. 2016. G20 institutional transition and global tax governance. *Pacific Review,* No. 29, Vol. 2.

■ **Bob Deacon** (UK) *is professor emeritus in international social policy at the University of Sheffield, UK and honorary professor of global social policy at the University of York, UK. He was founding editor of the journal* Global Social Policy, *author of several books on the subject, and has advised many UN and other international organizations on the subject of global social policy.*

46. The decline and recent uptick of income inequality in Latin America, 2002–13

Giovanni Andrea Cornia

This contribution discusses the exogenous and policy factors behind the large decline in income inequality recorded in Latin America in the 2000s. In particular, it relates the adoption of progressive policies to the election of left-of-centre regimes in most of the region. Finally, it discusses whether such a policy model is sustainable in a world affected by sluggish growth, falling terms of trade, some domestic policy mistakes, and a possible vanishing of middle-class support for the policy model of the 2000s.

Inequality trends during the last thirty years

The colonial origins of the high income inequality that has afflicted Latin America for centuries have been well analysed by Engerman and Sokoloff (2005). These authors argue that the high land, assets and power concentration inherited from the colonial era led to the development of institutions which perpetuated well into the post-Second World War period the privileges of a small agrarian and commercial oligarchy. This path-dependent situation continued until the last quarter of the twentieth century, a period during which Latin America suffered from slow growth, frequent financial crises and a Gini rise from 48.9 in the early 1980s to 54.1 in 2002 (Figure 46.1).

Figure 46.1 **Trend in the average regional Gini index, early 1980s to 2012**

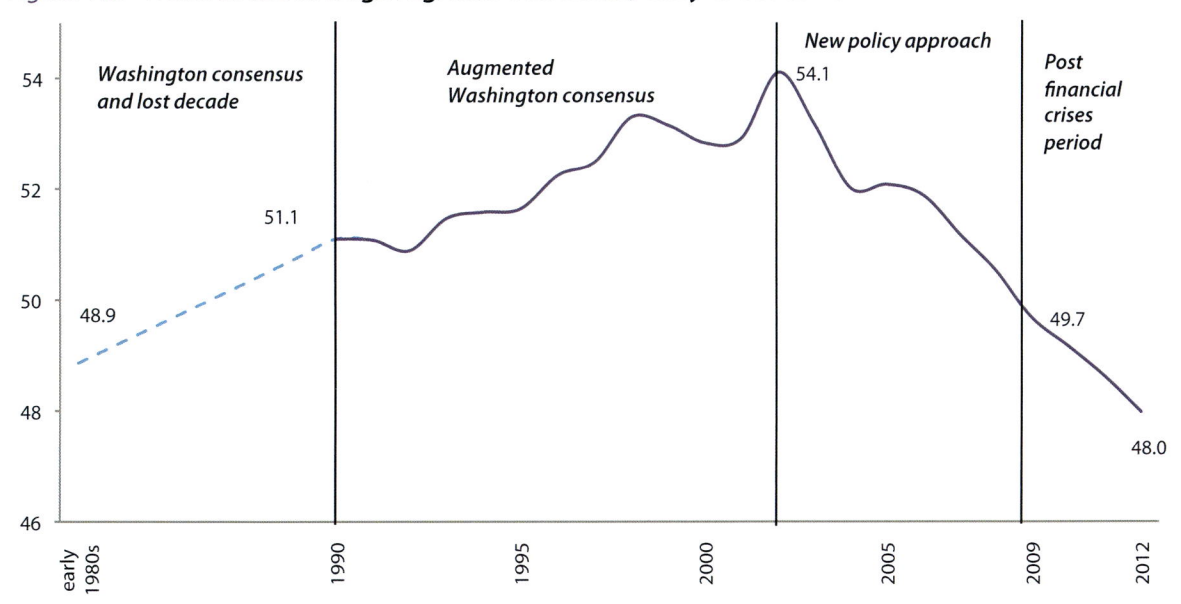

Note: The trend for 1990–06 covers eighteen countries. That for 2006–12 covers fifteen countries, as it excludes Venezuela, Guatemala and Nicaragua, for which there are no data. Source: author's elaboration on Cornia (2014) and Center for Distributional, Labor and Social Studies (CEDLAS) data.

Things changed significantly in the 2000s. After the turn of the century, the region enhanced its growth performance, reduced inequality and improved macroeconomic stability. The most striking change was a 6.1 point Gini decline over 2003–12, which more than offset in only ten years its increase of the two prior decades (*Figure 46.1*). The largest falls (twelve points) were recorded in Argentina and Brazil, while smaller or no gains were registered in conflict-affected countries (Colombia and Mexico) and Central America. It is important to underscore that the Latin American inequality fall stands out. During the same period the OECD nations, China, South Asia and the mining economies of sub-Saharan Africa recorded sizeable Gini rises (Cornia and Martorano, 2012).

Drivers of the recent inequality decline

What explains the inequality decline observed between 2002 and 2012? A decomposition of the Gini fall over 2002–10 for Chile, Ecuador, El Salvador, Honduras, Mexico and Uruguay shows that it was due (in order of importance) to a drop in the skilled–unskilled wage ratio, an increase in social transfers, and a lower concentration of capital incomes. In other economies, a fall in the urban–rural wage gap and increasingly better distributed remittances were also important (Cornia, 2014). The underlying causes of such changes are discussed below.

Impact of global economic conditions

Some have argued that the inequality decline of the 2000s was due to 'luck', in the sense of an improvement in global economic conditions. For sure, better terms of trade and growing remittances produced beneficial effects on growth. Furthermore, between 2002 and 2008 the region experienced yearly portfolio inflows amounting to 2.4 per cent of its GDP. Yet given the high concentration of assets in the export sector and the selective access to finance prevailing in the region, these improvements in external conditions did not reduce inequality. Instead they generated, all other things being unchanged, an un-equalizing effect on the distribution of market income. Such shocks also generated a positive income effect and relaxed the balance of payments constraint to growth. However, faster growth in itself is no guarantee of falling inequality, as is shown by the recent experience of China and India. In fact, in Latin America a more favourable global environment would not have reduced inequality in the absence of the policy changes discussed below. Regression analysis shows that until 2002 improvements in terms of trade and export volumes did not reduce inequality, while since then they have, thanks – among other factors – to the introduction of redistributive institutions financed by export proceeds.

Figure 46.2 **Trends in ideological orientation of eighteen Latin American governments, 1990–2013**

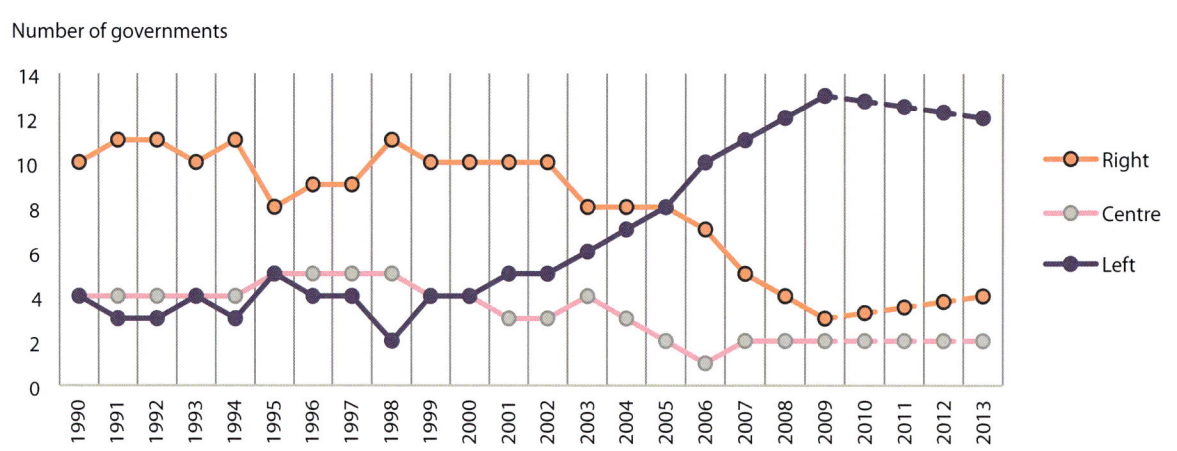

Source: Cornia (2014), updated to 2013.

New policy approaches

During the last twenty years the region experienced a return to and consolidation of democracy, and from the late 1990s a sudden shift in political orientation towards centre-left regimes,[1] whose number rose from two in 1998 to thirteen in 2009 (*Figure 46.2*). As suggested by the Latino Barometro, a major factor in this unprecedented turnaround was growing frustration with the sluggish growth, rising unemployment, and informalization of the economy brought about by the Washington consensus policies of the 1980s and 1990s.

The left turn of the 2000s was the result of retrospective economic voting and rising demand for a more active role of the state in the provision of public services and welfare, rather than marking an ideological realignment of the electorate. It was also the result of a reorganization of the left. As noted by Panizza (2005), the political coalitions supporting these new regimes included organizations of the urban and rural poor, unemployed, informal sector workers, indigenous groups and local communities that replaced the trade unions and traditional left parties at the forefront of social mobilization. The new coalitions also included parts of business and the middle class that had traditionally voted for conservative parties, but which switched allegiance after experiencing a decline in the level and share of their income.

As underscored by the recent debate, the middle class is seen as a source of equitable growth and political stability. To assess its incentives to back up the left regimes, we defined the middle class as the sixth to ninth income deciles. In this regard, the sluggish and unequal growth of 1990–2002 affected not only the low-income group (deciles 1 to 5) but also the middle class, which in six out of thirteen countries analysed in Cornia (2012) experienced the largest drop in income share. Symmetrically, the later gains of 2002–09 also benefited the middle class, if less markedly.

Policies adopted by the centre-left regimes

The new policy approach was inspired by the European social-democratic model, and is broadly consistent with the 'redistribution with growth' paradigm. In contrast, the radical-left policies are more in line with the 'redistribution before growth' paradigm that also emphasizes asset redistribution.

The main components of the social-democratic package are listed below, starting from those which had the greatest inequality impact.

First, a key role was played by an increase in public expenditure on education, which had already started in the 1990s, but which accelerated in the 2000s. The net effect was a massive increase in secondary enrolments, especially among the children of the poor. The resulting increase in the supply of skilled workers improved the distribution of human capital and reduced the skilled/unskilled wage ratio. The latter was also affected by a drop in the supply of unskilled workers (because of a prior slowdown of population growth), the educational upgrading of uneducated workers, a drop in the demand for skilled workers, a rise in that for unskilled workers, and changes in labour policies.

Next, during the 2000s, tax policy placed more emphasis on revenue collection, reduced exemptions, progressive taxation, reduced excise duties, and indirect taxes on luxuries. As a result, the regional tax/GDP ratio rose by 3.5 points over 2003–08. The surge in commodity prices contributed to its increase in six oil and metals exporters, but the revenue rise had begun before the commodity boom and also involved non-commodity exporters. These changes helped improve the progressivity of taxation, while higher revenues permitted the expansion of social assistance and education in a non-inflationary way.

Social assistance expenditure started to rise in the 1990s but accelerated its upward trend in the 2000s. All governments introduced measures to complement the uneven coverage of social insurance. These programmes absorbed less than 1 per cent of GDP, covered a large share of the target population, and benefited new political constituencies such as the urban and rural poor. Such programmes included cash transfers aimed at reducing child poverty and ensuring that children remain in school and have access to health services and proper nutrition (such as Brazil's famous Bolsa Familia). In addition, the centre-left regimes of Argentina, Bolivia, Brazil, Chile and Costa Rica introduced a progressive non-contributory social pension costing 0.18–1.3 per cent of GDP.

Labour policy explicitly addressed the problems inherited from the two previous decades: unemployment, job informalization, falling unskilled and minimum wages, and declining social security coverage. Most centre-left governments and a few conservative ones decreed hikes in minimum wages which further improved wage distribution.

These policies could not have been sustained in the absence of prudent and progressive macroeconomic policies that avoided the unequalizing effects of past crises. These included:

- Foreign macroeconomic policy aimed at reducing vulnerability to external shocks. Governments avoided the large balance of payments deficits and debt accumulation of the past by raising tax/GDP ratios and reducing dependence on foreign finance. With the exception of Brazil and Venezuela, they abandoned fixed pegs[2] in favour of more flexible exchange rate regimes, and encouraged central banks to accumulate reserves, which quadrupled between 2002 and 2010 for the region as a whole (ECLAC, 2014). Meanwhile, the region's gross foreign debt was cut in half.

- Domestic macroeconomic policy avoided the traditional procyclical fiscal and monetary biases of the past. Deficits were reduced below 1 per cent of GDP (ECLAC, 2014), and some governments created stabilization funds to draw upon when there were revenue shortfalls. There were also measures to control money supply, reduce interest rates, and expand lending by public banks in periods of crisis. The financial sector was re-regulated to avoid a repeat of the banking crises triggered by the deregulation of the 1980s. As a result, and unlike other regions, Latin America did not experience any financial crisis, even after the 2009 recession.

The 2013 break in the declining inequality trend

The US and EU financial crises, and the slowdown of East Asian growth, led to a fall in remittances, exports and commodity prices which caused a 2 per cent contraction of Latin American GDP in 2009, and a growth decline from 5 per cent over 2002–8 to 3 per cent over 2010–14 (ECLAC, 2014). Yet inequality continued to decline until 2012 (*Figure 46.1*). In 2013 inequality fell moderately in six countries but rose in nine, so that the regional Gini rose by 0.2 points (or by 0.55 if Honduras's exceptional 4.1 Gini drop is excluded). While the downward trend in inequality had not yet deviated substantially from its prior direction, a slow-growing world economy and domestic policy mistakes might have made it more difficult to continue lowering it. The possible decline of middle-class support for centre-left regimes might also threaten the continuation of redistributive policies.

Until 2013, the centre-left regimes continued to dominate the political scene (*Figure 46.2*), and until 2013–14 there were no signs that the centre-left policy package was going to be abandoned. However, policy mistakes, and the political choice to focus redistribution mainly on the poor (a key constituency of centre-left regimes) during the years of slow growth and stagnant revenue may have alienated the support of the middle class. This conjecture is supported by data showing that in countries affected by political tensions, the inequality decline of 2010–13 benefited only the low-income group. As discussed next in the case of Brazil, the lack of inequality gains by the middle class – which during these three years had borne a heavy tax burden to finance redistribution, without receiving in exchange adequate services and jobs – eroded its support for the centre-left regimes.

The 2013 Latino Barometro survey captures well the dissatisfaction emerging in several centre-left countries – in particular in Argentina, Brazil, Venezuela, Mexico, Paraguay and El Salvador – that experienced a drop of the income share of the middle class over 2010–13, a Gini rise in 2013, and in some cases an electoral reversal in 2015.

Brazil offers a good illustration of the relation between worsening economic conditions, policy mistakes, the weakening of distributive policies and the loss of middle-class support. As noted by Saad-Filho (2015), in 2015 hundreds of thousands of the middle class took to the streets to protest against their centre-left government. For a time, its policies had delivered growth, jobs, minimum wages and social transfers that reduced inequality. The commodity boom of 2003–08 sustained redistribution, a small expansion of infrastructure and the creation of 21 million low-wage jobs in services. The subsequent reduction in inequality was, however, hampered by global stagnation and a conservative macro policy that precluded fiscal expansion, industrial restructuring and devaluation of the reais. Because of its overvaluation, 4.5 million middle-class manufacturing jobs were lost in the 2000s, while urban infrastructure was neglected (Saad-Filho, 2015). The government did not drop its redistributive targets, but found it more difficult to finance them in a situation of falling commodity prices, zero growth and weakening middle-class support. Meanwhile, insufficient past investment in infrastructure led to a worsening of transport, water and health services which affected the middle class, who had paid substantial taxes during the golden years.

Conclusions: limitations of the new policy approach

Despite recent improvements, Latin America remains the region with the highest inequality in the world, paralleled only by Southern Africa. The battle for a more egalitarian society needs therefore to continue. In much of the region – and particularly in Central America and the Andean countries – the distributive gains of 2002–12 can be furthered by intensifying recent educational, tax, public expenditure, labour and macroeconomic reforms. Across the region, additional, if politically difficult, reforms should be tried to tackle the region's inheritance of unequal access to land, credit and tertiary education, and its low level of domestic savings. Inability to deal with these problems, if only in part, may prevent future inequality declines once the social-democratic reforms have run their course.

Finally, the 2008 crisis brought to the fore the limitations of the region's foreign-financed, export-led growth strategy introduced by the liberalization of the 1980s and 1990s. These reforms were not overturned in the 2000s. In years of low world growth, such a strategy has once more underscored the dependent nature of the Latin American economy. Even during the years of rapid growth, the region experienced large-scale deindustrialization which sacrificed middle-class jobs, led to the 're-primarization' of exports and output (Ocampo, 2012), and exposed the region to the risk of unstable terms of trade and sudden stops in capital inflows. Reversing the deindustrialization of the past three decades is a key policy challenge with important implications in terms of middle-class support for progressive policies. Such a challenge may be tackled with open-economy industrial policies that support labour-intensive manufacturing and services by means of competitive exchange rates, production support measures, technological upgrading, public–private partnerships to enter new sectors, regional cooperation, and a rebalancing of trade asymmetries with China.

Acknowledgement

This work is an author's update of Cornia (2014) based on recent data.

Notes

1. Some of them are social-democratic, as in Chile, Uruguay and Brazil. In turn, Venezuela, Bolivia and Nicaragua followed a radical populist approach which also entailed a redistribution of assets. The largest yearly Gini drops were recorded by the social-democratic regimes (0.96 Gini points), followed by radical and centrist regimes (both around 0.50).

2. In pegged exchange rate systems a country will fix ('peg') its currency to a major currency such as the US dollar, or to a basket of currencies.

Bibliography

Cornia, G. A. 2012. Inequality trends and their determinants: Latin America over 1990–2010. Working Paper no. 9. Helsinki, UNU-WIDER. https://www.wider.unu.edu/publication/inequality-trends-and-their-determinants (Accessed 1 February 2016.)

Cornia, G. A. (ed.). 2014. *Falling Inequality in Latin America Policy Changes and Lessons*. Oxford, Oxford University Press.

Cornia, G. A. and Martorano, B. 2012. Development policies and income inequality in selected developing regions, 1980–2010. Discussion Paper 210. Geneva, UNCTAD. http://unctad.org/en/PublicationsLibrary/osgdp20124_en.pdf (Accessed 1 February 2016.)

ECLAC (UN Economic Commission for Latin America and the Caribbean). 2014. *Preliminary Balance of the Latin American Economy*. Santiago, ECLAC.

Engerman, S. L. and Sokoloff, K. L. 2005. Colonialism, inequality and long run paths of development. Working Paper 11057. Cambridge, Mass., National Bureau of Economic Research. www.nber.org/papers/w11057 (Accessed 1 February 2016.)

Ocampo, J. A. 2012. The development implications of external integration in Latin America. Working Paper 48/2012. Helsinki, UNU/WIDER. https://www.wider.unu.edu/publication/development-implications-external-integration-latin-america (Accessed 1 February 2016.)

Panizza, F. E. 2005. Unarmed utopia revisited: the resurgence of left-of-centre politics in Latin America. *Political Studies*, Vol. 53, No. 4, pp. 716–34. http://onlinelibrary.wiley.com/doi/10.1111/j.1467-9248.2005.00553.x/abstract (Accessed 1 February 2016.)

Saad-Filho, A. 2015. A critical review of Brazil's recent economic policies. *Development Viewpoints*, No. 84. London, Centre for Development Policy Research, School of Oriental and African Studies. https://www.soas.ac.uk/cdpr/publications/brazil-in-focus/file101875.pdf (Accessed 1 February 2016.)

■ *Giovanni Andrea Cornia (Italy) has taught development economics at the University of Florence since 2000. Before that, he was the director of WIDER (Helsinki) and chief economist of UNICEF in New York. He has also served in various research capacities in other international agencies and the private sector. He has edited and partly written sixteen books and published ninety journal articles and working papers on growth, macroeconomics, political economy, inequality, poverty, mortality and child well-being.*

47. Taxation and inequality: lessons from Latin America

Juan Carlos Gómez Sabaíni, Bruno Martorano and Dalmiro Morán

Latin American policy-makers and society have become increasingly aware of the problems caused by inequality. Although this phenomenon has distant colonial origins and prevails thanks to the resistance of traditional and new elites, the consolidation of democracy during the 1990s and 2000s has encouraged several governments to correct some of these problems by promoting moderate fiscal reforms. Since most studies have focused on the distributive impact of social expenditure and income transfers, this contribution aims to complement these analyses by examining how favourable changes in taxation have contributed to the recent decline in income inequality observed throughout the region.

Introduction

Taxation is considered a useful policy tool, not only to mobilize revenue and to ensure macroeconomic stabilization, but also to promote redistribution. Whether or not this is true for developed countries, the possibility of using taxation to reduce inequality was historically believed to be both conceptually and practically more difficult for developing countries because of their weak administration and their large informal sectors. In addition, the historically fragile social contract between citizens and the state, the low credibility of political institutions, and their strong ties with the economic elite were considered further obstacles to the promotion of equality via taxation in these countries. There was a broad consensus that redistribution in developing nations could be achieved only by action on the public expenditure side.

Yet the past decade has witnessed some interesting lessons from Latin America. From the early 2000s to the present, income inequality has decreased in this region by around five Gini points (Cornia, 2014). Among other factors, taxation has played an important role thanks to the growing emphasis placed by governments on tax progressivity.[1] Although each context is different and has specific peculiarities, this contribution reviews the recent experience of Latin America, and argues that taxation could contribute to reducing inequalities in developing countries.

Taxation during the Washington consensus era (1980s and 1990s)

In the early 1980s, tax design in Latin American countries was affected by recommendations derived from neoliberal theory. In this setting, governments started to pay more attention to economic efficiency and simplicity, and less to equity. As part of this strategy, trade taxes were sharply reduced and replaced by value added tax (VAT) and other consumption taxes. Neoliberal tax reforms also promoted a simplification of personal income tax (PIT) because, as it was argued, of its negative effects on incentives, labour supply and investment. Moreover, the maximum marginal rates of PIT and corporate income tax (CIT) were reduced to between 30 and 40 per cent, and there were some extreme cases, such as Uruguay in 1974 and Paraguay in 1992, where PIT was abolished.

These tax policies failed to achieve their intended aims. The average tax/GDP ratio declined during the 1980s, reached a minimum close to 13 per cent by 1990 and took more than a decade to recover to its previous level of 15–16 per cent at the beginning of the 2000s. Tax policy changes also contributed to macroeconomic instability, which negatively affected economic growth. Finally, neoliberal reforms fuelled income inequality in a region which is historically considered among the most unequal in the world.

The great tax transformation (2000 onward)

The poor results of these neoliberal reforms, and the process of democratic consolidation, promoted important social and political changes. The growing social demand for redistribution provoked a shift in political preferences toward left parties, while a widespread sense of social responsibility among the middle class laid the foundations for a new social contract. In this framework, the new elected governments implemented a pragmatic set of policies aiming at achieving more inclusive growth. Accordingly, taxation reverted to its original role of boosting development, reducing volatility and promoting redistribution.

Latin American countries introduced a series of reforms aimed at strengthening and modernizing their tax systems, especially focused on income taxation. First, governments eliminated or reduced a long list of exemptions, deductions and tax holidays which had been found to cause large revenue losses and to have a regressive effect on income distribution. Furthermore, some countries incorporated a PIT dual system which combines a progressive tax schedule for labour-based income and a flat tax rate for capital income. Uruguay was the pioneer in the region in 2007; Peru and some Central American countries have followed a similar strategy since 2009. In more recent years, many countries continued to reform different aspects of income taxation, for example Colombia, Chile and Venezuela.

As a complement to these measures, new forms of taxation were introduced. The clearest example of this approach was the adoption and reform of simplified taxation regimes for the small business sector in almost all countries. In addition, some governments introduced a tax on financial transactions. In order to lower the cost of tax collection and reduce widespread tax evasion, most countries promoted further simplification of tax administration and the creation of semi-autonomous revenue authorities.

As a consequence, the average tax revenue/GDP ratio has risen steadily since the early 2000s, reaching one of its highest historical levels in 2008. After a halt in 2009 due to the global financial crisis, it has resumed a strong upward trend and continued to rise up to a level close to 21 per cent of GDP. Beyond that, these reforms have generated important consequences for tax composition. Indirect taxes still represent the bulk of total tax revenues, in marked contrast to the position in developed countries (*Table 47.1*). Yet taxes on income, profits and capital gains have grown more than other forms of taxation.

However, these general results hide complex regional diversity. Tax revenue in Brazil and Argentina exceeds 30 per cent of GDP, while in most Andean and Central American economies this ratio remains between 13 and 18 per cent of GDP. Furthermore some countries, including Bolivia, Chile, Peru and Venezuela, are endowed with large stocks of natural resources capable of generating substantial additional fiscal revenues.

Table 47.1 **Tax composition evolution in Latin American and OECD countries**

	Year	Taxes on income, profits and capital gains	Taxes on property	Taxes on sales	Excises	Taxes on international trade	Other taxes	Total
Latin America	1991	20.7	4.0	37.9	17.6	17.6	2.1	100
	2001	22.8	5.0	46.3	14.1	10.9	0.9	100
	2011	32.6	3.9	44.2	10.5	7.4	1.5	100
	Variation	57.3	-2.6	16.4	-40.5	-58.3	-29.0	
OECD	1991	50.9	7.5	24.8	12.5	2.8	1.5	100
	2001	50.1	7.4	28.0	12.4	0.9	1.2	100
	2011	49.5	8.0	29.2	11.6	0.6	1.1	100
	Variation	-2.8	7.3	17.8	-7.2	-77.5	-30.3	

Source: Authors' elaboration on ICTD (n.d.).

Changes in tax incidence

These reforms also generated interesting results for income distribution. Cornia and colleagues (2011) have shown that a greater reliance on direct taxes and the reduction in excise duties have promoted the redistributive role of taxation. The Gini coefficient of the distribution of household income has improved on average by 0.4–0.8 points. As pointed out by Gómez Sabaíni and Morán (2014), some recent studies suggest a general but not uniform trend where taxation has become more progressive (or less regressive) in most Latin American countries during the 2000s.

For instance, according to Cruces and Gasparini (2008), the tax system in Argentina became increasingly regressive in the 1990s, but the situation changed after the 2001 crisis. This was mostly due to the introduction of export duties, which have a very progressive redistributive effect.[2] In a similar way, Jorratt (2010) found that the Chilean tax system has become slightly progressive in the past decade, contradicting the results of previous studies that had shown it to be regressive.

Despite some methodological differences, this encouraging change might be attributed to the greater share of progressive income tax, which overcompensates for the regressivity of other taxes, especially VAT and excise duties. In Uruguay, the 2007 tax reform explicitly aimed to improve tax equity, and according to Burdín and colleagues (2014) it has achieved that objective. Martorano (2014) has shown that the new tax on income from employment has improved tax progressivity and lowered inequality by two Gini points.

Table 47.2 summarizes the estimated Reynolds–Smolensky (RS) indices – a commonly used measure of redistribution[3] – in a large body of available tax incidence studies for most Latin American countries, and shows how they have changed from the 1980s and 1990s to the present. Since these results rely on different methodologies and statistical assumptions, they are not strictly comparable. However, it can be observed that in all cases the RS indices turn positive or less negative. This could cautiously be interpreted as a slight but clear improvement in progressivity, caused by the redistributive power of taxation throughout the region.

Table 47.2 **Change in RS indices for taxes in selected Latin American countries**

Country	Washington consensus era Year	Washington consensus era RS	The great tax transformation era Year	The great tax transformation era RS
Argentina	1997	-0.020	2008	0.004
Bolivia[4]	2000	-0.011	2009	-0.007
Brazil	1999	-0.007	2009	0.016
Chile	1996	-0.008	2009	0.021
Costa Rica	1988	-0.010	2004	0.012
Ecuador	1998	-0.007	2003	0.007
El Salvador	2000	-0.014	2006	-0.008
Guatemala	2000	-0.008	2006	0.012
Honduras	2000	-0.028	2005	-0.001
Mexico	1989	-0.044	2010	0.017
Nicaragua	1998	-0.052	2001	0.002
Panama	2000	0.000	2003	0.009
Peru	2000	-0.008	2009	0.011
Uruguay	1996	-0.002	2011	0.020

Source: Authors' elaboration on the basis of Cornia et al. (2011) and Lustig (2015). Data for Argentina (2008) corresponds to Gómez Sabaíni and Morán (2014), Bolivia (2009) is from ECLAC and IEF (2014), and Uruguay (2011) is from Burdín et al. (2014).

Taxation and social spending

Taxation could also influence inequality in an indirect way by mobilizing resources to support social expenditure. And indeed, growing tax revenues have allowed Latin American countries to reform and improve their social protection systems. Almost all governments have introduced well-targeted conditional cash transfer programmes (such as the Bolsa Familia in Brazil and Oportunidades in Mexico) which are able to reach the most vulnerable families, more than 130 million people in 2013. In addition, new social pension schemes were implemented almost everywhere (for instance, Bono Solidario in Bolivia and Previdencia Rural in Brazil), extending protection to about 17 million people (in 2013) not previously covered by social insurance (Robles et al., 2015). Governments also enjoyed the necessary fiscal space needed to provide new cash transfers (such as Bono de Apoyo a la Familia in Chile) or to extend existing tools (such as the Programa de Apoyo Alimentario in Mexico) during the recent economic crisis. These measures have helped to partly overcome the problem of a truncated welfare system that has characterized the region (Lindert et al., 2006), and have helped to promote equity (Azevedo et al., 2013).

Conclusion and recommendations

Despite a large number of reforms, the tax system still shows structural weaknesses in several Latin American countries. Tax revenue is low, especially in Central America, limiting the redistributive capacity of fiscal policy. The contribution of PIT is still limited by the low level of maximum marginal tax rates; the narrowness of the tax base because of different tax treatment for income from different sources (for example, capital-based income may be taxed at lower rates than labour income); and high levels of evasion, particularly of income tax. A recent paper by ECLAC and IEF (2014) showed that there is room to expand the redistributive capacity of tax systems by reducing tax exemptions or by increasing the effective top tax rate. The additional revenue could be redistributed to the lower social classes, for example through cash transfer programmes.

However, Latin American countries have made extraordinary progress over the past decade. In the 1980s and 1990s taxation had a modest or even regressive effect on income distribution, while in the 2000s policy changes have contributed to promoting tax progressivity and redistribution through the tax system. Although each context is different and has specific peculiarities, the experience of Latin American countries provides important lessons. First, taxation could contribute to reducing inequalities in developing countries. Second, there is reason to believe that taxation could conciliate the goals of equality and efficiency as seen, for example, in Uruguay. Last, technological innovation presents a big opportunity for developing countries to improve the work and capacity of their public administration.

Notes

1. A progressive tax is a one in which the tax rate increases as the taxable amount increases. The opposite of a progressive tax is a regressive tax.

2. Progressivity and redistributive impact are different concepts. While the former refers to a greater tax burden as the taxable amount rises, the latter is associated with changes in income distribution once the effect of taxation is taken into account, which is finally related to the effective amount of tax revenue generated by a tax or an entire tax system.

3. The RS index measures the redistributive capacity of taxes. It arises from the comparison of the Gini index (for income distribution) before taxes and the concentration coefficient of taxes (also known as 'quasi-Gini') after their application. A positive value of this index indicates that taxes reduce inequality. A negative value of this index means that taxes increase inequality.

4. Data for Bolivia (2009) refer only to indirect taxes. The overall impact of taxes should not be different considering the small contribution of direct taxes.

Bibliography

Azevedo, J. P., Inchauste, G. and Sanfelice, V. 2013. Decomposing the recent inequality decline in Latin America. Policy Research Working Paper Series 6715. Washington DC, World Bank.

Burdín, G., Esponda, F. and Vigorito, A. 2014. Inequality and top incomes in Uruguay: a comparison between household surveys and income tax micro-data. CEQ Working Paper no. 21. Tulane, La., Center for Inter-American Policy and Research and Department of Economics, Tulane University and Inter-American Dialogue. *http://stonecenter.tulane.edu/uploads/CEQWPNo21_IneqTopIncomesUruguay_May_2014-1405720326.pdf* (Accessed 12 June 2016.)

Cornia, G. A. (ed.). 2014. *Falling Inequality in Latin America: Policy Changes and Lessons.* Oxford, Oxford University Press.

Cornia, G. A., Gomez Sabaini, J. C. and Martorano, B. 2011. A new fiscal pact, tax policy changes and income inequality. Working Paper 2011/70. Helsinki, UNU-WIDER.

Cruces, G. and Gasparini, L. 2008. A distribution in motion: the case of Argentina. Working Paper no. 0078. La Plata, Argentina, CEDLAS, Universidad Nacional de La Plata.

ECLAC and IEF (Instituto de Estudios Fiscales). 2014. Los efectos de la política fiscal sobre la redistribución en América Latina y la Unión Europea [The effects of tax policy on redistribution in Latin America and the European Union]. Colección Estudios Nº 8 (Serie Estados de la Cuestión). Madrid, EUROsociAL-FIIAPP.

Gómez Sabaíni, J. C. and Morán, D. 2014. *Tax Policy in Latin America: Assessment and Guidelines for a Second Generation of Reforms*. Macroeconomics of Development Series no. 133. Santiago de Chile, ECLAC.

ICTD (International Centre for Tax and Development). n.d. Government Revenue Dataset (*www.ictd.ac/news-events/109-the-ictd-government-revenue-dataset-best-option-for-researchers*) (Accessed 12 June 2016.)

Jorratt, M. 2010. Equidad fiscal en Chile: un análisis de la incidencia distributiva de los impuestos y el gasto social. Equidad fiscal en Brasil, Chile, Paraguay y Uruguay. [Fiscal equity in Chile: an analysis of the distributive impact of taxes and social spending. Fiscal equity in Brazil, Chile, Paraguay and Uruguay.] Washington DC, Inter-American Development Bank (IDB)/EUROsociAL.

Lindert, K., Skoufias, E. and Shapiro, J. 2006. *Redistributing Income to the Poor and the Rich: Public Transfers in Latin America and the Caribbean*. Washington DC, World Bank.

Lustig, N. 2015. Fiscal redistribution: analytical dimensions and results for middle income countries. Presentation for seminar at the Institute for Fiscal Studies, London, 10 July. www.ifs.org.uk/uploads/publications/conferences/presentations/Lustig_FiscalRedistribution_IFS_July%2010_2015.pdf (Accessed 12 June 2016.)

Martorano, B. 2014. The impact of Uruguay's 2007 tax reform on equity and efficiency. *Development Policy Review*, Vol. 32, No. 6, pp. 701–14.

Robles, M., Rubio, M. and Stampini, M. 2015. Have cash transfers succeeded in reaching the poor in Latin America and the Caribbean? IDB Policy Brief no. 246. Washington DC, International Development Bank.

■ **Juan Carlos Gómez Sabaíni** *(Argentina) is a senior economist and international consultant in the areas of public finance and tax systems. He is also a postgraduate professor at the University of Buenos Aires, Argentina. He is a former three-time deputy secretary of Tax Policy in Argentina. He has authored and co-authored numerous publications about tax policy in Latin America.*

■ **Bruno Martorano** *(Italy) holds a PhD in development economics from the University of Florence. He is currently based at the Institute of Development Studies (IDS) as ISSC-IDS Report Fellow, in charge of co-coordinating the preparation of this Report; and a research associate at Consortium pour la recherche économique et sociale (CRES) in Dakar, Senegal. Prior to this, Bruno worked at the UNICEF Office of Research in Florence and the University of Florence, and has held consultancies for the University of North Carolina at Chapel Hill, UNCTAD, UNU-WIDER and the World Bank. His research interests lie in the fields of development economics, fiscal policy, taxation, social protection, poverty and inequality.*

■ **Dalmiro Morán** *(Argentina) is an economist and consultant for the Economic Commission for Latin America and the Caribbean (ECLAC). Prior to that, he was a researcher at the Ministry of Economy of the Province of Buenos Aires, Argentina. His recent work focuses on tax reform, environmental and local government taxation, and natural resource fiscal management for Latin American countries.*

48. Global instruments for tackling inequality: the African experience

Adebayo O. Olukoshi

Global instruments tried in Africa have not addressed the structural roots of inequality and poverty; all have been based on the assumption that poverty and inequality can be tackled through technical and technocratic solutions. Yet inequality is rising in certain African countries, sometimes dramatically so, and there is growing recognition that inequality has all too often obstructed efforts at poverty reduction. To address rising inequality and persistent poverty in Africa it is necessary to acknowledge the central place of politics and domestic policy spaces for building an integrated, holistic agenda of development that reconciles economic policies with social vision and active participation.

Introduction

The theme of inequality has recently gained increased importance among the priority issues commanding the attention of scholars, policy officials and politicians worldwide. This includes Africa where for a long time the focus was almost exclusively on combatting poverty and its consequences. Although conceptually distinct from one another, poverty and inequality have tended all too often to be conflated in development policy thinking and practice globally. Across Africa, fighting poverty has been one of the most consistently avowed goals of a succession of postcolonial governments, and the central programme of the international development community for the continent. There was a longstanding assumption, sometimes silent and sometimes explicitly stated, that the fight against poverty was also part of an effort to tackle inequality. Instruments designed to tackle poverty both globally and regionally were also expected to help curb inequality.

This dominant approach was, of course, riddled with challenges, not least the fact that even where poverty has been successfully reduced, inequality has been known to grow, sometimes quite rapidly and dramatically. And although success in stemming inequality has been helpful under certain conditions in containing poverty, rising inequality in other countries such as South Africa has all too often obstructed efforts at poverty reduction.

Central to the contemporary emergence of inequality as a major source of concern among scholars and policy officials was the global shift in socio-economic policy-making and governance during the second half of the 1970s and into the early 1980s that ushered in the neoliberal era. The refraction of global neoliberalism into Africa through the conditionality and cross-conditionality clauses wielded by the International Monetary Fund (IMF), the World Bank, and some of the leading bilateral and other multilateral donors, was a critical turning point for the gradual emergence of inequality as a major source of concern on the continent. The structural adjustment programmes favoured by the international financial institutions effectively compelled African countries to abandon their postcolonial, state-led models of development and move under sustained donor pressure towards a liberalized free market regime that opened the floodgates to a massive policy bias tailored to favour the rich and powerful at the expense of the poor.

During the 1980s and 1990s, this context of all-round economic crises pushed many in the ranks of the working population back into poverty, and neoliberal structural adjustment exacerbated the situation through both its deflationary policies and the deliberate transfer of opportunity to the rich in the name of market liberalization and private-sector development. And since the dawn of the new millennium, the mostly commodity-driven growth of many African countries has spurred the 'Africa Rising' narrative.

Here inequality has been deepened by the clear absence of deeply rooted policies of redistribution, while the quality of growth itself has been so poor as to fail to make a dent in poverty. With the 'Africa Rising' expectations now severely dampened, attention will have to be shifted back to the fundamental question of the structural roots of the prolonged inability of African countries to overcome and contain growing social, spatial, gender, racial and intergenerational disparities.

Global instruments for redressing inequality in Africa

International aid

International aid is easily the oldest and most long-lasting instrument used by the international development community to try to reduce poverty in Africa and – in theory at least – to bridge global North–South inequalities. Introduced and packaged as development assistance in the face of the growing nationalist independence struggles against direct colonial rule in the post-war period, it has gone through many iterations in the hope that it could be made more effective in delivering to the poor. Although debates are rife over how more than half a century of development assistance has benefited African countries, it is a telling commentary on the overall aid experience that both recipient and donor countries feel a sense of frustration and even exasperation with the results registered to date.

The recurring question is simple: despite what would seem like huge resource commitments, why has poverty persisted and even grown, and why is it now compounded by growing inequality? Over the years, disappointment with the underperformance of aid in Africa has translated into an unending quest for a framework that can deliver mutually satisfactory outcomes. The quest has yielded lofty declarations – from Paris through Accra to Busan – but has not been successful in delivering the much-needed paradigm shift in the theory and practice of development cooperation.

Social dimensions of adjustment and safety nets

Beyond direct aid, the 1980s witnessed the introduction of a spate of initiatives aimed at mitigating what were referred to as the unintended costs and side-effects of painful but necessary market reform policies that had been imposed on African countries under the supervision of the Bretton Woods institutions. They included an assortment of hastily assembled and, for a period, ad hoc measures which were presented as an answer to critics of the huge toll which neoliberal market reform policies imposed on the working poor, to the point of reversing post-independence social welfare gains. From an initial focus on mitigating the costs of adjustment and cushioning the pain that the losers from structural adjustment had to bear, these initiatives soon became full-blown social policy instruments, spurring investments in the construction of social safety nets. Operationally, these initiatives were conceived defensively against the critics of the structural adjustment framework. They were very poorly funded and in policy terms occupied a residual category, which ruled out any possibility that they could make a meaningful difference.

The highly indebted poor country (HIPC) initiative

The HIPC initiative was introduced in 1996, at a time when the social dimensions of adjustment were being articulated in response to the poverty–inequality nexus in Africa during the 1980s. It recognized that the unsustainable debt overhang of African countries had become a burden which impeded recovery from economic crises, and ate too deeply into resources to make any meaningful dent in poverty and inequality. Under the initiative, a portion of the debt of eligible African countries was written off, and the repayment savings made were channelled into preferred social sectors and infrastructure development to improve welfare and well-being. Although it was launched with considerable fanfare and heralded as a bold new international approach to social and economic sustainability, eligibility for HIPC was tied to a rigorous adherence by African countries to the very same adjustment model that critics had suggested was, in part at least, at the heart of the problems that needed to be addressed.

The number of countries that were deemed qualified for HIPC was low, because the highly restrictive eligibility criteria eliminated many potential beneficiaries, the debt sustainability indicators used were both unrealistic and ill-conceived, and an inordinately long timespan would be needed for eligible countries to achieve completion point. The impact of the funds accruing from the HIPC initiative was more symbolic than substantive, and in time the initiative came to be seen as a tool geared more to protecting creditors than to helping the poor and vulnerable. Critics questioned the extent to which the initiative brought any meaningful debt relief, and worried that whatever assistance was offered by HIPC came from existing aid budgets rather than new money (Easterly, 2002; Issar, 2012).

Poverty reduction strategy papers

The limited social impact of these adjustment and safety net interventions, and the extremely slow pace of the HIPC initiatives, led in the face of persistent concerns about growing poverty and inequality to the introduction of the poverty reduction strategy papers (PRSPs) in the late 1990s. The PRSPs were marketed as an internationally supported initiative built on locally defined priorities that emanated from widespread multisectoral consultation, including engagements with local civil society groups. Local participation and ownership in the framing of the PRSPs was presented as offering legitimacy to the programme, while international financial and technical support would offer additional guarantees of success. Yet like other initiatives before it, the PRSPs were little more than an externally driven initiative subordinated to the neoliberal structural adjustment model, and like the adjustment programmes they operated as a one-size-fits-all instrument. What local consultation took place was little more than a pro forma exercise.

Significantly, the acceptance of the PRSPs was initially made a condition for the possible enjoyment of HIPC debt relief for many countries. They were later elevated to the status of a development strategy for participating African countries, leading critics to wonder how poverty reduction could be seen as the essence of development planning and structural transformation when it continued to be detached from the making of domestic development policy.

Given the deflationary macroeconomic foundation on which they were built, it was inevitably concluded over time that the PRSPs were a continuation by another name of the discredited structural adjustment policies of the 1980s and 1990s (AFRODAD, 2003; UNCTAD, 2002).

Formalization and titling for the poor

Even as the PRSPs were being rolled out as the new policy game in town for African countries in the 1990s, the World Bank and a number of influential bilateral donors invested in experiments designed to formalize the assets of the working and chronically poor scattered in Africa's sprawling slums through a process of land titling across the continent. Inspired by Hernando de Soto's writings and the work he did in his native Peru, resources were poured into initiatives designed to transform the 'dead assets' of the poor (worth over US$9 trillion globally by his estimate) into collateral that could be leveraged to enable them to access credit. All over Africa, an epidemic of land titling broke out, supported with financing from the World Bank, and de Soto himself was supported to experiment with making the poor more bankable through formalization in countries such as Tanzania and South Africa. The verdict was quick in coming: evidence of better access to credit through titling and formalization was very thin. Instead, titling became a shortcut to dispossession, physical displacement and marginalization among the poor, resulting in worse poverty and widening inequality (Gravois, 2005; van der Molen, 2012).

Millennium villages and MDGs

Exasperation at the fact that the world had enough wealth, knowledge and technological know-how to eradicate poverty permanently, and yet grinding poverty continued to be the lot of hundreds of millions of people in Africa, Asia and elsewhere, propelled the plea by Jeffrey Sachs for the launching of millennium villages. Proposed as an integrated approach to tackling the problems of hunger and want, the millennium villages particularly targeted rural poverty. The villages were also marketed as being integral to the MDGs that had been adopted by the UN General Assembly. But as experiments, the villages were too few and far apart relative to the challenges at hand. And being heavily donor-dependent, they were difficult to multiply for broader effect.

Although every country committed itself to the MDGs, links between the efforts to implement the goals and investment in the villages were weak, even in the countries where they were piloted. The MDGs themselves were mostly pursued outside the mainstream policy-making, development planning and budgeting frameworks of the majority of African countries, an outcome of the extreme donorization of their implementation and the concentrated localization of their impact across different sectors (Munk, 2013).

Social protection and local entrepreneurship

Amid the drive to implement the MDGs, donor interest in social protection measures was revived, as offering quick wins targeted at the most vulnerable in society. Multilateral and bilateral donors were joined in the promotion of social protection initiatives by international NGOs keen to address issues of individual welfare and help build communal resilience in Africa. However the initiatives, ranging from cash transfers to school-feeding schemes, once again tended to be heavily donor-dependent. This put them at risk of collapse once donor resources dried up, and this was a frequent occurrence. And as initiatives that were targeted rather than universal, they were liable to the problems of stigma and quality associated with targeted schemes. Exasperation among private entrepreneurs, who were concerned that a mentality of dependence might be fostered through social protection handouts, led to the introduction of competing microfinance and small-scale venture capital schemes designed to make self-sustaining entrepreneurs out of the working poor. The entrepreneurial approach is, however, still an enclave one, like the millennium villages. What Africa needs are more interventions that are systemic in their design and import and therefore able to generate multisectoral spin-offs which are beneficial for socio-economic progress (UNRISD, 2010).

Concluding reflections

Africa has not been short of global initiatives designed to support governments to reduce poverty and stem inequality, even if inequality has not received as much robust interest as might be expected, and indeed continues to be conflated with poverty. Regrettably, most of the global instruments that have been tried have been little more than experimental, and over the decades have seen African countries going round in circles led by global institutions that appear to be at a loss for workable solutions.

None of the global instruments have addressed the structural roots of poverty and inequality in Africa; all have been based on the assumption that poverty and inequality can be tackled through technical and technocratic solutions. Bringing politics back into the policy processes is a key priority if African countries are to be able to overcome the challenge of persistent poverty alongside growing inequality. A second priority, flowing from an acknowledgement of the central place of politics, will be the recovery of domestic policy space for building an integrated and holistic agenda of development that is able to reconcile economic policies with social vision and the active participation of an empowered citizenry.

Bibliography

AFRODAD. 2003. *Africa's Experience with the PRSP: Content and Process.* Harare, AFRODAD.

Easterly, W. 2002. How did heavily indebted poor countries become heavily indebted? Reviewing two decades of debt relief. *World Development*, Vol. 30, No. 10, pp. 1677–96. www.sciencedirect.com/science/article/pii/S0305750X02000736 (Accessed 2 March 2016.)

Gravois, John. 2005. The De Soto delusion. *Slate Magazine, Washington Post*, 29 January. www.slate.com/articles/news_and_politics/hey_wait_a_minute/2005/01/the_de_soto_delusion.html (Accessed 2 March 2016.)

Issar, S. 2012. Was the highly indebted poor country initiative (HIPC) a success? *Consilience*, Vol. 9, No. 1, pp. 107–22. www.consiliencejournal.org/index.php/consilience/article/viewFile/297/141 (Accessed 2 March 2016.)

Munk, N. 2013. *The Idealist: Jeffrey Sachs and the Quest to End Poverty.* New York, Doubleday.

UNCTAD. 2002. *Economic Development in Africa from Adjustment to Poverty Reduction: What is New?* Geneva, UNCTAD.

UNRISD (UN Research Institute for Social Development). 2010. *Combatting Poverty and Inequality: Structural Change, Social Policy and Politics.* Geneva, UNRISD.

Van der Molen, P. 2012. *After ten years of criticism: what is left of de Soto's ideas?* Mimeo. Rome.

■ **Adebayo O. Olukoshi** *(Nigeria) is regional director Africa and West Asia, International IDEA, and distinguished visiting professor, University of Johannesburg, South Africa.*

POSTCARD

49. Financial liberalization and global inequality

Stephany Griffith-Jones and E. A. Brett

The increasingly deregulated, liberalized and globalized financial system created over the past thirty years has been a major cause of inequality, nationally and internationally, through a number of channels.

Finance tends to increase inequality in boom times, when excessive credit is given. There is a bias towards financing the largest companies, the richest individuals and the richest economies, while small and medium-sized enterprises tend to suffer from lack of finance, especially in poorer countries. In such a context, the risk of crisis increases as rising credit and debt levels are thought necessary to maintain a high rate of growth (Turner, 2015). Indeed, when credit is given to poorer people or countries it is often done in an unsustainable way, leaving them often poorer after the bust, and undermining financial stability.

The USA is an illustrative case. Financial liberalization has contributed to financial sector growth from 2.8 per cent of GDP in the 1950s to 7.6 per cent in the mid-2000s (Stiglitz, 2015). This has further increased inequality, since the sector's high profits represent a very high share of total corporate profits, and it pays senior employees very high incomes (*Figure 49.1*).

Figure 49.1 **Bank failures, regulation and inequality in the USA**

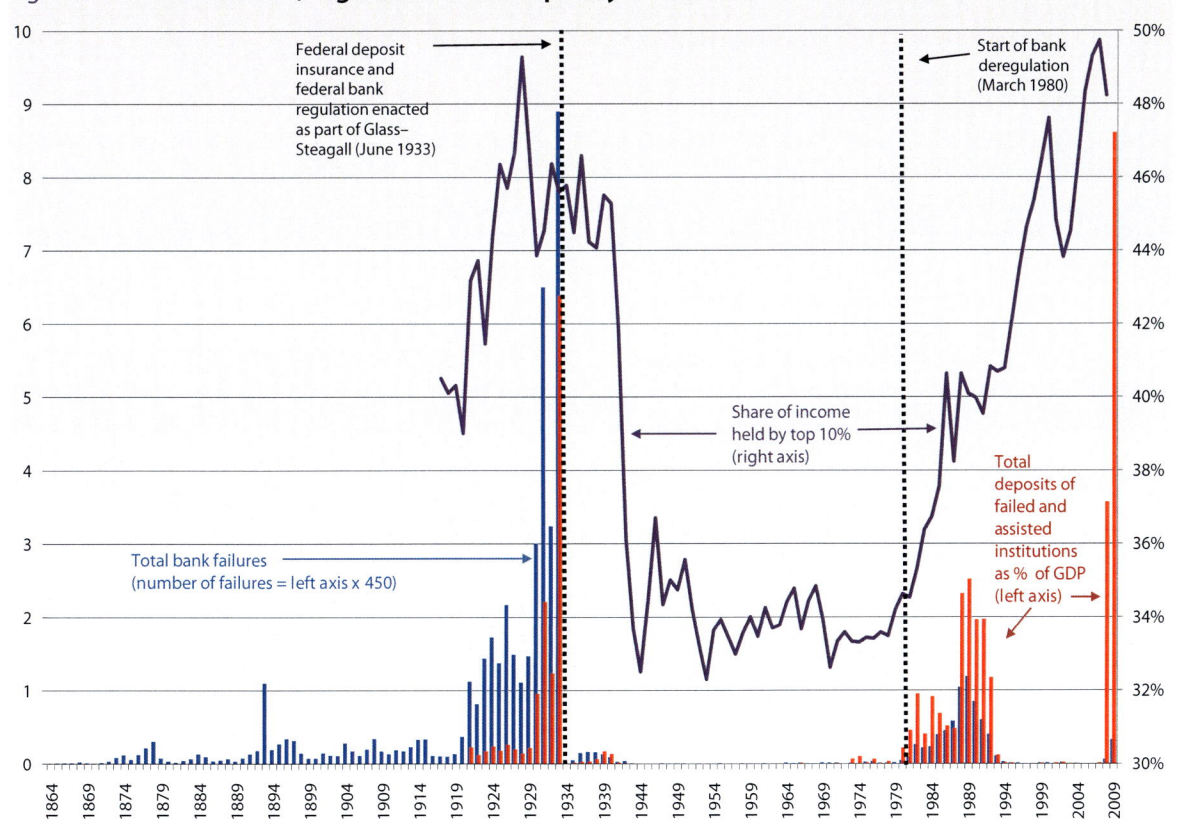

Source: Moss (2010).

On the other hand, the number of bank failures dramatically increased after the process of financial regulation in the 1980s (*Figure 49.1*).

Booms have increasingly been followed by busts, resulting in crises which damage development and impoverish nations. The rich can often protect themselves, through capital flight and other measures, but the poor cannot, so they suffer the losses. Further, financial crises are often managed by imposing austerity on crisis countries. These have historically been developing and emerging economies, and most recently Eurozone countries such as Greece and Spain. This not only damages employment and investment, but disproportionately hurts the poor, through wage and pension cuts, and reductions in public health, education and welfare spending.

A radical restructuring of the finance sector and its regulation is required to reverse this trend. This essential step is politically difficult, since the growth of the finance sector has increased its political influence and power. This can only be overcome by progressive social and political forces pushing a clear reform agenda.

The necessary changes include tighter regulation of the private financial sector, and a larger role for public development banks which can fund public infrastructure and the businesses needed to generate sustainable and equitable development.

Bibliography

Moss, D. 2010. Comments on bank failure/regulation/inequality chart. *www.tobinproject.org/sites/tobinproject.org/files/assets/BankFailures_ChartwithComments_Moss.pdf* (Accessed 24 February 2016.)

Stiglitz, J. E. 2015. *Rewriting the Rules of the American Economy: Agenda for Growth and Shared Prosperity.* New York, W.W. Norton.

Turner, A. 2015. *Between Debt and the Devil: Money, Credit, and Fixing Global Finance.* Princeton, N.J., Princeton University Press.

■ **Stephany Griffith-Jones** *(USA) is financial markets programme director, the Initiative for Policy Dialogue, Columbia University.*

■ **E. A. (Teddy) Brett** *(UK) is visiting professor, Department of International Development, London School of Economics and Political Science, London.*

POSTCARD

50. Could changes in the international tax system be a strategy for dealing with inequality?

Mick Moore

At the level of tax design, the answer to this question is clear and positive. It would be easy, for example, to draft the international treaty and the national legislation required to implement Thomas Piketty's (2014) proposal for a global tax on wealth. The obstacles to acceptance and implementation of those proposals are merely political – but at the same time they are formidable. There has been a steady, worldwide movement away from wealth taxes of any kind in recent decades, and the many previous calls for international cooperation to establish some kind of global tax have failed (Bird, 2015). Political realism suggests that we start somewhere else.

There is one slightly more promising launch pad: the considerable progress that has been made very recently in establishing a system for the automatic exchange of financial account information in tax matters (see OECD, n.d.). This sounds very technical. The system essentially increases and eases the flow of information to national tax authorities about the financial assets held by individuals and companies in other jurisdictions. China could discover, for example, what bank accounts its citizens hold in Portugal. This initiative is not transformative. Having access to more information is one thing, and having the resources and political incentives to make use of it to plug tax gaps is another. Many governments are unenthusiastic about taxing their rich friends, and there are still many legal devices to keep secret or obscure the real ownership of assets. At present, the information flows relate only to financial assets, not to real estate, gold bars, jewellery or Picassos. Few developing countries have yet qualified to join the system. Nevertheless, in the long term automatic information exchange provides a basis for the more effective taxation of rich people.

But what about companies, especially larger, transnational corporations? They are well placed to avoid taxes through more or less legal devices. One of the main techniques used is transfer mispricing. When companies within the same transnational group trade with one another across international borders, they may not account for these transactions at the 'real' market price for the goods and services involved. Instead, they may try to choose prices that are designed to shift group accounting profits to low-tax or no-tax locations. Transfer pricing is now illegal in most countries. However, it remains widespread, because it is very hard to police. It is a cause of significant tax losses, especially to governments of low-income countries.

It is easy to design changes to international tax rules that would reduce these losses. The obstacles to doing so are political. The resistance comes mainly from the rich countries. Some of the most significant tax haven activities are located in rich countries, rather than in small tropical islands. The OECD, acting under a mandate from the G20, has just spent two years trying to agree reforms to narrow the scope for legal tax avoidance by transnationals. The agreement, announced in October 2015, is rather modest in scope (see OECD, 2016).

Any positive, direct impact of the OECD's proposed measures will be more on government finances than on the distribution of income. In most countries, a strategy to reduce income inequality should put as much emphasis on effective taxation of the local rich as on reducing tax evasion and avoidance by companies. In many poor countries, little attention has yet been paid to taxing the personal incomes of the growing ranks of the rich and mega-rich.

So the answer to the opening question is that any changes to the international system that currently seem politically feasible are likely to contribute only marginally to reducing inequality. They could, however, be very helpful to national governments that are serious about the issue. When will they get serious? A good winning combination is a government that is really hungry for more revenue and a political movement that is well informed about the inequities of existing patterns of revenue raising.

Bibliography

Bird, R. 2015. *Global Taxes and International Taxation: Mirage and Reality.* Working Paper no. 28. Brighton, UK, International Centre for Tax and Development (ICTD), IDS. *http://www.ictd.ac/publication/2-working-papers/21-global-taxes-and-international-taxation-mirage-and-reality* (Accessed 13 June 2016.)

OECD. n.d. Automatic exchange of information. Global Forum on Transparency and Exchange of Information for Tax Purposes, OECD. *www.oecd.org/tax/transparency/automaticexchangeofinformation.htm* (Accessed 12 June 2016.)

OECD. 2016. Base erosion and profit shifting. *www.oecd.org/ctp/beps.htm* (Accessed 13 June 2016.)

Piketty, T. 2014. *Capital in the Twenty-First Century*. Cambridge, Mass., Harvard University Press.

■ **Mick Moore** *(UK) is a political economist. He has done extensive field research in Asia and Africa, especially Sri Lanka, India and Taiwan, China. He has taught at the Massachusetts Institute of Technology. His broad research interests are in the domestic and international dimensions of good and bad governance in poor countries. He focuses specifically on taxation and governance, and is the founding chief executive officer of the International Centre for Tax and Development.*

51. A seat at the table is not enough: gender and political inclusion

Sohela Nazneen

Women's political inclusion is promoted as a strategy for creating inclusive political institutions and attaining gender justice. The number of women at all levels of government is rising around the world, because of affirmative action and the creation of participatory spaces. However, easing women's access into political spaces does not automatically lead to the promotion of gender-equity concerns in policy-making. The effective participation of women in politics is influenced by the terms on which women are included, by the interplay between formal and informal rules in the political system, and by the presence of autonomous women's movement actors who have broad-based alliances with other state, social and political actors. How these factors play out in differing contexts and how they affect what women do once they enter politics and policy spaces require further analysis.

Many countries in the world recognize equal political rights for women. But in practice, women experience gendered barriers to entering and participating in the political arena, and in influencing decisions to address gender inequity in the distribution of social and economic resources. Intersecting economic and social inequalities further undermine women's ability to exercise political power and access public institutions. Many scholars and activists argue that women's political inclusion, particularly measures for increasing women's participation and representation, would lead to the creation of inclusive political institutions and help attain social justice (Phillips, 1995).

The number of women in government has been rising around the world in recent decades. The global average for women parliamentarians has nearly doubled in the past twenty years, and currently stands close to 22 per cent (UN Women, 2014). In many countries women have made effective inroads in local government, and populate the bureaucracy at all levels in increasing numbers. Women are increasingly gaining a seat at the table where political and policy decisions are made.

What has led to this increase in the number of women in government? Are women becoming accepted as actors in political institutions? Does having a seat at the table allow them to participate effectively in decision-making processes and attain gender justice?

What influences women's political inclusion?

While the number of women representatives in parliament is rising, progress towards attaining gender parity in representation has been slow. The Scandinavian countries take the lead at 41 per cent female parliamentarians, with some Latin American and sub-Saharan African countries performing well at over 30 per cent. Europe, Latin America and Africa take the top three places, while the Middle East and the Pacific lag behind all other regions (UN Women, 2014).

These regional variations can be explained by the presence of gender quotas, the structure of electoral systems, and the measures taken by political parties to include women. In many countries, the adoption of affirmative action measures such as reserved seats and gender quotas on party electoral lists, bureaucracies and state-created community user groups has facilitated women's entry in larger numbers into legislative assemblies, local government, state agencies and participatory citizen's forums. Evidence shows that proportional representation electoral systems lead to more women being elected than first-past-the-post systems with single member constituencies (UN Women, 2014).

Sanctions imposed on political parties for not complying with electoral rules on women's inclusion in party lists are also effective. The requirement to select women expands the pool of potential candidates and creates opportunities for nominating women who might have been overlooked (Krook, 2013).

Beside these factors, a country's political history also matters. Women's participation in critical political movements such as anti-colonial struggles, anti-authoritarian movements, independence movements and armed struggles legitimizes their claim for political inclusion. The examples of Chile, South Africa and Rwanda show that in the post-transition period, women's movement actors and their allies were able to negotiate a better deal for women's inclusion in political offices, and demand gender-equitable reforms, by framing their claims in light of the role played by women during political struggles (Waylen, 2008).

Women's determination and ability to enter politics and participate actively are influenced too by their access to material resources and social and political networks, by social and cultural norms regarding women's participation in formal and informal institutions (such as community spaces),[1] and by the allocation of care responsibilities.[2]

Different types of formal and informal institutional arrangements strengthen or limit women's participation in politics. Studies of women's political recruitment using the supply–demand model reveal gender biases in candidate selection processes and the lack of political opportunities inside political parties (Franceschet et al., 2012). Goetz and Hassim's (2003) comparative study of Uganda and South Africa shows that opportunities for women to participate effectively in electoral and party politics depend on party type (whether informal or rule-based), party ideology (conservative or liberal), the commitment of the senior party leadership to promote women's inclusion, the presence of a strong women's wing inside a party, and the nature and culture of political competition.

Rising levels of campaign finance adversely affect women, as they have a weaker resource base than men. Addressing this imbalance requires strict monitoring of election expenditure caps by state agencies. Lower candidate registration fees for women, and state funding for women candidates, may also increase the number of women candidates.

Political violence also constrains women's participation (UN Women, 2014), which indicates the need to create a level playing field for women and men in the political arena.

The action of senior party leadership to promote women's political inclusion is motivated by both instrumental and ideational concerns (Nazneen and Mahmud, 2012). In many developing countries, the decision-making process in political parties is highly centralized and the parties operate in an informal and personalized manner. Here the promotion of women's representation largely depends on the instrumental and ideational concerns of the senior party leadership. These types of party are able to overcome resistance quickly and include a large number of women. Women representatives are able to promote a gender-equity agenda within the party and in politics if they have close personal relationships and networks with the central leadership. However, studies on Uganda show that gains made by women from these forms of inclusion may be limited and short-lived (Goetz and Hassim, 2003).

Impact of women's inclusion in political spaces

Women's entry into political spaces changes social perceptions of their presence in the political arena, creates positive role models for other women to emulate, and over time, reduces prejudice about women's leadership, in the long run promoting their inclusion in politics (Agarwal, 2010). However, evidence is mixed as to whether women's inclusion leads to influence in policy-making. Evidence from Scandinavian countries supports the contention that a critical mass of women in legislatures creates space for raising issues linked to women's concerns. Examples are violence against women, child care and social welfare (Weldon, 2002). The presence of such a critical mass has allowed women parliamentarians in South Africa, Uganda and other developing countries to form a gender caucus or a cross-party alliance to advocate for issues linked to women's rights (Goetz and Hassim, 2003). Research on local government and community forums in developing countries shows that when women have a greater voice, public resources are used to address women's needs such as child health, access to water and employment for women (UN Women, 2014).

However, easing women's access to political office does not automatically guarantee that a gender equity agenda will be promoted in policy-making. Women are not a homogenous group. Class, caste, ethnic and racial interests influence the actions of women representatives. Like their male counterparts, they may or may not raise gender-equity concerns, depending on the context, the available opportunities, the existence of a gender mandate, their links with the women's wing of the party and women's movement actors, and the possible electoral consequences of promoting gender equity concerns (Childs and Krook, 2009).

Another open question is whether greater gender inclusion in formal political institutions leads to a spillover effect in addressing other forms of inequality. In Latin America, women parliamentarians have led resistance to legislation intended to strengthen the rights of domestic workers, the majority of whom are female and from disadvantaged ethnic and racial groups. They needed domestic workers to work long hours for the parliamentarians to be able to participate in politics. However, domestic workers were able to overcome this resistance by building strategic alliances with women's movement organizations, pro-labour political parties and other social movement groups. Cross-country research by Htun and Weldon (2010) shows that the presence of autonomous women's movement organizations that have strong relations with the state bureaucracy, political parties and other social movements, is key to bringing about gender-equitable policy changes. Over the years, broad-based alliances among women's movement actors have promoted formal policy changes that address gender inequality affecting different groups of women.

Gender and political inclusion – what we need to know more about

Most of the scholarly work on 'women in politics' has focused on the effectiveness of quotas and other macro-level institutional arrangements for increasing women's representation. Understanding why women's inclusion is promoted in a specific political context, and the influence it has, requires a broader understanding of the historical context, the interactions between the formal and the informal rules operating in a political system, and the negotiations that take place between the political elites and various social-political actors, including women's movement actors (Nazneen and Mahmud, 2012). The weight of these factors varies in different political contexts.

Our current knowledge of how women gain inclusion and how they influence policy outcomes is partial, and we need to generate evidence in the following areas.

Most studies of links between women's inclusion and influence have a narrower focus, and take women's entry as a starting point. This leaves out the broader range of factors that facilitate women's inclusion and the complex pathways through which gender-equitable policy change takes place. Methodologically, tracking backwards from the successful promotion of gender-equity policies and reforms to a wider range of political actors may offer a more nuanced picture of political agency, particularly of how the coalitions and alliances between various actors, and personal relations and networks, influence the terms of women's inclusion and their ability to promote gender-equitable changes in different contexts.

There are also gaps in our knowledge of women's inclusion, in terms of geographical coverage and the level of government. The Scandinavian countries, and Latin and Central America, are well researched. Recently, some African countries have also drawn attention (Krook, 2013), but Asia, with the exception of a few countries, remains largely under-researched. There are also fewer studies of women's inclusion in community-level organizations and local government. Systematic analysis of how women's inclusion affects the functioning of local government and the impact of decentralization on women's inclusion is needed.

We also need to know whether women's inclusion in politics creates gender-inclusive institutions, which in turn depends on the interplay between the formal and informal rules of the political system and how these rules are gendered. There is a need to investigate how informal institutions, such as norms based on customs, illegitimate practices and backdoor deals, shape women's inclusion and subvert or create women's rights in politics and policy-making. Feminist institutionalists have recently started to move in this direction (Chappell and Waylen, 2013). This burgeoning body of work will need to further unpack the impact of clientelist politics on women's inclusion.

These knowledge gaps indicate that while gender inclusion as a strategy has increased women's numbers in formal political institutions, what women do once they enter politics and policy spaces, and how and when they address gender and other forms of inequity, requires further analysis.

Notes

1. Social and cultural norms dictate which public spaces are open to women. For example, community meetings in mosques are inaccessible to women in South Asia. Norms also dictate the kinds of issues women may raise in public and how women should articulate demands.

2. A recent study on women representatives in local government in Bangladesh (Nazneen et al., 2014) revealed that women decided to enter politics after their children had entered their teens or if they were able to employ household help or delegate care and household responsibilities to another family member. The findings indicate that class plays a significant role in women's ability to enter politics.

Bibliography

Agarwal, B. 2010. *Gender and Green Governance*. Oxford, Oxford University Press.

Chappell, L. and Waylen, G. 2013. Gender and the hidden life of institutions. *Public Administration*, Vol. 91, No. 3, pp. 599–615. *http://onlinelibrary.wiley.com/doi/10.1111/j.1467-9299.2012.02104.x/abstract* (Accessed 8 February 2016.)

Childs, S. and Krook, M. L. 2009. Analysing women's substantive representation: from critical mass to critical actors. *Government and Opposition*, Vol. 44, No. 2, pp. 125–45. *http://onlinelibrary.wiley.com/doi/10.1111/j.1477-7053.2009.01279.x/abstract* (Accessed 8 February 2016.)

Franceschet, S., Krook, M. L. and Piscopo, J. (eds). 2012. *The Impact of Gender Quotas*. New York, Oxford University Press.

Goetz, A. M. and Hassim, S. 2003. *No Short Cuts to Power: African Women in Politics and Policy Making*. London, Zed Books.

Htun, M. and Weldon, S. L. 2010. When and why do governments promote sex equality? Violence against women, reproductive rights, and parental leave in cross-national perspective. *Perspectives on Politics*, Vol. 8, No. 1, pp. 206–17. *www.researchgate.net/publication/231808600_When_Do_Governments_Promote_Women's_Rights_A_Framework_for_the_Analysis_of_Sex_Equality_Policy* (Accessed 8 February 2016.)

Krook, M. L. 2013. Gender quotas and democracy: insights from Africa and beyond. *Women's Studies International Forum*, Vol. 41, part 2, pp. 160–63. *www.sciencedirect.com/science/article/pii/S0277539513001040* (Accessed 8 February 2016.)

Nazneen, S., Ehsan, I. and Hasan, B. 2014. Exceptional women: reserved councillors in municipal corporations in Bangladesh. M. Tadros (ed.), *Women in Politics: Gender, Power and Development*. London, Zed Books, pp. 74–100.

Nazneen, S. and Mahmud, S. 2012. *Gendered Politics of Securing Inclusive Development*. Working Paper no. 13. Manchester, Effective States and Inclusive Development (ESID) Research Centre, University of Manchester.

Phillips, A. 1995. *The Politics of Presence*. Oxford, Oxford University Press.

UN WOMEN. 2014. Women in Politics map. UN Women. *http://ipu.org/pdf/publications/wmnmap14_en.pdf* (Accessed 8 February 2016.)

Waylen, G. 2008. Enhancing the substantive representation of women: lessons from transitions to democracy. *Parliamentary Affairs*, Vol. 61, No. 3, pp. 518–34. *http://pa.oxfordjournals.org/content/61/3/518* (Accessed 8 February 2016.)

Weldon, S. L. 2002. Beyond bodies: institutional sources for women in democratic policymaking. *Journal of Politics*, Vol. 64, No. 4, pp. 1153–74. www.jstor.org/stable/1520080?seq=1#page_scan_tab_contents (Accessed 8 February 2016.)

■ **Sohela Nazneen** *(Bangladesh) is a fellow based at the Gender and Sexualities Cluster at the Institute of Development Studies (IDS), Brighton, UK. Her research largely focuses on gender and governance, rural livelihoods, and social and women's movements. She is currently leading a six-country research project to understand the relationship between women's inclusion in politics and their influence on education policy and domestic violence legislation in selected South Asian and sub-Saharan African countries for the Effective States and Inclusive Development (ESID) Research Center (www.effective-states.org/gender-political-settlement/).*

POSTCARD

52. Land redistribution: opportunities and traps

Michael Lipton

In the places where the poor farm, a heavy concentration of land ownership is a major cause of poverty. Land reform – legislation to redistribute farmland ownership, claims or rights, thus raising poor people's status, power and income – has a continuous, worldwide history from Messenia, Sparta, in around 540 BCE (Buckley, 2010; Powelson, 1987). In modern times, radicals and liberals alike have backed equal, small-scale farms: 'No man made the land. It is no hardship to be excluded from what others have produced. But it is some hardship to be born and to find all nature's gifts previously engrossed' (J. S. Mill).[1] Supporters claim that land reform equalizes opportunity. Opponents retort that it violates legitimate incumbents' security, makes returns uncertain and deters investment.

Settling this stand-off in a particular case depends on whether unequal opportunity or insecure property is the graver problem; on whether the poor have few or many off-farm opportunities; and on whether smaller-scale farming is more, or less, efficient and innovative after reform. Small-scale farms have lower transaction costs, but this applies only to low-income, labour-intensive agriculture in principally farming economies. That makes a strong equity and efficiency case for individually redistributive land reforms there.

Following Korea and Taiwan, China (1945–53), many Asian and Latin American countries have enacted ceilings on individual ownership. They have also brought in tenurial controls, for example on rents and evictions. Despite evasion and avoidance, ceilings on land ownership have created incentives to sell or bequeath land in small units, with massive redistributive effects. Tenurial controls, however, created incentives to shift land from rental to larger-scale owner-farming – often damaging the poor unless ownership ceilings were also enforced.

Alongside these effects are those of collective and state farming. Even when they have been equalizing in motive, both have transferred power from farmers to distant bureaucrats and to urban extractors of farm surplus. This process has disempowered the poor, and killed many millions in state-induced famines, but has also led to efficient reform after the failure of the centralized approach. Russia (1917), China (1948) and (North) Viet Nam (1954–58) enlisted peasant support for communism by redistributing big private farms. These were seized for collective or state farming from 1928, from 1956–59 and from 1958–60 respectively, with awful results. But farming in China between 1981 and 1984, from 1990 in Viet Nam and in some ex-communist countries in Eastern Europe and the former USSR, reverted for the second time to small-scale family farming: a relatively happy end to a terrible double detour.

In much of Asia and Latin America, land reforms preceded a 'green revolution'. Hundreds of millions of smallholders, often created by land reforms and their aftermath, massively improved yields and incomes. Small-scale farming and carefully managed land reform are powerful solvents of deep-seated inequalities in low-income countries, and the argument that they militate against agricultural efficiency and progress cannot be sustained. Enough is known for land reforms that are efficiency-inducing and politically sustainable to be designed for specific cases. However, land distribution, tenure, reform and alienation in the form of land grabs are all political and corruptible: as in chess, the mistakes are all there, waiting to be made.

Note

1. Mill is cited in Lipton (2009), which provides a fuller account of these and other economic and moral issues associated with land reform as a means towards greater equality.

Bibliography

Buckley, T. 2010. *Aspects of Greek History 750–323 BC: A Source-Based Approach.* London, Routledge.

Lipton, M. 2009. *Land Reform in Developing Countries: Property Rights and Property Wrongs.* London, Routledge.

Powelson, J. 1987. *The Story of Land – A World History of Land Tenure and Agrarian Reform.* Cambridge, Mass., Lincoln Institute of Land Policy.

■ ***Michael Lipton*** *(UK) is an emeritus professor at the University of Sussex, emeritus fellow at the Institute of Development Studies (IDS) and a fellow of the British Academy.*

53. Legal rights as instruments for challenging inequality

Celestine Nyamu Musembi

This contribution discusses the possibilities and limits of using legal rights to challenge inequality. Between two extremes – an optimistic liberal legalist ideal of law as neutral, and a sceptical dismissal of law as an instrument of domination – the article discusses insights drawn from writings on law and power. Legal rights can be effective in challenging inequality if they are deployed as counter-hegemonic strategies, are entwined with movement-building, are aware of the risks of piecemeal litigation, take account of broader normative bases for rights claims beyond narrow formal legal rights, and do not underestimate the transformative potential of legal rights at a symbolic, cultural level.

Legal rights tend to be viewed in liberal democracies as the default instrument for redressing patterns of inequality. In the liberal democratic ideal of the 'rule of law', rights are depicted as the rational regulator of the exercise of power, so that rule-defined behaviour is entrenched, rather than the interests of particular groups or individuals. Beyond the pages of legal theory and in the minds of social change activists including public interest lawyers, the idea of law as justice, in particular justice for the subordinated, has become something of an 'implicit popular jurisprudence' (Simon, 2004, p. 27; Calmore, 1999, p. 1936), whether consciously or subconsciously (Kostiner, 2003, p. 361).

A sceptical view denies altogether the possibility of engaging legal strategies to fight inequality, charging that far from being a neutral regulator of power, law is the very medium in which inequality is encoded and sanctioned. In Marxist thought, for instance, law's formal egalitarianism serves only to mask and deepen substantive inequalities, presenting the narrow interests of the dominant class as 'hold[ing] good for all' (Marx, excerpted in McLellan, 1977, p. 200). Law is only independent of unequal material conditions 'in the imagination of the ideologist' (Marx, excerpted in McLellan, 1977, p. 201). A similarly deterministic view of law as domination is expressed in radical feminism (MacKinnon, 1987).

Lying between the liberal legalist ideal and the Marxist dismissal of law and rights as domination are a range of views which call attention to the possibilities and limits of legal rights in challenging inequality. These writings on the relationship between law and power make the point that while there is no denying that legal orders do embody asymmetrical power relations, law should not be viewed simply as an instrument of domination. Rather it should be seen as an ideological force. The relationship between law and power is paradoxical: law is centrally implicated in the production of hegemony, but it can and does facilitate resistance, by becoming the vehicle through which something that had apparently congealed into hegemony is challenged and subjected to open contestation (Hirsch and Lazarus-Black, 1994; Hunt, 1990). While law is centrally implicated in skewing the distribution of resources, it also plays a role in efforts to make distribution fairer (Kennedy, 1991). These writings demonstrate that law does constrain the actions of the dominant groups and enable popular struggles, albeit in limited instances (Thompson, 1975) 'at the very perimeter of what the authorities are obliged to permit or unable to prevent' (Scott, 1985).

Rights as counter-hegemonic strategies

Rights will be effective in challenging inequality when they are deployed as 'counter-hegemonic' strategies (Hunt, 1990, p. 312).

While goals such as the concrete redistribution of resources are important, rights struggles must go beyond these to engage at the virtual level of thoughts, ideas and assumptions. Rights struggles serve as counter-hegemonic strategies when they engage in the long-term process of challenging the dominant hegemony and articulating an alternative to it. Engaging at this level makes it possible to expose and challenge 'biases that are deeply ingrained in the general social consciousness' (Kostiner, 2003, p. 342) and which feed inequality.

Sally Engle Merry (2006) illustrates the power of generating an alternative hegemony, drawing from a campaign against domestic violence in Hawaii. The advocates deliberately employed the term 'battering', reframing the issue as being about a crime rather than simply part of the reality of intimate relationships. This reframing articulated an alternative hegemony which forced a change in the law and in the attitude of law enforcement.

A legal strategy to challenge inequality should not naively treat legal rights as 'accomplished social facts or moral imperatives', but rather as 'political resources of unknown value in the hands of those who want to alter the course of public policy' (Stryker, 2007, p. 77, citing Scheingold, 2004, pp. 6–7).

Rights as movement-building

Legal strategy needs to be closely entwined with building a social movement, or else risk becoming abstract and failing to consolidate its gains in real life (Stryker, 2007, pp. 77–8, 88; Handler, 1978). The lawyers involved must 'work *with* and not just *for* the client community'. Lessons have also been learned on the advantages of collective over individual litigation in terms of movement-building. In contexts where the legal framework provides for it, class action or public interest litigation accomplishes this more effectively than individual cases. Data drawn from US Supreme Court decisions in Title VII (employment discrimination) cases showed that women were more likely to win in a class action than in individual suits (Stryker, 2007, pp. 82, 88). With publicity, even small victories are likely to translate into greater opportunities for mobilizing diversely situated citizens into a social movement (McCann, 1998, pp. 99–100). Even high-profile losses can have a positive effect on mobilization (Abel, 1995, pp. 25–43).

Inherent risk in piecemeal legal victories

In some instances, a law or regulation may confer tangible and immediate benefits to individuals in subordinated groups, yet rest on stereotypes of that subordinated group. Examples include indigenous peoples attempting to fit an idealized narrative so as to win land claims (Clifford, 1988; Robins, 2001); reprieve for female prisoners only, citing child-care justifications, thus reinforcing stereotypical gender roles (Cusack, 2013); and welfare benefits which transform claimants into 'supplicants', pitied but not entitled (Hunt, 1990, p. 311). In these instances, rights-claiming confers immediate benefits while solidifying and legitimizing the very ideology the subordinated are trying to resist. A legal rights strategy therefore calls for reflection on when piecemeal legal victories have the potential to contribute towards transformation, and when they risk reinforcing subordinate status.

Legal rights and their relation to entitlements

In some contexts, custom and religion may confer certain entitlements. One example is the protection of a spouse's undocumented rights to customary land. A narrow view of rights, as only formal legal rights, denies the possibility that these customary entitlements could play a role in mounting an internal challenge to unequal social relations. A broader view enables the aggrieved to articulate the injustice in terms that resonate with the context of norms that they have to live in (Musembi, 2013). Sally Engle Merry makes a similar point about 'layering' the bases for rights claims: people may take on a rights framing for their claim, but that does not mean that they abandon other bases for entitlement, such as a duty of care owed by their kin (Merry, 2006, p. 180).

Thinking broadly about entitlements multiplies the options and sites for rights claiming. It would enable advocates to maximize their use of forums that attract less social stigma, such as religious courts (Hirsch, 1998) and customary forums (Nyamu-Musembi, 2002). Informal spaces and seemingly humdrum administrative spaces (such as municipal housing authorities; see WLSA, 1995) all become sites for rights claims that challenge inequality.

Legality in relation to legitimacy

Ideally, the effectiveness of legal rights as a strategy for challenging inequality is enhanced when those rights resonate with existing social norms. Formal legality on its own inevitably proves to be an ineffective tool in the hands of the subordinated. However, legality and legitimacy do not always overlap. In some instances, establishing a claim in formal law is indispensable in boosting the social bargaining position of the subordinated person or group. Non-discrimination laws, for instance, can serve to embolden those who might be opposed to inequality but fail to speak up because the cost of positive deviance (or 'norm entrepreneurship') is too high, as was the case with civil rights laws in the USA (Sunstein, 1996, p. 2043). Law can and does challenge inequality by playing an expressive function, radiating messages about desirable social norms (Sunstein, 1996).

Conclusion

A review of the scholarship suggests that there is reason to be sceptical about the effectiveness of legal rights, certainly as the primary instrument for challenging inequality (McCann, 1998; Stryker, 2007). However, any assessment of whether legal rights are an effective instrument to challenge inequality must be multidimensional (Stryker, 2007, p. 75). Assessments that only take account of the instrumental (such as whether a specific court decision led to desegregation; see Rosenberg, 1991) will miss out on the subtle restructuring of power relations at the cultural or symbolic level. Securing 2 acres of land through participating in an MST[1] land occupation might not radically transform someone's economic prospects in rural Brazil, but its symbolic value against the backdrop of a long history of disenfranchisement through the twinning of land ownership with political power should not be underestimated (Navarro, 2005). An exclusively instrumental assessment also underestimates what rights subjectivity might do for the transformation of personal and collective identity that is necessary to galvanize and sustain a social movement (Williams, 1991; Kostiner, 2003).

Note

1. MST (Portuguese Movimento dos Trabalhadores Rurais Sem Terra) refers to a movement of the landless poor in Brazil, who acquire land through a combination of physical occupation and litigation.

Bibliography

Abel, R. 1995. *Politics by Other Means: Law in the Struggle against Apartheid, 1980–1994*. New York, Routledge.

Calmore, J. O. 1999. A call to context: the professional challenges of cause lawyering at the intersection of race, space, and poverty. *Fordham Law Review*, Vol. 67, No. 5, pp. 1927–57. http://ir.lawnet.fordham.edu/cgi/viewcontent.cgi?article=3552&context=flr (Accessed 8 February 2016.)

Clifford, J. 1988. *Identity in Mashpee. The Predicament of Culture: Twentieth-Century Ethnography, Literature, and Art*. Cambridge, Mass., Harvard University Press.

Cusack, S. 2013. The CEDAW as a legal framework for transnational discourses on stereotyping. A. H. and H. S. Aasen (eds), *Women's Human Rights: CEDAW in International, Regional and National Law*. Cambridge, UK, Cambridge University Press, pp. 124–57.

Handler, J. 1978. *Social Movements and the Legal System: A Theory of Law Reform and Social Change*. New York, Academic Press.

Hirsch, S. 1998. *Pronouncing and Persevering: Gender and the Discourses of Disputing in an African Islamic Court*. Chicago, Ill., University of Chicago Press.

Hirsch, S. F. and Lazarus-Black, M. 1994. Introduction – performance and paradox: exploring law's role in hegemony and resistance. S. F. Hirsch and M. Lazarus-Black (eds), *Contested States: Law, Hegemony and Resistance*. London, Routledge, pp. 1–31.

Hunt, A. 1990. Rights and social movements: counter-hegemonic strategies. *Journal of Law and Society*, Vol. 17, No. 3, pp. 309–28. www.jstor.org/stable/1410156?seq=1#page_scan_tab_contents (Accessed 8 February 2016.)

Kennedy, D. 1991. The stakes of law, or Hale and Foucault! *Legal Studies Forum*, Vol. 15, No. 4, pp. 327–66. http://duncankennedy.net/documents/The%20Stakes%20of%20Law%20or%20Hale%20and%20Foucault%20_%20J%20Leg%20Stud.pdf (Accessed 8 February 2016.)

Kostiner, I. 2003. Evaluating legality: toward a cultural approach to the study of law and social change. *Law and Society Review*, Vol. 37, No. 2, pp. 323–68. http://onlinelibrary.wiley.com/doi/10.1111/1540-5893.3702006/abstract (Accessed 8 February 2016.)

MacKinnon, C. 1987. *Feminism Unmodified: Discourses on Life and Law*. Cambridge, Mass., Harvard University Press.

McCann, M. 1998. How does law matter for social movements? B. G. Garth and Austin Sarat (eds), *How Does Law Matter?* Chicago, Ill., Northwest University Press, pp. 76–108.

McLellan, D. 1977, 2000. *Karl Marx: Selected Writings*. Oxford, Oxford University Press, pp. 200–1.

Merry, S. E. 2006. *Human Rights and Gender Violence: Translating International Law into Local Justice*. Chicago, Ill., University of Chicago Press.

Musembi, C. 2013. Pulling apart? Treatment of pluralism in CEDAW and Maputo Protocol. A. Hellum and H. S. Aasen (eds), *Women's Human Rights: CEDAW in International, Regional and National Law*. Cambridge, UK, Cambridge University Press, pp. 183–213.

Navarro, Z. 2005. Transforming rights into social practices? The landless movement and land reform in Brazil. *IDS Bulletin*, Vol. 36, No. 1, pp. 129–37. www.drc-citizenship.org/system/assets/1052734497/original/1052734497-navarro.2005-transforming.pdf?1289507836 (Accessed 8 February 2016.)

Nyamu-Musembi, C. 2002. Are local norms and practices fences or pathways? The example of women's property rights. A. An-Na'im (ed.), *Cultural Transformation and Human Rights in Africa*. London, Zed Books, pp. 126–50.

Robins, S. 2001. NGOs, 'bushmen' and double vision: the Khomani San land claim and the cultural politics of 'community' and 'development' in the Kalahari. *Journal of Southern African Studies*, Vol. 27, No. 4, pp. 833–53. http://r4d.dfid.gov.uk/PDF/Outputs/CentreOnCitizenship/robins.pdf (Accessed 8 February 2016.)

Rosenberg, G. N. 1991. *The Hollow Hope: Can Courts Bring About Social Change?* Chicago, Ill., University of Chicago Press.

Scott, J. 1985. *Weapons of the Weak: Everyday Forms of Peasant Resistance*. New Haven, Conn., Yale University Press.

Simon, W. H. 2004. Solving problems vs. claiming rights: the pragmatist challenge to legal liberalism. *William and Mary Law Review*, Vol. 46, No. 1, pp. 127–212. http://scholarship.law.wm.edu/cgi/viewcontent.cgi?article=1269&context=wmlr (Accessed 8 February 2016.)

Stryker, R. 2007. Half empty, half full, or neither: law, inequality, and social change in capitalist democracies. *Annual Review of Law and Social Science*, Vol. 3, No. 1, pp. 69–97. https://www.researchgate.net/publication/228190777_Half_Empty_Half_Full_or_Neither_Law_Inequality_and_Social_Change_in_Capitalist_Democracies (Accessed 8 February 2016.)

Sunstein, C. 1996. On the expressive function of law. *University of Pennsylvania Law Review*, Vol. 144, pp. 2021–53. http://papers.ssrn.com/sol3/papers.cfm?abstract_id=2622561 (Accessed 8 February 2016.)

Thompson, E. P. 1975. *Whigs and Hunters: The Origins of the Black Act*. New York, Pantheon.

Williams, P.J. 1991. *The Alchemy of Race and Rights*. Cambridge, Harvard University Press.

WLSA (Women and Law in Southern Africa). 1995. Beyond Research: WLSA in Action. Working Paper No. 10. Harare, WLSA Trust. https://searchworks.stanford.edu/view/4260139 (Accessed 8 February 2016.)

■ **Celestine Nyamu Musembi** *(Kenya) is a senior lecturer at the University of Nairobi, School of Law and a former research fellow at the Institute of Development Studies (IDS), Brighton, UK.*

POSTCARD

54. Reducing inequality through transformative institutional policies: the case of the Industrial Court of Nigeria

Caroline Joelle Nwabueze

International labour standards promote opportunities for all workers to obtain decent and productive work in conditions of freedom, equity, security and dignity. They are essential ingredients for ensuring equality for all in the workplace. Ratification of the International Labour Organization (ILO) Declaration on Fundamental Principles and Rights at Work (ILO, 1998) and its follow-up, the Addis Ababa Declaration (ILO, 2015) commits Member States to respect and promote principles and rights at work in four categories: 'freedom of association and the effective recognition of the right to collective bargaining, the elimination of forced or compulsory labour, the abolition of child labour and the elimination of discrimination in respect of employment and occupation' (ILO, 1998). International labour standards constitute a viable legal force which influences equality in labour market structure, both in providing a frame of reference for positive behaviours and social policy, and by placing a veto on negative practices which work against the establishment of equality for all in the marketplace. Standards promoting equality in the workplace will, however, be a vain slogan if they are not enforceable.

Nigeria is one of the few countries in Africa with a national, specialized Labour Law Court to which any individual, or group of individuals, may have access for the purpose of enforcing their rights as contained in the Declaration. The National Industrial Court of Nigeria[1] has since the third alteration of the National Constitution of 2010 been conferred with exclusive jurisdiction over matters relating to international labour law, best practices in labour, and the application or interpretation of international labour standards. The implication of this is that the standards can be enforced without having to be translated and passed as national law.

The basic and fundamental ILO Declaration concerning principles and rights at work creates a legal framework for regulating labour practices, together with the following Conventions: No. 100 Equal Remuneration Convention, 1951; No. 111 Discrimination (Employment and Occupation) Convention, 1958; No. 156 Workers with Family Responsibilities Convention, 1981; and No. 159 Vocational Rehabilitation and Employment (Disabled Persons) Convention, 1983.

A case illustrating the statutory protection afforded to those who seek redress of their rights at work

The case in question is Adebusola Adedayo Omole *v.* Mainstreet Bank Microfinance Bank LTD [2015] 53 N.L.L.R.[2]

The claimant filed a lawsuit against her employer for reasons to do with her salary having been reduced or withheld by her employer. The judge noted:

> *It is important for it to be said here and now that at the global level a unilateral reduction in the wages and salaries of workers is not acceptable. We must bear in mind that no nation can be an island to herself and any nation that seeks to do so will be doing so at its own peril. Thus the need to ensure that the Nigerian labour jurisprudence is in tandem with what is obtainable at the international scene found reflection in the National Industrial Court Act, 2006.*

He ordered the defendant to pay the claimant the sum of 1,386,652 Nigerian naira, corresponding to the total amount taken by the defendant from the claimant's salary without her consent, plus 15 per cent interest on this sum for the specified period.

Through enforcing international labour standards, the Nigerian Industrial Court creates the conditions for reducing inequality,[3] and participates in furthering ILO aims and the transformation of Africa through decent labour practices and rights at work.[4]

Acknowledgement

The ideas raised here were first presented at the World Social Science Forum 2015 in Durban, South Africa.

Notes

1. *http://nicn.gov.ng/jurisdiction.php#*

2. For full particulars of this case, see *http://judgment.nicn.gov.ng/pdf.php?case_id=676* and for others related to the argument here *http://judgment.nicn.gov.ng/courtRuling.php*

3. See Okafor (2010).

4. See the 2015 Addis Ababa Declaration for 'Transforming Africa through Decent Work for Sustainable Development' which involved governments, employers and workers from forty-five African countries (ILO, 2015).

Bibliography

ILO. 1998. ILO Declaration on Fundamental Principles and Rights at Work. *www.ilo.org/declaration/lang--en/index.htm* (Accessed 13 June 2016.)

ILO. 2015. Addis Ababa Declaration. *www.ilo.org/global/meetings-and-events/regional-meetings/africa/arm-13/reports/WCMS_432579/lang--en/index.htm* (Accessed 13 June 2016.)

National Industrial Court of Nigeria. 2010. National Industrial Court of Nigeria's Jurisdiction. *http://nicn.gov.ng/jurisdiction.php#* (Accessed 13 June 2016.)

Okafor, O. C. 2010. What should organized human rights activism in Africa become? Contributory insights from a comparison of NGOs and labor-led movements in Nigeria. *Buffalo Human Rights Law Review*, Vol. 16, pp. 113–53.

■ ***Caroline Joelle Nwabueze** (Cameroon) is lecturer in industrial law at Enugu State University of Science and Technology Faculty of Law, Enugu, Nigeria.*

55. Social protection, inequality and social justice

Keetie Roelen, Rachel Sabates-Wheeler and Stephen Devereux

Social protection refers to a range of policies that explicitly aim to reduce poverty and vulnerability, and which have the potential to be redistributive. This contribution argues that social protection can significantly contribute to reducing inequality and social injustice, particularly when it is designed and delivered in conjunction with complementary initiatives. Emerging evidence from middle and low-income countries makes a compelling case for social protection's positive impacts on addressing both material and non-material inequalities.

Introduction

Social protection is a suite of policy instruments that explicitly aims to reduce poverty and vulnerability and has the potential to be redistributive. While narrow 'residual' definitions focus on its safety net and social welfare functions, expanded 'rights-based' conceptualizations emphasize its ability to address social injustices, by reducing material and non-material inequalities and promoting social inclusion and universal access to essential social services. This contribution makes the case that social protection can be a powerful tool for reducing inequality and social injustice, particularly when it is designed and delivered in conjunction with complementary initiatives. We review the evidence for social protection impacts on both material and non-material inequalities.

Evolution of social protection

In the past decade, social protection has become an essential element of development interventions and social policy. *Figure 55.1* shows that by 2012, the number of countries in the 'developing world' with social assistance programmes had risen to over 160, from under 20 in 1990. Since the 1990s, social protection has evolved to include a wide set of policies that aim to offer protection against the experience of poverty, to prevent people from falling into poverty, to promote people out of poverty, and to address structural inequalities that lock people into poverty (Devereux and Sabates-Wheeler, 2004).

Popular instruments include social transfers, encompassing unconditional cash or in-kind transfers (including child grants, social pensions and school feeding); conditional cash transfers (CCTs); public works; social insurance schemes; and more recently, broader graduation programmes. The current popularity of graduation programmes reflects the growing acknowledgement that the desired impacts of traditional social protection instruments are best achieved when they are delivered in conjunction with a variety of other multisectoral interventions such as nutrition support, savings and loan programmes, and training.

Social protection, and social transfers in particular, are being called upon as a tool in the fight against inequality, from both a material (income and consumption) and a non-material (such as access to services, social exclusion) perspective.

Material inequality

Evidence about the impact of social transfers on material inequality in low and middle-income countries is scarce but expanding, particularly in middle-income countries. South Africa's longstanding experience with social grants offers compelling evidence. The combination of social grants (including the old age pension, child support grant and disability grant) has a modest but significant impact on inequality. Samson and colleagues (2004) found that social grants reduced the national Gini coefficient from 0.63 to 0.60 in 2000 (see *Figure 55.2*).

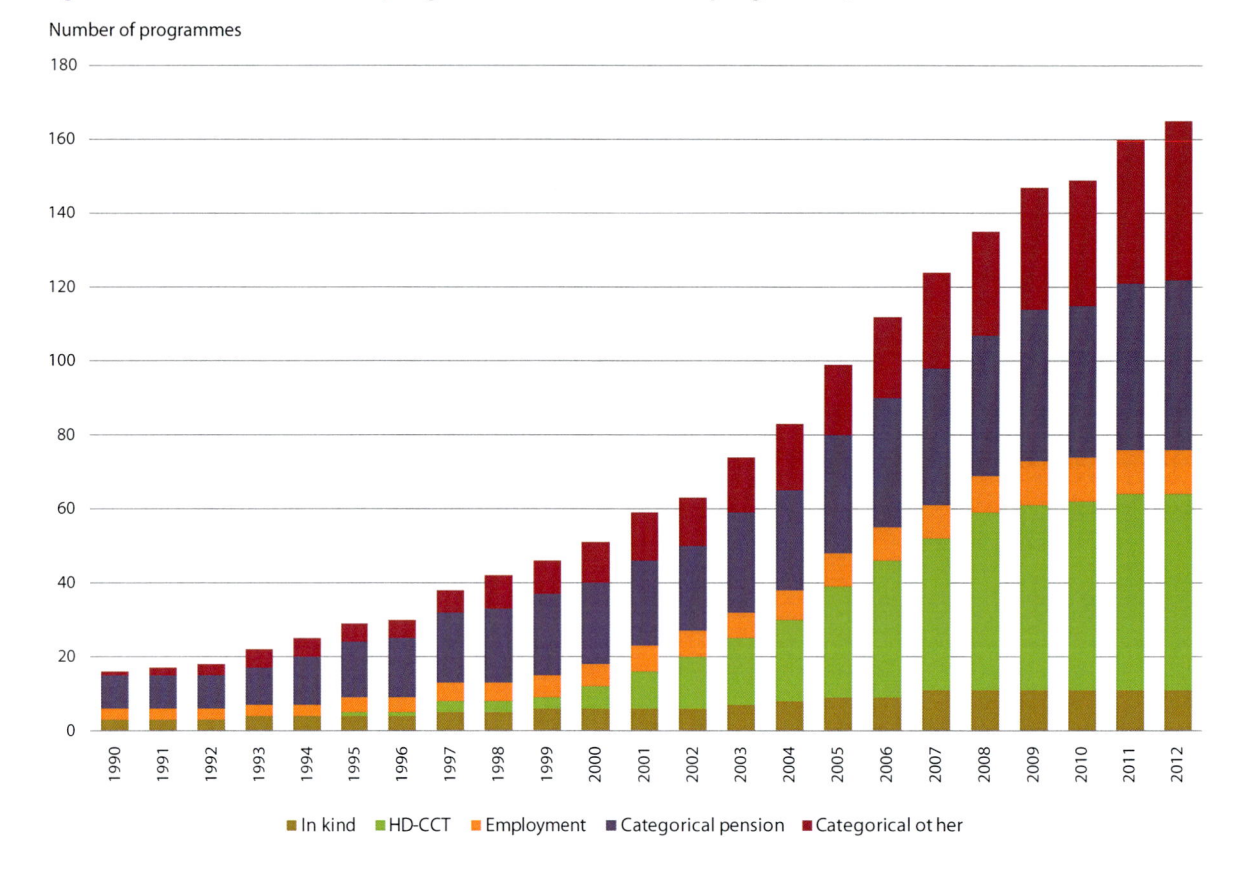

Figure 55.1 **Social assistance programmes in the 'developing world', 1990 to 2012**

Number of programmes

■ In kind   ■ HD-CCT   ■ Employment   ■ Categorical pension   ■ Categorical other

Note: HD-CCT = human development-conditional cash transfers.
Source: Barrientos et al. (2010).

This impact increased over time, with social grants contributing to an overall reduction in the Gini coefficient of 0.02 in 1995 compared with 0.05 in 2005. The impact has been differentiated for specific population groups. In 2005, the Gini coefficient among the White and Asian population was reduced by 0.01 compared with 0.04 for the Coloured[1] population and 0.10 for the African population as a result of social grants (Bhorat et al., 2009).

Latin America's experiences with CCTs also suggest an important role for social transfers. In Mexico and Brazil, the Oportunidades and Bolsa Família programmes were responsible for 21 per cent of the reduction in income inequality between the mid-1990s and mid-2000s (Soares et al., 2009). This makes CCTs the second most powerful driving force behind decreasing inequality after labour income (Soares et al., 2009).

The distributional impact of social transfers on income relies heavily on coverage and levels of spending. Significant transfer values, adequate coverage of the poorest population and effective targeting (Lustig et al., 2012; Bastagli, 2015) can ensure that social protection makes a significant contribution to reducing inequality. In Argentina, 90 per cent of the poor and indigenous population receive some form of cash transfer (Lustig et al., 2012), contributing to a reduction of vertical and horizontal income inequalities. In South Africa, the increasing impact of social transfers on inequality over time can be attributed to expansion of coverage, and increased expenditures on social spending (Bhorat et al., 2009).

By contrast, limited reductions in material inequality are to be expected from schemes with relatively low coverage of poor and vulnerable groups and modest transfer values, typical of low-income countries. Yet the continuing expansion of social protection shows promise for its role in tackling inequality. Ethiopia's Productive Safety Net Programme (PSNP) is a case in point. The PSNP provides food-insecure households with a transfer in lean times to avoid asset depletion and protect livelihoods.

Figure 55.2 **The impact of social grants on income inequality in South Africa**

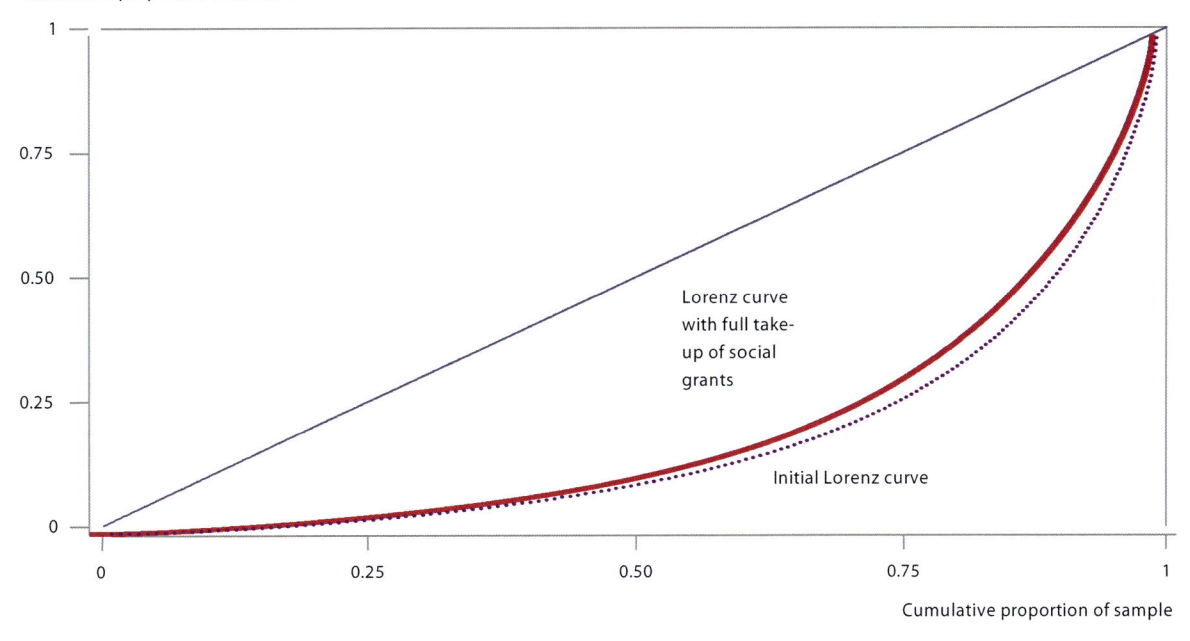

The diagonal line illustrates perfect equality: 10 per cent of the population get 10 per cent of national income, 50 per cent of the population get 50 per cent of national income, and so on. The outer 'initial Lorenz curve' shows how unequal the distribution of income is in South Africa without social grants – the poorest 75 per cent of the population get less than 25 per cent of national income, while the richest 25 per cent get more than 75 per cent, for instance. The inner 'Lorenz curve with full take-up of social grants' shows how the distribution of income moves visibly towards the line of perfect equality, thanks to income transfers to the poor.

Source: Samson et al. (2004) based on Statistics South Africa Income and Expenditure 2000 data.

Transfers are provided directly or through a public works component. Spending on PSNP transfers and food security programmes is the most progressive of all types of social spending in Ethiopia: 58 per cent of transfers go to households below the national poverty line and 66 per cent of all transfers are concentrated in the bottom two quintiles of the income distribution (World Bank, 2015). The joint distributional impact of tax and social welfare in Ethiopia reduces the Gini coefficient by 2 percentage points, largely due to the progressivity of social spending and the PSNP in particular (ibid.). As this impact on inequality is achieved against a backdrop of wide coverage (10 million people, or 11 per cent of the population), modest transfer amounts, and imminent tax reform, the potential for social protection to reduce inequality in low-income countries becomes evident.

Non-material inequality

The ability of social protection to tackle non-material inequalities is much more complex than the issue of social transfers. This is because vulnerability and exclusion are grounded in social norms that dictate access to resources in terms of social categories. Access constraints exist because of a range of factors, including lack of income, self-exclusion, lack of knowledge of processes, lack of information, positive discrimination and cultural norms. Different social protection interventions and programme design features can be successful in removing some of these constraints, enabling otherwise excluded and marginalized individuals to participate, and claim benefits and services.

Unequal access to knowledge and information leads to inequities in the uptake of social protection. In fact, 'specified [social protection] entitlements and rights are only as useful as the access structures that surround them. Much of this turns on the ability of individuals/households to establish and persuade providers of their eligibility for the resource' (MacAuslan and Sabates-Wheeler, 2011, p. 83). In other words, the sociopolitical structures that allow access to social protection are highly relevant to marginalized and excluded groups, and are often much more difficult to overcome than material barriers.

Sensitization and training events are critical to ensuring that households know what they are entitled to, how to access it and how to use their resources effectively and efficiently. Information barriers to social provision also apply to simple instructions about how to use a health-care provider, or how and where to register for a programme. For instance, potential beneficiaries often fail to access social protection programmes because they are unaware of the registration procedures. In Colombia's Familias en Acción, for example, local officers of the national registration agency are present at the enrolment of new beneficiaries by the programme agency in order to speed up and facilitate participant households in meeting this requirement. Parents or care givers can obtain the certificates needed for enrolment in the programme without spending additional resources on travelling to different places (Barrientos et al., 2013).

Notwithstanding the complexities, a recent qualitative study on the South African child support grant (CSG) (Adato et al., 2016) highlights how material provision is closely connected with non-material status, and how improvements in material status can alleviate social barriers. The CSG is able to partly counteract the powerful non-material drivers of education choice for adolescents. 'One of these drivers is shame related to poverty: for poor children, the food they bring (or don't bring) to school, the quality of their clothing and shoes, and their hairstyles can be significant sources of embarrassment, even keeping them away from school' (Adato et al., 2016, p. 1133). Adolescents can convert social protection in the form of cash into symbolic capital which facilitates inclusion into social networks and ultimately into opportunities that convert to economic capital. 'That is, these status goods potentially increase the likelihood that children will show up and stay in school, allowing them access to the economic opportunities that education provides' (Adato et al., 2016, p. 1134).

But while material transfers can be used to overcome social barriers, there are also cases in which social barriers inhibit the translation of material transfers into reductions in inequalities. In Mexico the conditional cash transfer programme Oportunidades has increased access to education for children in participating households. However, evidence suggests that indigenous people face discrimination in the labour market that counteracts their education attainments. So improving the education of indigenous children does not necessarily translate into better job prospects and higher incomes in adulthood (Ulrichs and Roelen, 2012).

Kabeer (2010) pointed out that socially excluded groups face multiple, intersecting and mutually reinforcing inequalities, which operate at the cultural, spatial, economic and political levels (among others). One implication is that interventions that address only one source of inequality are unlikely to reduce poverty and promote social inclusion if other sources remain unaddressed. Research in Ghana and Rwanda has found that although cash transfers support the provision of kinship care to orphans, they do not address the existing inequalities between biological children and orphans (Roelen, 2016). Another implication is that targeted interventions are required to redress 'inherited inequalities'. These might include affirmative action measures and specially designed social protection programmes.

Sometimes positive discrimination (affirmative action), or simply removing a source of discrimination, can be sufficient to promote social inclusion and reduce inequalities. In India, programmes that target 'BPLs' (below poverty line) and scheduled castes attempt to reverse practices of social and economic exclusion (Kabeer, 2010). In South Africa, legislation was passed that prohibits discrimination against anyone on the basis of their HIV status. Because it prevents employers from requiring job applicants to take an AIDS test, HIV-positive people can now access work opportunities on equal terms with everyone else. Nonetheless, South Africa's extensive social grants system has been criticized as providing material compensation for systematic inequalities, rather than addressing these fundamental determinants of poverty and inequality directly, or being complemented by social and economic policies that do so.

Conclusion

In high-income and middle-income countries, social transfer programmes can be sufficiently comprehensive and generous to achieve measurable reductions in poverty and income inequality. In low-income countries, the coverage of social transfers is less comprehensive, and the amounts transferred to beneficiaries are too small to lift them out of poverty or to substantially reduce income inequality. Nonetheless, the Sustainable Development Goals (SDGs) reflect the emerging consensus that social protection can make a more significant contribution. SDG 1 refers to national social protection floors, which guarantee income security to all throughout the life cycle, as an instrument for poverty reduction. SDG 10 advocates adopting social protection policies for progressively achieving greater equality.

Even when social protection leads to positive impacts on measurable distribution outcomes, a more radical question worth exploring is whether, and to what extent, social protection programmes primarily serve a political function to placate the poor and their demands for economic and social justice, rather than being a genuinely effective mechanism for redistribution.

In terms of non-material inequalities, sensitively designed social protection interventions have some potential to help poor people overcome social exclusion and access barriers. SDG 5 sees social protection as a tool for achieving gender equality. But given the complex nature of the 'intersecting inequalities' that are faced by poor and socially excluded people, social protection alone should not be expected to achieve social transformation. Social protection must be complemented by other social and economic policies to achieve maximum impact in reducing both material and non-material inequalities.

Note

1. In Southern Africa, the term 'Coloured' is a contested ethnic label for people of mixed ethnic origin who possess ancestry from Europe, Asia and various Khoisan and Bantu ethnic groups.

Bibliography

Adato, M., Devereux, S. and Sabates-Wheeler, R. 2016. Accessing the 'right' kinds of material and symbolic capital: the role of cash transfers in reducing adolescent school absence and risky behaviour in South Africa. *Journal of Development Studies*, Vol. 52, No. 8, pp. 1132–46.

Barrientos, A., Byrne, J., Villa, J. M. and Pena, P. 2013. *Social Transfers and Child Protection*. Working Paper no. 2013-05. Florence, Italy, UNICEF Office of Research. www.unicef-irc.org/publications/pdf/iwp_2013_05.pdf (Accessed 1 February 2016.)

Barrientos, A., Niño-Zarazúa, M. and Maitrot, M. 2010. Social Assistance in Developing Countries Database Version 5, Report. Manchester, UK, Brooks World Poverty Institute.

Bastagli, F. 2015. *Bringing Taxation into Social Protection Analysis and Planning,* Working Paper 421. London, Overseas Development Institute (ODI). www.odi.org/sites/odi.org.uk/files/odi-assets/publications-opinion-files/9700.pdf (Accessed 1 February 2016.)

Bhorat, H., van der Westhuizen, C. and Jacobs, T. 2009. *Income and Non-Income Inequality in Post-Apartheid South Africa: What are the Drivers and Possible Policy Interventions?* Pretoria, Trade and Industrial Policy Strategies (TIPS), Development Policy Research Unit (DPRU). www.tips.org.za/files/u65/income_and_non-income_inequality_in_post-apartheid_south_africa_-_bhorat_van_der_westhuizen_jacobs.pdf (Accessed 1 February 2016.)

Devereux, S. and Sabates-Wheeler, R. 2004. *Transformative Social Protection*. Working Paper no. 232. Brighton, UK, IDS. http://opendocs.ids.ac.uk/opendocs/bitstream/handle/123456789/4071/Wp232.pdf?sequence=1 (Accessed 1 February 2016.)

Kabeer, N. 2010. *Can the MDGs Provide a Pathway to Social Justice? The Challenges of Intersecting Inequalities.* New York and Brighton, UN MDG Achievement Fund and IDS. www.ids.ac.uk/idspublication/can-the-mdgs-provide-a-pathway-to-social-justice-the-challenges-of-intersecting-inequalities (Accessed 1 February 2016.)

Lustig, N., Pessino, C. and Scott, J. 2012. *The Impact of Taxes and Social Spending on Inequality and Poverty in Argentina, Bolivia, Brazil, Mexico, and Peru: A Synthesis of Results.* Working Paper 311. Washington DC, Center for Global Development. www.cgdev.org/publication/impact-taxes-and-social-spending-inequality-and-poverty-argentina-bolivia-brazil-mexico (Accessed 1 February 2016.)

MacAuslan, I. and Sabates-Wheeler, R. 2011. Structures of access to social provision for migrants. R. Sabates-Wheeler and R. Feldman (eds), *Migration and Social Protection: Claiming Rights beyond Borders*. New York, Palgrave Macmillan, pp. 61–90.

Niño-Zarazúa, M. 2015. Social assistance in sub-Saharan Africa. Will the green shoots blossom? Presentation at UNU-WIDER 30th Anniversary Conference, Mapping the Future of Development Economics, Helsinki, 17–19 September 2015. www1.wider.unu.edu/30thanniversary/sites/default/files/IGA/Nino-Zarazua.pdf (Accessed 1 February 2016.)

Roelen, K. 2016. *Cash for Care: Making Social Protection Work for Children's Care and Well-being*. London, Family for Every Child/IDS/Challenging Heights/Uyisenga Ni Manzi/Children in Distress Network.

Samson, M., Lee, U., Ndlebe, A., Mac Quene, K., van Niekerk, I., Gandhi, V., Narigaya, T. and Abrahams, C. 2004. *The Social and Economic Impact of South Africa's Social Security System*. Cape Town, Economic Policy Research Institute (EPRI). *http://allafrica.com/download/resource/main/main/idatcs/00010352:3ca37b223f2ad1b0dc6479ccca726034.pdf* (Accessed 1 February 2016.)

Soares, S., Osório, R. G., Soares, F. V., Medeiros, M. and Zepeda, E. 2009. Conditional cash transfers in Brazil, Chile and Mexico: impacts upon inequality. *Estudios Económicas*, Special Issue, pp. 207–44. *http://carnegieendowment.org/files/conditional_cash_transfers1.pdf* (Accessed 1 February 2016.)

Ulrichs, M. and Roelen, K. 2012. *Equal Opportunities for All? – A Critical Analysis of Mexico's Oportunidades*. IDS Working Paper no. 413/CSP Working Paper no. 007. Brighton, UK, IDS. *www.ids.ac.uk/publication/equal-opportunities-for-all-a-critical-analysis-of-mexico-s-oportunidades* (Accessed 1 February 2016.)

World Bank. 2015. *Ethiopia Poverty Assessment*. Addis Ababa, World Bank. *http://documents.worldbank.org/curated/en/2015/01/24190845/ethiopia-poverty-assessment* (Accessed 1 February 2016.)

■ **Keetie Roelen** (Netherlands) *is a research fellow at the Institute of Development Studies (IDS), Brighton, UK and a co-director of the Centre for Social Protection.*

■ **Rachel Sabates-Wheeler** (UK) *is a research fellow at IDS and a co-director of the Centre for Social Protection.*

■ **Stephen Devereux** (South Africa) *is a research fellow at IDS and a co-director of the Centre for Social Protection.*

POSTCARD

56. Unconditional basic income

Erik Olin Wright

The idea of an unconditional basic income (UBI) is quite simple: every legal resident in a country receives a monthly stipend sufficient to live above the poverty line. Let's call this the 'no frills culturally respectable standard of living'. The grant is unconditional on the performance of any labour or other form of contribution, and it is universal – everyone receives the grant, rich and poor alike. Grants go to individuals, not families. Parents are the custodians of under-age children's grants, which may be smaller than the grants for adults.

Universalistic programmes such as public education and healthcare, that provide services to people rather than cash, continue alongside UBI, but most other redistributive transfers are eliminated since the UBI provides everyone with a decent subsistence. This means that in welfare systems that already provide generous anti-poverty income support through a patchwork of specialized programmes, the net increase in cost represented by UBI is not large. Special needs subsidies of various sorts continue – for example, for people with disabilities – but they are also smaller than now since the basic cost of living is covered by UBI. Minimum wage rules are relaxed, since there is little need to prohibit below-subsistence wages if all earnings in effect generate discretionary income. While everyone receives the grant, most people at any given point in time are probably net contributors since their taxes rise by more than the basic income they receive.

UBI has potentially profound ramifications for inequality. Poverty is eliminated, the labour contract becomes more nearly voluntary, and the power relations between workers and employers become less unequal since workers have the option of exit.

The possibility of people forming cooperative associations to produce goods and services to serve human need outside the market increases since such activity no longer needs to provide the basic standard of living for participants.

Sceptics of basic income typically raise two main objections: that UBI would reduce incentives to work and reduce the supply of labour, and that the tax rates needed to fund UBI would be prohibitively high.

Two things can be said about the incentive issue. First, means-tested income support programmes are plagued by poverty traps in which people lose their benefits when their earned income crosses some threshold. By contrast, a UBI creates no disincentive to work. Paid work always increases the discretionary income of people with a UBI. Second, while no country has adopted a full basic income, there have been a few limited experiments in various places in the world which enable us to examine the effects of UBI on labour force participation. In the United States and Canada in the 1970s there were a number of randomized controlled trials, most notably in Seattle and Denver, in which randomly selected low-income individuals received a UBI. More recently, in India in 2011, eight villages were selected in which all residents were given a basic income. In all of these experiments, receiving a UBI significantly improved the lives of people while having at most a modest effect on labour force participation.

The level of taxation needed to pay for a basic income is, of course, an important issue. But the sustainable level of taxation in any country is not mainly an economic issue. It is a political issue that depends on the administrative capacity to extract taxes and the political will to do so.

Bibliography

Ackerman, B., Allstott, A. and van Parijs, P. 2006. Redesigning distribution: basic income and stakeholder grants as cornerstones of an egalitarian capitalism. E. O. Wright (ed.), *The Real Utopias Project*, Vol. V. London, Verso.

Standing, G. 2015. India's experiment in basic income grants. *Global Dialogues*, Vol. 5, No. 4. http://isa-global-dialogue.net/indias-great-experiment-the-transformative-potential-of-basic-income-grants/ (Accessed 1 February 2016.)

Van Parijs, P. 1995. *Real Freedom for All*. Oxford, Oxford University Press.

■ **Erik Olin Wright** (USA) *is professor of sociology at the University of Wisconsin-Madison, Wisconsin, USA. His research interests include: rethinking the Marxist tradition of social science; class structure and its transformations in contemporary capitalism; and 'real utopias', understood as viable emancipatory alternatives to contemporary institutions. His most recent publications include* Alternatives to Capitalism *(with Robin Hahnel, New Left Project, 2016),* Understanding Class *(Verso, 2015),* American Society: How It Really Works *(with Joel Rogers, W. W. Norton, 2015), and* Envisioning Real Utopias *(Verso, 2010).*

POSTCARD

57. Universal health coverage as a powerful social equalizer

Rüdiger Krech

Wide disparities in the health status of different population groups persist in all countries, whether low, middle or high-income. The poorest of the poor have the highest risk of bad health. Health inequalities arise from differences in social and economic conditions, and also intersect with and compound other inequalities, for example by affecting an individual's ability to study, work and earn.

Dr Margaret Chan, director-general of the World Health Organization, has said that 'Universal Health Coverage (UHC) is the single most powerful concept that public health has to offer to address persistent health inequalities'. It operationalizes the highest ethical principles of public health. It is a powerful social equalizer and an expression of fairness. And it is the best way to cement the health gains made during the previous decade.

But the aspiration of UHC will only be realized with consistent, immediate and comprehensive health system strengthening (HSS) efforts. Health systems must deliver on health outcomes and on the well-being of the populations they serve. But recent health emergencies such as the Ebola and Zika virus outbreaks, and natural disasters in Nepal or the Philippines, illustrate the point that health systems must also be prepared to guarantee the health security of the population. Moreover, bugs don't respect borders. The interconnectedness of this world means that health security becomes an ever bigger issue. Therefore, it is in every country's interest that all countries strive for universal health coverage and have health systems that can adapt to changing situations, speedily detect threats, and act.

UHC is defined as ensuring that all people and communities receive the quality health services they need without fear of financial hardship. This includes prevention, promotion, treatment, rehabilitation and palliation. With the adoption of the Sustainable Development Goals (SDGs), governments around the globe have embraced this concept.

In most countries, there are stark differences in the availability, accessibility, acceptability and quality of health services between population groups, often according to their socio-economic condition. Access for all to the health system calls for a UHC strategy to analyse, and when possible address, the societal conditions preventing access by specific population groups. Community engagement and consistent political will are needed to support the implementation of UHC in national policies.

To deliver, a health system needs workers, facilities, money, information, medicines and technologies, communications and transport, as well as overall leadership and direction. It also needs to put people at the centre, while providing services that are responsive and financially affordable. There is no predefined set of services, or one approach to financial protection mechanisms that is applicable to all countries. Policies and plans for UHC need to be sensitive to local and national contexts, as well as to epidemiological trends. But the design, implementation and monitoring of UHC in different country contexts tend to involve these elements:

● A specific set of health services (often known as a 'benefit package' including health promotion, prevention, treatment, rehabilitation and palliative services) aimed at ensuring integrated care and continuity across levels of care;

● Financial pre-payment mechanisms to prevent financial hardship of the population as a result of health expenditures;

● Criteria for system performance based on effective coverage rather than nominal service availability, highlighting the need to ensure equity in access for all and to monitor and address health inequities. This is important for ultimately attaining universal coverage.

Determinants outside the health sector can prevent, as well as enable, the success of a UHC strategy.

Not understanding the key determinants of access by specific populations would significantly undermine the goals of UHC, as they all influence the acceptability of services and access to them. Issues here might include social, political, commercial, economic, environmental and cultural factors, poverty, gender, education, national and local governance, trade policies, cultural dynamics and so on. Other determinants from outside the health sector (such as water and sanitation, and agriculture) are also relevant to specific health conditions. Agriculture influences food supply and nutrition, and subsequently diet, obesity and malnutrition.

By constantly improving service provision to vulnerable groups, for example through patient-centred approaches or responsive opening hours, the health system can reduce inequities in access through its managerial functions.

Additionally, the health system can reduce these inequities through its stewardship function, by using instruments coming from the fields of health promotion, social epidemiology and policy analysis. Ministries of health are increasingly feeling the need to adapt their core agendas at national and local levels to implement UHC and deliver equitable health outcomes.

In short, UHC is 'actionable': actions can be taken both within and outside the health sector, by the health sector alone or by partnering with other sectors.

For more detail on the World Health Organization's work on UHC see *www.who.int/universal_health_coverage/en/*

■ *Rüdiger Krech (Germany) is director, health systems and innovation at the World Health Organization.*

58. Critical elements for ensuring the success of more inclusive social policies

Michael Woolcock

Making social policy and implementing social policy are two different things. To be effective and reduce inequality, inclusive social policies must be carefully designed and politically supported. Crucially, they must also be implemented, by the agencies designated to do so. Yet most debates give this issue vastly inadequate attention. This contribution offers two constructive ways in which strategies for enhancing capability for implementation might be enhanced.

An array of social policies have been put in place in different countries with the objective of improving the well-being of all, including the most vulnerable, and reducing inequality, but they have not all been as effective as expected. As a result, identifying the critical elements that could facilitate the success of inclusive social policies is a key question. The success of such policies is not easy to determine when everyone (or a specific target group) is eligible to participate; when there is wide demographic and geographic variation in effectiveness; when the benefits might not materialize for long periods of time; when a given policy is as much a reflection of a society's values as it is of its welfare strategies; and when the truth of any empirical claim regarding a social programme's success or lack of it is filtered through people's ideological preconceptions. For example, there is an abundance of high-quality empirical evidence showing that raising minimum wages and providing universal health care is good for both low-income workers and society in general. But that evidence simply has no policy traction in contexts ideologically opposed to the very possibility of such initiatives.

I argue here that the critical elements ensuring the realization of a social policy are largely to do with implementation. The key questions are: can the agency designated to implement the social policy actually do so? Does it have the necessary funding, staff, local legitimacy and organizational capability to do what is being asked of it?

If it lacks any of these elements, what is its strategy for acquiring them, or optimizing in their absence? This contribution addresses these questions and highlights the salience of implementation issues with two examples, one at an analytical level, from a regional study of the quality of service delivery in the Middle East and North Africa region, and a second at the operational level, from attempts to improve learning outcomes in rural India.

Learning from variation in the quality of service delivery[1]

For historical reasons, most countries in the Middle East and North Africa have highly centralized systems for providing services to their citizens. This means that the same structures and policies guide the actions of teachers, health personnel and mid-level officials across any given country. In Jordan, for example, teachers across the country are trained, hired and promoted on the same criteria, they implement the same curriculum using the same pedagogical techniques, and students are assessed using the same examination methods. Yet when we examine how well these policies are implemented, we find enormous subnational variation in the provision of inputs and attainment of outcomes, even after allowing for obvious factors that might explain these differences, such as a community's wealth or proximity to roads. Some schools and health clinics are exemplary, most perform poorly even by local standards, and many are utterly failing.

This variation cannot be a function of policy or resources, since the policies and resource provision across the country are essentially identical. In seeking to explain this variation and identify possible entry points for reform and improvement, policy in itself matters but is surely of secondary importance.

An initial implication is that reform efforts should focus on mapping, explaining and learning from this variation as a basis for seeking to move the performance distribution in a positive direction. Moreover, it is highly likely that the underlying sources of performance variation at any given unit of analysis will be a combination of observable and unobservable factors. The first group should be assessed via household surveys and other quantitative approaches, and the second via qualitative methods whose comparative advantage is in engaging with questions of process, context and social relations. Using quantitative methods to map the nature and extent of subnational variation in policy implementation outcomes, and qualitative methods to explain how and why certain places and facilities are so much better or worse than others, enables local practitioners (including political leaders) to have a coherent and usable evidence base on which to convene an informed dialogue on where and how opportunities for improvement might be sought.

For complex social policies which have a strong impact on equality, such as education and health care, successful delivery requires the continuous combining of 'thin' (readily measurable) information and 'thick' (context-specific) knowledge. Because the ways in which this combining occurs are likely to be unique to each context, the most credible ideas for improvement are likely to come from a country's own experience, and not from the adoption of 'best practices' from abroad, verified by global 'experts'. Helping implementation systems themselves to become learning organizations which implement social policies to learn iteratively and adaptively, in real time, on the basis of their existing experience, is a frontier issue for those seeking to enhance the effectiveness of social policies.

In Yemen, for example, absenteeism of nurses and doctors from health clinics on any given day ranges from 8 per cent to 93 per cent. Similarly wide variation is seen at all levels, especially in large countries such as Egypt.[2] Interestingly, there is little correlation between different input and outcome factors.

Places where nurse absenteeism is high are not also those places where medical supplies are lacking, or where there are too few beds. There is unlikely to be a singular technical fix to these problems. Each will likely require a customized response.

In the Palestinian Territories, analysis of the performance of schools across the country on a standardized international test enabled our team to identify one school in a rural township (Jenin) whose students attained average scores by global standards, which in the local circumstances was an extraordinary achievement. How was this happening? Subsequent in-depth analysis of this school revealed that beyond generalizations such as 'effective leadership', 'capacity' and 'political will' was a deep commitment on the part of everyone, from mid-level education officials and the school principal to teachers and students themselves, to create an environment focused on learning and problem-solving. One specific innovation was a commitment by the school and the community alike to bring parents into this learning process. Many parents were illiterate, having themselves never attended school, and therefore intimidated merely by being on a school campus, an alien environment to them. Their illiteracy meant they were unable to provide their children with basic assistance on homework, or monitor whether their child was actually learning, for example to read, or to do basic mathematics. Identifying these issues as a 'binding constraint' on student learning, the school initiated a programme focused specifically on parents, inviting them onto campus after school hours to see what their children are doing each day, and giving them simple ideas for how they might be able to assist their children with homework.[3] This innovation was this school's solution to this school's problem; the people there nominated and prioritized it themselves, and thus it had full local legitimacy. Something like it may or may not be a solution elsewhere; the crucial point is that the community had built, in a tense and militarized setting, a high-capability local problem-solving system to implement education policy.[4] The next frontier is to discern whether and how such approaches to problem-solving can be established and routinized not just in Palestine, but elsewhere too.

Improving education in Bihar, India: Pratham's 'Teaching at the Right Level' programme[5]

The genius of bureaucracies is their capacity to enable routine activities to function at scale. Providing pensions and car insurance, for example, is possible across entire national populations because most of the necessary information is relatively uniform, visible, non-controversial, readily available and independently verifiable. Bureaucracies struggle, however, when the problem to be solved requires qualitatively different kinds of information. Providing education to all is one such problem (and was enshrined as such in the Millennium Development Goals (MDGs)); ensuring that learning by all actually happens is an even harder one (which is the aspiration of its successor, the Sustainable Development Goals (SDGs)).

In very large but very poor countries such as India, the challenge of ensuring learning for all is immense. In such settings, the prevailing level of capability for policy implementation is low. It risks falling even lower when designated agencies (in this case ministries of education) are asked to perform tasks at an even larger scale (for instance, to expand enrolments massively). Faced with such mandates but already overwhelmed, implementing agencies need to continue to convey legitimacy externally and secure a continued flow of resources. One way to do this is to monitor and measure progress exclusively on 'thin' information: the number of inputs provided and procedures correctly followed. Pritchett (2014) argues that this description aptly characterizes the situation in India: the District Information System for Education (DISE), which provides annual reports on the state of education, in 2011/12 provided '817 pieces of information [but] not a single one could be construed as a direct measure of learning of any kind'. Similarly, the Right to Free and Compulsory Education Act (of 2009) identified seven characteristics that would be used to accredit (and thus fund) schools, all of them 'thin'.[6] A school that ticked these seven boxes was deemed to be 'good', irrespective of what its students actually learned, while schools attaining even spectacular learning accomplishments but unable to meet all seven criteria were deemed unacceptable.

Pratham, a large education NGO in India, strives to work within such systems to put the focus back on student learning, especially in the younger grades, on the grounds that if children fail to acquire basic literacy and numeracy skills they will forever be behind.

A prevailing feature of these systems was (and the most part remains) that children moved through the school system each year, irrespective of whether they had acquired grade-appropriate skills. They would be asked to solve mathematics problems at Standard Five no matter whether they had demonstrably mastered Standard Two, and so on. For their part, teachers were instructed to teach the textbook, no matter what the students in their classroom actually knew: a good teacher was one who completed the textbook over the course of the year, not one whose students had learned its contents. Over time in the state of Bihar, the poorest state in India, Pratham discovered that daily attendance steadily declined, not because of endemic poverty but because students simply couldn't follow the material being presented to them. Unable to do even the most routine addition problems or read a simple sentence, yet each year being automatically promoted to a higher grade, students increasingly found schooling a frustrating and humiliating experience (especially when order was maintained via physical punishment and verbal abuse). Thus they ceased attending.

Rather than blaming teachers or students for this state of affairs, Pratham's strategy has been to focus on changing one feature of the implementation system: its requirement to promote each student to a higher grade each year, irrespective of their knowledge. With the support of the chief minister and local officials, selected schools have taken an approach which focuses on measuring what students actually know via short, simple, regularly administered tests of reading and arithmetic, and using child-friendly pedagogical strategies tailored to their current state of demonstrated learning, no matter what their age.

The effectiveness of this approach has been assessed via several formal and rigorous evaluations, but is perhaps best captured by the response of a startled official.

> 'Children who never came regularly to school before are coming now. Children who could not do anything earlier, are able to do so much. Look at this child', he said with shining eyes, 'ten days ago she could not even recognize words and today she wants to write her favourite word! We have achieved more in 10 days than in 5 years! How is all this happening?' ... 'There is nothing here', I [the director of Pratham] said. 'It is you – you have made the children able and now they are learning'. (Banerji, 2015, pp. 9–10)

Clearly there are good, bad and indifferent social policies, whether assessed on normative or technical grounds, and policy-makers should surely strive to make good ones. A closely related frontier issue, however, in high and low income countries alike,[7] is whether and how any given policy can actually be implemented, especially when doing do requires deftly combining 'thin' information and 'thick' knowledge for entire populations. Making social policy and implementing social policy are two different things. As more countries become larger and richer in the coming decades, the capabilities of their states to implement social policies beneficial to all will have a major bearing on whether hard-won gains are consolidated, and whether lingering challenges are confidently and competently embraced.

Notes

1. This section briefly summarizes evidence and arguments from Brixi and colleagues (2015).

2. I have heard fascinating presentations on health outcomes in Africa that explore this logic all the way down to individual clinics, documenting and explaining the variation in the cleanliness of birthing rooms, some of which are spotless while others are unspeakably awful, all under the same roof.

3. Even if this was doing seemingly obvious things like ensuring the house was relatively quiet for an hour each afternoon so that homework could be completed.

4. For a more complete discussion of these analytical issues as it pertains to building implementation capability, see Andrews and colleagues (2013).

5. The section draws on Banerji (2015) and Pritchett (2014).

6. The seven characteristics are teacher/enrolment ratio; buildings; working days/instructional hours; minimum working hours; learning equipment; library; play equipment.

7. On the challenges of reforming public schools in a disadvantaged community in the USA, despite a huge injection of targeted funds and technical expertise, see Russakoff (2015).

Bibliography

Andrews, M., Pritchett, L. and Woolcock, M. 2013. Escaping capability traps using Problem-Driven Iterative Adaptation (PDIA). *World Development*, Vol. 51, No. 1, pp. 234–44.

Banerji, R. 2015. How do systems respond to disruptive pedagogic innovations? The case of Pratham in Bihar. Working Paper 15/02, Research on Improving Systems of Education (RISE). www.riseprogramme.org/sites/www.riseprogramme.org/files/151026_BanerjiWP.pdf (Accessed 13 June 2016.)

Brixi, H., Lust, E. and Woolcock, M. 2015. *Trust, Voice and Incentives: Learning from Local Success Stories in Service Delivery in the Middle East and North Africa*. Washington DC, World Bank.

Pritchett, L. 2014. The risks to education from design mismatch and global isomorphism. Working Paper no. 2014/039. Helsinki, UNU-WIDER.

Russakoff, D. 2015. *The Prize: Who's in Charge of America's Schools?* Boston, Mass., Houghton Mifflin.

■ **Michael Woolcock** *(Australia) is lead social development specialist in the World Bank's Development Research Group, and a part-time lecturer in public policy at Harvard University's Kennedy School of Government. He also represents the Asia-Pacific Region on the Scientific Advisory Committee of UNESCO's Management of Social Transformation (MOST) programme.*

59. Inequality and corruption
Bo Rothstein

Corruption generally hurts poor people more than the rich, and therefore serves as a regressive tax. An additional negative effect of widespread corruption is that it destroys support for policies that can decrease economic inequality. Such policies, for instance universal health care, education and social insurance systems, will be difficult to establish in countries with widespread corruption. The reason is that corruption destroys both social and political trust. Citizens who are in principle in favour of policies for increased economic equality will refrain from supporting such policies if they perceive that corruption in the public sector is widespread.

For the vast majority of people, human well-being could be improved if inequality is decreased in their society (Radcliff, 2013). It is important to consider the necessary amount and type of solidarity needed to produce public policies that enhance social and economic equality, and whether this solidarity can be politically manufactured. We take as our starting point the notion that the level of social solidarity in a society is not culturally determined. The Nordic countries are not more equal than, for example, the UK or the USA because there is something special about the Nordic culture. Instead, the unusually broad-based political support for the welfare state has been politically constructed 'from above' by the universal (or near universal) design of the policies concerned (Rothstein, 2015). The recent introduction of a more universal type of social policy reform in several Latin American countries in areas such as health care, pensions and education shows the existence of the same causal logic as in the Nordic countries (Pribble, 2013), as does the contingent support for the National Health Service in the UK and the social security system in the USA. In sum, it is the specific design of the institutions, not history or culture, that matters for the possibility of establishing sustainable policies that reduce inequality.

Social solidarity and 'human nature'

When trying to gain political support for decreasing inequality, it is important to start from a correct understanding of 'human nature', especially if you want your policies to have a lasting impact.

Needless to say, ideas about 'basic human nature' have a long history in the social sciences. The empirically most compelling theory is the work done in experimental research based on the idea of reciprocity (Fehr and Fischbacher, 2005). This research has refuted the idea of man as a *homo economicus* (the rational self-interested individual assumed by classic economics). The results from laboratory, fieldwork and survey research that speaks against humans as utility-maximizing rational agents are by now overwhelming. Self-interest is for sure an important ingredient when people decide how to act, but it is far from being as dominating as has been portrayed in neoclassical economics. Moreover, it would be impossible to create solidaristic or cooperative institutions of any kind, including democracy, the rule of law and the control of corruption, if individual utility-maximizing self-interest is the only game in town. The reason is that individuals who adopt this approach would sooner or later fall for the temptation to 'free-ride', and if the majority do this, such institutions will never be established. If they exist, they will soon be destroyed (Miller, 2000). If all agents act out of the template prescribed in neoclassical economic theory, they will sooner or later outsmart themselves into a suboptimal equilibrium. Also known as a 'social trap', this is a situation where all agents will be worse off despite knowing that they would all gain from cooperation. They abstain from cooperation because they do not trust others to cooperate (Rothstein, 2005).

Understanding reciprocity

However, this new experimental (and to some extent field) research does not present humans as benevolent altruists. True, there is altruistic behaviour, but it is usually restricted to very small circles of family and close friends. Or it is simply too rare and unpredictable for building sustainable systems for solidarity at a societal level. This lesson is important, since it tells us that trying to mobilize political support for increased equality by referring only to people's altruistic motives is likely to fail. What comes out from this research is instead that reciprocity is the basic human orientation. The central idea here is that people are not so much motivated 'from the back' by utility-based calculations or culturally induced norms. Instead, human behaviour is to a large extent determined by forward-looking strategic thinking in the sense that what agents do, depends on what they think the other agents are going to do. Experimental studies show that people are willing to do 'the right thing', like paying their taxes and refraining from corruption, but only if they can be convinced that most others are willing to do the same (Bicchieri and Xiao, 2009). The idea of reciprocity fundamentally recasts how we should understand and explain human behaviour.

Institutional design and control of corruption

Regarding the prospects for social solidarity, results from empirical research show that most people are willing to engage in cooperation for goals such as universal social insurance systems, even if they will not benefit personally benefit from them (Rothstein, 2015). But for this to happen, three specific conditions have to be in place. First, people have to be convinced that the policy is morally justified (substantial justice). Second, people have to be convinced that most other agents can also be trusted to cooperate (solidaristic justice): that is, that other agents are likely to abstain from 'free-riding' such as cheating on taxes and getting special favours by paying bribes. Third, people have to be convinced that the policy can be implemented in an uncorrupt and fair manner (procedural justice).

For the first issue, political ideology certainly plays a role. The second and third requirements, however, have to be resolved by institutional design, and this is where knowledge from research into policy implementation and anti-corruption is needed.

For example, it is not difficult to argue that universal access to high-quality health care and sickness insurance is a policy that caters to basic ideas about social justice. However, if a majority cannot be convinced that most people will pay the increased taxes required for producing these goods, that the goods will be delivered in a manner that is free from corruption and respectful, and that policies such as sickness insurance will not be abused or overused, they are not likely to support these policies (Rothstein, 2011). If health personnel are known to be corrupt, unprofessional or disrespectful, support for this policy will dwindle even if people in general would be in favour of the policy as such. In other words, solidarity for increasing social justice is conditional on the institutional design of systems that are supposed to bring about the policies that will enhance equality. In particular, corruption is 'enemy number one'. This has been formulated in the following words by the political philosopher John Rawls:

> *A just system must generate its own support. This means that it must be arranged so as to bring about in its members the corresponding sense of justice, an effective desire to act in accordance with its rules for reasons and justice. Thus, the requirements of stability and the criterion of discouraging desires that conflict with the principles of justice put further constraints on institutions. They must not only be just but framed so as to encourage the virtue of justice in those who take part in them. (Rawls, 1971, p. 261)*

The central idea of this quote comes when Rawls specifies that for making a solidaristic system sustainable, we have to be aware of the existence of a feedback mechanism between people's support for just principles and their perceptions of the quality of the institutions set up to implement these principles.

Why institutional design trumps ideology

Recent empirical research strongly supports Rawls's argument that individuals' perception of corruption or similar forms of malpractice in the public services influences their support for social solidarity. Using survey data for twenty-nine European countries that includes questions about the fairness of public authorities (in the health sector and tax authorities), as well as questions about ideological leanings and policy preferences, Svallfors (2013) has shown the following.

Citizens who have a preference for more economic equality but live in a country where they perceive that the quality of government institutions is low, will in the same survey indicate that they prefer lower taxes and less social spending. However, the same 'ideological type' of respondent who happens to live in a European country where they believe that the authorities that implement policies are basically just and fair, will answer that they are willing to pay higher taxes for more social spending. This result is supported in a study using aggregate data about welfare state spending and corruption in the public sector for Western liberal democracies (Rothstein, 2011). The higher the quality of government, the more countries will spend, controlled for variables that measure political mobilization and electoral success by left parties.

To summarize, citizens who live in a country where they perceive that corruption or other forms of unfairness in the public administration are common are likely to be less supportive of the idea that the state should take responsibility for policies for increased social justice, even if they support the goals of such policies ideologically. This has been formulated by Fehr and Fischbacher in the following way: 'If people believe that cheating on taxes, corruption and abuses of the welfare state are widespread, they themselves are more likely to cheat on taxes, take bribes or abuse welfare state institutions' (2005). What can prevent this is high quality in the government institutions responsible for implementing social policies. Widespread notions of favouritism, lack of impartiality, corruption and incompetence will result in declining support for policies that alleviate inequality, even in the part of the electorate that is ideologically in favour of a society with more equality.

Bibliography

Bicchieri, C. and Xiao, E. 2009. Do the right thing: but only if others do so. *Journal of Behavioral Decision Making*, Vol. 22, No. 2, pp. 191–208. *http://psychsource.bps.org.uk/details/journalArticle/3045291/Do-the-right-thing-but-only-if-others-do-so.html* (Accessed 20 February 2016.)

Fehr, E. and Fischbacher, U. 2005. The economics of strong reciprocity. H. Gintis, S. Bowles, R. Boyd and E. Fehr (eds), *Moral Sentiments and Material Interests. The Foundations for Cooperation in Economic Life.* Cambridge, Mass., MIT Press, pp. 151–93.

Miller, G. J. 2000. Rational choice and dysfunctional institutions. *Governance*, Vol. 13, No. 4, pp. 535–47. *http://onlinelibrary.wiley.com/doi/10.1111/0952-1895.00145/abstract* (Accessed 20 February 2016.)

Pribble, J. E. 2013. *Welfare and Party Politics in Latin America.* New York, Cambridge University Press.

Radcliff, B. 2013. *The Political Economy of Human Happiness.* New York, Cambridge University Press.

Rawls, J. 1971. *A Theory of Justice.* Oxford, Oxford University Press.

Rothstein, B. 2005. *Social Traps and the Problem of Trust.* Cambridge, Cambridge University Press.

Rothstein, B. 2011. *The Quality of Government: Corruption, Social Trust and Inequality in a Comparative Perspective.* Chicago, Ill., University of Chicago Press.

Rothstein, B. 2015. The moral, economic, and political logic of the Swedish welfare state. J. Pierre (ed.), *The Oxford Handbook of Swedish Politics.* Oxford, Oxford University Press, pp. 69–86.

Svallfors, S. 2013. Government quality, egalitarianism, and attitudes to taxes and social spending: a European comparison. *European Political Science Review*, Vol. 5, No. 3, pp. 363–80. *https://www.cambridge.org/core/journals/european-political-science-review/article/government-quality-egalitarianism-and-attitudes-to-taxes-and-social-spending-a-european-comparison/DD99ADD1ADC81D7E254FBAAB6C2D9507* (Accessed 20 February 2016.)

■ **Bo Rothstein** *(Sweden) is professor in government and public policy at the Blavatnik School of Government, Oxford, and professorial fellow at Nuffield College, University of Oxford (UK).*

**World
Social
Science
Report**

Chapter 6
Mobilizing for change

60. Why social movements matter for addressing inequalities and ensuring social justice
    Leandro Vergara-Camus

61. POSTCARD • Inequalities and protests
    Isabel Ortiz and Sara Burke

62. POSTCARD • Africa's uprisings: no end in sight
    Adam Branch and Zachariah Mampilly

63. POSTCARD • Representing and challenging inequality through the arts
    Mike van Graan

64. Grass-roots pathways for challenging social and political inequality
    Alison Mathie with Eileen Alma, Asier Ansorena, Jagat Basnet, Yogesh Ghore, Sebastián Jarrín, Julien Landry, Nanci Lee, Bettina von Lieres, Valerie Miller, Malena de Montis, Salome Nakazwe, Stutlina Pal, Brianne Peters, Rehana Riyawala, Vicky Schreiber, Mohammed A. Shariff, Aster Tefera and Nani Zulminarni

65. POSTCARD • Equality as a valued social norm, inequality as an injustice
    Sakiko Fukuda-Parr

66. A historical view of the politics of inequality
    Duncan Green

67. POSTCARD • Rising extreme inequality is a concern for us all
    Winnie Byanyima

60. Why social movements matter for addressing inequalities and ensuring social justice

Leandro Vergara-Camus

This contribution examines our academic and political understandings of social movements, and the ways in which social movements in the developing world have recently tackled social inequalities and struggled for social justice. It highlights the importance of social mobilization, and critically examines the relationship between movements, political parties and the state. Constitutional moments are shown to be crucial for the establishment of an agenda and a discursive framework enabling the development or the critique of state policies. The author concludes by advising against romanticizing social movements, but recognizes the essential role that they play when they are relatively autonomous from the state.

History is replete with moments of intense social mobilization where people rise up against injustice, replacing the existing social order with the objective of establishing a more socially just society. The romantic and mythical aspects of these revolutionary moments have been captured in art and popular culture, including paintings, murals, novels, plays and films. Revolutionary moments are often at the core of the foundation myths of modern nation-states across the world, and the myth of the revolution often unconsciously informs our understanding of power, the state and social movements.

The 1980s were marked by the retreat of grand narratives and grand theories of social change, which were replaced by a single one, that of neoliberalism or the Washington consensus (Harvey, 2005). The free-market, pro-capital and anti-state orientation of this new discourse is well known. But less often mentioned is its corollary negative discourse on collective action. Following Adam Smith, Milton Friedman argued that collective action was subjected to a law of unintended consequences. Each time groups of individuals or the state acted in what was understood as the common good, for instance by addressing inequalities in society or the market, an invisible hand led the measures adopted to produce the opposite results to those initially intended.

This was the companion view to a conception of the state as inherently inefficient or as an object of corruption or rent-seeking. *Only* the individual working through the market could take charge of the common good.

But the 1980s and early 1990s saw the rise of numerous social movements and civil society organizations intended to tackle the negative consequences of neoliberal market restructuring through self-help local initiatives. This triggered a move to a post-Washington consensus phase in neoliberalism. Here the market and state in the developing world were still understood in the same way, but civil society actors were now cast as capable of keeping state officials in check (World Bank, 2001). The privileged actors were not, however, social movements but a new brand of NGOs funded by international aid and philanthropy, which quickly became synonymous with civil society. NGOs were naively deemed to be benevolent actors, closer to the population and better equipped than bureaucrats to address the needs and preoccupations of the local population (Kamat, 2004). Civil society organizations would improve governmental policy-making, implementation and monitoring.

The literature spoke of state–society synergy, complementarity, embeddedness and good governance (Evans, 1994). Since then, NGOs have become partners, stakeholders and even service providers to states or international development agencies, while social movements, often still seen through the myth of the revolution as too radical, are left out of the analysis of policies. However, as will be shown below, social movements and political conflicts can greatly influence the direction that policies take.

Social movements, politics, policies and inequalities[1]

In the past twenty years, social movements have forced their way back into policy discussion as numerous citizen groups and political coalitions have emerged to oppose mega-development projects (hydro-electric dams, open-cast mining), demand their right to access and control of resources (land, forest, mangroves, sea), and to social services (education, health, justice or employment) or even to implement their own vision of development, as with the Zapatista movement in Chiapas and the Landless Rural Workers' movement in Brazil. There are several ways in which social movements can tackle inequalities broadly conceived, including social, political, economic, racial, ethnic, gender, religious and generational inequalities. They do so first and foremost by demanding respect for basic rights and by politically organizing and representing marginalized groups. In this role, social movements can take a variety of actions (demonstrations, marches, occupations, blockades, civil disobedience, legal activism, military action and so on) to directly confront their oppressors, push their agenda into the public debate, or negotiate with the state. Social movements very often engage in coalition-building with other movements, political parties and politicians with the aim of influencing policy, or if possible the institutional framework of their countries.

Constitutional moments are privileged moments not only for political parties but also for social movements, because they are the point at which more inclusive political settlements and more progressive policy orientations can be embedded into the higher law of the nation. The 1950 Constitution of India abolished 'untouchability' and established legal safeguards for discriminated groups, castes and tribal people.

More recently, the 1988 Brazilian Constitution was partly the result of the influence of a broad coalition of political parties, social movements and civil society organizations that was able to push for certain social rights (education, health, agrarian reform) to be embedded into the constitution.

Similarly, peasant and indigenous movements that had brought down presidents participated in the constituent assemblies that culminated in the 2008 Constitution of Ecuador and the 2009 Constitution of Bolivia. They were largely responsible for enshrining principles like pluri-nationality of the state, food sovereignty, environmental sustainability, and even the rights of nature in the case of Ecuador, in these constitutions (Arauco et al., 2014, pp. 28–40).

Constitutional social rights do not guarantee that the state will comply. The Brazilian Constitution was only mobilized to justify more active state social policies under the first government of Luis Inácio 'Lula' da Silva in 2004, fifteen years after its adoption. Similarly, the concept of food sovereignty in the constitutions of Bolivia and Ecuador has not guided their agricultural policies, which mainly support large-scale industrial agriculture for export. Nor have clauses on environmental sustainability and the rights of nature impeded the Bolivian and Ecuadorian states from increasing gas, oil and mineral extraction, encroaching on indigenous peoples' territories, and criminalizing social movement opposition (Bebbington and Humphreys Bebbington, 2011). Constitutional clauses only lead to progressive policies when there is sustained and autonomous political pressure from social movements, civil society organizations and progressive political forces, as well as political will from governing parties or sectors within the state. Progressive constitutional principles, or court decisions, provide social movements with the ability to struggle for or against policies that have an impact on inequality, by mobilizing the foundational myths of the nation-state or exposing the contradictions of state discourse about progress and development.

The case of India, with its long history of legal activism, is an excellent example. The social movement around the National Rural Employment Guarantee Act (NREGA) of 2005, building on earlier decisions from India's Supreme Court in favour of social rights, contributed to the creation of a legal and judiciable basis for members of poor rural households to demand paid work from their local government (Arauco et al., 2014, p. 43).

The movement against the UK's Vedanta mining company represents another successful case in which tribal peoples from the state of Odisha managed to mobilize legal rights related to religious beliefs and tribal peoples to reverse the granting of mining rights over bauxite deposits to Vedanta on the Nayamgiri Hills that they held sacred (Temper and Martinez-Alier, 2013).

In many cases, social movement mobilization does not produce immediate effects, but instead establishes social and institutional foundations that are subsequently activated by political actors or new waves of social movement mobilization. The examples above of the attitude of the state towards social movements in South America and India highlight the point that social movement activism has not only short-term but also long-term consequences. At the same time it underlines the fundamentally conflictive nature of development policies.

For instance, the most progressive policies of the Partido dos Trabalhadores (PT) government under Lula in Brazil (universal cash transfer payments, quotas in higher education for discriminated groups, anti-discrimination laws, formalization of work and so on) were a response to decades of activism that began with the struggle against dictatorship in the early 1980s. This wave of social mobilization produced an extremely active, politicized and dense civil society, even though by the 1990s it was showing advanced signs of institutionalization and 'NGO-ization' (Alvarez, 2009). At the same time, its most conservative policies, such as its weak agrarian reform and its support for large landlords and large-scale export-oriented agribusiness, point to the PT's inability or unwillingness to disturb vested interests, upon which it depended in the Congress.

The state, civil society, autonomy and social movements

The myth of the revolution weighs heavily on our positive or negative assessment of social movements. Many tend to see them as being driven by a will for social change that is fundamentally democratic. However, social movements are not always revolutionary or democratic in their objectives or their internal decision-making.

There are numerous experiences of states across the world that have been formed around corporatist and clientelist networks in which social movements were a key instrument of social control. Even though they may oppose a specific state policy or measure, social movements do not necessarily seek autonomy from the state, but often seek to participate in its decision-making.

Some social movements participated in left-wing governments by accepting that their leaders should take government positions: in Bolivia under Evo Morales, in Brazil under Lula de Silva and to a lesser extent in Ecuador under Rafael Correa. Social movements in these countries have also pushed for the creation of alternative participative political spaces, such as fora, councils and national conferences (Arauco et al., 2014). These have increased the politicization of popular sectors but have not radically transformed national politics.

Policy-oriented scholars and policy-makers continue to view social movements with suspicion, as many continue to work within the good governance framework that privileges NGOs. At the opposite end, more radical scholars tend to over-emphasize the radical potential of social movements because they believe that the world today requires social injustice to be tackled through fundamental social change. I believe this to be the case. But fundamental social change and social justice are not reached in one moment of catharsis. Instead they are produced through the ebb and flow of political struggles, which only sometimes involve revolutions.

As we have seen, social mobilization, combined with specific alliances with political forces, can translate into more inclusive political settlements, legal principles and rights. These can promote policies that tackle inequalities in the short and medium term, and become the discursive foundations of future struggles for equality and social justice. However, no gain towards social justice is guaranteed, even when it has been enshrined in a constitution, and no single actor, such as the state, can take total responsibility for this agenda. As regimes continue to violate fundamental rights, social movements are easily subjected to repression, co-optation of their leaders or exhaustion of their membership. They need to be relatively autonomous in their sources of funding, their ideology and their constituency. Only this allows them to challenge powerful interests, governing parties and the state, and play a leading role in the battle against inequality and for social justice.

Note

1. This section takes examples from the Overseas Development Institute (ODI) report *Strengthening Social Justice to Address Intersecting Inequalities Post-2015* (Arauco et al., 2014), in which I participated as one of the co-authors.

Bibliography

Alvarez, S. 2009. Beyond NGOization? Reflections from Latin America. *Development*, Vol. 52, No. 2, pp. 175–84. *http://r4d.dfid.gov.uk/Output/180610/* (Accessed 21 February 2016.)

Arauco, V. P., Gazdar, H., Hevia-Pacheco, P., Kabeer, N., Lenhardt, A., Masood, S. Q., Naqvi, H., Nayak, N., Norton, A., Sabharwal, N. S., Scalise, E., Shepherd, A., Thapa, D., Thorat, S., Tran, D. H., Vergara-Camus, L., Woldehanna, T., and Mariotti, C. 2014. *Strengthening Social Justice to Address Intersecting Inequalities Post-2015*. London, Overseas Development Institute. *www.odi.org/sites/odi.org.uk/files/odi-assets/publications-opinion-files/9213.pdf* (Accessed 21 February 2016.)

Bebbington, A. and Humphreys Bebbington, D. 2011. An Andean avatar: post-neoliberal and neoliberal strategies for securing the unobtainable. *New Political Economy*, Vol. 16, No. 1, pp. 131–45. *www.tandfonline.com/doi/abs/10.1080/13563461003789803#.VsohgkDp5HI* (Accessed 21 February 2016.)

Evans, P. 1994. Government action, social capital and development: reviewing the evidence on synergy. *World Development*, Vol. 24, No. 6, pp. 1119–32. *http://econpapers.repec.org/article/eeewdevel/v_3a24_3ay_3a1996_3ai_3a6_3ap_3a1119-1132.htm* (Accessed 21 February 2016.)

Harvey, D. 2005. *A Brief History of Neoliberalism*. Oxford, Oxford University Press.

Kamat, S. 2004. The privatization of public interest: theorizing NGO discourse in a neoliberal era. *Review of International Political Economy*, Vol. 11, No. 1, pp. 155–76. *www.jstor.org/stable/4177492?seq=1#page_scan_tab_contents* (Accessed 21 February 2016.)

Temper, L. and Martinez-Alier, J. 2013. The god of the mountain and Godavarman: net present value, indigenous territorial rights and sacredness in a bauxite mining conflict in India. *Ecological Economics*, Vol. 96, pp. 79–87. *www.sciencedirect.com/science/article/pii/S0921800913002978* (Accessed 21 February 2016.)

World Bank. 2001. *World Development Report 2000/2001. Attacking Poverty: Opportunity, Empowerment and Security*. Washington DC, World Bank. *https://openknowledge.worldbank.org/handle/10986/11856* (Accessed 21 February 2016.)

■ **Leandro Vergara-Camus** *(UK) is senior lecturer in theory, policy and practice of development at the School of Oriental and African Studies, University of London. His latest book is* Land and Freedom: The MST, the Zapatistas and Peasant Alternatives to Neoliberalism *(Zed Books, 2014).*

POSTCARD

61. Inequalities and protests

Isabel Ortiz and Sara Burke

In recent years, the world has been shaken by protests, from the Arab Spring to the 'Indignant' in Europe, from Occupy to food riots. There have been periods in history when large numbers of people rebelled about the way things were, demanding change, such as in 1848, 1917 or 1968; today we are experiencing another period of rising outrage and discontent, and some of the largest protests in world history.

An analysis of 843 recent world protests reflects a steady increase in the overall number of protests every year, from 2006 (59 protests) to mid-2013 (112 protests in only half a year). Following the onset of the global financial and economic crisis, there has been a major increase in protests, beginning in 2010 with the adoption of austerity measures in all world regions. The major grievances of protestors relate to economic and social justice, and range from demanding real democracy, public services and civil rights to opposing international financial institutions, corporate rent-seeking and corruption (*Figure 61.1*).

Not only is the number of protests increasing, but also the number of protesters. Crowd estimates suggest that thirty-seven events had 1 million or more protesters; some of those may well be the largest protests in history (for instance, 100 million in India in 2013, and 17 million in Egypt, also in 2013).

A profile of demonstrators reveals that it is not only traditional protesters such as activists and union members who are demonstrating. On the contrary, middle classes, young people, older persons and other social groups are actively protesting in most countries because of lack of trust and disillusionment with the current political and economic system. They are increasingly joining activists from all kinds of movements, not only in marches and rallies (the most common methods of civil protest, in 437 events), but also in a new framework of civil disobedience that includes occupation of squares and road blockades to raise awareness about their demands (a total of 219 occupations of public spaces).

Contrary to public perception, violence and vandalism or looting appears in only 8.9 per cent of world protests. Of violent riots, 48 per cent occurred in low-income countries, mostly prompted by spikes in food and energy prices.

Demonstrators mostly address their grievances to national governments, as they are the legitimate policy-making institutions that should respond to citizens. But it is also worth noting the rising number of protests on global issues. Protesters demand that policy-makers at national and global levels take public responsibility for economic, social and environmental policies that benefit all, instead of just the few.

However, governments often respond to protest with repression. Repression leading to arrests, injuries and deaths is well documented in over half of the protest episodes between 2006 and 2013.

If governments aim to be legitimate, they need to listen to the messages coming from protesters and act on their demands. The majority of grievances, from reducing inequalities and corporate influence to promoting jobs, social protection, public services and racial justice, are in full accordance with United Nations proposals and the Universal Declaration of Human Rights.

Acknowledgement

This contribution is based on *World Protests 2006–2013* by Isabel Ortiz, Sara Burke, Mohamed Berrada and Hernán Cortés, published by the Initiative for Policy Dialogue at Columbia University and the Friedrich-Ebert-Stiftung New York in 2013.

■ **Isabel Ortiz** *(Spain) is director of the Global Social Justice Program at the Initiative for Policy Dialogue, Columbia University, New York.*

■ **Sara Burke** *(USA) is senior policy analyst at the Friedrich-Ebert-Stiftung, New York.*

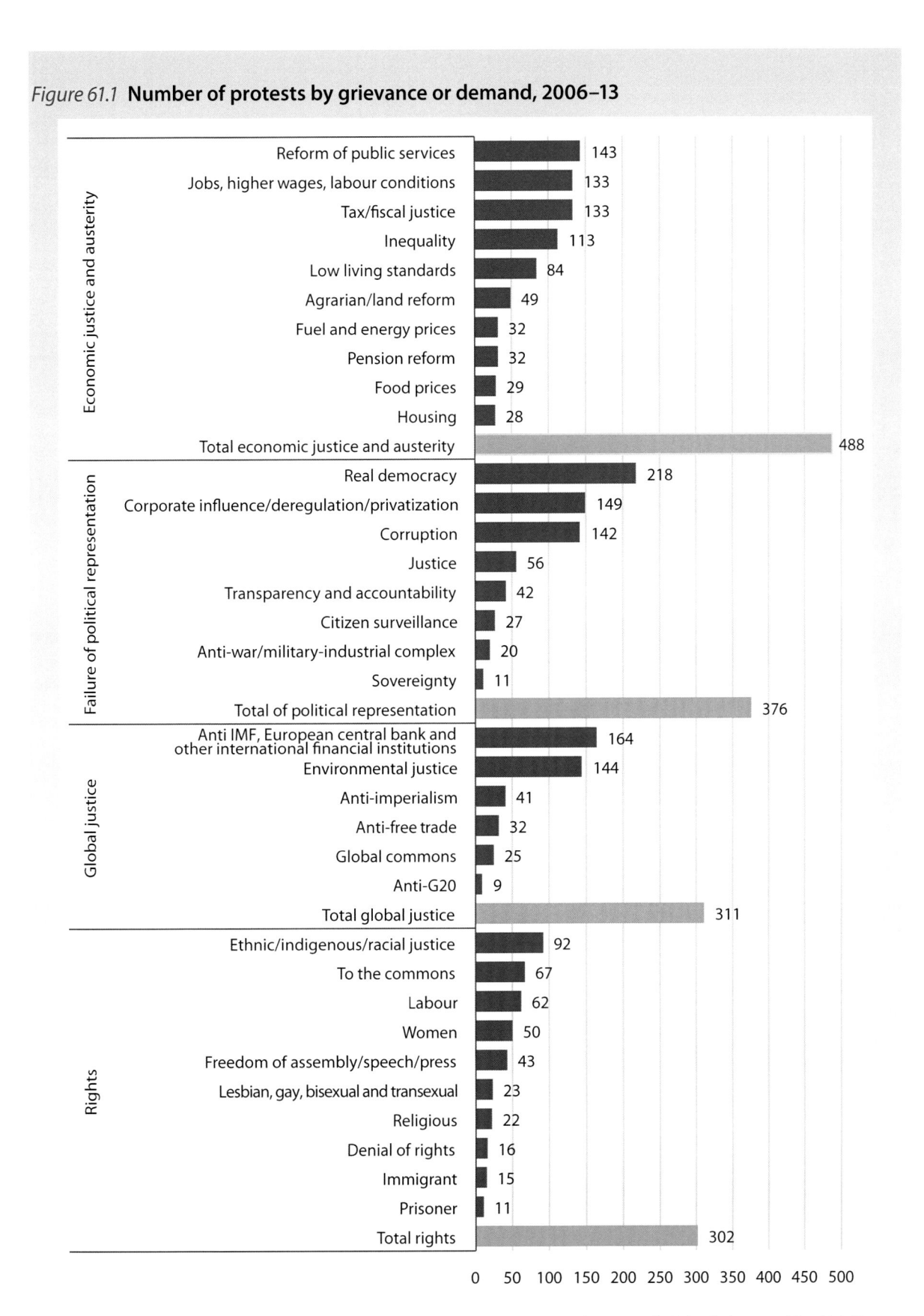

Figure 61.1 **Number of protests by grievance or demand, 2006–13**

Category	Grievance/Demand	Count
Economic justice and austerity	Reform of public services	143
	Jobs, higher wages, labour conditions	133
	Tax/fiscal justice	133
	Inequality	113
	Low living standards	84
	Agrarian/land reform	49
	Fuel and energy prices	32
	Pension reform	32
	Food prices	29
	Housing	28
	Total economic justice and austerity	**488**
Failure of political representation	Real democracy	218
	Corporate influence/deregulation/privatization	149
	Corruption	142
	Justice	56
	Transparency and accountability	42
	Citizen surveillance	27
	Anti-war/military-industrial complex	20
	Sovereignty	11
	Total of political representation	**376**
Global justice	Anti IMF, European central bank and other international financial institutions	164
	Environmental justice	144
	Anti-imperialism	41
	Anti-free trade	32
	Global commons	25
	Anti-G20	9
	Total global justice	**311**
Rights	Ethnic/indigenous/racial justice	92
	To the commons	67
	Labour	62
	Women	50
	Freedom of assembly/speech/press	43
	Lesbian, gay, bisexual and transexual	23
	Religious	22
	Denial of rights	16
	Immigrant	15
	Prisoner	11
	Total rights	**302**

Source: I. Ortiz, S. Burke, M. Berrada and H. Cortes. 2013. *World Protests 2006–2013*. New York, Initiative for Policy Dialogue and Friedrich-Ebert-Stiftung. Data correct to 31 July 2013.

POSTCARD

62. Africa's uprisings: no end in sight

Adam Branch and Zachariah Mampilly

Tunis, Cairo, Khartoum, Dakar, Ouagadougou, Lagos, Kinshasa, Kampala, Lilongwe, Cape Town – these are only a few of the African cities that have been convulsed by major urban uprisings over the past five years. Today's wave of popular protests is erupting in response to the rapidly rising inequality experienced by Africa's urban poor under the current neoliberal dispensation, occurring even as many countries register positive GDP growth. For these swelling, largely young urban populations, electoral democracy – which arrived in much of Africa simultaneously with structural adjustment – appears to offer no answers to their predicament. And so the young and other urban dwellers take to the streets in large numbers, often with little formal organization or leadership, but motivated by powerful slogans: *Y'en a marre! Ash-sha'b yurīd isqāt. an-niz.ām* – the people want to bring down the regime! #FeesMustFall!

As we argue in our recent book, *Africa Uprising: Popular Protest and Political Change*, this current protest wave is not the first Africa has seen. Precariousness, staggering inequality and a lack of political voice have characterized the daily lives of Africa's urban poor since the colonial period. These continuities in Africa's urban economic and political conditions have given rise to previous protest waves: first in the late colonial period, when popular protests were channelled into nationalist movements throughout the continent; and then in the late 1980s and early 1990s, when protests against the austerity imposed by international financial institutions, and against years of authoritarian rule, forced the inception of multiparty democracy in dozens of African states. As that order enters into crisis today, proposed solutions to inequality that ignore the often radical demands coming from young, urban Africans will be insufficient. Politicians and policy-makers must take seriously the voices of protesters in the streets who are asserting their own understanding of economic inequality and putting their own solutions into practice.

Bibliography

Branch, A. and Mampilly, Z. 2015. *Africa Uprising: Popular Protest and Political Change*. London, Zed Books.

■ **Adam Branch** *(USA) is a lecturer in African politics at the University of Cambridge, where he specializes in questions of political violence and human rights, principally in East Africa. He was previously senior research fellow at the Makerere Institute of Social Research in Kampala, Uganda. His most recent book is* Africa Uprising: Popular Protest and Political Change *(Zed, 2015).*

■ **Zachariah Mampilly** *(USA) is director of the Program in Africana Studies and associate professor of political science at Vassar College, N.Y., USA. He is the author of several books and edited volumes including* Rebel Rulers: Insurgent Governance and Civilian Life during War *(Cornell, 2011) and most recently,* Rebel Governance in Civil War *(Cambridge, 2015).*

POSTCARD

63. Representing and challenging inequality through the arts

Mike van Graan

It was the way he lay: asleep, terminal, so profoundly sad – as if by lying in supplication before the waves that killed him, he was asking for a replay, with a different outcome this time; and his socks and little shoes told us he was ready to try life again. But his cheek on the soft sand whispered otherwise, it made us choke. Shamed and disgraced, the world wept before the body of this little boy.
Zeid Ra'ad Al Hussein,
the UN High Commissioner for Human Rights

The photograph of one drowned Syrian refugee, Aylan al Kurdi, on the shores of Greece in 2015 provoked shock and sympathy around the world. Through one image, the world was confronted, not only with the maldistribution of wealth and income, but with the extremely unequal distribution of human misery, suffering and hardship, and indeed inequality in the means to inflict misery. The image provoked citizen responses that obliged authorities to act in more humane ways, but thus far, these actions have addressed the symptoms rather than the structural causes.

We live in a world characterized by two essential fault lines: inequality in the distribution of income, material wealth and political power, and in the military means to assert and defend them; and inequality in culture – values, belief systems, traditions and worldviews – and the means to project these as vehicles of soft power to manufacture consent. And yet we do not pay sufficient attention to culture and its relationship to development, conflict, peace-building, human rights and addressing inequality.

UNCTAD has showed that Africa's share of the global creative economy stands at less than 1 per cent. This points not only to huge inequalities in the trade of cultural goods and services, but more importantly, to inequalities in the projection and consumption of culture.

In 2005 UNESCO adopted the Convention on the Protection and Promotion of the Diversity of Cultural Expressions as a response to the World Trade Organization's emphasis on trade liberalization in the 1990s.

So what does all this have to do with the arts and the representation of inequality?

First, the arts are located within the realm of culture, within the battle for hegemony of ideas, worldviews and belief systems. They are not neutral players, and may be actively deployed or silently co-opted in the promotion, defence or challenging of inequality.

Second, the arts sector is itself unequal. Who has access to skills, resources, networks and cultural infrastructure often determines who creates and distributes art. And it is those with disposable income who are most able to enjoy the fundamental human right enshrined in Article 27 of the Universal Declaration of Human Rights: 'everyone shall have the right freely to participate in the cultural life of the community and to enjoy the arts'. They will largely determine whose stories are told, and whose narratives reach the screens, the stages and the gallery walls.

Third, it is not only that the arts are not neutral in themselves; it is also about the context in which they are produced and distributed, contexts that are determined by grave inequalities in economic, cultural and military power. A piece of orchestral music that is enjoyed for its own sake in Vienna might be associated with elitism in South Africa, with its high Gini coefficient, while the same piece played by an orchestra from Afghanistan in Washington might, on the orchestra's return to Afghanistan, place a target on their backs as agents of Western cultural imperialism.

This shows that there are important but often overlooked relationships between art, broader culture, and social and economic inequalities. These in turn impact on and shape such culture. These inequalities are manifested within the production of art (who has the skills, resources and distribution to produce and disseminate art) and the reception and consumption of art (who has resources to purchase access to art). There is no one particular role for art, not is art predetermined to reinforce – or counter – hegemonic ideas. Depending on where artists, arts administrators and institutions locate themselves, art production and distribution can perpetuate or challenge social and other inequalities.

There is an annual festival that takes place in Darling, a little town an hour north of Cape Town. Called the Voorkamerfees (the 'Front Room Festival'), it literally happens in the front rooms of people's homes. Audience members purchase a ticket for various routes, but no one knows what they will see on the route, which comprises stopovers at three different houses. They might be watching a stand-up comic one moment, an operatic tenor the next, a hip-hop dance group the next.

The interesting aspect of this festival is that it does not happen in city-based, purpose-built infrastructure, but in the homes of poorer people who reap economic benefits from hosting performances, and who are integrated into a broader social project, rather than remaining on the margins.

This cultural intervention integrates human, social and economic development, taking place at a very local level. Social inequality is addressed too, since communities traditionally marginalized from the main tourism routes and from cultural production in the town are now at the centre of cultural dissemination.

Those who produce and distribute art, and who support others in the same effort, should be made more aware of the global, regional and national contexts in which they work, of the role that their art might play in perpetuating social, economic and community inequalities, and how their art could challenge those inequalities. It is also imperative that governments recognize the fundamental human right asserted in Article 27 for all to participate in the cultural life of the community and to enjoy the arts. This would place an obligation on the state to ensure that all have access to skills, resources and other means to produce and distribute creative works, thereby giving voice to their hopes, their anxieties, their concerns and their interests.

■ *Mike van Graan (South Africa) is former executive director of the African Arts Institute, Cape Town, South Africa.*

64. Grass-roots pathways for challenging social and political inequality

Alison Mathie with Eileen Alma, Asier Ansorena, Jagat Basnet, Yogesh Ghore, Sebastián Jarrín, Julien Landry, Nanci Lee, Bettina von Lieres, Valerie Miller, Malena de Montis, Salome Nakazwe, Stutlina Pal, Brianne Peters, Rehana Riyawala, Vicky Schreiber, Mohammed A. Shariff, Aster Tefera and Nani Zulminarni

This contribution reports on a project to identify strategies for narrowing the inequality gap from below. Examples from India, Ethiopia, Brazil and Indonesia were selected to shed light on the dynamic between people's capacity to act in public and political spheres (their political or civic agency) and their ability to act in economic spheres (their economic agency). These studies illustrate the importance of linkages of mutual responsibility and accountability, as well as the capacity to claim rights and entitlements from the state. The authors discuss how these play out through individual and collective expression, and how skills in the economic sphere transfer to the civic or political, and vice versa.

Introduction

In the past few years, public attention has been drawn to escalating inequalities in the distribution of wealth within and between countries. Proponents of alternative economic futures have proposed a number of policy changes to redirect economies towards social justice and sustainability, citing the threats to democracy, social stability and environmental sustainability of the inequalities we see today.

Less well known are actions taken at the grass-roots level that push for political, economic and social inclusion, and evolve into precursors of a new economy. This contribution reports on a project to fill this gap through a series of scoping studies from India, Ethiopia, Brazil and Indonesia which were selected to shed light on the dynamic between people's capacity to act in public and political spheres (their political or civic agency) and their ability to act in economic spheres (economic agency).[1] Through these examples, we can see how people achieve the inclusion and agency in political and economic life that make the narrowing of the inequality gap possible (see the box overleaf).

The relevance of these cases to deliberations on how to address inequality has several dimensions.

They move the discussion of inequality beyond the economic, and draw attention to the inequalities of voice and participation in private and public decision-making which correlate with economic inequality. They move beyond issues of inclusion in economies shaped by the external forces of globalization, and into debates about how to shape and control democratized economies that are socially just and environmentally sustainable. As a result, they also call into question what is being measured as wealth, by assigning value to stocks and flows of environmental resources, local knowledge and social capital; to the sense of control associated with being a producer; and to livelihood, well-being and physical security. These cases show that intersecting forms of inequality are challenged not by segregating the economic from the political and social, an approach often favoured by non-governmental organizations (NGOs) and government agencies, but by treating them as intertwined, just as they are in real life.

These cases are striking examples of pathways for transforming inequality. We point to ways in which marginalized women have organized to get a toe-hold on economic security in India, Indonesia and Ethiopia – all places of significant economic growth and growing inequalities, but with varying degrees of political openness.

> ## Cases of grass-roots initiatives for a fairer economy from the global South
>
> **Self-Reliant Action through Joint Action (Srijan), India**: Srijan works with lowest caste, below-poverty-line (BPL) women who organize in self-help groups. Through its work in Rajasthan, women have become milk producers and shareholders in a dairy producer company with a stronger ability to advocate for basic services from the state.
>
> **Self Employed Women's Association (SEWA), India**: a member-based organization, SEWA is both a trade union and a development organization of self-employed women in the informal economy. SEWA is able to marshal its members to exert political pressure as well as supporting local women to achieve 'economic freedom'. In the agriculture sector, SEWA members resist urban expansion and corporate land purchase while at the same time strengthening economic agency, by linking producers and consumers in a sustainable land-based local economy.
>
> **PEKKA, Indonesia**: a member-based NGO working with female heads of households facing stigma as divorced, widowed or abandoned women. Supporting their economic empowerment through cooperatives, and their full participation as community leaders with paralegal training, PEKKA addresses cultural barriers to inclusion in decision-making in public as well as private domains.
>
> **WISE, Ethiopia**: an organization dedicated to supporting women's economic and social empowerment, primarily through savings and credit and entrepreneurship support.
>
> **Banco Palmas, Brazil**: the neighbourhood of Conjunto Palmeiras on the outskirts of Fortaleza has a fifty-year history of citizens organizing to claim rights to basic infrastructure, and then to build a local solidarity economy. A local social currency, 'palmas', is issued through the neighbourhood's community bank, Banco Palmas. This community banking model has since been replicated in over 100 Brazilian communities.

They vary in the degree to which public and political space is wide enough for marginalized populations to participate, and therefore in the degree to which skills acquired for economic agency transfer into the political realm.

We also look at the neighbourhood of Conjunto Palmeiras in Brazil and its fifty-year history of community organizing. This involves both political action to claim the rights to basic infrastructure, and economic action to create and sustain a viable local economy. It now faces new challenges to active participation, including urban violence. Finally we offer some closing reflections on the significance of these cases.

Pathways towards inclusion from the grass roots

The initiatives in India, Indonesia and Ethiopia have a similar focus: encouraging women to organize in groups to save, borrow and invest in micro-enterprises, to gradually achieve a sustainable livelihood and status in community life, and to use their collective strength for mutual solidarity.

The starting point is to reach out to vulnerable women in both the urban informal economy, and the agricultural sector. In the Indonesian case, the NGO PEKKA has a specific focus within this vulnerable category: women heads of households, often widowed or divorced, or left behind by the migration of male family members.

Such groups enable women to build and diversify income streams in an otherwise precarious household situation. Equally important is their function as a platform for NGOs and government agencies to build capacity and solidarity, and raise awareness about social and political rights and new economic opportunities. In Rajasthan, India, Srijan works with women's self-help groups among low-caste women. From these small beginnings, value chains for organized women to sell, process and market milk, and maximize returns at source, are being realized through a dairy producer company in which women hold shares. As a hybrid between a cooperative and a private company, the producer company complements the blend of collective and individual initiative nurtured in the self-help groups.

This in turn translates into collective claims for the services to which they are entitled, such as better schools, and on which their income-earning potential depends, such as veterinary services. As with SEWA, the ability of women to make demands on the state, or hold officials to account, is essential in a context where India's claims to democracy are confounded by high levels of corruption in its public distribution system.

In Indonesia, where space has been opened up through democratic reforms and decentralized governance, the female heads of households in PEKKA's programmes emerge as economic producers in community-based cooperatives and also as community leaders with paralegal training. Equipped with a progressive interpretation of Islamic teachings, these leaders have been able to support women through the village court system especially in marriage cases, and assert legal status for families headed by women. They also assist in birth registration, fundamental to claiming entitlements for women and children alike.

In Ethiopia, the women who get involved in WISE experience a social and economic boost through group-based savings and credit activities. They also make political gains in existing spaces for participation. They begin to be recognized, and are invited to participate in the deliberations of the local administration or in local community associations providing informal social safety nets. Nevertheless, the economic gains made by these women are still far from matched by their participation in other spaces, for example where market governance issues are negotiated, or by their influence in traditional associations. Economic agency seems to be a necessary but not a sufficient condition for equivalent levels of capacity to influence decisions in the public sphere.

There is no simple linear trajectory for such grass-roots citizen-led initiatives, and the characteristics of each of these are unique. Consider for example, the role of SEWA, which has grown in its forty-four-year history to 1.9 million women members across twelve Indian states. As a trade union it strives to achieve 'voice, visibility and validation' for women workers, and has the legitimacy to champion their rights and entitlements and to press for legislative changes that acknowledge women's contribution to the economy as a whole. Recent examples of its achievements have been the legalization of street vending in 2014, and its role in preventing an amendment to the Land Acquisitions Bill which would have made acquisition of land for urban expansion or corporate agriculture possible without the permission of rural owners.

As a member-based organization, SEWA's leadership works closely with members at the local level to support their economic empowerment. At the same time, recognizing the political nature of economic freedom, SEWA membership is a mobilizing force to be reckoned with when issues of common concern need to be addressed.

It is important to acknowledge the roots of SEWA's approach in Gandhi's idea of economic freedom as economic self-reliance and full employment. Applying this insight to rural areas, SEWA has embarked upon a strategy of linking producers to consumers, starting a private company that purchases from SEWA producers, employs SEWA members and sells packaged and processed commodities through individual retailers in the villages, who are also SEWA members. Such deliberate strengthening of the local economy goes hand in hand with support to agricultural producers, so they can adopt technical innovations, adapt to the unpredictable consequences of climate change, and protect their land from acquisition. SEWA now advocates a minimum support income, partly so that producers can invest time in protecting and regenerating the quality of the land they work on, and partly as a strategy to ensure basic economic security, so that full participation in political and public life can be realized.

Transforming inequality from below

Many of the cases we have explored show promise as pathways to inclusion in economic and political spaces, to a more equitable distribution of public goods, or to the consideration of our responsibility to future generations in our use and valuing of environmental resources. They share too the conviction that economic transformation is intrinsic to narrowing the gap between rich and poor. The SEWA case is an example, while in north-east Brazil the case of Conjunto Palmeiras and Banco Palmas illustrates the phases of a similar transformative strategy. When coastal people were relocated to wasteland on the periphery of Fortaleza, they first agitated to secure basic infrastructure for a liveable neighbourhood, then proceeded to build a local economy, and eventually established a solidarity economy of 'prosumers' with its own local currency. The demonstration effect of this action has helped create similar initiatives throughout north-east Brazil, with local currencies being replicated in community banks across the region.

Such grass-roots initiatives start small and take decades, even generations, to come to fruition. Not all succeed, and in success they face new challenges, but they set a precedent in their own context, showing the way forward for a restructuring of economic and political life.

Conclusion

These cases provide insights into the potential and the limits of collective political and economic agency for addressing inequality. They speak to the balance between maintaining associational linkages locally and establishing effective relationships with state actors. Each dimension – horizontal or vertical – demands relationships of responsibility and accountability. In the face of fragile livelihoods, collective action, mutual responsibility, and alliance-building to strengthen local economic relationships are as critical for security as shaping local decision-making and holding institutions to account. How such collective economic and political agency is sequenced and sustained, and how individual economic gain affects the propensity towards collective action, are questions to pursue further. If 'thin' one-dimensional solutions to global poverty and inequality need to be replaced by thicker strategies (Edwards, 2011), these cases, still unfolding, are context-specific examples of how that is being done.

Notes

1. See Coady International Institute (2014) for preliminary work. A final synthesis paper is due in 2016.
This research was carried out in a series of scoping studies. For each study the four to five-person team was composed of academics and NGO practitioners, including a representative of the local host organization, and was also mixed in terms of country of origin and disciplinary background. The opportunity for South-to-South peer learning was considered to be a priority.

Bibliography

Coady International Institute. 2014. *Exploring the Dynamic between Political and Economic Citizenship*. St Francis Xavier University, Antigonish, Nova Scotia, Canada. *http://coady.stfx.ca/tinroom/assets/file/Exploring%20the%20DynamicReport.pdf* (Accessed 15 June 2016).

Edwards, M. 2011. *Thick Problems and Thin Solutions: How NGOs can Bridge the Gap*. The Hague, Hivos Knowledge Programme. *www.thebrokeronline.eu/var/broker/storage/original/application/960b295f2838b63a6609cea4fdf0a51f.pdf* (Accessed 22 February 2016).

■ **Alison Mathie** *(Canada), Coady International Institute, St Francis Xavier University, Antigonish, Canada.*

■ **Eileen Alma** *(Canada), Coady International Institute.*

■ **Asier Ansorena** *(Spain), Instituto Banco Palmas, Fortaleza, Brazil.*

■ **Jagat Basnet** *(Nepal), Community Self Reliance Centre (CSRC), Kathmandu, Nepal.*

■ **Yogesh Ghore** *(India), Coady International Institute.*

■ **Sebastián Jarrín** *(Ecuador), Sub-National Governance Extractive Industries project, Grupo FARO, Quito, Ecuador.*

■ **Julien Landry** *(Canada), Coady International Institute.*

■ **Nanci Lee** *(Canada) is an independent consultant from Halifax, Nova Scotia, Canada.*

■ **Bettina von Lieres** *(South Africa), University of Toronto, Ontario, Canada.*

■ **Valerie Miller** *(USA), Just Associates (JASS), USA.*

■ **Malena de Montis** *(Nicaragua), Just Associates (JASS), Managua, Nicaragua.*

■ **Salome Nakazwe** *(Zambia), EMPOWER programme, Women for Change, Zambia.*

■ **Stutlina Pal** *(India), Self Reliant Initiatives through Joint Action (Srijan), India.*

■ **Brianne Peters** *(Canada), Coady International Institute.*

■ **Rehana Riyawala** *(India), Self Employed Women's Association (SEWA), India.*

■ **Vicky Schreiber** *(Canada), Coady International Institute.*

■ **Mohammed A. Shariff** *(Uganda), Kabarole Research and Resource Centre (KRC), Fortportal, Uganda.*

■ **Aster Tefera** *(Ethiopia), EMPOWER programme, WISE, Ethiopia.*

■ **Nani Zulminarni** *(Indonesia), PEKKA and JASS, Jakarta, Indonesia.*

POSTCARD

65. Equality as a valued social norm, inequality as an injustice

Sakiko Fukuda-Parr

Social attitudes to inequality are a critical factor in the politics of change. Unless inequality itself is seen as a problem, and equality is held as a social value by politicians, activists and the public at large, there will be no agitation or support for corrective measures. Is inequality bad in and of itself, and is equality a valuable end? Few would argue for a society of completely equal outcomes. Inequality that results from differences in effort and ability is widely accepted as legitimate, as both a just reward and a necessary incentive for hard work. So what kind and what level of inequality is unacceptable? At what point does public opinion turn to finding inequality excessive or extreme?

In much of the economics literature, these questions have been approached on the basis of self-interested median voters framed in rational choice theory, whose support for redistribution depends on their relative income position. People at the lower end of the income distribution are more likely to vote for redistributive policies which, when supported by the 'median voter', would lead to policy change (see e.g. Alesina and Rodrik, 1994). They reject inequality caused by unfair advantages of birth and connection (Alesina and Angeletos, 2005). This approach neglects two important and interrelated factors: social norms valuing equality, and the effect of income inequality on political power.

Inequality is inherently about fairness and social justice. Regardless of their position on income distribution, many view extreme inequality as morally wrong and unfair, a position that forms part of their ethical values (Sen, 2000). Such views are often socially constructed, and shaped by cultural norms. Societies vary in the value they place on equality, and in their rejection or tolerance of inequality.

Inter-country variations – consistently observed in surveys[1] – can be explained less by factors such as levels of economic development, levels of inequality, and the nature of active redistributive policies, than by history and cultural beliefs. Using data from twenty-six countries, Lubker (2006) found that intolerance for inequality and public support for redistribution are not driven by the level of inequality, but instead by social justice norms. Suhrcke (2001), in a study of Europe, found important differences between East and West, attributable to a historically entrenched cultural norm. Reducing inequality and winning public support for redistribution therefore requires shifts in cultural values.

Inequality regarded as social injustice is concerned with wealth that leads to political capture. Indeed, contemporary advocates for attacking inequality, from the protesters (Ortiz et al., 2014) to Joseph Stiglitz (2012) to Oxfam (2014), do not argue that inequality is excessive in the abstract, but as it relates to structures of power and the working of markets and politics. The grievance is not just against the distribution of income and wealth in itself, but with the perception that it is driven by policies and institutions that are unfair, pitted in favour of the wealthy, and active in perpetuating a vicious circle of ever-increasing inequality.

Note

1. Such as the World Values Survey (*www.worldvaluessurvey.org/wvs.jsp*) and the Social Inequality Survey of the International Social Survey Programme (ISSP) (*www.issp.org/*).

Bibliography

Alesina, A. and Angeletos, G.-M. 2005. Fairness and redistribution. *American Economic Review*, Vol. 95, No. 4, pp. 960–80. *www.jstor.org/stable/4132701?seq=1#page_scan_tab_contents* (Accessed 21 February 2016.)

Alesina, A. and Rodrik, D. 1994. Distributive politics and economic growth. *Quarterly Journal of Economics*, Vol. 109, No. 2, pp. 465–90. *https://www.mtholyoke.edu/courses/epaus/econ213/rodrikalesina.pdf* (Accessed 21 February 2016.)

Lubker, M. 2006. Inequality and the demand for redistribution: are the assumptions of the new growth theory valid? *Socio-Economic Review*, Vol. 4, No. 2, pp. 117–48. *http://papers.ssrn.com/sol3/papers.cfm?abstract_id=888722* (Accessed 15 February 2016.)

Ortiz, I., Burke, S. L., Berrada, M. and Cortes, H. 2013. World Protests 2006–2013. Working Paper no. 2013. New York, Initiative for Policy Dialogue and Friedrich-Ebert-Stiftung. *http://ssrn.com/abstract=2374098* (Accessed 15 February 2016.)

Oxfam. 2014. *Working for the Few: Political Capture and Economic Inequality*. Briefing Paper 178. London, Oxfam. *www.ipu.org/splz-e/unga14/oxfam.pdf* (Accessed 15 February 2016.)

Sen, A. 2000. Social justice and the distribution of income. A. B. Atkinson and F. Bourguignon (eds), *Handbook of Income Distribution*. Amsterdam, North-Holland.

Stiglitz, J. E. 2012. *The Price of Inequality*. New York, Norton.

Suhrcke, M. 2001. *Preferences for Inequality: East Vs. West*. Working Paper no. 89. Florence, UNICEF Innocenti Research Centre.

■ ***Sakiko Fukuda-Parr** (Japan) is professor of international affairs at the New School, New York.*

66. A historical view of the politics of inequality

Duncan Green

Discussions on development frequently take place in a historical vacuum. Debates are based largely on prevalent theoretical and conceptual paradigms and iconic (usually Northern) case studies. Seldom do they draw systemically on the lessons of history. Yet looking at the origins of historical success on any given topic liberates us to propose a wider range of policy options than whatever is the received wisdom of the day. To illustrate the value of such an approach, this article briefly surveys four countries that have experienced prolonged periods of redistribution at some point in the past fifty years: Bolivia, Brazil, Malaysia and Mauritius.

The historical narrative we currently use on inequality, redistribution and social justice is a limited one. The New Deal in the USA and the origins of the UK welfare state are far too prominent. History is much richer than that. In diverse cases where inequalities have declined, this outcome has depended on the interactions between policy and politics; between top-down leadership and bottom-up action; between deliberate responses and others unrelated to inequality in itself; and between measures aimed at both vertical and horizontal inequalities. One change can open up or close down possibilities for another.

To explore the potential of this approach, I identified four countries that had experienced prolonged periods of redistribution at some point in the last fifty years: Bolivia, Brazil, Malaysia and Mauritius. While a complete analysis would consider multiple dimensions of inequality, such as nutrition, health, education, security, wealth and land ownership, I concentrate here on income redistribution, for reasons of space.

Bolivia and Brazil have been at the forefront of Latin America's impressive recent achievements in reducing inequality. Over the past decade, the incomes of the poorest Brazilians have risen more than five times faster than those of the richest. Women's incomes are rising faster than men's, black people's faster than whites', the impoverished north-east faster than the rich south-east (Ivins, 2013). Beyond income inequality, Brazil has made stellar progress in achieving 'zero hunger'.

The political drivers of **Brazil**'s turnaround include:

- The transition from military rule to democracy, encompassing a constitution and political process attuned to the importance of basic rights, such as the right to food. The new charter also sought to restrict the power of the military and strengthen people power by establishing citizen oversight councils and mass-participation policy conferences, and by extending formal avenues of political participation and representation. These include greater freedom to propose new laws and initiate referenda (PDA, n.d.);

- The election of the centre-left government of the Workers' Party (PT), which assembled a coalition of working-class and progressive middle-class Brazilians behind a programme tackling poverty and inequality;

- A high level of public participation, for example in holding nineteen different ministries to account on Brazil's 'zero hunger' effort to achieve universal access to food (FAO, 2011).

Promising political and economic conditions paved the way for redistributive policies, including:

- Brazil's renowned and widely imitated Bolsa Familia social protection system (World Bank, n.d.), with cash transfers for women in return for getting their children vaccinated and keeping them in school;

- Labour policies that promoted a reduction of unemployment and job informality as well as an increase of social security coverage, average wages and reinstated tripartite wage bargaining (Cornia, 2014).

Also the reduction of the skill premium thanks to the increasing supply of educated workers (Lustig et al., 2011);

- Major increases in the minimum wage, and the introduction of a universal pension, particularly important in deprived rural households;

- The maintenance of political and economic stability, for example the avoidance of high inflation, throughout the period of reforms.

As of early 2016, however, there were signs that Brazil's recent economic model of progressive social policies combined with growth led by commodity exports in a market system was losing energy. In its place were an economic slump, calls for presidential impeachment, and mass public protests calling for deeper structural reforms (see e.g. Trebeck, 2014) and improvements in the country's health and education services (Mason, 2013).

Bolivia has seen a much sharper fall in inequality than Brazil, stemming from a seismic shift in Bolivia's social and political identity akin to the end of apartheid in South Africa. In 2006 Evo Morales took office as the country's first ever indigenous president, at the head of a new political movement, the Movement for Socialism (MAS).

The Morales government instigated talks on a radical new constitution enshrining a series of political, economic and social rights, intended to ensure that 'people power' became a driver of redistribution. This helped build momentum for new progressive spending programmes which the government funded by renegotiating the country's oil and gas contracts.

The new government used this windfall to invest in infrastructure, targeted social programmes and a universal pension entitlement. It has raised the minimum wage and presided over an expansion of the formal economy. There has been a substantial increase in public spending on health and education, which has had the biggest redistributive impact (Lustig et al., 2013) by providing the poorest with urgently needed 'virtual income' (Seery, 2014). Traumatic memories of Bolivia's 1980s hyperinflation have also ensured a degree of spending restraint, although little progress has been made in increasing the size or progressivity of the non-hydrocarbon tax take.

Malaysia's combination of stellar growth and high-speed redistribution in the 1970s and 1980s was born out of widespread rioting in 1969, as the country's ethnic Malay majority protested about its economic and social marginalization compared with the country's ethnic Chinese and Indian minorities. This prompted the introduction of the New Economic Policy (NEP) the following year. The NEP sought:

- a decisive reduction in urban and rural poverty for all Malaysians irrespective of race

- a definitive reduction in racial economic imbalances in terms of income, employment and wealth

- high growth rates with an annual target of 6.4 per cent per capita for 1970–85

- full employment, with the state guiding industrialization towards labour-intensive sectors

- state intervention to support small farmers (overwhelmingly Malays) and ensure asset redistribution, for example ownership of shares by ethnic Malays

- social policies in areas such as housing, education and health to reduce the likelihood of communal conflicts and build a sense of common identity

- comprehensive data gathering to monitor and adapt policies as they evolved.

Increased spending on essential services, and job creation through rapid industrialization in manufacturing (Malays had largely been employed in agriculture), led to a boom period of 'growth with equity', rapidly reducing poverty among ethnic Malays. However, inequality has risen since 1990, with signs that the government finds it harder to tackle intra-Malay inequality than inter-ethnic divisions.

At independence in 1968, the prospects for **Mauritius** looked grim: there was almost total dependence on sugar (93 per cent of its exports) in a racially fragmented society with serious ethnic tensions. Yet political leadership ensured a 'one nation' strategy, including a constitution that guaranteed parliamentary seats to the various ethnic minorities. Mauritius's first post-independence leader, Sir Seewoosagure Ramgoolam (1967–82), pursued 'consociational' coalition governments that ensured social stability.

Social peace aided an extraordinary economic take-off based on heterodox policies. First the government negotiated preferential access for Mauritian sugar to the European Union, while at the same time pursuing labour-intensive manufacturing through the introduction of export processing zones based on the experiences of Singapore, Hong Kong and Taiwan, China. When those showed signs of losing momentum, the government moved to promote services such as tourism, although in this latest phase, inequality has started to rise again.

The government also developed 'OECD-style social protection', working with a large and active trade union movement to introduce centralized wage bargaining, price controls on socially sensitive items, and generous social security, especially for the elderly. Income taxes, while progressive, are low and have 'negligible impact' on overall distribution.

One academic study concluded that 'strong domestic institutions have contributed substantially to Mauritian success and are a good candidate for underlying explanations of the Mauritian miracle' (Subramanian and Roy, 2003).

Some common factors behind these redistributive episodes warrant further study. They include the importance of new political parties in Brazil and Bolivia, in both cases linked to social movements. New constitutions have changed the nature of politics in these two countries. Big political shocks were important in Malaysia, in the form of race riots, and in Brazil with the end of military rule.

Factors that turned out not to be problematic include the curse of wealth – big commodity booms in Bolivia and Brazil coincided with redistribution. Another factor is ethnic diversity: Malaysia and Mauritius were both ethnically divided, but proved able to redistribute. In fact it may even be the case that having political and economic power in the hands of different groups can lead to them having to negotiate, although it can also lead to conflict, and we need to understand what determines the final outcome.

These initial thoughts have led to a joint and ongoing research programme with David Hudson and Niheer Dasandi from University College, London. Using the Gini index figures in the Standardized World Income Inequality Database, covering 173 countries from 1960 to 2012,[1] they identified twenty-three countries that have experienced redistribution over seven years or more.

The timeframe follows the literature on growth episodes, but is somewhat arbitrary and throws up anomalies. Nevertheless, the list provides a useful starting point for a more systematic review of the politics of redistribution.

A conference in Birmingham, UK (in February 2015) added a number of further avenues for exploration. One is decentralization in the run-up to the distribution period, which helped develop tools such as cash transfers and participatory budgeting in Brazil. Another is the way in which 'coalitions of commitment' have brought together state insiders and grass-roots outsiders to push through redistributive programmes. Also important is the use of narratives, national myths and symbols to generate momentum and weaken opposition to reforms.

The spread of secondary and tertiary education is seen to be important in reducing the return to skills for more educated people, so the wage differential between skilled and unskilled falls, bringing down income inequality. There is also a complex connection between horizontal and vertical inequalities. Horizontal inequalities affect groups – based on ethnicity, gender, region and other factors – whereas vertical inequalities are those between individuals. Stewart (2015) argued that horizontal inequalities are often the triggers for redistribution (such as race riots in Malaysia), but the impact of subsequent reforms affects both types of inequality.

This initial work raises other questions. Was falling inequality a conscious aim of the government, or an unintended consequence of something else, for example a shift to labour-intensive manufacturing in pursuit of growth in Mauritius and Malaysia? Are there particular historical windows of opportunity, when the prevailing economic and policy winds are favourable for national redistribution? (Of my four examples, two are from the 1970s, while two fall in the present century, after the global Washington consensus had already passed its high water mark.) How much of this was about a fortunate combination of circumstances, rather than conscious politics or policy?

Those concerned with international development too often operate in a historical vacuum, supplementing contemporary empiricism by falling back on either disciplinary 'priors' or an impoverished set of historical reference points. This is unfortunate, because a more rigorous consideration of a breadth of historical examples can greatly enrich discussions on a range of pressing contemporary challenges.

Note

1. The Standardized World Income Inequality Database is available at http://myweb.uiowa.edu/fsolt/swiid/swiid.html. Although questions have been raised about the accuracy of some of the data points in the database, for the purposes of this exercise, the author considered it good enough to provide a 'long list' of countries to consider. Subsequent analysis will weed out rogue data and erroneous candidates.

Bibliography

Cornia, G. A. 2014. *Falling Inequality in Latin America*. Oxford, Oxford University Press.

FAO (Food and Agriculture Organization). 2011. *The Fome Zero (Zero Hunger) Program: The Brazilian Experience*. www.fao.org/docrep/016/i3023e/i3023e.pdf (Accessed 4 February 2016.)

Ivins, C. 2013. Inequality matters: BRICS inequalities fact sheet. Rio de Janeiro, BRICS Policy Center/Oxfam. www.oxfam.org/sites/www.oxfam.org/files/brics-inequality-fact-sheet-oxfam-03-14-2013_0.pdf (Accessed 4 February 2016.)

Lustig, N., Pessino, C. and Scott, J. 2013. *The Impact of Taxes and Social Spending on Inequality and Poverty in Argentina, Bolivia, Brazil, Mexico, Peru and Uruguay: An Overview* Working Paper no. 13. Tulane, La., Commitment to Equity Institute, Tulane University. www.commitmentoequity.org/publications_files/CEQWPNo13%20Lustig%20et%20al.%20Overview%20Arg,Bol,Bra,Mex,Per,Ury%20April%202013.pdf (Accessed 22 February 2016.)

Lustig, N., Lopez-Calva, L. F. and Ortiz-Juarez, E. 2011. *The Decline in Inequality in Latin America: How Much, Since When and Why*. Economics Working Paper no. 1118. Tulane, La., Tulane University. http://econ.tulane.edu/RePEc/pdf/tul1118.pdf (Accessed 4 February 2016.)

Mason, P. 2013. Why are the BRICs crumbling? Welcome to the permanent revolution. *Independent*. www.independent.co.uk/voices/comment/why-are-the-brics-are-crumbling-welcome-to-the-permanent-revolution-8668803.html (Accessed 22 February 2016.)

PDA (Political Database of the Americas). http://pdba.georgetown.edu/constitutions/brazil/english96.html.

Seery, E. 2014. *Working for the Many*. Oxford, Oxfam. www.oxfam.org/sites/www.oxfam.org/files/bp182-public-services-fight-inequality-030414-en.pdf (Accessed 22 February 2016.)

Stewart, F. 2015. Inequality, justice and policy. Adrian Leftwich Memorial Lecture, Birmingham, UK, 12 February 2015. www.dlprog.org/events/the-politics-of-inequality-dlp-annual-conference-2015.php (Accessed 22 February 2016.)

Subramanian, A. and Roy, D. 2003. Who can explain the Mauritian miracle? D. Rodrik (ed.), *In Search of Prosperity*. Princeton, N.J., Princeton University Press.

Trebeck, K. 2014. Is Brazil's social/economic miracle running out of steam just as the World Cup arrives? Blog. https://oxfamblogs.org/fp2p/is-brazils-socialeconomic-miracle-running-out-of-steam-just-as-the-world-cup-arrives/ (Accessed 22 February 2016.)

World Bank. n.d. *Bolsa Família: Changing the Lives of Millions in Brazil*. http://web.worldbank.org/WBSITE/EXTERNAL/NEWS/0,,contentMDK:21447054~pagePK:64257043~piPK:437376~theSitePK:4607,00.html

■ **Duncan Green** (UK) is senior strategic adviser at Oxfam GB, professor in practice in international development at the London School of Economics and a visiting fellow at the Institute of Development Studies (IDS).

POSTCARD

67. Rising extreme inequality is a concern for us all

Winnie Byanyima

The richest 1 per cent of the world's population now own as much as the rest of the world put together, affirming Oxfam's assertion that extreme economic inequality is spiralling out of control.

This phenomenon is unfair and morally lacking, and its consequences are corrosive for everyone. Extreme inequality corrupts politics, hinders economic growth and stifles social mobility. It fuels crime and violent conflict. It touches a moral nerve in threatening the very health of our democracies when political and economic power is captured by elites. The rapid rise of extreme economic inequality is standing in the way of eliminating global poverty.

If India were to reduce inequality by 36 per cent, it could virtually eliminate extreme poverty by 2019 (Oxfam, 2014). Our research has indicated that inequality is the missing link that explains how the same rate of growth in different countries can lead to different rates of poverty reduction.

According to the Overseas Development Institute, 200 million of the 1.1 billion people living in extreme poverty in 2010 could have escaped extreme poverty if poor people benefited equally from the proceeds of growth during the Millennium Development Goals (MDGs) period (Hoy and Samman, 2015). Projections by World Bank economists find that to eliminate extreme poverty by 2030, the poorest must benefit from growth 2 percentage points higher than the rest of the population (Lakner et al., 2014). An equal share in growth is not enough, and would leave almost 200 million additional people trapped in extreme poverty (Oxfam, 2015).

A high level of inequality constitutes a barrier to future economic growth because it obstructs productive investment, limits the productive and consumptive capacity of the economy, and undermines the institutions necessary for fair societies. Researchers at the International Monetary Fund (IMF) found that an increase in the income share of the poor and the middle class in fact increases growth, while doing the same for the top 20 per cent results in lower growth (Dabla-Norris et al., 2015).

Inequality extremes are, in the words of Cambridge economist Ha-Joon Chang, 'a source of needless human and economic waste' (quoted in Oxfam, 2014, p. iii). Extreme inequality is an immediately pressing concern for us all, and it must be addressed without delay.

International bodies and governments must pay more attention to the gap between the richest and poorest, and track wealth and income transfers at the top and bottom of the inequality extremes. Access to good-quality data is imperative, to produce more in-depth research on the drivers of extreme wealth and income inequality, and their impact on poverty.

Inequality is not inevitable. Governments can reduce economic extremes by adopting a package of redistributive measures, including more progressive tax systems that redistribute incomes fairly, and by increasing investment in universal, good-quality and free public services and social protection programmes.

Increasing the number of decent jobs for decent pay is also essential. Good-quality jobs are inherently those that pay a living wage, provide job security and respect for workers' rights, and ensure equal pay for women.

There is, however, a power dynamic to address, and civil society must hold decision-makers to account. Governments and public institutions must realize they are first and foremost servants to their citizens, not to vested interests. Governments are obliged to protect human rights, which involves preventing commercial interests from emasculating those rights. Only then will we successfully tackle the scourge of extreme economic inequality.

Bibliography

Dabla-Norris, E., Kochhar, K., Suphaphiphat, N., Ricka, F. and Tsounta, E. 2015. *Causes and Consequences of Income Inequality: A Global Perspective.* IMF Staff Discussion Note. https://www.imf.org/external/pubs/ft/sdn/2015/sdn1513.pdf (Accessed 15 February 2016.)

Hoy, C. and Samman, E. 2015. *What if Growth had been as Good for the Poor as Everyone Else?* Overseas Development Institute. www.odi.org/publications/9588-income-inequality-poverty-growth (Accessed 15 February 2016.)

Lakner, C., Negre, M. and Prydz, E. B. 2014. *The Role of Inclusive Growth in Ending Extreme Poverty.* www.ecineq.org/ecineq_lux15/FILESx2015/CR2/p191.pdf (Accessed 15 February 2016.)

Oxfam. 2014. *Even It Up.* https://www.oxfam.org/sites/www.oxfam.org/files/file_attachments/cr-even-it-up-extreme-inequality-291014-en.pdf (Accessed 15 February 2016.)

Oxfam. 2015. *Inequality and the End of Extreme Poverty.* https://www.oxfam.org/sites/www.oxfam.org/files/inequality_and_the_end_of_poverty_oi_media_brief_final.pdf (Accessed 15 February 2016.)

■ **Winnie Byanyima** *(Uganda) is executive director of Oxfam International. She is a leader on women's rights, democratic governance and peace-building. She served eleven years in the Ugandan Parliament, and has served at the African Union Commission and as director of gender and development at the UNDP. She co-founded the sixty-member Global Gender and Climate Alliance and chaired a UN task force on gender aspects of the MDGs and on climate change.*

Part III

Part IV

TRANSFORMATIVE KNOWLEDGE FOR A JUST WORLD

68. A global research agenda on inequality for the next ten years
    The World Social Science Report 2016 Editorial Team

69. Knowledge divides: social science production on inequalities and social justice
    Françoise Caillods

70. The use of big data in the analysis of inequality
    Mike Savage

71. Tax and legal havens: a priority for inequality research
    Alain Deneault

72. POSTCARD • Increasing childhood equality in cities: a practical intervention through policy, research and advocacy
    Alberto Minujin

73. POSTCARD • Local knowledge as a common good
    Kemly Camacho Jiménez

74. POSTCARD • A proposal to monitor intersecting inequalities in the post-2015 Agenda
    Deborah S. Rogers

SAHBI ('My friend'), Daniel Eime
(Rabat, Morocco, 2016)
© Chadi Ilyass

68. A global research agenda on inequality for the next ten years

The World Social Science Report 2016 *Editorial Team*

This Report has demonstrated that inequality is already the subject of rich social science research. It has also helped identify important gaps in our awareness of inequalities. In this final Part of the report, we look towards future social science agendas, asking what new kinds of research and knowledge are needed to deepen and extend our understanding of inequalities. And crucially, what are the roles of social science in identifying and building transformative pathways towards greater equality?

Multiple, intersecting inequalities require multidimensional knowledge. In the following pages, we consider key elements of a research agenda which acknowledges all seven dimensions of inequality defined and discussed earlier in this Report – economic, social, cultural, political, spatial, environmental and knowledge – and which could improve understanding of their intersecting dynamics and their consequences over time and around the world.

To make progress in these areas means going well beyond current technical debates, such as that on the measurement of economic inequality, important as these are. This first means a shift towards integrating a far wider range of disciplinary lenses when setting agendas and defining frameworks for research, including not only anthropology, sociology, psychology, geography, political science and legal studies, but also the arts and humanities.

Even when research addresses issues such as education, health, political participation and gender, which range beyond income, consumption, employment and wealth, there is often an implicit push towards the quantification of these dimensions. This trend may well be reinforced by the need to monitor the indicators of the Sustainable Development Goals (SDGs). A second shift is needed, one that goes beyond quantification, integrating well-designed and conducted qualitative and participatory methods, and developing innovative combinations of quantitative and qualitative research to better understand why and how inequalities persist.

The improvement of our knowledge of inequalities also implies analysis of how social science can be used to challenge them, and in doing so contribute to a more equal and just world. Transformative pathways, we suggest, require transformative knowledge; transformative in what it covers, how and by whom it is produced and communicated, and how it interlinks with action and change. There are key opportunities for a transformative knowledge agenda that is co-constructed with those who are experiencing inequalities and are in a position to influence change through policies, practices and politics. At the same time, others argue that the role of the researcher is different from the role of the activist, and that social science and political practice cannot be reduced to each other. The relationships between research and action will necessarily vary by issue and context. The challenge now is to configure those relationships collectively to chart a transformative agenda towards equality.

The production of social science research on inequality

Inherent in this challenge is knowledge inequality itself, and how knowledge inequalities link to other intersecting inequalities. These include inequalities in the construction of knowledge – which kinds of knowledge are produced, by whom and where. They also include inequalities of access to formal, organized, published knowledge, as well as that available online amidst digital divides. And they include inequalities in whose knowledge counts. These include the tendency for economic knowledge to be prioritized over that from other disciplines, for technical, quantitative measures to be given more weight than studies rooted in lived experiences, and for expert knowledge to predominate over indigenous ways of knowing.

The bibliographic data assembled here (Caillods, 69 and *Annexes*) on the number of journal articles on inequality published in the past twenty years (1993–2012) provide interesting insights into these themes. First, we notice a dramatic increase in the number of social science journal publications on inequality.

Not only is the volume of publications increasing, but these publications are employing new and innovative methods, for instance in accessing and using big data to uncover broad patterns and linkages between different forms of inequality, as Savage (70) points out.

A second trend is for inequalities to become a concern for a broader range of disciplines. Even though economics, political science, sociology, and more recently education predominate, social psychology and gender studies make important contributions. This broad spectrum of disciplines confirms inequality as a theme of interest for social science in general. Interestingly, however, the social sciences (including economic and behavioural sciences) are no longer the only dominant voices on the topic. The health sciences are now producing nearly as many articles on inequality as all the social science disciplines put together.

A third feature, regional disparities in the production of social research on inequality, constitutes arguably the most problematic trend. Over 80 per cent of publications on inequality in the past twenty years are by researchers based in North America and Western Europe. It is positive to see an emerging middle-income country such as South Africa, with its particular historical legacy and current levels of wealth inequality, among the leading countries in terms of research produced. But very few articles are produced by researchers in India, China and Brazil, let alone in the poorest countries, where those most affected by the bottom end of global inequality live. Despite efforts to overcome this gap with this Report, which counts contributors from some forty countries, we recognize that we have succeeded only partially in bringing together the global perspective required to understand a complex phenomenon such as inequality in all of its diversity.

Towards a new agenda

In a world in which knowledge shapes power and voice, and vice versa, the fundamental inequality in the production of knowledge about inequality itself must be addressed. In addition, the contributions to this Report, as well as the process of compiling it, have pointed to a number of other gaps in the study of inequality which need attention in the future. On the basis of this Report, and additional suggestions from a survey of contributing authors, we point to seven key priorities for social science research and action.

Priority 1 – Increase support for knowledge production about inequality, and processes of social inclusion and exclusion, in those places most affected by them

The places at the lower ends of the inequality scales are often those where there is the least published social science knowledge on the theme. To put it another way, there is knowledge inequality in the production of knowledge about inequalities. It is an urgent priority to provide intellectual and financial support for the capacity of researchers who can collect, organize and analyse data on inequalities in such places, and how they evolve.

Action areas include:

- Expanding collective wisdom about inequality in the most affected areas, through support for geographically focused research efforts;

- Supporting researchers and institutions in poorer parts of the world to study inequality in their settings and from their perspectives. This includes supporting the capacity of state statistical agencies, which are often heavily under-resourced in poorer countries;

- Developing inclusive international networks of inequality researchers, thereby,

- Strengthening cross-country and cross-regional comparative work on inequality, its mechanisms and consequences;

- Developing and supporting open data sources, with open access publishing and open access software to enable researchers to contribute to and engage with multidimensional social science debates;

- Support for training and capability enhancement in the poorest parts of the world, including state-of-the-art methodologies, alongside links between research and practical change.

Priority 2 – Improve our ability to assess, measure and compare the dimensions of inequality over time and across the world

Social science understanding of inequality depends very much on our ability to measure and compare it across countries, across population groups and over time. This remains difficult across the multiple dimensions of inequality. With respect to the SDGs, Rogers (74) emphasizes the need to monitor inequalities across the full spectrum of factors that may contribute to human well-being, combining indicators of economic inequality with those for political participation, health, education, access to clean air or water, safety and security, and so on. While there has been a great deal of work over the past two decades on multidimensional indicators of poverty (e.g. Alkire and Foster, 2011; OPHI), there is now growing interest in the construction of multidimensional indicators of inequality (Aaberge and Brandolini, 2015), including single indices that aggregate different dimensions into one number such as the Inequality-adjusted Human Development Index (IHDI). So far this is very much work in progress, but it offers rich possibilities for advancing our future understanding of inequality changes, causes and consequences across the world.

Action areas include:

● Supporting further work on understanding the multiple dimensions of inequality and their interactions;

● Fostering comparative studies of the evolution of key dimensions of inequality in different groups of developed and developing countries; taking forward large-scale longitudinal projects which capture both actual and perceived inequalities between individuals and groups over time in various settings, including low-income countries in Africa and Asia;

● Increasing coverage of panel surveys in Africa and Asia. Few are currently carried out and they are often not longitudinal;

● Using the enormous capacities offered by big data technologies (Savage, 70) to track correlations between practices, habits, and diverse inequality indicators for specific population groups.

Priority 3 – Deepen our understanding of diverse experiences of inequality

While we need more and better data on trends in inequality, we also need a far deeper understanding of how it is experienced by different groups in different settings. For instance, several authors in this Report point to the need to understand further the stress and psychosocial impacts of inequality for those left at the bottom, including such aspects as fear, feelings of powerlessness and inferiority, and limited aspirations. We must complement statistical measurement with subjective assessments of people's relative well-being across a range of indicators (social acceptance, personal safety, health, education, housing, employment, financial stability, community influence and others), disaggregated by characteristics relevant to discrimination. Anthropological and participatory approaches go further, encouraging people themselves to define key concepts, criteria and meanings, according to local language, experience, history and identity. Yet while studies of subjective experience have been conducted for decades with a focus on poverty (e.g. Anderson and Broch-Due, 1999; Narayan et al., 1999), very few have an explicit focus on inequality.

Action areas include:

● Exploring how groups most affected by inequality make sense of their realities, including the notions, values, or narratives used to explain their conditions. How do these vary by social differences, such as gender, and according to people's diverse identities?

● Addressing how perceived inequalities and subjective assessments of relative well-being may lead to varying consequences, such as violence, unrest, conflict or migration, in different settings;

● Deepening understanding of how different dimensions of inequality are transmitted or mitigated intergenerationally;

● Identifying how inequality is affecting the middle classes in emerging economies and in high-income countries.

Priority 4 – Deepen our understanding of how multiple inequalities are created, maintained and reproduced

Another gap to be filled concerns the mechanisms through which multiple inequalities interact and are created, maintained and reproduced. We know remarkably little about the nature of these interactions. Those untangling them will need to attend to culture, social norms and values, and religion, as well as to material economy, politics and resources. Studies can examine the interacting effects of policies and practices intended to address inequalities, not just by looking downwards at those negatively affected by inequalities, but looking up as well. For instance, interdisciplinary research on tax and legal havens would help us understand how those at the top develop and maintain their privilege, including through their hidden power and wealth.

Action areas include:

- Conducting case studies and historical research on inequalities in specific contexts, and on how new trends in inequalities develop. Such studies can combine various approaches and methods, for instance integrating feminist and political ecology analyses to track interactions between gender and environmental inequalities;

- Exploring how those at the top develop and maintain their privilege and power, while also improving the transparency, availability and comprehensiveness of data on wealth;

- Conducting comparative studies of how inequalities are created and reproduced under multiple modernities and varieties of capitalism;

- Examining how recent, rapid technological change (for example, in robotics, machine learning and biotechnology) affects forms of inequality;

- Investigating the nature and role of corruption of various kinds, and of tax and legal havens, in creating new inequalities and maintaining existing ones.

Priority 5 – Deepen our understanding of how local and global forms of inequality connect and interact

The question of scale is closely related to mechanisms for the creation and reproduction of inequality. Understandings of inequalities need to shift from global to local contexts and patterns and back again. They need to encompass international and national processes, but also local experiences, effects and agency, drawing on local knowledge and taking into account local variables. They need to examine how power, operating across multiple scales and in multiple forms, shapes, sustains and transforms configurations of inequality. This calls for research approaches that are rooted locally and connected globally. There are roles for global research networks and partnerships, for new modes of global–local participatory research, and for adapting approaches attuned to dealing with multiple overlapping scales to the question of inequalities. Examples might include multi-sited ethnography (Marcus, 1995) and complex systems analysis (Gunderson and Holling, 2002).

Action areas include:

- Exploring the effects of extreme economic inequality on new forms of inequality in power, on a range of scales. For instance, how do global political economic actors and globally connected media grip and shape perceptions, imaginations and debates in local contexts?

- Identifying how concepts and discourses related to inequality travel and are adapted on different scales, and with what effects;

- Analysing how global power relations produce and reproduce various forms of inequality in interaction with local contexts.

Priority 6 – Promote research on how to move towards greater equality

The research focus on inequality has arguably obscured visions of better futures. Research needs to move from understanding inequality to identifying moves towards greater equality, and how transformation towards it might be achieved. This in turn demands a shift of language and framing. There is much to be done to understand the policies and interventions that work to promote more equal societies, as well as the forms of mobilization and intervention that develop the will to do so. While lessons might be drawn from the past, we also need to look to the future.

Action areas include:

- Elucidating how transformative pathways towards greater equality have unfolded historically in localities, countries and regions. What drivers and dynamics lead to greater equality in specific contexts, and what are the roles of non-linear change?

- Identifying what kinds of policies can lead to effective, deep and lasting change towards greater equality in specific contexts, for instance in relation to gender;

- Tracking how global, national and local initiatives interact and complement each other in reducing inequality, asking for instance how successful policies and initiatives came about and were implemented, and how transferable and scalable local initiatives are;

- Tracking the possible trade-offs between policies aiming at fostering greater equality and those aimed at other important development goals, such as sustainability;

● Exploring how deficits in accountability and of trust in institutions are impeding demands for and actions towards greater equality. What measures have contributed to improving accountability?

Priority 7 – Support cross-cutting syntheses and theory on inequality and equality

While empirical studies and data are vital, the integration of knowledge into new syntheses on inequality and pathways towards equality, and ultimately into new theory, will be critical. A global research agenda would combine the production of new data on inequalities and equality with finer understandings of their mechanisms and effects on people, alongside the development of new research capacity and infrastructures that can integrate these into higher-level conceptual advances. These new syntheses will have to integrate quantitative data, correlation analysis and qualitative assessments; they will need to offer convincing understandings of how the various inequalities interact at different scales; and they will have to cover a much broader scope of countries and regions than today's analyses. The recourse to more data, and the production of better data, does not hail the end of theory. But surely theories must be revisited and reassessed. When necessary, new words and categories must be created to depict new realities, and volatile indices must be improved (Deneault, 71). Working towards this kind of synthesis will also contribute to the achievement of the SDGs by providing countries with the evidence necessary to inform action.

Action points include

● Developing and promoting new synthetic approaches to research on inequality, which link across knowledge, policy and practice, and across disciplines and scales;

● Encouraging new conceptualizations of the meanings and consequences of inequality, in the light of rapid change and new realities;

● Creating and maintaining new data sets and collaborative research platforms on inequality and equality. These would be open to researchers around the world and would integrate quantitative and qualitative sources across countries and regions.

Towards a more transformative social science

While the above priorities are important, even taken together, they are not enough. Transformative pathways for reducing inequality, we suggest, demand a transformative social science, one that treats inequality and equality not just as a matter for analysis, but also as a normative concern, seeking to inform struggles for social justice. It moves beyond the mainstream to seek out alternative perspectives, and to combine methods and perspectives in new ways. And fundamentally, it engages society, often by co-designing agendas, co-constructing knowledge and co-communicating findings with different groups, including those positioned to bring about change.

Moving forward with such an agenda requires us to challenge and overcome knowledge inequalities within the research enterprise on inequality. As we have seen, these are many, with certain kinds of study – by region, discipline, or quantitative–qualitative orientation – dominating. Addressing inequality through the social sciences does not just mean producing more social science on the subject. Simultaneously, it is also about addressing inequalities in our knowledge of inequality – of access, of construction and co-construction, of whose knowledge counts.

These are not new themes in the social sciences. There are long traditions of social science research which try to overcome knowledge inequalities, whether approaching this from feminist perspectives, critical sociologies and philosophies of knowledge, participatory action research, or other angles. Here, Cooperative Sulá Batsú (Jiménez, 73) exemplifies a successful approach to challenging prevailing knowledge hierarchies by including and legitimizing indigenous knowledge and protecting its holders from expropriation. Minujin (72) describes a collaborative action research process in Latin American cities, in which co-constructed knowledge about childhood inequalities was translated into municipal action. Contemporary literature and practice contain many further examples, from bringing citizen knowledge to challenge the dominance of medical and humanitarian knowledge in the 2014–15 Ebola crisis, transforming the response and its effect on health inequalities (Martineau et al., 2016), to bringing the knowledge and perspectives of activists and lawyers together to transform gendered knowledge around sexuality and social justice (Lalor et al., 2016).

In such cases, researchers often co-construct knowledge with relevant members of society – community members, civil society organizations, activists, policy-makers or practitioners. Here the role of the researcher, community actor or political activist remains different and distinct, but at the same time, new relationships are forged between them. Co-design and co-production in research have received growing attention in many fields over the past decade. Much has been learned about when and how it can be effective, and what it can achieve in terms of relevance, impact and links with action and change. What is clear though is that the playing field is rarely level. Successful co-construction usually requires acknowledging and overcoming political and knowledge inequalities amongst the participants.

Co-construction is just one valid approach, and transformative social science works through other modes as well. Research can make a difference by being committed to and informing processes of change undertaken by others, even if it is not the task of social scientists themselves to mandate or make that change. Knowledge can be mobilized to inform action through many routes, from written, verbal and online briefings and dialogues, to impact-oriented communication strategies with policy-makers and practitioners, and to new ways of visualizing and communicating that combine 'data, theory and politics' (Savage, 70). While moves to 'evidence-based policy' often imply that such linkages are immediate and direct, research on knowledge, power and policy processes tells us that time lags and political interests often intervene. Informing change effectively can therefore mean finding the right moment, or the right ear to listen to and take up key messages. It can mean forging the right networks, relationships or alliances between researchers and groups of societal actors. Nor should we forget that it is not just evidence, but also theoretical and conceptual research, that can drive transformative change. The concepts and analysis of gender produced by feminist scholars over the past two decades have profoundly defined and then advanced research and action around gender inequalities.

A step change

We could add to these gaps in the study of inequality and equality many more specific ones. There is clearly need for more work on the strengths and weaknesses of particular measures of inequality, or for the study of one particular dimension or another of inequality.

As well as researching the perceptions of the poor, we need to identify the circumstances under which the better-off come to perceive poverty and inequality as impairing their well-being. The list could go on, and become quite long. However, simply continuing as is with more and more specific studies without rising to the larger challenges discussed above might make only marginal contributions to our understanding. A step change is needed, one which will result in a truly global research agenda that is far more interdisciplinary, methodologically pluralistic, multiscaled and globally inclusive than we see today, and which contributes towards more equal and just futures. What is needed are not only transformative pathways for challenging inequality, but transformative forms of social science that help take us there. The question is, can social science rise to this challenge? It is a big ask, but the level, consequences and scale of the inequalities documented in this Report by researchers from across regions, methods and traditions demand no less.

Bibliography

Aaberge, R. and Brandolini, A. 2015. Multidimensional poverty and inequality. A. B. Atkinson and F. Bourguignon (eds), *Handbook of Income Distribution*, Vol. 2. Amsterdam, Elsevier.

Alkire, S. and Foster, J. 2011. Counting and multidimensional poverty measurement. *Journal of Public Economies*, Vol. 95, No. 7, pp. 476–87.

Anderson, D. M. and Broch-Due, V. (eds). 1999. *The Poor are Not Us: Pastoralism and Poverty in East Africa*. Athens, Ohio: Ohio University Press.

Atkinson, A. and Bourguignon, F. 1982. The comparison of multi-dimensioned distributions of economic status. *Review of Economic Studies*, Vol. 49, pp. 183–201.

Gunderson, L. H. and Holling, C. S. (eds). 2002. *Panarchy: Understanding Transformations in Human and Natural Systems*. Washington DC, Island Press, pp. 63–102.

Kolm, S. C. 1977. Multidimensional egalitarism. *Quarterly Journal of Economics*, Vol. 91, pp. 1–13.

Lalor, K., Mills, E., Sánchez García, A. and Haste, P. 2016. *Gender, Sexuality and Social Justice: What's Law Got to Do with It?* Brighton, UK, IDS.

Marcus, G. 1995. Ethnography in/of the world system: the emergence of multi-sited ethnography. *Annual Review of Anthropology*, Vol. 24, pp. 95–117.

Martineau, F., Wilkinson, A. and Parker, M. 2016. Epistemologies of Ebola: reflections on the experience of the Ebola Response Anthropology Platform. *Anthropological Quarterly*, forthcoming.

Narayan, D., Chambers, R., Shah, M. K. and Petesch, P. 1999. *Global synthesis. Prepared for the Global Synthesis Workshop: Consultations with the Poor*. Washington DC, World Bank,

OPHI (Oxford Policy and Human Development Index). *www.ophi.org.uk/research/multidimensional-poverty/alkire-foster-method/*.

PART IV · TRANSFORMATIVE KNOWLEDGE FOR A JUST WORLD

69. Knowledge divides: social science production on inequalities and social justice

Françoise Caillods

This contribution discusses the extent of the knowledge divide by analysing through bibliometric data who the researchers are who study inequality and social justice, in which disciplines they specialize and the region and country where they are located.

The study of inequality and social justice is the research domain *par excellence* of social scientists. In the second half of the twentieth century, numerous books were published by sociologists, economists and political scientists which animated a large debate on inequality in Northern countries. However, no reliable bibliometric statistics on the production of social research are available for this period. Recent statistics from the Web of Science (WOS) on articles published after 1991 show that the number of social science and humanities publications on inequalities and social justice increased steadily throughout the period (*Figure 69.1b*). The number of publications on inequalities and social justice increased in absolute and in relative terms, growing from 4.3 to 5.9 per cent of all social science and humanities publications in just ten years, from 2003 to 2013. This illustrates an increasing interest in the topic. This contribution analyses who the researchers are who study inequality and social justice in the largest numbers. In which domain and fields of study do they specialize? An important knowledge divide is geographical: where, in which region and country, are researchers writing on inequality and social justice located? Are they located where they are most needed, in areas where inequalities are most acute? The analysis presented here is based on a series of tables prepared by Science-Metrix using the Web of Science data. The full tables and a methodological note are presented in *Annexes A and B*.[1]

Distribution of articles produced by disciplines and fields of study: a knowledge divide?

In which domains and fields of study are studies on equality and social justice conducted? A first surprise result is the large number of articles published on equality and social justice in the health science domain. Nearly as many articles are produced here as in the economic, social and behavioural sciences. If we leave psychology and cognitive sciences in the health sciences domain, as does the classification of Science-Metrix, the number of articles published in health science surpasses those in the economic and social sciences from 2004. The number of articles under health sciences – notably in public health and health policy – increased particularly rapidly from 2000. The exact reason is unknown. Is it related to the need to implement and monitor the MDG on health?

Arts and humanities specialists also write on the subject of inequalities and social justice, notably historians, anthropologists and philosophers. But as *Figure 69.1a* illustrates, the number of articles in this area published in the arts and humanities increased only slowly during the same period.

Researchers in the economic, social and behavioural sciences publish the highest number of articles on inequalities and social sciences. The number of publications increased throughout the period, with a sudden acceleration from 2007/08.

Knowledge divides: social science production on inequalities and social justice | *Françoise Caillods*

Figure 69.1a **Worldwide publications on inequality and social justice per year, 1991–2014**

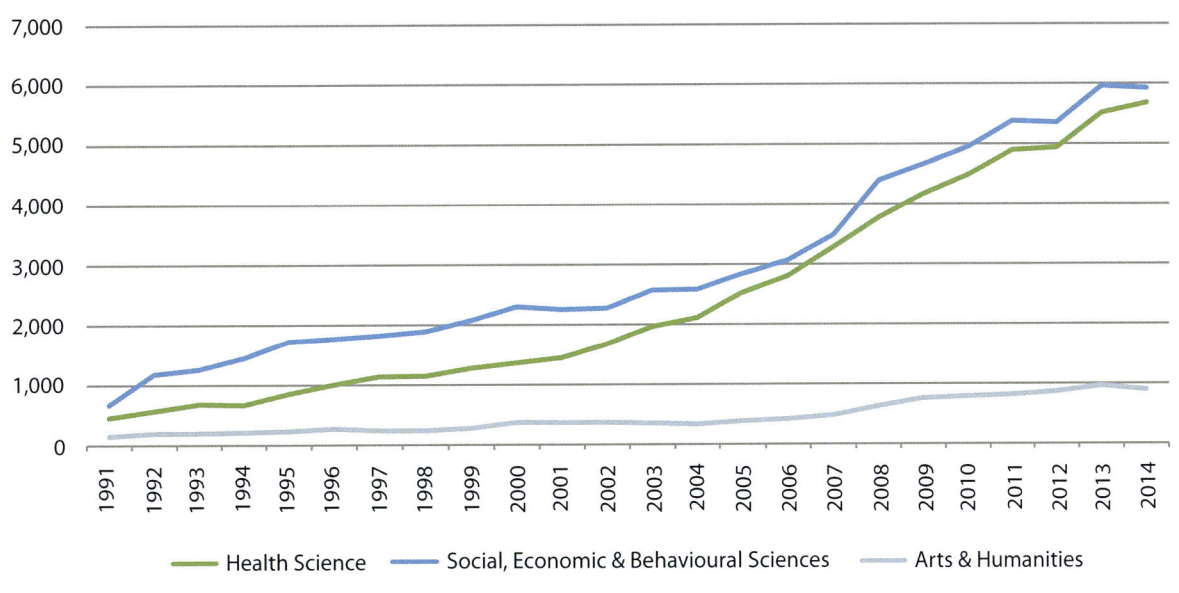

— Health Science — Social, Economic & Behavioural Sciences — Arts & Humanities

Source: Table B1, Annex B.

Figure 69.1b **Number of social science and humanities publications on inequalities and social justice produced worldwide per year, 1992–2013**

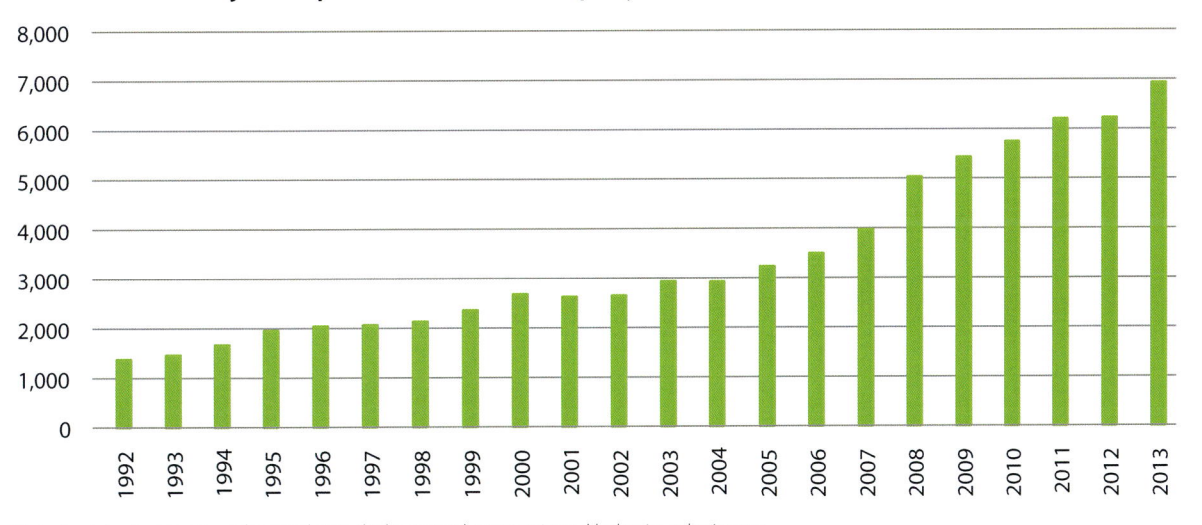

Note: Social sciences are understood as including social economic and behavioural sciences.
Source: Table B2, Annex B.

Research has subsequently been carried out on social and human sciences (SHS) to integrate publications produced in philosophy, history and anthropology into one larger field.

Economics, political science, sociology, education, social psychology and gender studies are the six subfields that dominated the production of SHS articles on inequality and social justice between 1992 and 2013.

At the beginning of the period, sociology and economics were producing more or less the same number of publications, ahead of all other SHS subfields. But since 1994 economics has been the subfield that produces the largest number of articles. Political science overtook sociology in 2000 and became the second largest subfield under which inequality articles are written, until 2011 when education became the second most important field after economics.

PART IV · TRANSFORMATIVE KNOWLEDGE FOR A JUST WORLD

Figure 69.2 **Number of SHS publications produced worldwide on inequality and social justice per subfield, 1992–2013 (fractional counting)**

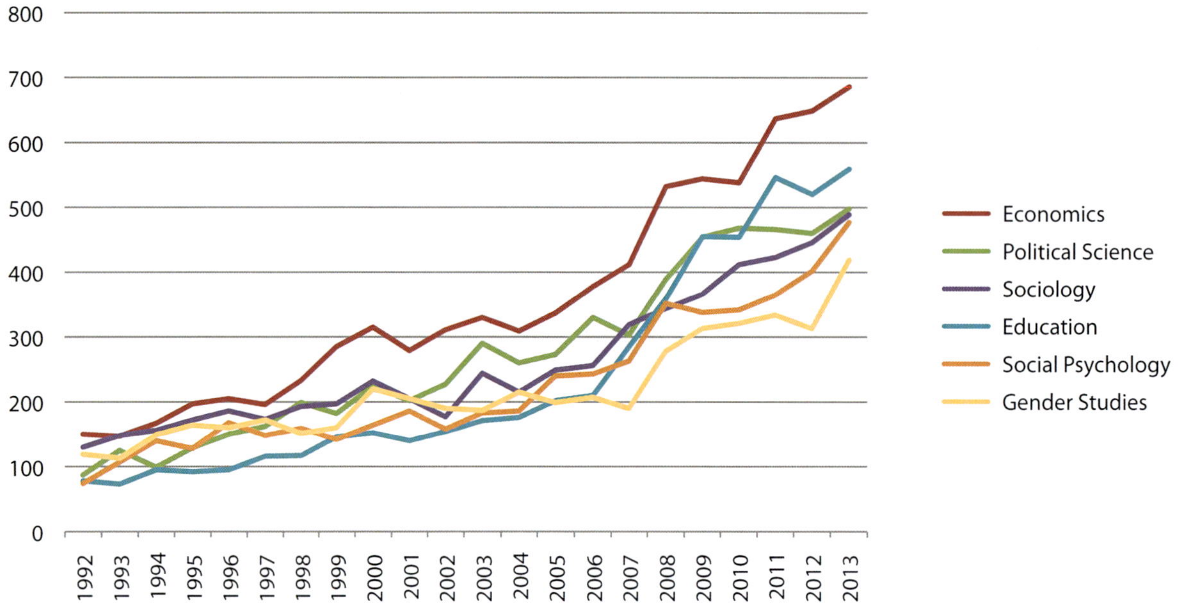

Source: Table B3, Annex B.

It is not easy to measure the extent to which multidisciplinary work is taking place through bibliometric statistics. The disciplinary orientations of research still seem quite strong. In certain areas of study, possibly those that are more action-oriented – education, health studies, gender studies – multidisciplinary teams involving economists, sociologists, education specialists, psychologists and political scientists are found more frequently. Intellectual links and cross-fertilization between disciplinary traditions occur more frequently in policy-oriented research, such as between economics, sociology and political science, which contributes to loosening disciplinary boundaries (Lebaron, in ISSC and UNESCO (2010), *World Social Science Report 2010: Knowledge Divides*).

Knowledge inequality: where is research on inequality produced?

Regional disparities in social science and humanities production have always been very high, with North American and European journals and researchers dominating the production of social science knowledge.

Regional disparities in the production of publications on inequalities and social justice are also very high, as shown in *Figures 69.3* and *69.4*. Nearly half of all SHS publications (49.3 per cent) on the theme of inequality and social justice[2] between 1992 and 2013 were produced in North America. Another 32.4 per cent was produced in Western Europe. Far behind came Oceania (4.6 per cent), sub-Saharan Africa (3.2 per cent), East and Southern Europe, and Latin America (*Figure 69.3*). All other regions, including East Asia and Southern Asia, produced relatively few articles on this theme. The dominance of North America has diminished slightly in the past decade as the number of articles increased more rapidly in almost all other regions (*Figure 69.3b*). Europe nearly caught up with North America between 1994–2003 and 2004–13.

In terms of country, the USA produced the largest number of SHS publications during the period 1992–2013 (43.8 per cent) followed by the UK (13.7 per cent), Canada, Australia, Germany and South Africa. In other words, the institutions of two countries produced 57 per cent of all publications on this theme between 1994–2003 and 2004–13.

Figure 69.3a **Number of social and human science publications on inequality and social justice per region, 1992–2013 (fractional counting)**

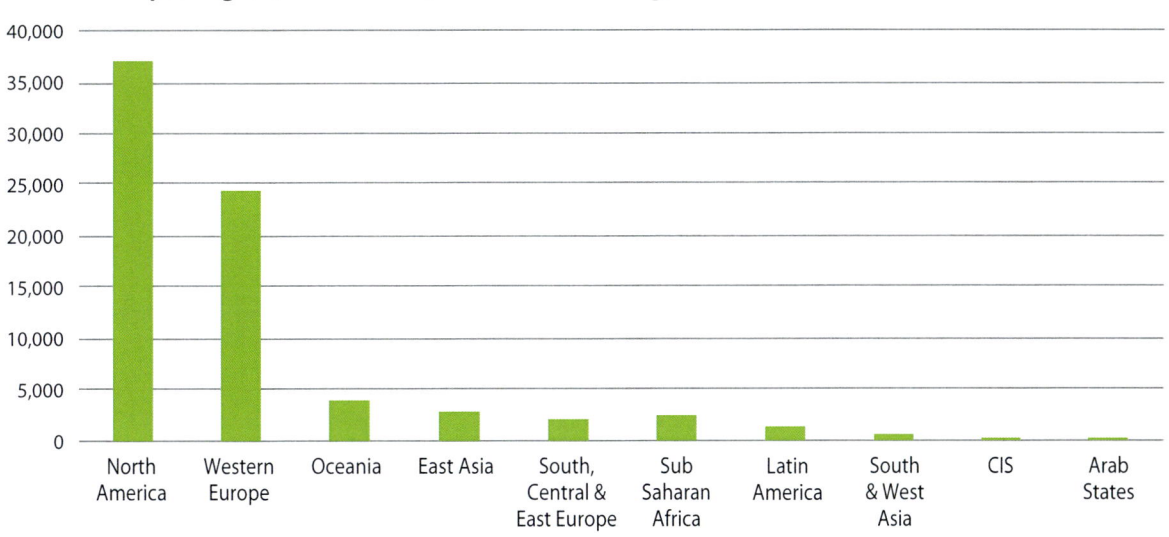

Source: Table B4, Annex B.

Figure 69.3b **Number of social and human science publications on inequality and social justice per region for two periods, 1994–2003 and 2004–13**

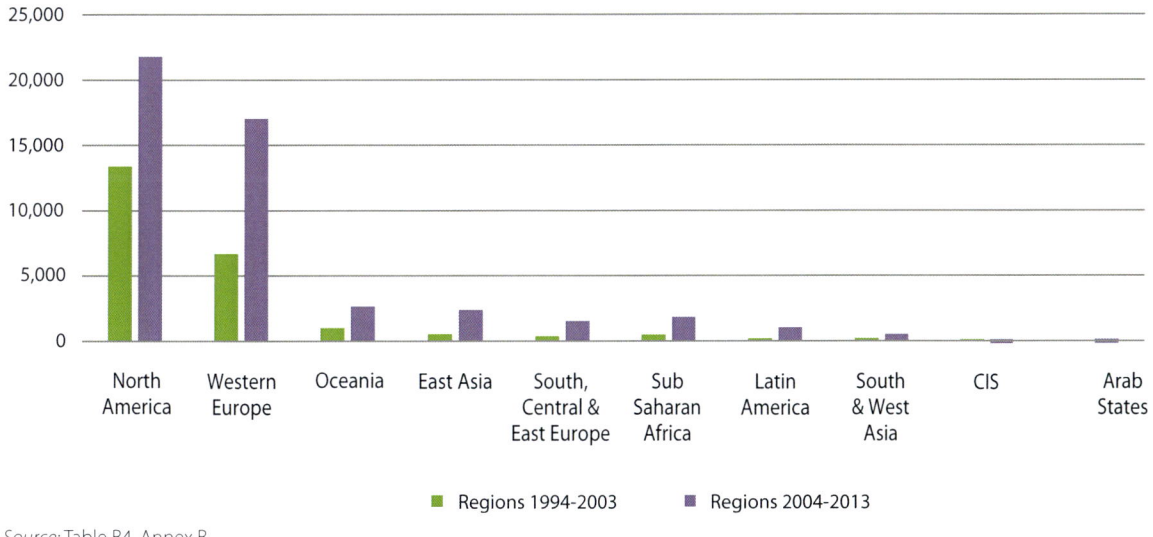

■ Regions 1994-2003   ■ Regions 2004-2013

Source: Table B4, Annex B.

An interesting point to note is the relatively high number of publications from South Africa, which produces more publications on this theme than France, the Netherlands and other European countries, and more than three times as many as India, China and Brazil. South Africa is the sixth largest producer of articles on this theme, while it is only the eighteenth largest producer in the social sciences altogether.[3]

On the other hand China, which is the second largest producer of articles in the sciences overall and the sixth largest producer of social science articles, is producing relatively few articles on the topic of inequality and social justice.

Figure 69.4 **Number of social and human science publications on inequality and social justice per country, 1992–2013 (fractional counting)**

Country	Publications
USA	~33,000
UK	~10,300
Canada	~4,200
Australia	~3,200
Germany	~2,700
South Africa	~1,900
Netherlands	~1,800
Spain	~1,400
France	~1,300
Sweden	~1,100

Source: Table B4, Annex B.

What are the possible explanations for such disparities? There may be several, including the higher importance attached by some countries (such as China, India and the Republic of Korea) to the natural sciences than to the social sciences.[4]

Another is the brain drain. A good number of African researchers from all over the continent work in South Africa; a high number of Indian specialists working on this theme are based in the UK or in the USA. In addition, the theme of inequality and social justice can be politically sensitive. A lack of funds in local universities to conduct research, and the lack of academic freedom, may explain why researchers on this topic often work outside their native countries.

A final possible reason may be that in some countries, especially the francophone nations, social scientists stand to gain greater prestige from publishing book-length monographs rather than articles. Books are read by a wider audience outside academic circles and may be discussed in traditional media. The bibliographical databases, such as WOS, are much better at counting articles in peer-reviewed journals than monographs. They are also well known for their linguistic and geographical bias. Language is part of the knowledge divide. These reasons were discussed for all social science publications in the 2010 *WSSR* (ISSC and UNESCO, 2010). As discussed above, they are even more valid for the theme of inequality and social justice, which is of considerable popular interest.

Conclusion

Three main lessons can be drawn. First, social scientists are not the only scientists writing on issues of inequality and social justice. Other scientists are writing on this topic, particularly health scientists. Over the past twenty years, social science research on the theme has largely been dominated by economics, and to a lesser extent political science, but in recent years new fields – and possibly more interdisciplinary fields – have emerged as important producers of knowledge. Education is an example of this trend. Third, the research and academic knowledge available on this theme is very much dominated by research in the North (by northern researchers, institutions and reviews). Yet inequalities are a major issue worldwide. The geographical divide in the study of inequality and social justice remains a major challenge.

Notes

1. See *Annex B* for the results of the bibliometric analysis of social science and humanities research into inequalities and social justice, detailed statistics, and the methodological note. Science-Metrix carried out the bibliometric analysis on social and human science publications using Web of Science (WOS Thomson Reuters) data. A publication is considered to be part of the social sciences if the journal in which it has appeared is classified in the 'Economic and Social Sciences' domain in the Science-Metrix data. For the purpose of this project the fields of 'Psychology & Cognitive Sciences' and 'Anthropology' were added to the domain of 'Economic & Social Sciences'. Scientific publications relevant to the field of inequalities and social justice were retrieved using keyword searches in the titles, author keywords and abstracts of scientific publications indexed in the WOS database. More details on the method used are provided in the methodological note in Annex B.

2. In the fractional counting method, each publication is attributed to the institutions which appear in the address fields on the basis of the number of authors from that institution. In the full counting method each paper is attributed fully to all institutions appearing in the address field. As a result there is some double counting. In the full counting method, more than half of all publications (51.9 per cent) would be attributed to North America.

3. Source, Tables A6 and B4 in *Annex A and B*. Data for 2008–13.

4. This is evident in Table A6 in *Annex A*.

Bibliography

ISSC and UNESCO. 2010. *World Social Science Report: Knowledge Divides*. Paris, UNESCO.

■ **Françoise Caillods** *(France) is ISSC senior adviser to the* 2016 World Social Science Report.

70. The use of big data in the analysis of inequality

Mike Savage

Like it or not, big data is happening. How should social scientists engage with it?

There is a lively debate these days about how social scientists should engage with 'big data'. For some, it is a distraction which detracts from rigorous causal analysis. For others it offers more promise (Savage and Burrows, 2007). Like it or not, big data is happening.[1] It is part of the emergent world of new kinds of data assemblage which forms the terrain on which contemporary social science needs to stand. Failure to join in will leave social scientists without a foothold in the emerging devices which will produce knowledge and information in the twenty-first century. Big data is, and will be, particularly relevant to the analysis of inequalities.

We have seen a striking shift towards data-driven analysis in the past few years. In place of grand theories of inequalities, the highest-profile works have been based on large-scale data analysis, including the work of Robert Putnam (2000) on the impoverishment of our connections with each other, Wilkinson and Pickett (2009) on why more equal societies almost always do better, and Thomas Piketty (2013) on wealth and inequality in the twenty-first century. These authors, and the ways they describe the phenomena they are concerned with, make the social science of the past appear overly burdened by theory, philosophy and history, and social scientists' pronouncements too abstract to inform more than academic debates about an issue.

Figure 70.1 **Health and social problems are worse in more unequal countries**

Source: Wilkinson and Pickett (2009).

Figure 70.2 **Income inequality in the USA, 1910–2010**

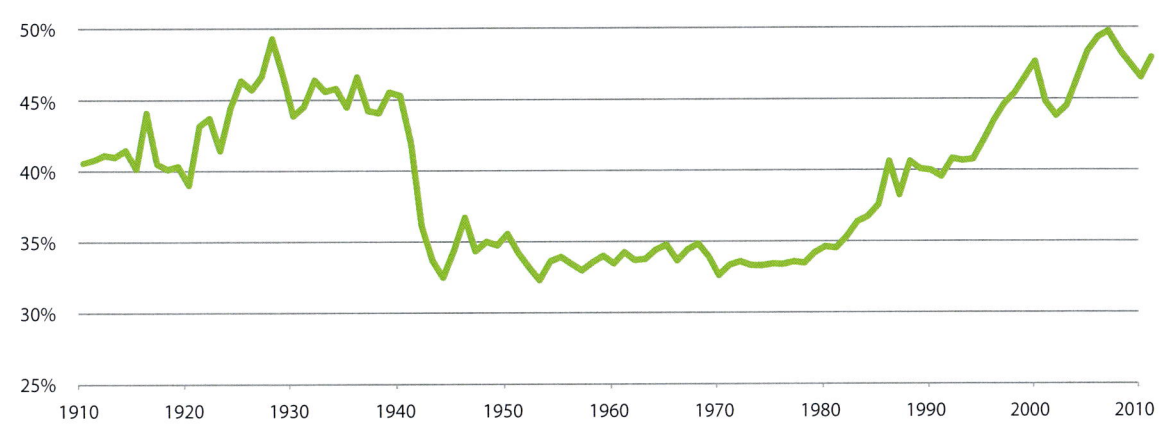

Share of top decile in national income

Sources: See http://piketty.pse.ens.fr/fr/capital21c.

The current crop of influential social scientists make innovative use of multiple data sources. Some of these are digitally stored data, others are more conventional data sets, but regardless of format, these 'data assemblages' now form the vanguard of social scientific analysis. They have been used to great effect to relate important facts about our world and the inequalities of today. A good example is the graphic representations in the work of Wilkinson and Pickett (*Figure 70.1*), who plot one set of data (income inequality across countries), against other indices within a country (such as rates of drug abuse and imprisonment, or decreases in physical and mental health) and show the pattern of this covariation.

Social science has been at best ambivalent and at worst dismissive of the power of visualizations, and has characteristically preferred to deploy textual and numerical assemblages. Yet every picture can tell a story that a thousand words cannot. Piketty has become influential in part because of his skilful use of the U-shaped curve to tell a powerful story of the fall and rise of inequality over the past 120 years.

The fundamental challenge in analysing big data is to reduce its complexity to a clear pattern, and to depict this graphically in a succinct way. Putnam, Wilkinson and Pickett, and Piketty succeed in this regard not only by using new sets of data – though without calling it big data – but also in finding simple visualization tools which summarize complex data.

In order to clarify this, we need to recognize that there are different issues involved in what 'big data' means. I draw a distinction between data sources (such as tax returns), the power of descriptive analytic strategies, and the big vision (see e.g. Oxfam, 2015).

Data sources

Putnam uses changes in the membership of clubs and trade unions in the USA over time to grasp and demonstrate a decline in civic engagement. Wilkinson and Pickett's data sources are records of income inequality and various health and social problems. Piketty uses taxation data to plot, for example, the relationship over time between the top percentiles of earners as a proportion of the national income. This and other comparisons of a similar kind support his argument that we are now moving towards income inequality last seen in the nineteenth century. More particularly, he uses available data sources on tax returns to show that when the rate of return on capital is greater than the rate of economic growth over the long term, the result is further concentration of wealth. In all cases, the bedrock of the analysis is the skilful deployment of multiple data sources, which often exceed standard national representative surveys.

Descriptive analytic strategies

The ways in which the diverse data assemblages are woven together and analysed, most typically using simple univariate and bivariate techniques, get to the heart of the new style of data-based social science.

The data sources and data points are big in that they reach across time (Putnam), across space (Wilkinson and Pickett), and across both space and time (Piketty), compared with the kind of data gathered and methods of analysis typical of older social science. Conventional social science emphasizes the need to focus analyses on specific 'dependent variables', which are then explicated through examining the potential causal power of numerous 'independent variables'. But here there are a great number of 'dependent variables', but only one main 'independent variable' (such as inequality). Rather than the 'parsimony' championed in mainstream social science, what matters here is 'prolixity', with the piling-up of examples of the same kind of relationship, punctuated by telling counterfactuals.

The big vision

The skill in using big data on inequality effectively is to stand back from the data, not get too involved in the detail, and allow the overall patterns, such as Piketty's U-shaped curves, to tell the story of a certain pernicious relationship between the structure of our world and the consequences. Rhythms of change have accelerated since the great social theorists of the past such as Marx, Durkheim and Weber first wrote about the structure of societies. The strength of the new style of doing social science depends on repeat visualizations with a recurring theme, each linked to an overarching story that effectively captures the central argument of the author, to deploy concepts with wide intellectual resonance and political implications. In doing this, social scientists can establish themselves as noteworthy commentators on our realities, and thus motivate change or transformation. This is in contrast to the often narrow and specialized ways in which big data is deployed by non-social scientists.

In conclusion, this is not the last word on the uses of big data (see Chang et al., 2014; González-Bailón, 2013) or the ways in which social scientists could use big data to inform citizens, policy-makers and debates more widely about the inequalities that mark our world. The most effective kinds of social science now are 'data-rich'. However, they are also theoretically sophisticated and offer an alternative form of data analysis to technocratic models derived from computation and information sciences.

The authors highlighted above are also deeply 'objective' in that they carefully report their data sources, their analysis of them, and thus where their findings come from. Yet all three also take a passionate, even politicized, view of their purposes. Putnam makes it clear that he wants to halt the decline of social capital. Wilkinson and Pickett are deeply perturbed by how socially damaging inequality is, while Piketty's concern to document the dynamics of wealth and income inequality throughout the past century and to reform capitalism is also clear. Data, theory and politics are richly and fruitfully combined in these three works. As we look to the future, it is important for social scientists to demonstrate their effectiveness in knowing how best to present and select data, in contrast to the data-driven and empiricist models often used in more technocratic visions of the 'big data' world, which are poorly placed to analyse inequality. Social scientists should not feel threatened by 'big data'. They should embrace their skills and sophistication in knowing how to deploy it to best effect.

Note

1. For a very short history of 'big data' see Press (2013).

Bibliography

Chang, R. M., Kauffman, R. J. and Kwon, Y. 2014. Understanding the paradigm shift to computational social science in the presence of big data. *Decision Support Systems*, Vol. 63, pp. 67–80.

González-Bailón, S. 2013. Social science in the era of big data. *Policy and Internet*, Vol. 5, No. 2, pp. 147–60.

Oxfam. 2015. *Wealth: Having it All and Wanting More.* Oxford, UK, Oxfam GB for Oxfam International.

Piketty, T. 2013. *Capital au XXIe siècle* [*Capital in the Twenty-First Century*]. Paris, Editions du Seuil. (In French.)

Press, G. 2013. A very short history of big data. Forbes. www.forbes.com/sites/gilpress/2013/05/09/a-very-short-history-of-big-data/#2715e4857a0b180a284b55da (Accessed 16 June 2016.)

Putnam, R. 2000. *Bowling Alone: The Collapse and Revival of American Community.* New York, Simon & Schuster.

Savage, M. and Burrows, R. 2007. The coming crisis of empirical sociology. *Sociology*, Vol. 41, No. 5, pp. 885–99.

Wilkinson, R. and Pickett, K. 2009. *The Spirit Level: Why More Equal Societies Almost Always Do Better.* London, Allen Lane.

■ **Mike Savage** (UK) is professor of sociology at the London School of Economics (LSE) and co-director of the International Inequalities Institute at LSE. www.lse.ac.uk/sociology/whoswho/academic/savage.aspx

71. Tax and legal havens: a priority for inequality research

Alain Deneault

Tax havens exacerbate inequality by depriving governments and their citizens of resources that would support services for the benefit of all. As a first step, basic concepts and economic jurisdictional vocabulary must be updated to better reflect the realities of accommodating jurisdictions.

Tax havens exacerbate inequality in terms of equal opportunity and income, by depriving citizens of the government support they need to achieve access to education, advanced training, health care, culture and professionalization. Elementary logic tells us that when wealthy multinationals and individuals are able to remove billions of dollars' worth of assets from the jurisdiction of traditional states' tax authorities, there will be a shortfall in the public funds of these states. This shortfall leads to increased taxation of captive taxpayers (wage-earners, real estate owners, small businesses and the like) and reduces government services. Statistical data corroborate this intuition (Shaxson et al., 2012).

This reduction of state revenues is the most visible aspect of the existence of tax havens. More fundamentally, tax havens generate unequal status for the various members of a national community. They lead to the emergence of two categories of social actor: those who are subject to the laws, regulations, standards and penalties prevailing in their jurisdiction under the rule of law, and those who have the means to shift their assets to tax havens and remove themselves from the constraints that the state enforces throughout its territory, even though all members of the community should in principle be subject to these constraints on an equal basis.

Tax havens do more than offer very low or zero tax rates to multinationals and wealthy individuals who open bank accounts or create trusts, holding companies, subsidiaries or private banks. They also provide a normless space, where impunity in all things is guaranteed. Offshore states such as the Bahamas, the Cayman Islands, Liberia, Luxembourg, Jersey and Singapore are not just tax shelters.

They are accommodating jurisdictions which enable private companies, financial institutions and wealth-holders in many areas, including insurance, high-risk finance, manufacturing and industry, maritime transportation, extractive industries, offshore oil production, medical research, medicine, the financial management of drug trafficking and gambling, to operate without having the state intervene in any way. For almost any area or sector, there is an accommodating jurisdiction willing to give free rein to practices that are highly controversial if not downright criminal. Like a photographic negative, tax and legal havens replicate traditional states, with legal systems that blithely authorize what traditional states forbid.

Understanding these accommodating jurisdictions and how they generate, perpetuate and reinforce inequality of revenue and status calls for interdisciplinary research. We must take offshore activity seriously enough not to reduce it to a mere parallel economy, although some estimates of offshore assets exceed $21,000 billion (Henry, 2012). But if we view accommodating jurisdictions as being central to a series of problems that go beyond tax issues and affect areas such as public policy, labour law, national security and the symbolic representation of states, then we cannot but acknowledge the extent of the work lying before us. Far from being explicable solely in terms of accounting and criminology, accommodating jurisdictions also require the attention of sociologists, philosophers, psychologists, students of literature, geographers and anthropologists.

The first task must be to reconsider the political and jurisdictional vocabulary customarily employed to describe these political and economic realities. The categories of political, economic and legal thought are distorted by the reality of accommodating jurisdictions. Political and legal concepts such as jurisdiction, political sovereignty, justice, law, crime, border, company from such-and-such a country and so on find their meaning so altered by accommodating jurisdictions that they no longer signify what they once did. The same is true of our economic vocabulary: what is an 'insurance company' when it directly covers the corporation that created it? What is a 'trust' when the settler, the trustee and the beneficiary are the same person? What is a 'charitable foundation' when it owns all the planes of a major airline? We need to update those basic concepts, and develop new ones better suited to describing the new realities induced by the offshore phenomenon. This is a vast project that social science must undertake.

Bibliography

Henry, J. 2012. *The Price of Offshore Revisited*. London, Tax Justice Network.

Shaxson, N., Christensen, J. and Mathiason, N. 2012. *Inequality: You Don't Know the Half of It (or Why Inequality is Worse than We Thought)*. London, Tax Justice Network.

■ **Alain Deneault** *(Canada) is researcher at the Réseau Justice fiscale (Québec/Canada) and programme director at the Collège international de philosophie in Paris. Several books he has written on tax havens and industrial criminality have been translated into English:* Offshore: Tax Havens and the Rules of Global Crimes *(New York, New Press);* Canada: A New Tax Haven *(Vancouver, BC, Talonbooks);* Imperial Canada Inc.: The Legal Haven of Choice for the World Mining Industries *(Vancouver, BC, Talonbooks) and* Paul Martin and Companies *(Vancouver, BC, Talonbooks).*

POSTCARD

72. Increasing childhood equality in cities: a practical intervention through policy, research and advocacy

Alberto Minujin

All of us are different, but that doesn't mean that we shouldn't all have the same opportunities.
Amanda, 9 years old [1]

By 2050, nine out of ten Latin Americans will live in cities characterized by increasing social inequalities, a deteriorating environment, and a growing number of people living in irregular settlements (UN-Habitat, 2012). Intra-urban inequalities are also growing. Three out of every four Latin American children are growing up in cities, but many lack access to the 'urban advantage'. Almost three out of every ten Latin American children live in highly deprived households (Born and Manujin, 2015). Everything is available – just not for them.

Malnutrition in urban areas, and the number of children without birth registration, are both nearly three times greater for children from deprived households. Save the Children's ninety-one-country Under 5 Mortality Rate (U5MR) research shows inequality increasing in forty-five of those countries (2015).

In 2014 the Colombian government legislated to improve the situation of disadvantaged young children through a national programme called 'From Zero to Forever'. In this context, Equity for Children, the Corona Foundation and Como Vamos conducted a research and advocacy project to increase early childhood well-being in Bogotá and six other Colombian cities, where 30 per cent of all Colombian children reside.

The project team analysed existing government data, augmented by qualitative information provided by NGO networks, to mobilize local authorities and civil society. Collaborators included leaders of municipal and local initiatives who are concerned with early childhood well-being, and stakeholders such as local community groups, citizens, young people, policy-makers and government officials. Each believed that urban inequalities, which exist in situations where available resources exist for all, must be addressed and eliminated, especially in light of Colombia's nationally legislated programme mandating resource distribution to all small children.

The project had a number of important findings. For instance, the under-5 mortality rate maps by locality in Bogotá and Medellín show that the probability of dying before the age of 5 is almost five times more in the most disadvantaged areas of Bogotá, and almost four times in Medellín, than in the least disadvantaged areas. In Cali, children from the county where the Embera Katio indigenous community live had a seventeen times greater chance of dying before the age of 5 than those in areas without an indigenous population.

Equally important was how the research process helped to generate awareness and action on inequality. The project also involved:

- translating the evidence into simple, user-friendly social media materials and posting them online to promote information broadly

- disseminating findings continuously to media and social networks and discussing them in the context of available policies for young children

- working with local committees to develop action plans linked to national and municipal policies, such as prevention and protection, in areas with a high prevalence of adolescent mothers

- promoting civil action committees in some deprived communities of Bogotá

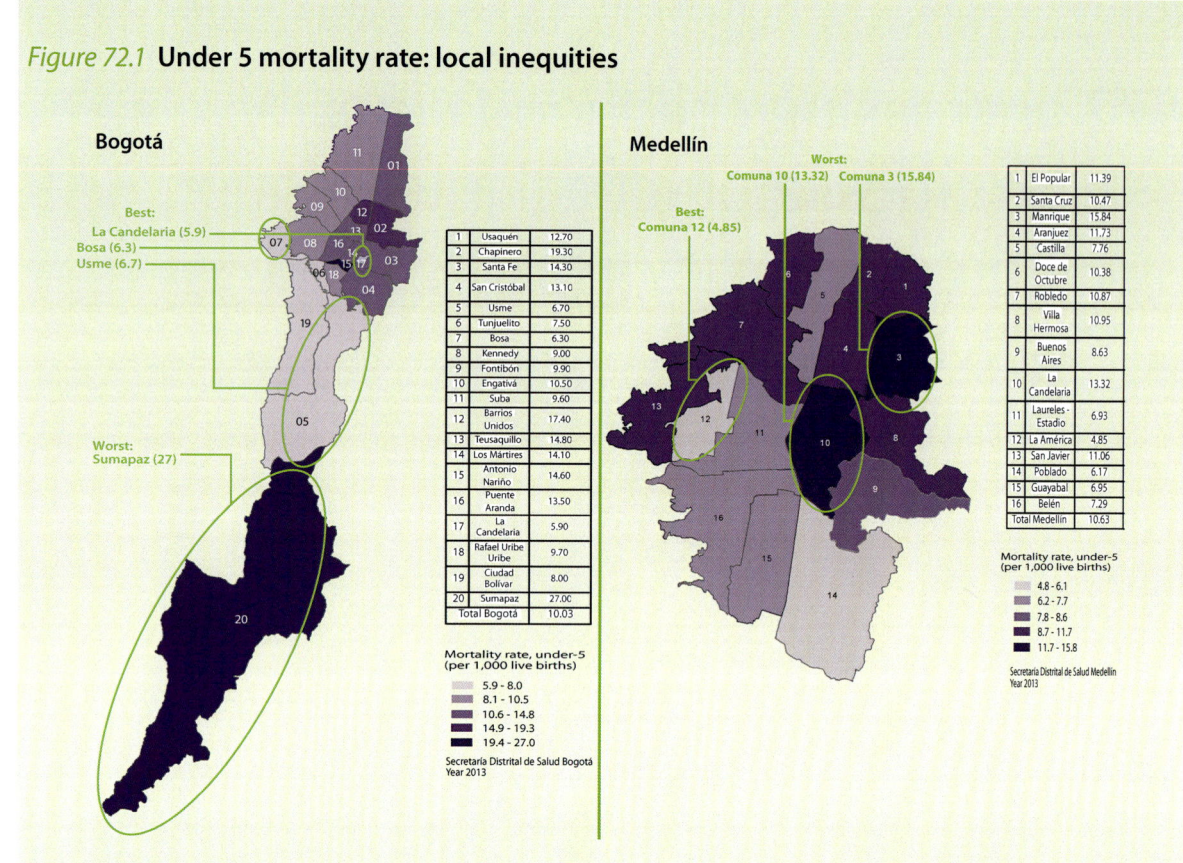

PART IV · TRANSFORMATIVE KNOWLEDGE FOR A JUST WORLD

Figure 72.1 **Under 5 mortality rate: local inequities**

Bogotá

1	Usaquén	12.70
2	Chapinero	19.30
3	Santa Fe	14.30
4	San Cristóbal	13.10
5	Usme	6.70
6	Tunjuelito	7.50
7	Bosa	6.30
8	Kennedy	9.00
9	Fontibón	9.90
10	Engativá	10.50
11	Suba	9.60
12	Barrios Unidos	17.40
13	Teusaquillo	14.80
14	Los Mártires	14.10
15	Antonio Nariño	14.60
16	Puente Aranda	13.50
17	La Candelaria	5.90
18	Rafael Uribe Uribe	9.70
19	Ciudad Bolívar	8.00
20	Sumapaz	27.00
	Total Bogotá	10.03

Best: La Candelaria (5.9), Bosa (6.3), Usme (6.7)
Worst: Sumapaz (27)

Mortality rate, under-5 (per 1,000 live births)
- 5.9 – 8.0
- 8.1 – 10.5
- 10.6 – 14.8
- 14.9 – 19.3
- 19.4 – 27.0

Secretaría Distrital de Salud Bogotá
Year 2013

Medellín

1	El Popular	11.39
2	Santa Cruz	10.47
3	Manrique	15.84
4	Aranjuez	11.73
5	Castilla	7.76
6	Doce de Octubre	10.38
7	Robledo	10.87
8	Villa Hermosa	10.95
9	Buenos Aires	8.63
10	La Candelaria	13.32
11	Laureles – Estadio	6.93
12	La América	4.85
13	San Javier	11.06
14	Poblado	6.17
15	Guayabal	6.95
16	Belén	7.29
	Total Medellín	10.63

Best: Comuna 12 (4.85)
Worst: Comuna 10 (13.32), Comuna 3 (15.84)

Mortality rate, under-5 (per 1,000 live births)
- 4.8 – 6.1
- 6.2 – 7.7
- 7.8 – 8.6
- 8.7 – 11.7
- 11.7 – 15.8

Secretaría Distrital de Salud Medellín
Year 2013

Source: Minujin et al. (2014).

- creating a public debate with the mayoral candidates for the October 2015 election, recommending strategies for inequality reduction

- monitoring progress annually in order to highlight previously invisible living situations for children.

The project team will replicate this action research approach in other Latin American cities, actively including the voice and participation of children and young people to resolve the inequities that affect them.

Notes

1. Pers. comm., June 2015.

Bibliography

Born, D. and Minujin, A. 2015. Inequalities on child well-being in Latin American cities in Ciudades Divididas, EDUNTREF, Argentina. www.equityforchildren.org/special-feature-urban-inequalities-in-childhood-and-adolescence/ (Accessed 16 June 2016.)

Minujin, A., Bagnoli, V., Osorio Mejía, A. and Aguado Quintero, L. 2014. Primera infancia cómo vamos: identificando desiguadades para impulsar la equidad en la infancia colombiana [How we are doing in early childhood: identifying inequities to promote equality among Colombian children.] www.equidadparalainfancia.org/informe-colombia-como-vamos-en-primera-infancia/ (Accessed 16 June 2016.)

The Save the Children Fund. 2015. *The Lottery of Birth: Giving all children an equal chance to survive.* https://everyone.savethechildren.net/sites/everyone.savethechildren.net/files/library/STC_The_Lottery_of_Birth_Final-2b_0.pdf (Accessed 6 September 2016.)

UN-Habitat. 2012. *State of Latin American and Caribbean Cities 2010: Towards a New Urban Transition.* State of Cities Regional Report no. HS/064/12E. UN-Habitat. http://unhabitat.org/books/state-of-latin-american-and-caribbean-cities-2/ (Accessed 16 June 2016.)

■ **Alberto Minujin** *(Argentina/USA) is professor at the New School University's Graduate Program of International Affairs in New York. He is executive director of Equity for Children/Equidad para la Infancia, a non-profit programme also housed in the Graduate Program in International Affairs. Minujin's research, teaching and advocacy are centred on improving the living conditions of poor, marginalized children; child poverty and social policy; and child rights. He teaches in Argentina at the Universidad Nacional Tres de Febrero (UNTREF) and before moving into higher education, spent 15 years as senior policy officer for UNICEF.*

POSTCARD

73. Local knowledge as a common good

Kemly Camacho Jiménez

Vulnerable people suffer multiple inequalities which thwart their development. These inequalities are mainly sustained by unequal relations with groups that hold economic, social, political, environmental and cultural power, and which impose an exclusive way of constructing knowledge. We can speak of 'unequal knowledge', where some knowledges are considered more valid than others. Social life is approached from only one way of knowing-that and knowing-how, imposed by educational, religious and legal institutions. When other knowledges are integrated into this institutionalized way of knowing, it is in a decontextualized way, as if knowledge were a commodity that can be taken out of where it is produced and consumed.

In Latin America, the knowledges of the most vulnerable populations have traditionally been made invisible by economically and politically powerful groups. The knowledge of indigenous people, *campesinos/as* (peasants or rural people), women, and people of African descent has been devalued by being categorized as tacit knowledge which is transmitted through experience, orality, practice and imitation. In these same populations, 'unequal knowledge' is practised whereby gender, age and ethnic origin affect the value assigned to knowledge.

But more recently, efforts to challenge global problems such as climate change, chronic disease, water management and new agricultural methods have begun to prioritize the 'extraction of local knowledge' through research processes studying collective wisdom.

The work of Cooperativa Sulá Batsú in Costa Rica is based on the principle that local knowledges belong to the people who have generated them, and as such are common goods that must be safeguarded.

The problem is highly complex because knowledge is an intangible asset and very difficult to appropriate in this way. A key condition is the existence of community collectives responsible for making knowledge dynamic, safeguarding it and appropriating it, and this is the main focus of Cooperativa Sulá Batsú.

Sulá Batsú supports the horizontal exchange of common knowledge between local collectives. This exchange allows the knowledge produced by those communities throughout their history to be recognized, documented and visualized. Information and communications technologies (ICT) play a key role in this process.

The cooperative works with young people, children and women from indigenous, *campesino*, rural, border and coastal communities in Central America, using ICTs to create and retrieve the telling of local stories through images, sound and text. The documentation and recovery of this community know-how is as vital as the organizational processes themselves, which are led by groups of young people, children and women in their communities. The local knowledge now being documented is able to be recognized, re-encountered and reappropriated as a common good of the people.

This process has strengthened local groups, allowing them to limit the indiscriminate extraction of local knowledge, to negotiate the way research is carried out, to have a say in terms of intellectual property of local knowledge, and to defend local knowledge as their own treasure which belongs to their communities.

■ *Kemly Camacho Jiménez (Costa Rica) works with Cooperativa Sulá Batsú [Sulá Batsú Cooperative], San José, Costa Rica.*

POSTCARD

74. A proposal to monitor intersecting inequalities in the post-2015 Agenda

Deborah S. Rogers

Sustainable Development Goal (SDG) 10 is specifically directed at reducing inequalities within and among countries. Beyond this, however, the need to reduce inequalities is also reflected in the requirement for disaggregated monitoring data, and in the declaration presenting the new goals, which states that 'no one will be left behind'. Indeed, tackling inequality is a primary theme that permeates nearly every one of the goals and many of the targets. SDG 1 calls for eradicating extreme poverty and halving poverty as defined nationally, SDG 2 calls for ending hunger, SDG 3 calls for universal health coverage, SDG 4 calls for ensuring inclusive and equitable quality education, and so on. To ensure achievement for all, the data for monitoring progress towards most goals must be disaggregated by relevant groups, including socio-economic class, gender and sexual orientation, age, ethnicity, disability, rural or urban location, legal status, and other characteristics that can lead to discrimination.

Inequalities are multidimensional, and various dimensions often interact in the form of a vicious cycle. We cannot focus on just one or two of the dimensions, for example economic inequality or gender discrimination, but must monitor disparities across the spectrum of factors contributing to human well-being. Because political inequalities often serve to perpetuate other inequalities, the key to reducing and overcoming inequalities of all kinds may be broad-based participation in decision-making, monitoring and accountability processes.

Many inequality-related indicators have been proposed, and no set of indicators has been settled on as of the time of writing. Space does not permit an analysis of each proposal. While the development of one synthetic indicator would greatly simplify matters, there can in fact be no objective indicator that is synthetic across the range of dimensions of inequality.

A subjective indicator could come closer, however: for example, asking individuals how they perceive and feel about their own well-being and prospects, compared with those of others in their community and society.

If we could choose three indicators for monitoring progress on reducing inequality, I would suggest the following:

Economic: I recommend using the Palma ratio for each nation (ratio of the income share of the top 10 per cent to that of the bottom 40 per cent) before and after transfers. The Palma ratio is thought to be the most sensitive to changes in economic inequality, because the income of those between the fiftieth and the ninetieth percentiles is relatively stable.

Social: I recommend a subjective assessment of relative well-being across a range of indicators (social acceptance, personal safety, health, education, housing, employment, financial stability, community influence and so on), disaggregated by characteristics relevant to discrimination. This would not be a measure of perceived happiness or optimism, but rather a set of questions concerning subjective perceptions of relative well-being along multiple dimensions (for example, do I feel that I am safer or less safe than others?), to determine whether different groups in society answer differently, and whether these differences are internally consistent.

Political: Political participation is a key leverage point in reducing inequalities. I recommend measuring representation in various local, national and international decision-making bodies, disaggregated by characteristics relevant to discrimination. While this does not measure actual political participation by all groups, it measures the outcome of that participation: the numbers of people from various social groups who end up in positions of decision-making power.

These three indicators are relevant to every nation on Earth, making the new equality-and-justice-focused SDGs much more powerful than the old poverty-and-aid-focused MDGs. However, monitoring these indicators will be difficult in terms of cost, credibility and political will. It is unlikely that most individual nations, or the United Nations itself, will allocate the funds needed to conduct scientific surveys for all these social indicators.

The most efficient means of monitoring would be a participatory, citizen-initiated monitoring and accountability approach, as recommended in the United Nations' 2014 Consultation on Participatory Monitoring and Accountability (see UNICEF, UN Women and UNDP, 2015).[1] Rather than utilizing a centralized, staff-based research approach, participatory monitoring relies on civil society actors to facilitate subjective feedback and monitoring by members of poor and marginalized communities. Community findings and priorities are then brought forward through organized citizen initiatives to hold governments accountable for progress towards the development goals.

At least two such civil society proposals are already being tested: the Frontline project by the Global Network of Civil Society Organisations for Disaster Reduction (GNDR) and the Field Hearings project by Initiative for Equality (IfE). Two other initiatives, the World Values Survey and the regional Barometer series (including Afrobarometer, Asia Barometer and so on), also provide data on citizen views, but are staff-based and do not engage in accountability activities.

Governments and private stakeholders that benefit from the status quo will probably not have the political will or motivation to monitor progress toward reducing inequalities, and may not accept citizen monitoring results as credible. But this is a matter of political interests rather than any lack of resources or technical proficiency.

Assessments of transparency and accountability initiatives suggest that the participatory monitoring and accountability approach recommended above, if well organized, can be effective in empowering citizens to demand more equitable development, as well as other public goods and policies, from their governments. In the end, this political pressure from below will be more effective than SDGs without teeth to give them bite.

Note

1. See Initiative for Equality's report on its Participatory Monitoring project, submitted to the UN Consultation on Participatory Monitoring and Accountability: Rogers et al. (2014).

Bibliography

Rogers, D., Balazs, B., Clemente, T., da Costa, A., Obani, P., Osaliya, R. and Vivaceta de la Fuente, A. 2014. *The Field Hearings Participatory Monitoring for Accountability Platform: Utilizing Initiative for Equality's 'Equity & Sustainability Field Hearings' Network to Help Achieve More Equitable and Sustainable Development.* New York, UNICEF, UN Women, UNDP Participatory Monitoring for Accountability Consultation. *https://www.worldwewant2030.org/node/462562* (Accessed 16 June 2016.)

UNICEF, UN Women, and UNDP. 2015. *Participatory Monitoring and Accountability: Critical Enablers for the Successful Implementation of the Post-2015 Sustainable Development Goals. Final report on the UN's Consultation on Participatory Monitoring and Accountability.* New York, UNICEF. *https://www.worldwewant2030.org/file/483948/download/527364* (Accessed 16 June 2016.)

■ **Deborah S. Rogers** *(USA) is affiliated scholar, Institute for Research in the Social Sciences, Stanford University, and president, Initiative for Equality. Her research interests include socio-economic inequality, citizen participation in decision-making, and achieving sustainable human well-being.*

ANNEXES

ANNEXES

Annex A ■ Basic statistics on the production of social science research

Annex B ■ Bibliometric analysis of social and human science research into inequalities and social justice

Annex C ■ Acronyms and abbreviations

Annex D ■ Glossary

Mock favela, created as part of the social and cultural project Morrinho, Cindy Ramos, Cirlan Souza de Oliveira and Raniere Dias (Rio de Janeiro, Brazil, 2013)
© Morrinho project

**World
Social
Science
Report**

Annex A

Basic statistics on the production of social science research

Methodological note for Tables A1 to A7

Tables A1 to A5 were prepared by the UNESCO Institute for Statistics.

Tables A6 and A7 were prepared by Science-Metrix using the Web of Science (WOS) (Thomson Reuters) (Tables A6 and A7), and Scopus for Table A7.

Definition of scientific domains

For this project, the Science-Metrix classification of journals was used to define the different domains presented. The domain of 'Arts and Humanities' was defined as the same domain as in the Science-Metrix classification, excluding the subfield of 'Anthropology', while the domain of 'Natural Sciences' was defined by the aggregation of the domains of 'Natural Sciences', 'Applied Sciences' and 'Health Sciences', excluding the field of 'Psychology and Cognitive Sciences'. Finally, the domain of 'Social Sciences' was defined by the aggregation of the domain of 'Economic and Social Sciences', the field of 'Psychology and Cognitive Sciences' and the subfield of 'Anthropology'. The journal classification by domains, fields and subfields of science can be consulted and downloaded at the following link: *http://science-metrix.com/en/classification*

Number of publications (full counts)

Using the full-counting method each paper is counted once for each different entity involved in the publication (an entity can be a country, an institution or an author, depending on the level of the analysis). For example, at the country level, if a paper is authored by two authors based in France, one based in the USA and one in China, the paper will be counted once for France, once for the USA and once for China. It will also be counted once at the world level.

Number of publications (fractional counts)

Fractional counting gives each entity involved in a publication its respective fraction of the publication (an entity can be a country, an institution or an author, depending on the level of analysis). For example, at the country level, if a paper is authored by two researchers based in France, one researcher based in the USA and one based in China, half of the paper is attributed to France, one quarter to the USA and one quarter to China.

Ideally, each author (or author's address) for a paper should be attributed a fraction of the paper that corresponds to the individual's participation in the research. Unfortunately, no reliable means exists for calculating the relative effort of different authors, and thus each author/address is granted the same fraction of the paper.

Additionally, data might be presented based on shares of publications, as in *Table A7* (e.g. Canada's share of world publications), using fractional counts of papers so that the sum across countries adds up to 100 per cent.

Annex A | Basic statistics on the production of social science research

Table A1 • Socio-economic indicators, 2014 or latest available year

Country	Population millions	Gross domestic product PPP$ billions	Gross domestic product/capita PPP$ thousand	Gross national income PPP$ billions	Gini index	Human Development Index
Arab states						
Algeria	39.7 +1	552.6	14.2	540.5	...	0.736
Bahrain	1.4 +1	62.0	45.5	50.8	...	0.824
Egypt	91.5 +1	943.5	10.5	920.7	31 -6	0.690
Iraq	35.9 +1	524.2	15.1	525.6	30 -2	0.654
Jordan	6.7 +1	79.6	12.1	78.7	34 -4	0.748
Kuwait	3.9 +1	274.9	73.2	299.7	...	0.816
Lebanon	4.6 +1	79.4	17.5	80.0	...	0.769
Morocco	34.4 +1	258.3	7.5	251.5	41 -7	0.628
Palestine	4.4 +1	19.4	4.5	21.5	34 -5	0.678
Oman	4.5 +1	163.6	38.6	156.0	...	0.793
Qatar	2.2 +1	305.5	140.6	292.0	...	0.850
Saudi Arabia	31.5 +1	1 606.4	52.0	1 549.8	...	0.837
Sudan	40.2 +1	160.1	4.1	154.4	35 -5	0.479
Tunisia	11.1 +1	125.8	11.4	121.2	36 -4	0.721
United Arab Emirates	9.2 +1	614.9	67.7	615.3	...	0.835
Yemen	26.8 +1	96.6	3.8	93.3	36 -9	0.498
Central and Eastern Europe						
Albania	2.9 +1	32.2	11.1	31.8	29 -2	0.733
Belarus	9.4 +1	172.2	18.2	166.8	26 -2	0.798
Bosnia and Herzegovina	3.8 +1	39.8	10.4	40.3	33 -7	0.733
Bulgaria	7.2 +1	124.3	17.2	121.6	36 -2	0.782
Croatia	4.2 +1	91.7	21.6	88.6	32 -3	0.818
Czech Republic	10.5 +1	328.2	31.2	302.5	26 -2	0.870
Estonia	1.3 +1	37.0	28.1	36.1	33 -2	0.861
Former Yugoslav Republic of Macedonia	2.1 +1	28.1	13.5	27.3	44 -6	0.747
Hungary	9.8 +1	247.3	25.1	236.3	31 -2	0.828
Latvia	2.0 +1	46.9	23.5	46.6	35 -2	0.819
Lithuania	2.9 +1	81.2	27.7	77.4	35 -2	0.839
Moldova, Republic of	3.6 +1	17.7	5.0	19.6	29 -1	0.693
Montenegro	0.6 +1	9.4	15.1	9.5	33 -2	0.802
Poland	38.0 +1	960.2	25.3	928.4	32 -2	0.843
Romania	19.8 +1	405.0	20.3	397.1	27 -2	0.793
Russian Federation	143.8 +1	3 358.6	23.0	3 237.4	42 -2	0.798
Serbia	7.1 +1	96.9	13.6	93.0	30 -4	0.771
Slovakia	5.4 +1	153.5	28.3	148.5	26 -2	0.844
Slovenia	2.1 +1	62.7	30.4	62.6	26 -2	0.880
Turkey	76.8 +1	1 502.5	19.8	1 485.2	40 -2	0.761
Ukraine	45.2 +1	370.5	8.7	366.2	25 -3	0.747
Central Asia						
Armenia	3.0 +1	24.3	8.1	25.4	32 -1	0.733
Azerbaijan	9.7 +1	167.1	17.5	161.3	17 -9	0.751
Georgia	3.7 +1	34.1	9.2	33.8	40 -1	0.754

Table A1 • **Socio-economic indicators, 2014 or latest available year** (continued)

Country	Population (millions)	Gross domestic product (PPP$ billions)	Gross domestic product/capita (PPP$ thousand)	Gross national income (PPP$ billions)	Gini index	Human Development Index
Kazakhstan	17.5 +1	418.9	24.2	375.3	26 -1	0.788
Kyrgyzstan	5.9 +1	19.4	3.3	18.8	27 -2	0.655
Mongolia	3.0 +1	34.8	11.9	32.4	34 -2	0.727
Tajikistan	8.5 +1	22.3	2.7	22.1	31 -5	0.624
Uzbekistan	31.2 +1	171.4	5.6	179.4	35 -11	0.675
East Asia and the Pacific						
Australia	23.8 +1	1 077.9	45.9	1 049.1	35 -4	0.935
Brunei Darussalam	0.4 +1	29.7	71.2	29.3 -2	...	0.856
Cambodia	15.6 +1	50.0	3.3	47.2	31 -2	0.555
China	1 370.8 +1	18 017.1	13.2	17 966.9	42 -4	0.728
China, Hong Kong Special Administrative Region	7.3 +1	398.9	55.1	409.7	...	0.910
China, Macao Special Administrative Region	0.6 +1	80.8	139.8	69.4	...	...
Indonesia	257.6 +1	2 676.1	10.5	2 592.3	36 -4	0.684
Japan	126.8 +1	4 655.5	36.6	4 846.7	32 -6	0.891
Korea, Republic of	50.6 +1	1 683.9	33.4	1 697.0	...	0.898
Lao People's Democratic Republic	6.8 +1	35.6	5.3	33.8	38 -2	0.575
Malaysia	30.3 +1	766.6	25.6	740.8	46 -5	0.779
Myanmar	53.9 +1	...	...	...	...	0.536
New Zealand	4.5 +1	169.9	37.7	163.3	...	0.914
Philippines	100.7 +1	690.9	7.0	837.6	43 -2	0.668
Singapore	5.6 +1	452.7	82.8	439.0	...	0.912
Taiwan, China	23.5 +1	1 078.8	46.0	...	...	...
Thailand	68.0 +1	1 065.7	15.7	1 006.9	39 -2	0.726
Viet Nam	91.7 +1	510.7	5.6	485.2	39 -2	0.666
Latin America and the Caribbean						
Argentina	43.4 +1	...	...	...	42 -1	0.836
Bermuda	0.1	3.4	52.3	4.3	...	...
Bolivia, Plurinational State of	10.7 +1	70.0	6.6	66.4	48 -1	0.662
Brazil	207.8 +1	3 275.2	15.9	3 209.4	53 -1	0.755
Chile	17.9 +1	392.0	22.1	378.7	50 -1	0.832
Colombia	48.2 +1	638.4	13.4	616.9	53 -1	0.720
Costa Rica	4.8 +1	71.0	14.9	68.6	49 -1	0.766
Cuba	11.4 +1	234.2	20.6	211.0 -3	...	0.769
Ecuador	16.1 +1	180.8	11.4	178.0	47 -1	0.732
El Salvador	6.1 +1	51.0	8.4	48.9	44 -1	0.666
Guatemala	16.3 +1	119.4	7.5	116.1	52 -3	0.627
Mexico	127.0 +1	2 171.0	17.3	2 111.2	48 -2	0.76
Nicaragua	6.1 +1	29.6	4.9	28.8	46 -5	0.631
Panama	3.9 +1	80.8	20.9	77.1	52 -1	0.780
Paraguay	6.6 +1	58.4	8.9	55.5	48 -1	0.679
Peru	31.4 +1	371.3	12.0	354.2	45 -1	0.734
Puerto Rico	3.5 +1	125.6	34.9	86.2	...	...
Trinidad and Tobago	1.4 +1	43.3	32.0	43.3	...	0.77

Table A1 • Socio-economic indicators, 2014 or latest available year (continued)

Country	Population millions	Gross domestic product PPP$ billions	Gross domestic product/capita PPP$ thousand	Gross national income PPP$ billions	Gini index	Human Development Index
Uruguay	3.4 [+1]	71.4	20.9	69.1	42 [-1]	0.793
Venezuela, Bolivarian Republic of	31.1 [+1]	553.3	18.3	535.7	47 [-8]	0.762
North America and Western Europe						
Austria	8.6 [+1]	407.5	47.7	404.9	30 [-2]	0.885
Belgium	11.3 [+1]	487.8	43.4	495.2	28 [-2]	0.890
Canada	35.9 [+1]	1 601.8	45.1	1 576.5	34 [-4]	0.913
Cyprus	1.2 [+1]	25.8	30.2	24.9	34 [-2]	0.850
Denmark	5.7 [+1]	256.8	45.5	264.2	29 [-2]	0.923
Finland	5.5 [+1]	222.2	40.7	221.9	27 [-2]	0.883
France	66.5 [+1]	2 604.2	39.3	2 655.5	33 [-2]	0.888
Germany	80.9 [+1]	3 757.1	46.4	3 843.2	30 [-3]	0.916
Greece	10.8 [+1]	291.9	26.9	296.6	37 [-2]	0.865
Iceland	0.3 [+1]	14.4	44.0	13.5	27 [-2]	0.899
Ireland	4.6 [+1]	228.0	49.4	197.7	33 [-2]	0.916
Israel	8.4 [+1]	276.9	33.7	273.6	43 [-4]	0.894
Italy	60.8 [+1]	2 155.8	35.5	2 155.2	35 [-2]	0.873
Luxembourg	0.6 [+1]	54.8	98.5	36.5	35 [-2]	0.892
Malta	0.4 [+1]	12.5	29.5	11.6	...	0.839
Netherlands	16.9 [+1]	813.8	48.3	824.1	28 [-2]	0.922
Norway	5.2 [+1]	337.1	65.6	344.7	26 [-2]	0.944
Portugal	10.4 [+1]	299.1	28.8	295.1	36 [-2]	0.830
Spain	46.5 [+1]	1 562.9	33.6	1 556.6	36 [-2]	0.876
Sweden	9.8 [+1]	439.2	45.3	454.4	27 [-2]	0.907
Switzerland	8.3 [+1]	487.5	59.5	484.4	32 [-2]	0.930
United Kingdom of Great Britain and Northern Ireland	65.0 [+1]	2 597.4	40.2	2 550.1	33 [-2]	0.907
United States of America	321.2 [+1]	17 419.0	54.6	17 823.2	41 [-1]	0.915
South and West Asia						
Bangladesh	161.0 [+1]	496.8	3.1	529.9	32 [-4]	0.570
India	1 311.1 [+1]	7 384.1	5.7	7 292.8	34 [-5]	0.609
Iran, Islamic Republic of	79.1 [+1]	1 352.1	17.3	1 280.2	37 [-1]	0.766
Pakistan	188.9 [+1]	890.3	4.8	941.1	30 [-4]	0.538
Sri Lanka	20.9 [+1]	230.8	11.1	214.0	39 [-2]	0.757
Sub-Saharan Africa						
Angola	25.0 [+1]	152.5 [-3]	6.9 [-3]	139.1 [-3]	43 [-6]	0.532
Benin	10.9 [+1]	21.5	2.0	21.4	43 [-3]	0.480
Botswana	2.3 [+1]	35.7	16.1	35.6	60 [-5]	0.698
Burkina Faso	18.1 [+1]	28.5	1.6	28.2	40 [-5]	0.402
Burundi	11.2 [+1]	8.3	0.8	8.3	33 [-8]	0.400
Cameroon	23.3 [+1]	67.7	3.0	67.1	43 [-7]	0.512
Cabo Verde	0.5 [+1]	3.4	6.5	3.2	47 [-7]	0.646
Central African Republic	4.9 [+1]	2.9	0.6	2.9	56 [-6]	0.350
Congo, Democratic Republic of	77.3 [+1]	55.8	0.7	48.8	42 [-2]	0.433
Côte d'Ivoire	22.7 [+1]	72.2	3.3	69.4	43 [-6]	0.462

Table A1 • **Socio-economic indicators, 2014 or latest available year** (continued)

Country	Population millions	Gross domestic product PPP$ billions	Gross domestic product/capita PPP$ thousand	Gross national income PPP$ billions	Gini index	Human Development Index
Ethiopia	99.4 +1	145.4	1.5	145.0	33 -4	0.442
Gabon	1.7 +1	32.8	19.4	29.0	42 -9	0.684
Gambia	2.0 +1	3.1	1.6	3.0	47 -11	0.441
Ghana	27.4 +1	109.3	4.1	104.5	43 -9	0.579
Kenya	46.1 +1	132.5	3.0	131.8	49 -9	0.548
Lesotho	2.1 +1	5.6	2.6	6.6	54 -4	0.497
Madagascar	24.2 +1	33.9	1.4	33.0	41 -4	0.510
Malawi	17.2 +1	13.7	0.8	13.2	46 -4	0.445
Mali	17.6 +1	27.3	1.6	25.8	33 -5	0.419
Mauritius	1.3 +1	23.4	18.6	22.9	36 -2	0.777
Mozambique	28.0 +1	30.7	1.1	30.3	46 -6	0.416
Namibia	2.5 +1	23.9	10.0	23.6	61 -5	0.628
Niger	19.9 +1	17.9	0.9	17.4	31 -3	0.348
Nigeria	182.2 +1	1 049.1	5.9	1 013.7	43 -5	0.514
Senegal	15.1 +1	34.2	2.3	33.8	40 -3	0.466
Seychelles	0.1 +1	2.4	26.4	2.3	43 -8	0.772
South Africa	54.8 +1	704.7	13.0	685.7	63 -3	0.666
Tanzania, United Republic of	53.5 +1	127.7	2.5	126.3	38 -3	0.521
Togo	7.3 +1	10.2	1.4	9.2	46 -3	0.484
Uganda	39.0 +1	66.9	1.8	65.0	42 -2	0.483
Zambia	16.2 +1	61.4	3.9	57.9	56 -4	0.586
Zimbabwe	15.6 +1	27.3	1.8	25.2	...	0.509

Sources: World Bank; World Development Indicators, as of June 2016; UNDP, Human Development Report, 2015.

Notes:

... Data not available

-n Data refer to n year(s) prior to the reference year

+n Data refer to n year(s) in advance of the reference year

Annex A | Basic statistics on the production of social science research

Table A2 • Expenditure on research and development, 2014 or latest available year

Country	GERD PPP$ millions	GERD/capita PPP$	GERD/GDP %	GERD in NSE/GERD %	GERD in SSH/GERD %	GERD in NEC/GERD %
Arab States						
Algeria	242.3[-9,t]	7.3[-9,t]	0.07[-9,t]	...	...	...
Bahrain	61.8	45.4	0.10	57.1	37.3	5.6
Egypt	6 401.7	71.5	0.68	...	...	...
Iraq	205.4	5.8	0.04	82.8	17.0	0.2
Jordan	263.3[-6]	43.8[-6]	0.43[-6]	...	...	...
Kuwait	830.5[-1,h]	231.1[-1,h]	0.30[-1,h]	44.2[-3,j]	2.8[-3,j]	53.0[-3,j,u]
Morocco	1 483.6[-4]	46.2[-4]	0.71[-4]	...	...	...
Palestine	...	...	...	...	...	...
Oman	267.8	68.6	0.17	76.3	8.2	15.5
Qatar	1 282.1[-2]	636.1[-2]	0.47[-2]	69.7[-2]	30.3[-2]	.[-2]
Saudi Arabia	842.7[-5,t]	30.7[-5,t]	0.07[-5,t]	...	...	...
South Sudan	...	...	...	...	...	...
Sudan	281.3[-9,a,u]	8.8[-9,a,u]	0.30[-9,a,u]	...	...	...
Tunisia	806.1	72.4	0.64	...	...	...
United Arab Emirates	4 304.3	473.7	0.70	...	...	...
Central and Eastern Europe						
Albania	39.8[-6,t]	13.4[-6,t]	0.15[-6,t]	...	...	...
Belarus	1 125.4	118.5	0.67	95.1	4.9	.
Bosnia and Herzegovina	98.6	25.8	0.26	55.3	37.8	6.8
Bulgaria	954.5	132.5	0.80	92.1	7.9	.
Croatia	710.2	166.9	0.79	86.5	13.5	.
Czech Republic	6 383.5[y]	605.5[y]	2.00[y]	93.4	6.6	...
Estonia	508.4	386.3	1.44	44.6[h,u]	11.9[h,u]	43.5[c,u]
Former Yugoslav Republic of Macedonia	114.0	55.0	0.44	80.7[-6]	19.3[-6]	.[-6]
Hungary	3 341.6	337.9	1.37	92.3	6.5	1.3
Latvia	314.3[y]	158.0[y]	0.69[y]	86.0[-3]	14.0[-3]	.[-3]
Lithuania	794.9[y]	272.5[y]	1.01[y]	54.0[-1,h,u]	20.5[-1,h,u]	25.5[-1,c,u]
Montenegro	32.4	51.8	0.36	74.8[-3]	25.2[-3]	.[-3]
Poland	8 842.4	229.0	0.94	89.8	10.2	...
Republic of Moldova	65.8	16.2	0.37	84.3	15.7	...
Romania	1 480.9	75.4	0.38	91.2	8.8	...
Russian Federation	44 451.5	309.9	1.19	95.9	4.1	...
Serbia	700.2	78.7	0.78	78.6	21.4	.
Slovakia	1 330.7	245.4	0.89	83.5	16.5	...
Slovenia	1 474.6	713.7	2.39	93.4	6.6	...
Turkey	14 682.5	189.4	1.01	84.7	15.3	...
Ukraine	2 440.8	54.2	0.66	89.0	6.6	4.4
Central Asia						
Armenia	58.4[h,t]	19.4[h,t]	0.24[h,t]	72.9[h,r]	18.6[h,r]	8.5
Azerbaijan	350.7	36.4	0.21	84.7	15.3	.
Georgia	33.6[k]	8.3[k]	0.10[k]	51.2[k,u,w]	32.7[k,u,w]	3.5[k,w]
Kazakhstan	691.4	40.4	0.17	89.8	10.2	.

Table A2 • **Expenditure on research and development, 2014 or latest available year** (continued)

Country	GERD PPP$ millions	GERD/capita PPP$	GERD/GDP %	GERD in NSE/ GERD %	GERD in SSH/ GERD %	GERD in NEC/ GERD %
Kyrgyzstan	24.5	4.2	0.13	89.8	10.2	.
Mongolia	79.0[t]	27.2[t]	0.23[t]	77.9[t]	17.8[t]	4.3[t]
Tajikistan	24.3[-1,h]	3.0[-1,h]	0.12[-1,h]	68.8	31.2	.
Uzbekistan	339.0	11.5	0.20	82.2	17.8	.
East Asia and the Pacific						
Australia	21 990.3[-1,u]	945.0[-1,u]	2.20[-1,u]	92.5[-6]	7.5[-6]	...[-6]
Brunei Darussalam	8.7[-10,t]	24.5[-10,t]	0.04[-10,t]	...	...	...
Cambodia	7.9[-12,t,u]	0.6[-12,t,u]	0.05[-12,t,u]	...	...	...
China	368 635.9	269.2	2.05	97.9[-7]	1.4[-7]	0.7[-7]
China, Hong Kong Special Administrative Region	2 800.3	390.9	0.73	...	...	...
China, Macao Special Administrative Region	70.1[t]	121.3[t]	0.09[t]	33.9[t]	18.8[t]	47.4
Indonesia	2 131.9[-1,u]	8.5[-1,u]	0.08[-1,u]	...	...	...
Japan	165 981.3	1 309.1	3.58	94.7[-13]	5.3[-13]	...[-13]
Korea, Republic of	74 346.2	1 484.7	4.29	96.4	3.6	...
Lao People's Democratic Republic	4.3[-12,t]	0.8[-12,t]	0.04[-12,t]	...	...	...
Malaysia	9 679.6	323.7	1.26	91.8	8.2	.
Myanmar	...	...	0.16[-12,t]	...	...	...
New Zealand	1 828.5	409.5	1.17	...	...	...
Philippines	884.7	9.1	0.14	86.9	6.9	6.1
Singapore	8 672.7	1 604.6	2.00	93.5	...	6.5
Taiwan, China	32 429.6	1 383.9	3.01	96.7	3.3	...
Thailand	5 145.7	76.0	0.48	74.9	10.6	14.5
Viet Nam	789.1[-3]	8.8[-3]	0.19[-3]	...	...	...
Latin America and the Caribbean						
Argentina	5 696.5[-1,u]	133.9[-1,u]	0.61[-1,u]	57.5[-1,h]	17.5[-1,h]	25.0[-1,c]
Bermuda	7.7[-1,a,r]	117.7[-1,a,r]	0.22[a]	97.6	.	2.4
Bolivia, Plurinational State of	78.3[-5]	8.0[-5]	0.16[-5]	99.0[-5]	1.0[-5]	.[-5]
Brazil	39 704.5	194.4	1.24	...	...	...
Chile	1 505.4[y]	84.8[y]	0.38[y]	90.3[y]	9.7[y]	...
Colombia	1 246.9	26.1	0.20	46.1	11.6	42.3
Costa Rica	379.4	80.6	0.56	38.4	13.1	48.6
Cuba	1 111.6	97.8	0.41	...	...	...
Ecuador	512.1[-3]	33.7[-3]	0.34[-3]	35.1[-3,h]	6.8[-3,h]	58.1[-3,c]
El Salvador	28.4	4.7	0.06	74.1	26.1	.
Guatemala	48.0[-2,t]	3.1[-2,t]	0.04[-2,t]	78.1[-2,t]	21.9[-2,t]	.[-2]
Mexico	11 543.1[u,y]	92.1[u,y]	0.54[u,y]	82.0[-11]	18.0[-11]	...[-11]
Panama	109.7[-3]	29.8[-3]	0.18[-3]	...	...	...
Paraguay	41.9[-2]	6.6[-2]	0.09[-2]	92.1[-2]	7.4[-2]	0.5[-2]
Peru	263.1[-10]	9.6[-10]	0.16[-10]	...	...	...
Puerto Rico	547.3	148.3	0.44	95.5	1.1	3.4
Trinidad and Tobago	22.0	16.3	0.05	91.2	8.7	0.0
Uruguay	218.4	64.1	0.32	60.6	14.0	25.4
Venezuela, Bolivarian Republic of	...	...	...	...	...	...

Annex A | Basic statistics on the production of social science research

Table A2 • Expenditure on research and development, 2014 or latest available year (continued)

Country	GERD PPP$ millions	GERD/capita PPP$	GERD/GDP %	GERD in NSE/GERD %	GERD in SSH/GERD %	GERD in NEC/GERD %
North America and Western Europe						
Austria	11 779.7[u,y]	1 383.1[u,y]	2.99[u,y]	90.6[-16]	9.4[-16]	…[-16]
Belgium	11 779.9[u]	1 049.3[u]	2.46[u]	…	…	…
Canada	25 233.6[y]	709.1[y]	1.61[y]	89.6[y]	10.4[y]	…
Cyprus	124.6[y]	108.0[y]	0.47[y]	74.9	25.1	.
Denmark	7 814.4[u]	1 383.8[u]	3.08[u]	…	…	…
Finland	6 933.0	1 265.2	3.17	…	…	…
France	58 023.4[y]	904.9[y]	2.26[y]	…	…	…
Germany	106 276.7[u,y]	1 317.8[u,y]	2.87[u,y]	94.8[-15,w]	5.0[-15,w]	…[-15]
Gibraltar	…	…	…	…	…	…
Greece	2 377.5	216.1	0.84	80.2[-3]	19.8[-3]	…[-3]
Iceland	268.2	819.5	1.89	76.9[-5]	23.1[-5]	…[-5]
Ireland	3 415.9[u]	730.6[u]	1.52[u]	93.8[-3]	5.8[-3]	0.3[-3]
Israel	11 216.0[s]	1 412.7[s]	4.11[s]	…	…	…
Italy	27 397.1[y]	458.2[y]	1.29[y]	…	…	…
Luxembourg	682.2[u,y]	1 225.6[u,y]	1.26[u,y]	…	…	…
Malta	111.2[y]	266.3[y]	0.85[y]	81.4	17.0	1.6
Netherlands	15 847.7[y]	939.5[y]	1.97[y]	87.2	12.8	…
Norway	5 697.3	1 106.7	1.71	85.4[-1]	14.6	…
Portugal	3 794.0[y]	364.7[y]	1.29[y]	81.4	18.6	…
Spain	18 977.7	410.2	1.23	92.3[-12]	7.7[-12]	.[-12]
Sweden	13 838.5[y]	1 426.2[y]	3.16[y]	…	…	…
Switzerland	13 251.4[-2]	1 651.8[-2]	2.97[-2]	…	…	…
United Kingdom of Great Britain and Northern Ireland	43 623.9[u,y]	678.1[u,y]	1.70[u,y]	21.9[-2,u]	12.9[-2,u]	…[-2]
United States of America	456 977.0[-1,r,y]	1 440.9[-1,r,y]	2.73[-1,r,y]	…	…	…
South and West Asia						
India	48 063.0[-3,u]	38.5[-3,u]	0.82[-3,u]	91.6[-9,w]	2.9[-9,w]	1.7[-9,w]
Iran, Islamic Republic of	4 170.4[-2]	54.8[-2]	0.33[-2]	…	…	…
Pakistan	2 454.3[-1,h]	13.5[-1,h]	0.29[-1,h]	…	…	…
Sri Lanka	219.5	10.7	0.10	94.8	4.9	0.2
Sub-Saharan Africa						
Angola	…	…	…	…	…	…
Benin	…	…	…	…	…	…
Botswana	76.7[-2]	36.0[-2]	0.25[-2]	95.4[-2]	4.6[-2]	.[-2]
Burkina Faso	39.7[-5]	2.6[-5]	0.20[-5]	…	…	…
Burundi	8.5[-3,t]	0.9[-3,t]	0.12[-3,t]	95.2[-4,t]	…[-4]	4.8[-4]
Cameroon	…	…	…	…	…	…
Cabo Verde	2.2[-3,k,t]	4.5[-3,k,t]	0.07[-3,k,t]	…	…	…
Central African Republic	…	…	…	…	…	…
Congo, Democratic Republic of	28.4[-5,j]	0.4[-5,j]	0.08[-5,j]	…	…	…
Ethiopia	785.9	8.3	0.60	74.1[-4]	10.1[-4]	15.8[-4]
Gabon	128.5[-5]	85.2[-5]	0.58[-5]	…	…	…

Table A2 • **Expenditure on research and development, 2014 or latest available year** (continued)

Country	GERD	GERD/capita	GERD/GDP	GERD in NSE/GERD	GERD in SSH/GERD	GERD in NEC/GERD
	PPP$ millions	PPP$	%	%	%	%
Gambia	3.5⁻³,ᵃ	2.0⁻³,ᵃ	0.13⁻³,ᵃ	...	...	...
Ghana	276.7⁻⁴	11.4⁻⁴	0.38⁻⁴	...	...	...
Kenya	788.2⁻⁴	19.5⁻⁴	0.79⁻⁴	89.8⁻⁴	10.2⁻⁴	0.1⁻⁴
Lesotho	0.6⁻³,ᵏ,ᵗ	0.3⁻³,ᵏ,ᵗ	0.01⁻³,ᵏ,ᵗ	76.9⁻⁵,ᵗ	13.8⁻⁵,ᵗ	9.3⁻⁵,ᵗ
Madagascar	5.3ʲ,ᵗ	0.2ʲ,ᵗ	0.02ʲ,ᵗ	75.1⁻³	12.1⁻³	12.7⁻³
Malawi	...	...	...	...	...	...
Mali	153.4⁻⁴,ʰ	10.1⁻⁴,ʰ	0.67⁻⁴,ʰ	...	...	...
Mauritius	38.6⁻²,ʰ	30.7⁻²,ʰ	0.18⁻²,ʰ	88.1⁻²,ʰ	11.9⁻²,ʰ	.⁻²
Mozambique	92.0⁻⁴,ʰ	3.8⁻⁴,ʰ	0.42⁻⁴,ʰ	74.1⁻⁴	25.9⁻⁴	.⁻⁴
Namibia	25.5⁻⁴,ⁱ,ᵗ	11.6⁻⁴,ⁱ,ᵗ	0.14⁻⁴,ⁱ,ᵗ	...	...	...
Nigeria	1 374.8⁻⁷,ʰ	9.3⁻⁷,ʰ	0.22⁻⁷,ʰ	85.8⁻⁷	14.2⁻⁷	.⁻⁷
Senegal	150.2⁻⁴	11.6⁻⁴	0.54⁻⁴	...	...	...
Seychelles	4.0⁻⁹	44.7⁻⁹	0.30⁻⁹	...	...	...
South Africa	4 824.2⁻²	91.3⁻²	0.73⁻²	85.2⁻³	14.8⁻³	...⁻³
Tanzania, United Republic of	622.7⁻¹,ʰ	12.4⁻¹,ʰ	0.53⁻¹,ʰ	...	...	...
Togo	27.4ʰ	3.9ʰ	0.27ʰ	61.7ʰ	36.8ʰ	1.6ʰ
Uganda	240.0⁻⁴	7.2⁻⁴	0.48⁻⁴	56.1⁻⁴	43.9⁻⁴	.⁻⁴
Zambia	101.2⁻⁶	7.7⁻⁶	0.28⁻⁶	...	...	...
Zimbabwe	...	...	...	...	...	...

Source: UNESCO Institute for Statistics (UIS), June 2016.

GDP and PPP conversion factor (local currency per international $): World Bank; World Development Indicators, as of February 2016.

Population: United Nations, Department of Economic and Social Affairs, Population Division, (2015); World Population Prospects: The 2015 Revision.

Notes:
- -n Data refer to n year(s) prior to the reference year
- +n Data refer to n year(s) in advance of the reference year
- ... Data not available
- . Magnitude nil or negligible
- a Overestimated or based on overestimated data
- b Including other classes
- c Including business enterprise sector
- d Including government sector
- e Including higher education sector
- f Including private non-profit sector
- g Included elsewhere
- h Excluding business enterprise sector
- i Excluding government sector
- j Government sector only
- k Higher education sector only
- l Included in business enterprise sector
- m Included in government sector
- o Included in higher education sector
- p Excluding social sciences
- q Excluding humanities
- r Excluding most or all capital expenditures
- s Excluding defence (all or mostly)
- t Underestimated or partial data
- u Estimation
- v Break in series with previous year for which data are available
- w The sum of the breakdown does not equal the total
- x University graduates instead of researchers
- y Provisional data

Please note that, for some countries, the sum of the breakdowns by sector and/or by field of science does not correspond to the total because of changes in the reference year.

Abbreviations:

- **NSE** Natural Sciences and Engineering (this includes the following fields: Natural Sciences, Engineering and Technology, Medical and Health Sciences, and Agricultural Sciences)
- **SSH** Social Sciences and Humanities (this includes the following fields: Social Sciences, and Humanities)
- **NEC** not elsewhere classified
- **GERD** Gross domestic expenditure on research and development
- **GDP** Gross domestic product
- **PPP$** Purchasing power parity in US Dollars (dollar amounts are in current prices)

For more information, please refer to the UIS Data Centre (http://data.uis.unesco.org/).

Table A3 • Researchers by sector of employment and field of science (in headcounts, HC, and full-time equivalents, FTE), 2014 or latest available year

Country		Total					Business enterprise				
		Total	Total*	NSE	SSH	NEC	Total	Total*	NSE	SSH	NEC
Arab States											
Algeria	FTE	5 593[-9,t]	...	4 510[-9,t]	1 083[-9,t]	.[-9]	...[-9]	...	...[-9]	...[-9]	...[-9]
	HC	13 805[-9,t]	...	10 829[-9,t]	2 976[-9,t]	.[-9]	...[-9]	...	...[-9]	...[-9]	...[-9]
Bahrain	FTE	493	...	219	261	13	2	...	2	.	.
	HC	1 560	...	826	700	34	6	...	6	.	.
Egypt	FTE	61 059	...	44 955[h]	12 742[h]	3 362[c]	3 362	...	...	...	3 362
	HC	124 976	...	90 537	34 439	.	4 653	...	4 026	627	.
Iraq	FTE	2 394	...	1 604	790	.	51	...	50	1	.
	HC	4 765	...	3 069	1 696	.	51	...	50	1	.
Jordan	FTE	9 090[-16]	...	...	...	...	...	...	...	...	...
	HC	11 310[-6,t]	...	4 810[-6]	2 502[-6]	3 998[-6]	...[-6]	...	...[-6]	...[-6]	...[-6]
Kuwait	FTE	...	...	...	...	...	...	...	...	...	...
	HC	4 025[-1,h]	...	1 800[-1,h]	890[-1,h]	1 335[-1,h]	...	...	...	...	...
Morocco	FTE	28 265[-2,v]	27 714[-3,t]	14 317[-3]	13 397[-3]	.[-3]	2 633[-2]	...	...[-3]	...[-3]	...[-3]
	HC	38 946[-2,v]	36 732[-3,t]	19 638[-3]	17 094[-3]	.[-3]	2 633[-2]	...	...[-3]	...[-3]	...[-3]
Palestine	FTE	2 492[-1,h]	...	...	...	...	...	...	...	...	...
	HC	4 533[-1,h]	992[-6,i,t]	1 728[-1,h]	2 805[-1,h]	.[-1,h]	...	236[-6]	106[-6]	130[-6]	.[-6]
Oman	FTE	497[-1,h]	604[-2]	388[-1,h]	104[-1,h]	5[-1,h]	...	122[-2]	122[-2]	.[-2]	.[-2]
	HC	1 235[-1,h]	1 301[-2]	745[-1,h]	463[-1,h]	27[-1,h]	...	122[-2]	122[-2]	.[-2]	.[-2]
Qatar	FTE	1 203[-2]	...	998[-2]	186[-2]	20[-2]	337[-2]	...	326[-2]	10[-2]	.[-2]
	HC	1 725[-2]	...	1 374[-2]	329[-2]	22[-2]	357[-2]	...	342[-2]	15[-2]	.[-2]
Saudi Arabia	FTE	...	...	...	...	...	...	...	...	...	...
	HC	1 271[-5,j,t]	...	802[-5,t]	6[-5,t]	463[-5,j]	...[-5]	...	...[-5]	...[-5]	...[-5]
Sudan	FTE	...	...	...	...	...	...	...	...	...	...
	HC	11 208[-9,a,u]	...	8 218[-9,u]	2 708[-9,u]	282[-9,u]	224[-9,u]	...	164[-9,u]	54[-9,u]	6[-9,u]
Tunisia	FTE	15 922	...	...	...	...	734	...	...	...	...
	HC	31 108	...	...	...	...	1 526	...	...	...	...
Central and Eastern Europe											
Albania	FTE	467[-6,t]	...	414[-6,t]	53[-6,t]	.[-6]	...[-6]	...	...[-6]	...[-6]	...[-6]
	HC	1 721[-6,t]	...	873[-6,t]	848[-6,t]	.[-6]	...[-6]	...	...[-6]	...[-6]	...[-6]
Belarus	FTE	...	...	...	...	...	...	...	...	...	...
	HC	18 353	...	16 539	1 814	...	11 073	...	10 715	358	...
Bosnia and Herzegovina	FTE	1 018	...	535	483	.	58	...	52	6	.
	HC	1 831	...	895	936	.	74	...	53	21	.
Bulgaria	FTE	13 201	12 275	9 535	2 740	.	3 559	2 760	2 680	80	.
	HC	16 095	...	12 005	4 090	.	3 186	...	3 089	97	.
Croatia	FTE	6 117	6 529	5 008	1 521	.	923	1 058	1 049	9	.
	HC	11 168	11 454[-3]	8 493	2 675	.	1 251	1 314[-3]	1 240	11	.
Czech Republic	FTE	36 040[y]	34 271	29 949	4 322	...	18 281[y]	16 766	16 511	255	...
	HC	51 455	...	42 731	8 724	...	19 882	...	19 527	356	...
Estonia	FTE	4 323	...	2 048[h,u]	1 008[h,u]	1 268[c,u]	1 268	...	...	...	1 268[u]
	HC	7 515	...	3 563[-1,h,u]	2 086[-1,h,u]	1 866[-1,c,u]	1 866	...	...	...	1 866[-1,u]
Former Yugoslav Republic of Macedonia	FTE	1 740	...	913	828	.	204	...	204	.	.
	HC	3 793	...	1 991	1 802	.	228	...	228	.	.

Table A3 | *Researchers by sector of employment and field of science, 2014 or latest available year*

Government					Higher education					Private non-profit					Not elsewhere classified (NEC)	
Total	Total*	NSE	SSH	NEC	Total	Total*	NSE	SSH	NEC	Total	Total*	NSE	SSH	NEC	Total	Total*
730⁻⁹,ᵗ	...	700⁻⁹	30⁻⁹	.⁻⁹	4 863⁻⁹,ᵗ	...	3 810⁻⁹	1 053⁻⁹	.⁻⁹	...⁻⁹	...⁻⁹	...⁻⁹	...⁻⁹	...⁻⁹	.⁻⁹	...
730⁻⁹,ᵗ	...	700⁻⁹	30⁻⁹	.⁻⁹	13 075⁻⁹,ᵗ	...	10 129⁻⁹	2 946⁻⁹	.⁻⁹	...⁻⁹	...⁻⁹	...⁻⁹	...⁻⁹	...⁻⁹	.⁻⁹	...
38	...	6	32	.	449	...	211	225	13	4	...	.	4	.	.	...
58	...	16	42	.	1 492	...	804	654	34	4	...	.	4	.	.	...
22 134	...	21 786	348	.	35 563	...	23 169	12 394	.	.	...	.	.	.	.	...
22 992	...	22 643	349	.	97 331	...	63 868	33 463	.	.	...	.	.	.	.	...
693	...	688	5	.	1 650ᵗ	...	866ᵗ	784ᵗ	.	.	...	.	.	.	.	...
814	...	808	6	.	3 900ᵗ	...	2 211ᵗ	1 689ᵗ	.	.	...	.	.	.	.	...
...	...	...	...	...	...	...	...	...	...	...	...	...	...	...	...	...
11 310⁻⁶,ᵉ	...	4 810⁻⁶,ᵉ	2 502⁻⁶,ᵉ	3 998⁻⁶,ᵉ	.⁻⁶,ᵐ	...	.⁻⁶,ᵐ	.⁻⁶,ᵐ	.⁻⁶,ᵐ	...⁻⁶	...⁻⁶	...⁻⁶	...⁻⁶	...⁻⁶	.⁻⁶	...
465	...	414	51	.	...	...	...	...	.	...	...	...	...	...	...	...
465	...	414	51	.	2 225	...	1 386	839	.	...	...	...	...	...	1 335	...
976⁻²	1 410⁻³	916⁻²	60⁻²	.⁻²	24 656⁻²	26 304⁻³	12 994⁻²	13 310⁻³	.⁻³	...⁻²	.⁻³	.⁻³	.⁻³	.⁻³	...⁻²	.⁻³
1 362⁻²	1 410⁻³	1 256⁻²	106⁻²	.⁻²	34 951⁻²	35 322⁻³	18 315⁻³	17 007⁻³	.⁻³	...⁻²	.⁻³	.⁻³	.⁻³	.⁻³	...⁻²	.⁻³
734	...	...	...	...	1 390	...	...	...	...	368	...	...	...	...	.	.
1 486	...⁻⁶	369	1 116	.	2 434	615⁻⁶	996	1 439	.	613	141⁻⁶	363	250	.	.	...⁻⁶
280	275⁻²	254	26	.	217	207⁻²	134	78	5	.⁻²	...	.⁻²	.⁻²	.⁻²	.⁻²	.⁻²
302	295⁻²	255	47	.	933	884⁻²	490	416	27	.⁻²	...	.⁻²	.⁻²	.⁻²	.⁻²	.⁻²
402⁻²	...	328⁻²	55⁻²	19⁻²	465⁻²	...	344⁻²	120⁻²	1⁻²	.⁻²	...	.⁻²	.⁻²	.⁻²	.⁻²	.⁻²
559⁻²	...	484⁻²	56⁻²	19⁻²	809⁻²	...	548⁻²	258⁻²	3⁻²	...⁻²	...	.⁻²	.⁻²	.⁻²	.⁻²	.⁻²
...	...	...	...	...	...	...	...	...	...	...	...	...	...	...	...	...
1 271⁻⁵	...	802⁻⁵	6⁻⁵	463⁻⁵	...⁻⁵	...	...⁻⁵	...⁻⁵	.⁻⁵	...⁻⁵	...	.⁻⁵	.⁻⁵	.⁻⁵	.⁻⁵	.⁻⁵
...	...	...	...	...	...	...	...	...	...	...	...	...	...	...	...	...
2 242⁻⁹,ᵘ	...	1 644⁻⁹,ᵘ	542⁻⁹,ᵘ	56⁻⁹,ᵘ	8 742⁻⁹,ᵘ	...	6 410⁻⁹,ᵘ	2 112⁻⁹,ᵘ	220⁻⁹,ᵘ	...⁻⁹	...	.⁻⁹	.⁻⁹	.⁻⁹	.⁻⁹	...
1 333	...	...	...	...	13 855	...	...	...	...	...	...	...	...	...	.	...
1 575	...	...	...	...	28 007	...	...	...	...	...	...	...	...	...	.	...
271⁻⁶,ᵗ	...	258⁻⁶	13⁻⁶	.⁻⁶	196⁻⁶,ᵗ	...	156⁻⁶	40⁻⁶	.⁻⁶	...⁻⁶	...	.⁻⁶	.⁻⁶	.⁻⁶	.⁻⁶	...
376⁻⁶,ᵗ	...	296⁻⁶	80⁻⁶	.⁻⁶	1 345⁻⁶,ᵗ	...	577⁻⁶	768⁻⁶	.⁻⁶	...⁻⁶	...	.⁻⁶	.⁻⁶	.⁻⁶	.⁻⁶	...
...	...	...	...	...	...	...	...	...	...	...	...	...	...	...	...	...
5 444	...	4 317	1 127	.	1 829	...	1 506	323	.	7	...	1	6	.	.	...
63	...	41	22	.	895	...	440	455	.	3	...	2	1	.	.	...
69	...	47	22	.	1 684	...	793	891	.	4	...	2	2	.	.	...
5 038	5 305	4 220	1 085	.	4 498	4 045	2 501	1 544	.	106	165	134	31	.	.	.
5 414	...	4 296	1 118	.	7 278	...	4 440	2 838	.	217	...	180	37	.	.	.
1 857	1 945	1 308	637	.	3 337	3 526	2 651	875	.	...	11⁻³	.⁻³	11⁻³	.⁻³	.	.
2 780	2 901⁻³	1 968	812	.	7 137	7 222⁻³	5 285	1 852	.	...	17⁻³	.⁻³	17⁻³	.⁻³	.	.⁻³
6 590ʸ	6 326	5 038	1 288	...	10 965ʸ	10 995	8 319	2 676	...	204ʸ	184	81	103	...	.	.
8 413	...	6 653	1 760	...	22 957	...	16 469	6 488	...	202	...	82	120	...	.	.
533	...	303	231	.	2 443	...	1 709	734	.	79	...	36	43	.	.	.
738	749	410	328	.	4 811	4 792	3 136	1 675	.	111	108	54	57	.	.	.
354	...	92	261	.	1 165	...	617	549	.	18	...	.	18	.	.	...
612	...	126	486	.	2 935	...	1 637	1 298	.	18	...	.	18	.	.	...

309

Table A3 • **Researchers by sector of employment and field of science (in headcounts, HC, and full-time equivalents, FTE), 2014 or latest available year** (continued)

Country		Total					Business enterprise				
		Total	Total*	NSE	SSH	NEC	Total	Total*	NSE	SSH	NEC
Hungary	FTE	26 213	25 038	21 335	3 703	...	15 577	14 317	14 062	255	...
	HC	37 803	...	29 363	8 440	...	16 010	...	15 696	314	...
Latvia	FTE	3 748[y]	3 947[-3]	2 875[-3]	1 072[-3]	.[-3]	776[y]	553[-3]	482[-3]	71[-3]	.[-3]
	HC	7 448	...	4 274[-1,h,u]	2 057[-1,h,u]	1 117[-1,c,u]	1 117	...	...	...	1 117[-1,u]
Lithuania	FTE	8 638	8 557	4 036[-1,h,u]	2 758[-1,h,u]	1 763[-1,c,u]	1 997	1 763	...	...	1 763[-1,u]
	HC	18 083	...	8 360[-1,h,u]	7 272[-1,h,u]	2 451[-1,c,u]	2 451	...	...	...	2 451[-1,u]
Moldova, Republic of	FTE	2 655	...	2 071	584	.	176[t]	...	176	.	.
	HC	3 315	...	2 503	812	.	269[t]	...	269	.	.
Montenegro	FTE	421	474[-3]	266[-3]	141[-3]	67[-3,u]	80	85[-3]	85[-3]	.[-3]	.[-3]
	HC	1 546[-3]	...	946[-3]	600[-3]	.[-3]	125[-3]	...	111[-3]	14[-3]	.[-3]
Poland	FTE	78 622	71 472	54 111	17 361	...	24 960	20 606	20 333	273	...
	HC	109 611	...	78 138	31 473	...	24 781	...	24 494	287	...
Romania	FTE	18 109	18 576	16 401	2 175	...	5 244	5 333	5 314	19	...
	HC	27 600	...	23 162	4 438	...	5 738	...	5 702	36	...
Russian Federation	FTE	444 865	...	...	...	...	207 593	...	...	...	...
	HC	373 905[t]	...	342 635[t]	31 270[t]	...	196 320[t]	...	193 248[t]	3 072[t]	...
Serbia	FTE	13 026	...	9 251	3 776	.	1 421	...	1 400	21	.
	HC	15 163	...	10 696	4 467	.	1 467	...	1 442	25	.
Slovakia	FTE	14 742	...	10 446	4 296	...	2 645	...	2 625	21	...
	HC	25 080	...	16 458	8 622	...	3 382	...	3 350	32	...
Slovenia	FTE	8 574	8 707	7 570	1 136	...	4 637	4 664	4 500	164	...
	HC	12 111	...	10 231	1 881	...	5 619	...	5 408	212	...
Turkey	FTE	89 657	...	71 617	18 040	...	41 847	...	41 213	634	...
	HC	181 544	...	131 557	49 987	...	48 247	...	47 519	728	...
Ukraine	FTE	46 191[t]	52 626[-1,t]	43 279	5 546	3 800	15 154	18 562	17 984	130	448
	HC	58 695	...	48 102	5 998	4 595	20 238	...	19 664	152	422
Central Asia											
Armenia	FTE	...	...	...	...	...	...	...	...	...	...
	HC	4 144[h,t]	...	3 122[h]	1 022[h]	.[h]	...	...	...	...	...
Azerbaijan	FTE	...	...	...	...	...	...	...	...	...	...
	HC	16 337	...	11 144	5 193	.	870	...	767	103	.
Georgia	FTE	2 362[k]	...	...	...	...	...	...	...	...	...
	HC	2 893[k]	8 112[-9]	5 315[-9]	2 309[-9]	488[-9]	...	...[-9]	...[-9]	...[-9]	...[-9]
Kazakhstan	FTE	12 552	...	...	...	...	...	...	...	...	...
	HC	17 195	...	13 305	3 890	.	3 155	...	2 920	235	.
Kyrgyzstan	FTE	...	...	...	...	...	...	...	...	...	...
	HC	3 013	...	1 874	1 137	2	86	...	69	16	1
Mongolia	FTE	...	...	...	...	...	...	...	...	...	...
	HC	1 903[t]	...	1 454[t]	449[t]	.	112[t]	...	112[t]	.	.
Tajikistan	FTE	...	...	...	...	...	...	...	...	...	...
	HC	2 152[-1,h]	...	1 561	591	.	...	...	...	...	...
Uzbekistan	FTE	15 029[-3,a]	...	5 954[-3]	958[-3]	8 117[-3,a]	1 931[-3,a]	...	1 835[-3]	96[-3]	.[-3]
	HC	30 785	...	19 036	11 749	.	1 545	...	1 437	108	.

Table A3 | *Researchers by sector of employment and field of science, 2014 or latest available year*

	Government					Higher education					Private non-profit					Not elsewhere classified (NEC)	
	Total	Total*	NSE	SSH	NEC	Total	Total*	NSE	SSH	NEC	Total	Total*	NSE	SSH	NEC	Total	Total*
	4 776	4 782	3 478	1 304	...	5 860	5 939	3 795	2 144	...	...	...	...	...	...	...	...
	5 770	...	4 035	1 735	...	16 023	...	9 632	6 391	...	...	...	...	...	...	...	...
	681[y]	707	665	42	.	2 291[y]	2 348	1 606	742	.	...	...	...	...	...	.	.
	944	...	865	79	.	5 387	...	3 409	1 978	.	...	...	...	...	...	...	...
	1 400	1 395	943	452	.	5 241	5 399	3 093	2 306	.	...	...	...	...	...	...	...
	1 696	...	1 139	557	.	13 936	...	7 221	6 715	.	...	...	...	...	...	...	...
	1 912	...	1 524	388	.	567[t]	...	371	196	.	...	...	...	...	...	...	...
	2 046	...	1 628	418	.	1 000[t]	...	606	394	.	...	...	...	...	...	...	...
	97	137[-3]	90[-3]	19[-3]	29[-3,u]	226	242[-3]	92[-3]	113[-3]	37[-3,u]	19	9[-3]	.[-3]	9[-3]	.[-3]	.	.[-3]
	494[-3]	...	475[-3]	19[-3]	.[-3]	918[-3]	...	360[-3]	558[-3]	.[-3]	9[-3]	...	.[-3]	9[-3]	.[-3]	.[-3]	...
	13 847	13 571	11 864	1 708	...	39 695	37 167	21 858	15 309	...	120	129	57	72	...	...	...
	15 633	...	13 588	2 045	...	69 027	...	39 984	29 043	...	170	...	72	98	...	...	...
	6 409	6 583	5 253	1 330	...	6 378	6 578	5 766	812	...	78	82	68	14	...	...	...
	6 859	...	5 371	1 488	...	14 884	...	11 998	2 886	...	119	...	91	28	...	...	...
	144 700	...	...	...	...	91 501	...	...	...	...	1 071	...	...	...	...	...	...
	132 796[t]	...	119 912[t]	12 884[t]	...	44 342[t]	...	29 200[t]	15 142[t]	...	447[t]	...	275[t]	172[t]	...	...	...
	2 874	...	2 214	660	.	8 728	...	5 636	3 091	.	4	...	1	3	.	...	...
	2 920	...	2 244	676	.	10 769	...	7 007	3 762	.	7	...	3	4	.	...	...
	3 123[s]	...	2 233[s]	890[s]	...	8 959	...	5 577	3 382	...	15	...	11	4	...	...	...
	3 975[s]	...	2 712[s]	1 263[s]	...	17 668	...	10 350	7 318	...	55	...	46	9	...	...	...
	1 744[y]	1 825	1 330	494	...	2 180	2 201	1 727	474	...	13[y]	17	13	4	...	...	...
	2 165	...	1 609	556	...	4 310	...	3 201	1 109	...	17	...	13	4	...	...	...
	6 541	...	6 336	205	...	41 269	...	24 067	17 202	...	...	...	...	...	...	...	...
	7 251	...	6 978	273	...	126 046	...	77 060	48 986	...	...	...	...	...	...	...	...
	26 377	29 103	23 373	5 139	591	4 660	4 961	1 922	278	2 761	.	.	.	.	.	.	.
	32 484	...	26 664	5 493	327	5 973	...	1 774	353	3 846	.	...	.	.	.	.	...
	...	...	...	...	...	...	...	...	...	...	...	...	...	...	...	...	...
	2 924	...	2 364	560	.	1 220	...	758	462	.	...	...	...	...	...	.	...
	...	...	...	...	...	...	...	...	...	...	...	...	...	...	...	...	...
	11 850	...	7 739	4 111	.	3 593	...	2 614	979	.	24	...	24	.	.	.	...
	...	...	...	...	...	2 362	...	...	...	...	...	...	...	...	...	...	...
	...	4 692[-9]	3 361[-9]	1 181[-9]	150[-9]	2 893	3 420[-9]	1 954[-9]	1 128[-9]	338[-9]	...	...[-9]	...[-9]	...[-9]	...[-9]	...	.[-9]
	...	...	...	...	...	...	...	...	...	...	...	...	...	...	...	...	...
	3 855	...	3 154	701	.	9 208	...	6 522	2 686	.	977	...	709	268	.	.	...
	...	...	...	...	...	...	...	...	...	...	...	...	...	...	...	...	...
	1 677	...	1 467	210	.	1 250	...	338	911	1	...	...	...	...	...	.	...
	...	...	...	...	...	...	...	...	...	...	...	...	...	...	...	...	...
	1 578	...	1 209	369	.	213[t]	...	133[t]	80[t]	.	...	...	...	...	...	.	...
	...	...	...	...	...	...	...	...	...	...	...	...	...	...	...	...	...
	1 504	...	1 131	373	.	648	...	430	218	.	...	...	...	...	...	.	...
	4 926[-3,a]	...	4 077[-3]	849[-3]	.[-3]	8 117[-3]	...	...[-3]	...[-3]	8 117[-3]	55[-3,a]	...	42[-3]	13[-3]	.[-3]	.[-3]	...
	4 743	...	4 095	648	.	24 417	...	13 451	10 966	.	80	...	53	27	.	.	...

311

Annexes

Table A3 • **Researchers by sector of employment and field of science (in headcounts, HC, and full-time equivalents, FTE), 2014 or latest available year** (continued)

Country		Total					Business enterprise				
		Total	Total*	NSE	SSH	NEC	Total	Total*	NSE	SSH	NEC
East Asia and the Pacific											
Australia	FTE	100 414[-4,u]	73 173[-12]	…[-12]	…[-12]	…[-12]	39 065	20 451[-12]	…[-12]	…[-12]	…[-12]
	HC	…	…	…	…	…	…	…	…	…	…
Brunei Darussalam	FTE	102[-10,t,v]	98[-11,t]	…[-11]	…[-11]	…[-11]	…[-10]	16[-11]	…[-11]	…[-11]	…[-11]
	HC	244[-10,t,v]	292[-11,t]	…[-11]	…[-11]	…[-11]	…[-10]	32[-11]	…[-11]	…[-11]	…[-11]
Cambodia	FTE	223[-12,t,u]	…	…	…	…	35[-12,t,u]	…	…	…	…
	HC	744[-12,t,u]	…	…	…	…	113[-12,t,u]	…	…	…	…
China	FTE	1 524 280	1 592 420[-6]	1 484 481[-6]	73 217[-6]	34 722[-6]	946 077	1 092 213[-6]	1 092 213[-6]	…[-6]	…[-6]
	HC	2 069 650[-2]	…	…	…	…	1 176 429[-2]	…	…	…	…
China, Hong Kong Special Administrative Region	FTE	22 466	…	…	…	…	8 962[-1,f]	…	…	…	…
	HC	26 835	…	…	…	…	12 119[-1,f]	…	…	…	…
China, Macao Special Administrative Region	FTE	609[t]	…	260[t]	348[t]	1	12[t]	…	12[t]	.[t]	.
	HC	1 379[t]	…	524[t]	853[t]	2	12[t]	…	12[t]	.[t]	.
Indonesia	FTE	21 349[-5,t,u]	…	…	…	…	7 588[-5,u]	…	…	…	…
	HC	41 143[-5,t,u,v]	35 564[-9,t]	15 242[-9,i]	9 069[-9,i]	11 253[-9]	7 588[-5,u,v]	673[-9]	273[-9]	288[-9]	112[-9]
Japan	FTE	682 935	…	…	…	…	506 134	…	…	…	…
	HC	926 671	…	792 777	102 942	30 951	560 466	…	554 148	6 317	…
Korea, Republic of	FTE	345 463	100 210[-15,p,q]	…[-15]	…[-15]	…[-15]	274 638	65 474[-15,p,q]	…[-15]	…[-15]	…[-15]
	HC	437 447	410 333	364 276	46 057	…	304 808	281 874	288 355	16 453	…
Lao People's Democratic Republic	FTE	87[-12,t]	…	…	…	…	26[-12]	…	…	…	…
	HC	209[-12,t]	…	…	…	…	59[-12]	…	…	…	…
Malaysia	FTE	61 351	52 052[-2]	42 530[-2]	9 522[-2]	.[-2]	6 290	5 596[-2]	5 596[-2]	.[-2]	.[-2]
	HC	84 516	75 257[-2]	60 873[-2]	14 384[-2]	.[-2]	6 581	6 247[-2]	6 247[-2]	.[-2]	.[-2]
Myanmar	FTE	837[-12,t]	…	…	…	…	…	…	…	…	…
	HC	4 725[-12,t]	…	2 600[-12]	2 125[-12]	.[-12]	…	…	…	…	…
New Zealand	FTE	17 900	…	…	…	…	6 100	…	…	…	…
	HC	29 300	…	…	…	…	7 800	…	…	…	…
Philippines	FTE	21 593	…	18 306	2 774	514	11 682	…	11 574	91	17
	HC	26 558	…	22 068	3 688	802	13 843	…	13 715	108	20
Singapore	FTE	36 025	…	34 128	…	1 897	18 329	…	17 642	…	687
	HC	40 385	…	38 181	…	2 204	19 826	…	19 110	…	716
Taiwan, China	FTE	142 983	…	132 981	10 002	…	97 019	…	95 479	1 540	…
	HC	182 119	…	163 209	18 910	…	109 221	…	107 239	1 982	…
Thailand	FTE	65 965	…	21 601[h]	15 883[h]	28 481[c]	28 440	…	…	…	28 440[b]
	HC	101 356	…	43 462[h]	27 768[h]	30 126[c]	30 029	…	…	…	30 029[b]
Viet Nam	FTE	9 328[-12]	…	…	…	…	968[-12]	…	…	…	…
	HC	105 230[-3]	…	…	…	…	14 990[-3]	…	…	…	…
Latin America and the Caribbean											
Argentina	FTE	50 785[-1]	…	…	…	…	3 569[-1]	…	…	…	…
	HC	81 964[-1]	…	52 745[-1,h]	25 059[-1,h]	4 160[-1,c]	4 160[-1]	…	…[-1]	…[-1]	4 160[-1]
Bermuda	FTE	…	…	…	…	…	…	…	…	…	…
	HC	31	…	31	.	.	4	…	4	.	.
Bolivia (Plurinational State of)	FTE	1 646[-4]	…	1 301[-4]	345[-4]	.[-4]	6[-4]	…	…	…	…
	HC	2 153[-4]	…	1 675[-4]	478[-4]	.[-4]	6[-4]	…	…	…	…

Table A3 | *Researchers by sector of employment and field of science, 2014 or latest available year*

	Government					Higher education					Private non-profit					Not elsewhere classified (NEC)	
	Total	Total*	NSE	SSH	NEC	Total	Total*	NSE	SSH	NEC	Total	Total*	NSE	SSH	NEC	Total	Total*
	8 311[-2]	8 036[-12]	...[-12]	...[-12]	...[-12]	65 772[-2]	42 780[-12]	25 462[-12]	17 317[-12]	...[-12]	3 416[-2]	1 906[-12]	1 812[-12]	94[-12]	...[-12]	...[-2]	...[-12]
	...	...	...	...	...	...	...	...	...	...	...	...	...	...	...	...	...
	...[-10]	24[-11]	...[-11]	...[-11]	...[-11]	...[-10]	58[-11]	...[-11]	...[-11]	...[-11]	...[-10]	...[-11]	...[-11]	...[-11]	...[-11]	...[-10]	.[-11]
	...[-10]	62[-11]	...[-11]	...[-11]	...[-11]	...[-10]	198[-11]	...[-11]	...[-11]	...[-11]	...[-10]	...[-11]	...[-11]	...[-11]	...[-11]	...[-10]	.[-11]
	113[-12,t,u]	...	...	...	...	28[-12,t,u]	...	...	...	...	47[-12,t,u]	...	...	...	...	.[-12]	
	394[-12,t,u]	...	...	...	...	88[-12,t,u]	...	...	...	...	149[-12,t,u]	...	...	...	...	.[-12]	
	295 899	238 970[-6]	196 096[-6]	8 152[-6]	34 722[-6]	282 304	261 237[-6]	196 172[-6]	65 065[-6]	...[-6]		...[-6]	...[-6]	...[-6]	...[-6]		...[-6]
	339 576[-2]	...	...	...	...	553 645[-2]	...	...	...	...	...[-2]					...[-2]	
	493	...	...	...	...	13 011	...	...	...	...	...[-1,l]						
	1 063	...	...	...	...	13 653	...	...	...	...	...[-1,l]						
	...	...	...	...	...	578	...	229	348	1	14[t]	...	14[t]	.[t]	.	5	...
	...	...	...	...	...	1 348	...	493	853	2	14[t]	...	14[t]	.[t]	.	5	...
	6 291[-5,u]	...	...	...	...	7 470[-5]	...	...	...	...	...[-5]	...	...	...	...	...[-5]	...
	11 114[-5,u]	11 141[-9]	...[-9]	...[-9]	11 141[-9]	22 411[-5,v]	23 750[-9]	14 969[-9]	8 781[-9]	.[-9]	...[-5]	...[-9]	...[-9]	...[-9]	...[-5,9]	...[-5]	...[-9]
	30 373		28 712	1 661	...	137 586	...	96 380	41 206	...	8 842	...	7 892	950	...		
	34 067	...	31 272	2 795	...	321 571	...	198 032	92 588	30 951	10 567	...	9 325	1 242	...		
	24 750	11 745[-15,p,q]	...[-15]	...[-15]	...[-15]	41 938	21 723[-15,p,q]	21 723[-15]	...[-15]	...[-15]	4 137	1 268[-15,p,q]	1 268[-15]	...[-15]	...[-15]		...[-15]
	27 508	26 153	22 742	4 766	...	99 317	97 319	70 706	26 613	...	5 814	4 987	4 808	1 006	...		
	31[-12]	...	...	...	...	30[-12]	...	...	...	...	...[-12]					...[-12]	
	109[-12]	...	...	...	...	41[-12]	...	...	...	...	...[-12]					...[-12]	
	3 964	3 533[-2]	3 454[-2]	80[-2]	.[-2]	51 097	42 920[-2]	33 477[-2]	9 442[-2]	.[-2]	.	3[-2]	3[-2]	.[-2]	.[-2]	.	.[-2]
	4 550	4 045[-2]	3 952[-2]	93[-2]	.[-2]	73 385	64 962[-2]	50 671[-2]	14 291[-2]	.[-2]	.	3[-2]	3[-2]	.[-2]	.[-2]	.	.[-2]
	...	...	...	...	...	...	...	...	...	...	...	...	...	...	...	...	...
	...	...	...	...	...	...	...	...	...	...	...	...	...	...	...	...	...
	2 000	...	...	...	...	9 800	...	...	...	...	...	...	...	...	...	...	...
	2 500	...	...	...	...	19 000	...	...	...	...	...	...	...	...	...	...	...
	2 572	...	2 382	182	7	7 176	...	4 249	2 437	490	163	...	100	63	.	.	...
	2 887	...	2 674	205	8	9 652	...	5 572	3 306	774	176	...	107	69	.	.	...
	1 843	...	1 742	...	102	15 853	...	14 745	...	1 109	...	...	...	...	...	...	...
	2 588	...	2 365	...	223	17 971	...	16 706	...	1 265	...	...	...	...	...	...	...
	14 753	...	13 957	797	...	30 621	...	23 107	7 514	...	590	...	439	151	...	...	...
	19 725	...	18 685	1 040	...	52 302	...	36 640	15 662	...	871	...	645	226	...	...	...
	10 045	...	9 491	554	.	26 970	...	11 775	15 156	39	510	...	335	173	2	.	...
	14 042	...	12 557	1 485	.	56 775	...	30 570	26 110	95	510	...	335	173	2	.	...
	5 272[-12]	...	...	...	...	3 020[-12]	...	...	...	...	68[-12]	...	...	...	...	...[-12]	...
	36 048[-3]	...	...	...	...	52 997[-3]	...	...	...	...	1 195[-3]	...	...	...	...	.[-3]	...
	23 444[-1]	...	...	...	...	23 220[-1]	...	...	...	...	552[-1]	...	...	...	...	.[-1]	...
	24 369[-1]	...	19 301[-1]	5 068[-1]	.[-1]	52 533[-1]	...	32 829[-1]	19 704[-1]	.[-1]	902[-1]	...	615[-1]	287[-1]	.[-1]	.[-1]	...
	...	...	...	...	...	...	...	...	...	...	...	...	...	...	...	...	...
	.	.	.	.	.	.	.	.	.	.	27	.	27	.	.	.	...
	73[-4]	...	...	...	...	1 370[-4]	...	...	...	...	197[-4]	...	...	...	...	.[-4]	...
	140[-4]	...	...	...	...	1 776[-4]	...	...	...	...	231[-4]	...	...	...	...	.[-4]	...

313

Table A3 • **Researchers by sector of employment and field of science (in headcounts, HC, and full-time equivalents, FTE), 2014 or latest available year** (continued)

Country		Total					Business enterprise				
		Total	Total*	NSE	SSH	NEC	Total	Total*	NSE	SSH	NEC
Brazil	FTE	138 653[-4]	...	...	...	...	35 970[-4]	...	...	...	...
	HC	234 797[-4]	...	...	...	...	41 317[-4,w]	...	...	...	...
Chile	FTE	7 602[y]	...	6 435[y]	1 167[y]	...	2 265[y]	...	2 215[y]	50[y]	...
	HC	12 320[y]	10 582[-6]	8 097[-6]	2 485[-6]	...[-6]	3 063[y]	1 831[-6]	1 698[-6]	133[-6]	...[-6]
Colombia	FTE	7 193	...	3 986	3 207	0	60	...	52[-1,w]	8[-1,w]	.
	HC	15 131	...	8 291	6 840	.	120	...	99[-1,w]	21[-1,w]	.
Costa Rica	FTE	1 684[-1,h]	527[-9]	410[-9]	117[-9,t]	.[-9]	4 225[-3,a]	30[-9]	31[-9]	.[-9]	.[-9]
	HC	4 291[-1,h]	1 444[-9]	2 882[-1,h]	1 288[-1,h]	121[-1,h]	4 686[-3,a]	49[-9]	47[-9]	2[-9,t]	.[-9]
Cuba	FTE	...	...	...	...	...	...	...	...	...	...
	HC	4 355	...	...	...	...	...	...	...	...	...
Ecuador	FTE	2 736[-3]	1 491[-6]	1 631[-3]	1 105[-3]	0[-3]	...[-3]	223[-6]	...[-3]	...[-3]	...[-3]
	HC	4 027[-3]	2 623[-6]	2 312[-3]	1 715[-3]	.[-3]	...[-3]	811[-6]	...[-3]	...[-3]	...[-3]
El Salvador	FTE	...	...	...	...	...	...	...	...	...	...
	HC	792	...	623	169	.	19	...	17	2	.
Guatemala	FTE	411[-2,t]	...	287[-2,t]	124[-2,t]	.[-2]	...[-2]	...	...[-2]	...[-2]	...[-2]
	HC	666[-2,t]	...	498[-2,t]	168[-2,t]	.[-2]	...[-2]	...	...[-2]	...[-2]	...[-2]
Mexico	FTE	38 823[-3]	33 558[-11]	25 334[-11,w]	8 150[-11,w]	...[-11]	14 641	8 663[-11]	8 276[-11,w]	450[-11,w]	...[-11]
	HC	...	44 577[-11]	33 016[-11]	11 561[-11]	...[-11]	16 141	10 688[-11]	10 136[-11]	552[-11]	...[-11]
Panama	HC	552[-3,v]	463[-6]	223[-6]	83[-6,t]	157[-6]	...[-3]	...[-6]	...[-6]	...[-6]	...[-6]
Paraguay	FTE	1 081[-2,v]	466[-6]	...[-2]	...[-2]	...[-2]	...[-2]	...[-6]	...[-2]	...[-2]	...[-2]
	HC	1 704[-2]	850[-6]	522[-6]	282[-6]	46[-6]	...[-2]	21[-3]	...[-3]	...[-3]	...[-3]
Peru	FTE	...	...	...	...	...	...	...	...	...	...
	HC	5 737[y]	4 965[-10]	...[-10]	...[-10]	...[-10]	...	688[-10]	...[-10]	...[-10]	...[-10]
Puerto Rico	FTE	960	...	...	...	...	904	...	...	...	...
	HC	1 976	...	...	...	...	1 332	...	1 333	1	.
Trinidad and Tobago	FTE	...	...	...	...	...	...	...	...	...	...
	HC	1 244	...	917	327	.	...	...	...	...	...
Uruguay	FTE	1 724	...	1 173	550	.	17	...	10	6	1
	HC	2 288	...	1 476	810	2	31	...	20	11	.
Venezuela, Bolivarian Republic of	FTE	8 686[-2,t]	5 209[-5,t]	3 376[-5,t]	1 833[-5,t]	.[-5]	393[-2,t]	20[-5,t]	18[-5]	2[-5,t]	.[-5]
	HC	10 256[-2,t]	6 829[-5,t]	4 355[-5,t]	2 474[-5,t]	.[-5]	776[-2,t]	46[-5,t]	38[-5,t]	8[-5,t]	.[-5]
North America and Western Europe											
Austria	FTE	41 005[u,y]	40 426	...	...	...	26 122[u,y]	25 752	...	...	...
	HC	71 448	...	...	...	...	33 643	...	...	...	...
Belgium	FTE	46 880[u]	46 355	...	...	...	23 812	23 759	...	...	...
	HC	66 724	63 207[-3]	...[-3]	...[-3]	...[-3]	30 374	28 325[-3]	...[-3]	...[-3]	...[-3]
Canada	FTE	159 190	...	129 560	29 630	...	89 170[-1,p,q,y]	...	89 170[-1,p,q,y]	...	...
	HC	...	...	...	...	...	...	...	...	...	...
Cyprus	FTE	865[y]	881	607	274	.	180[y]	172	159	13	.
	HC	2 209	...	1 286	923	.	320	...	285	35	.
Denmark	FTE	40 647[u]	40 316	...	...	...	24 193[u]	23 812	...	...	...
	HC	57 654	...	...	...	...	28 030	...	...	...	...

Table A3 | *Researchers by sector of employment and field of science, 2014 or latest available year*

Government					Higher education					Private non-profit					Not elsewhere classified (NEC)	
Total	Total*	NSE	SSH	NEC	Total	Total*	NSE	SSH	NEC	Total	Total*	NSE	SSH	NEC	Total	Total*
7 667[-4]	...	...	...	...	94 003[-4]	...	...	...	...	1 013[-4]	...	...	...	...	.[-4]	...
7 667[-4,w]	...	...	...	...	188 003[-4,w]	...	...	...	...	1 013[-4,w]	...	...	...	...	.[-4]	...
769[y]	...	571[y]	198[y]	...	3 600[y]	...	2 728[y]	872[y]	...	968[y]	...	921[y]	48[y]	...	...	...
1 060[y]	883[-6]	697[-6]	186[-6]	...[-6]	7 143[y]	7 372[-6]	5 342[-6]	2 030[-6]	...[-6]	1 054[y]	496[-6]	360[-6]	136[-6]	...[-6]	...	.[-6]
74	...	43[-1,w]	31[-1,w]	.	6 469	...	3 443[-1,w]	3 026[-1,w]	.	591	...	489[-1,w]	102[-1,w]	.	.	.
135	...	82[-1,w]	53[-1,w]	.	13 771	...	7 278[-1,w]	6 493[-1,w]	.	1 105	...	884[-1,w]	221[-1,w]	.	.	.
447	49[-9]	49[-9]	1[-9,t]	.[-9]	1 201	421[-9]	309[-9]	113[-9,t]	.[-9]	36	27[-9]	24[-9]	4[-9,t]	.[-9]	.	.[-9]
1 312	133[-9]	1 037	265	10[-1,w]	2 893	1 199[-9]	1 775	996	122[-1,w]	86	63[-9]	70[-1,w]	27[-1,w]	.[-1,w]	.	.[-9]
...	...	...	...	...	...	...	...	...	...	...	...	...	...	...	...	...
...	...	...	...	...	...	...	...	...	...	...	...	...	...	...	...	...
489[-3]	...[-6]	442[-3]	48[-3]	.[-3]	2 160[-3]	1 268[-6]	1 128[-3]	1 031[-3]	.[-3]	88[-3]	...[-6]	64[-3]	24[-3]	.[-3]	.[-3]	.[-6]
580[-3]	...[-6]	507[-3]	73[-3]	.[-3]	3 350[-3]	1 812[-6]	1 732[-3]	1 618[-3]	.[-3]	97[-3]	...[-6]	73[-3]	24[-3]	.[-3]	.[-3]	.[-6]
...	...	...	...	...	...	...	...	...	...	...	...	...	...	...	...	...
32	...	29	3	.	644	...	484	160	.	5	...	4	1	.	92	...
119[-2,t]	...	101[-2,t]	18[-2,t]	.[-2]	292[-2,t]	...	186[-2,t]	106[-2,t]	.[-2]	...[-2]	...	...[-2]	...[-2]	.[-2]	...	...
188[-2,t]	...	166[-2,t]	22[-2,t]	.[-2]	478[-2,t]	...	332[-2,t]	146[-2,t]	.[-2]	...[-2]	...	...[-2]	...[-2]	.[-2]	...	...
9 154[-3]	6 397[-11]	5 889[-11,w]	487[-11,w]	...[-11]	16 691[-3]	17 135[-11]	10 137[-11,w]	6 654[-11,w]	...[-11]	1 326[-3]	1 363[-11]	1 032[-11,w]	559[-11,w]	...[-11]	.[-3]	...[-11]
...	7 217[-11]	6 666[-11]	551[-11]	...[-11]	...	24 183[-11]	14 599[-11]	9 584[-11]	...[-11]	...	2 489[-11]	1 615[-11]	874[-11]	...[-11]	...	...[-11]
268[-3]	...[-6]	...[-6]	...[-6]	...[-6]	...[-13]	...[-6]	...[-6]	...[-6]	...[-6]	82[-3]	...[-6]	...[-6]	...[-6]	...[-6]	202[-3]	...[-6]
...[-2]	116[-6]	...[-2]	...[-2]	...[-2]	...[-2]	282[-6]	...[-2]	...[-2]	...[-2]	...[-2]	32[-6]	...[-2]	...[-2]	...[-2]	...[-2]	36[-6]
376[-2]	64[-3]	...[-3]	...[-3]	.[-3]	1 052[-2]	861[-3]	...[-3]	...[-3]	.[-3]	122[-2]	93[-3]	...[-3]	...[-3]	.[-3]	154[-2]	244[-3]
...	...	...	...	...	...	...	...	...	...	...	...	...	...	...	...	...
...	2 276[-10]	...[-10]	...[-10]	.[-10]	...	1 996[-10]	...[-10]	...[-10]	.[-10]	5	5[-10]	...[-10]	...[-10]	.[-10]	...	...[-10]
44	...	...	...	.	...	...	...	...	.	12	...	...	...	.	.	...
97	...	73	19	5	519	...	...	...	.	28	...	22	6	.	.	...
...	...	...	...	...	...	...	...	...	...	...	...	...	...	...	...	...
116	...	106	10	.	1 128	...	811	317	.	...	...	...	...	.	...	...
214	...	185	30	.	1 369	...	886	482	1	64	...	59	4	1	60	...
288	...	239	49	.	1 794	...	1 095	698	1	78	...	72	6	.	97	...
1 113[-2,t]	443[-5,t]	420[-5]	23[-5,t]	.[-5]	7 106[-2,t]	4 698[-5,t]	2 900[-5,u]	1 798[-5,t,u]	.[-5]	74[-2,t]	25[-5,t]	16[-5,u]	9[-5,t,u]	.[-5]	.[-2]	23[-5,t]
1 367[-2,t]	669[-5,t]	624[-5,t]	45[-5,t]	.[-5]	8 005[-2,t]	6 028[-5,t]	3 626[-5,t]	2 402[-5,t]	.[-5]	108[-2,t]	46[-5,t]	36[-5,t]	10[-5,t]	.[-5]	.[-2]	40[-5,t]
1 589[u,y]	1 567	720	847	.	13 030[u,y]	12 846	9 559	3 287	.	264[u,y]	261	180	81	.	...	...
3 472	...	1 578	1 894	.	33 781	...	23 046	10 735	.	552	...	376	176	.	...	...
3 724	3 657	3 225	432	.	19 148[u]	18 750	13 414	5 336	.	196[u]	189	176	12	.	...	...
4 061	3 215[-3]	2 778[-3]	437[-3]	.[-3]	32 077	31 353[-3]	22 293[-3,u]	9 060[-3,u]	.[-3]	212	314[-3]	312[-3]	2[-3]	.[-3]	...	.[-3]
9 100	...	7 730	1 370	...	60 270	...	32 010	28 260	...	660[-1,p,q]	...	660	...	...	...	...
...	...	...	...	...	...	...	...	...	...	...	...	...	...	...	...	...
80[y]	86	55	31	.	520[y]	549	333	216	.	85[y]	73	60	13	.	...	...
188	...	124	64	.	1 586	...	782	804	.	115	...	95	20	.	...	...
1 250[u]	1 254	620	634	.	15 012[u]	15 057	11 574	3 483	.	193[u]	194	156	37	.	...	...
2 289	...	1 285	1 004	.	27 080	...	19 270	7 810	.	255	...	197	58	.	...	...

315

Annex A | Basic statistics on the production of social science research

Table A3 • **Researchers by sector of employment and field of science (in headcounts, HC, and full-time equivalents, FTE), 2014 or latest available year** (continued)

Country		Total	Total*	NSE	SSH	NEC	Business enterprise Total	Total*	NSE	SSH	NEC
Finland	FTE	38 281	…	…	…	…	21 369	…	…	…	…
	HC	56 720	…	…	…	…	27 977	…	…	…	…
France	FTE	269 377[y]	…	…	…	…	162 724[y]	…	…	…	…
	HC	366 299	…	…	…	…	220 321	…	209 725	3 667	6 929
Germany	FTE	353 276[u,y]	354 463	…	…	…	198 076	198 585	…	…	…
	HC	549 283	…	…	…	…	221 362	…	…	…	…
Greece	FTE	29 877	24 674[-3]	18 900[-3]	5 774[-3]	…[-3]	4 938	4 021[-3]	3 852[-3]	168[-3]	…[-3]
	HC	53 744	45 239[-3]	34 341[-3]	10 898[-3]	…[-3]	6 004	5 858[-3]	5 595[-3]	263[-3]	…[-3]
Iceland	FTE	1 950	…	…	…	…	735	…	…	…	…
	HC	3 458	…	…	…	…	1 261	…	…	…	…
Ireland	FTE	17 448[u]	16 844	…	…	…	11 246[u]	10 793	…	…	…
	HC	25 393	…	…	…	…	13 750	…	…	…	…
Israel	FTE	…	63 521[-2,s,u]	…	…	…	51 727[-1,s]	53 157[-2,s]	…	…	…
	HC	…	…	…	…	…	54 672[-1,s]	…	…	…	…
Italy	FTE	119 977[y]	116 163	…	…	…	45 966[y]	43 116	…	…	…
	HC	163 925	…	…	…	…	…	52 710	…	…	…
Luxembourg	FTE	2 548[u,y]	2 504	…	…	…	1 028[y]	1 001	…	…	…
	HC	2 713	…	…	…	…	1 097	…	…	…	…
Malta	FTE	891[y]	857	688	155	14	533[y]	548	516	20	12
	HC	…	1 437	1 002	413	22	…	605	562	27	16
Netherlands	FTE	75 536[y]	76 670	66 479	10 192	…	45 959[y]	46 838	44 291	2 547	…
	HC	110 535	…	95 855	14 681	…	74 632	…	69 482	5 149	…
Norway	FTE	29 237	28 312	22 938	5 374	…	14 314[x]	13 553[-1,x]	13 470[-1,x]	83[-1,x]	…
	HC	47 795	…	36 241	11 426	128	18 857[-1,x]	…	18 822	35	…
Portugal	FTE	38 487[y]	37 813	28 090	9 724	…	10 533[y]	10 025	9 374	650	…
	HC	78 290	…	53 777	24 513	…	20 621	…	18 630	1 991	…
Spain	FTE	122 235	123 225	…	…	…	44 689	44 714	…	…	…
	HC	208 767	220 254[-3]	…	…	…	59 360	59 391[-3]	…	…	…
Sweden	FTE	66 643[t,y]	45 995[-13]	…[-13]	…[-13]	…[-13]	44 433[y]	27 884[-13,x]	…[-13]	…[-13]	…[-13]
	HC	101 820[-1,t]	…	…	…	…	48 961	…	…	…	…
Switzerland	FTE	35 950[-2]	…	…	…	…	16 595[-2]	…	…	…	…
	HC	60 278[-2]	…	…	…	…	17 904[-2]	…	…	…	…
United Kingdom of Great Britain and Northern Ireland	FTE	273 560[u,y]	254 009[-8,u]	…[-8]	…[-8]	…[-8]	104 484[u,y]	93 844[-8]	…[-8]	…[-8]	…[-8]
	HC	466 689[-1,u]	…	…	…	…	123 684	…	…	…	…
United States of America	FTE	1 265 064[-2,u]	1 047 242[-12,u]	…	…	…	869 000[-2]	…[-12]	…	…	…
	HC	…	…	…	…	…	…	…	…	…	…
South and West Asia											
India	FTE	192 819[-4]	154 827[-9]	113 379[-9]	2 796[-9]	38 652[-9]	74 672[-4]	57 360[-9,f]	56 082[-9]	1 278[-9]	…[-9,f]
	HC	…	…	…	…	…	…	…	…	…	…
Iran, Islamic Republic of	FTE	52 656[-2]	54 268[-6]	41 369[-6]	11 840[-6]	1 059[-6]	…[-2]	8 121[-6]	7 954[-6]	139[-6]	28[-6]
	HC	95 200[-2]	107 810[-6]	77 164[-6]	28 067[-6]	2 579[-6]	…[-2]	9 669[-6]	9 446[-6]	189[-6]	34[-6]
Pakistan	FTE	30 244[-1,h]	…	22 177[-1,h]	7 236[-1,h]	831[-1,h]	…	…	…	…	…
	HC	60 699[-1,h]	…	42 198[-1,h]	16 393[-1,h]	2 108[-1,h]	…	…	…	…	…

Table A3 | *Researchers by sector of employment and field of science, 2014 or latest available year*

	Government					Higher education					Private non-profit					Not elsewhere classified (NEC)	
	Total	Total*	NSE	SSH	NEC	Total	Total*	NSE	SSH	NEC	Total	Total*	NSE	SSH	NEC	Total	Total*
	4 089	...	...	...	...	12 381	...	...	...	...	441	...	...	...	...	...	...
	5 732	...	5 042[-1,b]	1 297[-1,b]	...	22 404	...	14 077	8 327	...	607	...	...[-1,g]	...[-1,g]	...	...	...
	29 390[y]	...	...	...	...	73 393[y]	...	...	...	...	3 870[y]	...	...	...	...	...	...
	28 520	...	...	...	...	113 058	...	...	...	...	4 400	...	...	...	...	...	...
	55 000[u,y]	56 755	48 775	7 980	...	100 200[u,y]	99 123	69 603	29 520	...	...	...	...	...	...	...	...
	66 264	...	56 462	9 802	...	261 657	...	176 639	85 018	...	...	...	...	...	...	...	...
	5 844	5 778	3 635	2 143	...	18 801	18 957	11 892	7 064	...	294	296	166	130	...	...	...
	8 567	6 094[-3]	5 164	3 403	...	38 724	32 842[-3]	24 282	14 442	...	449	445[-3]	274	175	...	...	...[-3]
	178	...	20	19	...	1 011	...	544	467	...	26	...	26	.	...	...	...
	222	...	186	36	...	1 910	...	1 167	743	...	65	...	65	.	...	...	...
	455[u]	437	363	74	.	5 747[u]	5 614	4 195	1 383	35	...	...	...	...	...	...	...
	516	...	427	89	...	11 127	...	7 071	4 002	55	...	...	...	...	...	...	...
	...	503[-2,s,u]	...	...	...	9 614[-1,s,u]	9 433[-2,s,u]	...	...	...	...	428[-2,s,u]	...	...	...	...	...[-2]
	...	...	...	...	...	...	...	...	...	...	...	...	...	...	...	...	...
	21 621[y]	21 313	19 244	2 069	...	48 203[y]	47 526	29 207	18 108	211	4 188[y]	4 208	3 485	723	...	...	...
	27 820[y]	27 621	24 832	2 789	...	...	77 737	48 685	28 645	407	5 852[y]	5 857	4 488	1 369	...	...	...
	742[u,y]	733	495	238	...	778[u,y]	769	441	328	...	...	...	...	...	...	...	...
	788	...	532	256	...	828	...	463	365	...	...	...	...	...	...	...	...
	16[y]	17	14[y]	1[y]	[y]	342[y]	292	196[y]	143[y]	3[y]	[y]	.	.	.	.	.	.
	23[y]	26	21[y]	2[y]	[y]	849[y]	806	453[y]	388[y]	8[y]	...	.	.	.	.	.	.
	8 127[b,y]	8 616[-1,b]	7 344[-1,b]	1 272[-1,b]	...	21 450[y]	21 216	14 843	6 373	...	...[g]	...[-1,g]	...[-1,g]	...[-1,g]	...	...	...
	11 315[-1,b]	...	9 167[-1,b]	2 147[-1,b]	...	24 589	...	17 205	7 384	...	...[-1,g]	...	...[-1,g]	...[-1,g]	...	...	...
	4 627	4 705	3 172	1 533	...	10 296	10 054	6 296	3 758	...	...	...	...	...	...	...	...
	6 350	...	4 351	1 999	...	22 588	...	13 068	9 392	128	...	...	...	...	...	...	...
	1 394[y]	1 386	1 245	141	...	25 848[y]	25 760	16 866	8 894	...	711[y]	642	604	38	...	...	...
	4 101	...	3 762	339	...	52 827	...	30 709	22 118	...	741	...	676	65	...	...	...
	20 180	20 673	19 152	1 521	...	57 156	57 641	34 876	22 765	...	210	242[-3]	188[-3]	55[-3]	...[-3]	...	...[-3]
	31 018	33 278[-3]	28 727	2 291	...	117 925	127 085[-3]	70 392	47 533	...	464	500[-3]	401[-3]	99[-3]	...[-3]	...	...[-3]
	2 304[t,y]	2 260[-13,x]	...[-13]	...[-13]	...[-13]	19 616[y]	15 851[-13]	10 488[-13]	3 639[-13]	1 724[-13]	290[y]	...[-13]	...[-13]	...[-13]	...[-13]	...	...[-13]
	9 527[-1,t]	...	6 040[-1,t]	1 042[-1,t]	2 445[-1,t]	42 894	...	26 733	15 249	912	438	...	...	...	...	...	...
	430[-2]	...	...	...	...	18 760[-2]	...	...	...	...	...[-2]	...	...	...	...	...[-2]	...
	980[-2]	...	...	...	...	41 395[-2]	...	...	...	...	...[-2]	...	...	...	...	...[-2]	...
	7 640[u,y]	8 936[-8]	7 946[-8]	990[-8]	...[-8]	158 491[u,y]	147 304[-8,u]	...[-8]	...[-8]	...[-8]	2 945[u,y]	3 925[-8,u]	...[-8]	...[-8]	...[-8]	...	...[-8]
	8 714	...	7 401	1 313	...	330 382[-1,u]	...	198 084[-1,u]	121 907[-1,u]	10 391	3 909[-1,u]	...	...	...	...	...	...
	...[-2]	47 822[-12,s]	...	...	...	...[-2]	186 049[-15]	...	...	...	...[-2]	11 800[-15,t]	...	...	...	...[-2]	...[-15]
	...	...	...	...	...	...	...	...	...	...	...	...	...	...	...	...	...
	87 905[-4]	75 367[-9]	57 297[-9]	1 518[-9]	16 552[-9]	22 100[-4,u]	22 100[-9,u]	...[-9]	...[-9]	22 100[-9]	8 142[-4]	.[-9,l]	.[-9]	.[-9]	.[-9,l]	.[-4]	.[-9]
	...	...	...	...	...	...	...	...	...	...	...	...	...	...	...	...	...
	...[-2]	18 217[-6]	12 805[-6]	4 976[-6]	436[-6]	...[-2]	27 930[-6]	20 610[-6]	6 725[-6]	595[-6]	...[-2]	.[-6]	.[-6]	.[-6]	.[-6]	...[-2]	.[-6]
	...[-2]	23 089[-6]	15 670[-6]	6 842[-6]	577[-6]	...[-2]	75 052[-6]	52 048[-6]	21 036[-6]	1 968[-6]	...[-2]	.[-6]	.[-6]	.[-6]	.[-6]	...[-2]	.[-6]
	8 183	...	7 387	473	323	22 061	...	14 790	6 763	508	...	...	...	...	...	...	...
	8 183	...	7 387	473	323	52 516	...	34 811	15 920	1 785	...	...	...	...	...	...	...

Table A3 • **Researchers by sector of employment and field of science (in headcounts, HC, and full-time equivalents, FTE), 2014 or latest available year** (continued)

Country		Total					Business enterprise				
		Total	Total*	NSE	SSH	NEC	Total	Total*	NSE	SSH	NEC
Sri Lanka	FTE	2 276	...	1 920	203	154	698	...	544	26	130
	HC	5 705	...	4 599	707	400	1 204	...	914	117	173
Sub-Saharan Africa											
Angola	FTE	1 150[-3]	...	...	...	...	...[-3]	...	...	...	...
	HC	1 482[-3]	...	948[-3]	534[-3]	.[-3]	...[-3]	...	...[-3]	...[-3]	...[-3]
Benin	FTE	...	...	...	...	...	...	...	...	...	...
	HC	1 000[-7,t,u]	...	...	...	...	...	...	...	...	...
Botswana	FTE	352[-2]	...	328[-2]	9[-2]	15[-2]	37[-2]	...	28[-2]	3[-2]	6[-2]
	HC	690[-2]	...	629[-2]	16[-2]	45[-2]	39[-2]	...	28[-2]	4[-2]	7[-2]
Burkina Faso	FTE	742[-4]	...	628[-4]	75[-4]	40[-4]	...	...	...	...	...
	HC	1 144[-4]	...	950[-4]	156[-4]	38[-4]	...	...	...	...	...
Burundi	FTE	...	...	...	...	...	...	...	...	...	...
	HC	379[-3,t]	...	75[-3,t]	4[-3,t]	300[-3,e]	...[-3]	...	.[-3]	.[-3]	.[-3]
Cameroon	FTE	...	...	...	...	...	...	...	...	...	...
	HC	4 562[-6]	...	...	...	...	156[-6]	...	...	...	...
Cabo Verde	FTE	25[-3,k,t]	...	13[-3,k]	12[-3,k]	.[-3]	...[-3]	...	.[-3]	.[-3]	.[-3]
	HC	128[-3,k,t]	...	73[-3,k]	55[-3,k]	.[-3]	...[-3]	...	.[-3]	.[-3]	.[-3]
Central African Republic	FTE	...	...	...	...	...	...	...	...	...	...
	HC	134[-5,t]	...	84[-5,t]	45[-5,t]	5[-5,t]	5[-5,t]	...	.[-5]	.[-5]	5[-5]
Ethiopia	FTE	4 267	...	3 379	808	80	21	...	13	7	.
	HC	8 221	...	6 043	1 975	203	39	...	23	13	3
Gabon	FTE	...	...	...	...	...	...	...	...	...	...
	HC	531[-5,t]	...	162[-5,t]	188[-5,t]	181[-5,t]	...	...	...	...	...
Gambia	FTE	59[-3,t]	...	59[-3,t]	...[-3]	.[-3]	.[-3]	...	.[-3]	.[-3]	.[-3]
	HC	60[-3,t]	...	60[-3,t]	...[-3]	.[-3]	...[-3]	...	.[-3]	.[-3]	.[-3]
Ghana	FTE	941[-4]	...	603[-4]	315[-4]	24[-4]	9[-4]	...	8[-4]	1[-4]	.[-4]
	HC	2 542[-4]	...	1 545[-4]	918[-4]	79[-4]	17[-4]	...	15[-4]	2[-4]	.[-4]
Kenya	FTE	9 305[-4]	...	8 330[-4]	975[-4]	.[-4]	1 062[-4]	...	886[-4]	176[-4]	.[-4]
	HC	13 012[-4]	...	10 848[-4]	2 164[-4]	.[-4]	1 226[-4]	...	1 015[-4]	211[-4]	.[-4]
Lesotho	FTE	12[-3,k,t]	46[-5,t]	12[-3,k,t]	0[-3,k,t]	.[-3]	...[-3]	2[-5,t]	2[-5,t]	...[-5]	...[-5]
	HC	42[-3,k,t]	229[-5,t]	41[-3,k,t]	1[-3,k,t]	.[-3]	...[-3]	11[-5,t]	11[-5,t]	...[-5]	NEC
Madagascar	FTE	1 106[-3,t]	...	746[-3]	278[-3]	82[-3]	...[-3]	...	...[-3]	...[-3]	...[-3]
	HC	1 828[t]	...	1 247[h]	410[h]	171	85	...	...	...	...
Malawi	FTE	732[-4,h]	406[-7]	524[-4,h]	208[-4,h]	.[-4]	...[-4]	7[-7]	...[-7]	...[-7]	...[-7]
	HC	1 843[-4,h]	733[-7]	1 315[-4,h]	528[-4,h]	.[-4]	...[-4]	27[-7]	...[-4]	...[-4]	...[-4]
Mali	FTE	443[-4]	513[-8,t]	411[-8]	102[-8]	.[-8]	217[-4]	...[-8]	...[-8]	...[-8]	...[-8]
	HC	898[-4]	1 236[-8,t]	990[-8]	246[-8]	.[-8]	249[-4]	...[-8]	...[-8]	...[-8]	...[-8]
Mauritius	FTE	228[-2,h]	...	187[-2,h]	39[-2,h]	2[-2,h]	...[-2]	...	...[-2]	...[-2]	...[-2]
	HC	353[-2,h]	...	268[-2,u]	79[-2,u]	6[-2,u]	...[-2]	...	...[-2]	...[-2]	...[-2]
Mozambique	FTE	912[-4,h]	...	579[-4]	334[-4]	.[-4]	...[-4]	...	...[-4]	...[-4]	...[-4]
	HC	1 588[-4,h]	...	1 007[-4]	581[-4]	.[-4]	...[-4]	...	...[-4]	...[-4]	...[-4]

Table A3 | *Researchers by sector of employment and field of science, 2014 or latest available year*

Government					Higher education					Private non-profit					Not elsewhere classified (NEC)	
Total	Total*	NSE	SSH	NEC	Total	Total*	NSE	SSH	NEC	Total	Total*	NSE	SSH	NEC	Total	Total*
1 030	...	899	131	.	534	...	472	46	14	14	...	5	.	9	.	...
1 819	...	1 310	354	156	2 668	...	2 368	229	71	14	...	7	7	.	.	...
234⁻³	...	...	...	...	916⁻³	...	...	...	...	...⁻³	...	...	...	...	.⁻³	...
259⁻³	...	244⁻³	15⁻³	.⁻³	1 223⁻³	...	704⁻³	519⁻³	.⁻³	...⁻³	...	...⁻³	...⁻³	...⁻³	.⁻³	...
...	...	...	...	...	...	...	...	...	...	...	...	...	...	...	...	...
...	...	...	...	...	...	...	...	...	...	...	...	...	...	...	...	...
168⁻²	...	164⁻²	1⁻²	3⁻²	120⁻²	...	111⁻²	5⁻²	5⁻²	26⁻²	...	25⁻²	.⁻²	1⁻²	.⁻²	...
186⁻²	...	179⁻²	4⁻²	3⁻²	422⁻²	...	380⁻²	8⁻²	34⁻²	43⁻²	...	42⁻²	.⁻²	1⁻²	.⁻²	...
...	...	...	...	...	...	...	...	...	...	...	...	...	...	...	...	...
...	...	...	...	...	...	...	...	...	...	...	...	...	...	...	...	...
68⁻³	...	68⁻³	.⁻³	.⁻³	298⁻³	...	...⁻³	...⁻³	298⁻³	13⁻³	...	7⁻³	4⁻³	2⁻³	.⁻³	...
...	...	...	...	...	...	...	...	...	...	...	...	...	...	...	...	...
298⁻⁶	...	...	...	...	4 108⁻⁶	...	...	...	...	...⁻⁶	...	...	...	...	...⁻⁶	...
...⁻³	...	...⁻³	...⁻³	...⁻³	25⁻³,ᵗ	...	13⁻³	12⁻³	.⁻³	...⁻³	...	...⁻³	...⁻³	...⁻³	...⁻³	...
...⁻³	...	...⁻³	...⁻³	...⁻³	128⁻³,ᵗ	...	73⁻³	55⁻³	.⁻³	...⁻³	...	...⁻³	...⁻³	...⁻³	...⁻³	...
...	...	...	...	...	...	...	...	...	...	...	...	...	...	...	...	...
29⁻⁵,ᵗ	...	24⁻⁵	5⁻⁵	.⁻⁵	90⁻⁵,ᵗ	...	50⁻⁵	40⁻⁵	.⁻⁵	10⁻⁵,ᵗ	...	10⁻⁵	.⁻⁵	.⁻⁵	.⁻⁵	...
2 407	...	2 099	296	11	1 731	...	1 177	485	69	109	...	89	19	.	.	...
2 555	...	2 209	334	12	5 475	...	3 697	1 590	188	152	...	114	38	.	.	...
...	...	...	...	...	...	...	...	...	...	...	...	...	...	...	...	...
...	...	...	...	...	...	...	...	...	...	...	...	...	...	...	...	...
33⁻³	...	33⁻³,ᵗ	...⁻³	.⁻³	...⁻³	...	...⁻³	...⁻³	...⁻³	26⁻³	...	26⁻³,ᵗ	...⁻³	.⁻³	.⁻³	...
33⁻³	...	33⁻³,ᵗ	...⁻³	.⁻³	...⁻³	...	...⁻³	...⁻³	...⁻³	27⁻³	...	27⁻³,ᵗ	...⁻³	.⁻³	.⁻³	...
360⁻⁴	...	262⁻⁴	98⁻⁴	.⁻⁴	564⁻⁴	...	331⁻⁴	211⁻⁴	22⁻⁴	8⁻⁴	...	2⁻⁴	4⁻⁴	2⁻⁴	.⁻⁴	...
450⁻⁴	...	327⁻⁴	123⁻⁴	.⁻⁴	2 037⁻⁴	...	1 194⁻⁴	764⁻⁴	79⁻⁴	38⁻⁴	...	9⁻⁴	29⁻⁴	.⁻⁴	.⁻⁴	...
1 883⁻⁴	...	1 747⁻⁴	136⁻⁴	.⁻⁴	5 647⁻⁴	...	5 084⁻⁴	563⁻⁴	.⁻⁴	713⁻⁴	...	613⁻⁴	100⁻⁴	.⁻⁴	.⁻⁴	...
3 624⁻⁴	...	3 202⁻⁴	422⁻⁴	.⁻⁴	7 370⁻⁴	...	5 951⁻⁴	1 419⁻⁴	.⁻⁴	792⁻⁴	...	680⁻⁴	112⁻⁴	.⁻⁴	.⁻⁴	...
...⁻³	5⁻⁵,ᵗ	3⁻⁵,ᵗ	1⁻⁵	1⁻⁵,ᵗ	12⁻³,ᵗ	39⁻⁵,ᵗ	12⁻³,ᵗ	0⁻³,ᵗ	.⁻³	...⁻³	...⁻⁵	...⁻⁵	...⁻⁵	...⁻⁵	...⁻³	.⁻⁵
...⁻³	25⁻⁵,ᵗ	17⁻⁵,ᵗ	4⁻⁵	4⁻⁵,ᵗ	42⁻³,ᵗ	193⁻⁵,ᵗ	41⁻³,ᵗ	1⁻³,ᵗ	.⁻³	...⁻³	...⁻⁵	...⁻⁵	...⁻⁵	...⁻⁵	...⁻³	.⁻⁵
...⁻³,⁰	...	...⁻³,⁰	...⁻³,⁰	...⁻³,⁰	1 106⁻³,ᵈ	...	746⁻³,ᵈ	278⁻³,ᵈ	82⁻³,ᵈ	...⁻³	...	...⁻³	...⁻³	...⁻³	...⁻³	...
276	...	265	11	.	1 467	...	982	399	86	...	...	...	...	...	...	...
497⁻⁴	173⁻⁷	354⁻⁴	143⁻⁴	.⁻⁴	225⁻⁴	147⁻⁷	160⁻⁴	65⁻⁴	.⁻⁴	10⁻⁴	79⁻⁷	10⁻⁴	.⁻⁴	.⁻⁴	.⁻⁴	.⁻⁷
507⁻⁴	247⁻⁷	361⁻⁴	146⁻⁴	.⁻⁴	1 324⁻⁴	349⁻⁷	942⁻⁴	382⁻⁴	.⁻⁴	12⁻⁴	110⁻⁷	12⁻⁴	.⁻⁴	.⁻⁴	.⁻⁴	.⁻⁷
151⁻⁴	227⁻⁸,ᵗ	182⁻⁸	45⁻⁸	.⁻⁸	75⁻⁴	286⁻⁸,ᵗ	229⁻⁸	57⁻⁸	.⁻⁸	...⁻⁴	...⁻⁸	...⁻⁸	...⁻⁸	...⁻⁸	.⁻⁴	.⁻⁸
339⁻⁴	257⁻⁸,ᵗ	206⁻⁸	51⁻⁸	.⁻⁸	310⁻⁴	979⁻⁸,ᵗ	784⁻⁸	195⁻⁸	.⁻⁸	...⁻⁴	...⁻⁸	...⁻⁸	...⁻⁸	...⁻⁸	.⁻⁴	.⁻⁸
146⁻²	...	131⁻²	15⁻²	.⁻²	79⁻²	...	53⁻²	24⁻²	2⁻²	2⁻²	...	2⁻²	.⁻²	.⁻²	.⁻²	...
150⁻²	...	133⁻²	17⁻²	.⁻²	199⁻²	...	131⁻²,ᵘ	62⁻²,ᵘ	6⁻²,ᵘ	4⁻²	...	4⁻²	.⁻²	.⁻²	.⁻²	...
324⁻⁴	...	276⁻⁴	48⁻⁴	.⁻⁴	556⁻⁴	...	284⁻⁴	272⁻⁴	.⁻⁴	32⁻⁴,ᵗ	...	18⁻⁴	14⁻⁴	.⁻⁴	.⁻⁴	...
564⁻⁴	...	481⁻⁴	83⁻⁴	.⁻⁴	968⁻⁴	...	495⁻⁴	473⁻⁴	.⁻⁴	56⁻⁴,ᵗ	...	31⁻⁴	25⁻⁴	.⁻⁴	.⁻⁴	...

Table A3 • Researchers by sector of employment and field of science (in headcounts, HC, and full-time equivalents, FTE), 2014 or latest available year (continued)

Country		Total					Business enterprise				
		Total	Total*	NSE	SSH	NEC	Total	Total*	NSE	SSH	NEC
Namibia	FTE	...	...	...	...	...	...	...	...	...	...
	HC	748⁻⁴	...	472⁻⁴	162⁻⁴	114⁻⁴	21⁻⁴	...	.⁻⁴	18⁻⁴	3⁻⁴
Nigeria	FTE	5 677⁻⁷,ʰ,ᵗ	...	...	...	...	...⁻⁷	...	...	...	...
	HC	17 624⁻⁷,ʰ,ᵗ,ᵛ	28 533⁻⁹,ᵗ	...⁻⁹	...⁻⁹	...⁻⁹	...⁻⁷	...	...⁻⁹	...⁻⁹	...⁻⁹
Senegal	FTE	4 679⁻⁴	...	1 948⁻⁴	2 622⁻⁴	109⁻⁴	4⁻⁴	...	4⁻⁴	.⁻⁴	.⁻⁴
	HC	8 170⁻⁴	...	3 365⁻⁴	4 663⁻⁴	142⁻⁴	4⁻⁴	...	4⁻⁴	.⁻⁴	.⁻⁴
Seychelles	FTE	13⁻⁹,ᵗ	...	12⁻⁹,ᵗ	...⁻⁹	1⁻⁹	...⁻⁹	...	...⁻⁹	...⁻⁹	...⁻⁹
	HC	14⁻⁹,ᵗ	...	13⁻⁹,ᵗ	...⁻⁹	1⁻⁹	...⁻⁹	...	...⁻⁹	...⁻⁹	...⁻⁹
South Africa	FTE	21 383⁻²	...	...	...	...	4 556⁻²	...	...	...	...
	HC	42 828⁻²	...	...	...	...	6 191⁻²	...	...	...	...
Tanzania, United Republic of	FTE	929⁻¹,ʰ,ᵗ	...	...	...	...	...	...	...	...	...
	HC	3 064⁻¹,ʰ,ᵗ	...	...	...	...	...	...	...	...	...
Togo	FTE	272ʰ	...	167ʰ	103ʰ	2ʰ	...	...	...	...	...
	HC	729ʰ	...	411ʰ	312ʰ	6ʰ	...	...	...	...	...
Uganda	FTE	1 263⁻⁴	...	567⁻⁴	696⁻⁴	.⁻⁴	639⁻⁴	...	167⁻⁴	472⁻⁴	.⁻⁴
	HC	2 823⁻⁴	...	1 444⁻⁴	1 378⁻⁴	.⁻⁴	1 431⁻⁴	...	597⁻⁴	833⁻⁴	.⁻⁴
Zambia	FTE	536⁻⁶	...	...	...	...	26⁻⁶	...	...	...	...
	HC	612⁻⁶	...	...	...	...	35⁻⁶	...	...	...	...
Zimbabwe	FTE	1 305⁻²,ʰ	...	756⁻²,ʰ	481⁻²,ʰ	69⁻²,ʰ	...⁻²	...	...⁻²	...⁻²	...⁻²
	HC	2 739⁻²,ʰ	...	1 574⁻²,ʰ	1 031⁻²,ʰ	134⁻²,ʰ	...⁻²	...	...⁻²	...⁻²	...⁻²

Source: UNESCO Institute for Statistics (UIS), June 2016.

Notes:
- -n   Data refer to n year(s) prior to the reference year
- +n   Data refer to n year(s) in advance of the reference year
- ...   Data not available
- .   Magnitude nil or negligible
- a   Overestimated or based on overestimated data
- b   Including other classes
- c   Including business enterprise sector
- d   Including government sector
- e   Including higher education sector
- f   Including private non-profit sector
- g   Included elsewhere
- h   Excluding business enterprise sector
- i   Excluding government sector
- j   Government sector only
- k   Higher education sector only
- l   Included in business enterprise sector
- m   Included in government sector
- o   Included in higher education sector
- p   Excluding social sciences
- q   Excluding humanities
- r   Excluding most or all capital expenditures
- s   Excluding defence (all or mostly)
- t   Underestimated or partial data
- u   Estimation
- v   Break in series with previous year for which data are available
- w   The sum of the breakdown does not add to the total
- x   University graduates instead of researchers
- y   Provisional data

Please note that, for some countries, the sum of the breakdowns by sector and/or by field of science does not correspond to the total because of changes in the reference year.

Abbreviations:
- NSE   Natural Sciences and Engineering (this includes the following fields: Natural Sciences, Engineering and Technology, Medical and Health Sciences, and Agricultural Sciences)
- SSH   Social Sciences and Humanities (this includes the following fields: Social Sciences, and Humanities)
- NEC   not elsewhere classified
- HC   headcounts
- FTE   full-time equivalents
- Total   Total figure for the latest available year
- Total*   Total figure, if the reference year of the figure presented under 'Total' differs from the reference year of sum of breakdowns (either by sector and/or field of science).

For more information, please refer to the UIS Data Centre (http://data.uis.unesco.org/).

Table A3 | Researchers by sector of employment and field of science, 2014 or latest available year

	Government					Higher education				Private non-profit					Not elsewhere classified (NEC)	
	Total	Total*	NSE	SSH	NEC	Total	Total*	NSE	SSH	NEC	Total	Total*	NSE	SSH	NEC	Total	Total*
	...	...	...	...	...	...	...	...	...	...	...	...	...	...	...	...	...
	280[-4]	...	270[-4]	8[-4]	2[-4]	447[-4]	...	202[-4]	136[-4]	109[-4]	...[-4]	...	...[-4]	...[-4]	...[-4]	.[-4]	...
	1 112[-7,t]	...	...	...	...	4 564[-7,t]	...	...	...	...	...[-7]	...	...	...	...	.[-7]	...
	1 885[-7,t,v]	1 051[-9,t]	810[-9]	99[-9]	142[-9,t]	15 739[-7,t,v]	27 482[-9,t]	...[-9]	...[-9]	...[-9]	...[-7]	...[-9]	...[-9]	...[-9]	...[-9]	.[-7]	...[-9]
	191[-4]	...	100[-4]	24[-4]	67[-4]	4 443[-4]	...	1 804[-4]	2 597[-4]	42[-4]	41[-4]	...	40[-4]	1[-4]	.[-4]	.[-4]	...
	191[-4]	...	100[-4]	24[-4]	67[-4]	7 934[-4]	...	3 221[-4]	4 638[-4]	75[-4]	41[-4]	...	40[-4]	1[-4]	.[-4]	.[-4]	...
	8[-9,t]	...	7[-9,t]	...[-9]	1[-9]	...[-9]	...	...[-9]	...[-9]	...[-9]	5[-9,t]	...	5[-9,t]	...[-9]	.[-9]	.[-9]	...
	8[-9,t]	...	7[-9,t]	...[-9]	1[-9]	...[-9]	...	...[-9]	...[-9]	...[-9]	6[-9,t]	...	6[-9,t]	...[-9]	.[-9]	.[-9]	...
	2 789[-2]	...	...	...	...	13 744[-2]	...	...	...	...	295[-2]	...	...	...	...	...[-2]	...
	3 288[-2]	...	...	...	...	32 955[-2]	...	...	...	...	394[-2]	...	...	...	...	...[-2]	...
	266[-1,t]	...	...	...	...	662[-1,t]	...	...	...	...	...	...	...	...	...	.	...
	324[-1,t,w]	...	...	...	...	2 680[-1,t,w]	...	...	...	...	...	...	...	...	...	.	...
	53	...	53	.	.	219	...	114	103	2	...	...	...	...	...	.	...
	66	...	66	.	.	663	...	345	312	6	...	...	...	...	...	.	...
	265[-4]	...	210[-4]	55[-4]	.[-4]	325[-4]	...	184[-4]	141[-4]	.[-4]	34[-4]	...	7[-4]	28[-4]	.[-4]	.[-4]	...
	404[-4]	...	271[-4]	133[-4]	.[-4]	880[-4]	...	550[-4]	330[-4]	.[-4]	108[-4]	...	26[-4]	82[-4]	.[-4]	.[-4]	...
	142[-6]	...	...	...	...	356[-6]	...	...	...	...	12[-6]	...	...	...	...	.[-6]	...
	198[-6]	...	...	...	...	366[-6]	...	...	...	...	13[-6]	...	...	...	...	.[-6]	...
	135[-2]	...	106[-2]	1[-2]	29[-2]	1 170[-2]	...	651[-2]	480[-2]	40[-2]	...[-2]	...	...[-2]	.[-2]	...[-2]	.[-2]	...
	228[-2]	...	178[-2]	1[-2]	49[-2]	2 511[-2]	...	1 396[-2]	1 030[-2]	85[-2]	...[-2]	...	...[-2]	.[-2]	...[-2]	.[-2]	...

Annex A | Basic statistics on the production of social science research

Table A4 • Student enrolments, by level, total, social science, business and law, and gender for three years circa 2006, 2011 and 2014

	Year	ISCED 5-8 All fields	ISCED 5-8 SSBL	ISCED 5-8 % SSBL	ISCED 5-8 % Female in SSBL	ISCED 8 All fields	ISCED 8 SSBL	ISCED 8 % F SSBL	Source
Arab states									
Algeria	2006	817 968	318 136	38.9	57.6	m	m	m	UIS
	2011	1 188 562	m	m	m	m	m	m	UIS
	2014	1 245 478	434 690	34.9	58.0	m	17 421	50.6	UIS
Bahrain	2006	18 403	9 536	51.8	70.2	5	a	a	UIS
	2011	40 175	m	m	m	m	m	m	UIS
	2014	38 113	20 171	52.9	59.3	135	39	56.4	UIS
Egypt	2006	2 402 860	m	m	m	27 201	m	m	UIS
	2011	2 246 244	m	m	m	35 746	m	m	UIS
	2014	2 544 107	927 254	36.4	34.7	46 729	5 801	28.2	UIS
Jordan	2006	220 103	57 186	26.0	39.8	2 318	308	12.3	UIS
	2011	252 446	78 992	31.3	42.3	2 319	859	33.5	UIS
	2014	m	m	m	m	m	m	m	UIS
Lebanon	2006	173 123	77 103	44.5	52.3	1 574	165	41.2	UIS
	2011	216 851	97 035	44.7	51.2	1 608	516	35.5	UIS
	2014	228 954	100 281	43.8	51.4	3 778	904	43.3	UIS
Oman	2006	55 956	m	m	m	2	m	m	UIS
	2011	89 230	18 862	21.1	51.5	41	n	a	UIS
	2014	84 954	26 480	31.2	54.1	71	2	100.0	UIS
Qatar	2006	10 161	m	m	m	m	m	m	UIS
	2011	15 352	m	m	m	a	m	m	UIS
	2014	25 255	8 469	33.5	62.4	37	7	57.1	UIS
Saudi Arabia	2006	636 445	105 734	16.6	53.2	2 410	184	51.1	UIS
	2011	1 021 288	233 312	22.8	42.2	4 784	290	41.7	UIS
	2014	1 496 730	443 603	29.6	40.0	5 607	442	31.2	UIS
Tunisia	2006	339 363	112 649	33.2	m	m	m	m	UIS
	2011	361 930	m	m	m	m	m	m	UIS
	2014	331 802	87 930	26.5	66.9	11 408	2 686	69.7	UIS
United Arab Emirates	2007	80 296	m	m	m	n	m	m	UIS
	2011	113 648	48 585	42.8	50.0	196	56	67.9	UIS
	2014	143 060	65 243	45.6	47.9	653	267	49.4	UIS
Central and Eastern Europe									
Albania	2006	74 747	m	m	m	m	m	m	UIS
	2011	134 877	46 133	34.2	55.4	2 094	376	65.2	UIS
	2014	173 819	66 117	38.0	56.1	4 553	1 888	59.0	UIS
Belarus	2006	544 328	210 359	38.6	70.2	5 173	1 128	58.8	UIS
	2011	584 846	219 905	37.6	74.0	5 043	928	61.2	UIS
	2014	517 578	176 225	34.0	72.9	5 507	1 325	62.3	UIS
Bosnia and Herzegovina	2006	91 263	m	m	m	m	m	m	UIS
	2011	107 537	41 412	38.5	57.8	m	m	m	UIS
	2014	111 970	37 586	33.6	57.5	709	309	33.0	UIS
Bulgaria	2006	243 464	103 395	42.5	60.3	5 163	1 094	57.4	UIS
	2011	285 265	117 807	41.3	63.3	4 095	1 003	56.8	UIS
	2014	283 294	111 197	39.3	62.0	6 055	1 515	54.3	UIS

Table A4 | Student enrolments, by level, total, social science, business and law, and gender for three years circa 2006, 2011 and 2014

Table A4 • Student enrolments, by level, total, social science, business and law, and gender for three years circa 2006, 2011 and 2014 (continued)

	Year	ISCED 5-8 All fields	ISCED 5-8 SSBL	ISCED 5-8 % SSBL	ISCED 5-8 % Female in SSBL	ISCED 8 All fields	ISCED 8 SSBL	ISCED 8 % F SSBL	Source
Croatia	2006	136 646	55 341	40.5	64.3	1 316	95	55.8	UIS
	2011	153 960	64 967	42.2	65.7	3 451	574	55.6	UIS
	2014	166 061	56 018	33.7	63.8	3 219	595	58.0	UIS
Czech Republic	2006	338 009	93 217	27.6	61.1	22 646	3 682	43.2	UIS
	2011	446 158	144 048	32.3	63.5	26 361	4 449	48.0	UIS
	2014	418 624	125 407	30.0	62.4	25 090	3 728	48.7	UIS
Estonia	2006	68 286	26 605	m	65.4	1 971	419	56.1	UIS
	2011	69 113	23 333	33.8	65.3	2 928	588	59.5	UIS
	2013	64 806	20 705	31.9	65.1	3 044	570	64.0	UIS
Former Yugoslav Republic of Macedonia	2006	48 368	15 758	32.6	60.6	n	n	a	UIS
	2012	63 318	24 080	38.0	56.6	457	300	57.3	UIS
	2013	60 682	22 445	37.0	57.3	226	57	57.9	UIS
Hungary	2006	438 702	182 453	41.6	65.2	7 965	1 640	52.3	UIS
	2011	381 927	152 109	39.8	64.1	7 167	1 500	53.3	UIS
	2014	329 455	117 453	35.7	63.2	7 347	1 508	54.8	UIS
Latvia	2006	131 125	71 049	54.2	66.7	1 809	606	61.4	UIS
	2011	103 856	47 775	46.0	66.6	2 418	757	64.3	UIS
	2014	89 671	35 880	40.0	63.1	2 406	772	56.7	UIS
Lithuania	2006	198 868	83 165	41.8	67.9	2 878	909	62.6	UIS
	2011	187 117	86 883	46.4	66.5	2 974	941	69.2	UIS
	2014	148 389	65 218	44.0	66.0	2 686	707	69.9	UIS
Moldova, Republic of	2006	143 750	m	m	m	1 935	m	m	UIS
	2011	128 988	m	m	m	1 833	m	m	UIS
	2013	122 464	50 779	41.5	m	1 767	731	56.2	UIS
Poland	2006	2 145 687	877 299	40.9	62.4	32 725	7 901	44.6	UIS
	2011	2 080 334	796 379	38.3	64.0	37 492	7 582	50.4	UIS
	2013	1 902 718	678 958	35.7	64.9	42 295	12 499	54.0	UIS
Romania	2006	834 969	417 599	50.0	61.8	21 694	3 800	47.6	UIS
	2011	871 842	427 217	49.0	63.3	27 485	5 150	55.5	UIS
	2014	578 706	214 903	37.1	64.6	19 992	4 035	54.1	UIS
Russian Federation	2006	9 167 277	m	m	m	147 181	m	m	UIS
	2011	8 652 607	m	m	m	161 855	m	m	UIS
	2014	6 995 732	m	m	m	136 574	39 278	50.9	UIS
Serbia	2011	228 531	86 914	38.0	59.8	5 206	747	56.2	UIS
	2014	242 848	83 806	34.5	60.0	7 721	1 064	60.2	UIS
Slovakia	2006	197 943	56 056	28.3	63.1	10 739	2 125	44.7	UIS
	2011	226 305	70 071	31.0	65.9	12 182	2 589	49.7	UIS
	2014	197 854	60 856	30.8	65.3	10 009	2 135	48.1	UIS
Slovenia	2006	114 794	49 903	43.5	65.9	1 057	167	52.7	UIS
	2011	107 134	37 134	34.7	67.7	3 985	888	58.0	UIS
	2014	90 622	28 536	31.5	66.8	3 016	485	52.8	UIS
Turkey	2006	2 342 898	1 110 426	47.4	44.8	32 575	7 914	34.2	UIS
	2011	3 817 086	2 089 795	54.7	45.7	43 405	10 827	40.7	UIS
	2013	4 975 690	2 704 948	54.4	45.6	80 494	15 870	38.3	UIS

Table A4 • Student enrolments, by level, total, social science, business and law, and gender for three years circa 2006, 2011 and 2014 (continued)

	Year	ISCED 5-8 All fields	ISCED 5-8 SSBL	ISCED 5-8 % SSBL	ISCED 5-8 % Female in SSBL	ISCED 8 All fields	ISCED 8 SSBL	ISCED 8 % F SSBL	Source
Ukraine	2006	2 740 342	1 157 556	42.2	m	31 181	9 371	m	UIS
	2011	2 566 279	983 503	38.3	64.5	36 825	12 013	67.7	UIS
	2014	2 146 028	692 887	32.3	63.1	33 959	10 472	68.6	UIS
Central Asia									
Armenia	2006	127 499	m	m	m	1 562	m	m	UIS
	2011	141 455	m	m	m	1 289	m	m	UIS
	2014	113 090	m	m	m	1 277	498	58.4	UIS
Azerbaijan	2006	181 293	m	m	m	1 559	m	m	UIS
	2011	181 057	50 579	27.9	31.5	877	227	19.4	UIS
	2014	195 401	53 812	27.5	37.5	2 496	1 188	51.5	UIS
Georgia	2006	144 991	43 924	30.3	44.2	1 112	231	45.0	UIS
	2011	110 557	m	m	m	3 825	m	m	UIS
	2014	120 923	54 145	44.8	54.9	3 213	1 304	55.0	UIS
Kazakhstan	2006	879 623	m	m	m	5 021	m	m	UIS
	2011	794 557	m	m	m	980	m	m	UIS
	2014	727 401	201 362	27.7	57.1	1 892	490	58.6	UIS
Kyrgyzstan	2006	233 463	80 468	34.5	52.8	2 368	909	53.4	UIS
	2011	258 869	110 614	42.7	56.2	2 299	681	59.9	UIS
	2014	267 920	x	m	m	2 286	685	66.0	UIS
Mongolia	2006	138 019	54 401	39.4	64.5	1 980	485	59.6	UIS
	2011	171 165	58 649	34.3	64.6	2 476	698	54.0	UIS
	2014	175 205	60 160	34.3	64.5	3 407	983	55.6	UIS
Tajikistan	2006	165 139	m	m	m	980	265	m	UIS
	2011	191 198	m	m	m	1 606	542	26.6	UIS
	2014	209 170	45 098	21.6	26.6	1 778	570	34.4	UIS
Uzbekistan	2006	280 837	59 001	21.0	23.8	2 163	337	43.6	UIS
	2014	m	m	m	m	m	m	m	UIS
East Asia and the Pacific									
Australia	2006	1 040 153	394 673	37.9	54.5	40 417	9 264	53.9	UIS
	2011	1 324 257	498 795	37.7	55.3	49 973	11 283	54.6	UIS
	2014	1 453 521	507 975	34.9	55.2	56 360	11 846	56.5	UIS
Brunei Darussalam	2006	5 094	707	13.9	62.7	16	a	a	UIS
	2011	6 626	1 405	21.2	64.7	102	23	17.4	UIS
	2014	11 292	2 825	25.0	66.4	212	28	28.6	UIS
China	2006	23 360 535	m	m	m	m	m	m	UIS
	2011	31 308 378	m	m	m	m	m	m	UIS
	2014	41 924 198	m	m	m	306 651	m	m	UIS
China, Hong Kong Special Administrative Region	2006	155 324	56 194	36.2	59.4	5 508	894	53.6	UIS
	2011	270 512	m	m	m	8 031	m	m	UIS
	2014	304 886	120 259	39.4	56.4	8 426	1 965	41.2	UIS
China, Macao Special Administrative Region	2006	23 291	16 137	69.3	40.1	492	414	22.9	UIS
	2011	30 519	19 044	62.4	48.0	648	416	26.9	UIS
	2014	29 521	14 961	50.7	55.2	1 013	515	46.0	UIS

Table A4 • Student enrolments, by level, total, social science, business and law, and gender for three years circa 2006, 2011 and 2014 (continued)

	Year	ISCED 5-8 All fields	ISCED 5-8 SSBL	ISCED 5-8 % SSBL	ISCED 5-8 % Female in SSBL	ISCED 8 All fields	ISCED 8 SSBL	ISCED 8 % F SSBL	Source
Indonesia	2006	3 657 429	m	m	m	64 600	m	m	UIS
	2011	5 364 301	2 722 070	50.7	m	m	m	m	UIS
	2014	6 463 297	2 096 205	32.4	46.8	20 592	6 567	43.2	UIS
Japan	2006	4 084 861	1 198 169	29.3	35.5	75 028	9 927	36.4	UIS
	2011	3 880 544	1 119 174	28.8	35.9	74 606	9 195	40.1	UIS
	2013	3 862 749	1 081 083	28.0	36.8	74 480	8 819	39.9	UIS
Korea, Republic of	2006	3 204 036	691 884	21.6	35.6	43 443	8 449	28.3	UIS
	2011	3 356 011	749 565	22.3	39.2	59 699	10 994	33.0	UIS
	2013	3 342 264	739 829	22.1	40.0	65 938	11 966	34.3	UIS
Malaysia	2006	737 267	201 040	27.3	62.8	m	2 248	54.2	UIS
	2011	1 036 354	347 553	33.5	63.8	m	10 790	47.4	UIS
	2014	860 144	290 107	33.7	63.2	34 187	10 060	41.3	UIS
Myanmar	2007	507 660	m	m	m	3 769	m	m	UIS
	2011	659 510	229 535	34.8	58.6	2 971	449	79.7	UIS
New Zealand	2006	237 784	82 690	34.8	56.2	5 325	1 089	55.0	UIS
	2011	262 230	90 370	34.5	56.5	8 073	1 734	59.3	UIS
	2014	260 847	88 776	34.0	57.2	8 666	1 867	58.7	UIS
Philippines	2006	2 483 988	m	m	m	8 939	m	m	UIS
	2011	2 951 195	941 629	31.9	63.2	12 841	3 419	53.1	UIS
	2014	3 563 396	1 149 499	32.3	65.2	21 756	5 366	53.9	UIS
Singapore	2006	m	m	m	m	m	m	m	UIS
	2011	236 891	91 220	38.5	57.8	7 794	787	52.4	UIS
	2013	255 348	104 163	40.8	56.6	8 515	934	50.1	UIS
Thailand	2006	2 338 572	m	m	m	11 462	m	m	UIS
	2011	2 497 323	1 337 273	53.5	58.1	22 823	5 819	46.1	UIS
	2014	2 433 140	944 442	38.8	60.6	25 467	6 416	44.6	UIS
Viet Nam	2006	1 427 046	m	m	m	m	m	m	UIS
	2011	2 229 494	770 984	34.6	59.1	4 683	1 598	35.7	UIS
	2014	2 692 124	m	m	m	8 870	4 642	39.3	UIS
Latin America and the Caribbean									
Argentina	2006	2 202 032	872 820	39.6	58.9	10 880	2 554	49.3	UIS
	2011	2 660 514	980 851	36.9	59.9	21 246	7 719	52.0	UIS
	2013	2 768 211	980 079	35.4	59.4	24 595	9 292	54.5	UIS
Barbados	2007	11 405	m	m	m	62	11	27.3	UIS
	2011	12 421	6 894	m	70.9	133	13	69.2	UIS
	2014	m	m	m	m	m	m	m	UIS
Brazil	2007	5 272 877	2 133 113	40.5	52.4	49 668	n	a	UIS
	2011	6 929 324	m	m	m	71 890	m	m	UIS
	2013	7 541 112	m	m	m	88 575	m	m	UIS
Chile	2006	661 142	170 129	25.7	51.8	2 753	266	41.0	UIS
	2011	1 061 527	271 553	25.6	55.4	3 955	483	46.8	UIS
	2014	1 205 182	311 592	25.9	56.2	4 775	682	45.4	UIS
Colombia	2006	1 314 972	563 394	42.8	56.6	1 131	251	27.9	UIS
	2011	1 849 466	842 179	45.5	55.2	2 784	485	41.9	UIS
	2014	2 137 795	1 022 094	47.8	61.5	4 257	814	42.0	UIS

Annex A | Basic statistics on the production of social science research

Table A4 • Student enrolments, by level, total, social science, business and law, and gender for three years circa 2006, 2011 and 2014 (continued)

	Year	ISCED 5-8 All fields	ISCED 5-8 SSBL	ISCED 5-8 % SSBL	ISCED 5-8 % Female in SSBL	ISCED 8 All fields	ISCED 8 SSBL	ISCED 8 % F SSBL	Source
Cuba	2006	681 629	m	m	m	4 129	m	m	UIS
	2011	664 775	204 779	30.8	63.9	5 776	3 029	39.4	UIS
	2014	301 773	m	m	m	4 576	m	m	UIS
Ecuador	2006	m	m	m	m	m	m	m	UIS
	2012	572 721	243 479	42.5	61.2	236	188	36.7	UIS
	2013	586 105	260 472	44.4	m	242	198	m	UIS
El Salvador	2006	124 956	58 828	47.1	57.3	10	n	a	UIS
	2011	160 374	64 203	40.0	58.3	179	n	a	UIS
	2014	176 293	69 297	39.3	57.9	70	48	50.0	UIS
Honduras	2012	174 935	71 110	40.6	60.5	30	30	36.7	UIS
	2014	185 876	73 866	39.7	59.7	98	86	57.0	UIS
Mexico	2006	2 446 726	968 044	39.6	56.9	13 458	3 308	41.1	UIS
	2011	2 981 313	1 247 139	41.8	57.3	23 122	5 922	45.6	UIS
	2014	3 419 391	1 372 528	40.1	56.9	29 355	7 528	46.0	UIS
Panama	2006	130 838	51 861	39.6	65.3	112	57	68.4	UIS
	2011	133 497	49 235	36.9	64.0	87	45	44.4	UIS
	2013	124 375	43 872	35.3	64.0	177	82	69.5	UIS
North America and Western Europe									
Austria	2006	253 139	88 589	35.0	55.3	16 819	6 379	48.5	UIS
	2011	361 797	132 203	36.5	55.4	26 031	9 966	50.8	UIS
	2014	421 225	142 678	33.9	56.1	24 579	8 163	50.2	UIS
Belgium	2006	394 427	108 352	27.5	53.3	7 482	1 465	43.8	UIS
	2011	462 419	136 096	29.4	54.0	13 323	2 821	50.0	UIS
	2014	495 910	157 141	31.7	54.3	15 604	3 260	52.0	UIS
Canada	2006	m	m	m	m	36 705	8 256	58.0	UIS
	2011	m	m	m	m	47 616	11 025	61.0	UIS
	2014	m	m	m	m	m	m	m	UIS
Cyprus	2006	20 587	9 763	47.4	47.8	302	64	48.4	UIS
	2011	32 118	15 603	48.6	43.1	589	112	59.8	UIS
	2014	33 674	15 014	44.6	54.4	929	219	59.4	UIS
Denmark	2006	228 893	67 618	29.5	50.4	4 751	610	48.9	UIS
	2011	258 932	87 072	33.6	52.8	8 857	1 207	48.9	UIS
	2014	301 399	98 190	32.6	53.9	9 869	1 294	56.0	UIS
Finland	2006	308 966	69 459	22.5	62.7	22 145	4 994	56.9	UIS
	2011	308 336	70 978	23.0	59.5	20 895	4 469	58.9	UIS
	2014	306 080	72 566	23.7	59.3	20 283	4 367	59.2	UIS
France	2006	2 201 201	759 984	34.5	61.4	69 831	21 423	48.7	UIS
	2011	2 259 448	828 003	36.6	60.1	71 121	20 222	51.1	UIS
	2014	2 388 880	903 013	37.8	58.9	68 938	18 197	51.6	UIS
Germany	2006	m	m	m	m	m	m	m	UIS
	2011	m	m	m	m	200 400	42 100	45.1	UIS
	2014	2 912 203	859 367	29.5	53.3	214 700	39 300	47.3	UIS
Greece	2006	653 003	m	m	m	22 483	m	m	UIS
	2011	660 741	209 362	31.7	52.3	22 628	5 017	48.3	UIS
	2013	659 284	210 884	32.0	52.7	23 011	4 604	49.4	UIS

Table A4 • Student enrolments, by level, total, social science, business and law, and gender for three years circa 2006, 2011 and 2014 (continued)

	Year	ISCED 5-8 All fields	ISCED 5-8 SSBL	ISCED 5-8 % SSBL	ISCED 5-8 % Female in SSBL	ISCED 8 All fields	ISCED 8 SSBL	ISCED 8 % F SSBL	Source
Iceland	2006	15 721	5 969	38.0	58.8	156	27	44.4	UIS
	2011	18 845	6 797	36.1	59.7	478	86	61.6	UIS
	2014	m	m	m	m	m	m	m	UIS
Ireland	2006	186 044	m	m	m	5 146	m	m	UIS
	2011	196 321	48 695	24.8	52.3	8 658	1 400	61.5	UIS
	2013	199 428	49 920	25.0	51.2	8 171	1 345	59.7	UIS
Israel	2006	310 014	119 923	38.7	55.7	9 715	1 609	57.5	UIS
	2011	365 665	139 005	38.0	56.8	10 590	1 750	58.6	UIS
	2014	376 952	134 472	35.7	58.5	10 719	2 081	57.3	UIS
Italy	2006	2 029 023	741 190	36.5	57.2	38 262	7 535	51.7	UIS
	2011	1 967 569	684 804	34.8	57.7	36 313	6 899	54.1	UIS
	2013	1 872 693	638 242	34.1	57.8	34 928	6 139	53.8	UIS
Liechtenstein	2006	636	m	m	m	n	m	m	UIS
	2011	984	742	75.4	28.3	78	46	21.7	UIS
	2014	830	605	72.9	28.8	119	67	25.4	UIS
Luxembourg	2006	2 692	1 218	45.2	m	m	m	m	UIS
	2012	6 085	2 820	46.3	50.9	390	111	61.3	UIS
Malta	2006	8 922	3 335	37.4	56.6	64	m	m	UIS
	2011	11 491	3 759	32.7	57.8	73	11	36.4	UIS
	2014	12 610	4 329	34.3	57.6	95	12	50.0	UIS
Netherlands	2006	579 622	217 163	37.5	46.8	7 475	m	m	UIS
	2011	780 014	306 558	39.3	47.9	11 029	2 832	56.8	UIS
	2014	m	m	m	m	13 849	m	m	UIS
Norway	2006	214 711	m	m	m	5 047	m	m	UIS
	2011	229 743	72 951	31.8	57.8	8 112	1 370	55.5	UIS
	2014	264 207	80 198	30.4	58.3	7 327	1 298	56.4	UIS
Portugal	2006	367 312	115 808	31.5	59.4	20 512	6 189	54.5	UIS
	2011	396 268	126 102	31.8	57.8	18 370	4 222	55.6	UIS
	2014	362 200	114 619	31.6	58.5	20 245	4 951	52.9	UIS
Spain	2006	1 789 254	570 202	31.9	58.8	77 056	18 422	49.7	UIS
	2011	1 950 482	608 467	31.2	58.1	68 865	15 306	50.1	UIS
	2014	1 982 162	603 759	30.5	56.8	24 317	4 993	49.1	UIS
Sweden	2006	422 614	110 665	26.2	61.0	21 377	2 651	51.2	UIS
	2011	463 530	125 130	27.0	61.3	20 642	2 542	53.9	UIS
	2014	429 444	114 568	26.7	62.8	21 590	2 680	54.9	UIS
Switzerland	2006	204 999	76 022	37.1	46.3	17 234	4 531	39.8	UIS
	2011	257 696	92 129	35.8	47.7	20 953	5 138	44.1	UIS
	2014	289 570	101 071	34.9	49.0	23 237	5 559	47.6	UIS
United Kingdom of Great Britain and Northern Ireland	2006	2 336 111	630 423	27.0	55.2	94 180	19 653	51.3	UIS
	2011	2 492 284	691 880	27.8	54.8	90 028	19 495	54.6	UIS
	2014	2 352 933	625 719	26.6	52.8	111 395	19 431	47.6	UIS
United States of America	2006	17 487 475	m	m	m	388 685	m	m	UIS
	2011	21 016 126	5 819 228	27.7	54.9	492 345	101 815	55.5	UIS
	2014	19 700 221	5 418 518	27.5	54.3	391 915	78 054	54.0	UIS

Annex A | Basic statistics on the production of social science research

Table A4 • **Student enrolments, by level, total, social science, business and law, and gender for three years circa 2006, 2011 and 2014** (continued)

	Year	ISCED 5-8 All fields	ISCED 5-8 SSBL	ISCED 5-8 % SSBL	ISCED 5-8 % Female in SSBL	ISCED 8 All fields	ISCED 8 SSBL	ISCED 8 % F SSBL	Source
South and West Asia									
Bangladesh	2006	1 053 566	m	m	m	3 183	m	m	UIS
	2011	2 008 337	968 951	48.2	45.0	7 090	1 949	49.4	UIS
	2014	2 068 355	908 960	43.9	42.8	7 092	1 886	49.4	UIS
India	2006	12 852 684	m	m	m	m	m	m	UIS
	2011	26 650 953	m	m	m	m	m	m	UIS
	2013	28 175 135	15 048 548	53.4	48.5	97 630	21 012	45.7	UIS
Iran, Islamic Republic of	2006	2 398 811	645 824	26.9	55.7	19 309	2 387	21.5	UIS
	2011	4 117 208	1 319 252	32.0	56.5	39 525	4 636	24.8	UIS
	2014	4 685 386	1 513 616	32.3	52.6	73 437	10 805	29.8	UIS
Nepal	2006	202 076	72 731	36.0	34.1	246	51	7.8	UIS
	2011	385 454	123 855	32.1	39.0	508	61	11.5	UIS
	2014	458 621	156 728	34.2	m	183	n	m	UIS
Sri Lanka	2006	m	m	m	m	m	m	m	UIS
	2011	242 300	47 539	19.6	55.3	2 858	69	27.5	UIS
	2014	323 866	91 435	28.2	46.8	m	86	45.3	UIS
Sub-Saharan Africa									
Botswana	2006	21 738	m	m	m	m	m	m	UIS
	2011	37 859	m	m	m	m	m	m	UIS
	2014	60 583	23 408	38.6	65.7	208	16	37.5	UIS
Burkina Faso	2006	30 472	16 211	53.2	30.8	n	m	m	UIS
	2011	60 998	32 397	53.1	39.2	2 163	283	36.0	UIS
	2013	74 276	37 805	50.9	39.3	m	m	m	UIS
Cabo Verde	2006	4 567	m	m	m	m	m	m	UIS
	2011	11 769	6 551	55.7	m	m	m	m	UIS
	2014	13 397	6 839	51.0	67.1	10	10	50.0	UIS
Cameroon	2006	120 298	77 588	64.5	m	2 169	655	m	UIS
	2011	244 233	84 741	m	42.7	m	m	m	UIS
	2014	m	m	m	m	m	m	m	UIS
Congo	2006	m	m	m	m	m	m	m	UIS
	2011	33 928	m	m	m	389	m	m	UIS
	2013	37 037	25 601	69.1	47.5	261	33	3.0	UIS
Côte d'Ivoire	2007	156 772	75 363	48.1	40.8	m	m	m	UIS
	2011	66 232	36 136	54.6	54.9	284	m	m	UIS
	2014	176 504	88 974	50.4	45.1	4 493	1 259	24.5	UIS
Ethiopia	2005	191 212	72 064	37.7	29.3	47	n	a	UIS
	2011	632 344	m	m	m	789	m	m	UIS
	2014	757 175	m	m	m	1 983	831	6.7	UIS
Ghana	2006	110 184	m	m	m	123	m	m	UIS
	2011	285 862	144 444	50.5	39.1	721	280	26.1	UIS
	2014	402 142	144 052	35.8	42.1	1 221	440	25.7	UIS
Madagascar	2006	49 680	28 667	57.7	49.8	2 351	773	49.9	UIS
	2011	85 548	48 258	56.4	50.6	m	m	m	UIS
	2013	97 056	54 230	55.9	51.1	761	34	44.1	UIS

Table A4 • **Student enrolments, by level, total, social science, business and law, and gender for three years circa 2006, 2011 and 2014** (continued)

	Year	ISCED 5-8 All fields	ISCED 5-8 SSBL	ISCED 5-8 % SSBL	ISCED 5-8 % Female in SSBL	ISCED 8 All fields	ISCED 8 SSBL	ISCED 8 % F SSBL	Source
Mali	2006	m	m	m	m	m	m	m	UIS
	2011	87 653	57 183	65.2	32.5	343	130	9.2	UIS
	2014	m	m	m	m	m	m	m	UIS
Mauritius	2006	22 221	m	m	m	260	m	m	UIS
	2011	35 906	18 643	51.9	57.9	92	52	21.2	UIS
	2014	40 457	22 720	56.2	57.9	280	210	41.0	UIS
Mozambique	2005	28 298	12 424	43.9	40.9	a	a	a	UIS
	2011	113 464	50 192	44.2	47.4	m	m	m	UIS
	2014	157 431	71 142	45.2	50.3	120	48	18.8	UIS
Niger	2006	11 208	4 335	38.7	29.7	n	n	a	UIS
	2011	18 328	10 538	57.5	29.1	285	43	2.3	UIS
	2014	m	m	m	m	m	m	m	UIS
South Africa	2006	m	m	m	m	m	m	m	UIS
	2012	1 005 721	504 119	50.1	59.5	14 020	4 119	45.7	UIS
	2013	1 035 594	517 433	50.0	59.3	16 067	4 835	45.3	UIS

Source: UIS online Data Centre (*http://stats.uis.unesco.org*)

Notes:

1. symbols used:

* Population data come from the UN Population Division

m = data missing or not available

n = quantity nil

a = not applicable

2. UIS = UNESCO Institute for Statistics

SSBL: Social Science, Business and Law

ISCED 5–8 corresponds to tertiary education, which comprises ISCED 5, 6, 7 and 8, according to the International Standard Classification of Education (ISCED) 2011.

ISCED 5 corresponds to short-cycle tertiary education.

ISCED 6 corresponds to Bachelor's or equivalent programmes.

ISCED 7 corresponds to Master's or equivalent programmes.

ISCED 8 corresponds to Doctoral or equivalent programmes.

Annex A | Basic statistics on the production of social science research

Table A5 • Student graduation, by level, total, social science, business and law, and gender, selected years circa 2001 2006 and 2011

	Year	ISCED 5-8 All fields	ISCED 5-8 SSBL	ISCED 5-8 % SSBL	ISCED 5-8 % Females in SSBL	ISCED 8 All fields	ISCED 8 SSBL	ISCED 8 Number of female graduates from SSBL	Population*	Source
Arab states										
Algeria	2007	120 168	56 525	47.0	62.0	m	m	m	34 261 971	UIS
	2011	208 536	85 531	41.0	66.8	m	m	m	36 717 132	UIS
	2014	311 511	123 264	39.6	63.8	m	m	m	38 934 334	UIS
Bahrain	2006	2 881	1 193	41.4	70.8	n	a	a	940 808	UIS
	2011	10 497	m	m	m	m	m	m	1 306 014	UIS
	2014	5 466	3 098	56.7	62.0	13	4	1	1 361 930	UIS
Egypt	2006	m	m	m	m	m	m	m	76 274 285	UIS
	2012	510 390	m	m	m	6 150	m	m	85 660 902	UIS
	2014	547 925	182 328	33.3	38.0	6 877	811	222	89 579 670	UIS
Jordan	2006	47 110	m	m	m	295	4	n	5 530 218	UIS
	2011	60 686	9 405	28.1	42.5	473	69	19	6 760 371	UIS
	2014	m	m	m	m	m	m	m	7 416 083	UIS
Lebanon	2006	30 462	14 845	48.7	52.4	911	66	35	4 057 041	UIS
	2011	34 007	15 811	46.5	51.5	171	56	14	4 591 698	UIS
	2014	m	m	m	m	m	m	m	5 612 096	UIS
Oman	2007	9 129	1 562	17.1	63.6	n	n	n	2 593 750	UIS
	2010	13 734	3 377	24.6	55.6	n	n	n	2 943 747	UIS
	2014	18 462	5 555	m	53.0	m	n	n	4 236 057	UIS
Palestine	2007	21 851	7 226	33.1	44.9	a	a	a	3 754 693	UIS
	2011	31 702	9 778	30.8	47.4	1	a	a	4 181 135	UIS
	2014	37 383	13 056	34.9	51.1	n	n	n	4 542 059	UIS
Qatar	2007	1 484	731	m	60.1	a	a	a	1 178 955	UIS
	2011	2 100	716	34.1	68.9	a	a	a	1 905 437	UIS
	2014	2 569	999	38.9	69.7	a	a	a	2 172 065	UIS
Saudi Arabia	2006	94 837	16 859	17.8	55.1	228	18	17	25 419 994	UIS
	2011	120 780	20 005	16.6	54.6	394	31	21	28 788 438	UIS
	2014	148 841	40 484	27.2	43.0	377	18	4	30 886 545	UIS
Tunisia	2006	56 559	18 865	33.4	m	368	m	m	10 196 441	UIS
	2011	77 301	m	m	m	959	m	m	10 758 870	UIS
	2014	65 332	16 528	25.3	72.4	825	146	87	11 130 154	UIS
United Arab Emirates	2007	13 060	m	m	m	n	m	m	6 010 100	UIS
	2011	19 366	9 828	50.7	53.3	5	n	n	8 734 722	UIS
	2014	28 553	13 937	48.8	44.3	31	n	n	9 086 139	UIS
Central and Eastern Europe										
Albania	2006	7 724	m	m	m	m	m	m	3 050 741	UIS
	2011	23 046	9 817	42.6	59.7	28	n	n	2 886 010	UIS
	2014	29 191	11 908	40.8	66.0	57	15	8	2 889 676	UIS
Belarus	2006	105 273	39 985	38.0	m	1 325	265	m	9 594 233	UIS
	2011	122 134	46 111	37.8	75.5	912	218	146	9 487 674	UIS
	2014	134 934	52 936	39.2	76.3	1 216	227	155	9 500 422	UIS

Table A5 • **Student graduation, by level, total, social science, business and law, and gender, selected years circa 2001 2006 and 2011** (continued)

	Year	ISCED 5-8 All fields	ISCED 5-8 SSBL	ISCED 5-8 % SSBL	ISCED 5-8 % Females in SSBL	ISCED 8 All fields	ISCED 8 SSBL	ISCED 8 Number of female graduates from SSBL	Population*	Source
Bosnia and Herzegovina	2007	12 763	m	m	m	136	m	m	3 840 418	UIS
	2011	19 680	m	m	m	205	m	m	3 832 310	UIS
	2014	21 368	8 531	39.9	59.9	81	8	4	3 817 554	UIS
Bulgaria	2007	45 353	21 700	47.8	64.9	583	99	57	7 568 378	UIS
	2011	64 043	33 459	52.2	67.3	638	155	95	7 355 231	UIS
	2014	63 373	31 134	49.1	65.9	1 363	320	182	7 201 308	UIS
Croatia	2006	20 687	8 153	39.4	68.1	439	67	36	4 368 518	UIS
	2011	38 789	m	m	m	1 072	m	m	4 302 073	UIS
	2014	m	m	m	m	m	m	m	4 255 853	UIS
Czech Republic	2006	69 312	19 914	28.6	64.3	2 023	290	120	10 271 476	UIS
	2011	107 118	36 772	34.3	68.5	2 462	396	183	10 533 985	UIS
	2014	104 671	34 177	32.7	67.1	2 484	371	184	10 542 666	UIS
Estonia	2006	11 546	4 226	36.6	74.2	143	18	7	1 349 369	UIS
	2011	11 828	4 316	36.5	73.1	250	50	28	1 328 068	UIS
	2014	10 190	3 174	31.1	74.2	213	27	17	1 316 203	UIS
Former Yugoslav Republic of Macedonia	2006	6 501	1 746	26.9	68.6	85	19	9	2 047 330	UIS
	2011	11 293	4 640	41.1	57.7	197	83	39	2 065 888	UIS
	2013	11 363	4 804	42.3	60.9	219	90	54	2 072 543	UIS
Hungary	2006	72 154	30 833	42.7	69.5	1 012	165	86	10 078 461	UIS
	2011	67 857	27 661	40.5	69.7	1 234	211	115	9 988 846	UIS
	2014	72 465	28 190	38.9	68.9	1 154	187	104	9 889 540	UIS
Latvia	2006	26 414	14 792	56.0	72.0	106	24	13	2 199 105	UIS
	2011	24 853	11 809	47.5	73.4	297	56	47	2 063 661	UIS
	2014	17 345	7 205	41.5	70.5	264	61	43	1 989 354	UIS
Lithuania	2006	43 343	17 739	40.9	73.5	326	77	52	3 305 529	UIS
	2011	43 419	20 426	47.0	72.6	353	104	67	3 070 593	UIS
	2013	39 265	16 860	42.9	71.7	441	108	76	2 963 810	UIS
Moldova, Republic of	2006	22 998	m	m	m	368	m	m	3 581 110	UIS
	2011	36 026	m	m	m	524	m	m	3 559 541	UIS
	2013	34 806	14 241	40.9	65.6	488	200	118	3 557 634	UIS
Poland	2006	504 051	214 939	42.6	69.1	5 917	745	377	38 478 763	UIS
	2011	648 045	262 443	40.5	68.9	3 055	m	m	38 594 217	UIS
	2014	557 769	203 947	36.6	69.4	3 376	682	363	38 619 974	UIS
Romania	2006	174 821	84 205	48.2	63.2	3 180	619	294	21 205 977	UIS
	2011	259 634	141 843	54.6	65.8	5 615	924	537	20 111 664	UIS
	2014	153 515	63 723	41.5	66.5	3 777	781	440	19 651 554	UIS
Russian Federation	2006	1 870 973	847 023	45.3	m	34 978	m	m	143 338 407	UIS
	2011	2 075 040	m	m	m	35 022	m	m	143 211 476	UIS
	2014	m	m	m	m	m	m	m	143 429 435	UIS
Serbia	2007	31 473	10 213	32.5	61.1	401	77	29	7 365 507	UIS
	2011	46 162	15 811	34.3	60.5	596	119	45	7 216 649	UIS
	2014	50 728	17 947	35.4	59.6	741	138	58	m	UIS

Annex A | Basic statistics on the production of social science research

Table A5 • Student graduation, by level, total, social science, business and law, and gender, selected years circa 2001 2006 and 2011 (continued)

	Year	ISCED 5-8 All fields	ISCED 5-8 SSBL	ISCED 5-8 % SSBL	ISCED 5-8 % Females in SSBL	ISCED 8 All fields	ISCED 8 SSBL	ISCED 8 Number of female graduates from SSBL	Population*	Source
Slovakia	2006	40 190	11 026	27.4	63.8	1 218	202	105	5 387 734	UIS
	2011	74 556	25 375	34.0	69.1	1 672	355	193	5 411 377	UIS
	2013	70 031	22 378	32.0	68.5	2 119	453	239	5 419 288	UIS
Slovenia	2006	17 145	8 504	49.6	67.7	395	76	41	2 005 566	UIS
	2011	20 461	8 945	43.7	70.8	523	89	48	2 059 023	UIS
	2014	m	m	m	m	m	m	m	2 066 068	UIS
Turkey	2006	373 375	140 672	37.7	47.0	2 594	493	185	68 704 721	UIS
	2011	534 055	244 465	45.8	47.3	4 653	941	388	73 517 002	UIS
	2014	733 237	334 068	45.6	48.0	4 516	911	424	77 523 788	UIS
Ukraine	2006	521 772	230 567	44.2	m	6 717	1 816	m	46 502 718	UIS
	2011	670 080	283 693	42.3	m	8 918	2 737	1 773	45 477 690	UIS
	2014	593 803	237 973	40.1	63.9	9 081	2 801	1 807	45 002 497	UIS
Central Asia										
Armenia	2006	23 741	m	m	m	389	m	m	3 002 161	UIS
	2011	37 466	m	m	m	453	m	m	2 967 984	UIS
	2014	36 335	7 326	20.2	52.6	247	99	26	3 006 154	UIS
Azerbaijan	2006	m	m	m	m	m	m	m	8 666 071	UIS
	2011	47 345	13 566	28.7	26.2	468	107	24	9 235 085	UIS
	2014	47 524	14 327	30.1	38.9	138	50	20	m	UIS
Georgia	2006	28 733	6 338	22.1	44.3	604	144	17	4 429 186	UIS
	2011	26 589	m	m	m	917	m	m	4 196 401	UIS
	2014	20 408	9 035	44.3	62.7	450	113	62	4 034 774	UIS
Kazakhstan	2006	m	m	m	m	m	m	m	15 603 072	UIS
	2011	m	m	m	m	m	m	m	16 554 305	UIS
	2014	238 013	93 819	39.4	57.0	373	146	81	17 371 621	UIS
Kyrgyzstan	2006	32 577	14 070	43.2	51.0	566	179	98	5 166 644	UIS
	2011	45 420	20 212	44.5	57.4	592	191	126	5 553 827	UIS
	2013	50 228	12 605	25.1	78.3	590	146	90	5 745 698	UIS
Mongolia	2006	23 628	10 210	43.2	67.1	111	17	6	2 558 484	UIS
	2011	35 847	14 544	40.6	64.6	94	17	10	2 759 074	UIS
	2014	33 850	13 492	39.9	66.6	118	29	16	2 909 871	UIS
Tajikistan	2006	m	m	m	m	204	52	m	6 949 566	UIS
	2012	37 800	8 212	21.7	m	331	110	m	7 930 929	UIS
	2014	40 175	8 859	22.1	m	382	92	m	8 295 840	UIS
Uzbekistan	2006	58 697	13 209	22.5	25.9	852	181	57	26 242 947	UIS
	2011	77 217	15 006	19.4	23.0	838	296	138	28 158 395	UIS
	2014	m	m	m	m	m	m	m	29 469 913	UIS
East Asia and the Pacific										
Australia	2006	282 854	122 812	42.4	55.1	5 559	1 207	628	20 606 228	UIS
	2011	386 625	177 788	45.1	56.0	6 547	1 411	767	22 542 371	UIS
	2014	422 842	179 841	42.5	56.3	8 400	1 892	1 049	23 622 353	UIS

Table A5 | *Student graduation, by level, total, social science, business and law, and gender, selected years circa 2001, 2006 and 2011*

Table A5 • Student graduation, by level, total, social science, business and law, and gender, selected years circa 2001 2006 and 2011 (continued)

	Year	ISCED 5-8 All fields	ISCED 5-8 SSBL	ISCED 5-8 % SSBL	ISCED 5-8 % Females in SSBL	ISCED 8 All fields	ISCED 8 SSBL	ISCED 8 Number of female graduates from SSBL	Population*	Source
Brunei Darussalam	2006	1 721	186	10.8	64.0	1	a	a	368 150	UIS
	2011	1 813	260	14.3	63.8	5	2	2	399 443	UIS
	2014	2 965	890	30.0	64.9	17	3	1	417 394	UIS
China	2006	5 622 795	m	m	m	m	m	m	1 312 600 877	UIS
	2011	8 733 298	m	m	m	m	m	m	1 348 174 478	UIS
	2014	11 380 503	m	m	m	54 218	m	m	1 369 435 670	UIS
China, Hong Kong Special Administrative Region	2006	41 079	13 450	32.7	63.7	1 746	268	145	6 855 818	UIS
	2011	m	m	m	m	m	m	m	7 044 211	UIS
	2014	m	m	m	m	m	m	m	7 226 869	UIS
China, Macao Special Administrative Region	2006	6 014	4 344	72.2	40.0	40	30	11	479 728	UIS
	2011	5 525	2 880	52.1	57.9	131	108	19	546 682	UIS
	2014	6 561	3 479	53.0	57.1	100	60	21	577 914	UIS
Indonesia	2006	492 802	m	m	m	m	m	m	229 263 980	UIS
	2012	867 822	m	m	m	4 104	m	m	248 037 853	UIS
	2014	948 638	303 703	32.0	47.9	3 591	1 132	512	254 454 778	UIS
Japan	2006	1 067 939	288 599	27.0	39.2	15 979	1 686	586	127 136 576	UIS
	2011	968 807	264 456	27.3	38.7	15 910	1 636	629	127 252 900	UIS
	2014	980 726	256 695	26.2	39.2	16 039	1 484	596	126 794 564	UIS
Korea, Republic of	2006	605 160	120 580	19.9	47.3	8 657	1 351	287	47 901 643	UIS
	2011	609 719	129 060	21.2	47.5	11 645	1 994	555	49 356 692	UIS
	2015	611 512	132 417	21.7	49.8	12 931	2 244	689	50 293 439	UIS
Malaysia	2006	208 998	51 391	24.6	65.1	687	164	44	26 263 048	UIS
	2011	204 782	67 102	32.8	69.0	2 853	1 644	1 017	28 572 970	UIS
	2014	190 453	67 458	35.4	69.3	2 983	653	242	29 901 997	UIS
Myanmar	2007	104 590	m	m	m	2 561	m	m	50 698 814	UIS
	2011	134 624	22 014	16.4	64.9	569	49	42	52 125 411	UIS
	2014	m	m	m	m	m	m	m	53 437 159	UIS
New Zealand	2006	59 320	22 301	37.6	57.3	638	136	81	4 187 584	UIS
	2011	67 749	23 884	32.7	56.9	1 109	262	143	4 404 483	UIS
	2014	m	m	m	m	m	m	m	4 495 482	UIS
Philippines	2006	410 067	m	m	m	1 612	m	m	87 592 899	UIS
	2011	496 949	148 078	29.8	63.7	1 976	522	247	94 501 233	UIS
	2014	585 288	199 809	34.1	66.2	3 427	744	403	99 138 690	UIS
Thailand	2006	483 924	m	m	m	1 604	m	m	66 174 486	UIS
	2012	443 648	m	m	m	2 119	m	m	67 164 130	UIS
	2014	345 899	m	m	m	1 577	336	159	67 725 979	UIS
Viet Nam	2007	242 026	66 886	27.6	51.1	m	m	m	85 770 717	UIS
	2012	417 436	140 349	33.6	38.1	401	129	23	90 335 547	UIS
	2014	420 607	142 489	33.9	55.7	826	192	88	92 423 338	UIS

Annex A | Basic statistics on the production of social science research

Table A5 • Student graduation, by level, total, social science, business and law, and gender, selected years circa 2001 2006 and 2011 (continued)

	Year	ISCED 5-8 All fields	ISCED 5-8 SSBL	ISCED 5-8 % SSBL	ISCED 5-8 % Females in SSBL	ISCED 8 All fields	ISCED 8 SSBL	ISCED 8 Number of female graduates from SSBL	Population*	Source
Latin America and the Caribbean										
Argentina	2006	223 116	70 371	31.5	58.6	825	136	58	39 558 750	UIS
	2011	222 000	76 576	34.5	56.3	1 674	407	193	41 655 616	UIS
	2013	225 285	80 410	35.7	60.9	2 088	551	259	42 538 304	UIS
Barbados	2007	1 733	1 051	60.6	74.1	7	2	1	276 154	UIS
	2011	2 389	1 180	49.4	71.4	9	1	1	280 602	UIS
	2014	m	m	m	m	m	m	m	283 380	UIS
Brazil	2007	820 473	312 151	38.0	54.5	9 919	m	m	189 953 924	UIS
	2011	1 072 267	430 130	40.1	57.1	12 321	n	n	195 242 800	UIS
	2014	1 097 494	461 979	42.1	58.6	16 745	2 032	997	203 190 852	UIS
Chile	2006	73 203	22 931	31.3	51.5	294	39	1	16 279 728	UIS
	2012	147 549	43 953	29.4	56.8	538	42	21	17 388 437	UIS
	2014	191 141	53 622	28.1	57.8	606	63	28	17 762 647	UIS
Colombia	2006	115 488	60 092	m	50.0	46	3	1	43 835 744	UIS
	2011	235 203	116 229	49.4	60.1	208	21	12	46 406 446	UIS
	2014	279 958	151 594	54.1	61.7	356	46	19	47 791 393	UIS
Costa Rica	2006	28 958	m	m	m	111	m	m	4 308 790	UIS
	2011	40 310	16 376	40.6	61.0	112	35	15	4 600 487	UIS
	2014	46 341	19 381	41.8	62.6	103	26	13	4 757 606	UIS
Cuba	2006	100 874	m	m	m	529	m	m	11 275 199	UIS
	2011	152 441	m	m	m	632	95	39	11 323 570	UIS
	2014	105 293	m	m	m	663	m	m	11 379 111	UIS
Ecuador	2007	62 972	27 440	43.6	58.4	m	m	m	14 205 479	UIS
	2012	79 189	32 607	41.2	60.4	13	12	6	15 419 493	UIS
	2013	91 344	39 283	43.0	61.3	14	11	n	15 661 312	UIS
El Salvador	2006	13 665	5 991	43.8	59.4	m	n	n	5 967 556	UIS
	2011	20 284	6 941	34.2	62.7	81	13	4	6 055 208	UIS
	2014	22 976	8 150	35.5	61.3	14	13	1	6 107 706	UIS
Honduras	2006	m	m	m	m	m	m	m	7 007 029	UIS
	2012	18 024	6 680	37.1	66.3	19	m	m	7 736 131	UIS
	2014	21 994	8 914	40.5	66.8	21	21	8	7 961 680	UIS
Mexico	2006	414 838	174 034	42.0	58.8	2 800	732	312	111 382 857	UIS
	2011	499 303	228 909	45.8	59.5	3 795	1 256	519	120 365 271	UIS
	2014	m	m	m	m	m	m	m	125 385 833	UIS
Panama	2006	19 679	6 177	31.4	73.4	9	5	5	3 378 600	UIS
	2011	22 172	7 814	35.2	62.6	10	n	n	3 681 979	UIS
	2013	23 752	8 239	34.7	67.1	59	36	22	3 805 683	UIS
Puerto Rico	2006	m	m	m	m	m	m	m	3 749 653	UIS
	2011	29 956	10 368	34.6	63.7	232	95	73	3 701 997	UIS
	2013	34 398	9 824	28.6	63.1	298	31	18	3 690 591	UIS

Table A5 • Student graduation, by level, total, social science, business and law, and gender, selected years circa 2001 2006 and 2011 (continued)

	Year	ISCED 5-8 All fields	ISCED 5-8 SSBL	ISCED 5-8 % SSBL	ISCED 5-8 % Females in SSBL	ISCED 8 All fields	ISCED 8 SSBL	ISCED 8 Number of female graduates from SSBL	Population*	Source
Uruguay	2006	8 485	2 796	33.0	65.8	11	n	n	3 331 041	UIS
	2010	7 551	3 086	40.9	66.7	39	6	3	3 374 414	UIS
	2014	m	m	m	m	m	m	m	3 419 516	UIS
North America and Western Europe										
Austria	2006	34 825	m	m	m	2 158	m	m	8 269 372	UIS
	2011	63 754	22 389	35.0	55.7	2 359	679	315	8 423 559	UIS
	2014	81 990	26 068	31.8	59.6	2 207	508	255	8 516 916	UIS
Belgium	2006	81 546	23 060	28.3	58.0	1 718	261	99	10 632 032	UIS
	2011	105 271	32 948	31.3	58.7	2 165	367	169	11 005 175	UIS
	2013	107 884	33 760	31.3	58.6	2 464	431	209	11 153 122	UIS
Canada	2006	m	m	m	m	4 608	993	564	32 611 436	UIS
	2011	m	m	m	m	5 906	1 119	677	34 499 905	UIS
	2014	m	m	m	m	m	m	m	35 587 793	UIS
Cyprus	2006	3 858	1 687	43.7	61.1	29	7	2	778 684	UIS
	2011	5 931	2 908	49.0	52.6	43	7	4	862 011	UIS
	2014	7 763	3 383	43.6	60.0	60	11	6	847 008	UIS
Denmark	2006	47 539	14 463	30.4	52.2	910	125	57	5 440 696	UIS
	2011	57 516	20 410	35.5	53.1	1 503	179	87	5 576 577	UIS
	2014	70 246	24 530	34.9	55.3	2 126	213	102	5 646 899	UIS
Finland	2006	40 472	9 451	23.4	71.1	1 846	m	m	5 266 600	UIS
	2011	51 441	12 675	24.6	65.3	1 850	365	228	5 395 816	UIS
	2014	53 878	13 556	25.2	64.3	2 013	379	232	5 479 660	UIS
France	2006	622 937	254 601	40.9	63.1	10 650	1 984	941	61 609 991	UIS
	2012	697 193	289 559	41.5	61.8	13 188	2 657	1 282	63 561 798	UIS
	2014	741 044	309 081	41.7	60.6	13 729	2 996	1 568	64 121 249	UIS
Germany	2006	m	m	m	m	24 946	4 451	1 628	81 055 904	UIS
	2011	m	m	m	m	26 981	4 390	1 804	80 424 665	UIS
	2014	521 845	151 092	29.0	56.0	28 147	4 246	1 837	80 646 262	UIS
Greece	2007	60 475	15 419	25.5	65.3	2 436	163	65	11 131 302	UIS
	2011	65 291	19 894	30.5	64.4	1 696	224	89	11 153 047	UIS
	2014	m	m	m	m	m	m	m	11 000 777	UIS
Iceland	2006	3 397	1 160	34.1	59.1	15	1	n	300 887	UIS
	2012	4 099	1 537	m	63.3	40	4	2	323 407	UIS
	2014	m	m	m	m	m	m	m	327 318	UIS
Ireland	2006	59 184	20 566	34.7	58.7	979	115	65	4 293 942	UIS
	2012	60 022	17 905	29.8	55.2	1 447	218	135	4 667 868	UIS
	2014	m	m	m	m	m	m	m	4 675 164	UIS
Israel	2006	m	m	m	m	1 210	190	93	6 754 836	UIS
	2011	m	m	m	m	1 530	226	138	7 563 334	UIS
	2014	m	m	m	m	1 546	241	148	7 939 483	UIS

Annex A | Basic statistics on the production of social science research

Table A5 • Student graduation, by level, total, social science, business and law, and gender, selected years circa 2001 2006 and 2011 (continued)

	Year	ISCED 5-8 All fields	ISCED 5-8 SSBL	ISCED 5-8 % SSBL	ISCED 5-8 % Females in SSBL	ISCED 8 All fields	ISCED 8 SSBL	ISCED 8 Number of female graduates from SSBL	Population*	Source
Italy	2006	400 860	134 644	33.6	57.9	10 188	1 877	970	58 918 471	UIS
	2011	388 837	123 673	31.8	58.5	11 270	2 125	1 179	59 678 993	UIS
	2014	m	m	m	m	m	m	m	59 788 667	UIS
Liechtenstein	2006	132	72	54.5	22.2	4	n	n	35 168	UIS
	2011	254	191	75.2	24.1	12	3	n	36 475	UIS
	2014	271	212	78.2	29.2	17	5	1	m	UIS
Luxembourg	2006	m	m	m	m	m	m	m	465 546	UIS
	2012	1 289	722	56.0	56.5	57	12	5	532 479	UIS
	2014	1 847	853	46.2	54.0	82	30	19	556 573	UIS
Malta	2006	2 676	1 182	44.2	57.8	4	n	n	399 892	UIS
	2011	3 393	1 159	34.2	57.1	19	2	n	414 075	UIS
	2014	m	m	m	m	m	m	m	417 723	UIS
Netherlands	2006	117 392	44 892	38.2	51.9	2 993	566	247	16 401 105	UIS
	2011	138 772	53 714	38.7	53.5	3 715	709	338	16 689 863	UIS
	2014	m	m	m	m	m	m	m	16 868 020	UIS
Norway	2006	33 529	m	m	m	882	m	m	4 667 105	UIS
	2011	40 379	12 063	29.8	57.5	1 297	151	76	4 953 945	UIS
	2014	47 742	12 943	27.1	58.7	1 442	209	108	5 147 970	UIS
Portugal	2006	71 828	23 102	27.4	66.0	5 342	1 574	950	10 516 559	UIS
	2011	87 129	26 128	30.0	62.4	2 314	443	281	10 558 909	UIS
	2014	88 503	26 951	30.5	61.8	4 008	821	432	10 402 343	UIS
Spain	2006	285 957	80 830	28.3	63.8	7 159	1 342	623	44 537 926	UIS
	2011	381 926	99 556	26.1	62.3	8 747	1 585	756	46 708 366	UIS
	2014	443 321	119 317	26.9	59.5	10 889	2 016	982	46 259 716	UIS
Sweden	2006	62 774	15 227	24.3	62.5	3 781	352	147	9 087 251	UIS
	2011	69 322	17 958	24.5	62.2	3 356	373	187	9 462 352	UIS
	2013	72 782	20 805	28.6	63.4	3 345	346	182	9 624 247	UIS
Switzerland	2006	68 607	27 022	39.4	44.1	3 381	602	231	7 480 317	UIS
	2011	78 918	29 095	36.9	47.5	3 709	683	274	7 925 813	UIS
	2014	85 750	30 893	36.0	48.1	3 847	683	318	8 211 383	UIS
United Kingdom of Great Britain and Northern Ireland	2006	640 246	195 516	30.5	56.1	16 465	2 977	1 529	60 648 850	UIS
	2011	754 310	238 040	31.6	54.5	20 076	4 170	2 296	63 164 949	UIS
	2014	772 362	230 522	29.8	53.2	25 020	3 928	1 836	64 331 348	UIS
United States of America	2006	2 639 006	1 005 047	38.1	56.1	56 067	10 912	6 221	298 860 519	UIS
	2011	3 164 951	1 178 182	37.2	55.7	73 041	13 444	7 967	312 390 368	UIS
	2014	3 813 956	1 223 850	32.1	55.8	67 449	13 408	7 821	319 448 634	UIS
South and West Asia										
Bangladesh	2006	m	m	m	m	m	m	m	144 839 238	UIS
	2011	302 965	129 528	42.8	m	1 134	n	m	153 405 612	UIS
	2014	329 181	141 815	43.1	43.7	1 449	396	191	159 077 513	UIS

Table A5 | *Student graduation, by level, total, social science, business and law, and gender, selected years circa 2001, 2006 and 2011*

Table A5 • **Student graduation, by level, total, social science, business and law, and gender, selected years circa 2001 2006 and 2011** (continued)

	Year	ISCED 5-8 All fields	ISCED 5-8 SSBL	ISCED 5-8 % SSBL	ISCED 5-8 % Females in SSBL	ISCED 8 All fields	ISCED 8 SSBL	ISCED 8 Number of female graduates from SSBL	Population*	Source
India	2006	m	m	m	m	m	m	m	1 162 088 305	UIS
	2011	m	m	m	m	m	m	m	1 247 446 011	UIS
	2013	8 846 030	4 563 385	51.6	50.4	24 300	5 627	2 274	1 279 498 874	UIS
Iran, Islamic Republic of	2006	357 031	78 876	22.1	50.6	2 537	159	23	70 923 164	UIS
	2011	607 121	161 372	26.6	44.2	4 788	466	91	75 184 322	UIS
	2014	718 801	211 374	29.4	52.6	6 842	681	177	78 143 644	UIS
Nepal	2006	28 928	9 554	33.0	m	50	5	m	25 794 344	UIS
	2011	48 162	13 350	27.7	m	65	7	m	27 179 237	UIS
	2014	58 802	17 397	29.6	m	x	x	x	28 174 724	UIS
Sri Lanka	2006	m	m	m	m	m	m	m	19 672 418	UIS
	2011	28 285	6 209	22.0	55.3	291	m	m	20 315 673	UIS
	2014	40 637	10 190	25.1	58.0	m	m	m	20 618 991	UIS
Sub-Saharan Africa										
Botswana	2006	m	m	m	m	m	m	m	1 895 671	UIS
	2011	m	m	m	m	m	m	m	2 089 706	UIS
	2014	15 594	5 423	34.8	m	14	x	x	2 219 937	UIS
Burkina Faso	2006	m	m	m	m	m	m	m	13 834 195	UIS
	2011	14 782	8 213	55.6	34.1	m	m	m	16 106 851	UIS
	2013	16 151	9 974	61.8	36.8	m	m	m	17 084 554	UIS
Cameroon	2006	27 838	17 454	62.7	m	888	241	m	18 597 109	UIS
	2011	36 310	10 498	m	m	m	m	m	21 119 065	UIS
	2014	m	m	m	m	m	m	m	22 773 014	UIS
Ghana	2006	m	m	m	m	m	m	m	21 951 891	UIS
	2012	72 071	34 727	m	38.4	109	51	12	25 544 565	UIS
	2014	79 345	30 353	38.3	41.7	74	6	3	26 786 598	UIS
Madagascar	2006	10 109	6 222	61.5	52.0	439	151	48	18 826 129	UIS
	2010	15 721	9 362	59.6	53.7	565	280	142	21 079 532	UIS
	2013	25 264	14 199	56.2	50.1	350	60	25	22 924 557	UIS
Mauritius	2006	m	m	m	m	m	m	m	1 227 714	UIS
	2011	m	m	m	m	m	m	m	1 253 089	UIS
	2014	5 621	2 518	44.8	64.7	10	2	2	1 268 567	UIS
Mozambique	2005	3 615	1 288	35.6	38.0	a	a	a	21 126 676	UIS
	2011	10 070	3 200	31.8	49.7	m	m	m	25 016 921	UIS
	2014	13 133	6 247	47.6	50.1	1	1	1	27 216 276	UIS
South Africa	2006	m	m	m	m	m	m	m	49 027 805	UIS
	2012	183 864	86 165	46.9	60.3	1 900	491	218	52 837 274	UIS
	2013	195 269	92 016	47.1	60.3	2 060	528	250	53 416 609	UIS

Source: UIS online Data Centre (http://stats.uis.unesco.org)

Notes:
Symbols used:
* Population data come from the UNs Population Division
m = data missing or not available
n = quantity nil
a = not applicable

SSBL : Social Science, Business and Law
ISCED 5–8 corresponds to tertiary education, which comprises ISCED 5, 6, 7 and 8, according to the International Standard Classification of Education (ISCED) 2011.
ISCED 5 corresponds to short-cycle tertiary education;
ISCED 6 corresponds to Bachelor's or equivalent programmes;
ISCED 7 corresponds to Master's or equivalent programmes;
ISCED 8 corresponds to Doctoral or equivalent programmes.

Annex A | Basic statistics on the production of social science research

Table A6 • Number of publications of the highest-producing countries in natural sciences, social sciences, arts and humanities, 2009 to 2013

Natural Sciences 2009-2013			Social Sciences 2009-2013			Arts and humanities 2009-2013		
Country	N° Pub. Full.	N° Pub. frac.	Country	N° Pub. Full.	N° Pub. frac.	Country	N° Pub. Full.	N° Pub. frac.
World	**5 588 368**	**5 588 368**	**World**	**446 810**	**446 810**	**World**	**133 850**	**133 850**
United States of America	1 468 309	1 192 895	United States of America	185 558	165 029	United States of America	48 286	46 182
China	890 077	787 337	United Kingdom of Great Britain and Northern Ireland	59 667	47 192	United Kingdom of Great Britain and Northern Ireland	19 478	18 000
Japan	361 987	307 542	Germany	29 092	22 359	Germany	7 627	6 931
Germany	417 211	287 952	Canada	27 392	21 062	Canada	7 038	6 449
United Kingdom of Great Britain and Northern Ireland	396 728	262 766	Australia	25 184	20 152	France	6 458	5 882
France	301 557	206 789	China	24 349	19 408	Spain	5 517	5 111
India	217 539	191 365	Spain	18 369	15 322	Australia	5 068	4 576
Italy	251 689	185 143	Netherlands	18 551	13 710	Italy	3 948	3 640
Korea, Republic of	210 793	179 687	France	13 940	10 296	China	3 798	3 441
Canada	246 075	172 945	Italy	12 299	9 334	Netherlands	3 163	2 746
Spain	215 102	155 565	Turkey	6 823	6 062	Belgium	2 818	2 527
Brazil	163 951	139 423	Japan	7 213	5 894	South Africa	1 894	1 631
Australia	184 842	129 567	Sweden	7 214	5 454	Israel	1 777	1 626
Russian Federation	135 257	108 943	Belgium	7 612	5 308	Sweden	1 652	1 477
Turkey	108 143	96 634	Switzerland	7 586	4 996	Switzerland	1 464	1 246
Netherlands	139 100	88 716	Israel	6 094	4 810	Russian Federation	1 385	1 336
Iran, Islamic Republic of	98 048	87 681	Rep. of Korea	6 229	4 571	Brazil	1 332	1 246
Poland	99 818	78 867	South Africa	4 946	4 094	Turkey	1 202	1 122
Switzerland	106 937	59 472	Norway	5 175	3 951	Romania	1 118	1 077
Sweden	93 729	57 380	Brazil	4 226	3 552	Romania	1 118	1 077
Belgium	78 970	46 720	New Zealand	4 793	3 487	New Zealand	1 107	939
Israel	51 203	35 987	Finland	4 212	3 292	Norway	1 101	966
Denmark	57 996	35 379	Denmark	4 298	3 106	Denmark	1 082	935
Greece	48 863	35 078	India	3 302	2 686	Czech Republic	1 071	1 038
Mexico	47 223	34 746	Austria	3 753	2 511	Chile	1 040	956
Portugal	48 121	32 955	Portugal	3 163	2 338	Japan	1 031	900
Austria	55 427	32 113	Singapore	3 453	2 293	Rep. of Korea	950	798
Czech Republic	44 081	30 347	Ireland	2 878	2 128	Austria	924	794
Finland	45 903	29 812	Croatia	2 274	2 080	Finland	885	793
Singapore	43 410	29 132	Russian Federation	2 365	2 030	Poland	869	799
Norway	44 185	27 637	Greece	2 540	1 983	Argentina	857	787
Argentina	35 918	26 417	Czech Republic	2 218	1 930	Ireland	770	679
Romania	32 256	24 889	Poland	2 173	1 792	Slovenia	629	589
Romania	32 256	24 889	Mexico	2 189	1 679	Greece	621	523
Malaysia	33 306	24 770	Chile	1 993	1 506	Portugal	549	462
South Africa	36 063	23 939	Malaysia	1 712	1 359	Mexico	510	431
Egypt	30 414	21 468	Ukraine	1 320	1 276	Singapore	502	427
New Zealand	32 030	20 502	Romania	1 475	1 269	Croatia	493	477
Ireland	30 386	19 423	Slovenia	1 399	1 212	Hungary	449	404
Thailand	26 915	19 420	Iran (Islamic Republic of)	1 339	1 114	Slovakia	401	390
Pakistan	25 066	19 335	Argentina	1 323	1 022	India	400	348

Table A7 • Number of social science publications per country, Scopus and Web of Science, 2008–13

Number of papers (full and fractional counts), share of output in the database (based on fractional counts), ratio of output shares between Scopus and WOS (based on fractional counts)

Country	No. of publications (full counting) Scopus	No. of publications (full counting) WOS	No. of publications (fractional counting) Scopus	No. of publications (fractional counting) WOS	% of world total (fractional counting) Scopus	% of world total (fractional counting) WOS
World	**827 863**	**524 542**	**827 863**	**524 542**	**100%**	**100%**
United States of America	325 502	220 532	294 862	196 765	35.6%	37.5%
United Kingdom of Great Britain and Northern Ireland	100 577	69 836	82 298	55 454	9.9%	10.6%
China	53 801	27 377	46 602	21 867	5.6%	4.2%
Germany	45 542	33 840	36 213	26 127	4.4%	5.0%
Canada	44 484	32 214	35 312	24 859	4.3%	4.7%
Australia	41 976	29 169	34 531	23 468	4.2%	4.5%
France	31 850	16 428	26 048	12 223	3.1%	2.3%
Spain	28 689	21 246	24 398	17 776	2.9%	3.4%
Netherlands	26 475	21 545	20 054	16 021	2.4%	3.1%
Italy	20 550	14 238	16 379	10 838	2.0%	2.1%
Japan	13 140	8 476	11 143	6 932	1.3%	1.3%
Brazil	12 902	4 975	11 665	4 187	1.4%	0.8%
Sweden	11 916	8 450	9 295	6 430	1.1%	1.2%
Turkey	11 864	7 713	10 706	6 848	1.3%	1.3%
India	11 755	3 847	10 513	3 156	1.3%	0.6%
Belgium	11 496	8 734	8 424	6 122	1.0%	1.2%
Switzerland	11 268	8 807	7 764	5 830	0.9%	1.1%
Israel	9 485	7 189	7 727	5 700	0.9%	1.1%
Korea, Republic of	8 798	6 978	6 446	5 120	0.8%	1.0%
New Zealand	8 619	5 653	6 534	4 128	0.8%	0.8%
Norway	8 332	5 958	6 539	4 558	0.8%	0.9%
South Africa	8 296	5 743	7 017	4 764	0.8%	0.9%
Finland	7 952	4 883	6 482	3 840	0.8%	0.7%
Denmark	6 807	4 918	5 052	3 572	0.6%	0.7%
Malaysia	6 176	1 818	5 401	1 441	0.7%	0.3%
Austria	6 138	4 327	4 433	2 932	0.5%	0.6%
Portugal	5 709	3 551	4 430	2 626	0.5%	0.5%
Greece	5 611	2 952	4 661	2 312	0.6%	0.4%
Singapore	5 530	3 951	3 858	2 635	0.5%	0.5%
Ireland	5 143	3 335	3 963	2 484	0.5%	0.5%
Romania	4 818	1 709	4 500	1 485	0.5%	0.3%
Mexico	4 461	2 600	3 562	1 991	0.4%	0.4%
Croatia	4 426	2 713	4 137	2 486	0.5%	0.5%
Czech Republic	4 011	2 618	3 526	2 290	0.4%	0.4%
Iran, Islamic Republic of	3 891	1 477	3 513	1 227	0.4%	0.2%
Chile	3 786	2 262	3 048	1 711	0.4%	0.3%
Poland	3 705	2 486	3 128	2 052	0.4%	0.4%
Russian Federation	3 084	2 686	2 535	2 303	0.3%	0.4%
Argentina	2 675	1 556	2 198	1 208	0.3%	0.2%
Hungary	2 657	1 465	2 173	1 079	0.3%	0.2%

Annex A | Basic statistics on the production of social science research

Table A7 • Number of social science publications per country, Scopus and Web of Science, 2008–13 (continued)
Number of papers (full and fractional counts), share of output in the database (based on fractional counts), ratio of output shares between Scopus and WOS (based on fractional counts)

Country	2008–2013 No. of publications (full counting) Scopus	WOS	No. of publications (fractional counting) Scopus	WOS	2008–2013 % of world total (fractional counting) Scopus	WOS
Slovenia	2 509	1 657	2 235	1 440	0.3%	0.3%
Colombia	2 308	943	1 802	674	0.2%	0.1%
Thailand	2 152	894	1 577	551	0.2%	0.1%
Nigeria	2 056	721	1 894	633	0.2%	0.1%
Serbia	1 749	1 172	1 542	1 010	0.2%	0.2%
Lithuania	1 623	800	1 501	717	0.2%	0.1%
Pakistan	1 575	659	1 349	543	0.2%	0.1%
Slovakia	1 478	971	1 268	818	0.2%	0.2%
United Arab Emirates	1 455	593	1 059	408	0.1%	0.1%
Cyprus	1 242	732	940	522	0.1%	0.1%
Jordan	1 135	196	984	135	0.1%	0.0%
Ukraine	1 076	1 358	989	1 300	0.1%	0.2%
Indonesia	976	463	610	246	0.1%	0.0%
Philippines	917	504	678	360	0.1%	0.1%
Estonia	912	635	702	474	0.1%	0.1%
Saudi Arabia	889	341	599	194	0.1%	0.0%
Egypt	850	391	587	237	0.1%	0.0%
Kenya	784	423	512	238	0.1%	0.0%
Venezuela	781	422	656	344	0.1%	0.1%
Tunisia	733	282	558	188	0.1%	0.0%
Bangladesh	627	249	442	156	0.1%	0.0%
Luxembourg	617	454	375	245	0.0%	0.0%
Ghana	599	265	422	177	0.1%	0.0%
Lebanon	548	255	415	173	0.1%	0.0%
Iceland	510	395	344	255	0.0%	0.0%
Bosnia and Herzegovina	474	390	342	273	0.0%	0.1%
Peru	451	311	281	197	0.0%	0.0%
Kuwait	451	173	342	117	0.0%	0.0%
Viet Nam	438	242	243	131	0.0%	0.0%
Bulgaria	425	188	293	119	0.0%	0.0%
Cuba	408	117	330	73	0.0%	0.0%
Uganda	401	220	247	118	0.0%	0.0%
Ethiopia	366	225	228	125	0.0%	0.0%
Latvia	359	119	306	89	0.0%	0.0%
Botswana	358	176	304	139	0.0%	0.0%
United Rep. of Tanzania	348	193	204	99	0.0%	0.0%
Kazakhstan	335	120	297	101	0.0%	0.0%
Uruguay	331	183	240	121	0.0%	0.0%
Sri Lanka	314	140	228	87	0.0%	0.0%
Qatar	299	124	203	71	0.0%	0.0%
Morocco	292	118	200	67	0.0%	0.0%
Macedonia	247	73	196	49	0.0%	0.0%

Table A7 • Number of social science publications per country, Scopus and Web of Science, 2008–13 (continued)

Number of papers (full and fractional counts), share of output in the database (based on fractional counts), ratio of output shares between Scopus and WOS (based on fractional counts)

Country	2008–2013 No. of publications (full counting) Scopus	WOS	2008–2013 No. of publications (fractional counting) Scopus	WOS	2008–2013 % of world total (fractional counting) Scopus	WOS
Costa Rica	242	155	150	95	0.0%	0.0%
Trinidad and Tobago	238	103	188	74	0.0%	0.0%
Oman	232	74	180	54	0.0%	0.0%
Jamaica	221	63	172	43	0.0%	0.0%
Zimbabwe	213	106	155	67	0.0%	0.0%
Malta	205	103	152	69	0.0%	0.0%
Fiji	192	115	131	77	0.0%	0.0%
Algeria	190	47	141	29	0.0%	0.0%
Cameroon	178	84	132	53	0.0%	0.0%
Palestinian Territory	166	0	113	0	0.0%	0.0%
Malawi	155	97	99	57	0.0%	0.0%
Georgia	154	61	94	36	0.0%	0.0%
Mauritius	152	66	125	49	0.0%	0.0%
Nepal	150	70	89	36	0.0%	0.0%
Ecuador	141	71	77	34	0.0%	0.0%
Bahrain	127	33	92	21	0.0%	0.0%
Senegal	122	71	77	39	0.0%	0.0%
Barbados	108	47	88	37	0.0%	0.0%
Panama	96	76	39	32	0.0%	0.0%
Zambia	91	55	53	32	0.0%	0.0%
Bolivia	84	77	38	32	0.0%	0.0%
Brunei Darussalam	80	21	58	14	0.0%	0.0%
Rwanda	79	35	43	16	0.0%	0.0%
Madagascar	77	64	33	27	0.0%	0.0%
Cambodia	76	39	41	21	0.0%	0.0%
Namibia	75	35	49	20	0.0%	0.0%
Syria	75	24	51	11	0.0%	0.0%
Mozambique	72	46	38	23	0.0%	0.0%
Albania	70	34	50	21	0.0%	0.0%
Belarus	70	62	56	51	0.0%	0.0%
Swaziland	68	17	41	12	0.0%	0.0%
Congo	67	14	35	5	0.0%	0.0%
Sudan	66	39	47	25	0.0%	0.0%
Côte d'Ivoire	66	29	47	18	0.0%	0.0%
Benin	66	33	33	18	0.0%	0.0%
Liechtenstein	66	24	33	10	0.0%	0.0%
Afghanistan	63	19	39	13	0.0%	0.0%
Iraq	61	27	42	19	0.0%	0.0%
Armenia	60	26	41	15	0.0%	0.0%
El Salvador	55	7	40	3	0.0%	0.0%
Azerbaijan	54	29	44	19	0.0%	0.0%
Guatemala	54	40	30	24	0.0%	0.0%

Annex A | Basic statistics on the production of social science research

Table A7 • Number of social science publications per country, Scopus and Web of Science, 2008–13 (continued)

Number of papers (full and fractional counts), share of output in the database (based on fractional counts), ratio of output shares between Scopus and WOS (based on fractional counts)

Country	2008–2013 No. of publications (full counting) Scopus	WOS	2008–2013 No. of publications (fractional counting) Scopus	WOS	2008–2013 % of world total (fractional counting) Scopus	WOS
Burkina Faso	51	28	26	12	0.0%	0.0%
Montenegro	50	37	37	26	0.0%	0.0%
Uzbekistan	49	20	32	12	0.0%	0.0%
Nicaragua	48	33	30	19	0.0%	0.0%
Yemen	46	15	33	7	0.0%	0.0%
Lao People's Dem. Rep.	46	25	22	13	0.0%	0.0%
Mongolia	43	18	22	7	0.0%	0.0%
Libya	41	19	28	11	0.0%	0.0%
Moldova, Republic of	40	15	32	11	0.0%	0.0%
Guyana	40	8	34	5	0.0%	0.0%
Mali	40	20	20	9	0.0%	0.0%
Papua New Guinea	38	20	22	12	0.0%	0.0%
Lesotho	38	19	32	14	0.0%	0.0%
Kyrgyzstan	37	22	20	11	0.0%	0.0%
Niger	34	14	23	7	0.0%	0.0%
Paraguay	32	7	23	5	0.0%	0.0%
Dominica	31	22	21	15	0.0%	0.0%
Dominican Republic	29	11	15	5	0.0%	0.0%
Bahamas	28	18	15	11	0.0%	0.0%
Gabon	26	20	12	7	0.0%	0.0%
Myanmar	21	12	10	5	0.0%	0.0%
Togo	20	6	14	6	0.0%	0.0%
Monaco	19	8	11	3	0.0%	0.0%
Sierra Leone	18	13	13	8	0.0%	0.0%
Honduras	17	10	7	5	0.0%	0.0%
Grenada	15	22	7	12	0.0%	0.0%
Burundi	14	6	8	4	0.0%	0.0%
Korea, Republic of	14	1	7	1	0.0%	0.0%
Angola	14	5	8	3	0.0%	0.0%
Liberia	13	4	9	2	0.0%	0.0%
Haiti	13	5	7	2	0.0%	0.0%
Bhutan	12	2	7	1	0.0%	0.0%
Solomon Islands	12	8	6	5	0.0%	0.0%
Central African Republic	12	10	6	4	0.0%	0.0%
Eritrea	11	9	7	5	0.0%	0.0%
Mauritania	10	2	5	1	0.0%	0.0%
Tajikistan	10	4	5	2	0.0%	0.0%
San Marino	9	4	3	2	0.0%	0.0%
Cape Verde	9	6	4	3	0.0%	0.0%
Congo, Dem. Rep. of	9	25	6	10	0.0%	0.0%
Samoa	9	1	5	0	0.0%	0.0%
Seychelles	8	6	3	2	0.0%	0.0%

Table A7 • Number of social science publications per country, Scopus and Web of Science, 2008–13 (continued)

Number of papers (full and fractional counts), share of output in the database (based on fractional counts), ratio of output shares between Scopus and WOS (based on fractional counts)

Country	2008–2013 No. of publications (full counting) Scopus	WOS	No. of publications (fractional counting) Scopus	WOS	2008–2013 % of world total (fractional counting) Scopus	WOS
Gambia	8	4	4	3	0.0%	0.0%
Belize	7	0	3	0	0.0%	0.0%
Vanuatu	6	3	4	1	0.0%	0.0%
Somalia	6	1	4	1	0.0%	0.0%
Saint Kitts and Nevis	6	0	4	0	0.0%	0.0%
Tonga	5	4	2	1	0.0%	0.0%
Kosovo	5	0	2	0	0.0%	0.0%
Antigua and Barbuda	4	1	2	1	0.0%	0.0%
Equatorial Guinea	4	0	3	0	0.0%	0.0%
Suriname	4	1	1	0	0.0%	0.0%
Turkmenistan	4	2	1	1	0.0%	0.0%
Maldives	4	1	2	1	0.0%	0.0%
Guinea	4	4	2	2	0.0%	0.0%
Chad	3	2	2	1	0.0%	0.0%
Guinea-Bissau	2	3	2	3	0.0%	0.0%
Marshall Islands	2	1	2	1	0.0%	0.0%
Tuvalu	2	0	1	0	0.0%	0.0%
Djibouti	1	0	1	0	0.0%	0.0%
Western Sahara	1	0	1	0	0.0%	0.0%
Comoros	1	0	1	0	0.0%	0.0%
Andorra	1	2	1	1	0.0%	0.0%
Palau	1	0	1	0	0.0%	0.0%
Cook Islands	1	1	0	0	0.0%	0.0%
Fed. States of Micronesia	1	5	0	4	0.0%	0.0%
Niue	1	0	0	0	0.0%	0.0%
Vatican	1	0	1	0	0.0%	0.0%
Saint Vincent and the Grenadines	1	1	0	1	0.0%	0.0%
Yugoslavia	0	0	0	0	0.0%	0.0%
Serbia and Montenegro	0	0	0	0	0.0%	0.0%
Unknown	7 422	3	4 291	2	0.5%	0.0%

Source: Prepared by Science-Metrix using the Web of Science (Thomson Reuters) and Scopus (Elsevier) databases.

Note: Since shares of output are prepared using fractional counts, the sum across countries adds up to 100%.
When the ratio of shares of output between both databases could not be prepared for a country because of a lack of output in the WOS database, N/A is displayed in the table.

**World
Social
Science
Report**

Annex B

Bibliometric analysis of social and human science research into inequalities and social justice

Methodological note for Tables B1 to B6

Tables B1 to B6 were prepared by Science-Metrix using the Web of Science (WOS) (Thomson Reuters).

Scientific publications on inequalities and social justice by main domain of study (Table B1)

For this project, the Science-Metrix classification of journals was used to define the different domains presented. The domain of 'Arts and Humanities' was defined as the same domain as in the Science-Metrix classification, excluding the subfield of 'Anthropology', while the domain of 'Natural Sciences' was defined by the aggregation of the domains of 'Natural Sciences', 'Applied Sciences' and 'Health Sciences', excluding the field of 'Psychology and Cognitive Sciences'. Finally, the domain of 'Social Sciences' was defined by the aggregation of the domain of 'Economic and Social Sciences', the field of 'Psychology and Cognitive Sciences' and the subfield of 'Anthropology'. The journal classification by domains, fields and subfields of science can be consulted and downloaded at the following link: *http://science-metrix.com/en/classification*

Social and human sciences publications on inequalities and social justice : fields and subfields (Tables B2 to B6)

In the Science-Metrix journal classification system, the corpus of the database (in this case WOS) is categorized into domains which are further divided into fields and subfields. For this analysis of Inequalities and Social Justice, two domains were included in the study: 'Arts and Humanities' and 'Social Sciences', with slight modifications.

The domain of 'Arts and Humanities' was defined as the same domain as in the Science-Metrix classification, excluding the subfield of 'Anthropology', while the domain of 'Social Sciences' was defined by the aggregation of the domain of 'Economic and Social Sciences', the field of 'Psychology and Cognitive Sciences' and the subfield of 'Anthropology'. The journal classification by domains, fields and subfields of science can be consulted and downloaded at the following link: *http://science-metrix.com/en/classification*

Scientific publications relevant to the field of inequalities and social justice
were retrieved using keyword searches in titles, author keywords and abstracts of scientific publications indexed in the WOS database. These keywords were identified by Science-Metrix analysts and tested to ensure that they retrieved only scientific publications relevant to the field of inequalities and social justice. A terms frequency-inverse document frequency (TF-IDF) statistic was also prepared using core articles of the field (identified with highly relevant keywords and specialized journals acting as a seed for the process) to help identify additional keywords that could have been missed at first in the analysis. This procedure was repeated several times until no new keyword bringing in additional scientific publications could be identified, which indicated that optimal coverage of the field had been attained. Here are a few examples of keywords used for the creation of the dataset: 'affirmative action', 'apartheid', 'economic justice', 'environmental racism', 'health disparity', 'poverty' and 'structural inequalities'. Additionally, about twenty specialized journals relevant to the topic of inequalities and social justice were fully included in the dataset, so that all their content was accounted for in the final dataset (examples of these specialized journals are *Gender and Society*, *International Journal for Equity in Health* and *Social Politics*).

Annex B — Bibliometric analysis of social and human science research into inequalities and social justice

Number of publications (full counts)

Using the full-counting method, each paper is counted once for each different entity involved in the publication (an entity can be a country, an institution, or an author, depending on the level of the analysis). For example, at the country level, if a paper is authored by two researchers based in France, one based in the USA and one in China, the paper will be counted once for France, once for the USA and once for China. It will also be counted once at the world level.

Number of publications (fractional counts)

Fractional counting gives to each entity involved in a publication its respective fraction of the publication (an entity can be a country, an institution, or an author, depending on the level of the analysis). For example, at the country level, if a paper is authored by two researchers based in France, one researcher based in the USA and one in China, half of the paper will be attributed to France, one quarter to the USA and one quarter to China.

Ideally, each author on a paper would be attributed a fraction of the paper that corresponds to their level of participation in the research. Unfortunately, no reliable means exists for calculating the relative effort of authors, and credit is spread equally among all the authors (or addresses) given.

Table B1 | *Evolution in the number of publications on inequalities and social justice by domain of study, 1991–2014*
Table B2 | *Number of publications in the social and human sciences on inequalities and social justice produced per year worldwide, 1992–2013*

Table B1 • Evolution in the number of publications on inequalities and social justice by domain of study, 1991–2014

Year	Health Sciences	Social, Economic and Behavioural Sciences	Arts and Humanities
1991	456	671	150
1992	569	1 180	195
1993	681	1 262	198
1994	667	1 452	212
1995	852	1 722	231
1996	1 005	1 769	270
1997	1 139	1 821	240
1998	1 146	1 890	239
1999	1 278	2 076	277
2000	1 364	2 301	373
2001	1 450	2 254	367
2002	1 678	2 275	369
2003	1 965	2 572	354
2004	2 113	2 585	335
2005	2 532	2 842	386
2006	2 809	3 070	419
2007	3 282	3 485	480
2008	3 773	4 394	630
2009	4 166	4 661	759
2010	4 488	4 952	789
2011	4 897	5 383	816
2012	4 938	5 355	867
2013	5 514	5 961	963
2014	5 680	5 925	895
1991–2014	58 442	71 858	10 814

Notes:

Heath Sciences comprises the domain of Health Sciences (according to the Science-Metrix classification) minus the field of Psychology and Cognitive Sciences.

Social, Economic and Behavioural Sciences was defined as including the domain of Economic & Social Sciences ((according to the Science-Metrix classification) plus the field Psychology and Cognitive Sciences and the subfield of Anthropology.

Arts and Humanities was defined as including the domain of Arts and Humanities (according to the Science-Metrix classification) minus the subfield of Anthropology.

Full counting and fractional counting results are equal when preparing data at the world level.

Source: Prepared by Science-Metrix using WOS (Thomson Reuters).

Table B2 • Number of publications in the social and human sciences on inequalities and social justice produced per year worldwide, 1992–2013

Year	Number of publications
1992	1 375
1993	1 460
1994	1 664
1995	1 953
1996	2 039
1997	2 061
1998	2 129
1999	2 353
2000	2 674
2001	2 621
2002	2 644
2003	2 926
2004	2 920
2005	3 228
2006	3 489
2007	3 965
2008	5 024
2009	5 420
2010	5 741
2011	6 199
2012	6 222
2013	6 924

Note: Full counting and fractional counting results are equal when preparing data at the world level, so the data is only presented once here.

Source: Prepared by Science-Metrix using WOS (Thomson Reuters).

Annex B | Bibliometric analysis of social and human science research into inequalities and social justice

Table B3 • Number of publications in the social and human sciences on inequalities and social justice produced worldwide by subfield (according to the Science-Metrix classification), 1992–2013

Subfield	1992–2013	1994–1998	1999–2003	2004–2008	2009–2013
Total	**75 031**	**9 846**	**13 218**	**18 626**	**30 506**
Economics	7 837	998	1 520	1 968	3 054
Political Science & Public Administration	5 977	739	1 125	1 555	2 346
Sociology	5 732	880	1 055	1 383	2 136
Education	5 195	515	763	1 232	2 534
Social Psychology	4 965	743	833	1 284	1 924
Gender Studies	4 779	796	962	1 089	1 700
Social Work	3 397	484	640	860	1 326
Geography	2 786	337	432	803	1 125
Development Studies	2 634	293	455	649	1 158
Developmental and Child Psychology	2 526	445	420	625	915
Criminology	2 351	300	418	594	982
History	2 044	221	397	510	836
Business & Management	1 797	209	317	418	794
Literary Studies	1 689	253	293	391	636
Law	1 493	234	249	350	566
Cultural Studies	1 436	142	240	352	659
Anthropology	1 315	198	247	342	460
Applied Ethics	1 259	101	229	289	612
Demography	1 130	165	199	292	436
Communication and Media Studies	1 013	129	143	205	504
International Relations	1 006	104	155	295	425
Agricultural Economics and Policy	983	99	157	295	406
Family Studies	975	178	201	249	283
Religions and Theology	950	160	209	209	325
Philosophy	894	146	158	196	359
Industrial Relations	822	114	170	177	326
Clinical Psychology	766	126	130	204	266
Experimental Psychology	652	63	77	153	340
Economic Theory	612	79	108	164	242
General Psychology & Cognitive Sciences	595	71	81	139	273
Languages and Linguistics	594	55	114	145	270
Logistics and Transportation	531	21	65	153	284
Sport, Leisure and Tourism	470	38	47	100	275

Table B3 | *Number of publications in the social and human sciences on inequalities and social justice produced worldwide per subfield (according to Science-Metrix classification), 1992–2013*

Table B3 • **Number of publications in the social and human sciences on inequalities and social justice produced worldwide by subfield (according to the Science-Metrix classification), 1992–2013** (continued)

Subfield	1992–2013	1994–1998	1999–2003	2004–2008	2009–2013
Social Sciences Methods	464	41	54	126	233
Information and Library Sciences	435	41	97	125	160
Marketing	420	45	47	104	211
Science Studies	330	45	65	72	141
History of Social Sciences	315	38	35	65	165
Archaeology	312	18	38	81	172
Behavioural Science and Comparative Psychology	227	38	42	60	78
History of Science, Technology and Medicine	193	15	23	40	112
Drama and Theatre	170	23	38	37	61
Finance	168	17	25	44	77
Econometrics	150	22	35	52	34
Psychoanalysis	141	19	31	39	47
Music	117	10	14	34	53
Art Practice, History and Theory	87	14	21	16	32
Human Factors	86	9	9	17	49
Folklore	79	3	17	24	32
Accounting	68	6	7	12	36
Classics	43	6	11	7	16
Unclassified	20	0	0	1	19
Paleontology	1	0	0	0	1

Note: Full counting and fractional counting results are equal when preparing data at the world level, so the data is only presented once here.

* Scales are not the same across different trend graphs.

Source: Prepared by Science-Metrix using WOS (Thomson Reuters).

Annex B | Bibliometric analysis of social and human science research into inequalities and social justice

Table B4 • Number of publications (fractional counting) on inequalities and social justice produced worldwide by region, country and time period, 1992–2013

Region	Fractional count				
	1992–2013	1994–1998	1999–2003	2004–2008	2009–2013
World	75 031	9 846	13 218	18 626	30 506
Arab states	169	10	20	47	89
Egypt	33	3	5	9	17
Kuwait	14	1	2	5	5
Lebanon	26	0	6	7	13
Morocco	14	1	4	5	5
Tunisia	21	0	1	7	14
United Arab Emirates	31	2	1	8	20
East Asia	2 959	197	344	726	1 662
China	557	15	23	125	393
China, Hong Kong Special Administrative Region	506	53	98	126	223
Indonesia	50	7	8	14	20
Japan	599	66	77	165	284
Korea, Republic of	453	17	59	110	263
Malaysia	78	7	8	8	55
Philippines	64	4	8	19	31
Singapore	201	9	27	51	110
Taiwan, China	357	14	29	81	231
Thailand	57	5	4	16	29
Viet Nam	27	0	1	8	19
CIS	246	41	71	41	80
Russian Federation	201	38	64	37	57
Ukraine	19	1	4	0	14
Latin America	1 278	77	127	304	737
Argentina	167	12	12	37	102
Brazil	377	22	42	98	203
Chile	197	9	16	41	130
Colombia	85	4	10	17	52
Costa Rica	17	1	2	3	11
Jamaica	11	4	4	1	2
Mexico	269	15	30	74	143
Peru	28	0	2	7	18
Uruguay	22	0	0	3	19
Venezuela	33	4	1	8	21
North America	37 040	6 048	7 336	9 057	12 731
Canada	4 165	623	734	1 052	1 576
United States of America	32 875	5 424	6 602	8 005	11 155
Oceania	3 794	418	600	918	1 749
Australia	3 171	353	480	739	1 509
New Zealand	604	63	119	172	233
South and West Asia	779	86	129	162	367
Bangladesh	58	8	9	13	26
India	592	71	109	128	254
Iran, Islamic Republic of	44	3	2	10	29
Nepal	13	0	2	0	10
Pakistan	54	4	6	4	40
Sri Lanka	15	0	1	7	6
Southern, Central, Eastern Europe	1 977	172	219	503	1 041
Bulgaria	21	7	4	6	5
Croatia	188	11	18	75	84

Table B4 • Number of publications (fractional counting) on inequalities and social justice produced worldwide by region, country and time period, 1992–2013 (continued)

Region	Fractional count 1992–2013	1994–1998	1999–2003	2004–2008	2009–2013
Czech Republic	338	41	65	88	144
Czechoslovakia	21	-	-	-	-
Estonia	36	3	3	10	20
Hungary	142	22	19	35	63
Lithuania	49	0	2	17	31
Poland	215	23	15	50	122
Romania	158	2	10	28	117
Slovakia	170	38	38	55	39
Slovenia	121	2	12	34	73
Turkey	478	19	28	100	328
Yugoslavia	13	4	3	2	0
Sub-Saharan Africa	**2 401**	**198**	**291**	**663**	**1 186**
Botswana	48	4	15	15	14
Cameroon	21	0	2	9	11
Ethiopia	31	1	4	9	18
Ghana	49	4	4	19	22
Kenya	74	5	14	15	39
Malawi	24	3	2	6	12
Nigeria	104	4	9	31	52
South Africa	1 899	171	224	514	945
Tanzania, United Republic of	27	2	3	10	13
Uganda	29	0	3	9	15
Zimbabwe	27	2	5	10	7
Western Europe	**24 345**	**2 597**	**4 081**	**6 197**	**10 828**
Austria	330	39	46	62	168
Belgium	610	43	79	164	316
Cyprus	38	2	4	10	22
Denmark	499	47	75	111	256
Finland	467	47	71	127	213
France	1 279	135	257	330	521
Germany	2 711	309	421	661	1 241
Greece	163	12	27	45	74
Iceland	27	5	3	7	10
Ireland	346	27	55	85	166
Israel	834	121	149	218	318
Italy	867	48	116	224	470
Luxembourg	30	0	3	4	22
Malta	12	0	4	1	7
Netherlands	1 804	197	298	435	812
Norway	696	85	110	171	314
Portugal	160	5	8	41	106
Spain	1 416	53	132	325	896
Sweden	1 176	124	170	282	575
Switzerland	533	39	77	134	269
United Kingdom of Great Britain and Northern Ireland	10 344	1 262	1 978	2 758	4 050
Unclassified	**43**	**1**	**1**	**7**	**34**

Note: Full counting and fractional counting results are equal when preparing data at the world level.
  * Scales are not the same across different trend graphs.

Source: Prepared by Science-Metrix using WOS(Thomson Reuters).

Annex B | Bibliometric analysis of social and human science research into inequalities and social justice

Table B5 • Number of social and human science publications (full and fractional counting) on inequalities and social justice produced worldwide by region and time period, 1992–2013

Regions	Fractional count				
	1992–2013	1994–98	1999–2003	2004–08	2009–13
World	**75 031**	**9 846**	**13 218**	**18 626**	**30 506**
Arab states	169	10	20	47	89
East Asia	2 959	197	344	726	1 662
Commonwealth of Independent States	246	41	71	41	80
Latin America	1 278	77	127	304	737
North America	37 040	6 048	7 336	9 057	12 731
Oceania	3 794	418	600	918	1 749
South and West Asia	779	86	129	162	367
Southern, Central, Eastern Europe	1 977	172	219	503	1 041
Sub-Saharan Africa	2 401	198	291	663	1 186
Western Europe	24 345	2 597	4 081	6 197	10 828

Note: Full counting and fractional counting results are equal when preparing data at the world level.
* Scales are not the same across different trend graphs.

Source: Prepared by Science-Metrix using WOS (Thomson Reuters).

Table B6 • Number of social and human science publications (fractional counting) on inequalities and social justice produced worldwide per subfield (according to the Science-Metrix classification) and region for the entire period, 1992–2013

Subfield	World	Arab states	East Asia	Commonwealth of Independent States	Latin America	North America	Oceania	South and West Asia	Southern, Central, Eastern Europe	Sub Saharan Africa	Western Europe
Total	**75 031**	**169**	**2 959**	**246**	**1 278**	**37 040**	**3 794**	**779**	**1 977**	**2 401**	**24 345**
Accounting	68	2	5	0	1	35	6	0	1	0	18
Agricultural Economics and Policy	983	5	60	1	28	441	53	32	22	67	274
Anthropology	1 315	4	27	6	27	742	70	83	64	49	243
Applied Ethics	1 259	1	39	2	32	631	73	14	26	28	413
Archaeology	312	0	8	0	28	142	15	2	10	13	93
Art Practice, History and Theory	87	0	1	0	2	40	2	0	3	4	35
Behavioural Science and Comparative Psychology	227	0	13	1	5	99	8	1	2	7	92
Business and Management	1 797	6	111	3	22	953	68	20	49	48	515
Classics	43	0	1	0	4	26	0	0	1	1	10
Clinical Psychology	766	1	13	0	6	531	54	3	5	1	153
Communication and Media Studies	1 013	9	38	1	10	603	50	3	10	30	260
Criminology	2 351	1	37	1	6	1 660	168	9	17	20	433
Cultural Studies	1 436	7	116	1	37	437	75	30	20	239	474
Demography	1 130	6	28	2	53	570	30	19	22	18	381
Development Studies	2 634	17	137	3	108	917	71	99	14	317	952
Developmental and Child Psychology	2 526	7	37	2	28	1 827	63	4	19	33	502
Drama and Theatre	170	1	6	0	0	98	11	0	2	8	44
Econometrics	150	0	3	0	1	87	9	4	1	0	46
Economic Theory	612	1	63	6	2	192	11	6	10	1	320
Economics	7 837	21	651	32	154	3 264	380	94	298	82	2 856
Education	5 195	4	171	15	55	2 471	386	20	148	314	1 608
Experimental Psychology	652	0	31	0	7	376	32	4	4	2	195
Family Studies	975	3	18	0	5	791	37	7	4	12	99
Finance	168	0	19	0	1	78	5	0	1	0	64
Folklore	79	0	22	0	0	25	2	0	10	3	17
Gender Studies	4 779	16	139	10	27	1 980	483	71	109	56	1 882
General Psychology and Cognitive Sciences	595	1	6	0	50	419	9	0	1	44	66
Geography	2 786	0	101	1	60	1 101	197	17	29	136	1 143
History	2 044	0	19	21	42	922	115	3	64	26	829
History of Science, Technology and Medicine	193	0	5	0	12	57	5	0	7	10	97
History of Social Sciences	315	0	6	0	7	106	14	0	2	5	176
Human Factors	86	2	6	0	3	17	3	3	2	2	48
Industrial Relations	822	2	34	2	9	250	76	12	10	12	415
Information and Library Sciences	435	1	38	2	19	188	18	11	4	47	105
International Relations	1 006	9	53	0	17	396	76	12	17	34	390
Languages and Linguistics	594	5	37	0	11	257	33	5	22	26	198
Law	1 493	0	21	0	11	1 140	24	14	5	39	238
Literary Studies	1 689	5	72	0	20	1 060	47	10	37	60	377
Logistics and Transportation	531	2	68	0	12	238	37	7	2	5	160
Marketing	420	3	41	0	4	236	21	1	11	7	96
Music	117	0	0	0	0	69	8	0	2	12	25
Paleontology	1	0	0	0	0	0	0	0	0	0	0
Philosophy	894	1	33	7	13	402	34	2	76	42	283
Political Science and Public Administration	5 977	2	128	92	212	2 198	245	15	247	102	2 732

Annex B | Bibliometric analysis of social and human science research into inequalities and social justice

Table B6 • Number of social and human science publications (fractional counting) on inequalities and social justice produced worldwide per subfield (according to the Science-Metrix classification) and region for the entire period, 1992–2013 (continued)

Subfield	World	Arab states	East Asia	Commonwealth of Independent States	Latin America	North America	Oceania	South and West Asia	Southern, Central, Eastern Europe	Sub Saharan Africa	Western Europe
Psychoanalysis	141	0	1	0	1	68	1	0	0	3	66
Religions and Theology	950	4	18	2	6	560	15	15	45	114	171
Science Studies	330	0	8	1	6	167	13	2	4	7	121
Social Psychology	4 965	13	154	27	49	2 813	243	27	179	175	1 275
Social Sciences Methods	464	1	60	0	4	258	11	2	8	12	106
Social Work	3 397	6	157	2	12	2 014	158	84	51	56	855
Sociology	5 732	4	70	4	40	2 860	164	10	281	61	2 238
Sport, Leisure and Tourism	470	0	27	0	2	225	58	2	4	12	140
Unclassified	20	0	0	0	7	1	0	0	0	0	12

Source: Prepared by Science-Metrix using WOS (Thomson Reuters).

Annex C
Acronyms and abbreviations

AAAA	Addis Ababa Action Agenda
AIIB	Asian Infrastructure Investment Bank
ANC	African National Congress
BAU	business as usual
BEE	Black Economic Empowerment
BPL	below the poverty line
BRICS	Brazil, Russia, India, China and South Africa
CCTs	conditional cash transfers
CEDLAS	Center for Distributional, Labor and Social Studies
CHIP	China Household Income Project
CIT	corporate income tax
CODESRIA	Council for the Development of Social Science Research in Africa
CRA	Contingent Reserve Arrangement
CSG	child support grant
CSO	Central Statistical Office
DAC	Development Assistance Committee
DFID	Department for International Development (UK)
DHS	demographic and health surveys
DPOs	disabled people's organizations
ESCWA	Economic and Social Commission for Western Asia
GCC	Gulf Cooperation Council
GDP	gross domestic product
GNP	gross national product
HIPC	highly indebted poor country
HSRC	Human Sciences Research Council
ICT	information and communications technologies
IDS	Institute of Development Studies
IHDI	Inequality-adjusted Human Development Index
ILO	International Labour Organization
IMF	International Monetary Fund
INGO	international non-governmental organization
IPCC	Intergovernmental Panel on Climate Change
ISSC	International Social Science Council
ITUC	International Trade Union Confederation
LAG	least advantaged group
MAG	most advantaged group
MAR	Minorities at Risk
MDG(s)	Millennium Development Goal(s)
MEB	minimum expenditure basket

Annex C | Acronyms and abbreviations

MICS	multiple indicator cluster surveys
NBER	National Bureau of Economic Research
NBS	National Bureau of Statistics China
NDB	New Development Bank
NEDLAC	National Economic Development and Labour Council
NEET	not in education, employment or training
NGO	non-government organization
OCHA	UN Office for Coordination of Humanitarian Affairs
PIT	personal income tax
PPP	purchasing power parity
PRSP	poverty reduction strategy paper
PSNP	Productive Safety Net Programme
RS	Reynolds–Smolensky (indices)
SAC	Scientific Advisory Committee
SDG(s)	Sustainable Development Goal(s)
SEWA	Self Employed Women's Association
SHS	social and human sciences
SOEs	state-owned enterprises
SPIAC-B	Social Protection Inter Agency Cooperation Board
SSA	sub-Saharan Africa
SSRN	Social Science Research Network
TTIP	Transatlantic Trade and Investment Partnership
TVEs	township-village enterprises
UBI	unconditional basic income
UCEs	urban collective enterprises
UHC	universal health coverage
UN	United Nations
UNCTAD	UN Conference on Trade and Development
UNDP	UN Development Programme
UNHCR	UN High Commissioner for Refugees
UNICEF	UN Children's Fund
UNRISD	UN Research Institute for Social Development
VAT	value added tax
VPN	virtual private networks
WFP	World Food Programme
WHO	World Health Organization
WIDE	World Inequality Database on Education
WOS	Web of Science
WSSD	World Summit for Social Development
WSSR	*World Social Science Report*
WTO	World Trade Organization

Annex D
Glossary

Atkinson index

A measure of income inequality developed by Anthony Atkinson, characterized by a weighting parameter ε (which measures aversion to inequality).

Attendance rate

The proportion of those in the theoretical age group for a given level of education who are attending schooling at that level at any time during the reference academic year (obtained from household surveys).

Concentration coefficient

A measure of dispersion computed with reference to the concentration curve. It ranges between -1 and 1, and takes a negative value when the curve lies above the line of equality (the 45-degree line).

Discretionary income

The balance of income available to spend or save once all essential expenditure (such as on food or shelter) has been deducted.

Disposable income

All income after direct taxes have been deducted.

Distribution-neutral growth

A situation in which economic growth does not produce any distributional change in income growth, so incomes at different levels grow at the same rate.

Gender Parity Index

The ratio of female-to-male (or male-to-female, in certain cases) values of a given indicator. A GPI of 1 indicates parity between the genders. A GPI above or below 1 indicates a disparity in favour of one gender over the other.

General entropy measures

A family of inequality measures. They are sensitive to changes at the different part of the distribution according to α. Special cases are the mean log deviation (α=0), the Theil index (α=1), and half the squared coefficient of variation (α=2).

Genuine progress indicator

An indicator of economic progress developed as an alternative to GDP. It is based on GDP data but adjusts for a number of other dimensions such as income distribution, pollution and dependence on foreign assets.

Gini coefficient

A measure of dispersion and the most frequently used measure of inequality. It ranges between 0 in the case of perfect equality and 1 in the case of perfect inequality. The income Gini coefficient is based on the comparison of cumulative proportions of the population with the cumulative proportions of total income they receive.

Global Gender Gap Index

Introduced by the World Economic Forum to provide information on the gap between males and females across four dimensions of inequality: economic participation and opportunity (based on salaries, participation levels and access to high-skilled employment); educational attainment (based on access to basic and higher-level education); political empowerment (based on representation in decision-making structures), and health and survival (based on life expectancy and gender ratio). See *http://reports.weforum.org/global-gender-gap-report-2014/part-1/the-global-gender-gap-index-2014/*

Annex D | Glossary of indicators

Global Sub-Index for Economic Participation and Opportunities

A subindex of the Global Gender Gap Index for differences between women and men in labour force participation rates, remuneration and high-skilled employment. See *http://reports.weforum.org/global-gender-gap-report-2014/part-1/the-global-gender-gap-index-2014/*

Global Sub-Index for Political Empowerment

A subindex of the Global Gender Gap Index for representation in decision-making structures (such as the ratio of women to men in parliamentary positions). See *http://reports.weforum.org/global-gender-gap-report-2014/part-1/the-global-gender-gap-index-2014/*

Growth elasticity of poverty (GEP)

The percentage reduction in poverty rates associated with a percentage change in mean (per capita) income.

Lorenz curve

A graphical representation of income or wealth distribution in a society. Income or wealth is represented on the y-axis, while the population is ranked from the poorest to the richest on the x-axis.

Market income

Total income before tax and minus income from social transfers.

Median income

The income value separating the population distribution in two equal parts: that is, the figure than which half of the population earns more, and half less.

Median wealth

The figure than which half of the population owns more and half less.

NEET rate

The proportion of young people of a specific age group who are not in education, employment or training.

Net enrolment rate in primary/secondary education

The percentage of the total population in the theoretical age group for a level of education who are actually enrolled in school at that level.

Palma index

The ratio of the income share of the top 10 per cent to that of the bottom 40 per cent.

Poverty line

A conventional threshold defined on the minimum acceptable standard of income required to secure the necessities of life in a given setting, established to define the poor as opposed to the non-poor population.

Poverty rate

The percentage of individuals (or households) whose income (or consumption) is below the established poverty line in a given setting.

Primary/secondary completion rate

The percentage of young people (aged between three and five years above primary/secondary school graduation age) who have completed that level of schooling (UNESCO-Institute for Statistics (UIS) and Global Education Monitoring Report (GMR)).

Progressive/regressive taxation

In a progressive tax scheme the tax rate increases as the amount subject to taxation increases. In contrast, a tax system is defined as regressive if the tax rate decreases as the taxable amount increases.

Reynolds–Smolensky index

A measure of the redistributive capacity of policy measures. For example, the Reynolds–Smolensky index of taxes is given by the comparison of the Gini index (for income distribution) before taxes with the concentration coefficient of taxes (also known as 'quasi-Gini') after their application. A positive value indicates that taxes are progressive and reduce inequality.

Trade union density

The number of wage and salary earners who are trade union members, divided by the total number of wage and salary earners.

Undernourishment rate

The proportion of a total population whose food intake does not meet a defined minimum level of dietary energy consumption.